INTERNATIONAL COUNTERTERRORISM LAW

International Counterterrorism Law is the first book to consider national terrorism legislation in every one of the 197 States worldwide. It explains how international counterterrorism law has become a distinct branch of international law, and what the different components are in both peacetime and armed conflict. The relevance and contribution of international humanitarian law, international criminal law, national criminal law, and international human rights law are examined in combination with global sectoral terrorism treaties and regional instruments to provide a thorough yet manageable account of the law's application. Real-life examples are used to inform the material, from Ukraine to Syria, to Iran and the unlawful actions of the Global War on Terror, so that the reader can understand how domestic and international terrorism has historically been treated by prosecutors and the courts.

Stuart Casey-Maslen is a Professor at the University of Pretoria where he teaches international humanitarian law (IHL), international human rights law, international counterterrorism law, *jus ad bellum*, and disarmament law. He established and maintains the global database of national terrorism legislation covering every State.

International Counterterrorism Law

STUART CASEY-MASLEN
University of Pretoria

Shaftesbury Road, Cambridge CB2 8EA, United Kingdom

One Liberty Plaza, 20th Floor, New York, NY 10006, USA

477 Williamstown Road, Port Melbourne, VIC 3207, Australia

314–321, 3rd Floor, Plot 3, Splendor Forum, Jasola District Centre,
New Delhi – 110025, India

103 Penang Road, #05–06/07, Visioncrest Commercial, Singapore 238467

Cambridge University Press is part of Cambridge University Press & Assessment,
a department of the University of Cambridge.

We share the University's mission to contribute to society through the pursuit of
education, learning and research at the highest international levels of excellence.

www.cambridge.org
Information on this title: www.cambridge.org/9781009309110

DOI: 10.1017/9781009309103

© Stuart Casey-Maslen 2024

This publication is in copyright. Subject to statutory exception and to the provisions
of relevant collective licensing agreements, no reproduction of any part may take
place without the written permission of Cambridge University Press & Assessment.

When citing this work, please include a reference to the DOI 10.1017/9781009309103

First published 2024

A catalogue record for this publication is available from the British Library.

A Cataloging-in-Publication data record for this book is available from the Library of Congress.

ISBN 978-1-009-30911-0 Hardback

Cambridge University Press & Assessment has no responsibility for the persistence
or accuracy of URLs for external or third-party internet websites referred to in this
publication and does not guarantee that any content on such websites is, or will remain,
accurate or appropriate.

Contents

Introduction		1
	The Context and the Aim of the Book	2
	The League of Nations' Terrorism Convention	3
	Terrorism Treaties within the United Nations	4
	The Layout of the Book	7
	A Brief History of Terrorism	8
1	**Defining Terrorism in International Law**	20
	1.1 Introduction	20
	1.2 Defining International Terrorism in Peacetime	21
	1.2.1 The Historical Background	21
	1.2.2 The Definition(s) of Terrorism in the UN Sectoral Terrorism Treaties	23
	1.2.3 Towards an Agreed Definition of Terrorism in Peacetime?	40
	1.3 Defining 'Domestic' Terrorism	43
	1.4 The Definition of Terrorism in Armed Conflict	46
	1.4.1 The definition of terrorism in Geneva Law	46
	1.4.2 The definition of terrorism in Hague Law	48
	1.5 Concluding Observations	50
2	**The Key Components of International Counterterrorism Law**	52
	2.1 Introduction	52
	2.2 The United Nations Sectoral Treaties	53
	2.2.1 The Global Hijacking and Counterpiracy Treaties	58
	2.2.2 The Prohibition and Interdiction of Terrorist Financing	62
	2.3 The Regional Terrorism Treaties	63
	2.3.1 The African Union Terrorism Treaties	63
	2.3.2 The Arab League Terrorism Treaty	64
	2.3.3 The ASEAN Terrorism Treaty	65
	2.3.4 The CIS Terrorism Treaties	66
	2.3.5 The Council of Europe Terrorism Treaties	66
	2.3.6 The Gulf Cooperation Council Terrorism Treaties	68
	2.3.7 The OAS Terrorism Treaties	68
	2.3.8 The OIC Terrorism Treaty	69
	2.3.9 The SAARC Terrorism Treaties	70
	2.3.10 The Shanghai Cooperation Organization Terrorism Treaties	71

2.4	Terrorism in Armed Conflict		71
	2.4.1	Terrorism under Geneva Law	72
	2.4.2	Terrorism under Hague Law	72
2.5	The Duty under International Law to Prevent Terrorism		73
	2.5.1	The Duty of Prevention under International Human Rights Law	73
	2.5.2	Terrorism under Jus ad Bellum	74
2.6	The Duty under International Law to Punish Terrorism		76

3 National Terrorism Legislation Worldwide — 78

3.1	Introduction		78
3.2	Constitutional Provisions on Terrorism		80
3.3	National Definitions of Terrorism Offences		82
	3.3.1	Predicate Offences for Terrorism	84
	3.3.2	Terrorism Motivation	99
	3.3.3	Jurisdictional Issues Pertaining to National Terrorism Laws	110
3.4	The Impact of National Terrorism Legislation on Fundamental Human Rights		118

4 Prosecution of Terrorism Suspects in Domestic Courts — 122

4.1	Introduction		122
4.2	Sentences for Terrorism in Domestic Law		123
	4.2.1	The Imposition of the Death Penalty	123
	4.2.2	Maximum Sentences of Imprisonment	125
	4.2.3	Other Prison Sentences for Terrorism Offences	126
	4.2.4	Sentences for Other Offences	130
4.3	The Prosecution of Terrorism in the Americas		132
	4.3.1	The Prosecution of Terrorism in Brazil	132
	4.3.2	The Prosecution of Terrorism in Canada	134
	4.3.3	The Prosecution of Terrorism in El Salvador	137
	4.3.4	The Prosecution of Terrorism in Mexico	140
	4.3.5	The Prosecution of Terrorism in the United States	142
4.4	The Prosecution of Terrorism in Asia and the Middle East		150
	4.4.1	The Prosecution of Terrorism in Australia	150
	4.4.2	The Prosecution of Terrorism in China	152
	4.4.3	The Prosecution of Terrorism in Iran	155
	4.4.4	The Prosecution of Terrorism in Iraq	156
	4.4.5	The Prosecution of Terrorism in Lebanon	158
	4.4.6	The Prosecution of Terrorism in Saudi Arabia	160
4.5	The Prosecution of Terrorism in Africa		161
	4.5.1	The Prosecution of Terrorism in Algeria	161
	4.5.2	The Prosecution of Terrorism in Kenya	164
	4.5.3	The Prosecution of Terrorism in Niger	167
	4.5.4	The Prosecution of Terrorism in Somalia	170
4.6	The Prosecution of Terrorism in Europe		171
	4.6.1	The Prosecution of Terrorism in Belgium	173
	4.6.2	The Prosecution of Terrorism in France	175
	4.6.3	The Prosecution of Terrorism in the United Kingdom	177

Contents

vii

5 Counterterrorism Action under International Law — 182

5.1 Introduction — 182
5.2 Surveillance and Data and the Rights to Privacy and to Family Life — 183
    5.2.1 The Rights to a Private and Family Life — 183
5.3 Tackling Terrorist Suspects in Law Enforcement — 186
    5.3.1 The Conduct of Investigations into Terrorism Suspects — 187
    5.3.2 Arresting Terrorist Suspects and the Rights to Life and to Freedom from Torture — 189
    5.3.3 Necessity for the Use of Force against Terrorist Suspects — 192
    5.3.4 Proportionate Force in Tackling Terrorists — 194
    5.3.5 The Duty of Precaution and Operations to Tackle Terrorist Suspects — 196
5.4 The Treatment of Terrorist Suspects in Custody — 198
    5.4.1 Deaths in Custody — 198
    5.4.2 Extraordinary Rendition — 200
5.5 Fair-Trial Rights — 201
    5.5.1 Terrorism Trials in Camera — 201
    5.5.2 Use of Evidence Obtained Using Coercion — 202
5.6 Preventive Detention and Other Restrictions on Terrorism Suspects — 203
    5.6.1 Preventive Detention — 203
    5.6.2 Control Orders and House Arrest — 204
    5.6.3 Revocation of Citizenship — 206
5.7 The Right of Burial of Terrorism Suspects — 207

6 Prosecution of Terrorism as an International Crime — 208

6.1 Introduction — 208
6.2 Elements of International Crimes and Modes of Liability — 211
    6.2.1 Modes of liability — 212
6.3 Terrorism as a Crime against Humanity — 213
6.4 Terrorism as a War Crime — 215
    6.4.1 Acts of Terrorism against Persons in the Power of the Enemy — 216
    6.4.2 Terrorism in the Conduct of Hostilities as a War Crime — 220
    6.4.3 Terror in a Situation of Armed Conflict: Other International Practice — 223
6.5 Terrorism as Genocide — 226
6.6 Terrorism as a Distinct International Crime in Peacetime — 228
6.7 Terrorism as an Act of Aggression — 229

7 State Responsibility for Terrorism — 231

7.1 Introduction — 231
7.2 The Key Components of State Responsibility — 233
7.3 The Duty to Prevent Terrorism — 235
    7.3.1 The Beslan School Siege — 235
7.4 State Perpetration of Terrorism — 237
    7.4.1 The Rainbow Warrior Bombing — 237
    7.4.2 Syrian Regime Infliction of Torture as Terrorism during the 'Arab Spring' in Syria — 240
    7.4.3 Russian Terrorism in Ukraine since the 2022 Invasion — 244
7.5 State Complicity in Acts of Terrorism — 248

	7.5.1	Liberia's State Responsibility for Acts of Terror in Sierra Leone	249
	7.5.2	Syria's Role in the Assassination of Rafik Hariri	250
7.6		The Labelling of Political Opposition as Terrorist	251

8 The Outlook for International Counterterrorism Law   254

Index   259

Introduction

Few words are more emotionally charged than 'terrorism' and 'terrorist'. They are used to denote conduct that is not only criminal but also – worse – action that strikes at the heart of the people or the fundament of the nation State. On occasion, condemnation in such egregious terms can disclose more about the user than it does about the target of their denunciation. Sometimes those designated as terrorists may bask in the descriptor, wearing it as a badge of honour. But far more often, the recipients reject their label on the basis that either their *raison d'être* or their tactics, or both, are dedicated to the achievement of lofty goals: freedom, religious purity, the quest for social justice, or the defence of the oppressed or the economically vulnerable. As Adam Roberts, an expert on political violence, says, the word terrorism is confusing and dangerous but also 'indispensable'.[1]

While the etymology of the root of the word to terrorize is found in ancient Greek, and terror tactics have been employed throughout human history,[2] we have the French of the late eighteenth century of the current era (CE) to thank for the transmission into English of contemporary understandings of terrorism. Along with his Revolutionary colleagues, Maximilien Robespierre – a lawyer by profession – espoused and vaunted '*La Terreur*' as a crucial mechanism in the sustenance of the French Revolution against the constant threats of its reversal by monarchists. Republican France thus employed brutality during the Reign of Terror not just as an incidental stratagem of governance but also as wilful, even *existential* State policy.[3]

Since then, whether in any given society it has been predominantly States or non-State armed groups that have engaged in terrorism has waxed and waned, at least in popular perception, at variance depending on the epoch and the regime. For instance, in the lead up to and throughout the Second World War, the Nazis used terror to maintain their control over Germany and the territories they forcibly occupied. This they did with relentless fervour right until the regime's bloody denouement in May 1945. In contrast, the 9/11 attacks have done much to imprint non-State Islamist terrorism as the predominant threat to Western civilization in the twenty-first century. First al-Qaeda, and then more recently the Islamic State that it spawned, have sought to replace democratic institutions with religious diktat and dedicated cruelty, moving from war crimes to crimes against humanity to genocide. Most frequently, however, the two types of

---

[1] A. Roberts, 'Countering Terrorism: A Historical Perspective', in A. Bianchi and A. Keller (eds.), *Counterterrorism: Democracy's Challenge*, Hart, Oxford, 2008, 3–41, at p. 5.

[2] M. Cherif Bassiouni, 'Legal Control of International Terrorism', *Harvard International Law Journal*, Vol. 43 (2001), 83–103, at p. 83.

[3] See, e.g., T. Tackett, *The Coming of the Terror in the French Revolution*, Harvard University Press, Cambridge, MA, 2017.

Introduction

armed entity – State and non-State – terrorize in ever-expanding lockstep: action provoking reaction and counteraction until the spiralling brutality wrought by each is almost symbiotic.

THE CONTEXT AND THE AIM OF THE BOOK

The aim of this book is to describe the content of a relatively new branch of international law. While, as discussed here, Member States of the League of Nations elaborated a treaty against terrorism in the second half of the 1930s, it never entered into force. Thereafter, it was not until the early 1970s that efforts were renewed with a view to defining and suppressing terrorism. Piecemeal and sporadic efforts at global and regional levels have generated a myriad of conventions but no unitary definition. International counterterrorism law is thus an amalgam of instruments and legal provisions, a complex set of sectoral treaties informed and influenced by international human rights law, international humanitarian law, and resolutions of the United Nations (UN) Security Council.[4]

Under the umbrella term of international counterterrorism law, terrorism itself can potentially be a targeted killing or an act of indiscriminate violence. In theory, any weapon can be used to commit an act of terrorism. It can be perpetrated by an insurgent, a traitor, the member of a drug cartel, or a lone wolf, as well as by an agent of a State. Indeed, even an act ostensibly of counterterrorism can itself be a terrorist act. What distinguishes a homicide from a terrorist murder under international law is a confluence of the status of the victim, the circumstances of the killing, and the intent of the killer.

Particular opprobrium is heaped on anyone deemed to be a terrorist, even though across national legal regimes such a person – man or woman, boy or girl – is defined in starkly different terms. But, howsoever any national jurisdiction prohibits terrorism in its domestic law, international law will still be relevant to that determination. It may sometimes deny the legitimacy of the label. It certainly regulates the treatment of anyone suspected of terrorist acts or inclinations, including their surveillance, the restriction of their rights, their detention and interrogation, their prosecution, and, upon conviction, their incarceration. International law will further determine the heavily constrained circumstances of if, when, and how a convicted terrorist may lawfully be executed.

Accordingly, this book describes the regulation of both terrorism and counterterrorism under international law. The legality of acts and measures to confront terrorism is to be assessed by reference to international human rights law and the law of law enforcement, as well as, when those acts and measures are directly related to armed conflict, international humanitarian law. Certain acts of terrorism rise to the level of international crimes, necessitating consideration of the personal responsibility of individuals under international criminal law. Especially (but not only) when force is used extraterritorially, *jus ad bellum* – the law on inter-State use of force – will also apply. In all cases where a State organ or agent has committed an internationally wrongful act, it will attract that State's responsibility under international law.

Counterterrorism overlaps substantially and substantively with counterinsurgency, counterpiracy, as well as efforts to tackle arms, drug, and human trafficking. Nonetheless, a relatively

---

[4] The first Security Council resolution to employ the term 'terrorism' was Resolution 579 of 1985. See B. Saul, 'Definition of "Terrorism" in the UN Security Council', *Chinese Journal of International Law*, Vol. 4, No. 1 (2005), 141–66, at p. 144. The resolution followed a Presidential Statement in the Council of 9 October 1985 that 'resolutely' condemned 'all acts of terrorism, including hostage-taking'. It urged 'further development of international co-operation among States in devising and adopting effective measures which are in accordance with the rules of international law to facilitate the prevention, prosecution and punishment of all acts of hostage-taking and abduction as manifestations of international terrorism'. UN Security Council Resolution 579, adopted on 18 December 1985 by unanimous vote in favour, operative para. 5.

The Context and the Aim of the Book

coherent (albeit fragmented) corpus of international law details the repression of terrorism and terrorist acts in criminal law and regulates the response of States in both law and practice. Articulating the contours and content of international counterterrorism law is the aim of this book. In so doing, however, the book is not a legal commentary on the 'Global War on Terror', for such a work has already been largely written.[5] That said, analysis of the lawfulness of actions taken by the United States and its allies does by necessity feature prominently in this book for, since the beginning of the twenty-first century, terrorism has indeed been 'the number one issue in international politics, security and law'.[6] But international counterterrorism law did not begin with the attacks against the United States on 11 September 2001, because – for the truism bears repeating – terrorism as a phenomenon did not start with 9/11.

The League of Nations' Terrorism Convention

Almost 100 years ago, Romania asked the League of Nations to consider drafting a 'convention to render terrorism universally punishable'. But the request made in 1926 was not acted upon at the time.[7] Yet only a decade would elapse before events of international significance in France would spur the negotiation by States of the day of a treaty to prevent and punish terrorism. The Convention for the Prevention and Punishment of Terrorism, concluded in 1937 under the auspices of the erstwhile League of Nations, is a landmark in international counterterrorism law, even though it would never become formally binding.[8] It required the criminalization of terrorism perpetrated against another State (not the territorial State), with terrorism motivation delineated as criminal acts 'intended or calculated to create a state of terror in the minds of particular persons, or a group of persons or the general public'.[9]

Specifically, the text stipulated that each State was obligated under a 'principle' of international law to refrain from *encouraging* terrorist activities directed against another State and to prevent and punish such activities and to criminalize offences against the life or bodily integrity of foreign diplomats or the property of a foreign State.[10] The implication was that terrorism was the preserve of non-State actors, even though the Convention did not exclude the possibility that an agent of a State could engage in acts of terrorism. The negotiation of the Convention had been prompted by the 1934 assassination by separatists in Marseilles of the King of Yugoslavia, Alexander I, and the associated, but perhaps not intended, killing[11] of the French Minister for Foreign Affairs, Jean Louis Barthou.[12]

---

[5] H. Duffy, *The 'War on Terror' and the Framework of International Law*, 2nd ed., Cambridge University Press, Cambridge, 2015.

[6] K. Nuotio, 'Terrorism as a Catalyst for the Emergence, Harmonization and Reform of Criminal Law', *Journal of International Criminal Justice*, Vol. 4 (2006), 998–1016, at p. 998.

[7] S. Kirsch and A. Oehmichen, 'Judges Gone Astray: The Fabrication of Terrorism as an International Crime by the Special Tribunal for Lebanon', *Durham Law Review Online*, Vol. 1 (2011), 1–20, at p. 11.

[8] M. D. Dubin, 'Great Britain and the Anti-terrorist Conventions of 1937', *Terrorism and Political Violence*, Vol. 5, No. 1 (1993), 1–29. Twenty-three States of the day signed it: Albania, Argentina, Belgium, Bulgaria, Czechoslovakia, the Dominican Republic, Ecuador, Egypt, Estonia, France, Greece, Haiti, India, Monaco, the Netherlands, Norway, Peru, Romania, Spain, the Soviet Union, Turkey, Venezuela, and Yugoslavia. Under Article 26(1) of the Convention, only three ratifications were needed to trigger its entry into force but these were never secured.

[9] Art. 1(2), Convention for the Prevention and Punishment of Terrorism; signed at Geneva, 16 November 1937; never entered into force.

[10] Arts. 1(1) and 2(1) and (2), 1937 Convention for the Prevention and Punishment of Terrorism.

[11] J. de Launay, *Les grandes controverses de l'histoire contemporaine 1914–1945*, Rencontre, Lausanne, 1964, p. 248.

[12] B. Saul, 'The Legal Response of the League of Nations to Terrorism', *Journal of International Criminal Justice*, Vol. 4, No. 1 (March 2006), 78–102.

4 *Introduction*

Even though, along with France, Britain had pushed hard for the Convention's successful conclusion, it never signed the fruit of the negotiations. In the event, nor did Germany or the United States – contested provisions on extradition and plans for prosecution of offenders at a proposed international criminal tribunal were the core of their opposition.[13] The League of Nations is of course no more, its impotence laid bare by the conflagrations of the Second World War it was supposed to prevent. Nevertheless, the articulation of the contours of terrorism and the motivation for terrorism in the 1937 Convention are certainly more than just historical curiosities, and their frequent citation by commentators today pays testament to the text's contemporary relevance.

Terrorism Treaties within the United Nations

The book traces the path of international law on terrorism and counterterrorism in the modern era ever since the abortive efforts of the League of Nations. Following the conclusion of two multilateral treaties under the auspices of the International Civil Aviation Organization[14] governing the hijacking and bombing of aircraft in 1970 and 1971, respectively,[15] the first UN treaty of particular salience to the issue was the 1973 Convention on Crimes against Internationally Protected Persons.[16] The Convention was negotiated in response to a spate of kidnappings and killings of diplomatic agents, including the assassination of Karl von Spreti, the Federal Republic of Germany's Ambassador to Guatemala, in 1970.[17] Again, therefore, the focus of burgeoning international counterterrorism law was on attacks against a foreign State. But the choice of theme for the first 'sectoral' terrorism treaty[18] was also a reflection of the inability of the international community to agree upon a general definition of international terrorism.

The conclusion of the Internationally Protected Persons Convention was followed in 1979 by another sectoral treaty, this time on hostage-taking, another common terrorist tactic in the 1970s.

---

[13] A separate treaty foresaw the establishment of an international criminal court to try terrorists, but this too would never see the light of day. Dubin dismisses the two Conventions as 'products of political theater'. Dubin, 'Great Britain and the Anti-terrorist Conventions of 1937', p. 1.

[14] ICAO was established in April 1947 pursuant to the 1944 Chicago Convention. Art. 43, Convention on International Civil Aviation; adopted at Chicago, 7 December 1944; entered into force, 4 April 1947 (hereafter, Chicago Convention). At the time of writing, 193 States were party to the Chicago Convention. The depositary for the Convention is the United States. Art. 91, Chicago Convention. ICAO is a United Nations (UN) specialized agency but it operates autonomously of the UN. ICAO, 'ICAO and the United Nations', undated but accessed 1 September 2023, at: https://bit.ly/3YTobA5.

[15] Convention on the Suppression of Unlawful Seizure of Aircraft; adopted at The Hague, 16 December 1970; entered into force, 14 October 1971 (185 States Parties); and Convention on the Suppression of Unlawful Acts against the Safety of Aviation, adopted at Montreal, 23 September 1971; entered into force, 26 January 1973 (188 States Parties). In both cases, the depositaries of the Convention are the Russian Federation (as successor State to the Soviet Union), the United Kingdom, and the United States.

[16] Convention on the Prevention and Punishment of Crimes against Internationally Protected Persons, including Diplomatic Agents; adopted at New York, 14 December 1973; entered into force, 20 February 1977. As of 1 January 2024, 180 of 197 States were party to the Convention. In addition, the Cook Islands is also bound to the Convention through New Zealand's ratification in 1985. Niue has adhered to the Convention in its own right.

[17] M. Wood, 'Convention on the Prevention and Punishment of Crimes against Internationally Protected Persons, Including Diplomatic Agents', UN Audiovisual Library of International Law, United Nations, 2008, at: https://bit.ly/3rusjuz, p. 1.

[18] See, e.g., A. R. Perera, 'The draft United Nations Comprehensive Convention on International Terrorism', chap. 9 in B. Saul (ed.), *Research Handbook on International Law and Terrorism*, 2nd ed., Edward Elgar, Cheltenham, 2021, p. 122. See also R. Perera, 'Declaration on Measures to Eliminate International Terrorism, 1994, and the 1996 Supplementary Declaration Thereto', UN Audiovisual Library of International Law, New York, 2008, at: https://bit.ly/3uGDgeA, p. 1.

The 1979 Hostage-Taking Convention[19] was the 'first attempt to prescribe an offence with a "terrorist motive"', that is to say, to seek to compel conduct by others through unlawful action.[20] That said, the Convention employs the term 'terrorism' only once, and only in the preamble, reflecting the polemic already affecting use of the term.[21] The putative States Parties thus declared themselves convinced of the 'urgent necessity' to improve international cooperation in support of effective measures to prevent, prosecute, and punish all acts of the taking of hostages – 'as manifestations of international terrorism'.[22] The distinction drawn between international terrorism and purely 'domestic' terrorism, where crime, victims, and offenders are all in the same State, is addressed in more detail in Chapter 1.

In the decades following the adoption of the Hostage-Taking Convention, UN Member States concluded a series of global treaties on different forms of terrorism within the auspices of the United Nations. Of particular note are the 1997 Terrorist Bombings Convention[23] and the 1999 Terrorism Financing Convention,[24] the latter being the most widely ratified UN counterterrorism treaty with 190 States Parties among the 197 that could adhere.[25] At the time of writing, the most recent global counterterrorism treaty was the Nuclear Terrorism Convention, concluded in 2005.[26] Its negotiation had begun in 1998 with a draft proffered by Russia,[27] which stated that the proposed convention was particularly significant insofar as it was the first international legal instrument in the domain of counterterrorism that was specially designed as a 'pre-emptive instrument'.[28]

What has still not been adopted under UN auspices is a 'comprehensive' convention on international terrorism, even though it has already been more than twenty years in the making.[29] The principal sticking point between States remains the precise contours of the definition of international terrorism, which continues to elude general agreement, let alone consensus. Consequently, as the International Criminal Tribunal for the former Yugoslavia (ICTY)

---

[19] International Convention against the Taking of Hostages; adopted at New York, 17 December 1979; entered into force, 3 June 1983 (1979 Hostage-Taking Convention). As of 1 January 2024, 176 of 195 States were party to the 1979 Hostage-Taking Convention. In addition, the Cook Islands and Niue are bound through New Zealand's ratification prior to their recognition as independent nations by the UN Secretary-General. See the UN Treaty Collection entry at: https://bit.ly/3KyjBmt.

[20] J. Atwell, 'Aviation and International Terrorism', chap. 4 in B. Saul (ed.), *Research Handbook on International Law and Terrorism*, 2nd ed., p. 51.

[21] B. Saul, 'International Convention against the Taking of Hostages', UN Audiovisual Library of International Law, 2014, at: https://bit.ly/3ouIVAl, p. 2.

[22] 1979 Hostage-Taking Convention, fifth preambular para. [added emphasis].

[23] International Convention for the Suppression of Terrorist Bombings; adopted at New York, 15 December 1997; entered into force, 23 May 2001. As of 1 January 2024, 170 States were party to the 1997 Terrorist Bombings Convention.

[24] International Convention for the Suppression of the Financing of Terrorism; adopted at New York, 9 December 1999; entered into force, 10 April 2002. As of 1 January 2024, 190 States were party to the 1999 Terrorism Financing Convention.

[25] As Pierre Klein recalls, however, at the time of the 9/11 attacks, only four States had adhered to the Convention, which was thus a long way from coming into force. P. Klein, 'International Convention for the Suppression of the Financing of Terrorism', UN Audiovisual Library of International Law, 2009, at: https://bit.ly/3uqmeRL, p. 4. A total of twenty-two contracting States were needed to trigger entry into force. Art. 26, 1999 Terrorism Financing Convention.

[26] International Convention for the Suppression of Acts of Nuclear Terrorism; adopted at New York, 13 April 2005; entered into force, 7 July 2007. As of 1 January 2024, 123 States were party to the 2005 Nuclear Terrorism Convention, the most adherence, at the time of writing, being by the Republic of Congo in November 2023.

[27] J. Boulden, 'The United Nations General Assembly and Terrorism', chap. 34 in B. Saul (ed.), *Research Handbook on International Law and Terrorism*, 2nd ed., p. 499.

[28] Nuclear Threat Initiative (NTI), 'International Convention on the Suppression of Acts of Nuclear Terrorism', last reviewed 29 April 2020, at: https://bit.ly/3gusq2Y.

[29] See, e.g., J. Cockayne, 'Challenges in United Nations Counter-Terrorism Coordination', chap. 41 in B. Saul (ed.), *Research Handbook on International Law and Terrorism*, 2nd ed., p. 601.

observed in 2003, the offence of international terrorism has 'never been singly defined under international law'.[30] Regrettably, this statement of more than twenty years' vintage remains true today. A number of generalized counterterrorism treaties have, though, been successfully concluded at regional levels, each with its own particular definition.

Although much – sometimes too much – is made of UN Security Council Resolution 1373, adopted in the aftermath of 9/11,[31] it nonetheless binds all UN Member States (and purports to bind all States), demanding that they put in place a wide range of regulatory and legislative measures to prevent terrorism.[32] This is so despite the 'far from satisfactory situation' in which the Council becomes the legislator[33] and albeit without it even clearly defining what terrorism is.[34] In 1998, following the terrorist bombings by al-Qaeda in Nairobi and Dar es Salaam in East Africa, the Council had declared that the suppression of acts of international terrorism was 'essential' for international peace and security.[35] But while primary responsibility for the maintenance of international peace and security is generally delegated to the Security Council,[36] the Council has continued to affirm that UN Member States have the primary responsibility for countering terrorist acts.[37]

The UN General Assembly too continues to be active on the issue. As Boulden observes, this global body adopted more than 110 resolutions on different aspects of terrorism between 1972 and 2020.[38] In September 2005, the World Summit Outcome document strongly condemned 'terrorism in all its forms and manifestations, committed by whomever, wherever, and for whatever purposes', terming it 'one of the most serious threats to international peace and security'.[39] In December 2021, in the 76th Session of the Assembly, three such resolutions were adopted, on each occasion without a vote, demonstrating a solidarity that is not always replicated in State practice. In 2022, the 77th Session of the Assembly passed a further four resolutions (two of which were contested). The resolutions concerned measures to eliminate international terrorism;[40] preventing the acquisition of radioactive sources by terrorists;[41] measures to prevent terrorists from acquiring weapons of mass destruction;[42] and the designation of an International Day for the Prevention of Violent Extremism as and When Conducive to

[30] ICTY, *Prosecutor* v. *Galić*, Judgment (Trial Chamber) (Case No. IT-98-29-T), 5 December 2003, para. 87, note 150.
[31] See on this issue Saul, 'Definition of "Terrorism" in the UN Security Council', p. 155; and N. Quénivet, 'You Are the Weakest Link and We Will Help You! The Comprehensive Strategy of the United Nations to Fight Terrorism', *Journal of Conflict and Security Law*, Vol. 11 (2006), 371–97, at p. 379.
[32] UN Security Council Resolution 1373, adopted on 28 September 2001 by unanimous vote in favour. See Boulden, 'The United Nations General Assembly and Terrorism', p. 499.
[33] L. M. Hinojosa Martínez, 'The Legislative Role of the Security Council in Its Fight against Terrorism: Legal, Political and Practical Limits', *International and Comparative Law Quarterly*, Vol. 57, No. 2 (2008)333–59, at p. 358.
[34] L. M. Hinojosa-Martínez, 'Security Council Resolution 1373: The Cumbersome Implementation of Legislative Acts', chap. 39 in B. Saul (ed.), *Research Handbook on International Law and Terrorism*, 2nd ed., p. 584.
[35] UN Security Council Resolution 1189, adopted on 13 August 1998 by unanimous vote in favour, third preambular para.
[36] Art. 24(1), Charter of the United Nations; adopted at San Francisco, 26 June 1945; entered into force, 24 October 1945.
[37] UN Security Council Resolution 2617, adopted on 30 December 2021 by unanimous vote in favour, ninth preambular para.
[38] Boulden, 'The United Nations General Assembly and Terrorism', p. 501.
[39] UN General Assembly Resolution 60/1: '2005 World Summit Outcome', adopted without a vote on 24 October 2005, para. 81. But as Adam Roberts observed, the document did not attempt to define terrorism. Roberts, 'Countering Terrorism', p. 8.
[40] UN General Assembly Resolution 77/113 ('Measures to eliminate international terrorism'), adopted on 7 December 2022 without a vote.
[41] UN General Assembly Resolution 77/77 ('Preventing the acquisition by terrorists of radioactive sources'), adopted on 7 December 2022 by 180 votes to nil with two abstentions (Iran and Syria).
[42] UN General Assembly Resolution 77/75 ('Measures to prevent terrorists from acquiring weapons of mass destruction'), adopted on 7 December 2022 without a vote.

Terrorism.[43] Over the course of the last fifty years, the General Assembly has also taken overall charge of the elaboration of most of the global treaties on terrorism, mandating committees and working groups to take responsibility for their drafting.

In sum, international counterterrorism law comprises a patchwork of treaties, along with a number of customary rules and a set of general principles of law. These are supplemented by a swathe of international, regional, and domestic caselaw and the doctrinal views of leading jurists, as well as soft law instruments and politically binding resolutions promulgated both within and outside the United Nations. By synthesizing and analysing these rules, norms, and decisions, it is sought to bring a modicum of clarity to a complex branch of international law. Descriptions of acts of terrorism and related judicial decisions serve as illustrations both of the existence of rules and of their breach.

THE LAYOUT OF THE BOOK

Following this Introduction, the book is organized in eight chapters. Chapter 1 is dedicated to the multiple definitions of terrorism that exist in the absence of the adoption of the long-discussed Comprehensive Convention against International Terrorism as well as other definitions outside that Convention's ostensible purview. The key components of international counterterrorism law are then articulated in Chapter 2, starting with a summary of the key UN treaties on terrorism along with an overview of the content and impact of human rights law, humanitarian law, *jus ad bellum*, refugee law, and international criminal law.

Coverage of international terrorism concerns especially the 1973 Internationally Protected Persons Convention, the 1979 Hostage-Taking Convention, the 1997 Terrorist Bombings Convention, the 1999 Terrorism Financing Convention, and the 2005 Nuclear Terrorism Convention, along with relevant aerial and maritime treaties. At the regional level, detailed consideration of relevant instruments includes the 1977 European Convention on the Suppression of Terrorism and the 2005 European Convention on the Prevention of Terrorism; the 1987 South Asian Association for Regional Cooperation (SAARC) Regional Convention on the Suppression of Terrorism; the 1998 Arab Convention on the Suppression of Terrorism; the 1999 Organisation of Islamic Cooperation (OIC) Convention on Combating International Terrorism; the 1999 Algiers Convention on the Prevention and Combating of Terrorism and its 2004 Protocol; the 2002 Inter-American Convention against Terrorism; and the 2007 Association of Southeast Nations (ASEAN) Convention on Counter Terrorism.

Analysis of national terrorism legislation in Chapter 3 covers the definitions of crimes and available sentences in domestic jurisdictions, drawing on the practice across every one of the 197 States[44] recognized by the UN Secretary-General in his capacity as treaty depositary. The unique nature and vastly varying breadth of terrorism across States is a remarkable feature of counterterrorism law. Chapter 4 moves on to consider the prosecution of terrorism suspects at national level. The chapter first considers sentences for terrorism in domestic law around the world, including the imposition of the death penalty and maximum sentences of imprisonment for terrorism offences. It then considers the conduct and outcome of selected terrorism cases,

---

[43] UN General Assembly Resolution 77/243 ('International Day for the Prevention of Violent Extremism as and When Conducive to Terrorism'), adopted on 20 December 2022 by 154 votes to nil with four abstentions (Iran, North Korea, Russia, and Syria). The date of 12 February was selected under operative paragraph 1 of the resolution.

[44] A global repository of terrorism law in each of these States has been established by the Centre for Human Rights and the Institute for International and Comparative Law in Africa (ICLA) at the University of Pretoria. See Laws on Countering Terrorism Worldwide, at: https://counterterrorlaw.info.

8   *Introduction*

grouped regionally: in Brazil, Canada, El Salvador, Mexico, and the United States in the Americas; in Australia, China, Iran, Iraq, Lebanon, and Saudi Arabia in Asia and the Middle East; in Algeria, Kenya, Niger, and Somalia in Africa; and in Belgium, France, and the United Kingdom in Europe.

Operational surveillance of criminal suspects and individuals 'of particular concern' raises significant human rights issues, especially pertaining to the right of privacy and later the right to fair trial. The use of force against terrorist suspects by law enforcement agencies, whether in custody or in an extra-custodial situation, also brings into play the rights to life and to freedom from torture. These issues are tackled in Chapter 5. As two judges of the European Court of Human Rights observed in 2008: 'States are not allowed to combat international terrorism at all costs. They must not resort to methods which undermine the very values they seek to protect.'[45]

Despite the plethora of rules governing terrorism under international law, it would be a mistake to presume that terrorism is, per se, a specific international crime. That said, many terrorist acts are subject to punishment, whether as a war crime, as a crime against humanity, as well as, potentially, as genocide. An act of aggression can involve an act or multiple acts of terror. Chapter 6 thus considers the prosecution of terrorism under international criminal law. Certainly, the victims of terrorism should receive assistance to support their recovery and compensation for their losses, as Chapter 7 considers when looking at the responsibility of States under international law.

Outlook, the final chapter of the book, looks at terrorist threats that have been emerging in recent years or are on the horizon and the extent to which they are covered by extant international counterterrorism law. These include cyberterrorism and the use of fully autonomous weapons in counterterrorism. The book concludes with an assessment of the potential for the successful conclusion of the UN Comprehensive Convention against International Terrorism in the near future as well as for the – more probable – greater fragmentation of international counterterrorism law in the years to come.

A BRIEF HISTORY OF TERRORISM

Before turning to the consideration of contemporary international counterterrorism law, however, a brief historical perspective of terrorism is offered. Naturally, no history of terrorism could ever hope to be comprehensive; what follows, therefore, is by definition a succinct and partial representation of selected key events and issues. Fear is a form of control and a means to maintain power, as regimes great and small have demonstrated for millennia. Others might legitimately have chosen different events.

Furthermore, one should really begin with the existence of *homo sapiens* as a species, for terror tactics are as old as the animal kingdom, and human history from its earliest moments is replete with examples. But given the etymology of the term terrorism, the classical world is perhaps as good a place as any to start. For the word is first found in ancient Greek and, more directly with regard to its contemporary meaning, in later-age Latin. While the term is often used loosely and with a degree of abandon, what is at the core of terrorism is the employment of certain tactics and/or the choice of a number of targets. This explains the term's foundation in the Latin word *terrere*, meaning to frighten; to alarm; or to deter by provoking great fear. The Latin, in turn, has a cognate in the Greek τρέω, meaning to flee in fear or to be afraid of. Homer, for instance, used

---

[45]   European Court of Human Rights, *Saadi* v. *Italy*, Judgment (Grand Chamber), 28 February 2008, p. 52, Concurring Opinion of Judge Myjer, joined by Judge Zagrebelsky.

A Brief History of Terrorism

the verb on numerous occasions in *The Iliad*.[46] Of course, the fact that I may feel terrorized as a result of the actions of a particular person does not mean that the perpetrator of that conduct is, in legal parlance, a terrorist. Indeed, his or her actions may not even be criminal in any objectively rational assessment. Hence, the legal interrelationship between the actions, intent, and perceptions of the subject and object is intricate, or, at the least, rather more nuanced than one might instinctively expect.

The Romans employed crucifixion as a brutal form of capital punishment in part to deter others from rising up against the empire, an early counterinsurgency/counterterrorism mechanism that employed terror as its modus operandi.[47] Jesus was thus crucified on the basis that he had instigated rebellion against Rome.[48] But the Romans did not invent crucifixion: responsibility is often attributed to the Persians who developed the technique somewhere between 400 and 300 BCE.[49] Crucifixion is a method of capital punishment in which the victim is tied or nailed to a large wooden cross or beam and left hanging until eventual death from either exhaustion or asphyxiation or a combination of the two. It is described by one commentator as 'quite possibly the most painful death ever invented by humankind'.[50] As a consequence, the word 'excruciating' in English is derived from crucifixion, reflecting the slow but extreme suffering it engenders.[51]

Fourteen centuries later, in medieval Europe, Vlad 'the Impaler' was a prince whose bloodthirsty acts would later inspire the fictional creation by Bram Stoker of the world's most famous vampire, Dracula.[52] Vlad III, whose epithet was only accorded to him post-mortem, had been held captive by the Turks for a while, a condition that weighed heavily on him. After his father was ousted as ruler of Wallachia, Vlad, now free again, launched a campaign to regain authority over his lands. During his captivity, he had seen how the Ottomans would sometimes impale their enemies.[53] He now used the technique to consolidate his power and strike fear into his

---

[46] Word Sense Dictionary, 'τρέω (Ancient Greek)', at: https://bit.ly/3415iGo.

[47] Crucifixion as a method of execution was practiced systematically by the Persians in the sixth century BCE but wooden crosses were not used until Roman times. Alexander the Great brought the practice to eastern Mediterranean countries in the fourth century BCE following his invasion of Persia, but Roman officials became aware of the practice only when fighting Carthage during the Punic Wars a hundred years later. They then practised and 'perfected' crucifixion until Constantine I abolished it in the fourth century CE. It was used especially for those who rebelled against the authority of Rome. See L. Geggel, 'Jesus Wasn't the Only Man to Be Crucified. Here's the History behind This Brutal Practice', *Live Science*, 19 April 2019, at: https://bit.ly/3nNai8i; and F. P. Retief and L. Cilliers, 'The History and Pathology of Crucifixion', *The South African Medical Journal*, Vol. 93, No. 12 (2003), 938–41, at: https://bit.ly/3rzNb29.

[48] Retief and Cilliers, 'The History and Pathology of Crucifixion', p. 939, citing Flavius Josephus, *The Jewish War*, Vol. III (Trans. by H. St. J. Thackeray, Harvard University Press, Cambridge, MA, 1957), 321, vv. 362–420.

[49] Alternatively, Daniel Manix suggested that it was 'probably' invented by the Phoenicians, who introduced it to their colony of Carthage. D. P. Mannix, *The History of Torture*, Sutton, Stroud, 1964, p. 35.

[50] Mannix notes, however, that in certain instances the executioner nailed spikes through the wrists in such a way as to cut the artery in which case death came quickly. Ibid., p. 37.

[51] C. Shrier, 'The Science of the Crucifixion', Azusa Pacific University, Azusa, 2002, at: https://bit.ly/3Y1ufsp. The piece describes graphically the suffering that Jesus would have undergone before his physical death.

[52] M. Lallanilla and C. McKelvie, 'Vlad the Impaler: The real Dracula', *Live Science*, 15 December 2021, at: https://bit.ly/3ItaPEw. The term comes from the induction by King Sigismund of Hungary of his father, Vlad II, into a knightly order, the Order of the Dragon. Vlad II gained a new name, Dracul, coming from the old Romanian word for dragon, *drac*. His son, Vlad III, would later be known as the 'son of Dracul' or, in old Romanian, *Drăculea*.

[53] As Marc Lallanilla graphically describes, impaling a person while still alive involves inserting a wood or metal pole through the body either front to back, or vertically, through the rectum or vagina. The exit wound could be near the victim's neck, shoulders, or mouth. In some cases, the pole was rounded, not sharp, to avoid damaging internal organs and thereby prolong the suffering of the victim. The pole was then raised vertically to display the victim's torment; hours or days could elapse before the impaled person finally died. M. Lallanilla, 'Vlad the Impaler: The real Dracula was absolutely vicious'', *NBC News*, 31 October 2013, at: https://nbcnews.to/3AmJKzS.

enemies.[54] On one occasion, he invited hundreds of querulous aristocrats – the exact number is uncertain – to a banquet. Knowing his authority would be challenged, he had his guests stabbed and, their bodies still twitching, impaled.[55] On another occasion, Vlad dined serenely amid an army of defeated warriors who were writhing in agony on impaled poles. At a later time, he had a reported 20,000 people impaled and displayed outside the city of Targoviste. The sight was so horrific that, when confronted with the thousands of decaying bodies being picked apart by crows, the invading Ottoman Sultan, Mehmed II, turned tail and headed back to Constantinople.[56]

Beginning in the late fifteenth century, the Spanish Inquisition used torture to terrify heretics to admit heretical practices. A thousand years earlier, Pope Gregory I had ordered judges not to accept any statement made under torture (although he remained comfortable with burning heretics alive).[57] But Friar Tomás de Torquemada, the first Inquisitor-General, believed that the devil had to be driven out of the body of heretics by force. He and others of similar persuasion devised a series of the most extreme suffering to be inflicted on the victims of the Inquisition, transmogrifying interrogation of troubled souls into torture 'as a fine art'. In so doing, 'he virtually exterminated the Spanish middle class and so crippled Spanish trade that it never completely recovered'. Among many other acts, changing one's underwear on a Saturday or cutting the fat off meat was clear evidence of heresy.[58]

Sometimes the intent behind terrorism is to retain power, while in other instances it is an attempt to overthrow a regime and seize power, whether on the basis of religious or ideological motivations. The Gunpowder Plot of 1605, the aim of which was to restore a Catholic to the throne of England, is sometimes cast as a planned act of terrorism. Poorly contrived and incompetently executed, it is doubtful the Plot could ever had succeeded. But the amount of decaying explosives hidden under the House of Lords, if actually detonated, could have killed hundreds if not thousands.[59] In 2005, David Starkey claimed that the 'parallels between the actions of the plotters and modern-day terrorists are terrifying and the motivation is the same – that religion is the only important thing and that if the Government does not subscribe to the idea that your religion is absolute it must be removed'.[60] No stranger to controversy,[61] the historian once described the Gunpowder Plot as the Tudor equivalent of 9/11:

> Look at what the plotters did. They put one ton of gunpowder in a room underneath the Houses of Parliament. Had it gone off, it would have killed the king, the chancellor, all the important bishops and judges. It was their Twin Towers and the effect would have been immense.[62]

But the undoubted starting point for discussion of the English term *terrorism* – as opposed to acts of terror – is the French Revolution. For, as noted above, despite its origins in classical languages, we have late-eighteenth-century CE France to thank for the arrival of 'terrorism' (and 'terrorist') into English. The words derive from the terms the French came to employ during the French

---

[54] About 2,000 years earlier, the Assyrians had used impaling of prisoners below the breast bone to terrify besieged populations into surrendering. Mannix, *The History of Torture*, p. 20.

[55] Lallanilla, 'Vlad the Impaler: The real Dracula was absolutely vicious'.

[56] Ibid.

[57] T. O'Connor, 'Our Legal Heritage: Gregory IX, the cat-killing pope who laid down the law', *Irish Legal News*, 14 October 2022, at: https://bit.ly/3VT4xWL.

[58] Mannix, *The History of Torture*, pp. 59, 61.

[59] A. Sherwin, 'Gunpowder plotters get their wish, 400 years on', *The Times*, 31 October 2005.

[60] N. Britten, 'Gunpowder Plot was England's 9/11, says historian', *Daily Telegraph*, 22 April 2005, at: https://bit.ly/3FRpx6n.

[61] See, e.g., H. Siddique, 'David Starkey says sorry for "deplorably inflammatory" remarks', *The Guardian*, 6 July 2020, at: https://bit.ly/45t30ZY.

[62] Britten, 'Gunpowder Plot was England's 9/11, says historian'.

Revolution to describe the newly installed Republican government's elimination of its vanquished monarchist foes and violent repression of its 'counter-revolutionary' enemies. Revolutionary goals were usually pursued through capital punishment at the guillotine.[63] On other occasions, revolutionary justice would be meted out on the streets in massacres at the hands of roving mobs.[64]

The Reign of Terror (*le Règne de la Terreur*, or simply '*la Terreur*') traversed two main periods, a first in 1792 and the second – the 'Great Terror'[65] – in 1793–94.[66] It was a 'gruesome and protracted' period of State violence, one that 'set the political tone for much of the use of these words ever since'.[67] Central to the Great Terror – its 'charter' in the words of the historian Simon Schama – was the Law of Suspects, a decree passed on 17 September 1793 by the euphemistically named 'Committee of Public Safety' (as illustrated on the cover of this book).[68] The Law authorized the creation of revolutionary tribunals to try those suspected of treason against the Republic and to punish the convicted with death.[69] Even hoarding food staples would be made a capital offence, while the criteria for arrest were so 'elastic' that the prisons would swell to around 7,000 in Paris alone.[70] The Committee of Public Safety would swiftly become the most concentrated State machine France had ever experienced, with revolutionary leaders engaging in 'unconscionable slaughter'.[71]

Indeed, Robespierre and the other revolutionary delegates to the French National Convention elected to draft the new Constitution had adopted terror as overt State policy.[72] Speaking before the Convention, the young jurist declared: 'Terror is merely justice; prompt, severe, and inflexible. It is therefore an emanation of virtue, and results from the application of democracy to the most pressing needs of the country.'[73] But terror was not only cruel by design – it was also arbitrary and vengeful in its application as Hibbert illustrates:

> Hundreds of innocent people suffered with those whom the Revolutionary Tribunal had some cause to consider guilty, some of them through clerical and administrative errors, or even

---

[63] The guillotine was a contraption that was 'brought to market' by a French physician (on the basis of the work of another surgeon at the College of Physicians). Ironically, it was intended as an act of relative mercy to its victims. Although personally opposed to capital punishment, Dr Joseph-Ignace Guillotin argued that decapitation by a lightning-quick machine would be more humane and egalitarian than sword and axe beheadings, which were often botched. Indeed, some among the public audiences for executions derided the guillotine as being excessively humane. R. Schurr, *Fatal Purity: Robespierre and the French Revolution*, Vintage Books, London, 2007, pp. 134, 201, 202; and see E. Andrews, '8 Things You May Not Know about the Guillotine', *History*, Last updated 30 August 2018, at: https://bit.ly/3qSuurC. More recently, Sophie Wahnich seemingly bemoans the 'limitations of the guillotine's lack of cruelty'. S. Wahnich, *In Defence of the Terror: Liberty or Death in the French Revolution* (Trans. by D. Fernbach), Verso, United Kingdom, 2012, p. 86.

[64] In her 2012 polemic, Wahnich argues that the Terror was actually a means by which the State sought to restrain the risk of unfettered mob violence, a 'deliberate self-constraint'. In her view, 'vengeance is not a more archaic form of justice than penal justice, but a form of justice corresponding to a different social configuration'. Wahnich, *In Defence of the Terror*, pp. 41 and 97; and *cf.* also pp. 51, 53, 59, 62, 65, 74, and 97. 'Revolutionary terror is not terrorism' she affirms. She does, though, concede that: 'Classically, it is easier to open a cycle of vengeance than to close it . . .'. Ibid., pp. 102 and 71.

[65] Wahnich, *In Defence of the Terror*, p. 57.

[66] Entry for 'la Terreur', *Larousse*, accessed 1 January 2022, at: https://bit.ly/3r1wlsW. See also Schurr, *Fatal Purity*, p. 258.

[67] 'The History of the Word "Terrorism"', *Merriam-Webster*, accessed 1 January 2022, at: https://bit.ly/3r5M61Q.

[68] S. Schama, *Citizens: A Chronicle of the French Revolution*, Penguin, United Kingdom, 2004, p. 651.

[69] 'The Law of Suspects', Liberty, Equality, Fraternity: Exploring the French Revolution, accessed 30 March 2022 at: https://bit.ly/3ISPDrf.

[70] Schama, *Citizens*, pp. 641, 670.

[71] Ibid., pp. 642–43 and 669.

[72] In a further irony, Robespierre himself had earlier pleaded for an end to the death penalty, before embracing it wholeheartedly as an essential Revolutionary tool. Schurr, *Fatal Purity*, pp. 134, 234.

[73] Cited by Schurr, *Fatal Purity*, p. 275.

because their accusers chose not to spare them. Others were denounced by jealous or vindictive neighbours. One victim was fetched from prison to face a charge which had been brought against another prisoner with a similar name. Her protests were silenced by the prosecutor who said casually, 'Since she's here, we might as well take her'.[74]

With dozens being guillotined daily at certain times – a macabre record was thirty-two severed heads in only twenty-five minutes[75] – terror was, Robespierre claimed, only a weapon of oppression when in the hands of despots.[76] In similarly noted language, Saint-Just, the political philosopher and fellow revolutionary leader, declared that the republic 'consists in the extermination of everything that opposes it'.[77] By 1794, however, delegates became increasingly fearful that they too would become victims to the orchestrated and seemingly relentless bloodletting from Robespierre and his Jacobin club allies.[78] As the revolutionary regime lapsed into factionalism, they accused Robespierre of criminal abuse of power (which, without a hint of irony, they called '*terrorisme*') and sent him to the guillotine.[79]

The term in French entered the *Dictionnaire de l'Académie française*, already in its fifth edition, in 1798 to describe a 'system, regime of terror'.[80] But despite its use in English since the French Revolution, only in Noah Webster's final revision of his famous dictionary (the edition of 1840) would he include a definition of terrorism: 'TERRORISM, n. A state of being terrified, or a state impressing terror'.

That same edition of 1840 also saw the addition of the word 'terrorist', drawing on the definition in the *Dictionnaire de l'Académie française*, with similarly explicit references to the French Revolutionary period: 'TERRORIST, n. [Fr. terroriste.] (Fr. Hist.) An agent or partisan of the revolutionary tribunal during the reign of terror in France'.[81] More than 130 years later, in 1973, a further meaning connected to terrorism was added to the relevant entry in Merriam-Webster's dictionary:[82] 'violent or destructive acts (such as bombing) committed by groups in order to intimidate a population or government into granting their demands'.[83] North American language and culture were thus placing non-State actors front and centre as the architects of terror.

The *Oxford English Dictionary* has retained the original sense of terrorism pertaining to the French Revolution, but likewise offers a second, more general meaning: 'A policy intended to strike with terror those against whom it is adopted; the employment of methods of intimidation; the fact of terrorizing or condition of being terrorized.'[84] More succinct is the corresponding definition in the *Cambridge English Dictionary*: '(threats of) violent action for political purposes'.[85]

---

[74] C. Hibbert, *The French Revolution*, Penguin, London, 1982, p. 227.

[75] Schama, *Citizens*, p. 661.

[76] Cited by Schurr, *Fatal Purity*, p. 275. Saint-Just would declare that opposition to the Terror was one of the three 'deadly sins' against the republic. Ibid., p. 276.

[77] Schama, *Citizens*, p. 665.

[78] R. Peckham, *Fear*, Profile Books, London, 2023, pp. 84–85. On 31 March 1794, Robespierre declared ominously before the Convention that 'anyone who trembles at this moment is culpable'.

[79] See S. Spector, 'The meaning of "terrorism"', OUP Blog entry, 18 November 2015, at: https://bit.ly/3qbmYaN.

[80] *Dictionnaire de l'Académie française*, 5th ed., 1798, Vol. I, p. 775, at: https://bit.ly/3rFAEdw. As Peckham observes, Denis Diderot's *Encyclopédie*, published in a series of volumes beginning in 1751, had defined terror as an emotion that heightened other people's suffering, linking it with compassion and pity. Peckham, *Fear*, p. 81.

[81] Spector, 'The meaning of "terrorism"'.

[82] Merriam-Webster is the oldest publisher of American English in the United States.

[83] Spector, 'The meaning of "terrorism"'.

[84] 'Terrorism', in *Oxford English Dictionary*, 2nd ed. (1989), at: https://bit.ly/33BQzle.

[85] Online Cambridge English dictionary, definition taken from *Cambridge Advanced Learner's Dictionary & Thesaurus*, Cambridge University Press, at: https://bit.ly/3uqi3FE.

In the twentieth century, the Nazis engaged in terrorism as State policy on an unparalleled scale across Europe both prior to and during the Second World War. While it may seem inappropriate to engage in comparative analysis, among the many pogroms perpetrated since the French Revolution, the terror inflicted by the Nazis across Europe beginning in the late 1930s and through to their ultimate defeat in April 1945 is totemic.[86] The Holocaust against the Jews is the greatest single crime of human history. In Eastern Europe, the atrocities perpetrated by the *Einsatzgruppen*, the Schutzstaffel (SS) paramilitary death squads, were based, in Benjamin Ferencz's words, on 'the principles of unmitigated terror and murder'.[87] In concluding his opening remarks for the prosecution in the trial of a chosen twenty-three of their commanders, which opened in September 1947, he stated:

> The judgment of the International Military Tribunal declares that two million Jews were murdered by the Einsatzgruppen and other units of the Security Police.[88] The defendants in the dock were the cruel executioners, whose terror wrote the blackest page in human history. Death was their tool and life their toy. If these men be immune, then law has lost its meaning and man must live in fear.[89]

Hitler's nemesis, Joseph Stalin, had himself perpetrated massacres on a massive scale in the 1930s. The Great Purge, also known as the 'Great Terror' (a retrospective term which historians have borrowed from the French Revolution),[90] was Stalin's campaign in 1936–38 to eliminate dissent within the Communist Party and anyone else he deemed a threat to his leadership. Although estimates vary widely, as many as 750,000 people are believed to have been executed and more than a million others were dispatched to gulags (forced labour camps).[91] Stalin signed a decree making families liable for crimes committed by a husband or father, meaning that children as young as twelve could be subject to the death penalty. As many as 81 of the 103 generals and admirals in the Soviet Union were executed, initially rendering the Soviet armed forces unable to resist Operation Barbarossa, the German invasion of Russia in 1941.[92] Millions of Soviet citizens would die unnecessarily as a result.

A Brief History of Terrorism since the Second World War

Outside the Soviet Union, terrorism persisted – and in many instances flourished – after the end of the Second World War. Sometimes terror has been the work of organs or agents of the State, while in other instances non-State armed groups have been its primary instigators. The targets have been political opponents, ethnic minorities, and adherents of other religions. Since then, however, the perception has become widespread that terrorism is primarily the work of non-State armed groups, a tendency that has been accentuated by prominent attacks in recent decades.

---

[86] In perhaps a subconscious throwback to the French Revolution, Hitler made the guillotine a State method of execution in Germany during the Third Reich. According to Nazi records, the guillotine was used to execute some 16,500 people between 1933 and 1945, many of them resistance fighters and political dissidents. Andrews, '8 Things You May Not Know about the Guillotine'.

[87] B. B. Ferencz, Opening Statement for the Prosecution in *United States of America* v. *Otto Ohlendorf and others*, *Trial of the Major War Criminals*, Vol. IV (1947), Nuremberg, at http://bit.ly/2JUPiLN, p. 36.

[88] *Trial of the Major War Criminals*, Vol. I (1947), Nuremberg, p. 292.

[89] Ferencz, Opening Statement for the Prosecution in *United States of America* v. *Otto Ohlendorf and others*, p. 53.

[90] L. Siegelbaum, 'The Great Terror', Seventeen Moments in Soviet History, at: https://bit.ly/35HSTYx.

[91] In 1989, with the Cold War over, a Soviet report alleged that twenty million had died as direct victims of Stalin. 'Major Soviet Paper Says 20 Million Died as Victims of Stalin', *The New York Times*, 4 February 1989, at: https://nyti.ms/3JotbNl.

[92] 'Great Purge', History, last updated on 7 July 2020, at: https://bit.ly/3HuHVUf.

14   *Introduction*

The 9/11 attacks made al-Qaeda the 'exemplar' of global terrorism in the first decade of the twenty-first century; in this it was replaced in the second decade by Islamic State.[93] Accordingly, although the origin of the term *terrorism* was State action, it has broadened to encompass any group that uses terror tactics as its modus operandi.

Genocide, the term coined by Raphael Lemkin in 1944 to describe the Holocaust against the Jews, was formally outlawed by United Nations treaty four years later.[94] But this 'odious scourge', as the Preamble to the 1948 Genocide Convention terms an attempt by a State or an armed group to destroy a minority group, would not be outlawed in practice. Since 1945, genocide has been perpetrated against, among others, Mayans in Guatemala (in 1982–83); Kurds in Iraq (in February–September 1988); Tutsis in Rwanda (in April–July 1994); Muslims in Bosnia and Herzegovina (in July 1995); Darfurians (belonging to Fur, Masalit and Zaghawa groups) in Sudan (in 2003–08); Yazidis in Iraq (in 2014–16); and Rohingya in Myanmar (in October 2016–January 2017 and subsequently). Wherever genocide has been perpetrated, terror is invariably at its heart.

The genocide in Rwanda in 1994 is perhaps the most notorious example of the second half of the twentieth century of the international 'crime of crimes'. Based on detailed analysis of data for one province, Verpoorten has estimated that between 600,000 and 800,000 Tutsis were murdered, with only some 30 per cent of the pre-genocide Tutsi population surviving.[95] Machetes were the weapon of choice for many of the Hutus responsible, particularly the *Interahamwe* militia.

Félicien Kabuga, a Rwandan businessman arrested in Paris in May 2020, had gone on trial before the UN Residual Mechanism that followed the closure of the International Criminal Tribunal for Rwanda (ICTR) accused of assisting and inciting the perpetration of genocide.[96] It had been widely reported that, in the months leading up to the genocide, 581 tonnes of machetes were imported by supporters of the Habyarimana regime. Mr Kabuga was accused of using his companies to import vast quantities of machetes for supply to the *génocidaires* for the purpose of genocide.[97] Although the charges relating to the importation of the machetes were later dropped (with the requisite mens rea difficult to prove), the prosecution was seeking to sustain in fact and in law that Kabuga was directly responsible for the content of broadcasts on Radio-Télévision des mille collines that incited genocide; that he provided moral, logistical, material, and financial support to the *Interahamwe* in the capital, Kigali, and in the prefectures of Gisenyi and Kibuye; and that he distributed machetes to the *Interahamwe* with complicit genocidal intent.[98] But in June 2023, Mr Kabuga's dementia brought the trial to a premature halt. In August, judges in the Appeals Chamber rejected an 'alternative finding procedure' whose aim would have been to provide some measure of justice for the victims. The Trial Chamber was instructed to impose an indefinite stay of proceedings 'in view of Mr Kabuga's lack of fitness to stand trial'.[99]

---

[93]   D. Fidler, 'Nuclear, biological and chemical terrorism in international law', chap. 10 in B. Saul (ed.), *Research Handbook on International Law and Terrorism*, 2nd ed., p. 94.

[94]   Convention on the Prevention and Punishment of the Crime of Genocide; adopted at Paris, 9 December 1948; entered into force, 12 January 1951. As of 1 January 2024, 153 States were party to the Convention, the latest to adhere being Zambia in April 2022.

[95]   M. Verpoorten, 'The Death Toll of the Rwandan Genocide: A Detailed Analysis for Gikongoro Province', *Population*, Vol. 60, No.4 (2005), 331–67, at: https://bit.ly/35GAzyX.

[96]   United Nations International Residual Mechanism for Criminal Tribunals, 'KABUGA, Félicien (MICT-13–38)', accessed 1 March 2023, at: https://bit.ly/3AZtEN4.

[97]   A. Guichaoua, 'Did machete imports to Rwanda prove that the genocide against the Tutsi was planned?', The Conversation, 2 September 2020, at: https://bit.ly/34BNO3E.

[98]   E. Rugiririza and E. S. Ruvugiro, 'Why Kabuga Is No Longer Accused of Importing Machetes for Genocide', Justice Info, 30 March 2021, at: https://bit.ly/3orug8U.

[99]   'Rwanda genocide suspect Kabuga should not face trial, UN judges say', *Aljazeera*, 7 August 2023, at: https://bit.ly/45qc4jG.

A far less well-known genocide is the slaughter of indigenous Mayans in Guatemala in the early 1980s. In the 1970s, the Maya had been protesting against the country's repressive government, calling for greater equality and inclusion of the Mayan language and culture. In 1980, the Guatemalan army instituted 'Operation Sophia',[100] which sought to end an insurgency by destroying the civilian base in which the guerrillas hid. The programme specifically targeted the Mayan population.[101] Over the next three years, the army destroyed 626 villages, killed or forcibly disappeared more than 200,000 people, and displaced a further 1.5 million internally. The army's scorched-earth policy involved the destruction or burning of buildings and crops, the slaughter of livestock, the fouling of water supplies, and the violation of sacred places and cultural symbols. In addition to the army's special units (known as the 'Kaibiles'), private death squads were employed for the operation. The US government gave significant support to the Guatemalan regimes in furtherance of its anti-Communist campaigns during the Cold War.[102] In February 1999, the UN-supported Commission of Historical Clarification released its report, *Guatemala: Memory of Silence*, which concluded the army had committed genocide against four specific groups: the Ixil Mayas; the Q'anjob'al and Chuj Mayas; the K'iche' Mayas of Joyabaj, Zacualpa, and Chiché; and the Achi Mayas.[103]

Terror has also been a common feature of crimes against humanity, that is to say, crimes committed in the course of a widespread or systematic attack against a civilian population. One of the means by which terror is perpetrated is in the course of indiscriminate bombing, whether that occurs within or outside international armed conflicts. Vietnam is one of the best known examples of a conflict where all sides carried out atrocities. North Vietnamese regular forces and Vietcong guerrillas engaged in widespread and systematic acts of terror across South Vietnam. For most of this period, the US Air Force was bombing North Vietnam as well as neighbouring Cambodia and Laos, cumulatively dropping more bombs than were used in the whole of the Second World War. Millions were killed or seriously injured, the majority civilians. Ground offensives in South Vietnam also killed many women and children. During the Tet offensive in 1968, one US commander is reported to have uttered the memorable phrase (or something akin to it): 'It became necessary to destroy the town in order to save it.'[104] The US bombing of Cambodia would give rise to the Khmer Rouge, whose Kampuchean regime under Pol Pot would see another two million murdered.

Terrorism would also flourish at home in the United States. But as Brian Michael Jenkins remarks, and despite the heavy toll of 9/11, the incidence of terrorism has declined dramatically since the 1970s. In that decade, 1,470 separate acts of terrorism unfolded within the nation's borders and 184 people were killed.[105] As Jenkins further noted:

Terrorists perfected their tactical repertoire in the 1970s. They employed six basic tactics, some of which had been practised for centuries: assassination, bombing, kidnapping, airline hijacking,

---

[100] See, e.g., 'Operation Sofia: Documenting Genocide in Guatemala', National Security Archive Electronic Briefing Book No. 297, Posted on 2 December 2009, at: https://bit.ly/3ouUO9s.

[101] Holocaust Museum Houston, 'Genocide in Guatemala', at: https://bit.ly/35Xek5f.

[102] Ibid.

[103] Commission of Historical Clarification, *Guatemala: Memory of Silence*, Report, February 1999: Conclusions and Recommendations, at: https://bit.ly/3B4tvrN.

[104] S. L. Carter, 'Destroying a Quote's History in Order to Save It', *Bloomberg Opinion*, 9 February 2018, at: https://bloom.bg/3J8GFqx. Peckham describes the inversion of the 1789 Declaration of the Rights of Man and of the Citizen, just a month after its promulgation by the National Assembly in France, to justify State terror against 'malefactors' who contravened those rights. Peckham, *Fear*, p. 87.

[105] B. M. Jenkins, 'The 1970s and the Birth of Contemporary Terrorism', Blog entry, The RAND Blog, 30 July 2015, at: https://bit.ly/35OAdqe.

16 *Introduction*

barricaded hostage situations and armed assaults. Assassination had emerged as a terrorist tactic in the 11th century. With the invention of dynamite in the 19th century, terrorist bombings became increasingly common – and remain the most common terrorist tactic.[106]

Palestinian groups and those supportive of the Palestinians engaged in terror attacks around the world from the early 1970s. The killing of Israeli athletes at the Munich Olympic Games in 1972 was only one of a number of incidents that shocked the world.[107] Members of the Black September group stormed the athletes' apartment in the Olympic Village, killing two of the group and taking nine others hostage. In return for the release of the hostages, they demanded that Israel release more than 230 Arab prisoners being held in Israeli jails as well as two German terrorists. In a later shootout at Munich airport, all nine Israeli hostages were killed along with five terrorists and one West German policeman.[108]

Carlos 'the Jackal', whose real name is Ilich Ramírez Sánchez, is a Venezuelan national currently serving a life sentence in prison in France for terrorist offences under French law. In September 2021, the life sentence given to the Marxist supporter of the Palestinian cause four years earlier for a deadly grenade attack on a Paris shop in 1974 was confirmed. A member of the Popular Front for the Liberation of Palestine at the time, Carlos denied responsibility for the attack at his trial. Prosecutor Remi Crosson du Cormier declared that democracy had 'two principal enemies – totalitarianism and terrorism', suggesting that Mr Ramírez Sánchez was among those 'who threaten democracy by their actions'. At his trial he told the judge, 'Yes, I have regrets – because I'm kind-hearted – that I did not kill people I should have killed.'[109]

Carlos, now in his early seventies, is serving separate life sentences for the murders in 1975 of two French policemen and a police informer, as well as for a series of bombings in Paris and Marseille in 1982 and 1983 that killed eleven people and left dozens more injured.[110] Carlos had become one of the world's most wanted fugitives as a result of leading the attack in Vienna in 1975 on a meeting of the OPEC (Organization of the Petroleum Exporting Countries) oil cartel.[111] The 'Arm of the Arab Revolution' group called for the liberation of Palestine. The targeting of Arab leaders led to their becoming rather more supportive of the development of both counterterrorism efforts and counterterrorism law under UN auspices.[112]

In the United States, the Oklahoma City bombing of April 1995 had been perpetrated by a domestic terrorist, Timothy McVeigh.[113] It was the worst act of home-grown terrorism in the nation's history, with 168 people killed, including 19 children, and hundreds more injured.[114] Six years later, the attacks on the United States by al-Qaeda changed the world. In the four aircraft

---

[106] Ibid.

[107] Although, as Ben Saul observes, it was not characterized as terrorism by the UN Security Council and no action was taken of 'Terrorism' in the UN Security Council, *Chinese Journal of International Law*, Vol. 4, No. 1 (2005), 141–66, *esp.* at p. 143.

[108] 'Massacre begins at Munich Olympics: 5 September 1972', *History*, at: https://bit.ly/3HmGtmV.

[109] Associated Press, 'Unrepentant "Carlos the Jackal" sentenced to life for deadly grenade attack on Paris in 1974', *The National Post*, 28 March 2017.

[110] France24, 'Paris court upholds life sentence for "Carlos the Jackal" in 1974 grenade attack', 23 September 2021, at: https://bit.ly/3L7Z1JY.

[111] R. Russell, 'Carlos the Jackal seeks reduced sentence for deadly 1974 Paris attack', *Sky News*, 22 September 2021, at: https://bit.ly/3Gm45ql.

[112] B. Blumenau, *The United Nations and Terrorism: Germany, Multilateralism, and Antiterrorism Efforts in the 1970s*, Palgrave Macmillan, United Kingdom, 2014, p. 123.

[113] McVeigh claimed that the building in Oklahoma City was targeted to avenge the more than seventy deaths (most of whom were burned alive) at the Branch Davidian religious sect in Waco, Texas, in 1993 when it was stormed by the FBI. See, e.g., S. Pruitt, 'How Ruby Ridge and Waco Led to the Oklahoma City Bombing', *History*, Last updated 2 April 2020, at: https://bit.ly/35Wd4SP.

[114] FBI, 'Oklahoma City Bombing', accessed 1 February 2022 at: https://bit.ly/3sdFEGB.

A Brief History of Terrorism

hijacked by the 19 terrorists, in the twin towers of the World Trade Center into which two of the aircraft crashed, and at the Pentagon, a cumulative total of almost 3,000 people from more than ninety nations died and thousands more were injured.[115] al-Qaeda, which means 'the Base' in Arabic, had already engaged in acts of terror in Africa, with the bombings of the US embassies in Nairobi and Dar es Salam on 7 August 1998. A total of 224 people died in the blasts and more than 4,500 were wounded, the vast majority Africans.[116]

Islamic State grew out of the unlawful invasion of Iraq in 2003 that was led by the United States with the support of a number of military allies, including the United Kingdom. In the run-up to the invasion, the United States had spoken before the UN Security Council of the significance of Abu Musab al-Zarqawi, a Jordanian national. In making the case for war in Iraq, Secretary of State Colin Powell mistakenly identified him as a crucial link between al-Qaeda and Saddam Hussein's regime. In fact, he was not even formally a member of al-Qaeda at the time, reportedly being closer to a number of Iranian groups.[117] But al-Zarqawi would go on to exploit his new-found prominence on the global stage to create al-Qaeda in Iraq. He was killed by a US drone strike in June 2006, shortly after the group had been rebranded the Islamic State of Iraq.[118] His would be a deadly legacy, for the organization he founded would evolve under the intellectual leadership of his number two, Abu Ali al-Anbari, into one that would drive Iraqi security forces out of key cities in Western Iraq, beginning with Fallujah in December 2013.[119]

In 2014, the group, by then renamed 'Islamic State', captured Mosul in Nineveh governorate. Islamic State was now being led by Abu Bakr al-Baghdadi, after the death of Abu Omar al-Baghdadi at the hands of Iraqi and US forces in a joint operation in April 2010.[120] On 4 July 2014, Abu Bakr al-Baghdadi had declared the establishment of an Islamic caliphate from the pulpit of Mosul's medieval al-Nuri mosque.[121] A month later, the 'Sinjar massacre' marked the beginning of genocide of Yazidis by Islamic State, with the killing and abduction of thousands of Yazidi men, women, and children in Sinjar city and the surrounding Sinjar district in Nineveh.[122]

Islamic State's reach penetrated deep into Syria with its nominal headquarters established in Raqqa. At its peak in January 2015, Islamic State controlled an area across Syria and Iraq equivalent to the size of the United Kingdom and had attracted tens of thousands of foreign fighters to its cause.[123] Its brutality was legendary. In November 2014, the Independent International Commission of Inquiry on the Syrian Arab Republic established by the UN Human Rights Council issued a report entitled 'Rule of Terror: Living under ISIS in Syria', in which it described Islamic State as a terrorist group that had 'become synonymous with extreme violence directed against civilians and captured fighters'.[124] It stated:

---

[115] 9/11 Memorial & Museum, '9/11 FAQs', accessed 1 February 2022 at: https://bit.ly/3gpEaDC.

[116] FBI, 'East African Embassy Bombings', accessed 1 February 2022 at: https://bit.ly/3uqMKdK.

[117] M. A. Weaver, 'The Short, Violent Life of Abu Musab al-Zarqawi', *The Atlantic*, July/August 2006, at: https://bit.ly/3rAulJL.

[118] Ibid.

[119] H. Hassan, 'The True Origins of ISIS', *The Atlantic*, 30 November 2018, at: https://bit.ly/3L8nkY8. In March 2016, Anbari was killed near the Syrian city of Shaddadi, along the border with Iraq. American soldiers are said to have tried to capture him in a raid but he blew himself up using a suicide belt.

[120] W. Ibrahim, 'Al Qaeda's two top Iraq leaders killed in raid', *Reuters*, 19 April 2010, at: https://reut.rs/3JoitQQ. Abu Bakr al-Baghdadi had pledged allegiance to al-Zarqawi in 2005.

[121] 'Who was ISIL's self-proclaimed leader Abu Bakr al-Baghdadi?', *Aljazeera*, 27 October 2019, at: https://bit.ly/3Hw5jRe.

[122] International Organization for Migration (IOM), 'Seven Years on from Sinjar Massacre, VR Film Honours Victims and Advocates for the Yazidi Community's Recovery', 3 August 2021, at: https://bit.ly/3urgMxJ.

[123] Ibid.

[124] Report of the Independent International Commission of Inquiry on the Syrian Arab Republic, Rule of Terror: Living under ISIS in Syria, UN doc. A/HRC/27/CRP.3, 19 November 2014, para. 1.

18 *Introduction*

> Civilians, including men, women and children, ethnic and religious minorities who remain in ISIS-controlled areas live in fear. Victims and witnesses that fled consistently described being subjected to acts that terrorise and aim to silence the population. . . . ISIS has beheaded, shot and stoned men, women and children in public spaces in towns and villages across north-eastern Syria. . . . By orchestrating systematic harm against a civilian population, ISIS has demonstrated its capacity and intent to wilfully apply measures of intimidation and terror, such as violence to life and inhuman treatment inflicting great suffering and injury to bodily integrity.[125]

Islamic State's overwhelming military defeat in Iraq and Syria in 2017 did not, however, end its use of terror tactics. According to the Syrian Observatory for Human Rights, at least 600 people were killed in dozens of attacks by Islamic State in Syria in 2021.[126] In Iraq, a double-suicide bombing in January in central Baghdad and a suicide bombing in July in Sadr city each killed more than thirty people.[127] In February 2022, its (then) latest leader, Abu Ibrahim al-Hashimi al-Qurayshi, was killed in the course of a US raid in Syria; he was reported to have detonated a suicide vest, killing his own children in the process.[128] In November 2022, Islamic State announced the appointment of his successor, Abu al-Husain al-Husaini al-Quraishi.[129] He in turn was killed only a few days later, in Syria.[130]

In Syria, the violent repression of peaceful protests during the Arab Spring led to civil war, and terror was a tactic routinely employed by the regime in Damascus. In February 2021, Eyad al-Gharib was convicted and sentenced to fifty-four months' imprisonment for aiding and abetting crimes against humanity. He had arrested anti-Assad protesters who were then transported to the Al-Khatib centre, a facility known as 'Hell on Earth'.[131] In January 2022, a German court sentenced a fifty-eight-year-old Syrian colonel, Anwar Raslan, to life in prison for crimes against humanity for his role in the torture of more than 4,000 people in the same facility. The court heard how detainees were beaten and doused in cold water. Others were raped or hung from the ceiling for hours on end. Torturers tore out the fingernails of their victims and administered electric shocks. One survivor told the media he could hear the screams of people being tortured all day, every day. Thousands died from their suffering.[132]

As this brief historical overview has illustrated, sometimes terrorism is directed at the general population or a segment of it, or a particular minority, while at others it is aimed at a nation's leadership. Peaceful protest is never to be deemed terrorism under international law, even though it is treated as such in a number of repressive national jurisdictions. Always relevant is the unlawful, often barbaric nature of the act and the intent of the perpetrator, whether that is expressed verbally or in writing or where it is otherwise manifest. These issues are explored in Chapter 1.

Debate though continues to surround the extent to which international law should address the conduct of State actors as terrorism. The United States is at the vanguard of those arguing that

---

[125] Ibid., paras. 19, 32, 45.
[126] S. Kajjo, 'Analysts: Islamic State Poised for More Attacks in Syria in 2022', Voice of America, 4 January 2022, at: https://bit.ly/3LdptBN.
[127] C. Bunzel, 'Explainer: The Islamic State in 2021', Wilson Center, 10 December 2021, at: https://bit.ly/3sbBC1w.
[128] D. Vergun, 'Leader of ISIS Dead Following U.S. Raid in Syria', *DOD News*, 3 February 2022, at: https://bit.ly/300gWSY.
[129] E. Kourdi, 'ISIS acknowledges the death of its leader, announces his successor', CNN, 30 November 2022, at: http://bit.ly/3XKqKWf.
[130] C. Lister, 'ISIS leader's death raises intriguing questions', Middle East Institute, 5 December 2022, at: http://bit.ly/3KlhWmG.
[131] C. Otto, T. Qiblawi, and S. Halasz, 'In world first, Germany convicts Syrian regime officer of crimes against humanity', CNN, Updated 24 February 2021, at: https://cnn.it/3AVwFxG.
[132] J. Hill, 'German court finds Syrian colonel guilty of crimes against humanity', BBC, 13 January 2022, at: https://bbc.in/300rHoq.

treaties should focus on the repression of the activities of non-State actors given that other rules of international law constrain the acts of States. But for a number of other States, especially many within the Non-Aligned Movement (NAM),[133] the actions of States (and particularly the United States) should also be the focus of attention and not those armed groups representing peoples engaged in a struggle for national liberation. Already in 1973, many States were arguing in the United Nations that State terrorism 'was the most harmful, noxious, cruel, pernicious or dangerous form of terrorism'.[134]

As a matter of law, it is clear that any entity (State or non-State) and indeed any individual can engage in terrorism, even absent membership of or adherence to an existing terrorist group. It is primarily the *intent* of the salient individual, group, or entity that distinguishes an 'ordinary' crime of murder from a terror attack. That intent may be expressed or it may be inferred from the nature and consequences of the act or acts that are perpetrated. And what is clear from practice is that terrorism may even be perpetrated when a State is ostensibly engaged in counterterrorism. Indiscriminate violence and, a fortiori, violence targeted at civilians is evidence of terror tactics. Such violence can occur on land, at sea, in the air, and even in cyberspace.

---

[133] Serbia's Ministry of Foreign Affairs explains that the Non-Aligned Movement 'emerged as an expression of the efforts of a large number of developing countries, mostly in the process of decolonisation, as a kind of political alternative to avoid opting for one military-political bloc during the Cold War division of the world and articulate an independent foreign policy approach'. The first Conference of Non-Aligned Countries was held in 1961 in Belgrade at the initiative of the Socialist Federal Republic of Yugoslavia (SFRY), to which Serbia is the successor State. During the Cold War, the Non-Aligned Movement 'played a significant role in preserving peace and calming the competition between the two blocks, and especially in accelerating the decolonisation process'. Republic of Serbia Ministry of Foreign Affairs, 'The Non-Aligned Movement', accessed 1 February 2022 at: https://bit.ly/3GOhA2z.

[134] B. Saul, 'United Nations Measures to Address the "Root Causes" and "Conditions Conducive" to Terrorism, and to Prevent Violent Extremism: 1972–2019', chap. 37 in B. Saul (ed.), *Research Handbook on International Law and Terrorism*, 2nd ed., pp. 532–33.

1

Defining Terrorism in International Law

1.1 INTRODUCTION

No unitary definition of terrorism exists in international law and it is unlikely that States will agree upon one in the future.[1] The salient definition (or definitions) that pertains to any set of facts is to be determined by reference to the prevailing context as well as to the nature of the criminal conduct itself. Hence, when considering how contemporary international law defines terrorism, it is first necessary to interrogate the specific scenario at issue. If a terrorist act is committed in peacetime, is it an act of international terrorism or of domestic terrorism? If instead terrorism in a situation of armed conflict is at issue, does this involve the perpetration of acts against persons detained by the enemy or against civilians by use of force in the conduct of hostilities? Each of these scenarios evinces particularities in the contours of terrorism under international law.

Fifty years ago, an unnamed State representative observed in relation to the definition of international terrorism that *omnis definitio in lege periculosa*[2] – 'every legal definition is perilous' in the vernacular. Yet the absence of a clear definition is indeed 'a normative black hole', and one that is not without consequence. For how, Saul asks, can the United Nations (UN) Security Council, 'credibly, and with a straight face', designate all terrorism as a threat to international peace and security and require legal measures to be taken against it, without explaining what it is?[3] The myriad obligations imposed upon States by Security Council Resolution 1373 pertain to 'terrorism' and 'terrorists' and thus the terms have 'operative legal significance'.[4]

Moreover, when – or rather *if* – the Comprehensive Convention against International Terrorism[5] is finally concluded by States,[6] it will not be all-encompassing, its claimed

---

[1] K. Ambos, 'Amicus Curiae brief on the question of the applicable terrorism offence in the proceedings before the Special Tribunal for Lebanon, with a particular focus on a "special" special intent and/or a special motive as additional subjective requirements', Special Tribunal for Lebanon (Re. Case No. STL-11-0111), Scheduling Order of the President, 21 January 2011, at: https://bit.ly/3sz5ipq, p. 6, para. 7.

[2] Report of the Ad Hoc Committee on International Terrorism, UN doc. A/9028, UN General Assembly, New York, 1973, at: https://bit.ly/3HLz54T, para. 35.

[3] B. Saul, *The Legal Black Hole in United Nations Counterterrorism*, IPI Observatory, New York, 2 June 2021, at: https://bit.ly/3GTe8nn.

[4] B. Saul, 'Definition of "Terrorism" in the UN Security Council', *Chinese Journal of International Law*, Vol. 4, No. 1 (2005), 141–66, *esp.* at pp. 159–60.

[5] Draft comprehensive convention against international terrorism, Coordinator's draft text, Appendix II to UN doc. A/59/894, 12 August 2005, at: http://bit.ly/2sVRhYm (hereafter, 2005 Draft Comprehensive Convention against International Terrorism).

[6] Writing back in 2006, for instance, Nuotio had claimed overoptimistically that the Ad Hoc Committee was 'relatively close to reaching an agreement' on the definition of international terrorism for the purpose of the Comprehensive

1.2 Defining International Terrorism in Peacetime

'comprehensive' scope notwithstanding. For a provision in the draft text excludes from the treaty's scope the activities of State and non-State armed forces during an armed conflict insofar as their conduct is governed by international humanitarian law (IHL). A further provision excludes application to the activities of a State's 'military force' in peacetime, insofar as the conduct is governed by other rules of international law.[7] Reflecting its proposed title – and as has typically been the case with the 'sectoral' counterterrorism conventions – what purely domestic terrorism also falls outside the purview of the Draft Comprehensive Convention against International Terrorism?[8]

In 2003, as the Introduction to this book recalled, the International Criminal Tribunal for the former Yugoslavia (ICTY) reflected that the offence of international terrorism has 'never been singly defined under international law'.[9] In its judgment in the *Galić* case, the ICTY was interested in terrorism during armed conflict (the material jurisdiction imposed by its founding Statute), an issue covered later in this chapter. Moreover, that an act of terrorism does not have a transnational element does not per se exclude the application of IHL.

This chapter thus considers the primary contexts for terrorism in turn. International terrorism perpetrated in peacetime is addressed first. The distinction with domestic terrorism is then clarified. Consideration next moves to terrorism committed amid a situation of armed conflict. It is already important to bear in mind, though, that under the relevant UN sectoral counterterrorism treaties, the demarcation between terrorism in peacetime and terrorism during and in connection with an armed conflict is neither strict nor especially crisp.

1.2 DEFINING INTERNATIONAL TERRORISM IN PEACETIME

1.2.1 *The Historical Background*

Early efforts to construct an overarching definition of terrorism were made prior to the Second World War under the League of Nations. The 1937 Convention for the Prevention and Punishment of Terrorism had defined 'acts of terrorism' as 'criminal acts directed against a State and intended or calculated to create a state of terror in the minds of particular persons, or a group of persons or the general public'.[10] The scope of the definition was not only limited to acts of violence against persons but also encompassed damage to (public) property.[11] The Convention's breadth of scope and the focus on terrorism directed at another State tracked the primary motivation for its elaboration – the slaying in France of the leader of another European nation three years earlier. There was no orientation with respect to the Convention's application during a state of war, but no formal exclusion either.

Four decades later, following the murder of the Israeli Olympic athletes at Munich in September 1972, the United States proposed a draft Convention for the Prevention and

---

Convention. K. Nuotio, 'Terrorism as a Catalyst for the Emergence, Harmonization and Reform of Criminal Law', *Journal of International Criminal Justice*, Vol. 4 (2006), 998–1016, at p. 1005.

[7] Art. 20(2) and (3), 2005 Draft Comprehensive Convention against International Terrorism.

[8] 'The present Convention shall not apply where the offence is committed within a single State, the alleged offender and the victims are nationals of that State, [and] the alleged offender is found in the territory of that State.' Art. 4, 2005 Draft Comprehensive Convention against International Terrorism.

[9] ICTY, *Prosecutor* v. *Galić*, Judgment (Trial Chamber) (Case No. IT-98-29-T), 5 December 2003, para. 87, note 150.

[10] Art. 1(2), Convention for the Prevention and Punishment of Terrorism; signed at Geneva, 16 November 1937; never entered into force.

[11] Art. 2(2), 1937 Convention for the Prevention and Punishment of Terrorism.

Punishment of Certain Acts of International Terrorism.[12] The heart of the 1972 US draft text was its Article 1(1), wherein it was stipulated that '[a]ny person who unlawfully kills, causes serious bodily harm or kidnaps another person ... commits an offence of international significance'. This applied where the act

- had an international element;
- was committed 'neither by or against a member of the armed forces of a State in the course of military hostilities'; and
- was 'intended to damage the interests or obtain concessions from a State or an international organization'.[13]

This is an intriguing text in a number of respects. It does not extend the notion of terrorism to damage to property or economic harm, as does the current draft of the ComprehensiveConvention against International Terrorism, but rather hones in on the infliction of bodily harm. The US draft also excluded from its scope certain conduct in hostilities in all armed conflicts (not only those which involved two States pitted against one another and thus were international in character). As a consequence, salient acts of an armed group engaged in armed struggle in furtherance of the right of a people to self-determination would have been exempted from treatment as international terrorism as long as the group was party to an armed conflict and that it targeted the armed forces of a State. Seemingly, the draft provision put forward by the United States would even have excluded from the treaty's ambit a civilian not belonging to an armed group who similarly attacked a soldier in a State armed forces. This would have been so, as long as the action occurred with sufficient nexus to the conduct of hostilities in an armed conflict.[14] The proposed provision also excluded domestic terrorism from its purview.[15]

Despite the proposed exclusions in the US draft, the formulation of international terrorism in the proposed text was generally opposed by Arab and African States as well as by China, all of whom perceived the initiative as a renewed attempt to criminalize national liberation movements.[16] A national liberation movement that was not party to an armed conflict under IHL – either for want of the requisite level of 'organization' of the armed group or owing to a lack of intensity of the violence – would still be captured by the definition of international terrorism.[17]

---

[12] 'US Draft Convention for Prevention and Punishment of Terrorism Acts', UN doc. A/C.6/L.850, reprinted in *International Legal Materials*, Vol. 11, No. 6 (November 1972), 1382–87 (hereafter, 1972 US Draft Convention for Prevention and Punishment of Terrorism Acts).

[13] Surprisingly, Friedrichs did not consider this to amount to any legal definition of international terrorism. J. Friedrichs, 'Defining the International Public Enemy: The Political Struggle behind the Legal Debate on International Terrorism', *Leiden Journal of International Law*, Vol. 19 (2006), 69–91, at p. 72.

[14] This approach is not, though, the way in which the law has developed in the sectoral treaties.

[15] Art. 1(1)(a) and (b), 1972 US Draft Convention for Prevention and Punishment of Terrorism Acts. The relevant text specifies that in order to constitute international terrorism, the salient act of violence must be committed in a State of which the offender is not a national *and* is committed against a State but outside its territory or against a person who the offender knows is not a national of the State where the attack occurs.

[16] B. Saul, 'United Nations Measures to Address the "Root Causes" and "Conditions Conducive" to Terrorism and to Prevent Violent Extremism (PVE)', Chap. 37 in Saul (ed.), *Research Handbook on International Law and Terrorism*, 2nd ed., Edward Elgar, Cheltenham, 2021, p. 531.

[17] Of course, these '*Tadić* judgment requirements for a non-international armed conflict are being transplanted even though they were only set out in the ICTY's Appeals Chamber twenty-three years later, in 1995. ICTY, *Prosecutor* v. *Tadić (aka 'Dule')*, Decision on the Defence Motion for Interlocutory Appeal on Jurisdiction (Appeals Chamber) (Case No. IT-94-1), 2 October 1995, at: https://bit.ly/2YR8mzd, para. 70. Also not yet adopted was the provision in Article 1(4) of the 1977 Additional Protocol I deeming as international in character 'armed conflicts in which peoples are fighting against colonial domination and alien occupation and against racist régimes in the exercise of their right of self-determination'. Art. 1(4), Protocol Additional to the Geneva Conventions of 12 August 1949, and relating to the Protection of Victims of International Armed Conflicts

1.2 Defining International Terrorism in Peacetime

The Non-Aligned Movement was seeking to have international law condemn Israel instead for its occupation of Palestine as well as South Africa for its policy and practice of *apartheid*.[18] The schism in the international community that persists to this day was manifest, despite occasional claims in literature that it has been largely overcome.

Seeking a compromise way forward, the UN Secretary-General at the time, Kurt Waldheim, proposed an agenda item in the General Assembly on measures to prevent terrorism.[19] UN General Resolution 3034 (XXVII) established an Ad Hoc Committee on International Terrorism,[20] one of whose tasks was to elaborate a general treaty on international terrorism. It would not be successful in this endeavour. Instead, the United Nations turned to the negotiation of more limited, sectoral treaties in order to bypass the ideological divide.

1.2.2 The Definition(s) of Terrorism in the UN Sectoral Terrorism Treaties

1.2.2.1 The Definition in the 1973 Internationally Protected Persons Convention

The 1973 Convention on Crimes against Internationally Protected Persons[21] is considered the first of the UN sectoral treaties repressing specific forms of terrorism, even though the word terrorism or terrorist appears nowhere within it.[22] The treaty text is based on the Convention to Prevent and Punish Acts of Terrorism Taking the Form of Crimes against Persons and Related

---

(Protocol I); adopted at Geneva, 8 June 1977, entered into force, 7 December 1978 (hereafter, 1977 Additional Protocol I). The threshold of violence necessary to meet this criterion is uncertain but the limited State practice that exists, with respect to the struggle between the Polisario Front and Morocco over Western Sahara, suggests that it is very low, potentially equating to the minimal threshold required for an international armed conflict between two existing States. The United States has strongly opposed the extension of scope of the Protocol to national liberation movements.

[18] In the words of Adam Roberts, the labelling of the African National Congress as 'terrorist' was a 'shallow and silly attribution even at the time'. Roberts, 'Countering Terrorism', p. 6. Whereas, as Saul notes, *apartheid* South Africa was justly accused of ruling by terror. Saul, 'United Nations Measures to Address the "Root Causes" and "Conditions Conducive" to Terrorism and to Prevent Violent Extremism (PVE)', p. 333. The 1973 International Convention on the Suppression and Punishment of the Crime of Apartheid terms *apartheid* a crime against humanity but also does not use the word terrorism in its provisions. International Convention on the Suppression and Punishment of the Crime of Apartheid; adopted at New York, 30 November 1973; entered into force, 18 July 1976. As of 1 January 2024, 109 States were party to the Convention. Kenya is the sole signatory that has never ratified the Convention. Of the five permanent members of the UN Security Council, States not party are France, the United Kingdom, and the United States.

[19] Saul, 'United Nations Measures to Address the "Root Causes" and "Conditions Conducive" to Terrorism and to Prevent Violent Extremism (PVE)', p. 531.

[20] UN General Assembly Resolution 3034 (XXVII), adopted on 18 December 1972 by 76 votes to 35 with 17 abstentions, operative para. 9.

[21] Convention on the Prevention and Punishment of Crimes against Internationally Protected Persons, including Diplomatic Agents; adopted at New York, 14 December 1973; entered into force, 20 February 1977. As of 1 January 2024, 180 of 197 States were party to the Convention. In addition, the Cook Islands and Niue are bound through New Zealand's ratification, meaning that 182 States in total are bound by its provisions. See the relevant UN Treaty Collection entry at: https://bit.ly/3BaEfVk.

[22] As noted in the Introduction to this book, the 1970 Hague Convention and the 1971 Montreal Convention, on air hijacking and the bombing of aircraft, respectively, were adopted within the International Civil Aviation Organization (ICAO), which is a specialized agency of the United Nations albeit with a significant degree of autonomy from it. Convention on the Suppression of Unlawful Seizure of Aircraft; adopted at The Hague, 16 December 1970; entered into force, 14 October 1971; and Convention the Suppression of Unlawful Acts against the Safety of Aviation, adopted at Montreal, 23 September 1971; entered into force, 26 January 1973. In both cases, the depositaries of the Convention are the Russian Federation (as successor State to the Soviet Union), the United Kingdom, and the United States and not the UN Secretary-General. The two treaties are discussed later in the present chapter.

Extortion that Are of International Significance,[23] which had been promulgated by the Member States of the Organization of American States (OAS) in 1971.[24]

An internationally protected person under the 1973 UN Convention covers, in particular, a head of State, the head of government, and the minister for foreign affairs, as well as their family members, when travelling abroad.[25] Similarly, falling within the ambit of the Convention are other State and government officials housed abroad who are entitled to special protection under international law (for instance, Embassy and consular diplomats), along with family members in their households.[26] There is no exemption for a prohibited act that is committed by an agent of a State.

Already, however, the problems that continue to bedevil the negotiation of the Comprehensive Convention against International Terrorism were laid bare following the conclusion of the 1973 Internationally Protected Persons Convention. To address the issue of national liberation movements, it was agreed that the 1973 Convention would be annexed to a UN General Assembly resolution that recognized that the provisions of the Convention

> could not in any way prejudice the exercise of the legitimate right to self-determination and independence, in accordance with the purposes and principles of the Charter of the United Nations and the Declaration on Principles of International Law concerning Friendly Relations and Cooperation among States in accordance with the Charter of the United Nations, by peoples struggling against colonialism, alien domination, foreign occupation, racial discrimination and apartheid.[27]

When depositing its instrument of ratification, Burundi formally declared that it would decline to criminalize such acts 'where the alleged offenders belong to a national liberation movement recognized by Burundi'. Italy responded with a declaration 'that the reservation expressed by the Government of Burundi is incompatible with the aim and purpose of the Convention', and that 'the Italian Government can not consider Burundi's accession to the Convention as valid as long as it does not withdraw that reservation'.[28] Iraq went a step further than Burundi, asserting that the protection of Article 1(1)(b) of the Convention (namely, government diplomats) 'shall cover the representatives of the national liberation movements recognized by the League of Arab States or the Organization of African Unity'. Israel, Italy, and the United Kingdom all objected to what it termed a reservation, while Germany declared that Iraq's statement 'does not have any legal effects for the Federal Republic of Germany'.[29]

---

[23] Convention to Prevent and Punish Acts of Terrorism Taking the Form of Crimes against Persons and Related Extortion that Are of International Significance; adopted at Washington DC, 2 February 1971; entered into force, 16 October 1973. As of 1 January 2024, eighteen States were party to the Convention leaving sixteen States not party of which three (Chile, Jamaica, and Trinidad and Tobago) were signatories. The status of adherence is available at: https://bit.ly/3YS2XFW. Cuba, the other member State, is not currently in a position to adhere to the Convention given its stand-off with the Organization, although it had ratified the OAS Charter in 1952. The 1971 OAS Convention has effectively been superseded by the 2002 Inter-American Convention against Terrorism, which explicitly considers the 1973 Internationally Protected Persons Convention as the basis for a terrorist offence.

[24] M. Sossai, 'The Legal Response of the Organization of American States in Combatting Terrorism', chap. 43 in Saul (ed.), *Research Handbook on International Law and Terrorism*, 2nd ed., p. 626.

[25] Art. 1(1)(a), 1973 Internationally Protected Persons Convention.

[26] Art. 1(1)(b), 1973 Internationally Protected Persons Convention.

[27] UN General Assembly Resolution 3166 (XXVIII), adopted without a vote on 14 December 1973, operative para. 4.

[28] Declarations available at: https://bit.ly/3rBRmvD.

[29] At ibid. In contrast to Burundi's declaration, it is something of a stretch to see Iraq's declaration as a reservation as it does not purport to 'exclude or to modify the legal effect of provisions of the treaty' but rather only to broaden the

1.2 *Defining International Terrorism in Peacetime* 25

The 1973 Convention does not exempt its application in a situation of armed conflict. Nevertheless, in accordance with IHL, certain senior State officials and diplomats may be lawful military objectives in the conduct of hostilities. Targeting them where this is the case would not amount to terrorism under this branch of international law. If they are combatant members of the armed forces or they meet the IHL criteria for direct participation in hostilities, neither their international protection under the 1973 Convention nor their presence on the territory of another State will render them personally immune from attack under the law of armed conflict. This is so, at the least in an international armed conflict, whose jurisdictional reach *ratione loci* is not geographically circumscribed.[30]

That said, in 2005, the Eritrea-Ethiopia Claims Commission held that the Eritrean Embassy residence was, in the midst of the international armed conflict between the two States, 'absolutely inviolable under Article 22 of the Vienna Convention on Diplomatic Relations',[31] even where it might have been used 'criminally' to stockpile weapons for the war effort.[32] Moreover, the 'person of a diplomatic agent shall be inviolable'.[33] The Commission's holding is very much open to question. For if it were correct, the 1973 Convention 'potentially raises a direct and irreconcilable conflict with IHL'.[34] It was certainly open to the Ethiopian authorities to have closed the Embassy, as the Claims Commission observed.[35] But the actions of Ethiopia at issue in the adjudication were to search and ransack the Embassy in search of weapons.

That said, should their forces have come under attack from within the Eritrean Embassy, they would have been entitled to respond forcibly. After all, a duty is imposed upon all persons enjoying the privileges and immunities of the 1961 Vienna Convention on Diplomatic Relations to 'respect the laws and regulations of the receiving State' and 'not to interfere in the internal affairs of that State'.[36] Moreover, 'the premises of the mission must not be used in any manner incompatible with the functions of the mission as laid down in the present Convention or by other rules of general international law'.[37]

1.2.2.2 The Definition in the 1979 Hostage-Taking Convention

In contrast to the UN Internationally Protected Persons Convention, the 1979 International Convention against the Taking of Hostages did refer to unlawful action within its scope as

---

protection afforded by the Convention to other categories of person. A reservation is defined in Art. 2(1)(d), Vienna Convention on the Law of Treaties; adopted at Vienna, 23 May 1969; entered into force, 27 January 1980.

[30] See on this issue S. Casey-Maslen, *Hague Law Interpreted: The Conduct of Hostilities under the Law of Armed Conflict*, Hart, Oxford, 2018, pp. 49–50.

[31] Vienna Convention on Diplomatic Relations; adopted at Vienna, 18 April 1961; entered into force, 24 April 1964. Article 22(1) of the Convention stipulates that '[t]he premises of the mission shall be inviolable. The agents of the receiving State may not enter them, except with the consent of the head of the mission'. Both Eritrea and Ethiopia were States Parties. As of 1 January 2024, 193 States were party to the 1961 Vienna Convention on Diplomatic Relations. The Cook Islands, Niue, Palau, and South Sudan are the four States that are not party. Status of adherence at: https://bit.ly/3QZvBD4.

[32] Eritrea-Ethiopia Claims Commission (EECC), *Partial Award: Diplomatic Claim – Eritrea's Claim 20*, *Reports of International Arbitral Awards*, Vol. XXVI (19 December 2005), 381–406, at: https://bit.ly/36Zc4hg, paras. 45–46; see B. Saul, 'From Conflict to Complementarity: Reconciling International Counterterrorism Law and International Humanitarian Law', *International Review of the Red Cross*, Vol. 103, Nos. 916–917 (February 2022), 157–202, at p. 176.

[33] Art. 29, 1961 Vienna Convention on Diplomatic Relations.

[34] Saul, 'From Conflict to Complementarity', p. 174.

[35] EECC, *Partial Award: Diplomatic Claim – Eritrea's Claim 20*, para. 47.

[36] Art. 41(1), 1961 Vienna Convention on Diplomatic Relations.

[37] Art. 41(3), 1961 Vienna Convention on Diplomatic Relations.

26 *Defining Terrorism in International Law*

a 'manifestation' of international terrorism, albeit only in a preambular paragraph.[38] The core of proscribed conduct is as follows:

> Any person who seizes or detains and threatens to kill, to injure or to continue to detain another person (hereinafter referred to as the 'hostage') in order to compel a third party, namely, a State, an international intergovernmental organization, a natural or juridical person, or a group of persons, to do or abstain from doing any act as an explicit or implicit condition for the release of the hostage commits the offence of taking of hostages ('hostage-taking') within the meaning of this Convention.[39]

The Convention thus applies to hostage-taking for private purposes (such as extortion) as well as for the purpose of terrorizing the public or coercing State conduct.[40]

The material scope of the Convention is not strictly limited to peacetime, even though proposals were made during the drafting for such a clear demarcation to be incorporated.[41] The text does explicitly exclude its application to certain acts of hostage-taking in armed conflict, but only where States Parties to the salient treaties of IHL are obligated to either prosecute or hand over for prosecution a hostage-taker.[42] This would pertain to international armed conflict, including, explicitly, situations where people were fighting in the exercise of their right of self-determination.[43] Taking as hostage a civilian in occupied territory or on the territory of the parties to armed conflict, where that civilian is a protected person,[44] is a grave breach of the 1949 Geneva Convention IV,[45] a treaty that binds all 197 States today.[46]

[38] International Convention against the Taking of Hostages; adopted at New York, 17 December 1979; entered into force, 3 June 1983 (1979 Hostage-Taking Convention), fifth preambular para. As of 1 January 2024, 176 States were party to the Convention. In addition, the Cook Islands and Niue are bound through New Zealand's ratification, meaning that 178 of 197 States able to adhere to the Hostage-Taking Convention are bound by its provisions. See the relevant UN Treaty Collection entry at: https://bit.ly/3KyjBmt.

[39] Art. 1(1), 1979 Hostage-Taking Convention.

[40] This implies that if I take my neighbour hostage and demand a ransom for his safe return, I am an ordinary criminal if we share the same nationality and where that nationality is of the territorial State but that if he is a foreign national, I am an international terrorist.

[41] W. Verwey, 'The International Hostages Convention and National Liberation Movements', *American Journal of International Law*, Vol. 75, No. 1 (1981), 69–92, at pp. 84–86; see also Saul, 'From Conflict to Complementarity', p. 177.

[42] Thus, Article 12 of the 1979 Hostage-Taking Convention stipulates: 'In so far as the Geneva Conventions of 1949 for the protection of war victims or the Additional Protocols to those Conventions are applicable to a particular act of hostage-taking, and in so far as States Parties to this Convention are bound under those conventions to prosecute or hand over the hostage-taker, the present Convention shall not apply to an act of hostage-taking committed in the course of armed conflicts as defined in the Geneva Conventions of 1949 and the Protocols thereto, including armed conflicts mentioned in article 1, paragraph 4, of Additional Protocol I of 1977, in which peoples are fighting against colonial domination and alien occupation and against racist regimes in the exercise of their right of self-determination, as enshrined in the Charter of the United Nations and the Declaration on Principles of International Law concerning Friendly Relations and Co-operation among States in accordance with the Charter of the United Nations'.

[43] Thus, if a relevant State is party to the 1977 Additional Protocol I to the four Geneva Conventions and has not made a reservation with respect to Articles 1(4) and 96(3) of the Protocol, the exclusion would apply. At the time of writing, this concerned only Morocco, which was deemed to be engaged in an international armed conflict with the Polisario Front, a national liberation movement representing the Sahrawi people in Western Sahara.

[44] Persons protected by the 1949 Geneva Convention IV are 'those who at a given moment and in any manner whatsoever, find themselves, in case of a conflict or occupation, in the hands of persons a Party to the conflict or Occupying Power of which they are not nationals. . . . Nationals of a neutral State who find themselves in the territory of a belligerent State, and nationals of a co-belligerent State, shall not be regarded as protected persons while the State of which they are nationals has normal diplomatic representation in the State in whose hands they are'. Art. 4, Convention (IV) relative to the Protection of Civilian Persons in Time of War; adopted at Geneva, 12 August 1949; entered into force, 21 October 1950 (hereafter, 1949 Geneva Convention IV).

[45] Arts. 34, 146, and 147, 1949 Geneva Convention IV. For further details of the prohibition of hostage-taking in a situation of armed conflict under IHL, see *infra* the discussion of the Geneva Law definition of terrorism.

[46] As of 1 January 2024, 196 States were party to the 1949 Geneva Convention IV (and the other three Geneva Conventions) while the 197th (Niue) remains bound by New Zealand's ratification of the 1949 Geneva Conventions, 'until such time as Niue accedes to the Conventions in its own right'. International Committee of

1.2 Defining International Terrorism in Peacetime

Thus, the exclusionary clause in the Hostage-Taking Convention would not apply in non-international armed conflict and incidents of hostage-taking in such conflicts would therefore fall within the Convention's scope.[47] That includes the taking as hostage of members of State armed forces or non-State armed groups in such a conflict.[48] That said, 'where the offence is committed within a single State, the hostage and the alleged offender are nationals of that State and the alleged offender is found in the territory of that State', a broader exclusion under the Convention applies. This is a generalized exclusion for acts of 'domestic' terrorism.[49]

There is no exemption from the Hostage-Taking Convention for acts by an agent of a State. In adhering to the Convention in 2006, Iran made an interpretative declaration whereby it categorically condemned 'each and every act of terrorism, including taking innocent civilians as hostages'. At the same time, Iran expressed its belief that 'fighting terrorism should not affect the legitimate struggle of peoples under colonial domination and foreign occupation in the exercise of their right of self-determination'. Austria, Canada, France, Germany, Italy, Japan, the Netherlands, Portugal, Spain, the United Kingdom, and the United States all objected to this declaration, with several of these States deeming it an unlawful 'reservation' to the provisions.[50]

1.2.2.3 The Definition in the 1997 Terrorist Bombings Convention

The first UN treaty to contain the word 'terrorist' in its title was the 1997 International Convention for the Suppression of Terrorist Bombings.[51] The Convention, which was negotiated at the instigation of the United States following a bombing of its air force personnel at the Khobar Towers in Dhahran, Saudi Arabia, in 1996,[52] requires the criminalization in domestic law of the act of intentionally delivering, placing, discharging, or detonating

> an explosive or other lethal device in, into or against a place of public use, a State or government facility, a public transportation system or an infrastructure facility, with the intent to cause death or serious bodily injury or to cause extensive destruction of such a place, facility or system, where such destruction results in or is likely to result in major economic loss.[53]

In addition to the explosive and incendiary devices its title indicates, the Convention also applies to weapons or devices that can cause serious physical harm or material damage through 'the release, dissemination or impact of toxic chemicals, biological agents or toxins or similar substances or radiation or radioactive material'.[54]

Witten has suggested: 'Like its predecessors, the Convention does not attempt to define "terrorism" but instead defines particular conduct that, regardless of its motivation, is condemned internationally and therefore is an appropriate subject of international law enforcement

---

the Red Cross (ICRC), States Parties to International Humanitarian Law and Other Related Treaties, available at: https://bit.ly/2OSD7Sg, p. 6.

[47] Dinstein, *Non-International Armed Conflicts in International Law*, 2nd ed., p. 224, para. 632.

[48] K. N. Trapp, *State Responsibility for International Terrorism*, Oxford University Press, Oxford, 2011, p. 111 note 149.

[49] Art. 13, 1979 Hostage-Taking Convention.

[50] Texts available at: https://bit.ly/3J9Pn7Q.

[51] International Convention for the Suppression of Terrorist Bombings; adopted at New York, 15 December 1997; entered into force, 23 May 2001. As of 1 January 2024, 170 States were party to the 1997 Terrorist Bombings Convention, while Burundi and Nepal were signatories. Status at: https://bit.ly/44tEGHw.

[52] Ibid., pp. 110–11. For details of the bombing which killed 19 US airmen and wounded almost 500, see, e.g., B. Riedel, 'Remembering the Khobar Towers bombing', The Brookings Institution, 21 June 2021, at: http://bit.ly/3IyX4a2.

[53] Art. 2(1), 1997 Terrorist Bombings Convention.

[54] Art. 1(3)(b), 1997 Terrorist Bombings Convention.

28   *Defining Terrorism in International Law*

cooperation.'[55] His claim is clearly open to question given the treaty nomenclature. Yet, it is true that the Convention does not demand any specific intent behind the delivery, placing, discharge, or detonation of the explosive or other lethal device. This must occur 'unlawfully and intentionally', but all offences within the Convention's scope must be criminalized, 'in particular' – but not only – 'where they are intended or calculated to provoke a state of terror in the general public or in a group of persons or particular person'.[56] One argument is that any use of an explosive device to kill, injure, or cause extensive property damage is inherently terrorizing and thus no mental element is needed.[57] Ben Saul's argument that a political or religious other ideological purpose behind a serious criminal offence is the crux of terrorism is, however, more persuasive.[58]

A number of exemptions and exclusions are set out in the Convention. Activities undertaken by the 'military forces of a State in the exercise of their official duties, inasmuch as they are governed by other rules of international law', are not governed by the Convention.[59] Thus, it is questionable whether the French secret service agents who blew up the Greenpeace boat, the *Rainbow Warrior*, in Auckland in 1985 would have been excluded from the scope of the Convention – had it existed at that time – as it appears they were not formally part of the French armed forces.[60] The General Directorate for External Security (la DGSE) is, however, answerable to the Minister of the Army[61] and the term 'military forces of a State' is explicitly defined as 'the armed forces of a State which are organized, trained and equipped under its internal law for the primary purpose of national defence or security and persons acting in support of those armed forces who are under their formal command, control and responsibility'.[62] In fact, while supporting the armed forces in certain respects, the DGSE also intervenes where the armed forces cannot.[63]

There is a broader exemption for acts *in bello*. Since targeting military objectives is not just permissible to parties to armed conflict but is also effectively *obligated* by the IHL principle of distinction,[64] an exclusion for the conduct of hostilities and for the actions of the parties in relations to persons protected under IHL is also set forth in the Convention.[65] Thus, it is stipulated that '[t]he activities of armed forces during an armed conflict, as those terms are understood under international humanitarian law, which are governed by that law, are not governed by this Convention'.[66] O'Donnell suggests that this exclusionary clause in the Convention might not apply to 'other situations' in which IHL applies, 'such as occupation'.

---

[55]   S. Witten, 'The International Convention for the Suppression of Terrorist Bombings', chap. 8 in Saul (ed.), *Research Handbook on International Law and Terrorism*, 2nd ed., p. 111.

[56]   Arts. 2(1) and 5, 1997 Terrorist Bombings Convention.

[57]   See, e.g., Trapp, *State Responsibility for International Terrorism*, p. 20.

[58]   B. Saul, *Defining Terrorism in International Law*, Oxford University Press, Oxford, 2006, p. 39.

[59]   Art. 19(2), 1997 Terrorist Bombings Convention.

[60]   But see *contra* the claim by O'Donnell that they were. D. O'Donnell, 'International treaties against terrorism and the use of terrorism during armed conflict and by armed forces', *International Review of the Red Cross*, Vol. 88, No. 864 (December 2006), 853–80, at p. 870.

[61]   See, e.g., 'Compte rendu de réunion n° 60 – Commission de la défense nationale et des forces armées', l'Assemblée Nationale (French Parliament), 12 April 2023, at: https://bit.ly/3qPFJni.

[62]   Art. 1(4), 1997 Terrorist Bombings Convention.

[63]   See, e.g., DGSE, 'La DGSE au cœur des cinq fonctions stratégiques : enjeux et perspectives', *Revue Défense Nationale*, Vol. 813, No. 8 (2018), pp. 14–19, at: https://bit.ly/3KZfe5J.

[64]   Thus, 'the Parties to the conflict shall at all times distinguish between the civilian population and combatants and between civilian objects and military objectives and accordingly *shall direct their operations only against military objectives*'. Art. 48, 1977 Additional Protocol I [added emphasis].

[65]   As Pierre Klein has observed: 'Compared with the majority of previous "sectoral" conventions, the 1997 Convention breaks new ground' through this exclusion. Klein, 'International Convention for the Suppression of the Financing of Terrorism', UN Audiovisual Library of International Law, p. 3.

[66]   Art. 19(2), 1997 Terrorist Bombings Convention.

1.2 Defining International Terrorism in Peacetime

But this is incorrect. A situation of international armed conflict includes a situation of belligerent occupation, as the Elements of Crime for the Rome Statute of the International Criminal Court make clear.[67] In contrast, O'Donnell correctly affirms that the exclusion in the Terrorist Bombings Convention would not specifically apply where resistance to occupation by a non-State armed group does not rise to the level of an armed conflict.[68]

The notion of 'armed forces' in the 1997 Convention encompasses both State armed forces and organized non-State armed groups, where they are party to an armed conflict (whether international or non-international in character).[69] Despite opposition from a small number of commentators to the notion that the term 'armed forces' excludes also non-State armed groups,[70] this appears clear from the text, which refers first to 'armed forces' and then to the 'military forces of a State' in the same provision.[71] It is also the position of the International Committee of the Red Cross (ICRC), which affirms that the reference in Article 3 common to the four 1949 Geneva Conventions to '[p]ersons taking no active part in the hostilities, including members of armed forces who have laid down their arms',[72] encompasses non-State armed groups as well as the State armed forces.[73]

A civilian, however, who decides to engage in prohibited conduct *in bello* but who is not a member of any armed forces would fall outside the exclusion for armed conflict.[74] This would mean, for instance, that Ukrainian civilians who threw Molotov cocktails[75] at Russian forces in

---

[67] Elements of Crimes under the Rome Statute of the International Criminal Court, reproduced from Official Records of the Assembly of States Parties to the Rome Statute of the International Criminal Court, First Session, New York, 3–10 September 2002, note 34.

[68] O'Donnell, 'International treaties against terrorism and the use of terrorism during armed conflict and by armed forces', p. 868. O'Donnell subsequently appears to equate a non-international armed conflict with the criteria related to territorial control laid down in Article 1(2) of the 1977 Additional Protocol II. Ibid., p. 869. This is wrong. No territorial control by a non-State armed group is necessary for a non-international armed conflict where the relevant hostilities are governed by customary IHL.

[69] Witten, 'The International Convention for the Suppression of Terrorist Bombings', p. 117. See also A. R. Perera, 'The draft United Nations Comprehensive Convention on International Terrorism' chap. 9 in Saul (ed.), *Research Handbook on International Law and Terrorism*, 2nd ed., p. 127; and Saul, 'From conflict to complementarity: Reconciling international counterterrorism law and international humanitarian law', p. 180.

[70] Saul cites two such outliers: M. Zwanenburg, 'Foreign Terrorist Fighters in Syria: Challenges of the Sending State', *International Legal Studies*, Vol. 92, No. 1 (2016), 204–34, at: https://bit.ly/3vBEat9, at pp. 216–17; and M. Hmoud, 'Negotiating the Draft Comprehensive Convention on International Terrorism: Major Bones of Contention', *Journal of International Criminal Justice*, Vol. 4, No. 5 (2006), at p. 1036. Saul, 'From conflict to complementarity: Reconciling international counterterrorism law and international humanitarian law', p. 179. See also the references in T. Van Poecke, F. Verbruggen and W. Yperman, 'Terrorist offences and international humanitarian law: The armed conflict exclusion clause', *International Review of the Red Cross*, Vol. 103, Nos. 916–917 (2021), 295–324, at p. 303, note 49. Zwanenburg argues that the determinant issue is whether members of the force enjoy combatant's privilege. In fact, terrorism under IHL is defined in more restrictive terms than is terrorism outside the realm of armed conflict; according to the sectoral treaties, acts of terrorism can be perpetrated against military objects or personnel and must be punished as such. These would be lawful military objectives under IHL within the confines of armed conflict.

[71] D. Kretzmer, 'Terrorism and the International Law of Occupation', chap. 15 in Saul (ed.), *Research Handbook on International Law and Terrorism*, 2nd ed., p. 216. The argument by Van Poecke, Verbruggen, and Yperman that the two terms 'operate in different legal spheres, and it seems that they should not be read in relation to one another' is unpersuasive. Van Poecke, Verbruggen, and Yperman, 'Terrorist offences and international humanitarian law: The armed conflict exclusion clause', p. 304. Acts of terrorism by a State in the context of a military occupation are expressly prohibited by Article 33 of the 1949 Geneva Convention IV, as discussed in Section 1.4.4.1.

[72] See, e.g., Art. 3(1), 1949 Geneva Convention IV.

[73] N. Melzer, *Interpretive Guidance on the Notion of Direct Participation in Hostilities under International Humanitarian Law*, ICRC, Geneva, 2009, pp. 28–30.

[74] Saul, 'From conflict to complementarity: Reconciling international counterterrorism law and international humanitarian law', p. 186; and see similarly O'Donnell, 'International treaties against terrorism and the use of terrorism during armed conflict and by armed forces', p. 869.

[75] On the issue of Molotov cocktails as lawful weapons under IHL, see S. Watts, 'Are Molotov Cocktails Lawful Weapons?' Blog Post, Lieber Institute for Law & Warfare at West Point, United States, 2 March 2022, at: https://bit.ly/3vBpbze.

March 2022 and beyond were engaging in international terrorism as defined in the 1997 Convention (and furthermore must be prosecuted by the authorities in accordance with that treaty's dictates).[76] The position of a member of a *levée en masse* – inhabitants of a non-occupied territory who, on the approach of the enemy, spontaneously take up arms to resist the invading forces – is not settled.[77] As Saul notes, while they are not strictly 'armed forces', a 'purposive interpretation' would argue in favour of their exclusion from the scope of the 1997 Convention.[78] Participants in a *levée en masse* are entitled to prisoner-of-war status and thus enjoy combatant's privilege from prosecution for lawful acts of war.[79]

Following the conclusion of the 1997 Convention, a distinction between criminal actions and legitimate struggle for self-determination outside the conduct of hostilities was again drawn by a contracting State. Pakistan made a declaration at the time of its adherence whereby 'nothing' in the Convention 'shall be applicable to struggles, including armed struggle, for the realization of right of self-determination launched against any alien or foreign occupation or domination, in accordance with the rules of international law'. Many States objected to this position.[80] Finland, for instance, was 'of the view that the declaration amounts to a reservation as its purpose is to unilaterally limit the scope of the Convention'. Finland further considered the declaration 'to be in contradiction with the object and purpose of the Convention, namely the suppression of terrorist bombings wherever and by whomever carried out'.[81] For its part Russia stated that 'the realization of the right of peoples to self-determination must not conflict with other fundamental principles of international law, such as the principle of the settlement of international disputes by peaceful means, the principle of the territorial integrity of States, and the principle of respect for human rights and fundamental freedoms'.[82]

1.2.2.4 The Definition in the 1999 Terrorism Financing Convention

The 1999 Terrorism Financing Convention[83] has particular resonance given that it is the most widely ratified sectoral treaty on the repression of terrorism, with 190 States Parties to it from the

[76] Art. 7(1) and (2), 1997 Terrorist Bombings Convention. In 2015, Ukraine informed the depositary of the Convention that 'from 20 February 2014 and for the period of temporary occupation by the Russian Federation of a part of the territory of Ukraine – the Autonomous Republic of Crimea and the city of Sevastopol – as a result of the armed aggression of the Russian Federation committed against Ukraine and until the complete restoration of the constitutional law and order and effective control by Ukraine over such occupied territory, as well as over certain districts of the Donetsk and Luhansk oblasts of Ukraine, which are temporarily not under control of Ukraine as a result of the aggression of the Russian Federation, the application and implementation by Ukraine of the obligations under the above [Convention], as applied to the aforementioned occupied and uncontrolled territory of Ukraine, is limited and is not guaranteed'. Communication of Ukraine to the UN Secretary-General in his capacity as treaty depositary, UN Ref. C.N.610.2015.TREATIES-XVIII.9 (Depositary Notification), Communication was received on 20 October 2015.

[77] For details on the legal status of a *levée en masse*, see, e.g., Y. Dinstein, *The Conduct of Hostilities under the Law of International Armed Conflict*, 4th ed., Cambridge University Press, Cambridge, 2022, pp. 68–69, paras. 189–92.

[78] Saul, 'From conflict to complementarity: Reconciling international counterterrorism law and international humanitarian law', p. 179.

[79] United Kingdom Ministry of Defence, *Joint Service Manual of the Law of Armed Conflict* (as amended in 2010), London, para. 4.2.2.

[80] Australia, Austria, Canada, Denmark, Finland, France, Germany, India, Ireland, Israel, Italy, Japan, Moldova, the Netherlands, New Zealand, Norway, Poland, Russia, Spain, Sweden, United Kingdom, and the United States.

[81] Declaration of Finland, 17 June 2003, at: http://bit.ly/2YbSI1g.

[82] Declaration of the Russian Federation, 22 September 2003, in Endnote 10 on the UN Treaty Series website entry for the 1997 Convention, available at: http://bit.ly/2YbSI1g.

[83] International Convention for the Suppression of the Financing of Terrorism; adopted at New York, 9 December 1999; entered into force, 10 April 2002.

1.2 Defining International Terrorism in Peacetime

197 that could adhere at the time of writing.[84] The core definition of international terrorism is set forth in its Article 2(1). Subparagraph (a) referred States Parties to the list of nine multilateral treaties on terrorism adopted at the time the Convention was concluded[85] and the offences provided for under those treaties as being applicable.[86] An opportunity was given to 'opt out of' definitions in treaties by any given State Party to the 1999 Convention.[87] Predictably, many States declared that those treaties to which they were not party upon adherence to the 1999 Terrorism Financing Convention would not be relevant to the scope of their obligations.

Subparagraph (b) of Article 2(1) contains what might conceivably be adopted as a general definition of a terrorist offence under international counterterrorism law. It is thus stipulated that it is also an offence 'within the meaning' of the 1999 Convention if funding is knowingly provided for:

> Any other act intended to cause death or serious bodily injury to a civilian, or to any other person not taking an active part in the hostilities in a situation of armed conflict, when the purpose of such act, by its nature or context, is to intimidate a population, or to compel a government or an international organization to do or to abstain from doing any act.[88]

A number of leading commentators expressly approve of the definition in the Terrorism Financing Convention. Yoram Dinstein, for instance, has termed it a most 'useful and relevant definition' and 'certainly the clearest'.[89] The focus is on harm to civilians or those *hors de combat* and not to property or to the environment per se. What is more, there is a purposive terrorism element: either to 'intimidate' the general public or to compel government conduct (or that of an international organization, such as the United Nations). While it expressly applies to a situation of armed conflict, the definition is not entirely consistent with the definitions of terrorism under international humanitarian law, being substantively broader than the IHL understanding of the term. This is so, given the requirement that mere intimidation – and not the spreading of 'terror' – suffices, along with, in the alternative, compelling government conduct.[90] This latter motivation is not relevant to IHL.

Di Filippo criticizes the Terrorism Financing Convention for adopting the 'lowest common denominator' approach.[91] Nevertheless, even this narrow scope did not attract universal support

---

[84] At the time of writing, only Burundi (a signatory), Chad, Eritrea, Iran, Somalia (also a signatory), the State of Palestine, and Tuvalu were States not party.

[85] The 1970 Hague Convention; the 1971 Montreal Convention; the 1973 Internationally Protected Persons Convention; the 1979 Hostage-Taking Convention; the 1979 Convention on the Physical Protection of Nuclear Material, adopted at Vienna, 28 October 1979; entered into force, 8 February 1987; the Protocol for the Suppression of Unlawful Acts of Violence at Airports Serving International Civil Aviation, supplementary to the Convention for the Suppression of Unlawful Acts against the Safety of Civil Aviation, adopted at Montreal, 24 February 1988; entered into force, 6 August 1989; the Convention for the Suppression of Unlawful Acts against the Safety of Maritime Navigation, adopted at Rome, 10 March 1988; entered into force, 1 March 1992; the Protocol for the Suppression of Unlawful Acts against the Safety of Fixed Platforms Located on the Continental Shelf, adopted at Rome, 10 March 1988; entered into force, 1 March 1992; and the 1997 Terrorist Bombings Convention.

[86] As Saul observes, the exceptions applicable in those treaties remain applicable in the context of the 1999 Terrorism Financing Convention. Saul, 'From conflict to complementarity: Reconciling international counterterrorism law and international humanitarian law', p. 178.

[87] Art. 2(2)(a), 1999 Terrorism Financing Convention. The provision stipulates, however, that any declaration 'shall cease to have effect as soon as the treaty enters into force for the State Party, which shall notify the depositary of this fact'.

[88] Art. 2(1)(b), 1999 Terrorism Financing Convention.

[89] Y. Dinstein, *Non-International Armed Conflicts in International Law*, 2nd ed., Cambridge University Press, Cambridge, 2021, p. 226, para. 637.

[90] This would cover almost funding linked to almost every direct attack on a civilian by a non-State armed group.

[91] M. Di Filippo, 'The definition(s) of terrorism in international law', chap. 1 in Saul (ed.), *Research Handbook on International Law and Terrorism*, 2nd ed., p. 6.

from States as the issue of national self-determination remained the sticking point. Thus, upon ratification of the 1999 Convention, Egypt entered an 'explanatory declaration', stating that '[w]ithout prejudice to the principles and norms of general international law and the relevant United Nations resolutions', Egypt 'does not consider acts of national resistance in all its forms, including armed resistance against foreign occupation and aggression with a view to liberation and self-determination, as terrorist acts within the meaning' of Article 2(1)(b) of the Convention. Jordan similarly declared that it 'does not consider acts of national armed struggle and fighting foreign occupation in the exercise of people's right to self-determination as terrorist acts' within the context of that provision. Syria made a 'reservation' inasmuch as it 'considers that acts of resistance to foreign occupation are not included under acts of terrorism'.[92] A considerable number of States objected to one or more of these declarations or reservations.[93]

Other States made more general observations on the ambit of the term *terrorism*. Namibia entered what it termed a reservation to its application of the Convention whereby 'a struggle waged by people in accordance with the principles of international law for their liberation or self-determination, including armed struggle against colonialism, occupation, aggression and domination by foreign forces, shall not be considered as terrorist acts'. When submitting its proposal for accession to the Convention in its Parliament, the Government of Nepal clarified that the meaning of the word 'terrorism' in the Convention does not encompass 'any acts which are related to political activities'.[94] Pakistan, however, which had entered a reservation to its adherence to the 1997 Terrorist Bombings Convention on the basis of the right of peoples to self-determination, did not do likewise when adhering to the 1999 Convention.

1.2.2.5 The Definition in the 2005 Nuclear Terrorism Convention

The 2005 International Convention for the Suppression of Acts of Nuclear Terrorism[95] took seven years to negotiate in the Ad Hoc Committee on Measures to Eliminate International Terrorism established under the UN General Assembly.[96] The last four years of these negotiations were dedicated to resolving disputes about the definition of terrorism. The solution was effectively to omit such a definition, at least overtly.[97]

Largely mirroring the approach in the 1997 Terrorist Bombings Convention, the 2005 Nuclear Terrorism Convention covers the unlawful and intentional possession of radioactive material and the making or possession of a device with the intent either to cause death, serious bodily injury, or substantial damage to property or to the environment.[98] It also applies to the 'unlawful and intentional' use of radioactive material or a device or damage to a nuclear facility in a manner that releases (or risks the release of) radioactive material. This is the case where the intent exists to cause death or serious bodily injury; or to inflict substantial damage on property or

---

92   The text of the various declarations is available on the UN Treaty Section webpage for the status of adherence to the Convention, at: https://bit.ly/3LiTzUJ.
93   Austria, Belgium, Canada, Czechia, Denmark, Estonia, Finland, France, Germany, Hungary, Ireland, Italy, Japan, Latvia, the Netherlands, Norway, Poland, Portugal, Spain, Sweden, the United Kingdom, and the United States.
94   At: https://bit.ly/3LiTzUJ.
95   International Convention for the Suppression of Acts of Nuclear Terrorism; adopted at New York, 13 April 2005; entered into force, 7 July 2007. As of 1 January 2024, 123 States were party to the 2005 Nuclear Terrorism Convention and a further 30 States were signatories.
96   The Ad Hoc Committee, which was established by General Assembly Resolution 51/210, adopted without a vote on 17 December 1996, concentrated first on the elaboration of the Terrorist Bombings Convention.
97   D. Joyner, 'Countering Nuclear Terrorism: A Conventional Response', *European Journal of International Law*, Vol. 18 (2007), 225–51, at p. 232.
98   Art. 2(1)(a), 2005 Nuclear Terrorism Convention.

to the environment; *or* to compel conduct by a natural or legal person, an international organization, or a State.[99] Hence, the aim of compelling conduct is only an alternative requirement (to two others) for an offence involving the use of radioactive material or a device (or damage to a nuclear facility). It is not even potentially part of the offence where the *possession* of such material or device is concerned. As with the Terrorist Bombings Convention, the actus reus of the offence in the 2005 Convention is implicitly considered to be inherently terrorizing.

There is a general exclusion for warfare directed against nuclear facilities in a situation of armed conflict under the 2005 Nuclear Terrorism Convention in almost identical terms to those set forth in the Terrorist Bombing Convention:

> The activities of armed forces during an armed conflict, as those terms are understood under international humanitarian law, which are governed by that law[,] are not governed by this Convention, and the activities undertaken by military forces of a State in the exercise of their official duties, inasmuch as they are governed by other rules of international law, are not governed by this Convention.[100]

In addition, unauthorized non-State actors are, indirectly, precluded from ever having access to a radiological device under UN Security Council Resolution 1540 (2004).[101] Under the Resolution, which pertains in both peacetime and armed conflict, the Security Council decided that *all* States *shall refrain* from providing any form of support to non-State actors that attempt to develop, acquire, manufacture, possess, transport, transfer, or use nuclear, chemical, or biological weapons and their means of delivery, in particular for terrorist purposes.[102]

1.2.2.6 The Proposed Definition in the Draft Comprehensive Convention against International Terrorism

Although the UN Comprehensive Convention against International Terrorism had not been adopted at the time of writing, it is important to review the definition in the current draft. This is set forth in draft Article 2(1), which provides that:

> Any person commits an offence within the meaning of the present Convention if that person, by any means, unlawfully and intentionally, causes:
>
> (a) Death or serious bodily injury to any person; or
> (b) Serious damage to public or private property, including a place of public use, a State or government facility, a public transportation system, an infrastructure facility or to the environment; or
> (c) Damage to property, places, facilities or systems referred to in paragraph 1 (b) of the present article resulting or likely to result in major economic loss;
>
> when the purpose of the conduct, by its nature or context, is to intimidate a population, or to compel a Government or an international organization to do or to abstain from doing any act.[103]

---

[99]   Art. 2(1)(b), 2005 Nuclear Terrorism Convention.
[100]   Art. 4(2), 2005 Nuclear Terrorism Convention.
[101]   The resolution defines non-State actors in a footnote in the following terms: 'Non-State actor: individual or entity, not acting under the lawful authority of any State in conducting activities which come within the scope of this resolution.' UN Security Council Resolution 1540, adopted on 28 April 2004 by unanimous vote in favour.
[102]   UN Security Council Resolution 1540, operative para. 1.
[103]   Art. 2(1), Draft comprehensive convention against international terrorism (Consolidated text prepared by the coordinator for discussion), Appendix II to Letter dated 3 August 2005 from the Chairman of the Sixth

The definition thus covers all means of inflicting physical harm or causing material damage but only when the requisite intent – coercing conduct by a government or international organization or intimidating a population – is present in relation to the actus reus. Trapp gives examples of polluting food or water or destroying railways without recourse to explosives as additional offences instituted by the Comprehensive Convention against International Terrorism.[104] Where explosives were used, however, the 1997 Terrorist Bombings Convention would be determinant. Thus, in the current draft text, it is stipulated that where the Convention and a sectoral treaty 'dealing with a specific category of terrorist offence' would apply to the same act as between States that are parties to both the Comprehensive Convention and the sectoral treaty, 'the provisions of the latter shall prevail'.[105]

The Comprehensive Convention is nevertheless also broad in scope insofar as it would extend not only to what one might naturally consider terrorist actions but also potentially to protests against a regime in power that involved violence. This would be so, at the least when the relevant protest involved foreign nationals (either as victims or as perpetrators),[106] and when the protests saw violence directed not only at law enforcement officials or the authorities but also against private property. Indeed, as O'Donnell has remarked: 'Expanding the material element to include serious damage to private property of any kind is a significant departure from existing definitions, since the main thrust of existing international standards against terrorism is to safeguard the public interest.'[107] He also suggests that the 'recognition of serious damage to the environment as a material element of the definition may be the most significant innovation contained in the present draft'.[108]

Certain exclusions are, however, incorporated to the definition of international terrorism, broadly similar to those under the Terrorist Bombings and Nuclear Terrorism Conventions. Draft Article 20(2) provides that '[t]he activities of armed forces during an armed conflict, as those terms are understood under international humanitarian law, which are governed by that law, are not governed by the present Convention'. The notion of 'armed forces' in the Draft Comprehensive Convention likewise encompasses not only State armed forces but also organized non-State armed groups, where they are party to an armed conflict. Seemingly, however, a civilian who decides to engage in prohibited conduct but who is not a member of any armed force that is party to the armed conflict would again fall outside that exclusion.

Article 20(3) of the Draft Comprehensive Convention further provides that '[t]he activities undertaken by the military forces of a State in the exercise of their official duties, inasmuch as they are governed by other rules of international law, are not governed by the present Convention'. This would exclude acts of 'law enforcement' by a State's armed forces, including counterterrorism operations, which do not amount to the conduct of hostilities, at the least where these acts fell to be regulated by the law on inter-State use of force or international human

Committee addressed to the President of the General Assembly, UN doc. A/59/894, 12 August 2005 (hereafter, 2005 Draft Comprehensive Convention against International Terrorism).

[104] Trapp, *State Responsibility for International Terrorism*, p. 22.
[105] Art. 3, 2005 Draft Comprehensive Convention against International Terrorism.
[106] Draft Article 4 stipulates in part that '[t]he present Convention shall not apply where the offence is committed within a single State, the alleged offender and the victims are nationals of that State, the alleged offender is found in the territory of that State and no other State has a basis under article 7, paragraph 1 or 2, of the present Convention to exercise jurisdiction'. Article 7 concerns inter alia an offence committed on national territory but within the embassy of a foreign State.
[107] O'Donnell, 'International treaties against terrorism and the use of terrorism during armed conflict and by armed forces', p. 873.
[108] Ibid.

rights law.[109] This is one of the sticking points precluding the finalization of the Convention. Acts such as the bombing of the Greenpeace vessel, *Rainbow Warrior*, in 1985 by French security service agents operating covertly (discussed in Chapter 7) would not be excluded from coverage of the Comprehensive Convention as, seemingly, the agents were not members of the French military forces.[110]

The main issue remains, however, the situation of peoples involved in armed struggle for their right of self-determination. Western nations oppose an exclusion on this basis. Members of the Non-Aligned Movement, and especially those who also belong to the Organisation of Islamic Cooperation (OIC),[111] insist that peoples seeking to achieve statehood and using force to do so shall not be treated as terrorists.[112] The current draft text of the Convention would exclude from its purview the actions of an armed group fighting on behalf of people struggling for self-determination when the group was a party to an armed conflict, but not other members of such people. Outside a situation of armed conflict, all would be considered terrorists if they engaged in armed struggle against the State. This is clearly problematic given the status as a peremptory (*jus cogens*) norm of international law of the right of self-determination,[113] even though the right to use force with a view to achieving self-determination does not enjoy customary law recognition.[114]

The OIC has proposed language to amend the draft text of the Comprehensive Convention. Thus:

2. The activities of the parties during an armed conflict, *including in situations of foreign occupation*, as those terms are understood under international humanitarian law, which are governed by that law, are not governed by this Convention.

3. The activities undertaken by the military forces of a State in the exercise of their official duties, *inasmuch as they are in conformity with international law*, are not governed by this Convention.[115]

This is not acceptable to many Western nations. In 2005, the Coordinator of the negotiations proposed to add a preambular paragraph to the Draft Comprehensive Convention.

---

[109] The United States, for example, rejects the extraterritorial application of the 1966 International Covenant on Civil and Political Rights. Fifth Periodic Report of the United States under the ICCPR, UN doc. CPR/C/USA/5, 19 January 2021, para. 14.

[110] See on the broader issue of State responsibility K. Trapp, 'Terrorism and the international law of State responsibility', in Saul (ed.), *Research Handbook on International Law and Terrorism*, 2nd ed., pp. 37–8; and infra Chapter 7.

[111] English language homepage of the OIC at: https://bit.ly/3JbGafg.

[112] The OIC Convention on Combatting International Terrorism exempts from the crime of terrorism 'Peoples' struggle including armed struggle against foreign occupation, aggression, colonialism, and hegemony, aimed at liberation and self-determination in accordance with the principles of international law'. Art. 2, Convention of the Organisation of the Islamic Conference on Combating International Terrorism; Annex to Resolution 59/26-P, adopted at Ouagadougou, 1 July 1999. A similar exemption was incorporated in the corresponding 1999 Organization of African Unity (OAU) Convention on Terrorism. Art. 3, OAU Convention on the Prevention and Combating of Terrorism; adopted at Algiers, 1 July 1999; entered into force, 6 December 2002. As of 1 January 2024, forty-three States were party to the OAU Convention and a further ten were signatories. Only Morocco and Zimbabwe are non-signatory States.

[113] International Law Commission (ILC), Annex to the text of the draft conclusions on peremptory norms of general international law (*jus cogens*), adopted by the ILC on first reading, in UN doc. A/74/10, 2019, point (h).

[114] See, e.g., S. Casey-Maslen, *Jus ad Bellum: The Law on Inter-State Use of Force*, Hart, Oxford, 2020, pp. 30–33, 51.

[115] UN doc. A/58/37, 11 February 2002, Annex IV, incorporated in Report of the Ad Hoc Committee established by General Assembly resolution 51/210 of 17 December 1996, UN doc. A/68/37, New York, 2013, at: https://bit.ly/3Jodm39, p. 18 [added emphasis]. Saul argues that the reference to 'parties' could 'conceivably' extend to disorganized armed groups, civilians directly participating in hostilities, and civilians participating indirectly in hostilities, although he also believes that the drafting of the OIC would fail to achieve these aims. Saul, 'From conflict to complementarity: Reconciling international counterterrorism law and international humanitarian law', pp. 186–87.

This was based on operative paragraph 15 of General Assembly Resolution 46/51 of 9 December 1991, whereby:

> *Reaffirming* that nothing in this Convention shall in any way prejudice the right to self-determination, freedom and independence, as derived from the Charter of the United Nations, of peoples forcibly deprived of that right or the right of these peoples to struggle to this end in conformity with international law.[116]

This did not suffice to break the impasse. In informal negotiations chaired by the Coordinator in July 2005, Jordan made a further proposal to amend the operative text of the Convention, whereby '[e]xcept for an offence under article 2, paragraph 1 (a), of this Convention committed against a protected civilian to which this Convention shall be applicable, the activities during an armed conflict, as those terms are understood under international humanitarian law, which are governed by that law, are not governed by this Convention'.[117] This likewise did not overcome the negotiating blockage. So there we stand. Two decades later, the draft Convention remains just that, an unadopted proposal for a new treaty.

For the OIC has shown no signs of backing down on its demands for legislative change to the salient article on exclusions from the text. As Samuel explains, the Organisation does not seek to amend international law governing violations of IHL by those engaged in the struggle for self-determination, but rather to exclude from the ambit of international terrorism other acts of resistance movements that use force.[118] This would seem to counterbalance the exclusion of acts in such situations by State armed forces. In relation to the corresponding provision in the Terrorist Bombings Convention, O'Donnell declared that 'the exemption for acts of terrorism committed by the armed forces of states even when international humanitarian law is inapplicable is an affront to the rule of law'.[119]

1.2.2.7 Maritime Terrorism

Acts of terrorism may also be perpetrated on the high seas. This is significant as around 90 per cent of the world's goods are transported by sea.[120] But just as there is no generally accepted definition of terrorism on land, so too an accepted definition of maritime terrorism remains elusive.[121] In addition, the interrelationship between terrorism and piracy is not straightforward, and the international legal framework is further complicated by drug and human trafficking, which may sometimes be carried out by terrorist groups in order to fund their military activities.[122]

---

[116] Report of the coordinator on the results of the informal consultations on a draft comprehensive convention on international terrorism, held from 25 to 29 July 2005, Appendix I to Letter dated 3 August 2005 from the Chairman of the Sixth Committee, pp. 3–4.

[117] Ibid., p. 5.

[118] K. Samuel, 'The legal response to terrorism of the Organization of Islamic Cooperation', chap. 44 in Saul (ed.), *Research Handbook on International Law and Terrorism*, 2nd ed., p. 648.

[119] O'Donnell, 'International treaties against terrorism and the use of terrorism during armed conflict and by armed forces', p. 879.

[120] Organisation for Economic Co-operation and Development (OECD), 'Ocean shipping and shipbuilding', accessed 1 February 2022 at: https://bit.ly/3HKKDFi.

[121] E. Papastravridis, 'Maritime terrorism in international law', chap 5 in Saul (ed.), *Research Handbook on International Law and Terrorism*, 2nd ed., p. 62.

[122] The procurement of explosives used for the 2004 Madrid train bombing, for instance, was in part funded by the provision of drugs. B. Saul, 'The legal nexus between terrorism and transnational crime', chap. 10 in Saul (ed.), *Research Handbook on International Law and Terrorism*, 2nd ed., p. 143. In December 2008, a Moroccan court convicted a drug trafficker, Hicham Ahmidan, of links to the bombing, which killed 191 people. He was sentenced to

1.2 Defining International Terrorism in Peacetime

No right is laid down in the UN Convention on the Law of the Sea[123] (UNCLOS) – or indeed customary international law – according to which warships may interfere with vessels on the basis that they have on board individuals who are reasonably suspected of having committed a terrorist offence on the high seas.[124] Two potential grounds from among those set forth in UNCLOS[125] may, though, be relevant: piracy and where a vessel is not flagged.

Under general international law, as codified in Article 101 of UNCLOS, piracy is defined as

any illegal acts of violence or detention, or any act of depredation, committed for private ends by the crew or the passengers of a private ship or a private aircraft, and directed:

(i) on the high seas, against another ship or aircraft, or against persons or property on board such ship or aircraft;

(ii) against a ship, aircraft, persons or property in a place outside the jurisdiction of any State.[126]

Given that the material elements of the offence of piracy – 'illegal acts of violence or detention' or any act of 'depredation' (i.e., robbery) – will typically exist in an act of maritime terrorism, the interplay between piracy and terrorism turns primarily on the interpretation of the notion of 'private ends'; that is to say, the motivation for the unlawful acts. Historically, a distinction was made in law between 'privateering' and 'piracy'. The former involved private individuals duly authorized by the State to capture merchant vessels belonging to another State.[127] The latter involved a private individual engaging in the same conduct but without possessing such lawful authority, meaning that the captain of the marauding ship did not possess a requisite 'letter of marque' from a government.[128]

Privateering was formally abolished in international law by the 1856 Paris Declaration Respecting Maritime Law.[129] The 1856 Declaration, which by the end of the nineteenth century was also codifying customary law, stated simply that '[p]rivateering is, and remains, abolished'.[130] This is a customary rule. The wording of 'private ends' appeared in the 1927 Report of the Sub-Committee of the League of Nations Committee of Experts for the Progressive Codification of International Law. This document stated: 'According to international law, piracy consists in sailing the seas *for private ends without authorisation from the Government of any State* with the object of committing depredations upon property or acts of violence against persons.'[131]

Some commentators argue that private ends refer to the aim of lucrative gain as opposed to a political motive.[132] The better view is that, reflecting the evolution of piracy under the law of

---

ten years' imprisonment. France24, 'Moroccan jailed for 20 years for Madrid bombings', 18 December 2008, at: https://bit.ly/34GCljo.

[123] United Nations Convention on the Law of the Sea; adopted at Montego Bay, 10 December 1982; entered into force, 16 November 1994. As of 1 January 2024, 169 States were party to UNCLOS and a further 13 were signatories. Among the permanent members of the UN Security Council, only the United States is a State not party. It did not sign the treaty when it was possible to do so. Art. 305, UNCLOS. See further W. Gallo, 'Why Hasn't the US Signed the Law of the Sea Treaty?' *VOA News*, 6 June 2016, at: https://bit.ly/3Lsztr2.

[124] Papastavridis, 'Maritime terrorism in international law', p. 64.

[125] Art. 110, UNCLOS.

[126] Art. 101(a), UNCLOS.

[127] See, e.g., Y. Dinstein, *The Conduct of Hostilities under the Law of International Armed Conflict*, 4th ed., Cambridge University Press, Cambridge, 2022, pp. 48–49, para. 132.

[128] See, e.g., Royal Museums Greenwich, 'Letters of marque', accessed 1 February 2022, at: https://bit.ly/3BhJl24.

[129] Declaration Respecting Maritime Law; adopted at Paris, 16 April 1856; entered into force the same day.

[130] Text available at: https://bit.ly/3Be79nG.

[131] League of Nations Document C.196.M.70 (1927) V, pp. 116–17 [added emphasis].

[132] For example, this is the understanding of the International Maritime Organization (IMO). See 'Introduction: Southeast Asian Piracy: Research and Developments', in G. G. Ong-Webb (ed.), *Piracy, Maritime Terrorism and*

nations, the requirement serves to distinguish the acts of private individuals from the acts of a State or its duly authorized agents.[133] Hostage-taking can be both piracy and terrorism. Hence, piratical acts by non-State actors may also amount to acts of terrorism where the requisite terrorist motive is satisfied. What is more, since the right of search pertaining to suspected piracy may allow a warship to board a piratical vessel and arrest individuals who are reasonably suspected of being pirates,[134] once in custody, the detainees may later be charged also with an act of terrorism in certain circumstances.

In an armed conflict, a military vessel of an adversary may lawfully be targeted under IHL as may a merchant vessel of an adversary that is transporting armaments on its behalf.[135] As discussed in Section 1.4.2, IHL provides that terrorism in the conduct of hostilities in armed conflict occurs where acts (or threats) of violence have as their primary purpose to spread terror among the civilian population.[136] This would include terror attacks against civilians on board ships.[137] Saul wisely suggests that terrorism treaties 'be harmoniously interpreted with IHL by applying the IHL rules to define whether an act is "unlawful"' under the salient terrorism treaty'. If this is not the case, no terrorism offence is committed.[138]

Piracy, however, only exists under international law where the crew of one vessel attacks another on the high seas.[139] The *Achille Lauro* hijacking in 1985 concerned four armed Palestinians who had boarded the Italian cruise ship, but not from another ship. The men, who belonged to the Popular Front for the Palestine Liberation Front (PLF), took control of the vessel and demanded that Israel release imprisoned PLF members. They sought the ship's entry to a Syrian port but when Syria denied the request, the hijackers killed a sixty-nine-year-old wheelchair-bound American Jew, Leon Klinghoffer, in cold blood. After being shot in the head, Mr Klinghoffer was thrown overboard.[140]

The United States prompted the International Maritime Organization[141] (IMO) to take action. In March 1988, a diplomatic conference in Rome adopted the Convention for the Suppression of Unlawful Acts against the Safety of Maritime Navigation[142] (SUA Convention). The Convention

---

    Securing the Malacca Straits, Institute of Southeast Asian Studies, Singapore, 2006, p. xiii. See also Papastravridis, 'Maritime terrorism in international law', p. 65.

[133] A. Priddy and S. Casey-Maslen, *Counterpiracy under International Law*, Academy Briefing No. 1, Geneva Academy of International Humanitarian Law and Human Rights, Geneva, August 2012, p. 12, and related citations.

[134] See similarly Papastravridis, 'Maritime terrorism in international law', p. 66.

[135] See, e.g., S. Haines, 'Naval Warfare', chap. 11 in Casey-Maslen, Hague Law Interpreted: The Conduct of Hostilities under the Law of Armed Conflict, 274–312; Y. Dinstein, *The Conduct of Hostilities under the Law of International Armed Conflict*, 4th ed., Cambridge University Press, Cambridge, 2022, pp. 151–52, para. 434.

[136] Art. 51(2), 1977 Additional Protocol I. See also ICRC, Customary IHL Rule 2: 'Violence Aimed at Spreading Terror among the Civilian Population', at: https://bit.ly/33ip53U.

[137] Art. 49(3), 1977 Additional Protocol I.

[138] Saul, 'From conflict to complementarity', p. 174.

[139] Art. 101(a), UNCLOS.

[140] '1985, October 7: Palestinian terrorists hijack an Italian cruise ship', *History*, last updated 6 October 2020, at: https://bit.ly/3BfN93S.

[141] The International Maritime Organization is the UN's specialized agency with responsibility for the safety and security of shipping and the prevention of marine and atmospheric pollution by ships. IMO, 'Introduction to IMO', 2019, at: https://bit.ly/3YSJzsh. In 1948, an international conference in Geneva adopted a convention formally establishing the Inter-Governmental Maritime Consultative Organization (IMCO), but the name was changed in 1982 to IMO. The Convention entered into force in 1958 and the new organization met for the first time the following year. Its mission is 'to promote safe, secure, environmentally sound, efficient and sustainable shipping' by 'adopting the highest practicable standards of maritime safety and security . . . as well as through consideration of the related legal matters and effective implementation of IMO's instruments with a view to their universal and uniform application'. IMO, 'Brief History of IMO', 2019, at: https://bit.ly/45pvRQ5.

[142] Convention for the Suppression of Unlawful Acts against the Safety of Maritime Navigation; adopted at Rome, 10 March 1988; entered into force, 1 March 1992. As of 1 January 2024, 166 States were party to the Convention.

1.2 Defining International Terrorism in Peacetime

prohibits the seizure of ships by force, acts of violence against persons on board ships, and the placing of devices on board a ship which are likely to destroy or damage it, obligating States Parties to either extradite or 'establish their jurisdiction over' these offences when the alleged perpetrators are found on their territory. Moreover, unlike the crime of piracy, which is limited to acts on the high seas (and in a State's exclusive economic zone),[143] the SUA Convention also applies in a State's territorial waters.[144]

In 2005, a Protocol to the SUA Convention was adopted to amend the Convention by its States Parties.[145] The Protocol adds a new Article 3*bis*, which provides that a person commits an offence within the meaning of the Convention if that person unlawfully and intentionally uses against or on a ship or discharges from a ship any explosive, radioactive material, or biological, chemical, nuclear weapon in a manner that causes or is likely to cause death or serious injury or damage (or uses a ship in a manner that causes death or serious injury or damage).[146] The offence is committed 'when the purpose of the act, by its nature or context, is to intimidate a population, or to compel a Government or an international organization to do or to abstain from any act'.

That the States Parties were concluding treaties on the repression of terrorism is clear from the text of the Convention and its Protocol. In the preamble to the 1998 SUA Convention, they expressed their 'deep concern about the worldwide escalation of acts of terrorism in all its forms, which endanger or take innocent human lives, jeopardize fundamental freedoms and seriously impair the dignity of human beings'.[147] In the second preambular paragraph to the 2005 SUA Protocol, the States Parties explicitly 'acknowledg[e] that terrorist acts threaten international peace and security'. They further express their belief that 'it is necessary to adopt provisions supplementary to those of the Convention, to suppress additional terrorist acts of violence against the safety and security of international maritime navigation and to improve its effectiveness'.[148]

A provision in the 2005 Protocol covers the procedures to be followed if a State Party seeks to board a ship flying the flag of a State Party when the requesting Party has reasonable grounds to suspect that the ship or a person on board the ship is, has been, or is about to be involved in, the commission of an offence under the Convention.[149] In other respects, neither the SUA Convention nor its 2005 Protocol amends the contours of the freedom of the high seas, which has been a customary rule of international law for centuries.

1.2.2.8 Terrorism and Transnational Organized Crime

With respect to transnational organized crime, such as drug smuggling or human trafficking, the key to understanding the overlap with, or differentiation from, terrorism is the intent requirement of a financial or material benefit.[150] That is not to say that terrorist groups are not interested in fundraising through illicit activities – in its Resolution 2195 (2014), the UN Security Council expressed its 'concern that terrorists benefit from transnational organized crime in some

---

[143] Art. 58(2), UNCLOS.

[144] Priddy and Casey-Maslen, *Counterpiracy under International Law*, p. 14.

[145] Protocol of 2005 to the Convention for the Suppression of Unlawful Acts against the Safety of Maritime Navigation; adopted at London, 14 October 2005; entered into force, 28 July 2010. As of 1 January 2024, fifty-three States were party to the 2005 SUA Protocol.

[146] Art. 4(5), 2005 SUA Protocol.

[147] 1988 SUA Convention, third preambular para.

[148] 2005 SUA Protocol, twelfth preambular paragraph.

[149] Art. 8 *bis* (5), 2005 SUA Protocol.

[150] Saul, 'The legal nexus between terrorism and transnational crime', p. 132.

regions"[151] – but their 'further, ulterior aim' is 'to use the proceeds of such crimes to fund terrorist acts'.[152] As Chapter 3 describes, a number of States have adopted dedicated national legislation that governs both terrorism and organized crime.

The UN Convention against Transnational Organized Crime[153] (also known as the Palermo Convention) defines a transnational organized group as 'a structured group of three or more persons, existing for a period of time and acting in concert with the aim of committing one or more serious crimes or offences established in accordance with this Convention, in order to obtain, directly or indirectly, a financial or other material benefit'.[154] This clearly encompasses certain terrorist groups. Indeed, in the UN General Assembly, in the resolution that adopted the Palermo Convention, noted 'with deep concern the growing links between transnational organized crime and terrorist crimes'.[155] As Saul remarks, the distinction between terrorism and transnational organized crime is 'slippery' because of the lack of an internationally accepted definition of what does and does not constitute terrorism and the 'diversity of terrorist-type offences' in treaties and national law.[156]

1.2.3 Towards an Agreed Definition of Terrorism in Peacetime?

Despite the impasse in the negotiation of the UN Comprehensive Convention on International Terrorism, in a 2011 decision the Appeals Chamber of the Special Tribunal for Lebanon, led by Judge Antonio Cassese, held that a definition existed in customary law of international terrorism in peacetime. This holding was surprising for a number of reasons.[157] First and foremost, of course, given the disagreement among States as to the definition of international terrorism, how could one credibly argue that the threshold of general agreement, including among 'specially affected States', had been reached? Second, the determination of any customary rules was materially irrelevant to the case at hand and was thus *obiter dicta*. The Special Tribunal for Lebanon was an ad hoc mechanism created in relation to the bombing that killed former Lebanese prime minister Rafik Hariri on 14 February 2005. Its mandate, which was issued by the UN Security Council, made it explicit that Lebanese law and not international law was the legal basis for the offences to be tried by the Tribunal.[158] Third, the Prosecution and the Defence before the Tribunal decision had been in agreement that no definition of terrorism existed in customary international law.[159]

---

[151] UN Security Council Resolution 2195, adopted without a vote on 19 December 2014, seventh preambular para. The Security Council identified as examples of activities of such transnational organized crime 'the trafficking of arms, persons, drugs, and artefacts' and 'the illicit trade in natural resources including gold and other precious metals and stones, minerals, wildlife, charcoal and oil', as well as 'kidnapping for ransom and other crimes including extortion and bank robbery'.

[152] Saul, 'The legal nexus between terrorism and transnational crime', p. 132.

[153] United Nations Convention against Transnational Organized Crime; adopted at New York, 15 November 2000; entered into force, 29 September 2003 (2000 Palermo Convention). As of 1 January 2024, 191 States were party to the Convention. A further two States (the Republic of Congo and Iran) were signatories. The other four States not party are Papua New Guinea, the Solomon Islands, Somalia, and Tuvalu. The European Union is also a party to the Convention having adhered in 2004.

[154] Art. 2(a), 2000 Palermo Convention.

[155] UN General Assembly Resolution 55/25, adopted without a vote on 15 November 2000, eighth preambular para.

[156] Saul, 'The legal nexus between terrorism and transnational crime', p. 133.

[157] That a Court led by Antonio Cassese should make such a determination is not the surprise. Cassese had already written an article in 2006 in which he affirmed that a customary rule detailing the elements of the [international] crime of international terrorism in time of peace had already crystallized. A. Cassese, 'The Multifaceted Criminal Notion of Terrorism in International Law', *Journal of International Criminal Justice*, Vol. 4 (2006), 933–58, at p. 935.

[158] Art. 2, Statute of the Special Tribunal for Lebanon, annexed to UN Security Council Resolution 1757, adopted on 30 May 2007 by ten votes to nil, with five abstentions (China, Indonesia, Qatar, Russia, and South Africa).

[159] Ibid., p. 590.

1.2 Defining International Terrorism in Peacetime

Notwithstanding these obstacles, the Appeals Chamber averred not only that international terrorism during peacetime was already defined under customary international law but also that the offence was criminalized under international criminal law. The Appeals Chamber opined that the international crime of international terrorism comprised the following three key elements:

(a) The perpetration of a criminal act (such as murder, kidnapping, hostage-taking, or arson);
(b) The intent to spread fear among the population or to coerce a national or international authority to take some action or to refrain from taking it; and
(c) The act involves a transnational element.[160]

The Tribunal's *Interlocutory Decision on the Applicable Law* received scant support from States and leading jurists. Mettraux described it as an 'extraordinary judicial pronouncement', noting the mixture of 'scepticism and disapproval' that greeted it.[161] Among that chorus was Saul, who authored an article unambiguously entitled 'The United Nations Special Tribunal for Lebanon *invents* an international crime of transnational terrorism'.[162] He pointed out that all the sources of custom relied upon by the Appeals Chamber – national legislation, judicial decisions, regional and international treaties, and UN resolutions – were 'misinterpreted, exaggerated, or erroneously applied'.[163] Kirsch and Oehmichen similarly termed the purported customary law crime a 'fabrication'.[164] Mettraux himself concludes that the Special Tribunal's 'discovery' of an international crime of international terrorism 'fails to convince', declaring that in its reasoning the Tribunal 'seems to have over-reached' using a 'recipe' of '*peel off, cherry-pick and bend*'.[165]

Cassese's attempt to rewrite both history and international law failed even to persuade fellow judges on the Special Tribunal itself. Thus, in its trial judgment of four accused, issued nine years later, the Tribunal not only recalled that the Appeals Chamber's consideration of the 'apparent existence of a customary international law definition of terrorism' was *obiter dicta* but also declared that it was 'not convinced that one exists'.[166] In her separate opinion, Judge Janet Nosworthy did argue that the definition was *de lege ferenda* as custom as of 2005,[167] but insufficient evidence was adduced to sustain even this more tentative assertion.

In rejecting the *customary law* nature of the Appeals Chamber's proposed definition, Ambos and Timmermann nonetheless aver that a 'current consensus' exists that terrorism 'requires the commission of any criminal act, which causes death or bodily injury to any person, or severe damage to public or private property' where an associated special intent exists to spread fear,

---

[160] Special Tribunal for Lebanon, Interlocutory Decision on the Applicable Law: Terrorism, Conspiracy, Homicide, Perpetration, Cumulative Charging (Appeals Chamber) (Case No. STL-11–01/I), 16 February 2011, para. 85.

[161] G. Mettraux, 'The UN Special Tribunal for Lebanon: defining international terrorism', chap. 40 in Saul (ed.), *Research Handbook on International Law and Terrorism*, 2nd ed., p. 589.

[162] B. Saul, 'Legislating from a radical Hague: The United Nations Special Tribunal for Lebanon invents an international crime of transnational terrorism', *Leiden Journal of International Law*, Vol. 24, No. 3 (2011), 677–700, available on SSRN at: https://bit.ly/3rHyRGb [added emphasis]. In 2005, Saul had concluded that arguments that terrorism is a customary international crime 'are premature'. B. Saul, *Defining Terrorism in International Law*, Oxford University Press, Oxford, 2006, p. 270.

[163] Saul, 'Legislating from a radical Hague: The United Nations Special Tribunal for Lebanon invents an international crime of transnational terrorism', p. 679.

[164] S. Kirsch and A. Oehmichen, 'Judges gone astray: The fabrication of terrorism as an international crime by the Special Tribunal for Lebanon', *Durham Law Review Online*, Vol. 1 (2011), 1–20 [added emphasis].

[165] Mettraux, 'The UN Special Tribunal for Lebanon: defining international terrorism', pp. 598, 589, and 592 [original emphasis].

[166] Special Tribunal for Lebanon, *Prosecutor v. Salim Jamil Ayyash and others*, Judgment (Trial Chamber) (Case No. STL-11–01/T/TC), 18 August 2020, para. 6192.

[167] Ibid., Separate Opinion of Judge Janet Nosworthy, paras. 124–25.

intimidate a population, or coerce an entity to do or abstain from doing any act.[168] Claiming that such a consensus exists is significantly overreaching. It flies in the face of State practice, including as set out in the sectoral treaties.

It is true, as Kent Roach observes,[169] that 'guidance' on the definition of international terrorism was provided by the United Nations Security Council Resolution 1566 (2004). It even 'came close' to a comprehensive definition of terrorism in an operative paragraph.[170] But the relevant paragraph was carefully drafted to allow those States that did not consider national liberation movements as terrorists to lay claim to a continued carve-out on that basis. Thus, the Resolution

> [r]ecalls that criminal acts, including against civilians, committed with the intent to cause death or serious bodily injury, or taking of hostages, with the purpose to provoke a state of terror in the general public or in a group of persons or particular persons, intimidate a population or compel a government or an international organization to do or to abstain from doing any act, which constitute offences within the scope of and as defined in the international conventions and protocols relating to terrorism, are under no circumstances justifiable by considerations of a political, philosophical, ideological, racial, ethnic, religious or other similar nature, and calls upon all States to prevent such acts and, if not prevented, to ensure that such acts are punished by penalties consistent with their grave nature[.][171]

What is also notable in the operative provision is the omission of reference to property or economic damage as being constitutive of an offence.[172] In any event, the terms of Resolution 1566 have had little influence on State practice.[173]

A broadly similar approach was taken by Fionnuala Ní Aoláin, the then UN Special Rapporteur on the promotion and protection of human rights and fundamental freedoms while countering terrorism, in her 2018 letter to Mark Zuckerberg, the Chief Executive Officer of Facebook. Therein, the Special Rapporteur offered the following 'model' definition of terrorism:

Terrorism means an action or attempted action where:

1. The action:

   (a) Constituted the intentional taking of hostages; or
   (b) Is intended to cause death or serious bodily injury to one or more members of the general population or segments of it; or
   (c) Involved lethal or serious physical violence against one or more members of the general population or segments of it; and

2. The action is done or attempted with the intention of:

   (a) Provoking a state of terror in the general public or a segment of it; or
   (b) Compelling a Government or international organization to do or abstain from doing something; and

---

[168]   K. Ambos and A. Timmermann, 'Terrorism and customary international law', chap. 2 in Saul (ed.), *Research Handbook on International Law and Terrorism*, 2nd ed., pp. 27–8.

[169]   K. Roach, 'Comparative Counter-Terrorism Law Comes of Age', in K. Roach (ed.), *Comparative Counter-Terrorism Law*, Cambridge University Press, Cambridge, 2015, p. 14.

[170]   Roberts, 'Countering Terrorism: A Historical Perspective', p. 7.

[171]   UN Security Council Resolution 1566, adopted on 8 October 2004 by unanimous vote in favour, operative para. 3.

[172]   B. Saul, *'The Legal Black Hole in United Nations Counterterrorism'*, IPI Observatory, New York, 2 June 2021, at: https://bit.ly/3GTe8nn.

[173]   Saul, 'From conflict to complementarity', p. 188.

(3) The action corresponds to:

    (a) The definition of a serious offence in national law, enacted for the purpose of complying with international conventions and protocols relating to terrorism or with resolutions of the Security Council relating to terrorism; or

    (b) All elements of a serious crime defined by national law.[174]

While not a perfect definition of terrorism in peacetime, the model definition proposed by the Special Rapporteur is certainly valuable.[175] It effectively excludes property damage and peaceful protest against the regime from the ambit of terrorism.[176] Thus, foreign nationals among the *gilets jaunes* ('yellow vest') protesters against President Emmanuel Macron's government in France in 2018–19[177] could not be deemed international terrorists under the definition, even had they defaced or damaged monuments in the capital.[178]

A further tweak to the language could usefully draw on the European Union's 2002 Framework Decision on Terrorism. Therein, one of the requisite intents for terrorist action includes reference to 'unduly compelling' the conduct of a government or international organization.[179] More problematic, however, is the delimiting reference in the Special Rapporteur's text to 'the general population or segments of it', which would appear to also exclude from the ambit of terrorism acts of violence against law enforcement officials. This is hard to square with the dictates of the 1997 Terrorist Bombings Convention, which certainly encompasses bombings directed against the police outside the conduct of hostilities in an armed conflict.[180]

1.3 DEFINING 'DOMESTIC' TERRORISM

As has been seen, a number of UN anti-terrorism treaties exclude from their scope what may be considered acts of purely domestic terrorism. The relevant provision in the 1979 Hostages Convention, for example, excludes consideration of a situation where the offence is committed within a single State, the hostage and the alleged offender are nationals of that State, and the alleged offender is found in the territory of that State.[181] Similar provisions are found in the 1997

---

[174] Mandate of the Special Rapporteur on the promotion and protection of human rights and fundamental freedoms while countering terrorism, Letter to Mr Mark Zuckerberg, UN doc. OL OTH 46/2018, 24 July 2018, at: https://bit.ly/34qJpkf, pp. 4–5. Small grammatical and typographical corrections have been made to the text for the sake of consistency, none of which is substantive.

[175] Compare the proposed definition with the one put forward by Ben Saul in 2006. *Defining Terrorism in International Law*, Oxford University Press, Oxford, 2006, pp. 65–6.

[176] Saul would include acts against property where they resulted in physical harm, and would include a specific exemption for the exercise of certain fundamental human rights. Ibid.

[177] See, e.g., J. Lichfield, 'Just who are the gilets jaunes?' Observer Special Report, *The Guardian*, 9 February 2019, at: https://bit.ly/3JspQaf.

[178] That does not make such acts lawful, of course, nor does it seek to preclude a State from prosecuting offenders for a crime in national law, just not one that falls under the rubric of terrorism and under cover of international counterterrorism law.

[179] Art. 1(1), EU Council Framework Decision of 13 June 2002 on combating terrorism, at: https://bit.ly/30LeoA1.

[180] The Convention stipulates that '[a]ny person commits an offence within the meaning of this Convention if that person unlawfully and intentionally delivers, places, discharges or detonates an explosive or other lethal device in, into or against a place of public use, a State or government facility'. Art. 2(1), 1997 Terrorist Bombings Convention. In turn, a 'State or government facility' is defined broadly as 'any permanent or temporary facility or conveyance that is used or occupied by representatives of a State, members of Government, the legislature or the judiciary or by officials or employees of a State or any other public authority or entity'. Art. 1(1), 1997 Terrorist Bombings Convention.

[181] Art. 13, 1979 Hostage-Taking Convention.

Terrorist Bombings Convention,[182] the 1999 Terrorism Financing Convention,[183] the 2005 Nuclear Terrorism Convention,[184] and the draft Comprehensive Convention against International Terrorism.[185]

As a consequence, where an offence is one of 'domestic' rather than international terrorism, a considerable measure of discretion is left to the national legislature in how it defines terrorism in its national law. This has engendered, in Duffy's words, a 'definitional deficit and the creeping reach of the terrorism label today'.[186] The risk is further that '[o]ld style repression of dissent could be legitimized through the language of modern counter-terrorism'.[187]

This does not, however, mean that the government of the day in any given State has *carte blanche* to adopt criminal law pertaining to terrorism in the manner it sees fit. International human rights law will act to render an overly broad crime of terrorism an internationally wrongful act, at the least where the purported offence directly contravenes a protected right. This is so, whether the right is laid down in a treaty to which the State in question is party or exists under customary international human rights law. Rights that would be of special concern as a result of overly broad definitions of offences include the right to life, the right to freedom from torture and other ill-treatment, the rights to liberty and to security, the right to a fair trial, and the right to freedom of peaceful assembly.

If, for example, the legislature in any given State renders all peaceful protests against the government of the day a criminal offence, this would be unlawful under international law. This principle pertains a fortiori to the establishment of terrorism offences. Hence, in relation to the right of peaceful assembly recognized under the 1966 International Covenant on Civil and Political Rights (ICCPR),[188] the Human Rights Committee has stated without caveat that '[t]he mere act of organizing or participating in a peaceful assembly cannot be criminalized under counterterrorism laws'.[189] A similar principle pertains to other fundamental rights, such as the right to freedom of association, the right to freedom of religion, and the right to freedom of speech.

A number of States safeguard national liberation movements from prosecution under domestic law for their involvement per se in armed struggle. In its 2004 Protection of Constitutional Democracy against Terrorist and Related Activities Act, South Africa had excluded from criminal prosecution and extradition as an act of terrorism

> any act committed during a struggle waged by peoples, including any action during an armed struggle, in the exercise or furtherance of their legitimate right to national liberation, self-determination and independence against colonialism, or occupation or aggression or domination by alien or foreign forces in accordance with the principles of international law, especially international humanitarian law, including the purposes and principles of the Charter of the United Nations and the Declaration on Principles of International Law concerning Friendly Relations and Cooperation among States in accordance with the said Charter.[190]

---

[182] Art. 3, 1997 Terrorist Bombings Convention.
[183] Art. 3, 1999 Terrorism Financing Convention.
[184] Art. 3, 2005 Nuclear Terrorism Convention.
[185] Art. 4, draft Comprehensive Convention against International Terrorism.
[186] H. Duffy, 'International human rights law and terrorism: An overview', chap. 22 in Saul (ed.), *Research Handbook on International Law and Terrorism*, 2nd ed., p. 332.
[187] K. Roach, 'Comparative Counter-Terrorism Law Comes of Age', p. 26.
[188] Art. 21, International Covenant on Civil and Political Rights; adopted at New York, 16 December 1966; entered into force, 23 March 1976. As of 1 January 2024, 173 States were party to the ICCPR.
[189] Human Rights Committee, General Comment No. 37 (2020) on the right of peaceful assembly (Article 21), UN doc. CCPR/C/GC/37, 17 September 2020, para. 68.
[190] Art. 1(4), Protection of Constitutional Democracy Against Terrorist and Related Activities Act, Act 33 of 2004, published in Government Gazette of the Republic of South Africa, Vol. 476, Cape Town, 11 February 2005, No. 27266, at: https://bit.ly/3GLqgX6.

1.3 Defining 'Domestic' Terrorism

The Act declared that any such act 'shall not, for any reason, including for purposes of prosecution or extradition, be considered as a terrorist activity'.[191] In December 2022, however, the South African Parliament revised the text of the 2004 Act. One of the amendments involved the deletion in its entirety of the above exclusion.[192]

Yemen's 2010 law on terrorist financing stipulates that '[c]ases of struggle by various means against foreign occupation and aggression for liberation and self-determination in accordance with the principles of international law shall not be considered as offences covered by this article'.[193]

Many other States explicitly include as an act of domestic terrorism an insurgency or rebellion on their territory. Under IHL, only in an international armed conflict do combatant members of the armed forces enjoy 'combatant's privilege'.[194] This is a customary rule[195] that, following their capture by the enemy, prohibits their trial on charges of direct participation in hostilities or for lawful acts of war.[196]

No corresponding privilege exists in non-international armed conflict. There is only an obligation – if one can call it that – to '*endeavour* to grant the broadest possible amnesty to persons who have participated in the armed conflict' at the 'end' of hostilities.[197] This does not preclude a prosecution being mounted by the authorities under *domestic* law: for example, for treason, for rebellion, or for terrorism, and for acts of violence by members of armed groups that are party to a non-international armed conflict.

In its judgment in *R* v. *Gul* in 2012, the Court of Appeal (Criminal Division) of England and Wales rejected the assertion that a domestic criminal law offence of terrorism in a non-international armed conflict could not be successfully prosecuted where the defendant was advocating attacks on lawful military objectives under IHL. Although the Court of Appeal's reasoning and certain of its conclusions are at times flawed, it was correct to hold that, under national law, in such a conflict 'there is nothing in international law which would exempt those engaged in attacks on the military during the course of an insurgency from the definition of terrorism'.[198] The following year, the UK Supreme Court confirmed this holding, declaring that

> [e]ven if it were the case that, because of the need to take into account the UK's international law obligations, the wide definition of terrorism had to be read down when it comes to construing those provisions [with extraterritorial effect], that would be of no assistance to a defendant such as the appellant, who is a UK citizen being prosecuted for offences allegedly committed in this country.[199]

---

[191] Ibid.

[192] S. 1(s), 2022 Protection of Constitutional Democracy against Terrorist and Related Activities Amendment Act (Act No. 23 of 2022).

[193] Art. 4, 2010 Law on Combating Money Laundering and Terrorist Financing (Law No. 1 on combating money laundering and terrorist financing).

[194] Thus, Article 43 of the 1977 Additional Protocol to the Geneva Conventions refers to combatant members of the armed forces as having the 'right to participate directly in hostilities'.

[195] See, e.g., G. D. Solis, *The Law of Armed Conflict, International Humanitarian Law in War*, 3rd ed., Cambridge University Press, Cambridge, 2021, p. 37. As Gary Solis recalls, the 1907 Hague Regulations (and indeed the earlier 1899 Regulations) expressed this in terms of the 'laws, rights, and duties of war'. Art. 1, Regulations concerning the Laws and Customs of War on Land, Annex to the Convention (IV) respecting the Laws and Customs of War on Land; adopted at The Hague, 18 October 1907; entered into force, 26 January 1910.

[196] ICRC, 'Internment in Armed Conflict: Basic Rules and Challenges', Opinion Paper, p. 4. See also Swiss Federal Department of Foreign Affairs, *ABC of International Humanitarian Law*, Bern, 2009, p. 13.

[197] Art. 6(5), Protocol Additional to the Geneva Conventions of 12 August 1949, and relating to the Protection of Victims of Non-International Armed Conflicts (Protocol II); adopted at Geneva, 8 June 1977, entered into force, 7 December 1978 (hereafter, 1977 Additional Protocol II).

[198] Court of Appeal (Criminal Division), *R* v. *Mohammed Gul*, Judgment, [2012] EWCA Crim 280, para. 49.

[199] UK Supreme Court, *R* v. *Mohammed Gul*, Judgment, [2013] UKSC 64, *esp.* paras. 56, 57.

1.4 THE DEFINITION OF TERRORISM IN ARMED CONFLICT

This segues into the international legal definitions of terrorism in situations of armed conflict. The two branches of IHL (also called the law of armed conflict) are Geneva Law and Hague Law. Geneva Law protects persons in the power of the enemy, in particular when they are detained or are civilians in territory occupied by a foreign State in an international armed conflict.[200] The other branch of IHL, Hague Law, regulates the conduct of hostilities: the combat between parties to an armed conflict.[201]

1.4.1 *The Definition of Terrorism in Geneva Law*

In international armed conflict, 'measures' of terrorism are explicitly prohibited against the civilian population. In non-international armed conflict, 'acts of terrorism' are similarly unlawful, but the prohibition also extends beyond civilians to those who formerly took a direct part in hostilities but no longer do so. These are addressed in turn.

1.4.1.1 Measures of Terrorism against Persons in the Power of the Enemy in International Armed Conflict

The 1949 Geneva Convention IV generally concerns the protection of civilians in international armed conflict. In addition to prohibiting hostage-taking, it contains an express prohibition of 'all measures' of 'terrorism' against civilians in occupied territories or against protected persons in the territory of a party to an armed conflict.[202] The ICRC's 1958 commentary on the provision offers little in the way of clarification of the unusual formulation, nor does it elucidate precisely what the provision envisages. The commentary does, however, observe that 'in resorting to intimidatory measures to terrorise the population, the belligerents hoped to prevent hostile acts. Far from achieving the desired effect, however, such practices, by reason of their excessive severity and cruelty, kept alive and strengthened the spirit of resistance. They strike at guilty and innocent alike'.[203]

The treatment meted out by the Nazis to civilians in occupied Europe during the Second World War does, however, offer an idea of what was envisaged. In 1948, former Field Marshal Erhard Milch was found guilty of war crimes pertaining to the 'slave labor and deportation to slave labor of the civilian populations of countries and territories occupied by the German armed forces, and in the enslavement, deportation, ill-treatment and terrorization of such persons'.[204] Mr Milch had been charged in connection with slave labour and deportation to slave labour of 'the civilian populations of Austria, Czechoslovakia, Italy, Hungary, and other countries and territories occupied by the German Armed Forces'.[205] In its judgment, the US

---

[200] Thus, in its 1987 commentary on the two 1977 Additional Protocols to the four Geneva Conventions, the ICRC noted that in 'the legal literature, the expression Geneva law is used fairly commonly to designate the rules of humanitarian law laying down the right of victims to protection'. ICRC, *Commentary on the Additional Protocols of 8 June 1977 to the Geneva Conventions of 12 August 1949*, Geneva, 1987, p. xxvii.

[201] ICRC, Commentary on the 1977 Additional Protocols, p. xxvii.

[202] Art. 33, Convention (IV) relative to the Protection of Civilian Persons in Time of War; adopted at Geneva, 12 August 1949; entered into force, 21 October 1950.

[203] ICRC Commentary on Article 33 of 1949 Geneva Convention IV, 1958, at: https://bit.ly/2LbfkLJ, p. 226.

[204] US Military Tribunal II, *US v. Milch*, Judgment, 31 July 1948, reprinted in *Trials of War Criminals Before the Nuernberg Military Tribunals under Control Council Law No. 10*, Vol. II (1997), available at: https://bit.ly/3sNmDLq, p. 790.

[205] Ibid., p. 360.

1.4 The Definition of Terrorism in Armed Conflict

Military Tribunal declared that 'it is an undoubted fact that the foreign workers were subjected to cruelties and torture and the deprivation of decent human rights merely because they were aliens'.[206]

The extermination of more than one million Jews perpetrated by the *Einsatzgruppen* in Eastern Europe, first in Poland and later in the Soviet Union, was mentioned in the Introduction to this book. Atrocities against civilians were also committed across occupied Western Europe. For example, on 10 June 1944 the SS Panzer Division *Das Reich* destroyed the French village of Oradour-sur-Glane, a small farming village near Clermont-Ferrand in Central France. The SS soldiers rounded up everyone they found in the village and concentrated them on the market square. Thereafter, they took the 197 men to several barns on the edge of town and locked them in, while the 240 women and 205 children were locked in the village church.[207] The soldiers set fire to the barns and threw grenades through the windows of the church, shooting those who sought to escape the flames.

After 642 inhabitants, including seven Jewish refugees, were dead, the company looted the empty dwellings and burned the village to the ground. Only seven villagers survived the massacre: six men and a woman, all injured. About fifteen other inhabitants of the village were able to escape the Germans before the massacre started or evade the round-up by hiding.[208] No reason was given for the barbarity, but the intimidatory message being communicated to the population of northern France was unmistakeable.

The 1977 Additional Protocol I, which applies also to 'armed conflicts in which peoples are fighting against colonial domination and alien occupation and against racist régimes in the exercise of their right of self-determination',[209] does not specifically refer to either measures or acts of terrorism. That said, in the fundamental guarantees that apply as a minimum standard to all who fall under the power of a party to an international armed conflict in accordance with the Protocol, many of the prohibited acts, such as murder, mutilation, torture, the taking of hostages, and collective punishments,[210] as well as arbitrary executions,[211] clearly constitute potential predicate offences for terrorism.[212] Surprisingly, in its detailed study of customary IHL issued in 2005, the ICRC did not identify a discrete rule prohibiting measures or acts of terrorism against those in the power of the enemy.

1.4.1.2 Acts of Terrorism against Persons in the Power of the Enemy in Non-international Armed Conflict

Article 3 common to the four 1949 Geneva Conventions, which applies to all situations of non-international armed conflict, does not specifically refer to acts of terrorism either, although similar to the fundamental guarantees referred to in Section 1.4.1.1, many of the prohibited acts, such as murder, mutilation, torture, the taking of hostages, and arbitrary executions, clearly

---

[206] Ibid., p. 790.

[207] United States Holocaust Memorial Museum, 'Oradour-sur-Glane', accessed 1 February 2022, at: https://bit.ly/3GDjLWs.

[208] Ibid.

[209] Art. 1(4), 1977 Additional Protocol I.

[210] Art. 75(2), 1977 Additional Protocol I.

[211] Art. 75(4), 1977 Additional Protocol I.

[212] In a separate section of its commentary on other provisions in the Protocol, the ICRC describes terrorism as being 'understood to be the systematic attack on non-military objectives in order to force the military elements of the adverse Party to comply with the wishes of the attacker by means of the fear and anguish induced by such an attack'. ICRC Commentary on Article 44(2) of the 1977 Additional Protocol I, para. 1690 note 27.

Defining Terrorism in International Law

constitute predicate offences. A specific, 'absolute' and 'unconditional' prohibition[213] of 'acts of terrorism' is, though, incorporated in the 1977 Additional Protocol II,[214] which binds parties to the non-international armed conflicts falling within its particular material scope.[215] The provision is broad in ambit, applying to protect '[a]ll persons who do not take a direct part or who have ceased to take part in hostilities, whether or not their liberty has been restricted'.[216] Hence, exceptionally, acts of terrorism may be committed against those who formerly participated directly in hostilities (e.g., by taking part in fighting) and not only against civilians.

In the view of the ICRC, the term 'acts of terrorism' in the Additional Protocol II covers 'not only acts directed against people, but also acts directed against installations which would cause victims as a side-effect'.[217] Thus, for example, the deliberate destruction of civilian homes, schools, or medical facilities, as well as the murder or torture of civilians or those *hors de combat*, at least where the intent or effect was to terrorize the population, would be encapsulated by the prohibition.

1.4.2 *The Definition of Terrorism in Hague Law*

Within the conduct of hostilities (the *fighting* in the vernacular), the use of terror tactics against the civilian population is explicitly prohibited in identical terms by the two 1977 Additional Protocols. It is thus stipulated that '[a]cts or threats of violence the primary purpose of which is to spread terror among the civilian population are prohibited'.[218] This is also a customary rule, as the ICRC confirms, applicable to all armed conflicts.[219]

The acts proscribed by the prohibition constitute, the ICRC avers, a 'special type of terrorism'.[220] As its commentary on the Additional Protocols explains: 'Air raids have often been used as a means of terrorizing the population, but these are not the only methods. For this reason, the text contains a much broader expression, namely 'acts or threats of violence' so as to cover all possible circumstances.'[221] The concept of 'terror' in the context of IHL was defined by the ICTY in its 2005 judgment at trial in the *Galić* case as 'extreme fear'.[222]

The ICRC commentary notes that acts of violence during conflict 'almost always give rise to some degree of terror among the population' and further that 'attacks on armed forces are purposely conducted brutally in order to intimidate the enemy soldiers and persuade them to surrender'. Accordingly, the Hague Law prohibition on terrorizing civilians is limited to acts of

---

[213] H. Gasser, 'Prohibition of Terrorist Acts in International Humanitarian Law', *International Review of the Red Cross*, No. 253 (1986), 200–12, at: https://bit.ly/3R3M4WR, at p. 200.

[214] Art. 4(2)(d), 1977 Additional Protocol II.

[215] These are where dissident armed forces or other organized armed groups fighting State armed forces have effective control of part of that State's territory such as to enable them to carry out sustained and concerted military operations and to implement the Protocol. Art. 1(1), 1977 Additional Protocol II. As of 1 January 2024, 169 States were party to the Protocol and a further three States were signatories.

[216] Art. 4(1), 1977 Additional Protocol II.

[217] ICRC, Commentary on the 1977 Additional Protocols, at: http://bit.ly/2IGhscP, para. 4538.

[218] Art. 51(2), 1977 Additional Protocol I; and Art. 13(2), 1977 Additional Protocol II.

[219] ICRC, Customary IHL Rule 2: 'Violence Aimed at Spreading Terror among the Civilian Population'.

[220] Y. Sandoz, C. Swinarski and B. Zimmermann (eds.), *Commentary on the Additional Protocols of 8 June 1977 to the Geneva Conventions of 12 August 1949*, Martinus Nijhoff, Geneva, 1987, para. 4538.

[221] ICRC commentary on the 1977 Additional Protocols, para. 4785.

[222] ICTY, *Prosecutor* v. *Galić*, Judgment (Trial Chamber) (Case No. IT-98-29-T), 5 December 2003, para. 135. This interpretation was effectively confirmed in the judgment at trial in the *Blagojević* case two years later, even though the charge itself was of persecution as a crime against humanity. ICTY, *Prosecutor* v. *Blagojević and Jokić*, Judgment (Trial Chamber) (Case No. IT-02-60-T), 17 January 2005, para. 590. In making its determination, the Trial Chamber explicitly referred to the IHL rule in the 1977 Additional Protocol I. Ibid., para. 589.

1.4 The Definition of Terrorism in Armed Conflict

violence whose primary purpose is to spread terror among the civilian population 'without offering substantial military advantage'.[223] As Dinstein has observed, large-scale aerial bombardments that are 'pounding' military objectives and 'breaking the back of the enemy armed forces' are not unlawful according to this rule, even if they lead to a 'collapse of civilian morale'.[224] Accordingly, in its judgment in the *Prlić* case, reversing the decision at trial, the ICTY Appeals Chamber held that the destruction of the Old Bridge at Mostar could not amount to terrorization of the civilian population since it constituted a lawful military objective in the circumstances prevailing at the time.[225]

Indiscriminate bombing of cities was widely practised in the Second World War, especially of German cities by the United States Air Force (USAF) and the British Royal Air Force (RAF) and of Japanese cities by the USAF. The bombing of Hamburg and later Dresden, in particular, killed tens of thousands of German civilians for negligible military advantage: less than 10 per cent of German industrial production is said to have been cut by the bombing.[226] After Dresden was bombed on 13 February 1945, even Churchill expressed doubts as to the value of the raid, writing in a memorandum: 'It seems to me that the moment has come when the question of bombing of German cities simply for the sake of increasing the terror, though under other pretexts, should be reviewed.'[227] That is not to downplay the illegality or inhumanity of the Blitz (the shortened German term used to describe the bombing of British cities from 1940) and the later use of the indiscriminate V-1 and V-2 weapons, which were equally criminal in intent and in operation. About 60,000 people, the overwhelming majority civilians, would be killed in the Blitz, around half of them in London.[228]

The dropping of the atomic bomb on Hiroshima and then on Nagasaki in August 1945 was designed to intimidate and coerce the Japanese into ending the war quickly and preserving American lives. A uranium fission bomb was dropped over Hiroshima on 6 August 1945, detonating directly over Shima Hospital in the centre of the city at 8:15 am. Every doctor, nurse, and patient in the hospital was killed instantly. Everything within a 500-metre radius of Ground Zero was charred; ground temperatures briefly attained 4,000 degrees Celsius.[229] Tens of thousands of people within a two-kilometre radius were 'burned, decapitated, disembowelled, crushed and irradiated'. The sudden, precipitate drop in air pressure 'blew their eyes from their sockets and ruptured their eardrums; the shockwave cleaved their bodies apart'.[230] There were minimal military objectives in Hiroshima. Strategic nuclear weapons are the epitome of indiscriminate terror weapons.

Terrorizing too can be conventional weapons. In the last decade, the link between acts carried out with a view to terrorize civilians, such as targeted or indiscriminate bombardment and crimes against humanity, has been widely seen in the armed conflicts in Syria. In 2014, the UN Commission of Inquiry on Syria found that the government had employed a military strategy targeting the civilian population, combining long-lasting sieges with continuous air and ground bombardment. In neighbourhoods around Damascus, civilians were targeted on the basis of their perceived opposition to the government. Innocent civilians would be attacked for merely

---

[223] ICRC commentary on the 1977 Additional Protocols, para. 1940.

[224] Dinstein, *The Conduct of Hostilities under the Law of International Armed Conflict*, 4th ed., pp. 168–69, para. 490.

[225] ICTY, *Prosecutor* v. *Prlić*, Judgment (Appeals Chamber) (Case No. IT-04–74-A), 29 November 2017, paras. 411 and 425–26.

[226] A. Marr, *The Making of Modern Britain*, Pan Books, London, 2009, p. 423.

[227] T. Luckhurst, 'Dresden: The World War Two bombing 75 years on', *BBC News*, 13 February 2020, at: https://bbc.in/2VdKhnk.

[228] Marr, *The Making of Modern Britain*, p. 354.

[229] P. Ham, *Hiroshima Nagasaki*, Macmillan, United Kingdom, 2011, p. 357.

[230] Ibid., p. 358.

residing in or originating from these neighbourhoods. The Commission of Inquiry concluded that the Syrian regime 'has carried out a widespread and systematic attack against the civilian population of Aleppo to punish and terrorize civilians for supporting or hosting armed groups, in an apparent strategy to erode popular support for those groups'.[231]

1.5 CONCLUDING OBSERVATIONS

This chapter has sought to lay bare the complexity of the nature of terrorism's definition under international law. In the absence of a Comprehensive Convention on International Terrorism, States are of course bound by the sectoral or regional terrorism treaties to which they are party. *Pacta sunt servanda* – the duty to interpret and apply treaties in good faith – is a fundamental rule of international law. There is, however, no customary law definition of international terrorism in peacetime (and a fortiori no corresponding international crime per se).[232] Whether those engaged in national liberation struggles outside armed conflict are international terrorists when they engage in certain acts thus remains unsettled as a matter of customary law.

On the high seas, a right of search of suspected piratical vessels exists, but not for vessels containing suspected terrorists who do not meet the customary law definition of pirates as codified in the UN Convention on the Law of the Sea. Gaps in the right of search are filled by the SUA Convention and its 2005 Protocol between States Parties to those treaties, but the corresponding rights of visit do not apply to States not party as a matter of custom.

Purely 'domestic' terrorism is within the bounds of municipal law, and a measure of discretion is afforded to the executive and the legislature in this regard. That said, international law will intervene where the scope of legislation is capricious or where it violates fundamental human rights. A State that renders the lawful exercise of fundamental human rights a terrorist offence in its domestic law engages its international responsibility.

In armed conflict, attacks by air, on the ground, and at sea whose primary purpose is to terrorize the civilian population are prohibited under the customary and treaty law of the Hague. Bombardment is an obvious means by which to do so. Attacking lawful military objectives in the conduct of hostilities, however, including so-called internationally protected persons when they meet the IHL definition of a military objective, does not constitute terrorism under the law of armed conflict.

The prohibition of acts of terrorism against detained civilians or of measures of terrorism against the population in an occupied territory is equally a customary rule of IHL, despite the ICRC's relative silence on the matter.[233] Hostage-taking is always unlawful under international

---

[231] Report of the Independent International Commission of Inquiry on the Syrian Arab Republic, UN doc. A/HRC/27/60, 13 August 2014, para. 104.

[232] Thus, the ILC's proposed text in 1995 of an international crime of international terrorism for the Statute of the International Criminal Court received significant pushback from States. See Draft Article 24, 'Draft Code of Crimes against the Peace and Security of Mankind', Thirteenth report on the draft code of crimes against the peace and security of mankind, by Mr. Doudou Thiam, Special Rapporteur, UN doc. A/CN.4/466, paras. 111 *et seq.* The draft crime read as follows: 'An individual who is an agent or representative of a State commits or orders the commission of any of the following acts: ... Undertaking, organizing, assisting, financing, encouraging or tolerating acts against another State directed at persons or property and of such a nature as to create a state of terror in the minds of public figures, groups of persons or the general public.'

[233] In confirming the customary rule prohibiting terror attacks in the conduct of hostilities, the ICRC avers that the rule is 'supported by the wider prohibition of "acts of terrorism" in Article 4(2)(d) of Additional Protocol II' and that the UN Secretary-General had 'noted that violations of Article 4 of Additional Protocol II have long been considered violations of customary international law'. ICRC, Customary IHL Rule 2: 'Violence Aimed at Spreading Terror among the Civilian Population'.

1.5 Concluding Observations

law, whether that occurs inside or outside armed conflict.[234] It may readily be considered as an act of terrorism wherever the object of the hostage-taking is civilians and the aim of the action is to strike extreme fear into the civilian population. In the context of armed conflict, the taking of hostages is unequivocally prohibited. In peacetime, the 1979 Hostage-Taking Convention fully applies.[235]

The customary rule of 'combatant's privilege' will not allow a party to an international armed conflict to prosecute an enemy combatant that it detains for his or her mere direct participation in hostilities, including for acts of terrorism under domestic law. Only if the combatant has committed a war crime may a prosecution be lawfully engaged. In a situation of non-international armed conflict, however, no combatant's privilege exists, and thus the State may potentially charge a detained fighter with terrorism offences under its domestic law even when they comply with the rules of international humanitarian law.

---

[234] It is the specific intent that characterizes hostage-taking, distinguishing it from the deprivation of liberty as an administrative or judicial measure. ICRC, Customary IHL Rule 96: 'Hostage-Taking', at: https://bit.ly/3GPHRgS.

[235] Torture and rape are similarly always prohibited under international law irrespective of the prevailing circumstances. Where the intent is to terrorize, they may justly be considered also as acts of terrorism. In certain cases, such acts also amount to international crimes.

2

The Key Components of International Counterterrorism Law

2.1 INTRODUCTION

The architecture of international counterterrorism law is the subject of this chapter. It is a branch of public international law that has emerged from an evolving 'special legal regime'[1] to regulate action to prevent and punish terrorism and to tackle terrorists. International counterterrorism law is a matrix of global terrorism treaties and dedicated United Nations (UN) Security Council resolutions that require the incorporation of offences into domestic law combined with the salient rules of international humanitarian law (IHL) and the law of law enforcement. These rules, which regulate when and against whom force may be used in counterterrorism, are supplemented by (though are sometimes inconsistent with) the content of regional treaties and domestic legislation.[2] The standards and laws are subject to the constraints and oversight of international human rights law.

Specific penalties may be imposed upon individuals following their conviction under international criminal law for the perpetration of terrorism as a war crime. Despite claims to the contrary,[3] terrorism per se is not yet a distinct international crime, although it is punishable as a form of war crime. Those who have engaged in an act of terrorism and who seek asylum abroad may lawfully be refused the status of refugee as a consequence of their conduct. Nonetheless, their deportation or extradition to the territory or control of another State is always subject to compliance with the rule of *non-refoulement* that is binding on all States as a matter of custom. Our communications and movements may be surveilled by the authorities where it is reasonably suspected that we are planning or conspiring to commit an act of terror. For dual nationals, citizenship may be withdrawn by one of the two States in exceptional circumstances. In certain cases, terrorist action by a State and, at the least when they act under its instruction as its proxy, also by a non-State armed group, may breach the law on inter-State use of force (*jus ad bellum*).

The endeavour of the chapter is to bring a degree of clarity to an international legal domain of complexity and fragmentation. But anyone seeking a simple, coherent, and consensual ensemble of norms will have to lower their expectations.[4] As sketched out in Chapter 1, the

---

[1] D. Moeckli, 'The Emergence of Terrorism as a Distinct Category of International Law', *Texas International Law Journal*, Vol. 44 (2008), 157–83, at p. 168.

[2] As Saul has written, some regional definitions are 'so broad as to be indistinguishable from other forms of political violence, or public order or national security offences'. Saul, Defining Terrorism in International Law, p. 190.

[3] See Chapter 6 on this issue.

[4] Saul, for instance, observes that terrorism 'is thick with law' but 'that does not mean that the law is coherent or legitimate'. B. Saul, 'Terrorism and International Criminal Law: Questions of (in)coherence and (il)legitimacy', chap. 8 in G. Boas, W. A. Schabas, and M. P. Scharf (eds.), *International Criminal Justice*, Edward Elgar, Cheltenham, 2012, 190–230, at p. 191.

definitional disputes as to the nature and scope of terrorism – and hence also the identification of terrorists – simply run too deep. The competing claims underpinning the ideological divides between States persist, seemingly without prospective resolution. Even the adoption of the UN Comprehensive Convention against International Terrorism, should ever it come to pass,[5] will merely construct a bridge between two opposing cliffs. The gorge below will surely remain.

2.2 THE UNITED NATIONS SECTORAL TREATIES

In the absence of a concluded UN Comprehensive Convention on International Terrorism, the phenomenon of international terrorism in peacetime is primarily regulated under international law by the sectoral global terrorism treaties and regional instruments. Any interrogation of the dictates of international counterterrorism law should begin with consideration of the many treaties concluded under UN auspices, but with due acknowledgement of the political and ideological disputes that negotiations and subsequent State practice reflect. A review of the materially inconsistent substance of regional treaties on the prevention and/or repression of terrorism follows.

In none of these instances, however, is terrorism instituted as an international crime: the focus is consistently on the implementation of offences defined in the global and regional treaties as criminal offences under domestic law. That municipal law status persists notwithstanding the extraterritorial or even universal criminal jurisdiction that the different treaties typically demand of their States Parties. The duty to either 'submit for the purpose of prosecution' the case of a suspected terrorism offender or to hand him or her over to another State for prosecution, while similar to the *aut dedere aut iudicare* obligations under the 1949 Geneva Conventions,[6] is legally distinct.[7]

---

[5] In December 1996, the UN General Assembly adopted a resolution in whose preamble Member States declared themselves to be '[b]*earing in mind* the possibility of considering in the future the elaboration of a comprehensive convention on international terrorism'. (Resolution 51/210: 'Measures to eliminate international terrorism', adopted without a vote on 17 December 1996, tenth preambular para.) Two years later, the General Assembly went beyond mere aspiration to call on the Ad Hoc Committee established by that resolution to consider 'on a priority basis', once it had concluded dedicated treaties on terrorist financing and nuclear terrorism, 'the elaboration of a comprehensive convention on international terrorism'. (Resolution 53/108, adopted without a vote on 8 December 1998, operative para. 11.) In fact, drafting did not wait for the conclusion of the nuclear terrorism treaty, which would only occur in 2005. Already in 2000, the Assembly had decided that the Ad Hoc Committee shall meet from 12 to 23 February 2001 to *continue* the elaboration of a draft comprehensive convention on international terrorism. (Resolution 55/158, adopted on 12 December 2000 by 151 votes to nil with 2 abstentions (Lebanon and Syria), operative para. 14 [added emphasis].) The work would not, however, be brought to fruition. Twenty-two years later the annual resolution on '[m]easures to eliminate international terrorism' was mandating the establishment of yet another working group, and still only 'with a view to finalizing the process on the draft comprehensive convention on international terrorism'. Resolution 77/113, adopted without a vote on 7 December 2022, operative para. 25.

[6] Art. 146, Convention (IV) relative to the Protection of Civilian Persons in Time of War; adopted at Geneva, 12 August 1949; entered into force, 21 October 1950 (hereafter, 1949 Geneva Convention IV): 'Each High Contracting Party shall be under the obligation to search for persons alleged to have committed, or to have ordered to be committed, such grave breaches, and shall bring such persons, regardless of their nationality, before its own courts. It may also, if it prefers, and in accordance with the provisions of its own legislation, hand such persons over for trial to another High Contracting Party concerned, provided such High Contracting Party has made out a prima facie case.'

[7] Trapp, *State Responsibility for International Terrorism*, pp. 82–86, 128, 266. The obligations in Article 7 of the 1984 UN Convention against Torture, which reflect to a significant extent the corresponding wording in the sectoral terrorism treaties, were held by the International Court of Justice (ICJ) to require that a national prosecution *be mounted* if the choice is made not to extradite a suspected perpetrator of terrorism: 'Extradition is an option offered to the State by the Convention, whereas prosecution is an international obligation under the Convention, the violation of which is a wrongful act engaging the responsibility of the State.' ICJ, *Questions Concerning the Obligation to Prosecute or Extradite (Belgium v. Senegal)*, Judgment, 20 July 2012, para. 95. Nevertheless, the obligation to submit the case to

As Chapter 1 outlined, the politically contested nature of the ambit and parameters of what constitutes terrorism was palpable in the early 1970s in the context of discussions and negotiations within the UN General Assembly. An agenda item in 1972 was initially termed 'Measures to prevent international terrorism which endangers or takes innocent human lives or jeopardizes fundamental freedoms'. But following an amendment moved by Saudi Arabia, and with the support of other members of the Non-Aligned Movement, the item was retitled with the addition of the following text: 'and study of the underlying causes of those forms of terrorism and acts of violence which lie in misery, frustration, grievance and despair and which cause some people to sacrifice human lives, including their own, in an attempt to effect radical changes'.[8] Disagreement about what drives a person to commit a terrorist act was in plain sight, with the implicit but underlying contestation as to whether acts of violence in pursuit of certain legitimate goals even amounted to terrorism.

The relevant Assembly resolution in the twenty-sixth session of the General Assembly in 1972 established an Ad Hoc Committee on International Terrorism,[9] a potentially significant achievement. But the fraught politics of the issue were reflected in the contested nature of the resolution's passage, achieved with only seventy-six votes in favour to thirty-five against. That was, in great measure, due to the incorporation in the operative text of the resolution of language that would become a lingua franca of terrorism debates: '*Reaffirms* the inalienable right to self-determination and independence of all peoples under colonial and racist régimes and other forms of alien domination and upholds the legitimacy of their struggle, in particular the struggle of national liberation movements, in accordance with the purposes and principles of the Charter and the relevant resolutions of the organs of the United Nations.'[10] The resolution went on to condemn the 'continuation of repressive and *terrorist* acts by colonial, racist and alien régimes'.[11] States were divided as to who the terrorist truly was.[12]

The United States tried and failed to push through a draft Convention for the Prevention and Punishment of Certain Acts of International Terrorism,[13] but this foundered on the basis of the ongoing struggles for national liberation from colonial rule and other forms of mass oppression around the world. And whereas in the 1950s the United States and its allies had effectively dominated the UN General Assembly, by the early 1970s almost three-quarters of its members were from the Global South.[14] This raised hackles in Richard Nixon's faltering administration at

---

the competent authorities under Article 7(1) of the Convention against Torture 'may or may not result in the institution of proceedings, in the light of the evidence before them, relating to the charges against the suspect'. Ibid. para. 94. See Art. 7, Convention against Torture and Other Cruel, Inhuman or Degrading Treatment or Punishment; adopted at New York, 10 December 1984; entered into force, 26 June 1987.

[8] On this issue, see Perera, 'The Draft United Nations Comprehensive Convention on International Terrorism', p. 122.

[9] UN General Assembly Resolution 3034 (XXVII), adopted on 18 December 1972 by 76 votes to 35 with 17 abstentions, operative para. 9.

[10] Ibid., operative para. 3 [original emphasis].

[11] Ibid., operative para. 4 [added emphasis].

[12] The thirty-five Member States voting against the adoption of Resolution 3034 (XXVII) were Australia, Austria, Barbados, Belgium, Bolivia, Brazil, Canada, Colombia, Costa Rica, Denmark, the Dominican Republic, Fiji, Greece, Guatemala, Haiti, Honduras, Iceland, Iran, Israel, Italy, Japan, Lesotho, Luxembourg, Malawi, the Netherlands, New Zealand, Nicaragua, Paraguay, the Philippines, Portugal, South Africa, Turkey, the United Kingdom, the United States, and Uruguay. Those abstaining were Argentina, El Salvador, Finland, France, Ireland, Ivory Coast, Jordan, Laos, Liberia, the Maldives, Nepal, Norway, Spain, Swaziland, Sweden, Thailand, and Zaire.

[13] 'US Draft Convention for Prevention and Punishment of Terrorism Acts', UN doc. A/C.6/L.850, reprinted in *International Legal Materials*, Vol. 11, No. 6 (November 1972), 1382–87.

[14] Blumenau, *The United Nations and Terrorism: Germany, Multilateralism, and Antiterrorism Efforts in the 1970s*, p. 90.

2.2 The United Nations Sectoral Treaties

the time (accompanied by more than a hint of racism, as Blumenau depicts in his 2014 work, *The United Nations and Terrorism. Germany, Multilateralism, and Antiterrorism Efforts in the 1970s*).[15]

Given the new mathematics of global diplomacy, it was decided in the West to seek to achieve agreement on the text of a convention far more limited in scope. The choice was ultimately made to work towards a treaty dedicated to the protection of diplomats working abroad. This would become the first of the global 'sectoral' terrorism treaties, even though, to minimize opposition, the 1973 Convention as adopted does not refer to 'terrorism' at any point. The framing of the treaty would, in part, set the stage for the approach that followed: a definition of the offences within the scope of each Convention together with a requirement that they be duly incorporated into domestic criminal law and then that the offenders be prosecuted. To seek to ensure there were no safe havens for terrorists, provision was further made for the inter-State cooperation needed to tackle the problem.

The 1973 Internationally Protected Persons Convention[16] obligates its States Parties to make it a criminal offence in their domestic law to murder, kidnap, or attack internationally protected persons (as defined under the Convention),[17] as well as to criminalize violent attacks on their official premises, private accommodation, and transport.[18] Attacks against not only the personal safety of diplomats but also certain State property abroad are to be criminalized as offences under the host nation's domestic law. A prosecution must be mounted by either the State where the protected diplomats are attacked or the State of the offenders' nationality, or else the criminal suspects must be handed over to another State for prosecution.[19] The inherently international nature of the offence meant that no corresponding exemption of the Convention's provisions for acts of 'domestic' terrorism against the protected persons could be appropriate. Ordinarily, such exclusions are otherwise the third leg of the tripartite approach that is common to other sectoral counterterrorism treaties.

In 1979, six years after the successful adoption of the Internationally Protected Persons Convention, it was a common tactic of terrorism rather than a common target that was at issue. The taking of hostages to raise international profile (and cash), as well as with a view to achieving short- and longer-term political objectives, was an especially regular phenomenon in the 1970s. The 1979 Hostage-Taking Convention, formally adopted by the UN General Assembly two weeks before the end of the decade, is one of the most widely ratified UN sectoral terrorism treaties, with only nineteen States not bound by its provisions.[20] Each State Party is required to make hostage-taking a domestic criminal offence punishable by 'appropriate penalties' that take account of its 'grave nature'.[21]

---

[15] Ibid., p. 91.

[16] Convention on the Prevention and Punishment of Crimes against Internationally Protected Persons, including Diplomatic Agents; adopted at New York, 14 December 1973; entered into force, 20 February 1977. As of 1 January 2024, 180 of 197 States were party to the Convention. In addition, the Cook Islands and Niue are bound through New Zealand's ratification, meaning that 182 States in total are effectively bound by its provisions. See the relevant UN Treaty Collection entry at: https://bit.ly/3BaEfVk.

[17] For further details on the definition, see supra Chapter 1 of this work.

[18] Art. 2(1) and (2), 1973 Internationally Protected Persons Convention.

[19] Art. 3, 1973 Internationally Protected Persons Convention.

[20] International Convention against the Taking of Hostages; adopted at New York, 17 December 1979; entered into force, 3 June 1983 (1979 Hostage-Taking Convention), fifth preambular para. As of 1 January 2024, 176 States were party to the Convention. In addition, the Cook Islands and Niue are bound through New Zealand's ratification, meaning that 178 of 197 States able to adhere are bound by its provisions. See the relevant UN Treaty Collection entry at: https://bit.ly/3KyjBmt.

[21] Art. 2, 1979 Hostage-Taking Convention.

In peacetime, the 1979 Hostage-Taking Convention fully applies, even absent what might ordinarily be considered a terrorism motivation. The limited exclusionary clause in the Convention for situations of armed conflict – where an obligation exists under a treaty of international humanitarian law to prosecute or hand over for prosecution an offender – would thus not apply in a situation of non-international armed conflict. That said, where cumulatively the substance of the offence is committed within a single State; the hostage and the alleged offender are nationals of that State; and the alleged offender is found in the territory of that State, a general exclusion of the Convention applies.[22] The rationale is that such a situation equates to domestic, rather than international terrorism, and hence that a prosecution, which is highly likely to be mounted by the municipal authorities, does not ordinarily require legal assistance from other States in order to be successful (such as through the extradition of a suspected offender).

The 1997 Terrorist Bombings Convention, negotiated at the insistence of the United States following the bombing targeting its air force personnel in Saudi Arabia the year before, similarly requires that its States Parties ensure that the cases of terrorist bombing defined in the Convention are made criminal offences under their domestic law and that they are likewise punishable by 'appropriate penalties which take into account the grave nature of those offences'.[23] No specific intent of the bomber is required: in effect, the nature of bombings is – rightly or wrongly – considered to be inherently terrorizing.

As is the case with the 1979 Hostage-Taking Convention, a general exclusion of the application of the 1997 Convention exists in a situation that equates to purely domestic terrorism.[24] But a broader exclusion of the application of the Terrorist Bombings Convention during an armed conflict than is the case in the 1979 Hostage-Taking Convention pertains to acts *in bello* by State armed forces or non-State armed groups. This is so where their acts are governed by international humanitarian law.[25]

Further excluded from the Convention's purview are acts of the military forces of a State 'in the exercise of their official duties', where this conduct is governed by other rules of international law.[26] This controversial omission concerns, among others, acts regulated by international human rights law, such as law enforcement operations, and could thus exclude certain targeted killings, including where perpetrated by remotely piloted aircraft (drones), as well as conduct regulated by *jus ad bellum*.[27] The corresponding provision in the draft Comprehensive Convention against International Terrorism[28] remains the subject of dispute, one of the issues effectively precluding its conclusion.

---

[22] Art. 13, 1979 Hostage-Taking Convention.

[23] Art. 4, International Convention for the Suppression of Terrorist Bombings; adopted at New York, 15 December 1997; entered into force, 23 May 2001. As of 1 January 2024, 170 States were party to the 1997 Terrorist Bombings Convention.

[24] Art. 3, 1997 Terrorist Bombings Convention.

[25] Art. 19(2), 1997 Terrorist Bombings Convention.

[26] Ibid.

[27] In 2005, the then UN Secretary-General Kofi Annan declared: 'It is time to set aside debates on so-called "State terrorism". The use of force by States is already thoroughly regulated under international law.' 'In larger freedom: Towards development, security and human rights for all', Report of the Secretary-General, UN doc. A/59/2005, 21 March 2005, para. 91. This statement is legally incorrect and morally questionable. Terrorism can be committed by organs or agents of the State domestically (where *jus ad bellum* does not ordinarily apply) and in a situation of armed conflict under IHL without reference to *jus ad bellum*.

[28] Art. 20(3), 'Draft comprehensive convention against international terrorism, Consolidated text prepared by the coordinator for discussion', Annex II to Report of the Coordinator of the draft convention, attached to the letter of the Chair of the Sixth Committee to the President of the General Assembly, dated 3 August 2005, UN doc. A/59/894.

2.2 The United Nations Sectoral Treaties

The 2005 Nuclear Terrorism Convention[29] is, at the time of writing, the most recent of the primary global sectoral treaties on terrorism.[30] Negotiated over a period of seven years, it requires, in particular, the criminalization in domestic law of the unlawful and intentional possession of radioactive material and the making or possession of a radiological device (i.e., a 'dirty bomb') where this act is intended either to cause death or serious bodily injury, or to inflict substantial damage on property or the environment.[31]

This provision expanded on the text of the 1979 Vienna Convention on the Physical Protection of Nuclear Material, adopted under the auspices of the International Atomic Energy Agency (IAEA), which required the criminalization of an intentional threat either to use nuclear material to cause death or serious injury to any person or substantial property damage, or to engage in theft or robbery of nuclear material in order to compel a natural or legal person, international organization, or State to do or to refrain from doing any act.[32] An amendment to the Convention, adopted in 2005, added as offences

> an act directed against a nuclear facility, or an act interfering with the operation of a nuclear facility, where the offender intentionally causes, or where he knows that the act is likely to cause, death or serious injury to any person or substantial damage to property or to the environment by exposure to radiation or release of radioactive substances, unless the act is undertaken in conformity with the national law of the State Party in the territory of which the nuclear facility is situated;
> an act constituting a demand for nuclear material by threat or use of force or by any other form of intimidation[.][33]

There is a broad exclusion for acts of warfare directed against nuclear facilities in a situation of armed conflict under the 2005 Nuclear Terrorism Convention in the same terms as the Terrorist

---

[29] International Convention for the Suppression of Acts of Nuclear Terrorism; adopted at New York, 13 April 2005; entered into force, 7 July 2007. As of 1 January 2024, 123 States were party to the 2005 Nuclear Terrorism Convention and a further 30 States were signatories.

[30] At the time of writing, work had begun in the United Nations on the elaboration of a cybercrime treaty, which could potentially encompass cyberterrorism. The initial draft negotiating text contains a proposed provision whereby '[e]ach State Party shall adopt such legislative and other measures as may be necessary to establish as criminal offences, when committed by means of information and communications technologies, the commission of terrorist acts, the incitement, recruitment or other involvement in terrorist activities, the advocacy and justification of terrorism or the collection or provision of funds for its financing, training for terrorist acts, the facilitation of communication between terrorist organizations and their members, including the establishment, publication or use of a website or the provision of logistical support for perpetrators of terrorist acts, the dissemination of methods for making explosives employed in particular in terrorist acts, and the spreading of strife, sedition, hatred or racism'. Draft Article 29, 'Consolidated negotiating document on the general provisions and the provisions on criminalization and on procedural measures and law enforcement of a comprehensive international convention on countering the use of information and communications technologies for criminal purposes', UN doc. A/AC.291/16, 7 November 2022.

[31] Arts. 2(1)(a) and 5, 2005 Nuclear Terrorism Convention.

[32] Art. 7, Convention on the Physical Protection of Nuclear Material; adopted at Vienna, 28 October 1979; entered into force, 8 February 1987. As of 1 January 2024, 164 States were parties to the Convention. The link with terrorism was made explicit in the 2005 Protocol to the Convention. A new preamble contained the following paragraphs:
'DEEPLY CONCERNED by the worldwide escalation of acts of terrorism in all its forms and manifestations, and by the threats posed by international terrorism and organized crime,
BELIEVING that physical protection plays an important role in supporting nuclear non-proliferation and counter-terrorism objectives'.
Amendment to the Convention on the Physical Protection of Nuclear Material; adopted at Vienna, 8 July 2005; entered into force, 8 May 2016, eighth and ninth preambular paras. A further preambular paragraph recalled the Declaration on Measures to Eliminate International Terrorism annexed to General Assembly Resolution 49/60 of 9 December 1994. Amendment to the Convention on the Physical Protection of Nuclear Material, sixth preambular para.

[33] Art. 7(e) and (f), 2005 Amended Convention on the Physical Protection of Nuclear Material. As of 1 January 2024, 135 States were parties to the amended Convention.

58   Components of International Counterterrorism Law

Bombings Convention.[34] And just as with the 1997 Convention, while the conduct of the main parties to an armed conflict would be excluded from its purview, relevant acts of civilians participating directly in hostilities would fall to be considered under the Nuclear Terrorism Convention as well as under IHL.

The same is true with the amended Convention on the Physical Protection of Nuclear Material, which provides that

> [t]he activities of armed forces during an armed conflict, as those terms are understood under international humanitarian law, which are governed by that law, are not governed by this Convention, and the activities undertaken by the military forces of a State in the exercise of their official duties, inasmuch as they are governed by other rules of international law, are not governed by this Convention.[35]

2.2.1 *The Global Hijacking and Counterpiracy Treaties*

A number of multilateral aerial and maritime treaties have also been adopted to address acts that may typically be considered terrorist in nature.[36] The aerial treaties were concluded within the auspices of the International Civil Aviation Organization (ICAO), a specialized UN agency established before the creation of the United Nations pursuant to the 1944 Chicago Convention, which regulates civil aviation around the world.[37] All States but four (as recognized by the UN Secretary-General) are party to the Chicago Convention.[38] The salient maritime treaties have been concluded under the auspices of the International Maritime Organization (IMO), the specialized UN agency responsible for regulating international shipping.[39] The UN Convention on the Law of the Sea (UNCLOS) addresses piracy and counterpiracy but not terrorism or counterterrorism.[40]

2.2.1.1 The Aerial Terrorism Treaties

The 1963 ICAO Tokyo Convention[41] was devised in order to address the hijacking of aircraft and it has been very widely ratified (with 189 States Parties at the time of writing). That said, it neither

---

[34] Art. 4(2), 2005 Nuclear Terrorism Convention.

[35] Art. 2(4)(b), 2005 Amended Convention on the Physical Protection of Nuclear Material.

[36] As noted in Chapter 1, the Annex to the 1999 Terrorism Financing Convention refers to the following six aerial and maritime treaties as instituting terrorism offences: the 1970 Hague Aircraft Hijacking Convention; the 1971 Montreal Convention and its 1988 Protocol; the 1979 (Vienna) Convention on the Physical Protection of Nuclear Material; the 1988 Suppression of Unlawful Acts against the Safety of Maritime Navigation (SUA) Convention; and the 1988 Fixed Platforms Protocol. Protocols to the latter two treaties, both adopted in 2005 after the conclusion of the Terrorism Financing Convention, would logically be added to the list.

[37] Art. 43, Convention on International Civil Aviation; signed at Chicago, 7 December 1944; entered into force, 4 April 1947.

[38] As of 1 January 2024, 193 States were party to the Convention. The four States not party are the Holy See, Liechtenstein, Niue, and Palestine. The Convention depositary is the United States.

[39] The IMO has 175 members (all States; see the list at: http://bit.ly/3Z4DnwA) and three associate members: the Faroes; Hong Kong, China; and Macao, China. The twenty-two States that have not joined the IMO are the following: Afghanistan, Andorra, Bhutan, Burkina Faso, Burundi, Central African Republic, Chad, the Holy See, Kyrgyzstan, Laos, Lesotho, Liechtenstein, Mali, Micronesia, Niger, Niue, Palestine, Rwanda, South Sudan, Swaziland, Tajikistan, and Uzbekistan.

[40] Arts. 102–107, UN Convention on the Law of the Sea; adopted at Montego Bay, 10 December 1982; entered into force, 16 November 1994. As of 1 January 2024, 169 States were party to UNCLOS and a further 13 were signatories.

[41] Convention on Offences and Certain Other Acts Committed On Board Aircraft; signed at Tokyo, 14 September 1963; entered into force, 4 December 1969. As of 1 January 2024, 187 States were party to the Convention.

2.2 The United Nations Sectoral Treaties

defined hijacking nor did it obligate the domestic criminalization of relevant offences.[42] These fundamental lacunae were rectified in the 1970 Hague Convention.[43] This treaty defined the act of unlawful seizure of aircraft as an offence, where force is used or attempted aboard the aircraft while it is in flight.[44] The Convention's preamble noted that the 'occurrence of such acts' was 'a matter of grave concern' though it did not employ the term terrorism.[45] The Convention obligated States Parties to make the unlawful seizure of aircraft a serious offence in their domestic criminal law.[46] It also made the State on whose territory the hijacked aircraft is found – with the alleged offender(s) still on board – responsible for either prosecuting the offenders or handing them over to another State for prosecution.[47]

Despite the normative progress it represented, the 1970 Convention, too, had limitations in its drafting. In particular, it required that the aircraft be registered in a foreign State for the Convention to apply. Technically, this would preclude its application to, for instance, the 9/11 attacks, since the two airlines whose aircraft were hijacked – American Airlines and United Airlines – were both registered in the United States. This issue was an important motivation for the negotiation and conclusion of the Beijing Convention in 2010.[48] The Convention makes using civil aircraft as a weapon an offence and does not contain the jurisdictional restriction of the Hague Hijacking Convention.[49] It also requires States Parties to criminalize the illicit transport of biological, chemical, and nuclear weapons and related material. These provisions reflect the obligations under the 2005 Nuclear Terrorism Convention as well as those emanating from the decisions taken by the UN Security Council, acting under Chapter VII of the UN Charter, in its Resolution 1540 (2004).[50]

At the same diplomatic conference that adopted the Beijing Convention, States Parties to the Hague Hijacking Convention adopted a Protocol to that latter Convention, explicitly amending its text in a number of important ways. This included the incorporation of an exclusion for the acts, in a situation of armed conflict, of armed forces (again encompassing also the military forces of non-State actors) when their conduct is regulated by IHL.[51] The Hague Convention was also changed to disqualify, for the purposes of extradition or mutual legal assistance, consideration of hijacking as a political offence, while allowing for compliance with the rule of *non-refoulement*. This would legitimate a refusal to extradite or assist where the request was 'made for the purpose of prosecuting or punishing a person on account of that person's race,

---

[42] See, e.g., H. M. Biernacki, 'Evolving Threat to Civil Aviation Is Countered by Legal Instruments as well as New Technology', *ICAO Journal*, December 1997, at: https://bit.ly/3Y1nl5r, p. 1. A Protocol to the Convention amending its text was adopted in 2014: Protocol to Amend the Convention on Offences and Certain Other Acts Committed On Board Aircraft; adopted at Montreal, 4 April 2014; entered into force, 1 January 2020. At the time of writing, only forty-five States had adhered to it.

[43] Convention for the Suppression of Unlawful Seizure of Aircraft; signed at the Hague, 16 December 1970; entered into force, 14 October 1971. As of 1 January 2024, 185 States were party to the Convention.

[44] Art. 1(a), 1970 Hague Aircraft Hijacking Convention.

[45] It was, however, listed as a terrorism treaty in the Annex to the 1999 Terrorism Financing Convention.

[46] Art. 2, 1970 Hague Aircraft Hijacking Convention.

[47] Art. 7, 1970 Hague Aircraft Hijacking Convention.

[48] Convention on the Suppression of Unlawful Acts Relating to International Civil Aviation; adopted at Beijing, 10 September 2010; entered into force, 1 July 2018. As of 1 January 2024, forty-seven States were party to the Convention and a further eighteen States were signatories.

[49] Art. 1(1)(f), 2010 Beijing Convention.

[50] UN Security Council Resolution 1540, adopted on 28 April 2004 by unanimous vote in favour, operative para. 2.

[51] Art. VI, Protocol Supplementary to the Convention for the Suppression of Unlawful Seizure of Aircraft; adopted at Beijing, 10 September 2010; entered into force, 1 January 2018. As of 1 January 2024, forty-seven States were party to the 2010 Beijing Protocol and a further eighteen States were signatories.

60 *Components of International Counterterrorism Law*

religion, nationality, ethnic origin, political opinion or gender, or that compliance with the request would cause prejudice to that person's position for any of these reasons'.[52]

The bombings of civilian passenger aircraft were also a persistent threat in the late 1960s and early 1970s. The 1971 Montreal Convention required the domestic criminalization of a range of offences, including the placing, or causing to be placed, on a civil aircraft of a device or substance likely to destroy or damage the aircraft.[53] A duty to prosecute or extradite for prosecution is incorporated in the Convention.[54] This issue was the subject of a contentious case launched in 1992 before the International Court of Justice by Libya against the United Kingdom and the United States concerning the Lockerbie bombing in 1988. Libya was seeking to ensure that, by virtue of the framing of the Montreal Convention, its nationals would be subject to its own criminal jurisdiction and not dragged before foreign courts.[55] The Convention's application is, however, limited, as was the Hague Hijacking Convention adopted a year earlier, to aircraft registered in a foreign State. A Protocol supplementary to the Montreal Convention 'for the Suppression of Unlawful Acts of Violence at Airports serving International Civil Aviation' was concluded in 1988, requiring the criminalization of violent, dangerous, or harmful acts in airports that serve civil aviation.[56]

2.2.1.2 The Maritime Terrorism Treaties

In March 1988, a diplomatic conference in Rome adopted the Convention for the Suppression of Unlawful Acts against the Safety of Maritime Navigation[57] (SUA Convention). The Convention prohibits the seizure of ships by force, acts of violence against persons on board ships, and the placing of devices on board a ship which are likely to destroy or damage it, obligating States Parties to either 'establish jurisdiction' over the offences or extradite for prosecution alleged offenders where they are present in their territory.

---

[52] Arts. XII and XIII, 2010 Beijing Protocol.

[53] Art. 1(1)(c), Convention for the Suppression of Unlawful Acts Against the Safety of Civil Aviation; signed at Montreal, 23 September 1971; entered into force, 26 January 1973. As of 1 January 2024, 188 States were party to the 1971 Montreal Convention. The nine States not party were Eritrea, the Holy See, Kiribati, Palestine, San Marino, Somalia, South Sudan, Timor-Leste, and Tuvalu.

[54] Arts. 5 and 7, 1971 Montreal Convention.

[55] Libya complained about the charging and indictment of two Libyan nationals by a Grand Jury of the United States and by the Lord Advocate of Scotland, respectively, for having caused a bomb to be placed aboard Pan Am flight 103. Libya stated that the acts alleged were an offence within the meaning of Article 1 of the Montreal Convention, which it claimed to be the only appropriate Convention in force between the Parties, and asserted that it had fully complied with its own obligations under that instrument, Article 5 of which required a State to establish its own jurisdiction over alleged offenders present in its territory in the event of their non-extradition; and that there was no extradition treaty between Libya and the respective other Parties, so that Libya was obliged under Article 7 of the Convention to submit the case to its competent authorities for the purpose of prosecution. Libya contended that the United States and the United Kingdom were in breach of the Montreal Convention through rejection of its efforts to resolve the matter within the framework of international law, including the Convention itself. In 2003, Libya and the two adverse parties informed the Court in writing that, by mutual agreement, they were discontinuing the case.

[56] Protocol for the Suppression of Unlawful Acts of Violence at Airports Serving International Civil Aviation, Supplementary to the Convention for the Suppression of Unlawful Acts against the Safety of Civil Aviation; adopted at Montreal, 24 February 1988; entered into force, 6 August 1989. As of 1 January 2024, 176 States were party to the Montreal Protocol. The twenty-one States not party were Afghanistan, Burundi, the Democratic Republic of Congo (a signatory), Eritrea, Eswatini, Haiti, the Holy See, Indonesia (a signatory), Kiribati, Malawi (a signatory), Nepal, Palestine, San Marino, Somalia, Solomon Islands, South Sudan, Timor-Leste, Tuvalu, Venezuela, and Zambia.

[57] Convention for the Suppression of Unlawful Acts against the Safety of Maritime Navigation; adopted at Rome, 10 March 1998; entered into force, 1 March 1992. As of 1 January 2024, 166 States were party to the Convention.

2.2 The United Nations Sectoral Treaties

Potentially, hostage-taking on the high seas may amount to both piracy and international terrorism.[58] Thus, piratical acts by non-State actors will also amount to international terrorism where the requisite terrorist motive, constructed in broad terms,[59] is satisfied and an international nexus exists. (This is a highly likely scenario given the multinational crews typically on board merchant vessels.) And since the right of search under UNCLOS pertaining to suspected piracy allows a warship to board a piratical or pirated vessel[60] and to detain individuals who are reasonably suspected of being pirates,[61] once in custody, the detainees could later be charged also with an act of terrorism in appropriate circumstances. Moreover, unlike the crime of piracy, which is limited to the high seas (and the exclusive economic zone, EEZ), the SUA Convention applies anywhere at sea, including in a State's territorial waters.[62]

In 2005, a Protocol to the SUA Convention was adopted to amend the Convention by its States Parties.[63] The Protocol adds a new Article 3bis, which provides that a person commits an offence within the meaning of the Convention if that person unlawfully and intentionally uses against or on a ship or discharges from a ship any explosive, radioactive material, or biological, chemical, nuclear weapon in a manner that causes or is likely to cause death or serious injury or damage (or uses a ship in a manner that causes death or serious injury or damage).[64] Again, this reflected both the negotiation of the Nuclear Terrorism Convention and the adoption of UN Security Council Resolution 1540 a year earlier. The offence under the 2005 SUA Protocol is committed 'when the purpose of the act, by its nature or context, is to intimidate a population, or to compel a Government or an international organization to do or to abstain from any act'.

In contrast to ICAO treaties, that States acting under IMO auspices were concluding treaties on the repression of terrorism is explicit in the text of both the 1988 SUA Convention and its 2005 Protocol. In the preamble to the Convention, States Parties expressed their 'deep concern about the worldwide escalation of acts of terrorism in all its forms, which endanger or take innocent human lives, jeopardize fundamental freedoms and seriously impair the dignity of human beings'.[65] In the second preambular paragraph to the 2005 SUA Protocol, the States Parties explicitly 'acknowledg[e] that terrorist acts threaten international peace and security'. They further express their belief that 'it is necessary to adopt provisions supplementary to those of the Convention, to suppress additional terrorist acts of violence against the safety and security of international maritime navigation and to improve its effectiveness'.[66]

Also in 1988 was adopted the Protocol to the SUA Convention 'for the Suppression of Unlawful Acts against the Safety of Fixed Platforms located on the Continental Shelf'.[67]

---

[58] Belgium specifically considers piracy as a terrorism offence. Art. 137 §2(6), Criminal Code of Belgium.

[59] This is defined as the taking and detention of a hostage 'in order to compel a third party, namely, a State, an international intergovernmental organization, a natural or juridical person, or a group of persons, to do or abstain from doing any act as an explicit or implicit condition for the release of the hostage'. Art. 1(2), 1979 Hostage-Taking Convention.

[60] A piratical vessel is one that is used by pirates to take over another vessel. A pirated vessel is the one that has been taken over by pirates. The crime of piracy, by definition, always involves at least two boats.

[61] See similarly Papastravridis, 'Maritime Terrorism in International Law', p. 66.

[62] Priddy and Casey-Maslen, Counterpiracy under International Law, p. 14.

[63] Protocol of 2005 to the Convention for the Suppression of Unlawful Acts against the Safety of Maritime Navigation; adopted at London, 14 October 2005; entered into force, 28 July 2010. As of 1 January 2024, fifty-three States were party to the 2005 SUA Protocol.

[64] Art. 4(5), 2005 SUA Protocol.

[65] 1988 SUA Convention, third preambular para.

[66] 2005 SUA Protocol, twelfth preambular paragraph.

[67] Protocol for the Suppression of Unlawful Acts against the Safety of Fixed Platforms Located on the Continental Shelf; adopted at Rome, 10 March 1988; entered into force, 1 March 1992. As of 1 January 2024, 157 States were party to the 1988 Fixed Platforms Protocol.

The 1988 Fixed Platforms Protocol concerns damage to a range of offshore fixed platforms, notably including oil platforms. Only a State that has adhered to the SUA Convention may adhere to the 1988 Protocol.[68] In 2005, a Protocol was adopted to the 1988 Protocol.[69] A new Article 2 *bis* broadens the range of offences included in the original Protocol. A person commits an offence if he or she unlawfully and intentionally uses against or on a fixed platform or discharges from a fixed platform any explosive or radioactive material or a biological, chemical, or nuclear weapon. The terrorism offence also involves a mental element: that the purpose of the act, by its nature or context, be to intimidate a population or to compel government conduct. A new Article 2 *ter* includes the offences of unlawfully and intentionally injuring or killing any person in connection with the commission of any of the offences.

2.2.2 *The Prohibition and Interdiction of Terrorist Financing*

The 1999 Terrorism Financing Convention is the most widely ratified UN counterterrorism convention, with a total of 190 States Parties.[70] At the time of writing, only Burundi (a signatory), Chad, Eritrea, Iran, Palestine, Somalia (also a signatory), and Tuvalu were States not party. On the day of the 9/11 attacks on the United States, however, only four States had adhered to the Convention,[71] which was a long way from becoming binding international law.[72] Among a plethora of measures sought by UN Security Council Resolution 1373, which was adopted a little over two weeks after the attacks on 11 September 2001, was a call to all States to become parties 'as soon as possible' to the relevant international treaties relating to terrorism. This included, specifically, the 1999 Terrorism Financing Convention.[73] Allied to firm pressure from the United States, this led to swift ratification by many States, with the 1999 Convention entering into force only a little more than six months later.

The 1999 Convention's definition of terrorism is broad, bringing into play the respective definitions set forth in nine UN sectoral terrorism treaties adopted until that time.[74] This composite definition combined with a specific prohibition in the 1999 Convention itself:

> Any other act intended to cause death or serious bodily injury to a civilian, or to any other person not taking an active part in the hostilities in a situation of armed conflict, when the purpose of such act, by its nature or context, is to intimidate a population, or to compel a Government or an international organization to do or to abstain from doing any act.

This supplemental definition thus encompasses not only peacetime acts of terrorism perpetrated against members of the public but also acts targeting civilians or those *hors de combat* in an

---

[68] Art. 5(4), 1988 Fixed Platforms Protocol.

[69] Protocol for the Suppression of Unlawful Acts against the Safety of Fixed Platforms Located on the Continental Shelf; adopted at London, 14 October 2005; entered into force, 28 July 2010 (the 2005 London Protocol).

[70] International Convention for the Suppression of the Financing of Terrorism; adopted at New York, 9 December 1999; entered into force, 10 April 2002.

[71] See P. Klein, 'International Convention for the Suppression of the Financing of Terrorism', UN Audiovisual Library of International Law, 2009, at: https://bit.ly/3uqmeRL, p. 4.

[72] A further eighteen ratifications/accessions were needed to trigger entry into force. Art. 26, 1999 Terrorism Financing Convention.

[73] UN Security Council Resolution 1373, adopted on 28 September 2001 by unanimous vote in favour, operative para. 3(d).

[74] The 1970 Hague Aircraft Hijacking Convention; the 1971 Montreal Convention and its 1988 Protocol; the 1973 Internationally Protected Persons Convention; the 1979 Hostage-Taking Convention; the 1979 (Vienna) Convention on the Physical Protection of Nuclear Material; the 1988 SUA Convention and the 1988 Fixed Platforms Protocol; and the 1997 Terrorist Bombings Convention. The treaties are listed in an annex to the 1999 Terrorism Financing Convention and referred to in Article 2(1)(a) of the Convention. States may declare that definitions in treaties to which they are not party do not apply to them. Art. 2(2)(a), 1999 Terrorism Financing Convention.

armed conflict where the aim is either to 'intimidate' the public or to seek to compel governmental conduct. This latter understanding of motivation would apply to the acts of almost any non-State armed group that is a party to any armed conflict. The overlap of the definition in the Terrorism Financing Convention with the relevant provisions of IHL is partial and not entirely consistent with those provisions which demand an intent to terrorize and not to change governmental action.[75] Notably, the Terrorism Financing Convention does not contain a general exclusion of acts *in bello* by parties to an armed conflict as does the 1997 Terrorist Bombings Convention.

The Terrorism Financing Convention requires that each State Party make it an offence under their domestic criminal law for any person, 'by any means, directly or indirectly, unlawfully and wilfully', to provide or collect funds 'with the intention that they should be used or in the knowledge that they are to be used, in full or in part, in order to carry out' the proscribed acts.[76] As is the case with the other sectoral terrorism treaties, the offences must be punishable 'by appropriate penalties which take into account' their 'grave nature'.[77] An exception to the Convention's application is likewise made for the purely domestic financing of terrorism.[78]

2.3 THE REGIONAL TERRORISM TREATIES

Most regions of the world, but not quite all, have concluded treaties governing different aspects of terrorism and counterterrorism. Those organizations that have adopted terrorism treaties include the following: the African Union (and formerly its predecessor, the Organization of African Unity), the Arab League, the Association of Southeast Asian Nations (ASEAN), the Commonwealth of Independent States (CIS), the Council of Europe, the Gulf Cooperation Council (GCC), the Organization of American States (OAS), the Organization of Islamic Cooperation (OIC), the Shanghai Cooperation Organization (SCO), and the South Asian Association for Regional Cooperation (SAARC).[79] The principal regional organization that has not elaborated a treaty on terrorism – at least not yet – is the Pacific Islands Forum.[80]

2.3.1 *The African Union Terrorism Treaties*

The African Union, which numbers fifty-five Member States,[81] has two terrorism treaties. The first, known as the Algiers Convention, was adopted in 1999 by the erstwhile OAU.[82]

---

[75] See further on this issue the discussion *supra* in Chapter 1 and *infra* the section in the present chapter concerning terrorism in armed conflict.

[76] Art. 4(a), 1999 Terrorism Financing Convention.

[77] Art. 4(b), 1999 Terrorism Financing Convention.

[78] Art. 3, 1999 Terrorism Financing Convention.

[79] See the detailed list in Report of the Special Rapporteur on the promotion and protection of human rights and fundamental freedoms while countering terrorism, Ben Saul, UN doc. A/HRC/55/48, 17 January 2024, para. 39, note 46.

[80] Already in 1992, the Forum (then known as the South Pacific Forum) 'recognised terrorism as a threat to the political and economic security of the region, and noted the various international conventions in the field. It identified areas of possible cooperation amongst Forum governments, particularly in intelligence gathering, training of personnel and joint exercises in dealing with serious incidents'. Forum Communiqué, Twenty-Third South Pacific Forum, Honiara, Solomon Islands, 8–9 July 1992, para. 16.

[81] Algeria, Angola, Benin, Botswana, Burkina Faso, Burundi, Cameroon, the Central African Republic, Cape Verde, Chad, Côte d'Ivoire, Comoros, the Republic of Congo, Djibouti, the Democratic Republic of Congo, Egypt, Equatorial Guinea, Eritrea, Ethiopia, Gabon, Gambia, Ghana, Guinea-Bissau, Guinea, Kenya, Libya, Lesotho, Liberia, Madagascar, Mali, Malawi, Morocco, Mozambique, Mauritania, Mauritius, Namibia, Nigeria, Niger, Rwanda, South Africa, the Sahrawi Arab Democratic Republic, Senegal, Seychelles, Sierra Leone, Somalia, South Sudan, Sao Tome & Principe, Sudan, Swaziland, Tanzania, Togo, Tunisia, Uganda, Zambia, and Zimbabwe.

[82] OAU Convention on the Prevention and Combating of Terrorism; adopted at Algiers, 14 July 1999; entered into force, 26 December 2002. As of 1 January 2024, forty-three of the fifty-five African Union Member States were party to

64   *Components of International Counterterrorism Law*

The second, a Protocol to the 1999 Convention, was concluded in 2005 by the African Union.[83]

The 1999 Algiers Convention (and the 2005 Protocol, which applies the same definition) considers as terrorism offences domestic criminal acts that involve a risk to life, physical integrity or freedom, or which may cause damage to public or private property, natural resources, or environmental or cultural heritage. This is so, where such acts are intended to intimidate the public or coerce government conduct; to disrupt a public service or create a public emergency; or to create a 'general insurrection' in a State.[84] States Parties undertake to establish criminal offences in domestic laws for these terrorist acts, making their commission punishable by 'appropriate penalties that take into account the grave nature of such offences'.[85] It is stipulated, however, that 'the struggle waged by peoples in accordance with the principles of international law for their liberation or self-determination, including armed struggle against colonialism, occupation, aggression and domination by foreign forces shall not be considered as terrorist acts'.[86]

The 2005 Protocol obligates its States Parties to take 'all necessary measures to protect the fundamental human rights of their populations against all acts of terrorism', to prevent the entry onto their territory of terrorist groups, and to interdict terrorist funding.[87] The Protocol declares it is, in and of itself, an adequate basis for permitting the extradition of terrorist suspects in the absence of a concluded bilateral agreement among States Parties.[88] The Protocol also mandates the AU Peace and Security Council continental responsibility for coordination of counterterrorism action.[89]

2.3.2 *The Arab League Terrorism Treaty*

The Arab League is composed of twenty-two States.[90] The Arab Convention on the Suppression of Terrorism, which it adopted in 1998, defines terrorism as:

> Any act or threat of violence, whatever its motives or purposes, that occurs in the advancement of an individual or collective criminal agenda and seeking to sow panic among people, causing fear by harming them, or placing their lives, liberty or security in danger, or seeking to cause damage to the environment or to public or private installations or property or to occupying or seizing them, or seeking to jeopardize a national resources.[91]

the Convention. The twelve States not party were the following: Botswana, the Central African Republic, Côte d'Ivoire, the Democratic Republic of Congo, Eswatini, Morocco, Sierra Leone, Somalia, South Sudan, Sao Tome & Principe, Zambia, and Zimbabwe. All of these States were signatories except for Morocco and Zimbabwe. The last ratification occurred in 2017.

[83] Protocol to the OAU Convention on the Prevention and Combating of Terrorism; adopted at Addis Ababa, 2 July 2004; entered into force, 26 February 2014. As of 1 January 2024, twenty-one African Union Member States were party to the Protocol: Algeria, Benin, Burkina Faso, Burundi, Cameroon, Ethiopia, Gabon, Guinea-Bissau, Guinea, Libya, Lesotho, Liberia, Mali, Mozambique, Mauritania, Niger, Rwanda, South Africa, Sahrawi Arab Democratic Republic, Togo, and Tunisia. For a useful review of the implementation of the two instruments, see D. U. Williams, 'The African Union (AU) Counterterrorism Framework and the Rhetoric of Regional Cooperation', *International Journal of Peace and Conflict Studies*, Vol. 4, No 2 (December 2017), 1–19.

[84] Art. 1(3), 1999 Algiers Convention.

[85] Art. 2(a), 1999 Algiers Convention.

[86] Art. 3(1), 1999 Algiers Convention.

[87] Art. 3(1)(a) to (c), 2005 Protocol to the Algiers Convention.

[88] Art. 8(1), 2005 Protocol to the Algiers Convention.

[89] Art. 4, 2005 Protocol to the Algiers Convention.

[90] Algeria, Bahrain, Comoros, Djibouti, Egypt, Iraq, Jordan, Kuwait, Lebanon, Libya, Mauritania, Morocco, Oman, Palestine, Qatar, Saudi Arabia, Somalia, Sudan, Syria, Tunisia, the United Arab Emirates, and Yemen.

[91] Art. 1(2), Arab Convention on the Suppression of Terrorism; adopted at Cairo by the Council of Arab Ministers of the Interior and the Council of Arab Ministers of Justice, 22 April 1998; entered into force, 7 May 1999.

Amnesty International has expressed its concern that 'this broad definition can be subject to wide interpretation and abuse, and in fact does not satisfy the requirements of legality in international human rights and humanitarian law'.[92] The Convention further stipulates that '[a]ll cases of struggle by whatever means, including armed struggle, against foreign occupation and aggression for liberation and self-determination, in accordance with the principles of international law, shall not be regarded as an offence'. The text clarifies, however, that this provision 'shall not apply to any act prejudicing the territorial integrity of any Arab State'.[93]

The States Parties to the 1988 Arab Convention on the Suppression of Terrorism 'undertake not to organize, finance, or commit terrorist acts or to be accessories thereto in any manner whatsoever'.[94] There is also a rather weakly framed provision under the rubric of 'measures of suppression' whereby the States Parties shall 'endeavour' to arrest the perpetrators of terrorist offences and either prosecute them 'in accordance with national law' or extradite them in accordance with the provisions of the Convention or any bilateral treaty between the requesting and requested States.[95] Article 6, however, provides that extradition is not permissible where, among other circumstances, the offence for which extradition is requested is regarded as an offence of a political nature under domestic law in the requested State or if the offence for which extradition is requested relates solely to a dereliction of military duties.[96]

2.3.3 *The ASEAN Terrorism Treaty*

At the time of writing, the Association of South East Asian Nations (ASEAN) still comprised ten Member States.[97] In 2007, members adopted the ASEAN Convention on Counter Terrorism, which uses as its definition of terrorism the composite of all those offences whose scope is set forth in fourteen named multilateral sectoral treaties.[98] For States Parties to the Convention that had not adhered to any given global treaty, they may declare they will not apply the respective definition(s) until they ratify or accede to the relevant treaty (or treaties).[99] Otherwise, the 2007 Convention obligates each State Party to exercise its jurisdiction over every terrorism offence that is committed in its territory or on board a vessel flying its flag or an aircraft registered under its laws (at the time the offence is committed), as well as when the offence is committed by one of its nationals.[100] The 2007 Convention has been in force for all ASEAN Member States since 2013.[101]

---

[92] Amnesty International, *The Arab Convention for the Suppression of Terrorism: A Serious Threat to Human Rights*, AI Index: IOR 51/001/2002, London, 2002, p. 22.

[93] Art. 2(a), 1998 Arab Convention on the Suppression of Terrorism.

[94] Art. 3, 1998 Arab Convention on the Suppression of Terrorism.

[95] Art. 3(II)(1), 1998 Arab Convention on the Suppression of Terrorism.

[96] Art. 6(a) and (b), 1998 Arab Convention on the Suppression of Terrorism.

[97] Brunei Darussalam, Cambodia, Indonesia, Lao PDR, Malaysia, Myanmar, Philippines, Singapore, Thailand, and Viet Nam. ASEAN, 'ASEAN Member States', at: http://bit.ly/3Y5CqD1. In November 2022, the leaders of ASEAN issued a statement agreeing 'in principle' to admit Timor-Leste as its eleventh member. ASEAN, 'ASEAN Leaders' Statement on the Application of Timor-Leste for ASEAN Membership', 11 November 2022, at: http://bit.ly/3SHDzQg. In May 2023, ASEAN adopted a roadmap for Timor-Leste's full membership. 'Chairman's Statement of the 42nd ASEAN Summit', Labuan Bajo, Indonesia, 10–11 May 2023, at: https://bit.ly/44znuQF, para. 25.

[98] Art. II(1), 2007 ASEAN Convention on Counter Terrorism. The treaties are: the 1970 Hague Aircraft Hijacking Convention; the 1971 Montreal Convention and its 1988 Protocol; the 1973 Internationally Protected Persons Convention; the 1979 Hostage-Taking Convention; the 1979 Vienna Convention on the Physical Protection of Nuclear Material and its 2005 Amendment; the 1988 SUA Convention and its 2005 Protocol and the 1988 Fixed Platforms Protocol and its 2005 Protocol; the 1997 Terrorist Bombings Convention; the 1999 Terrorism Financing Convention; and the 2005 Nuclear Terrorism Convention.

[99] Art. II(2), 2007 ASEAN Convention on Counter Terrorism.

[100] Art. VII(1), 2007 ASEAN Convention on Counter Terrorism.

[101] ASEAN 'Counter Terrorism', at: http://bit.ly/3Z84Uom.

66   *Components of International Counterterrorism Law*

2.3.4 *The CIS Terrorism Treaties*

The CIS brings together ten States from the former Soviet Union, although of these ten, Moldova is no longer a participating member.[102] A Treaty on Cooperation among the States Members of the CIS in Combating Terrorism was adopted in 1999.[103] It defines terrorism in very broad terms as a criminal act 'committed for the purpose of undermining public safety, influencing decision-making by the authorities or terrorizing the population, and taking the form of violence, property damage, threatening the life of a public figure with a view to putting an end to his public activity, or attacking a representative of a foreign State'. Also considered terrorism under the Convention are '[o]ther acts classified as terrorist under the national legislation of the Parties or under universally recognized international legal instruments aimed at combating terrorism'.[104]

The 1999 Convention is of limited effect. It stipulates that in cooperating to combat acts of terrorism, including in the extradition of 'persons committing them', the States Parties 'shall not regard the acts involved as other than criminal'.[105] But it otherwise defers to bilateral agreements on extradition. In June 2022, the CIS agreed to draft a new agreement on combating terrorism.[106] At the time of writing, the main thrust of the new instrument was not known, nor when it would be concluded. The draft of a revised treaty on combatting terrorist financing and the proliferation of mass destruction weapons was approved in Belarus in 2020.[107]

2.3.5 *The Council of Europe Terrorism Treaties*

The Council of Europe brought together forty-six European States at the time of writing,[108] with Russia suspended from membership following its launching of a war of aggression against Ukraine in late February 2022. Designated Observer States are the Holy See within Europe and four States from outside the continent.[109]

There are four Council of Europe terrorism treaties of which only three are currently in force. The 1977 Convention on the Suppression of Terrorism[110] has a supplemental 2003 Protocol

[102]   Armenia, Azerbaijan, Belarus, Georgia, Kazakhstan, Kyrgyzstan, Moldova, Russia, Tajikistan, Turkmenistan, Ukraine, and Uzbekistan. Turkmenistan and Ukraine did not ratify the CIS Charter, as a result of which they are not formally Member States of the CIS, but only as 'founding' or 'participating' States. Ukraine, which was one of the three States that created the CIS in 1991, suspended its participation in the Commonwealth after the Russian annexation of Crimea in 2014. Georgia joined the CIS in 1993 but officially withdrew in 2009.

[103]   Treaty on Cooperation among the States Members of the Commonwealth of Independent States in Combating Terrorism; adopted at Minsk, 4 June 1999; entered into force for each party upon signature of the Treaty or upon notification of domestic ratification where this is necessary under domestic law. Art. 22, 1999 CIS Treaty on Cooperation among Member States in Combating Terrorism. The following States were party to the Treaty: Armenia, Azerbaijan, Belarus, Kazakhstan, Kyrgyzstan, Moldova, Russia, and Tajikistan. Georgia was a signatory.

[104]   Art. 1, 1999 CIS Treaty on Cooperation among Member States in Combating Terrorism.

[105]   Art. 4(1), 1999 CIS Treaty on Cooperation among Member States in Combating Terrorism.

[106]   BelTA, 'CIS to draft agreements on combating terrorism, illegal migration', Minsk, 24 June 2022, at: http://bit.ly/3IZAdod.

[107]   Eurasian Group, 'Draft treaty of CIS states on combatting money laundering, terrorist financing and proliferation of mass destruction weapons approved in Belarus', 2 September 2020, at: https://bit.ly/3QSRCDD.

[108]   Albania, Andorra, Armenia, Austria, Azerbaijan, Belgium, Bosnia and Herzegovina, Bulgaria, Croatia, Cyprus, Czechia, Denmark, Estonia, Finland, France, Georgia, Germany, Greece, Hungary, Iceland, Ireland, Italy, Latvia, Liechtenstein, Lithuania, Luxembourg, Malta, Moldova, Monaco, Montenegro, the Netherlands, North Macedonia, Norway, Poland, Portugal, Romania, San Marino, Serbia, Slovakia, Slovenia, Spain, Sweden, Switzerland, Türkiye, Ukraine, and the United Kingdom.

[109]   Canada, the Holy See, Japan, Mexico, and the United States. Aside from Russia and the Holy See, Belarus is the only European State that is not a member of the Council of Europe.

[110]   European Convention on the Suppression of Terrorism; adopted at Strasbourg, 27 January 1977; entered into force, 4 August 1978. As of 1 January 2024, forty-six States were party to the Convention. Russia denounced the Convention in March 2022.

2.3 *The Regional Terrorism Treaties* 67

amending its provisions.[111] The Protocol has still to enter into force as eleven States Parties to the original Convention have yet to ratify it.[112] The 2005 Convention on the Prevention of Terrorism[113] has a 2015 Protocol that is in force.[114]

The 1977 Convention is designed to facilitate the extradition of individuals who have committed acts of terrorism. To this end, it lists offences that are not to be considered as political offences for the purpose of assessing a request for extradition, such as aircraft hijacking, kidnapping, hostage-taking, and the use of explosive devices, wherever their use endangers persons, along with the early UN global terrorism treaties.[115] Moreover, the Convention empowers Parties not to consider as a political offence any act of violence against the life, physical integrity, or liberty of a person.[116] Compliance with the rule of *non-refoulement* is expressly foreseen in the Convention, to the extent that a person who might be prosecuted or punished on the grounds of race, religion, nationality, or political opinion may not be handed over to that State.[117]

The 2003 Protocol to the Convention on the Suppression of Terrorism expands significantly the list of offences which may not be considered as 'political' for the purpose of extradition, covering also those offences set forth in global terrorism treaties.[118] A simplified amendment procedure is also incorporated to allow new offences to be added to the list in the future.[119] Article 4 of the Protocol amends the Convention to address the duty to refuse extradition where the person being handed over risks being subject to the death penalty. The possibility to adhere to the 1977 Convention is also granted to the Council of Europe Observer States. The Committee of Ministers may decide on a case-by-case basis to invite other States to join the Convention as well.[120]

The 2005 'Warsaw' Convention on the Prevention of Terrorism aims to strengthen Member State efforts to prevent terrorism by establishing as domestic criminal offences certain acts that may lead to the commission of terrorist offences, namely: public provocation (incitement to terrorism), recruitment by terrorist groups, and training for terrorism.[121] The Convention also contains a provision on the protection and compensation of victims of terrorism.[122] Of the forty-six members of the Council of Europe, all but five are party to the Warsaw Convention.[123] Russia is a non-member State Party. The European Union has adhered as an international organization.[124]

The 2015 Protocol makes a number of acts a criminal offence, including taking part in an association or group for the purpose of terrorism, receiving terrorist training, travelling abroad for

[111] Protocol amending the European Convention on the Suppression of Terrorism; adopted at Strasbourg, 15 May 2003; not yet in force.
[112] Austria, Bosnia and Herzegovina, Czechia, Greece, Hungary, Iceland, Ireland, Malta, San Marino, Sweden, and the United Kingdom.
[113] Council of Europe Convention on the Prevention of Terrorism; adopted at Warsaw, 16 May 2005; entered into force, 1 June 2007. As of 1 January 2024, forty-two States, including Russia as a non-Member State of the Council of Europe, were party to the Convention along with the European Union.
[114] Additional Protocol to the Council of Europe Convention on the Prevention of Terrorism; opened for signature at Riga, 22 October 2015; entered into force, 1 July 2017. As of 1 January 2024, thirty- States were party to the Protocol, including Russia as a non-Member State of the Council of Europe, along with the European Union. A further twelve States were signatories.
[115] Art. 1, 1977 European Convention on the Suppression of Terrorism.
[116] Art. 2(1), 1977 European Convention on the Suppression of Terrorism.
[117] Art. 5, 1977 European Convention on the Suppression of Terrorism.
[118] Art. 1, 2003 Protocol to the Convention on the Suppression of Terrorism.
[119] Art. 9, 2003 Protocol to the Convention on the Suppression of Terrorism.
[120] Art. 10(2) and (3), 2003 Protocol to the Convention on the Suppression of Terrorism.
[121] Arts. 5–7, 2005 Warsaw Convention.
[122] Art. 13, 2005 Warsaw Convention.
[123] Georgia, Greece, Iceland, Ireland, and the United Kingdom. All five States are signatories.
[124] This is permitted under Articles 23(1) and 25(1) of the Convention.

68   *Components of International Counterterrorism Law*

the purposes of terrorism, and financing or organizing travel for this purpose. At the time of writing, thirty States, including non-member Russia, along with the European Union, were party to the Protocol.[125]

2.3.6 *The Gulf Cooperation Council Terrorism Treaties*

The GCC was established by a 1981 treaty concluded in Riyadh among Bahrain, Kuwait, Oman, Qatar, Saudi Arabia, and the United Arab Emirates. Jordan and Morocco have both applied to join the GCC. With seventeen of the nineteen 9/11 hijackers coming from the Gulf, the Council members realized they had to react. In October 2002, GCC interior ministers met in Oman to draft the Muscat Declaration on Combating Terrorism, a document that recognized the importance of addressing the root causes of terrorism, and acknowledged the need for members to 'streamline their collective fight against terrorism'.[126] Then in May 2004, a treaty on mutual cooperation among the Member States to combat terrorism was concluded and signed by the six GCC members.[127] Abdul Rahman Al-Atiyah, the then Secretary-General of the Council, described the treaty as the 'most important' since the GCC was formed in 1981.[128]

The GCC Convention for the Suppression of Terrorism reproduces the main definitions of 'terrorism' contained in the 1998 Arab Convention on the Suppression of Terrorism with three significant expansions.[129] The first is an addition to the definition of 'terrorist offence' for 'incitement to terrorist crimes, or propagating for it or applauding making it, and printing or publishing or possessing leaflets, publications or recordings of any kind if it was prepared for distribution or for others to read and contained propagation or applauding for those crimes'. Second, terrorist financing – collecting and donating money knowingly to finance terrorism – is itself considered a terrorist crime.[130] Third, an offence amounting to material support to terrorism (including terrorist financing) is incorporated in the 2004 treaty.[131]

2.3.7 *The OAS Terrorism Treaties*

The OAS has concluded two treaties on terrorism. The 1971 Convention to Prevent and Punish the Acts of Terrorism Taking the Form of Crimes against Persons and Related Extortion that are

---

[125]   The twenty-nine Council of Europe Member States that have adhered to the Protocol are Albania, Andorra, Armenia, Belgium, Bosnia and Herzegovina, Croatia, Czechia, Denmark, Finland, France, Germany, Hungary, Italy, Latvia, Lithuania, Luxembourg, Moldova, Monaco, Montenegro, the Netherlands, Norway, Portugal, San Marino, Slovakia, Slovenia, Sweden, Switzerland, Türkiye, and Ukraine.

[126]   'GCC Declares Its Full Support to Terror Fight', *Arab News*, 10 October 2002, at: http://bit.ly/3ZfH0A3; see R. Miller, 'The Gulf Cooperation Council and Counter-Terror Cooperation in the Post-9/11 Era: A Regional Organization in Comparative Perspective', *Middle Eastern Studies*, Vol. 58, No. 3 (2022), 435–51.

[127]   GCC Convention on Combating Terrorism; signed in May 2004.

[128]   F. Al-Zaabi and A. Al-Awsat, 'GCC Countries Sign Landmark Counterterrorism Agreement', *Arab News*, 5 May 2004, at: http://bit.ly/41FuJXa.

[129]   Amnesty International, Saudi Arabia: Assaulting Human Rights in the Name of Counter-Terrorism, London, 2009, pp. 21–22.

[130]   Art. 1(3), 2004 GCC Convention for the Suppression of Terrorism.

[131]   'Every action that comprises gathering or receiving or delivering or allocation or transporting or transferring of funds or their revenues to any individual or collective terrorist activity inside or outside the country, or conducting any such activity or its components through banking or commercial transactions, or obtaining any monies, directly or through another medium, to be invested in terrorist activity interests, or propagating and promoting its principles or securing places for training or housing its elements, or providing those with any weapons or false documents, or knowingly offering them any other means of assistance, support or finance.' Art. 1(4), 2004 GCC Convention for the Suppression of Terrorism.

of International Significance,[132] to which eighteen States are party,[133] was the basis for the drafting of the 1973 UN Internationally Protected Persons Convention. In other respects, the OAS Convention has had little normative impact since its conclusion.

Of far more significance is the 2002 Inter-American Convention against Terrorism.[134] This treaty, to which twenty-four States are party,[135] covers the ten global UN terrorism treaties that had been adopted by 2002.[136] It obligates each of the States Parties, to the extent it had not already done so, to institute a domestic legal and regulatory regime to prevent, combat, and eradicate the financing of terrorism and for effective international cooperation.[137] For the purposes of extradition or mutual legal assistance, none of the offences within the scope of the Convention may be regarded as a political offence so that 'a request for extradition or mutual legal assistance may not be refused on the sole ground that it concerns a political offense, or an offense connected with a political offense or an offense inspired by political motives'.[138] It is further stipulated that each State Party shall not grant refugee status to any person in respect of whom serious reasons exist to consider that he or she has committed a terrorist offence.[139]

2.3.8 The OIC Terrorism Treaty

The Convention on Combating International Terrorism[140] was adopted in 1999 by the Organisation of the Islamic Conference, now renamed the Organisation of Islamic Cooperation and to which fifty-seven States belong.[141] The Convention defines terrorism in broad and rather vague terms as follows:

> [A]ny act of violence or threat thereof notwithstanding its motives or intentions perpetrated to carry out an individual or collective criminal plan with the aim of terrorizing people or threatening to harm them or endangering their lives, honour, freedoms, security or rights or exposing the environment or any facility or public or private property to hazards or occupying

[132] Convention to Prevent and Punish the Acts of Terrorism Taking the Form of Crimes against Persons and Related Extortion that are of International Significance; adopted at Washington, DC, 2 February 1971; entered into force for each State on the date of deposit of its instrument of ratification.

[133] Bolivia, Brazil, Colombia, Costa Rica, the Dominican Republic, Ecuador, El Salvador, Grenada, Guatemala, Honduras, Mexico, Nicaragua, Panama, Paraguay, Peru, United States, Uruguay, and Venezuela.

[134] Inter-American Convention against Terrorism; adopted at Bridgetown, Barbados, 6 March 2002; entered into force, 7 October 2003.

[135] Antigua and Barbuda, Argentina, Brazil, Canada, Chile, Colombia, Costa Rica, Dominica, the Dominican Republic, Ecuador, El Salvador, Grenada, Guatemala, Guyana, Honduras, Mexico, Nicaragua, Panama, Paraguay, Peru, Trinidad & Tobago, the United States, Uruguay, and Venezuela. States not party are Bahamas, Barbados, Belize, Bolivia, Haiti, Jamaica, St. Kitts & Nevis, St. Lucia, St. Vincent & Grenadines, and Suriname.

[136] The 1970 Hague Aircraft Hijacking Convention; the 1971 Montreal Convention and its 1988 Protocol; the 1973 Internationally Protected Persons Convention; the 1979 Hostage-Taking Convention; the 1979 Vienna Convention on the Physical Protection of Nuclear Material; the 1988 SUA Convention and the 1988 Fixed Platforms Protocol; the 1997 Terrorist Bombings Convention; and the 1999 Terrorism Financing Convention. Art. 2(1), 2002 Inter-American Convention against Terrorism.

[137] Art. 4(1), 2002 Inter-American Convention against Terrorism.

[138] Art. 11, 2002 Inter-American Convention against Terrorism.

[139] Art. 12, 2002 Inter-American Convention against Terrorism.

[140] Convention of the Organisation of the Islamic Conference on Combating International Terrorism; adopted at Ouagadougou, Burkina Faso, 1 July 1999; entered into force, 7 November 2002.

[141] Afghanistan, Albania, Algeria, Azerbaijan, Bahrain, Brunei-Darussalam, Bangladesh, Benin, Burkina Faso, Cameroon, Chad, Comoros, Côte d'Ivoire, Djibouti, Egypt, Gabon, The Gambia, Guyana, Guinea, Guinea-Bissau, Indonesia, Iran, Iraq, Jordan, Kazakhstan, Kuwait, Kyrgyzstan, Lebanon, Libya, Maldives, Mali, Malaysia, Morocco, Mauritania, Mozambique, Niger, Nigeria, Oman, Pakistan, Palestine, Qatar, Saudi Arabia, Senegal, Sudan, Syria, Suriname, Sierra Leone, Somalia, Tajikistan, Togo, Tunisia, Türkiye, Turkmenistan, Uganda, the United Arab Emirates, Uzbekistan, and Yemen.

or seizing them, or endangering a national resource, or international facilities, or threatening the stability, territorial integrity, political unity or sovereignty of independent States.[142]

The Convention lists the UN global treaties then adopted as amounting to terrorist crimes, including UNCLOS and its provisions on piracy.[143] It also declares that '[a]ll forms of international crimes, including illegal trafficking in narcotics and human beings, [and] money laundering aimed at financing terrorist objectives shall be considered terrorist crimes'.[144] The Convention stipulates that none of these terrorist crimes shall be considered political crimes but excludes from their scope '[p]eoples' struggle including armed struggle against foreign occupation, aggression, colonialism, and hegemony, aimed at liberation and self-determination in accordance with the principles of international law'.[145]

States Parties undertake to arrest the perpetrators of terrorist crimes and prosecute them according to national law or extradite them in accordance with the provisions of the Convention or existing agreements between the requesting and requested States.[146] In 2016, the OIC proposed an additional Protocol and updates to the provisions of the OIC Convention to include provisions on 'new trends' of terrorism: the fight against cyberterrorism, combating terrorist financing, addressing trans-boundary terrorist networks, and respect for human rights.[147] The Protocol had not been adopted at the time of writing.

2.3.9 The SAARC Terrorism Treaties

The SAARC has eight member States: Afghanistan, Bangladesh, Bhutan, India, Maldives, Nepal, Pakistan, and Sri Lanka. It has concluded two terrorism treaties: a 1987 Regional Convention on the Suppression of Terrorism, which entered into force upon ratification by all members,[148] and a 2004 Additional Protocol. The 1987 Convention applied to the 1970 Hague Convention, the 1971 Montreal Convention, the 1973 Internationally Protected Persons Convention, and any offence within the scope of any Convention to which SAARC Member States are parties and which oblige the parties to prosecute or grant extradition. Added to the list of terrorism offences are murder, manslaughter, assault causing bodily harm, kidnapping, hostage-taking, and offences relating to firearms, weapons, explosives, or dangerous substances 'when used as a means to perpetrate indiscriminate violence involving death or serious bodily injury to persons or serious damage to property'.[149]

The Convention requires either prosecution or acceding to a request for extradition to another State Party.[150] The Additional Protocol strengthens the Regional Convention by criminalizing the provision, collection, or acquisition of funds for the purpose of committing terrorist acts and taking further measures to prevent and suppress financing of such acts.[151]

---

[142] Art. 1(2), 1999 OIC Convention on Combating International Terrorism.

[143] Art. 1(4), 1999 OIC Convention on Combating International Terrorism.

[144] Art. 2(d), 1999 OIC Convention on Combating International Terrorism.

[145] Art. 2(b) and (a), 1999 OIC Convention on Combating International Terrorism.

[146] Art. 3(II)(B)(1), 1999 OIC Convention on Combating International Terrorism.

[147] OIC, 'OIC to Revisit Convention on Combating International Terrorism', 8 May 2016, at: https://bit.ly/3Ydikqu.

[148] SAARC Regional Convention on the Suppression of Terrorism; adopted at Kathmandu, 4 November 1987; entered into force, 22 August 1988.

[149] Art. I, SAARC Regional Convention on Suppression of Terrorism.

[150] Art. IV, SAARC Regional Convention on Suppression of Terrorism.

[151] Additional Protocol to the SAARC Regional Convention on Suppression of Terrorism; opened for signature at Islamabad, 4–6 January 2004; entered into force, 12 January 2006.

2.3.10 *The Shanghai Cooperation Organization Terrorism Treaties*

The SCO brings together eight States today, with India and Pakistan having joined in 2017. The overall definition in the 1999 Terrorism Financing Convention is used, with slight amendment, in the 2001 Shanghai Convention on Combating Terrorism, Separatism and Extremism, a treaty agreed upon by the then members China, Kazakhstan, Kyrgyzstan, Russia, Tajikistan, and Uzbekistan.[152] The principal change compared to the Terrorism Financing Convention is to add the motivation of violating public security to that of intimidating the public or compelling government conduct in the Shanghai Convention.[153] The 2001 Shanghai Convention is largely one providing for mutual assistance between its parties. It has been criticized from a human rights perspective for the breadth and vagueness of its concepts and definitions.[154]

In 2009, the SCO members adopted the Convention of the Shanghai Cooperation Organization against Terrorism.[155] Therein, the definitions differ materially to those in the 2001 Convention. 'Terrorism' is held to mean 'an ideology of violence and the practice of influencing decision-making by the authorities or international organisations either by committing or by threatening to commit acts of violence and/or other criminal acts intended to intimidate the population and cause harm to persons, to society or to the State'.[156] A terrorist act means 'an act to intimidate the population and endanger human life and health, intended to cause substantial damage to property, or trigger environmental disasters or other serious consequences in order to achieve political, religious, ideological and other aims by influencing the decisions of authorities or international organisations'.[157] States Parties are required to exercise domestic criminal jurisdiction where an offence (not further defined) was committed in its territory, on board a ship flying its flag, or an aircraft registered in accordance with its laws, or was committed by one of its nationals.[158]

2.4 TERRORISM IN ARMED CONFLICT

While the sectoral treaties often apply, at least to a certain extent, in a situation of armed conflict, IHL has dedicated provisions on terrorism in both the branch dedicated to the protection of persons in the power of the enemy (Geneva Law) and the branch concerning the conduct of hostilities (Hague Law). These provisions are narrower in scope than are the corresponding rules in the sectoral treaties, focusing almost entirely on the protection of civilians. This state of affairs is the result of the fundamental principle of distinction, which requires that military operations be directed against the armed forces of the enemy in an armed conflict. It makes the relationship between IHL and the sectoral terrorism treaties a difficult one.

---

[152] Shanghai Convention on Combating Terrorism, Separatism and Extremism; adopted at Shanghai, 15 June 2001; entered into force, 29 March 2003.

[153] Art. 1(1)(1)(b), 2001 Shanghai Terrorism Treaty.

[154] See on the human rights implications of the Convention: OSCE Office for Democratic Institutions and Human Rights, 'Note on the Shanghai Convention on Combating Terrorism, Separatism and Extremism', Opinion No. TERR-BiH/382/2020 [AlC], Warsaw, 21 September 2020, at: https://bit.ly/3KIEQEH.

[155] Convention of the Shanghai Cooperation Organization against Terrorism; opened for signature, 16 June 2009; entered into force, 14 January 2012 (hereafter, 2009 SCO Counterterrorism Convention).

[156] Art. 2(1)(2), 2009 SCO Counterterrorism Convention.

[157] Art. 2(1)(3), 2009 SCO Counterterrorism Convention.

[158] Art. 5(1), 2009 SCO Counterterrorism Convention.

2.4.1 *Terrorism under Geneva Law*

In international armed conflict, under the 1949 Geneva Convention IV, 'measures' of terrorism are explicitly prohibited against the civilian population in occupied territory and against alien civilians in the territory of the enemy (to the extent they meet the definition of protected persons under the Convention).[159] There is no directly corresponding provision in the 1949 Geneva Convention III on the protection of prisoners of war, although, of course, POWs must be treated humanely at all times.[160] In non-international armed conflict, 'acts' or 'threats' of terrorism are similarly unlawful, but the prohibition in Article 4 of the 1977 Additional Protocol II also extends to those who formerly took a direct part in hostilities, whether as soldiers in the State armed forces or as fighters in a non-State armed group.[161]

Perhaps surprisingly, given that the Statute of the International Criminal Tribunal for Rwanda and the Statute of the Special Court for Sierra Leone (SCSL) both inscribed the perpetration of acts of terrorism as a war crime falling within their jurisdiction, the International Committee of the Red Cross (ICRC) did not even conclude that this distinct IHL rule was of a customary nature. Indeed, as the ICRC notes in its otherwise detailed study of customary IHL,[162] in his report on the establishment of a SCSL issued in October 2000, the UN Secretary-General stated that violations of Article 4 of Additional Protocol II had 'long' been considered violations of customary international law.[163]

2.4.2 *Terrorism under Hague Law*

Within the conduct of hostilities (i.e., the fighting between adverse parties to an armed conflict), the use of terror tactics against the civilian population is explicitly prohibited, in identical terms, by the two 1977 Additional Protocols to the four Geneva Conventions. It is thus stipulated that '[a]cts or threats of violence the primary purpose of which is to spread terror among the civilian population are prohibited'.[164] This is also a specific customary rule, as the ICRC confirms, applicable to all armed conflicts.[165] It concerns both the targeting of civilians and indiscriminate attacks, where the primary purpose criterion is met, but not legitimate attacks against combatants.[166]

The ICRC determined in 2005 that the IHL rule was of a customary nature.[167] In its jurisprudence beginning with the judgment on appeal in the *Galić* case in 2003,[168] the International Criminal Tribunal for the former Yugoslavia (ICTY) has held consistently – and

---

[159] Arts. 4 and 33, Geneva Convention IV.

[160] Convention (III) relative to the Treatment of Prisoners of War; adopted at Geneva, 12 August 1949; entered into force, 21 October 1950.

[161] Art. 4(d) and (h), Protocol additional to the Geneva Conventions of 12 August 1949, and relating to the protection of victims of non-international armed conflicts (Protocol II); adopted at Geneva, 8 June 1977; entered into force, 7 December 1978.

[162] ICRC, Customary IHL Rule 2: 'Violence Aimed at Spreading Terror among the Civilian Population', at: http://bit.ly/2ONFTT7.

[163] Report of the Secretary-General on the Establishment of a Special Court for Sierra Leone, UN doc. S/2000/915, 4 October 2000, para. 14.

[164] Art. 51(2), 1977 Additional Protocol I; and Art. 13(2), 1977 Additional Protocol II.

[165] ICRC, Customary IHL Rule 2: 'Violence Aimed at Spreading Terror among the Civilian Population'.

[166] ICTY, *Prosecutor* v. *Galić*, Judgment (Trial Chamber) (Case No. IT-98-29-T), 5 December 2003, para. 135. See also on this point Dinstein, The Conduct of Hostilities under the Law of International Armed Conflict, pp. 168–69, para. 490.

[167] ICRC, Customary IHL Rule 2: 'Violence Aimed at Spreading Terror among the Civilian Population'.

[168] ICTY, *Prosecutor* v. *Galić*, Judgment (Appeals Chamber) (Case No. IT-98-29-A), 30 November 2006, paras. 86–98.

2.5 Duty under International Law to Prevent Terrorism

despite a dearth of strong evidence – that it is also a war crime under customary law, at the least when acts rather than threats are concerned.[169] General Stanislav Galić, as commander of the Bosnian Serb army around Sarajevo, was accused of having 'conducted a protracted campaign of shelling and sniping upon civilian areas of Sarajevo and upon the civilian population thereby inflicting terror and mental suffering upon its civilian population'.[170] The majority at trial were convinced by the evidence that civilians in government-held areas of Sarajevo were 'directly or indiscriminately attacked' from Bosnian Serb-controlled territory, and that, as a result and 'as a minimum, hundreds of civilians were killed and thousands others were injured'.[171] The existence of the customary law war crime has been reiterated most recently in the judgment on appeal of Ratko Mladic by the ICTY's Residual Mechanism in 2021.[172]

2.5 THE DUTY UNDER INTERNATIONAL LAW TO PREVENT TERRORISM

There is a duty upon every State under general international law to prevent terrorism. This duty could be seen to inhere in the right of the sovereign, which encompasses a general obligation to protect all those falling within a State's jurisdiction from harm. In 2001, in its Resolution 1373, cited in Section 2.2.2, the UN Security Council *decided* that all States 'shall . . . take the necessary steps' to prevent the commission of terrorist acts and prevent those who finance, plan, facilitate, or commit terrorist acts from using their territories for those purposes against other States or their citizens.[173] This was effectively phrased as a decision requiring action rather than as a reiteration of existing customary law, which it was.[174] The Security Council also urged States to cooperate, 'particularly through bilateral and multilateral arrangements and agreements', with a view to preventing terrorist attacks.[175] This was hortatory in nature, not even amounting to a Council decision requiring observance.[176]

2.5.1 *The Duty of Prevention under International Human Rights Law*

But the duty to prevent terrorism has also been expressed within the terms of the duty to protect life under international human rights law. Such a duty has been identified by the European Court of Human Rights and the Human Rights Committee, in both cases with respect to the right to life.[177] And, as noted in Section 2.3.1, in Africa the 2005 Protocol to the Algiers

---

[169] At trial, the ICTY had held, bizarrely, that the treaty prohibition was implicitly criminalized. ICTY, *Prosecutor v. Galić*, Judgment (Trial Chamber), paras. 69, 97, 98, and 113. Cassese claimed that the Trial Chamber had 'convincingly proved' the existence of a treaty-based war crime. A. Cassese, 'The Multifaceted Criminal Notion of Terrorism in International Law', 933–58, at p. 945. In contrast, Saul observed that the findings at trial that terrorization in the conduct of hostilities in international armed conflict *implicitly* amounts to a grave breach of the 1977 Additional Protocol I was 'not entirely persuasive'. Saul, Defining Terrorism in International Law, p. 305.

[170] Ibid., paras. 65, 66.

[171] Ibid., para. 591.

[172] International Residual Mechanism for Criminal Tribunals, *Prosecutor* v. *Ratko Mladic*, Judgment (Appeals Chamber) (Case No. MICT-13–56-A), 8 June 2021, para. 287.

[173] UN Security Council Resolution 1373, operative para. 2(b) and (d).

[174] Trapp, State Responsibility for International Terrorism, p. 76.

[175] UN Security Council Resolution 1373, operative para. 3(c).

[176] Thus, under the UN Charter, UN Member States 'agree to accept and carry out the decisions of the Security Council'. Art. 25, Charter of the United Nations; adopted at San Francisco, 26 June 1945; entered into force, 24 October 1945.

[177] Human Rights Committee, General Comment No. 36: Article 6: right to life, UN doc. CCPR/C/GC/36, 3 September 2019, paras. 20 and 70.

Convention obligates its States Parties to take 'all necessary measures to protect the fundamental human rights of their populations against all acts of terrorism'.[178]

In its 2017 judgment in the *Tagayeva* case, the European Court of Human Rights held that Russia had failed in its duty of due diligence to seek to prevent the act of terrorism that occurred at Beslan school in North Ossetia on 1–3 September 2004.[179] In particular, no plan was put in place to ensure additional security despite warnings of a terror attack against an educational facility in the district on a particular day. The terrorist group that perpetrated the atrocity was able to gather and train unnoticed close to a village and a major road, as well as to pass unhindered to the school in the centre of a town across the administrative border, which was supposed to have been under special protection.[180]

Ultimately, more than 330 children and teachers were killed when the Russian forces stormed the school. The Court's underlying reasoning was built on the landmark 1998 judgment in the *Osman* case. Therein, the Grand Chamber had held that in order to find a violation of the positive obligation to protect life, it must be established that the authorities knew, or ought to have known at the time, of the existence of a real and immediate risk to the life of identified individuals from the criminal acts of a third party and that they failed to take measures within the scope of their powers which, judged reasonably, might have been expected to avoid that risk.[181]

The nature of the duty to prevent terrorism involves the adoption of relevant domestic legislation as well as the institution of suitable capacity for general law enforcement and specific counterterrorism expertise. This will include surveillance of those reasonably suspected to be planning terrorism, as and where this is lawful, and prosecution where evidence of the commission of a crime exists. The interdiction of terrorist funding has been mentioned in Sections 2.2.2 and 2.3.1. Terrorists must also be prevented from accessing weapons, and especially any weapons of mass destruction.[182]

2.5.2 *Terrorism under Jus ad Bellum*

An act of terrorism may also be a violation of the rules governing the inter-State use of force. Under *jus ad bellum*, aggression is a serious violation of the prohibition on such a use of force. Aggression is committed by a State (or a proxy armed group) but not a non-State actor operating

---

[178] Art. 3(1)(a), 2005 Protocol to the Algiers Convention.

[179] European Court of Human Rights, Tagayeva v. *Russia*, Judgment (First Section), 13 April 2017, paras. 482, 492, 639, 659.

[180] Ibid., paras. 375, 491.

[181] European Court of Human Rights, *Osman* v. *United Kingdom*, Judgment (Grand Chamber), 28 October 1998, para. 116. This judgment in turn built on the 1991 decision in the *Dujardin* case in which the erstwhile European Commission on Human Rights determined that the duty to protect life in Article 2(1) of the European Convention on Human Rights 'can' create positive obligations for a Contracting State. European Commission on Human Rights, *Laurence Dujardin* v. *France*, Decision (admissibility), 2 September 1991.

[182] On this latter issue, UN General Assembly Resolution 76/28, adopted without a vote on 6 December 2021, concerned measures to prevent terrorists from acquiring weapons of mass destruction. UN General Assembly Resolution 76/28, adopted without a vote on 6 December 2021. This Assembly resolution furthers the intent and implementation of UN Security Council Resolution 1540. Under Council Resolution 1540 (2004), which was adopted by unanimous vote in favour, States are required to refrain from providing any form of support to non-state actors that seek to develop, acquire, manufacture, possess, transport, transfer, or use nuclear, chemical, or biological weapons and their means of delivery. UN Security Council Resolution 1540, adopted on 28 April 2004 by unanimous vote in favour, operative para. 1. General Assembly Resolution 76/28 urged all UN Member States to 'take and strengthen national measures' to 'prevent terrorists from acquiring weapons of mass destruction, their means of delivery and materials and technologies related to their manufacture'. UN General Assembly Resolution 76/28, operative para. 3.

2.5 *Duty under International Law to Prevent Terrorism* 75

on its own behalf. For instance, an act of aggression involving use by State armed forces of biological, chemical, or nuclear weapons against an area populated with civilians would be very likely to amount to a terror attack *ad bellum* as well as a serious violation of the law *in bello*. Under the UN Charter, the Security Council is obligated to determine the existence of any act of aggression or threat to the peace (which includes major terrorism attacks) and is further required to make recommendations, or decide what measures shall be taken to maintain or restore international peace and security.[183]

The 9/11 attacks cannot be considered aggression as al-Qaeda was not – and is not – a State. But the extent to which, under the law on inter-State use of force, a non-State actor may carry out an armed attack against one State without being under the effective control of another is far more disputed. Several commentators consider that UN Security Council Resolution 1373 constitutes recognition that the reference to armed attack in Article 51 of the UN Charter is not to be limited to States,[184] the views of the International Court of Justice in its 2004 Advisory Opinion in the *Wall* case notwithstanding.[185]

Judge Bruno Simma, in his separate opinion to the judgment of the International Court of Justice in the *Armed Activities* case in 2005 declared that 'Security Council resolutions 1368 (2001) and 1373 (2001) cannot but be read as affirmations of the view that large-scale attacks by non-State actors can qualify as "armed attacks" within the meaning of Article 51.'[186] That claim is, however, subject to contestation. The reference to the right of self-defence was in a preambular paragraph. It was certain that the United States had been attacked by someone and the impact of the attacks was very significant, justly giving rise to great sympathy worldwide among States. The United States would have received authorization to use force against al-Qaeda had it sought it from the Security Council.

But while the involvement of al-Qaeda was strongly suspected in the following days, there was no firm evidence for some time that the group was responsible and that it acted without State support. At the time, the attack could equally have been a State acting on its own or through a proxy armed group, which could serve as the legal basis for the resolution. Indeed, as is clear from Security Council Resolution 1530 on the Madrid bombings in March 2004, it is possible to be wholly mistaken about the author of a major terror attack.[187]

---

[183] Art. 39, UN Charter.

[184] See, e.g., J. D. Ohlin, 'The Unwilling and Unable Test for Extraterritorial Defensive Force', chap. 4 in C. Kress and R. Lawless (eds.), *Necessity and Proportionality in International Peace and Security Law*, Lieber Studies Vol. 5, Oxford University Press, New York, 2021, 113–30, at p. 114; Y. Dinstein, *War, Aggression and Self-defence*, 6th ed., Cambridge University Press, Cambridge, 2017, para. 647. See also K. Trapp, 'Can Non-state Actors Mount an Armed Attack?', in M. Weller (ed.), *The Oxford Handbook of the Use of Force in International Law*, Oxford University Press, Oxford, 2015, p. 690. But see *contra* Saul, 'Definition of "Terrorism" in the UN Security Council', 141–66, at p. 155; and Quénivet, 'You Are the Weakest Link and We Will Help You!' 371–97, at p. 379.

[185] Citing Article 51 of the UN Charter, the Court declared: 'Article 51 of the Charter *thus* recognizes the existence of an inherent right of self-defence in the case of armed attack by one State against another State.' International Court of Justice, *Legal Consequences of the Construction of a Wall in the Occupied Palestinian Territory*, Advisory Opinion, 9 July 2004, para. 139 [added emphasis]. As Ohlin notes, this claim was made 'without much evidence or legal analysis'.

[186] International Court of Justice, *Case Concerning Armed Activities on the Territory of the Congo (Democratic Republic of Congo v. Uganda)*, Judgment, 19 December 2005, Separate Opinion of Bruno Simma, para. 11.

[187] Spain, and the Council resolution itself, wrongly attributed responsibility to ETA when in fact it was a group linked to al-Qaeda. See UN Security Council Resolution 1530, adopted on 11 March 2004 by unanimous vote in favour, operative para. 1: 'Condemns in the strongest terms the bomb attacks in Madrid, Spain, perpetrated by the terrorist group ETA on 11 March 2004'. Also of note, the resolution did not mention the right of inherent self-defence. The Madrid train bombings are discussed in Chapter 5.

76   *Components of International Counterterrorism Law*

2.5.2.1 The Proscription of 'Safe Havens' for Terrorists

Even if non-State armed groups acting on their own accord cannot perpetrate armed attacks in the sense of Article 51 of the UN Charter and customary law, it is nevertheless a corollary of the duty on every State to prevent terrorism not to allow terrorists safe haven in one's territory. Already in the 1937 League of Nations treaty it was stipulated that it was a 'principle of international law' that 'every State' is obligated 'to refrain from any act designed to encourage terrorist activities directed against another State and to prevent the acts in which such activities take shape'.[188] In 1970, the UN Declaration on Friendly Relations between States stipulated that:

> Every State has the duty to refrain from organizing, instigating, assisting or participating in acts of civil strife or terrorist acts in another State or acquiescing in organized activities within its territory directed towards the commission of such acts, when the acts . . . involve a threat or use of force.[189]

The UN definition of aggression, which reflects customary law, also includes more narrowly the 'sending by or on behalf of a State of armed bands, groups, irregulars or mercenaries, which carry out acts of armed force against another State of . . . gravity'.[190]

UN sanctions are applied against individuals under a range of sanctions regimes, in particular those pertaining to al-Qaeda and Islamic State. This is intended to prevent their presence in a Member State where they may plan or perpetrate acts of terrorism. The 2005 African Union Protocol to the Algiers Convention obligates its States Parties to prevent the entry onto their territory of terrorist groups and to interdict terrorist funding.[191]

2.6 THE DUTY UNDER INTERNATIONAL LAW TO PUNISH TERRORISM

Where acts of terrorism are not prevented, there is a general duty under the relevant sectoral terrorism treaties to prosecute acts of terrorism in domestic law. UN Security Council resolutions similarly call for the prosecution and punishment of acts of terrorism with suitable criminal penalties.[192] This includes the Council's decision in its Resolution 2178 (2014) that all Member States shall establish serious criminal offences regarding the travel, recruitment, and financing of foreign terrorist fighters.[193] Such obligations are further set forth in the regional counterterrorism legal frameworks. There is a duty to suppress war crimes involving the use of terror. According to the ICRC, the following is a customary rule binding on all States: 'States must investigate war crimes allegedly committed by their nationals or armed forces, or on their territory, and, if appropriate, prosecute the suspects. They must also investigate other war crimes over which they have jurisdiction and, if appropriate, prosecute the suspects.'[194] Criminal sanctions for terrorism offences must, though, comply with the principles of international law governing fair trials. This concerns not only the conduct of the trial – including the exclusion of evidence elicited by or as

---

[188] Art. I(I), 1937 Convention for the Prevention and Punishment of Terrorism.

[189] Principle 1, para. 9 of the Declaration on Principles of International Law concerning Friendly Relations and Co-operation among States in accordance with the Charter of the United Nations, annexed to UN General Assembly Resolution 2625 (XXV), adopted without a vote on 24 October 1970 (1970 UN Friendly Relations Declaration).

[190] Art. 3(g), Definition of Aggression, annexed to UN General Assembly Resolution 3314 (XXIX), adopted without a vote on 14 December 1974.

[191] Art. 3(1)(b) and (c), 2005 Protocol to the Algiers Convention.

[192] See, e.g., UN Security Council Resolution 1373, operative para. 2(e).

[193] UN Security Council Resolution 2178, adopted on 24 September 2014 by unanimous vote in favour, operative para. 6.

[194] ICRC, Customary IHL Rule 158: 'Prosecution of War Crimes', at: https://bit.ly/3QWk3k9.

2.6 *Duty under International Law to Punish Terrorism*

a result of torture[195] – but also the appropriateness of the sentences. The mandatory death penalty, for instance, will always be a breach of international human rights law as its imposition precludes consideration of the particular circumstances of the offender, rendering pointless any appeal against sentence. In this regard, UN General Assembly Resolution 76/169 reaffirms the duty on States to ensure that 'any measure' taken to counterterrorism complies with their international legal obligations, in particular those under international human rights law, refugee law, and humanitarian law.[196]

[195] In August 2023, the confession made to federal agents by Abd al-Rahim al-Nashiri who is accused of having led the attack on the *USS Cole* in 2000, which killed seventeen American sailors, was thrown out as inadmissible by a judge at the US military commission at the Guantanamo Bay detention centre in Cuba. The judge held that his previous experiences of torture were still relevant: 'Any resistance the accused might have been inclined to put up when asked to incriminate himself was intentionally and literally beaten out of him years before', Acosta stated. M. Evans, 'Confession ruled out over past CIA torture at Guantanamo Bay', *The Times*, 28 August 2023. See further Chapter 5, §5.5.

[196] UN General Assembly Resolution 76/169, adopted without a vote on 16 December 2021, operative paras. 2 and 5. International refugee law provides that an asylum-seeker who has committed an international crime or a serious non-political crime is excluded from refugee status. This would include the commission of terrorism as a war crime. See for the exclusion: Art. 1(F), Convention relating to the Status of Refugees; adopted at Geneva, 28 July 1951; entered into force, 22 April 1954 (1951 Refugees Convention). As of 1 January 2024, 146 States were party to the 1951 Refugees Convention.

3

National Terrorism Legislation Worldwide

3.1 INTRODUCTION

A total of 188 States (of the total of 197 currently recognized by the Secretary-General of the United Nations in his capacity as treaty depositary)[1] have domestic legislation in place specifically criminalizing acts of terrorism. Despite certain commonalities, as this chapter examines, the definitions of these crimes are unique to each individual State.[2]

At the time of writing, only one State, Micronesia,[3] had no dedicated legislative provisions on terrorism of any form in its domestic law.[4] A further seven States – the Republic of Congo,[5] Dominica,[6] Eritrea,[7] Kuwait,[8] Sierra Leone,[9] Suriname,[10] and Yemen[11] – repress the financing

---

[1] There are 193 UN Member States, two Observer States (Holy See and the State of Palestine), and two other States (Cook Islands and Niue). As at 1 January 2024, the UN Secretary-General was the depository for more than 560 treaties of international law. UN Treaty Collection, 'Overview', at: http://bit.ly/3YrTwv7. This includes most of the global terrorism treaties discussed in Chapters 1 and 2.

[2] A repository of legislation in each State, along with a human rights analysis of the domestic legal regimes governing terrorism offences, is contained in a dedicated website managed by the University of Pretoria's Centre for Human Rights, at: https://counterterrorlaw.info.

[3] Micronesia's Parliament discussed a terrorism bill on two occasions in 2005 and 2008, but did not adopt legislation on the issue.

[4] There are, however, crimes of armed insurrection and aircraft piracy (among other predicate offences) in its criminal code. See, e.g., §402, Criminal Code of Micronesia, at: https://bit.ly/3KWFVbh.

[5] Loi n° 28–2021 du 12 mai 2021 portant régime juridique du gel des avoirs ou des actifs liés au terrorisme et à son financement, at: https://bit.ly/3T4JKy3.

[6] Suppression of the Financing of Terrorism Act, Act No. 3 of 2003 (as amended by the Act No. 5 of 2022). At the time of writing, a proposed new terrorism law had not been adopted. In 2020, the Human Rights Committee expressed concern about the 2018 Anti-terrorism Bill for its 'very broad' definition of terrorism and the danger that it might be used as a tool to intimidate political opposition. UN, 'Human Rights Committee asks Dominica about the use of force against political opposition and the infringement on the right of peaceful assembly', 11 March 2020, at: https://bit.ly/3IucaNF.

[7] 2014 Anti-Money Laundering and Combating Financing of Terrorism Proclamation. Eritrea's Criminal Code punishes murder as aggravated murder when it is committed for 'terroristic purposes', but these are not defined in the Code.

[8] Anti-Money Laundering and Combating the Financing of Terrorism Law, Law No. 106 of 2013. There are, however, 'State security crimes' punishable under the Criminal Code.

[9] 2012 Anti-Money Laundering and Combating of Financing of Terrorism Act.

[10] 2022 Money Laundering and Terrorism Financing Act.

[11] 2010 Law on Combating Money Laundering and Terrorist Financing (Law No. 1 on combating money laundering and terrorist financing). In addition, Yemen's parliament has had a draft counterterrorism bill before it for many years, but the armed conflicts and surrounding chaos across the country have contributed to preventing its successful passage into law. The United Nations Office on Drugs and Crime (UNODC) delivered a workshop in Aden in southern Yemen on the implementation of the international legal framework against terrorism in accordance with the rule of law and human rights on 20–21 November 2022. UNODC, 'UNODC Supports Yemen to Prevent and Counter Terrorism', undated but accessed 29 August 2023 at: https://bit.ly/45FCT3e.

3.1 Introduction

of terrorism with criminal sanction but do not also establish the perpetration of an act of terrorism as a distinct criminal offence. The Holy See has a 2010 law on terrorism financing[12] and a 2012 amendment decree that criminalizes the creation or leading of terrorist groups,[13] but not the perpetration of acts of terrorism per se. Palestine's criminal provisions on terrorism are from old Jordanian law from 1960, at that time applicable only to the West Bank,[14] although it also has a 2015 law on terrorism financing.[15]

This chapter describes and compares the plethora of legislative provisions on terrorism offences across all States, noting similarities and variations of definition. A total of 101 States currently criminalize terrorism within their respective Criminal Codes.[16] A further eighty-four have dedicated legislation on terrorism offences instead.[17] A small number have penal provisions repressing terrorism both in the Criminal Code and in a dedicated law; on occasion, the definition of terrorism differs between the two.[18] The Democratic Republic of Congo (DR Congo) criminalizes terrorism only in its military Criminal Code,[19] while in Fiji, terrorism offences are contained in public order legislation.[20] In Japan, a range of laws address terrorist offences although rarely are the words 'terrorism' or 'terrorist' specifically employed.[21] Among those States that set forth terrorist offences in their domestic Criminal Code, several also have a separate law on the financing of terrorism.[22]

---

[12] 2010 Prevention and Combating of Money Laundering and Financing of Terrorism Act.

[13] Art. 4, Terrorism (Amendment) Decree of January 2012.

[14] Art. 147, Criminal Code (Act No. 16 of 1960). See Initial report of Palestine on implementation the International Covenant on Civil and Political Rights, UN doc. CCPR/C/PSE/1, 26 August 2021, para. 108.

[15] Decree-Law No. 20 of 2015 on combating money laundering and the financing of terrorism, as amended.

[16] Albania, Algeria, Andorra, Argentina, Armenia, Australia, Austria, Azerbaijan, Belarus, Belgium, Benin, Bhutan, Bolivia, Bosnia and Herzegovina, Bulgaria, Burkina Faso, Burundi, Cabo Verde, Canada, Central African Republic, China, Colombia, Comoros, Costa Rica, Czechia, Denmark, Djibouti, Dominican Republic, Ecuador, Equatorial Guinea, Estonia, Ethiopia, Finland, France, Gabon, Georgia, Germany, Greece, Guatemala, Guinea, Guinea-Bissau, Honduras, Hungary, Iceland, Iran, Italy, Kazakhstan, Kyrgyzstan, Laos, Latvia, Lebanon, Lesotho, Liberia, Libya, Liechtenstein, Lithuania, Luxembourg, Malawi, Malaysia, Malta, Mexico, Moldova, Monaco, Mongolia, Montenegro, Morocco, the Netherlands, Nicaragua, Niger, North Korea, North Macedonia, Norway, Oman, Palau, Palestine, Panama, Poland, Qatar, Russia, San Marino, Senegal, Serbia, Sao Tome & Principe, Slovakia, Slovenia, Somalia, South Sudan, Spain, Sri Lanka, Switzerland, Tajikistan, Thailand, Timor-Leste, Togo, Türkiye, Turkmenistan, Ukraine, United States, Uzbekistan, and Zimbabwe.

[17] Afghanistan, Angola, Antigua and Barbuda, Bahamas, Bahrain, Bangladesh, Barbados, Belize, Botswana, Brazil, Brunei Darussalam, Cambodia, Cameroon, Chad, Chile, Cook Islands, Côte d'Ivoire, Cuba, Cyprus, Egypt, El Salvador, Eswatini, The Gambia, Ghana, Grenada, Guyana, Haiti, India, Indonesia, Iraq, Ireland, Israel, Jamaica, Jordan, Kenya, Kiribati, Madagascar, the Maldives, Mali, Marshall Islands, Mauritania, Mauritius, Mozambique, Myanmar, Namibia, Nauru, Nepal, New Zealand, Nigeria, Niue, Pakistan, Papua New Guinea, Paraguay, Peru, the Philippines, Portugal, Romania, Rwanda, Saint Kitts and Nevis, Saint Lucia, Saint Vincent & the Grenadines, Samoa, Saudi Arabia, Seychelles, Singapore, South Africa, Solomon Islands, South Korea, Sudan, Sweden, Syria, Tanzania, Tonga, Trinidad and Tobago, Tunisia, Türkiye, Tuvalu, Uganda, the United Arab Emirates, the United Kingdom, Uruguay, Vanuatu, Venezuela, Vietnam, and Zambia.

[18] This is the case, for instance, in Angola and Lesotho. Angola's 2017 Law on Preventing and Countering Terrorism has a different (and more detailed) definition of terrorism than does the 2020 Criminal Code. The definition in Lesotho's 2010 Penal Code differs from the one in the 2018 Prevention and Suppression of Terrorism Act.

[19] Arts. 157–160, Law No. 24/2002 concerning the Military Criminal Code (Loi N° 024/2002 du 18 novembre 2002 portant Code Pénal Militaire).

[20] S. 12 (A) to (O), 1969 Public Order Act (as amended by Decree 1 of 2012), at: http://bit.ly/3kZ44Ea.

[21] These include the 1954 Ordinance regarding establishment of the National Police Agency; the 2002 Act for Punishment of the Financing of Criminal Activities for the Purpose of Intimidation of the General Public and of Governments; and the 2013 Act on the Protection of Specially Designated Secrets.

[22] These include Guinea-Bissau, Guyana, Iran, Laos, Liechtenstein, Lithuania, Luxembourg, Malawi, Monaco, the Netherlands, North Macedonia, Somalia, South Sudan, Spain, Thailand, and Vanuatu. DR Congo has also had a law on terrorist financing since 2004, which its parliament most recently updated in November 2022. See Actualité. CD, 'RDC-Assemblée nationale: adoption du projet de loi portant lutte contre le blanchiment des capitaux et le financement du terrorisme, satisfecit du GAFI', 2 November 2022, at: https://bit.ly/3J5s1lc.

80   *National Terrorism Legislation Worldwide*

Thirty-one States also refer to terrorism in their respective national constitutional instrument,[23] although they do so in a markedly diverse manner. The chapter summarizes these constitutional provisions pertaining to terrorism before turning to the legal definitions of terrorism offences in national criminal law. The assessment includes consideration of the jurisdictional reach of municipal laws on terrorism (geographical, material, personal, and temporal), including their application in situations of armed conflict and the interrelationship between extant national legislation and fundamental human rights. A concluding section describes the negative consequences for the respect of human rights of certain expansive national laws on terrorism offences.

Indeed, new and increasingly repressive laws continue to be adopted to counter terrorism, even in States with existing legislative provisions on terrorism crimes. In March 2023, for instance, Somalia adopted a new anti-terrorism law that provides for a broadened definition of terrorism along with a separate law granting greater counterterrorism powers to the authorities.[24] Terrorism had long been criminalized in its penal code. Human Rights Watch criticized the new counterterrorism law, which grants the Somali National Security and Intelligence Agency sweeping powers over 'broad and vaguely defined definitions' of offences. These crimes encompass acts that are deemed to 'harm the security, reputation, independence, interests, and dignity of the Somali nation'.[25] Variations of some of these concepts are found in the counterterrorism legislation of a number of repressive States.

3.2 CONSTITUTIONAL PROVISIONS ON TERRORISM

As already mentioned, thirty-one States address terrorism in some manner in their respective constitutional instrument. This reference pertains variously to a duty to prevent or combat terrorism; the granting of exceptional measures to combat terrorism domestically, such as through the imposition of the death penalty for terrorist offenders; a commitment to cooperate internationally to confront terrorism; and that terrorism shall not amount to a political offence when considering a request from another State for extradition of a suspect present on national territory.

Three States impose a constitutional duty to prevent or combat terrorism, with two of these imposing the obligation on the State. Afghanistan's 2004 Constitution simply requires the State to 'prevent all kinds of terrorist activities'.[26] Iraq's 2005 Constitution, among other stipulations, provides that the 'State shall undertake to combat terrorism in all its forms'.[27] Bhutan's 2008 Constitution demands instead that every *person* take steps to prevent terrorism. In the article entitled 'fundamental duties', it is thus stipulated that a person – not merely a Bhutanese citizen, as is the case in other Constitutional provisions – 'shall not tolerate or participate in' terrorism and that each one 'shall take necessary steps to prevent such acts'.[28] Algeria's Constitution refers to the fact that the army has already protected the people from the 'plague' of terrorism.[29]

---

[23]   Afghanistan, Algeria, Angola, Bangladesh, Bhutan, Brazil, Cabo Verde, Chile, Côte d'Ivoire, DR Congo, Dominican Republic, Egypt, Equatorial Guinea, Gabon, Germany, Honduras, Hungary, India, Iraq, Kazakhstan, the Maldives, Myanmar, North Macedonia, Papua New Guinea, Peru, Portugal, South Sudan, Spain, Switzerland, Timor-Leste, and Türkiye.

[24]   M. O. Hassan, 'Somalia's Lower House Passes Historic Anti-terrorism Law', *VoA News*, Mogadishu, 8 March 2023, at: http://bit.ly/3TztogZ; and 'Somalia: President Mohamud signs the new anti-terrorism law', *Nova News*, 9 March 2023, at: https://bit.ly/42SwIHC; and Global State of Democracy Initiative, 'Somalia – March 2023: New national security laws threaten human rights', at: https://bit.ly/3I4DKAM.

[25]   Human Rights Watch, 'Somalia: Revamp Intelligence Agency Bill', 24 February 2023, at: https://bit.ly/3OasPJP.

[26]   Art. 7, 2004 Constitution of Afghanistan.

[27]   Art. 7(2), 2005 Constitution of Iraq.

[28]   Art. 8(5), 2008 Constitution of Bhutan.

[29]   Nineteenth preambular para., 2020 Constitution of Algeria.

3.2 *Constitutional Provisions on Terrorism*

Switzerland's Constitution expressly allows taxes on aircraft fuel to be used to prevent terrorism, including aircraft hijacking.[30]

Peru's Constitution specifically allows the imposition of capital punishment as a sentence for acts of terrorism.[31] Kazakhstan's likewise declares that the death penalty may 'exceptionally' be imposed for terrorism offences. In certain other instances, the need to confront terrorism is stipulated as the justification for the taking of other measures of unusual severity. Equatorial Guinea allows human rights to be comprehensively suspended with respect to suspected terrorists when the nation is confronted with a threat of terrorism.[32] The Sixth Amendment of Hungary's Fundamental Law, which entered into force in 2016, entitles the National Assembly to declare, pursuant to a proposal by the Executive and following a two-thirds majority vote in favour in the Assembly, a 'state of terror threat', authorizing the government to introduce extraordinary measures.[33] In Iraq, it is prohibited for the President to issue a special pardon where a person has been convicted of terrorism.[34] Under Papua New Guinea's Constitution, use of lethal force to suppress acts of terrorism is expressly permissible, although only where this is 'reasonable in the circumstances of the case'.[35] Brazil's Constitution specifies that a person charged with acts of terrorism cannot be released on bail pending trial.[36]

The Constitution of Myanmar declares that political parties that engage in terrorism (a notion that is very broadly defined in national law) have no right to exist.[37] Iraq's Constitution stipulates that an entity that glorifies terrorism is prohibited.[38] The Constitution of Bangladesh provides that no person shall have the right to establish or be a member of an association or union 'if it is formed for the purposes of organizing terrorist acts or militant activities against the State or the citizens or any other country'.[39] India's Constitution grants Parliament 'exclusive power' to make any law to prevent 'activities involving terrorist acts directed towards overawing the Government as by law established or striking terror in the people or any section of the people or alienating any section of the people or adversely affecting the harmony amongst different sections of the people'.[40]

Facing outwards, and reflecting one of the tenets of *jus ad bellum*, DR Congo's Constitution decrees that no individual or group may use national territory as a base for subversive or terrorist activities against either the Congo or any other State. Gabon's Constitution indirectly incorporates the prohibition in the 1981 African Charter on Human and Peoples' Rights precluding the State from allowing national territory to be used for terrorist activities against any other State.[41]

Several States stipulate that terrorism offences shall not be considered 'political', thereby forestalling this argument as a defence to the extradition of suspected offenders. This is the case

---

[30] Art. 86(3*bis*)(b), Federal Constitution of the Swiss Confederation of 18 April 1999.
[31] Art. 140, 1993 Constitution of Peru (as amended through 2021).
[32] Art. 42(5), Constitution of Equatorial Guinea. It is stipulated, however, that there must be 'necessary' judicial intervention and 'adequate' parliamentary oversight.
[33] Art. 51/A, Sixth Amendment of Hungary's Fundamental Law.
[34] Art. 73(1), 2005 Constitution of Iraq.
[35] S. 35(1)(b)(v), Constitution of the Independent State of Papua New Guinea.
[36] Art. 5(43), Constitution of the Federative Republic of Brazil, 3rd ed. (2010).
[37] S. 407(b), Constitution of the Republic of the Union of Myanmar (2008).
[38] 'Any entity or programme that adopts, incites, facilitates, glorifies, promotes, or justifies … terrorism … shall be prohibited'. Art. 7(1), 2005 Constitution of Iraq.
[39] Art. 38(c), Constitution of Bangladesh (as amended in 2011).
[40] Art. 248(a), 2018 Constitution of India (as amended through end-July 2018). The Constitutional amendment defines a terrorist act as 'any act or thing by using bombs, dynamite or other explosive substances or inflammable substances or firearms or other lethal weapons or poisons or noxious gases or other chemicals or any other substances (whether biological or otherwise) of a hazardous nature'. Explanation of Article 248 of the Constitution as amended.
[41] Art. 23(2)(b), 1981 African Charter on Human and Peoples' Rights, as referred to in the Preamble to the 1991 Constitution of Gabon (as amended through 2011).

with the Dominican Republic, North Macedonia, Peru, and Spain. Honduras and Portugal will, as an exception to their general practice, extradite their own citizens for prosecution on terrorist charges. Iraq decrees that political asylum 'shall not be granted to a person accused of committing international or terrorist crimes or to any person who inflicted damage on Iraq'.[42]

Other States emphasize the need for international cooperation to defeat terrorism, or designate the combatting of terrorism a priority for foreign policy. This is so under the constitutional instruments of Angola, Cabo Verde, Côte d'Ivoire, and South Sudan.[43] Finally, in a rare consideration of the rights of the victims, Iraq's Constitution stipulates that the State 'shall guarantee compensation to the families of the martyrs and those injured as a result of terrorist acts'.[44]

3.3 NATIONAL DEFINITIONS OF TERRORISM OFFENCES

The breadth of definitions of terrorism in national criminal law and the manifold differences between State practices are astonishing. No two laws are the same.[45] Accordingly, any attempt, on the basis of material jurisdiction across national legislation, to construct a particular notion of terrorism as a general principle of law – in the sense of Article 38(c) of the Statute of the International Court of Justice[46] – must surely fail.

The lack of an agreed definition under international law governing international terrorism in peacetime is part of the explanation for the variances between national legislation. Another element in certain States is the convenience of the terrorism label that can be attached to political opponents, which serves as a temptation to broaden the compass of terrorism laws. In contrast, the rare instances of even partial coincidence of definitions of terrorism owe much to those set forth in the global sectoral treaties (and, on occasion, the relevant regional treaty).

That said, there is a general similarity of approach to the overall framing of terrorism: in most cases, a crime of terrorism is perpetrated under domestic law when one of a series of ordinary criminal offences is committed for any of a range of stipulated terrorism motivations. Hence, it is typically the purpose – express or implied – for the commission of any of the enumerated crimes that transforms these predicate offences into acts of terrorism (and the perpetrators from 'ordinary' criminals into terrorists). Nevertheless, while this approach is indeed generalized, it is not universal.

In one category of exception, certain States do not specify any predicate offences, but refer more generally to 'acts of violence'. Laos, for example, cites as a terrorism offence 'violence that affects lives, health, freedom or that coerces [or] poses a physical and moral threat'.[47] Oman refers to 'any act of violence or threat of violence'.[48] Lebanon's Criminal Code defines terrorist acts more broadly as 'all acts intended to cause a state of terror and committed by means liable to create a public danger'.[49]

---

[42]   Art. 21(3), 2005 Constitution of Iraq.
[43]   Sudan's 2005 Constitution had stated that its foreign policy was to be conducted with a view to combating international and transnational terrorism but its latest Constitutional instrument has deleted the provision. S. 17(g), 2005 Constitution of Sudan.
[44]   Art. 132(2), 2005 Constitution of Iraq.
[45]   The closest laws in terms of definition of offences are found in the laws adopted in some of the Pacific Island nations.
[46]   The provision reads 'the general principles of law recognized by civilized nations'. Article 38(c), Statute of the International Court of Justice; adopted at San Francisco, 24 October 1945; entered into force, 24 October 1945. These days, when considering the notion of a general principle of law, the otiose term 'civilized', with its unfortunate colonial connotations, is often either omitted or implicitly replaced by 'democratic'.
[47]   Art. 120(1), Criminal Code of Laos.
[48]   Royal Decree No. 8 of 2007 on combating terrorism.
[49]   Art. 314, Criminal Code of Lebanon.

3.3 *National Definitions of Terrorism Offences* 83

A second category of exception is to consider any crime as a possible predicate offence for terrorism. Argentina thus makes any criminal offence in its Penal Code a crime of terrorism when committed with the requisite motivation.[50] Bahrain similarly refers in its 2006 law to 'a punishable crime'.[51] Poland's Criminal Code defines terrorism as any prohibited act committed with a terrorist aim.[52] Angolan law talks of 'criminal acts'.[53] In Luxembourg, it is any crime and misdemeanour punishable by imprisonment for at least three years that is the basis for a terrorism offence.[54]

A third category of exception involves the legal focus on predicate offences without requiring any specific intent. This is generally the case under Mali's 2008 counterterrorism law.[55] The same situation occurs in Myanmar, where many acts covered by global terrorism treaties are criminalized as terrorism in the 2014 counterterrorism law but without the accompanying need for any specific purpose or motivation. In a number of other States, certain offences are considered terrorism per se, similarly without the need for any *dolus specialis*. This is the case, for instance, under Belize law with respect to bombings (reflecting the tenor of the 1997 Terrorist Bombings Convention) and the use of firearms.[56]

In terms of the definition of terrorism offences, a number of approaches are evident. Sometimes, definitions in the global sectoral treaties are simply transplanted into national law. This can be achieved either directly or indirectly. Madagascar is an example of the broader approach: 'any act that constitutes an offence under the universal conventions and treaties on terrorism'.[57] Somalia reflects the formulation in Article 2(1)(a) of the 1999 UN Terrorism Financing Convention,[58] referring to all of the treaties listed in the Annex to that Convention.[59] Other States limit the contours of terrorism crimes to definitions in those treaties to which they have formally adhered. The Bahamas thus lists the sectoral treaties to which it is a State Party in an annex to its own national terrorism legislation, stipulating that offences delineated therein are also terrorism offences in its domestic law.[60] A similar approach is taken in Belize,[61] Barbados,[62] and St Vincent and the Grenadines.[63] Qatar recounts the relevant treaties in the operative provisions of its domestic law.[64]

Alternatively, the transposition of definitions from global sectoral treaties into domestic criminal law may be indirect or even implicit. Lithuania thus employs the term *terrorize* in its Criminal Code but without definition, whereas its separate terrorist financing law cites and applies the definition in Article 2 of the 1999 UN Terrorism Financing Convention.[65] The same

---

[50] Art. 41 *quinquies*, Penal Code of Argentina.
[51] Art. 1, 2006 Law on the Protection of Society from Terrorist Acts.
[52] Art. 115(20), Revised Penal Code of Poland.
[53] Art. 297(1), 2020 Penal Code of Angola.
[54] Art. 135(1), Criminal Code of Luxembourg.
[55] The 2008 Anti-terrorism Law thus defines terrorism in broad terms first as a series of offences without the need to prove any specific motivation. Art. 2, 2008 Anti-terrorism Law. See *infra*, however, the discussion of hostage-taking as a predicate offence.
[56] S. 2C(2), 2008 Money Laundering and Terrorism (Prevention) Act.
[57] Art. 1, 2014 Counterterrorism Act.
[58] Art. 2(1)(a), International Convention for the Suppression of the Financing of Terrorism; adopted at New York, 9 December 1999; entered into force, 10 April 2002 (1999 Terrorism Financing Convention).
[59] Art. 1, 2016 Somalia Financing of Terrorism Act.
[60] S. 14(1)(b), 2018 Anti-Terrorism Act.
[61] S. 2C(1)(a)(i), 2008 Money Laundering and Terrorism (Prevention) Act.
[62] S. 3(1)(a), 2002 Anti-Terrorism Act.
[63] S. 2, 2002 United Nations (Anti-Terrorism Measures) Act. The law also refers to the offences set forth in the UN sectoral treaties listed in an annex to the 2002 law.
[64] Art. 1, 2019 Law on Combatting Terrorism.
[65] Art. 2(20), Republic of Lithuania Law on the Prevention of Money Laundering and Terrorist Financing, No. VIII-275, 19 June 1997 (as amended through April 2021).

is true in Guinea-Bissau, which is another of the few States that do not explicitly define an act of terrorism in domestic criminal law but rather in a dedicated law on terrorism financing.[66] On rare occasion, a State refers in its criminal law to a particular form of terrorism offence proscribed in sectoral treaties but without defining it. This is the case with Togo, which proscribes 'hostage-taking' and offences against 'internationally protected persons', as well as 'terrorist bombings' and 'nuclear terrorism'[67] In such circumstances, if they are not inclined to find the criminal offence of the commission of an act of terrorism unconstitutional on the grounds of vagueness, domestic courts may choose to have recourse to the definitions in the corresponding sectoral treaty or treaties to which the State is party.

In the case of Eritrea, the broad definition of terrorism in the country's financing law could also potentially be used as the definition for the offence of terrorism under the Criminal Code. This raises great concern, however, as terrorism offences under the Criminal Code can attract the death penalty. Fair-trial rights should preclude any such prosecutorial overreach or judicial activism. Finally, in exceptionally rare cases, the law may not even overtly distinguish between distinct, albeit potentially related, offences. Zimbabwe thus addresses insurgency, banditry, sabotage, and terrorism in a single provision of its Criminal Code but without distinguishing between these distinct crimes and concepts.[68]

3.3.1 *Predicate Offences for Terrorism*

This section describes the common – and not so common – predicate offences for terrorism. A great variety of acts are encompassed in national laws, ranging from acts of violence against the person (the most common) to property damage (sometimes only to State facilities, in other instances to all property) to environmental harm. Hostage-taking and hijacking are very common predicate offences, as are offences involving the use of weapons, particular conventional bombs or weapons of mass destruction. Many States now also include cyberterrorism – criminal acts perpetrated in or through cyberspace for a terrorism purpose – in their domestic legislation. In a few cases, extortion is a predicate crime, as is, in fewer still, insulting the sovereign or criminal libel. Most exceptional of all, but nonetheless shocking, littering the streets or daubing graffiti have been designated as terrorism offences.

3.3.1.1 Homicide or Occasioning Bodily Harm as Terrorism

Offences against any person causing his or her death, when committed with the requisite intent, are among the most common predicate offences for terrorism. This is the case, among many others, in Albania,[69] Angola,[70] Austria,[71] the Bahamas,[72] Bahrain,[73] Belgium,[74] Chile,[75] Denmark,[76] Eritrea,[77]

---

[66] Art. 1(1), Law No. 3/2018 on Terrorism Financing.
[67] Art. 716, Criminal Code of Togo.
[68] S. 23(1), Criminal Code of Zimbabwe.
[69] Art. 230(a), Criminal Code of Albania.
[70] Art. 23, 2017 Law on Preventing and Countering Terrorism.
[71] S. 278c, Penal Code of Austria.
[72] S. 14(1)(b), 2018 Anti-Terrorism Act.
[73] S. 6(1)(a)(i), 2009 Anti-Terrorism Act (as amended).
[74] Art. 137 §2(1), Criminal Code of Belgium.
[75] Art. 2(1), 1984 Law on Terrorist Acts.
[76] S. 114(1), Criminal Code of Denmark.
[77] Art. 276(1)(d), Criminal Code of Eritrea.

Guatemala,[78] Japan,[79] Liechtenstein,[80] Moldova,[81] North Macedonia,[82] São Tomé and Príncipe,[83] Sierra Leone,[84] South Korea,[85] Togo,[86] and Tunisia.[87] As one would expect, the most serious penalties are reserved for terrorism which involves some form of homicide.

Sometimes, though, homicide of only certain categories of person is considered a predicate offence for terrorism (when combined with the requisite motivation). In Afghanistan, for instance, the killing of a 'detained' person is considered terrorism.[88] In Barbados, it is the killing of a 'civilian' that is considered terrorism.[89] Failed attempts to kill are also specifically cited as predicate offences in a few States.[90] Thus, attempts on the life of a person suffice under Venezuelan law,[91] while Slovenian law refers to 'assault on life'.[92]

Offences against a person occasioning grave or serious bodily injury are also very commonly proscribed predicate offences for terrorism. This is the case, among many instances, in Albania,[93] Afghanistan (again, only when it concerns a 'detained' person), Botswana,[94] Moldova,[95] North Macedonia,[96] São Tomé and Príncipe,[97] Sierra Leone,[98] South Korea,[99] the United Arab Emirates,[100] and Vietnam.[101] In a few cases, even slight injury[102] or attacks on the physical integrity of a person suffice. Thus, Slovenian law refers to an 'assault' on 'body or human rights and freedoms'.[103]

3.3.1.2 Hostage-Taking or Kidnapping as Terrorism

Most States consider the taking of hostages as a terrorism offence, reflecting the thrust of the 1979 sectoral treaty adopted in the United Nations (UN).[104] Typically, the crime must be committed with specific terrorism intent. In Uganda, for instance, a predicate offence is

---

[78] Art. 132(8), Criminal Code of Guatemala.
[79] S. 1, 2002 Act for Punishment of the Financing of Criminal Activities for the Purpose of Intimidation of the General Public and of Governments.
[80] S. 278c, Criminal Code of Liechtenstein.
[81] Art. 278(4), Criminal Code of Moldova.
[82] Art. 394-b (1), Criminal Code of North Macedonia.
[83] Art. 360(1), Criminal Code of São Tomé and Príncipe.
[84] S. 1, 2012 Terrorist Financing Act.
[85] Art. 2(1), 2016 Act on Counter-Terrorism for the Protection of Citizens and Public Security (as amended).
[86] Art. 716, Criminal Code of Togo.
[87] Art. 14, 2015 Counterterrorism Law.
[88] Art. 12(1) and (2), 2008 Law on Combat against Terrorist Offences (unofficial translation).
[89] S. 3(1)(a), 2002 Anti-Terrorism Act.
[90] Of course, inchoate offences are generally included in most national laws, but they are not made specific to homicide.
[91] Art. 4(1), 2012 Law on Organized Crime and Terrorist Financing.
[92] Art. 108(1), Criminal Code of Slovenia.
[93] Art. 230, Criminal Code of Albania.
[94] Section 2(1), 2014 Counterterrorism Act.
[95] Art. 278(4), Criminal Code of Moldova.
[96] Art. 394-b (1), Criminal Code of North Macedonia.
[97] Art. 360(1), Criminal Code of São Tomé and Príncipe.
[98] S. 1, 2012 Terrorist Financing Act.
[99] Art. 2(1), 2016 Act on Counter-Terrorism for the Protection of Citizens and Public Security (as amended).
[100] Art. 1 2014 Law on Combatting Terrorism.
[101] Art. 3(1), 2013 Anti-terrorism Act.
[102] Such is the case in Liechtenstein. S. 278c, Criminal Code of Liechtenstein.
[103] Art. 108(1), Criminal Code of Slovenia.
[104] International Convention against the Taking of Hostages; adopted at New York, 17 December 1979; entered into force, 3 June 1983 (1979 Hostage-Taking Convention).

86 *National Terrorism Legislation Worldwide*

direct involvement or complicity in the seizure or detention of and threat to kill, injure or continue to detain a hostage, whether actual or attempted, in order to compel a State, an international intergovernmental organisation, a person or group of persons, to do or abstain from doing any act as an explicit or implicit condition for the release of the hostage.[105]

In Mali, one of the specific motivations set forth in the 1979 Convention is needed for the offence of hostage-taking, whereas it is not for other terrorism offences.[106]

The predicate offence itself may be either generally or more narrowly construed. In Slovenia, the predicate offence is simply 'taking hostages'.[107] Comoros similarly refers to hostage-taking as an instance of a predicate offence.[108] Botswana amended its counterterrorism law in 2018, replacing the predicate offence of 'taking of hostages' with 'taking of hostage[s], *whether or not for ransom*'.[109] But sometimes threatening violence against the detainee is needed. Thus, Indian law considers a predicate offender anyone who detains, kidnaps, or abducts any person and threatens to kill or injure him or her.[110] Albanian law partially reflects the wording in Article 1(1) of the 1979 Hostage-Taking Convention, referring to 'taking hostage or kidnapping a person and threatening to kill, injure or continue holding him hostage' as the predicate offence.[111] Palau uses a similar formulation in its Criminal Code.[112]

Kidnapping is also regularly included as a predicate terrorism offence. In Latvia, for instance, the list of predicate terrorism offences include 'kidnapping of persons, taking of hostages'.[113] Belgium's Criminal Code covers hostage-taking or abduction.[114] Kidnapping or unlawful detention of a person is a predicate terrorism offence in Honduras.[115] In Bangladesh, confining or kidnapping any person are the predicate offences.[116] In Austria, it is kidnapping that is specifically proscribed,[117] while in Greece it is the abduction and kidnapping of minors.[118] In Nepal, a predicate terrorism offence is 'any act to detain or manhandle or terrorize any person in any place or any type of vehicle or to kidnap any person from such place and vehicle or kidnap any person who is travelling by such vehicle, with or without such vehicle'.[119]

Angolan legislation speaks rather of a crime against the liberty of a person, but this would certainly encompass hostage-taking and kidnapping.[120] In Iceland, unlawful deprivation of liberty is the predicate offence.[121] In Bosnia and Herzegovina, unlawful confinement or in some other manner depriving another of the freedom of movement or the taking of hostages

---

[105] S. 7(2)(e), 2002 Anti-Terrorism Act.
[106] '[T]he fact of seizing a person or detaining him and threatening to kill him, to injure him or to continue to detain him in order to compel a State, an international or intergovernmental organization, a natural or legal person or a group of persons to do or refrain from doing any act as an express or implied condition of the person's release.' Art. 3(1), 2008 Antiterrorism Law.
[107] Art. 108(1), Criminal Code of Slovenia.
[108] Art. 255, Criminal Code of Comoros.
[109] S. 2(1)(m)(iii), 2014 Counterterrorism Act (as amended) [added emphasis].
[110] S. 15(c), India 1967 Unlawful Activities (Prevention) Act (UAPA).
[111] Art. 230(g), Criminal Code of Albania.
[112] '[T]he seizing or detaining, and threatening to kill, injure, harm, or continue to detain, another person'. S. 4202(mm), Criminal Code of Palau.
[113] S. 79(1), Criminal Code of Latvia.
[114] Art. 137 §2(2) and (3), Criminal Code of Belgium.
[115] Art. 335, Criminal Code of Honduras.
[116] S. 6(1)(a)(ii), 2009 Anti-Terrorism Act (as amended).
[117] S. 278c, Penal Code of Austria.
[118] Art. 187A, Criminal Code of Greece.
[119] S. 3, 2002 Terrorist and Disruptive Acts (Prevention and Punishment) Act.
[120] Art. 23(1)(b), 2017 Law on Preventing and Countering Terrorism.
[121] Art. 100(a), Criminal Code of Iceland.

3.3 National Definitions of Terrorism Offences

are predicate offences for terrorism.[122] In North Korea, the Criminal Code stipulates that terrorism involves a person abducting people 'with anti-State purposes'.[123] In South Korea, a predicate terrorism crime is 'arresting, confining, kidnapping, inducing, or taking a person hostage'.[124]

3.3.1.3 Bombings as Terrorism

Most States consider bombings as a form of terrorism, in particular if they have adhered to the 1997 Terrorist Bombings Convention.[125] Article 2(1) of the Convention does not require a specific intent once the bomb is deliberately and unlawfully placed. Accordingly, under the law in force in the Dominican Republic, the fact of deliberately placing a bomb is inherently an act of terrorism without the need to prove any terrorism motivation.[126] The same is true in Lithuania: 'A person who places explosives in a place of people's residence, work or gathering or in a public place with the intent to cause an explosion [or] causes an explosion or sets on fire.'[127] Bosnia and Herzegovina speaks more broadly of the causing of explosions in its Criminal Code.[128]

Brunei is unusual in incorporating in its domestic legislation the exclusions from coverage set forth in Article 19(2) of the 1997 Convention. As discussed in Chapter 2, this pertains to the acts of armed forces in the course of an armed conflict (when their conduct is governed by international humanitarian law (IHL)) and the acts of the military forces of a State (when their conduct is governed by other rules of international law).[129]

3.3.1.4 Nuclear, Chemical, or Biological Terrorism

Many States consider offences relating to weapons of mass destruction as predicate terrorism crimes.[130] Much of the Bahamas' dedicated 2018 terrorism law, for instance, focuses on the development, possession, and use of weapons of mass destruction as predicate offences.[131] Bosnia and Herzegovina's Criminal Code specifies as predicate terrorism offences the 'manufacture, possession, acquisition, transport, supply, use of or training for the use of weapons, explosives, nuclear, biological or chemical weapons or radioactive material, as well as research into, and development of, biological and chemical weapons or radioactive material'.[132] Brazil's 2016 Terrorism Law includes as a predicate offence 'using or threatening to use, transporting, keeping, possessing, carrying or bringing explosives, toxic gases, poisons, biological, chemicals

---

[122] Art. 201(5)(c), Criminal Code of Bosnia and Herzegovina.

[123] Art. 60, Criminal Code of North Korea.

[124] Art. 2(1), 2016 Act on Counter-Terrorism for the Protection of Citizens and Public Security (as amended).

[125] Art. 4, International Convention for the Suppression of Terrorist Bombings; adopted at New York, 15 December 1997; entered into force, 23 May 2001. As of 1 January 2024, 170 States were party to the 1997 Terrorist Bombings Convention.

[126] Art. 435, Criminal Code of the Dominican Republic.

[127] S. 250(1), Criminal Code of Lithuania.

[128] Art. 201(5)(g), Criminal Code of Bosnia and Herzegovina.

[129] S. 18(2), 2011 Anti-Terrorism Order.

[130] That said, Afghanistan's national law is rare in defining in detail nuclear material. The law defines nuclear material as inter alia: plutonium; uranium not in the form of ore or ore residue that contains the mixture of isotopes in their natural form; enriched uranium; or uranium-233. Art. 3(9), 2008 Law on Combat against Terrorist Offences (unofficial translation).

[131] Ss. 6–8, 2018 Anti-Terrorism Act. Conventional weapons (firearms) and explosives are also covered in relation to the provision or receipt of weapons training. S. 5, 2018 Anti-Terrorism Act.

[132] Art. 201(5)(f), Criminal Code of Bosnia and Herzegovina.

or nuclear products or other means capable of causing damage or promoting mass destruction'.[133]

Other States' terrorism laws focus on the use or threat of use of a range of weapons of mass destruction. Guinean law, for example, refers to terrorism as anyone who 'uses or threatens to use viruses, bacteria, fungi, toxins or any other micro-organisms for the purpose of causing illness or death of beings humans, animals or plants'.[134] Latvia's Criminal Code defines terrorism as encompassing the use of 'nuclear, chemical, biological, bacteriological, toxic chemical, or other weapons of mass destruction'.[135]

Israeli law deems an act or threat carried out using a biological, chemical, or radioactive weapon or a harmful substance to be terrorism where, due to their quality or type, they are liable to cause serious harm to a large area or a wide public. This is so without any harm being caused and without the need to prove the intent to terrorize or to compel government conduct. It must, though, be proven that the act or threat was carried out with a political, religious, nationalistic, or ideological motive.[136] In Portugal, research and development of biological or chemical weapons are specifically listed offences but so too are crimes involving use of biological or chemical or explosive devices, 'where, by their nature or the context in which they are committed, such crimes are likely to seriously affect the State or the targeted population'.[137]

3.3.1.5 Targeting Internationally Protected Persons

Numerous States make targeting internationally protected persons a predicate offence for terrorism, consonant with the 1973 Convention on Crimes against Internationally Protected Persons, to which 180 States were formally party as of the beginning of 2024.[138] The Cook Islands, which is bound through New Zealand's ratification of the 1973 Convention, implemented its provisions in domestic law (along with those of the 1979 UN Hostage-Taking Convention) in a single Statute adopted in 1982.[139] Some, such as the Bahamas, simply refer to the Convention and its definition,[140] or, in the case of Afghanistan, 'a person who is entitled to special protection rights, based on international legal documents'.[141] Albania specifically defines an internationally protected person in its law 'unless international agreements ratified by the Albanian State provide for otherwise'.[142]

---

[133] Art. 2(1), 2016 Terrorism Law.
[134] Art. 575(1), Criminal Code of Guinea.
[135] S. 79(1), Criminal Code of Latvia.
[136] S. 2(a), 2018 Anti-Terrorism Law.
[137] Art. 2(1), 2002 Terrorism Law.
[138] Convention on the Prevention and Punishment of Crimes against Internationally Protected Persons, including Diplomatic Agents; adopted at New York, 14 December 1973; entered into force, 20 February 1977.
[139] The Cook Islands Crimes (Internationally Protected Persons and Hostages) Act, Act No. 6 of 1982.
[140] S. 29(7), 2018 Anti-Terrorism Act.
[141] Art. 3(5), 2008 Law on Combat against Terrorist Offences (unofficial translation).
[142] Art. 9, Criminal Code of Albania. In accordance with the Criminal Code, the term includes: 'a) the head of a State, including a member of the collegial body performing the functions of the head of State, under the constitution of that State, the head of the government or the minister for foreign affairs, where the latter are in another State, and the family members accompanying them; b) a representative or official of a State, or an official or agent of an international organisation having an intergovernmental character, who, at the time and venue of the commission of the offence against him, his office, private residence or means of transport, enjoys, in accordance with the international law, special protection against any assault on his person, freedom and dignity, as well as on the members of his family'.

3.3.1.6 Arson as Terrorism

In contrast, only a relatively small number of States, particularly from the former Soviet Union, include arson as a possible predicate offence for terrorism. Former USSR nations that do so include Armenia, Azerbaijan, Belarus, Croatia, Georgia,[143] Kazakhstan,[144] Kyrgyzstan,[145] Latvia,[146] Moldova,[147] North Macedonia,[148] Russia,[149] Tajikistan,[150] Turkmenistan,[151] and Ukraine.[152] Greece also considers arson a predicate terrorism offence,[153] as do Haiti,[154] Iceland,[155] and Spain.[156] Honduras amended its Criminal Code in 2017 to include arson as a predicate terrorism offence.[157] Bosnian law speaks more broadly of the 'causing of fires' in its Criminal Code provisions on terrorism,[158] as do the dedicated terrorism laws in the Philippines[159] and Venezuela.[160] Panama also uses the term 'fire',[161] as do Portugal[162] and São Tomé and Príncipe.[163] The Lithuanian Criminal Code refers to terrorizing a *person* by threatening to set him on fire.[164]

As described in Chapter 2, in 2011 the Appeals Chamber of the Special Tribunal for Lebanon had issued an Interlocutory Decision on the applicable international law covering terrorism, holding that arson was one of the predicate offences for the claimed customary law definition of the international crime of terrorism when committed in peacetime.[165] Even had there been sufficient evidence to hold that such an international crime existed in customary international law, the number of States that believed that arson was a constituent element of the crime fell far short of meeting the threshold of a 'general practice accepted as law'.[166]

3.3.1.7 Aircraft Hijacking as Terrorism

Many States, though by no means all, consider the hijacking of aircraft as a terrorism offence, typically when committed with specific intent. This amounts, in particular, to implementation of the 1970 Hague Aircraft Hijacking Convention, to which 185 States were party at the time of

---

[143] Art. 323(1), Criminal Code of Georgia.
[144] Art. 255(1), Criminal Code of Kazakhstan.
[145] Art. 252(2), Criminal Code of Kyrgyzstan.
[146] S. 79(1), Criminal Code of Latvia.
[147] Art. 278(1), Criminal Code of Moldova.
[148] Art. 313, Criminal Code of North Macedonia.
[149] Art. 205(1), Criminal Code of Russia.
[150] Art. 179(1), Criminal Code of Tajikistan.
[151] Art. 271(1), Criminal Code of Turkmenistan.
[152] Art. 258(1), Criminal Code of Ukraine.
[153] Art. 187A, Criminal Code of Greece.
[154] Art. 1(2), 2020 Decree for the Reinforcement of Public Security.
[155] Art. 100(a), Criminal Code of Iceland.
[156] Art. 573(1), Criminal Code of Spain.
[157] Art. 335, Criminal Code of Honduras.
[158] Art. 201(5)(g), Criminal Code of Bosnia and Herzegovina.
[159] S. 4(e), 2020 Terrorism Act.
[160] Art. 4(1), 2012 Law on Organized Crime and Terrorist Financing.
[161] Art. 293, Criminal Code of Panama.
[162] Art. 2(1), 2002 Terrorism Law.
[163] Art. 360(1), Criminal Code of São Tomé and Príncipe.
[164] S. 145(2), Criminal Code of Lithuania.
[165] Special Tribunal for Lebanon, Interlocutory Decision on the Applicable Law: Terrorism, Conspiracy, Homicide, Perpetration, Cumulative Charging (Appeals Chamber) (Case No. STL-11–01/I), 16 February 2011, para. 85.
[166] Art. 38(b), 1945 Statute of the International Court of Justice.

writing.[167] Canada, for example, in defining 'terrorist activity' in its Criminal Code[168] refers to the offences therein that implement Article 1(1) of the 1970 Convention, and in particular: 'Every one who, unlawfully, by force or threat thereof, or by any other form of intimidation, seizes or exercises control of an aircraft.'[169]

Domestic laws sometimes extend more broadly their compass. Thus, for instance, Czechia stipulates as a predicate offence a person who 'hijacks an aircraft, ship or another means of personal or cargo transportation or exercises control over it'.[170] Iceland's Criminal Code refers to hijacking of an aircraft or attacking international airport passengers[171] (reflecting the provisions of the 1988 Montreal Protocol).[172] Latvia designates the hijacking of air, land, or sea means of transport as predicate terrorism offences.[173] In Slovenia, it is the 'hijacking of an aircraft, ship or public transport'.[174] For Liechtenstein, it is 'air piracy'.[175]

3.3.1.8 Maritime Offences, including Piracy, as Terrorism

Maritime offences are quite widely deemed predicate terrorism offences in the national legislation of coastal States, reflecting two key International Maritime Organization (IMO) treaties: on the safety of maritime navigation and on attacks against fixed platforms located on the continental shelf.[176] Only rarely do States go beyond the particular scope of the two treaties. That said, in South Korea, predicate offences include more broadly any proscribed conduct 'related to a ship ... or a marine structure'.[177]

Myanmar's anti-terrorism law includes any intentional offence unlawfully committed in order to harm maritime travel.[178] In Togo, terrorism is generally defined in the Criminal Code as including offences relating to the security of maritime navigation, ports, and fixed platforms.[179] Guatemala's Criminal Code specifically punishes terrorist acts that concern maritime disasters.[180] In addition, Belgium specifically considers maritime piracy as a terrorism offence,[181] seemingly the only State to do so, while Greece has 'causing a shipwreck' as a predicate offence.[182]

---

[167] Convention for the Suppression of Unlawful Seizure of Aircraft; signed at the Hague, 16 December 1970; entered into force, 14 October 1971.

[168] S. 83.01 (1), Criminal Code of Canada.

[169] S. 76, Criminal Code of Canada.

[170] S. 311(e), Criminal Code of Czechia.

[171] Art. 100(a), Criminal Code of Iceland.

[172] Protocol for the Suppression of Unlawful Acts of Violence at Airports Serving International Civil Aviation; adopted at Montreal, 24 February 1988; entered into force, 6 August 1989 (Montreal Protocol). As of 1 January 2024, 176 States were party to the Montreal Protocol.

[173] S. 79(1), Criminal Code of Latvia.

[174] Art. 108(1), Criminal Code of Slovenia.

[175] S. 278c, Criminal Code of Liechtenstein.

[176] Convention for the Suppression of Unlawful Acts Against the Safety of Maritime Navigation; and Protocol for the Suppression of Unlawful Acts against the Safety of Fixed Platforms Located on the Continental Shelf; both adopted at Rome, 10 March 1988; entered into force, 1 March 1992. As of 1 January 2024, a total of 166 and 157 States, respectively, were party to the two treaties.

[177] Art. 2(1), 2016 Act on Counter-Terrorism for the Protection of Citizens and Public Security (as amended).

[178] chap. 1(3)(5), 2014 Counterterrorism Law.

[179] Art. 716, Criminal Code of Togo.

[180] Art. 391, Criminal Code of Guatemala.

[181] Art. 137 §2(6), Criminal Code of Belgium.

[182] Art. 187A, Criminal Code of Greece.

3.3.1.9 Endangering Life or Public Health

Numerous States provide for predicate offences that endanger life or public health. Australia, for instance, includes as a possible terrorism offence causing 'a serious risk to the health or safety of the public'.[183] In Singapore, the 2002 Terrorist Financing Act defines a terrorist act as the use or threat of action where it endangers a person's life or 'creates a serious risk to the health or the safety of the public or a section of the public'.[184] Azerbaijani law deems terrorism to encompass 'other actions threatening the lives of people or damaging their health, causing significant property damage or other hazardous consequences to the public'.[185] In Liechtenstein, it is 'wilful endangerment through pollution of water or air'.[186]

Several States specifically regard disrupting the safety of traffic (on land, in the air, and/or at sea) as a predicate terrorism offence. Disturbing traffic safety when committed in such a way as to endanger human life or cause great financial loss is a predicate offence in Iceland, for instance.[187] In Latvia, the spreading of epidemics or epizootic diseases is a predicate terrorism offence when committed with the requisite intent.[188] Under the Penal Code of Oman, whoever proceeds with a terrorist act that spreads fear and horror among people or frightens them using epidemic substances commits a terrorism offence.[189]

3.3.1.10 Property Damage as Terrorism

Damage or destruction of infrastructure is a predicate terrorism offence in many States. This includes Afghanistan, which has a broad definition of the term.[190] Albania limits the offence to 'heavy and large-scale destruction' of public property, public infrastructure, a transportation system, an information system, and private property, 'where it endangers the lives of people'.[191] Peru, which suffered from attacks on its electricity pylons during the conflict against Shining Path in the 1980s, has made such acts terrorism offences.[192] Togo covers serious damage to any property or less serious damage which causes or is likely to cause considerable economic costs.[193]

The destruction of private property is potentially a terrorism offence in several States. This includes, in addition to Afghanistan and Albania, Bangladesh,[194] Belize (where the damage is serious),[195] Cameroon (whose law refers generally to material damage),[196] China (which mentions simply 'property rights'),[197] Greece ('causing of significant damage to a third party's

---

[183]   S. 100.1, 1995 Criminal Code Act.
[184]   Art. 2(2)(a)(iii) and (iv), 2002 Terrorism (Suppression of Financing) Act.
[185]   Art. 1, 1999 Azerbaijan Law on Countering Terrorism.
[186]   S. 278c, Criminal Code of Liechtenstein.
[187]   Art. 100(a), Criminal Code of Iceland.
[188]   S. 79(1), Criminal Code of Latvia.
[189]   Art. 113, Penal Code of Oman.
[190]   Art. 16(1), 2008 Law on Combat against Terrorist Offences (unofficial translation). According to Article 3(6) of the same law, infrastructural establishments 'are governmental and non-governmental establishments that provide public services including production, storage and distribution of gas, fuel and water, water supply and canalization systems, generation of electricity, financial services, education, banking, health, fire-fighting and rescue services, transportation including land, air and sea, surveillance of roads and highways, protective, security and communication lines or other social and economic services'.
[191]   Art. 230(m), Criminal Code of Albania.
[192]   Art. 2, 1992 Terrorism Law.
[193]   Art. 716, Criminal Code of Togo.
[194]   S. 6(1)(a)(iii), 2009 Anti-Terrorism Act (as amended).
[195]   S. 2C(2)(b), 2008 Money Laundering and Terrorism (Prevention) Act.
[196]   S. 2(1), 2014 Law on Repression of Acts of Terrorism.
[197]   Art. 3, 2016 Counterterrorism Law of the People's Republic of China (as amended).

property'),[198] and Mexico (concerning property or services).[199] In Jamaica, 'substantial' property damage, whether to public or private property, is covered, but only if the damage is likely to result in physical harm.[200]

3.3.1.11 Cyberterrorism

Different forms of cyberterrorism are incorporated in many national laws but in materially distinct ways and with widely differing penal consequences. In Italy, for instance, the 2015 law on terrorism stipulates that the punishment for inciting terrorism shall be increased by up to two-thirds if the act is committed 'through internet or electronic tools'.[201] Cuba prescribes a penalty of between five and twenty years in prison for cyberterrorism.[202]

A common offence is disruption of online banking or financial services. In Antigua and Barbuda, for instance, cyberattacks to disrupt 'any computer system or the provision of services directly related to communications infrastructure, banking or financial services, utilities, transportation or other essential infrastructure' are considered as terrorism when committed with the requisite intent.[203] Similar (though not verbatim) language is used in The Gambia.[204] In Belize, the predicate offence concerns action 'designed or intended to seriously interfere with or seriously disrupt ... any electronic system, including a computer system or system for the provision of services directly related to communications, banking or financial services'.[205] Brazil criminalizes as terrorism in its dedicated 2016 legislation

> sabotaging the operation or taking total or partial control ... by making use of cyber mechanisms, albeit on a temporary basis, of the means of communication or transportation, of ports, airports, railway or bus stations, hospitals, nursing homes, schools, sports stadiums, public facilities or locations where essential public services are installed, power generation or transmission facilities, military facilities, exploration, refining and processing of oil and gas facilities and bank institutions and their service network.[206]

Sometimes mere disruption is sufficient, whereas in other States only serious disruption potentially qualifies as terrorism. In Brunei, acts designed 'to disrupt any public computer system' are predicate offences,[207] whereas in Australia, 'seriously' interfering with electronic systems affecting critical infrastructure is one of the predicate offences for terrorism. Similarly, in the Central African Republic, all acts that 'are designed in such a way as to interfere with or seriously disrupt an electronic system' are predicate offences for terrorism,[208] while in Grenada, the corresponding offence is an act 'designed seriously to interfere with or seriously to disrupt an electronic system'.[209]

---

[198] Art. 187A, Criminal Code of Greece.
[199] Art. 139(I), Federal Criminal Code of Mexico.
[200] S. 3(2), 2015 Terrorism Prevention Act.
[201] Law No. 43/2015; see Arnone & Sicomo, 'Italy: Italy Terrorism Legislation: Art. No. 270 of the Italian Criminal Code', mondaq, 8 January 2021, at: https://bit.ly/3IJqRwr.
[202] Art. 24(a) and (b), 2001 Terrorism Law.
[203] Definition of 'terrorist act' in S. 2(1), 2005 Prevention of Terrorism Act.
[204] '[I]s designed to disrupt any computer system or the provision of services directly related to communication infrastructure, banking and financial services, utilities, transportation or key infrastructure.' Art. 2(d). 2002 Terrorism Act.
[205] S. 2C(2)(e)(i), 2008 Money Laundering and Terrorism (Prevention) Act.
[206] Art. 2(1), 2016 Terrorism Law.
[207] S. 2, 2011 Anti-Terrorism Order.
[208] Art. 296, Criminal Code of the Central African Republic.
[209] S. 2, 2012 Terrorism Act.

3.3 National Definitions of Terrorism Offences

In Haiti, digital offences per se are predicate crimes for terrorism.[210] In Laos, a terrorism offence is 'causing damage and chaos to computers and communications, internet systems, or digital instruments of State organisations, legal persons, and natural persons'.[211] In the Marshall Islands, a predicate offence includes

> any act that is designed to disrupt or destroy an electronic system, including, without limitation:
>
> (i) an information system;
> (ii) a telecommunications system;
> (iii) a financial system;
> (iv) a system used for the delivery of essential government services;
> (v) a system used for, or by, an essential public utility;
> (vi) a system used for, or by, a transport system.[212]

In Austria, data corruption can be terrorism where it poses a risk to the life of another or of widespread damage to property.[213] Similarly, in Liechtenstein damage to data is considered a predicate offence for terrorism if life or property could thereby be greatly endangered.[214] In Belgium, 'unlawful interference with the integrity of a computer system and unlawful interference with the integrity of data in a computer system' are both per se predicate offences for terrorism.[215]

The Bahamas' dedicated anti-terrorism legislation makes 'cybercrime' – undefined – a predicate offence for terrorism.[216] This is also the case in Benin.[217] Panama talks more broadly of 'cyberoperations', but does not define them either.[218] In contrast, in Cuba, cyberterrorism is defined broadly and in detail as facilitating an act terrorism through the use

> of computer equipment, means, programmes, networks or any other computer application to intercept, interfere with, use, alter, damage, render useless or destroy data, information, electronic documents, software support systems, information, communication or telematic programmes or systems of public, social, administrative, emergency, national security or any other type of services of national or international entities or entities of another country.[219]

Sierra Leone's 2021 Cyber Crimes Act defines and criminalizes cyberterrorism as 'the unlawful use of computers and information technology to unlawfully attack or threaten to attack computers, networks and the information stored therein done to intimidate or coerce a government or its people in furtherance of political or social objectives and to cause severe disruption or widespread fear in society'.[220] Iran's cybercrime law establishes a committee whose task includes identifying online support for terrorist groups.[221]

---

[210] Art. 1(2), 2020 Decree for the Reinforcement of Public Security.
[211] Art. 120(3), Criminal Code of Laos.
[212] S. 105(38) (g), 2002 Counterterrorism Act.
[213] S. 278c, Penal Code of Austria.
[214] S. 278c, Criminal Code of Liechtenstein.
[215] Art. 137 §2, Criminal Code of Belgium.
[216] S. 14(1)(b)(ff), 2018 Anti-Terrorism Act.
[217] Art. 162(3), Criminal Code of Benin.
[218] Art. 293, Criminal Code of Panama.
[219] Art. 24(a) and (b), 2001 Terrorism Law.
[220] S. 70(2), 2021 Cyber Security and Cyber Crimes Act.
[221] Art. 22, 2009 Computer Crimes Law.

3.3.1.12 Environmental Harm as Terrorism

Environmental harm is addressed by more than fifty States as potential terrorism, but again they do so in a range of different ways. In Guinea, unlawful acts that cause damage to natural resources or the environment are predicate offences.[222] Canadian anti-terrorism law requires that environmental damage be 'major' and that the consequences be significant.[223] Paraguay phrases environmental harm as 'crimes against the natural foundations of human life' in its list of predicate terrorism offences, referring to relevant ordinary offences in the Criminal Code.[224] Algeria, however, considers environmental harm as a possible *motivation* for terrorism rather than a predicate offence.[225] In further contrast, Indonesia considers damage or destruction to the environment as a causal element of terrorism as opposed to a purposive one.[226] In Greece, causing a flood is a predicate offence for terrorism.[227]

Many States address the release of toxic substances into the natural environment. Antigua and Barbuda, for instance, includes as a terrorist act releasing into the environment any dangerous, hazardous, radioactive, or harmful substance; any toxic chemical; or any microbial or other biological agent or toxin.[228] A similar approach is taken in Brunei,[229] Vanuatu,[230] and Zambia,[231] among others. More narrowly, Afghanistan only considers environmental harm when it results from an offence involving a *radioactive* substance.[232]

Burundi deems as acts of terror the introduction into the natural environment any substance that may endanger human health or that of animals, when the act is perpetrated with terrorist intent.[233] Similar language is contained in the Comoros' Criminal Code: 'the fact of introducing into the atmosphere on the ground, in subsoil or in waters, including those of the territorial sea, a substance likely to endanger human or animal health or the natural environment'.[234] In France, the maximum sentence for acts of terrorism committed in or against the natural environment is twenty years in prison.[235] The same is true in Gabon.[236]

3.3.1.13 Terrorism Financing

The financing of acts of terrorism or terrorist groups is a criminal offence in the overwhelming majority of States. In many cases it is a distinct terrorism offence, while in some States an entire law is dedicated to addressing terrorism funding.[237] Germany, which does not have detailed terrorism legislative provisions, tackles most offences under its ordinary criminal law. Nevertheless, terrorism financing has been specifically proscribed in the Criminal Code.[238]

---

[222] Art. 574(1), Criminal Code of Guinea.
[223] S. 5, 2002 Terrorism Suppression Act.
[224] Art. 1, 2013 Law on Terrorism.
[225] Art. 87 bis, Penal Code of Algeria (as amended).
[226] Art. 1(2), 2018 Amendment to Terrorism Law.
[227] Art. 187A, Criminal Code of Greece.
[228] Definition of 'terrorist act' in S. 2(1), 2005 Prevention of Terrorism Act.
[229] S. 2, 2011 Anti-Terrorism Order.
[230] S. 3(1), 2005 Counterterrorism Act.
[231] S. 2(1), 2018 Anti-Terrorism and Non-Proliferation Act.
[232] Art. 3(10), 2008 Law on Combat against Terrorist Offences (unofficial translation).
[233] Art. 615, Criminal Code of Burundi.
[234] Art. 255, Criminal Code of Comoros.
[235] Art. 421–2, French Criminal Code.
[236] Art. 202, Criminal Code of Gabon.
[237] This is the case, for instance, in Andorra, Bhutan, Bulgaria, DR Congo, Liechtenstein, among others.
[238] Section 89c(1), Criminal Code of Germany.

3.3 *National Definitions of Terrorism Offences*

In Dominica, as noted in the introduction to this chapter, there is not yet a dedicated law on terrorism offences, but only on the financing of terrorism.[239] The same is true in the Holy See, which uses the definition from the 1999 Terrorism Financing Convention,[240] although a 2012 amendment decree does also criminalize the fact of creating or leading terrorist groups.[241] Kuwait uses the wording of the 1999 Convention verbatim in its domestic terrorism financing law of 2013.[242] The same approach is taken in Liechtenstein.[243]

In a few States, funding is subsumed within the broader notion of assisting or supporting terrorism. This is the case in Afghanistan, for instance.[244] Namibian law makes the 'payment of ransom to designated persons or organisations' a terrorism offence, 'except where such payment is approved or authorised by any government to secure the safety of a national of that country'.[245]

3.3.1.14 Offences in Relation to Arms or Ammunition

Frequent are the cases of States expressly considering offences in relation to arms or ammunition to be predicate terrorism crimes. Andorra explicitly makes the 'storage' of arms or ammunition a terrorism offence.[246] In Laos, however, it is weapons trafficking that is a terrorism offence.[247] In Montenegro, development, possession, procurement, transport, provision, or use of weapons or explosives are predicate terrorism offences.[248] In Myanmar, conduct 'to produce, transfer, keep, supply or offer to supply arms and ammunition' is per se a terrorism offence.[249] Spain refers to 'the holding, trafficking and depositing of weapons, ammunition or explosives' a terrorism offence.[250]

Slovakia has one of the most detailed provisions, stipulating in its Criminal Code that any person will be guilty of a terrorism offence who, when acting with the requisite intent,

> requires, produces, obtains, stores, owns, possesses, imports, exports, transports, has it trans-ported, delivers or otherwise uses an explosive, nuclear material, radioactive substance, chemical substance, biological agent or toxin, firearm, nuclear weapon, radiological weapon, biological weapon, chemical weapon or other weapon, means of combat or material of a similar nature, or performs research and development of a nuclear weapon, biological weapon, chemical weapon or other weapon or means of combat or an explosive, or a facility for the production, treatment, storage or use of nuclear materials, radioactive substances, chemical substances or biological agents and toxins.[251]

Also extremely broad in scoping terrorism is Sri Lanka's law from 1979, which covers anyone who 'without lawful authority imports, manufactures or collects any firearms, offensive weapons, ammunition or explosives or any article or thing used, or intended to be used, in the

---

[239] Terrorist financing carries a maximum penalty of twenty-five years in prison along with a fine. S. 5, 2003 Terrorist Financing Act.

[240] Art. 1(6), 2010 Terrorist Financing Law. Under the 2012 amendment decree, the Holy See provides for prison sentences for terrorists of five to fifteen years. Art. 4, Terrorism (Amendment) Decree of January 2012.

[241] Art. 4, Terrorism (Amendment) Decree of January 2012.

[242] Art. 1, 2013 Law on Terrorist Financing.

[243] Art. 2(2)), 1997 Terrorist Financing Law (as amended in 2021).

[244] Art. 3(4), 2008 Law on Combat against Terrorist Offences (unofficial translation).

[245] S. 1(1)(e), 2014 Terrorism Act.

[246] Art. 362(1), Criminal Code of Andorra.

[247] Art. 120(4), Criminal Code of Laos.

[248] Art. 447(1)5), Criminal Code of Montenegro.

[249] Chap. 1(3)(12), 2014 Counterterrorism Law.

[250] Art. 573(1), Criminal Code of Spain.

[251] S. 418(1), Criminal Code of Slovakia.

manufacture of explosives'; or 'possesses without lawful authority, within any security area, any firearms or any offensive weapon, ammunition or explosives or any article or thing used, or intended to be used, in the manufacture of explosives'.[252] The 2023 Anti-Terrorism Bill that was before Sri Lanka's Parliament, but not yet adopted at the time of writing, maintains this element.[253]

3.3.1.15 Subverting the Constitutional Order or Endangering National Security as Terrorism

Subverting the constitutional order or endangering national security are more often terrorism motivations, but they are sometimes considered as predicate terrorism offences instead. Thus, under a 1995 Executive Order, Algeria's Criminal Code criminalizes acts that disturb the functioning of the State or its territorial integrity or security.[254] Bolivia's Criminal Code makes 'crimes against common security' a terrorism offence when they are perpetrated with specific intent,[255] while Kenya does so when conduct concerns an act that 'prejudices national security or public safety'.[256]

3.3.1.16 Interrupting Public Services

Many States deem the interruption of public services as possible terrorism offences. Albania considers as a terrorist offence the act of intentionally interrupting electrical or water supply. Bolivia's Criminal Code makes 'crimes against ... public transportation' a terrorism offence when they are perpetrated with specific intent.[257] The details of the offences are not, however, made clear in the Code.

Algeria considers the interruption of public services as a motivation for terrorism offences rather than as a predicate offence. These issues potentially overlap with certain fundamental human rights, an issue discussed in Section 3.3.8.1 on the interrelationship between terrorism and the exercise of human rights, including the right to freedom of assembly and the right to strike.[258]

3.3.1.17 Public Order Offences as Terrorism

Two States deem relatively mild public order offences to be predicate terrorism crimes. Haiti considers blocking the streets or leaving rubbish in the streets as predicate terrorism offences pursuant to a 2020 decree.[259] Under Sri Lankan law still in force at the time of writing, anyone who 'without lawful authority erases, mutilates, defaces or otherwise interferes with any words, inscriptions, or lettering appearing on any board or other fixture on, upon or adjacent to, any highway, street, road or any other public place' commits a terrorism offence.[260] If adopted as drafted, however, the 2023 Anti-Terrorism Bill does not maintain this offence.

---

[252] S. 2(1), 1979 Prevention of Terrorism Act.
[253] S. 3(2)(m), 2023 Anti-Terrorism Bill.
[254] Art. 87 bis, Penal Code of Algeria (as amended).
[255] Art. 133, Criminal Code of Bolivia.
[256] S. 2(a)(ix), 2012 Prevention of Terrorism Act.
[257] Art. 133, Criminal Code of Bolivia.
[258] See generally on this issue J. Vogt et al., *The Right to Strike in International Law*, Hart, Oxford, 2021.
[259] Art. 1(12) and (13), 2020 Decree for the Reinforcement of Public Security.
[260] S. 2(1)(i), 1979 Prevention of Terrorism Act.

3.3.1.18 Extortion as Terrorism

Austria explicitly makes extortion a possible predicate offence for terrorism.[261] The same is true in France,[262] Haiti,[263] and Monaco.[264] A 2013 decree in Honduras considers acts of extortion by organized criminal groups to be acts of terrorism.[265] In Pakistan, predicate terrorism offences include 'extortion, intimidation, and barring public servants from their duties'.[266] Sri Lanka's 2023 Anti-Terrorism Bill as currently drafted includes extortion as a predicate offence.

3.3.1.19 Insulting or Attacking the Sovereign or Degrading National Honour as Terrorism

Belarus has made 'degrading national honour' a predicate offence for terrorism. In Saudi Arabia, the country's 2017 counterterrorism law includes criminal penalties of five to ten years in prison for portraying the king or crown prince, directly or indirectly, 'in a manner that brings religion or justice into disrepute'.[267]

In Russia, encroachment on the life of a statesman or a public figure, committed for the purpose of terminating his government or any other political activity, is potentially punishable by capital punishment (although the country has a de facto moratorium on the execution of the death penalty).[268] A similar crime exists in Turkmenistan, where it concerns 'an infringement on the life of the President of Turkmenistan, other statesman or a public figure'.[269]

3.3.1.20 Criminal Libel or Propagating False Information as Terrorism

Iran's terrorism laws include a range of offences against the State as acts of terrorism. This includes 'criminal libel', which attracts the mandatory death penalty upon conviction.[270] In Nigeria, the 'propagation and dissemination of information or information materials in any form or mode calculated to cause panic, evoke violence or intimidate a government, person or group of persons' are acts of terrorism.[271]

3.3.1.21 Inciting Racial Hatred

Sri Lankan law from 1979 provides that anyone who 'by words either spoken or intended to be read or by signs or by visible representations or otherwise causes or intends to cause commission of acts of violence or religious, racial or communal disharmony or feelings of ill-will or hostility between different communities or racial or religious groups' commits a terrorism offence.[272] Section 3(1)(e) of the 2023 Terrorism Bill before Sri Lanka's Parliament replaces this with 'advocat[ing] national, racial or religious hatred that constitutes incitement to discrimination,

---

[261] S. 278c, Penal Code of Austria.

[262] Art. 421–2, French Penal Code.

[263] Art. 1(2), 2020 Decree for the Reinforcement of Public Security.

[264] Art. 391–1(5), Criminal Code of Monaco.

[265] Art. 5, Decree No. 168–2013.

[266] S. 6(1), 1997 Anti-Terrorism Act.

[267] See on this issue Human Rights Watch, 'Saudi Arabia: New Counterterrorism Law Enables Abuse', 23 November 2017, at: https://bit.ly/3MM7tQS.

[268] Art. 277, Criminal Code of Russia.

[269] Art. 1(4), 2003 Law on the Fight against Terrorism.

[270] Art. 286, Criminal Code of Iran.

[271] S. 1(3), 2022 Terrorism (Prevention and Prohibition) Act.

[272] S. 2(1)(h), 1979 Prevention of Terrorism Act.

hostility or violence'. In Tunisia, inciting or advocating hatred or animosity between races and religions is a predicate terrorism offence.[273]

3.3.1.22 Complicating Foreign Relations as Terrorism

A small number of States render criminal acts that seek to complicate a State's foreign relations terrorism offences. Thus, in Jordan, amendments made in 2014 to the 2006 Prevention of Terrorism Act granted the State Security Court authority over non-violent offences by defining terrorist acts also as those which disturb 'relations with a foreign state'. In Laos, causing problems to the international relations of the State is a terrorism offence.[274] The same is true in neighbouring Vietnam, where this is sought to be achieved by terrorizing foreigners.[275]

3.3.1.23 Destroying Cultural Heritage

Several States make the destruction of cultural heritage a specific predicate offence for terrorism. That is the case with Cameroon, for instance.[276] The same is true in South Africa's 2022 law, which stipulates that significantly damaging cultural heritage in the exercise of fundamental human rights is not excluded from being treated as terrorism.[277] Section 3(2)(j) of Sri Lanka's 2023 Anti-Terrorism Bill would make it a predicate terrorism offence 'causing the destruction of, or serious damage to, . . . cultural property'.

3.3.1.24 Other Predicate Offences for Terrorism

There are a number of other predicate terrorism offences, not discussed in previous sections, that are unique to a particular State. Hazing in the armed forces is a predicate offence in Lithuania, where a member of the services humiliates or terrorizes another member by using physical violence or a weapon. The terrorism offence is punishable by imprisonment for a term of up to five years.[278] In Bahrain, the preventing of an academic institution from conducting its work is likewise a terrorist offence when it occurs with the requisite motivation.[279]

Israel's terrorism laws include causing serious harm to religious objects as a predicate offence for terrorism. The term 'religious objects' denotes either a place of worship or burial, or holy objects.[280] Morocco includes as a predicate offence 'the counterfeiting or falsification of coins or public credit instruments, State seals and hallmarks, stamps and marks'.[281] The minimum penalty for terrorism is ten years' imprisonment.[282] Although it is not yet on the Statute book, at the time of writing Brazil was moving to make territorial control by armed gangs a predicate terrorism crime.[283]

---

[273] Art. 14, 2015 Counterterrorism Law.
[274] Art. 120(1), Criminal Code of Laos.
[275] Art. 84(4), Criminal Code.
[276] S. 2, 2014 Law on Repression of Acts of Terrorism.
[277] 2022 Protection of Constitutional Democracy against Terrorist and Related Activities Amendment Act.
[278] S. 320(2), Criminal Code of Lithuania.
[279] Art. 1, 2006 Law on the Protection of Society from Terrorist Acts.
[280] S. 2(a), 2018 Anti-Terrorism Law.
[281] Art. 218(1)2), Criminal Code of Morocco.
[282] Art. 218(3), Criminal Code of Morocco.
[283] C. Silva, 'Senators define territorial control as terrorist activity', *The Brazilian Report*, 10 May 2023, at: https://bit.ly/ 45krnuL.

3.3.2 *Terrorism Motivation*

A broad range of motivations for the commission of the predicate offences are found in national legislation. The most common are intimidating the population or compelling government conduct, reflecting the specific definition set forth in the 1999 Terrorism Financing Convention.[284] Perhaps surprisingly, the specific aim of *terrorizing* the civilian population is only found in a minority of national terrorism laws, as recounted in Section 3.3.2.1.

Some national laws have exceptionally expansive motivations. One such case is Egypt, which deems that a terrorist act encompasses any 'use of force' or 'threat' that aims to 'disrupt general order or endanger the safety, interests or security of society; harm individual liberties or rights; harm national unity, peace, security, the environment or buildings or property; prevent or hinder public authorities, judicial bodies, government facilities, and others from carrying out all or part of their work and activity'.[285]

Certainly, the tendency over recent years has been to broaden the capture of terrorism laws. In 2022, South Africa amended its terrorism law to delete the exemption previously accorded to national liberation movements. Thus removed was the following savings clause:

> [A]ny act committed during a struggle waged by peoples, including any action during an armed struggle, in the exercise or furtherance of their legitimate right to national liberation, self-determination and independence against colonialism, or occupation or aggression or domination by alien or foreign forces, in accordance with the principles of international law, especially international humanitarian law, . . . shall not, for any reason, including for purposes of prosecution or extradition, be considered as a terrorist activity.[286]

Fighting *apartheid* would therefore be a terrorism offence under contemporary South African law.

3.3.2.1 Terrorizing the Civilian Population

Remarkably, only some thirty States make the intent to *terrorize* civilians a terrorism motivation, and only a few of the legal formulations pertaining thereto coincide. Argentina makes terrorizing the population one of the motivations for a terrorism offence.[287] So too does Kazakhstan.[288] In Tunisia, it is the intent to spread terror among the civilian population that is a possible terrorism motivation.[289] Spain's Criminal Code talks rather of 'provoking a state of terror among the population or part thereof'.[290] In Estonia, 'seriously terrorising the population' is a terrorism motivation.[291]

France's Criminal Code talks of 'seriously disturbing public order through intimidation or terror' as predicate offences.[292] The same language is used in Burundi,[293] Comoros,[294] the Democratic

---

[284] Art. 2(1)(b), 1999 Terrorism Financing Convention.
[285] Art. 2, Law 95 of 2015 for Confronting Terrorism.
[286] S. 1(4), 2004 Protection of Constitutional Democracy against Terrorist and Related Activities Act.
[287] Art. 41 *quinquies*, Penal Code of Argentina.
[288] Art. 255(1), Criminal Code of Kazakhstan.
[289] Art. 13, 2015 Counterterrorism Law.
[290] Art. 573(1), Criminal Code of Spain.
[291] S. 237, Criminal Code of Estonia.
[292] Art. 421–1, French Penal Code: 'ayant pour but de troubler gravement l'ordre public par l'intimidation ou la terreur'.
[293] Art. 614, Criminal Code of Burundi.
[294] Art. 255, Criminal Code of Comoros.

Republic of Congo,[295] Gabon,[296] and Senegal,[297] indicating the colonial (or post-colonial) link. Andorra similarly sets as a terrorism motivation 'a serious attack on public law and order through intimidation and terror'.[298] Burkina Faso has defined terrorist acts in a 2015 amended law pertaining to predicate offences as 'breaches that, by their nature, aim to intimidate or terrorise a population'.[299] In India, whoever does any act with intent to strike terror or likely to strike terror in the people or any section of the people in India or in any foreign country commits a terrorism offence.[300]

As already noted, Lebanon describes terrorism as 'all acts intended to cause a state of terror and committed by means liable to create a public danger'.[301] In Côte d'Ivoire, terrorist intent includes to 'provoke a situation of terror or to intimidate the population'.[302] Acts intended to 'intimidate' or 'provoke a situation of terror' in Guinea are likewise terrorism motivations.[303] In Indonesia, it is the causing of a 'widespread atmosphere of terror or fear' that is at issue.[304] In Cameroon, the requisite motivation is to 'intimidate the public' or 'provoke a situation of terror'.[305] In Chad, possible motivations are to 'intimidate' or 'cause terror'.[306] In Iran, the purpose of causing 'horror and fear among people and to create chaos to achieve terrorist goals' is set forth in the country's 2005 Anti-terrorism Law.[307]

In Sudan, 'any threat or act of violence, whatever its motives or purposes, that takes place in implementation of an individual or collective criminal project and aims to sow terror among people' is a terrorism offence.[308] Cuba's dedicated 2001 law defines terrorism as including acts whose means and methods 'evidence the specific purpose of causing states of alarm, fear, or terror in the population'.[309] Angola's 2017 Law on Preventing and Countering Terrorism makes provoking a state of terror in the population or a part of it a terrorism motivation.[310] In its 2020 Criminal Code, terrorism is then defined as 'criminal acts aimed at provoking a state of terror in the general public, in a group of people or individuals ... irrespective of political, philosophical, ideological, racial, ethnic, or religious considerations or of any other nature that may be invoked'.[311]

In Mexico, domestic terrorism is considered to exist when a certain act 'produces alarm, fear or terror in the population or in a group or sector of it'.[312] Mexico has a further definition that is specific to 'international terrorism' when these same acts are perpetrated 'which produce alarm, fear or terror in the population or in a group or sector of it, in order to put pressure on the

---

[295]   Art. 157, 2002 Military Criminal Code.
[296]   Art. 194, Criminal Code of Gabon.
[297]   '[T]o seriously disturb public order or the functioning of national or international institutions, through intimidation or terror'. Art. 279–1, Criminal Code of Senegal.
[298]   Art. 362(1), Criminal Code of Andorra.
[299]   Art. 2, Loi No. 084–2015/CNT, Portant Modification de la Loi No. 060–2009/AN du 17 décembre 2009 portant Repression d'Actes de Terrorisme au Burkina Faso. The same wording appears in the Criminal Code. Art. 361–1, Criminal Code of Burkina Faso.
[300]   S. 15, India 1967 Unlawful Activities (Prevention) Act (UAPA).
[301]   Art. 314, Criminal Code of Lebanon.
[302]   Art. 3, 2015 Anti-Terrorism Law (Law No. 2015–493 of 7 July 2015 on the suppression of terrorism).
[303]   Art. 574(1), Criminal Code of Guinea.
[304]   Art. 1(2), 2018 Amendment to Terrorism Law.
[305]   S. 2, 2014 Law on Repression of Acts of Terrorism.
[306]   Art. 2(1), 2020 Law on the Suppression of Terrorism.
[307]   Art. 1, 2005 Anti-Terrorism Law.
[308]   Sudan 2001 Counterterrorism Act.
[309]   Art.1(1), 2001 Terrorism Law.
[310]   Art. 23(1), 2017 Law on Preventing or Countering Terrorism.
[311]   Art. 297(1), 2020 Penal Code of Angola.
[312]   Art. 139(I), Federal Criminal Code of Mexico.

3.3 *National Definitions of Terrorism Offences* 101

authority of that foreign State or to oblige it or an international organization to take a particular decision'. Thus, it is the fact of causing terror that is devised by the perpetrators to compel action by a foreign State that is determinant.[313] A similar approach is taken in Monaco, which covers acts that are 'directed either against the Principality of Monaco or against any other State or against an international organization, and are of a nature, by means of intimidation or terror either to threaten their political, economic or social structures, to harm them or to destroy them; or to seriously disturb public order'.[314]

Namibian law describes a terrorist act as 'any act committed by a person with the intention of instilling terror and which is a violation of the criminal laws of Namibia' but it then adds alternative purposes, including to 'intimidate, instil fear, force, coerce or induce any government, body, institution, the general public or any segment thereof, to do or abstain from doing any act, or to adopt or abandon a particular standpoint, or to act according to certain principles'.[315] Nepal sees 'any act to terrorize the general public or passers-by or assembling people' as a means to meet the terrorism purpose of, inter alia, undermining the sovereignty or unity of the country.[316] In South Sudan, the Terrorism Financing Act defines terrorism as 'the use of organized intimidation or extreme fear to coerce a government or community'.[317]

3.3.2.2 Intimidation of the Population or Causing Panic

Far more common than terrorizing the population is the broader notion of *intimidating* the population or a segment of it, reflecting the particular wording in the 1999 Terrorism Financing Convention.[318] Again, different formulations exist in national legislation. Certain States use only the wording 'intimidating' or 'to intimidate' the population or the public.[319] Such wording is found, for instance, in Armenian,[320] Australian,[321] Barbados,[322] and Belize legislation,[323] as well as in the law in the Central African Republic,[324] The Gambia,[325] and Georgia.[326] In Brunei, if the relevant use or threat is not covered by a global sectoral terrorism treaty, it must be either intended or 'reasonably regarded as intending' to 'intimidate the public or a section of the public'.[327] The Cook Islands uses the same terminology.[328]

Kenya's dedicated law refers to 'intimidating or causing fear amongst members of the public or a section of the public'.[329] In Cabo Verde, a terrorist purpose can be to 'intimidate certain people, groups of people, or the general population'.[330] In Jamaica, the wording is 'intimidating the public, or a segment of the public, with regard to its security, including its economic

---

[313] Art. 148, Federal Criminal Code of Mexico.
[314] Art. 391–1, Criminal Code of Monaco.
[315] S. 1(1)(a)(i), 2014 Terrorism Act.
[316] S. 3(a), 2002 Terrorist and Disruptive Acts (Prevention and Punishment) Act.
[317] S. 5, 2012 Anti-Money Laundering and Counterterrorist Financing Act, Act No. 29 of 2012.
[318] Art. 2(1)(b), 1999 Terrorism Financing Convention.
[319] See, e.g., S. 3(1)(b), Barbados 2002 Anti-Terrorism Act.
[320] Art. 217(1), Penal Code of Armenia.
[321] S. 2C(1)(b)(ii), 2008 Money Laundering and Terrorism (Prevention) Act.
[322] S. 3(1)(b), 2002 Anti-Terrorism Act.
[323] S. 100.1, 1995 Criminal Code Act.
[324] Art. 296, Criminal Code of the Central African Republic.
[325] Art. 2(b), 2002 Anti-Terrorism Act.
[326] Art. 323(1), Criminal Code of Georgia.
[327] S. 2(2)(b)(ii), 2011 Anti-Terrorism Order.
[328] S. 4(2), 2004 Act on the Suppression of Terrorism (as amended).
[329] S. 2(b)(i), 2012 Prevention of Terrorism Act.
[330] Art. 2(1), 2013 Terrorism Law, Law No. 27/VIII/2013 of 21 January.

security'.[331] The latter element of 'economic security' greatly expands the breadth of the purpose. China's National Security Law, which is applicable to Hong Kong, defines 'Terrorist Activities' to include the aim of 'intimidating the public in order to pursue a political agenda'.[332]

Reflecting language in the preamble to the 2005 European Convention on the Prevention of Terrorism,[333] a number of European States refer rather to 'serious' or 'grave' intimidation. Thus, Austrian law talks of 'gravely' intimidating the population,[334] while Belgium's Criminal Code refers to 'seriously' intimidating the population.[335] So too do the Criminal Codes of Finland[336] and Germany.[337] Cyprus refers to the intention 'to seriously intimidate the public or sections of the public'.[338] Albania makes the causing of 'panic' among the population one of several alternative motivations for terrorism.[339] So too do Azerbaijan,[340] Bangladesh,[341] and Belarus.[342] Chinese law refers to 'social' panic.[343]

Terrorist motivation under Bolivian law is a predicate offence that is perpetrated in order to 'keep the population or a section of it in a state of collective anxiety, alarm, or panic'.[344] In Bulgaria, it is the aim of 'causing disturbance or fear among the population' that constitutes terrorism motivation.[345] Cambodia, which has a long-standing dedicated terrorism law, defines acts of terrorism in its 1992 law as acts of violence 'which create panic among the mass of the people and aim at causing strong turmoil to the public order and security and affecting political stability'.[346] Syria's 2012 law defines terrorism as '[a]ny act aimed at creating panic among people, disturbing public security or damaging the infrastructure or infrastructure of the State'.[347]

In Japan, legislation dating back to the 1950s defines terrorism as meaning violent subversive activities based on political or other principles, which are carried out with the intention of achieving the purpose by causing widespread fear or anxiety.[348] Guinea, which has the provoking of a situation of terror as one of its terrorism motivations, also refers to acts whose intent is to 'create a feeling of insecurity among the population' as well as to 'create a situation of crisis within the population'.[349] Kyrgyzstan's Criminal Code identifies violating public security and

---

[331] S. 3(4), 2015 Terrorism Prevention Act.

[332] Art. 24, National Security Law.

[333] Thus, the preamble to the 2005 European Convention on the Prevention of Terrorism recalls that 'acts of terrorism have the purpose by their nature or context to seriously intimidate a population.' Council of Europe Convention on the Prevention of Terrorism; adopted at Warsaw, 16 May 2005; entered into force, 1 June 2007, ninth preambular para.

[334] S. 278(c), Penal Code of Austria.

[335] Art. 137, Criminal Code of Belgium.

[336] S. 6, chap. 34(a), Criminal Code of Finland.

[337] Section 89c(1), Criminal Code of Germany.

[338] Art. 5, 2010 Combatting Terrorism Act.

[339] Art. 230, Criminal Code of Albania.

[340] Art. 1, 1999 Azerbaijan Law on Countering Terrorism.

[341] S. 6(1), 2009 Anti-Terrorism Act (as amended).

[342] Art. 3, 2002 Law on Terrorism.

[343] Art. 3, 2016 Counterterrorism Law.

[344] Art. 133, Criminal Code of Bolivia.

[345] Art. 108a(1), Criminal Code of Bulgaria.

[346] Art. 1, 1992 Law on the Punishment of Terrorism.

[347] Art. 1, 2012 Terrorism Act.

[348] Art. 40, 1954 Ordinance regarding establishment of the National Police Agency. More recently, a 2013 law described acts of terrorism as 'activities intended to kill or injure people or destroy important facilities or other objects for the purpose of forcing a political or other principle or belief upon the State or other persons or causing fear or terror in society based on such principle or opinion'. Art. 12(2), Act on the Protection of Specially Designated Secrets, Act No. 108 of 2013.

[349] Art. 574(1), Criminal Code of Guinea.

3.3 *National Definitions of Terrorism Offences* 103

frightening the population as terrorism motivations.[350] For Pakistan, it is predicate offences that are designed to 'create a sense of fear or insecurity in society' that constitute terrorism.[351]

The Netherlands' Criminal Code defines terrorist intent as 'the intent to harm the population or part of the population of a country to create *serious fear*, or to unlawfully compel a government or international organization to do or not to do something, or to seriously disrupt or destroy the fundamental political, constitutional, economic or social structures of a country or an international organization'.[352] Norway's law refers to 'causing serious fear in a population' as terrorism.[353]

3.3.2.3 Compelling Government Conduct

Reflecting the wording found in Article 2(1)(b) of the 1999 Terrorism Financing Convention, the overwhelming majority of States set efforts to compel the government to do or refrain from certain conduct as a terrorism motivation. The few exceptions to the general rule that exist include Lebanon, which, as already noted, describes terrorism as 'all acts intended to cause a state of terror and committed by means liable to create a public danger' but without a separate motivation of compelling government conduct.[354] Andorra determines rather that terrorism has the aim of 'subverting the constitutional order' (or terrorizing the public). A similar approach is taken in the Bolivian Criminal Code.[355] Furthermore, Afghanistan only requires the motivation of coercing government conduct with respect to certain predicate offences. Thus, bombings are per se terrorism offences without the need for a particular terrorism motivation.

As discussed further in Section 3.3.2.9, in Brazil, terrorism is perpetrated 'for reasons of xenophobia, discrimination or prejudice based on race, colour, ethnicity and religion', but the dedicated 2016 law does not cover political ends in articulating the parameters of a terrorism offence.[356] Papua New Guinea's 1993 Internal Security Act defines terrorism as 'the use of violence for political ends or any use of violence for the purpose of putting the public or any section of the public in fear'.[357] In Rwanda, terrorism is defined as committing or threatening to commit 'acts aimed at leading State organs into changing their functioning through taking hostages of one or more persons, killing, injuring or threatening the population by use of any means that may kill or injure a person'.[358] Comoros talks in its Criminal Code of 'blackmailing' a government.[359]

Romania has a particularly unusual definition of terrorism in its domestic law:

> the ensemble of actions and/or threats that represent a public danger and affect national security, with the following characteristics:
>
> a) they are committed with premeditation by terrorist entities, motivated by extremist beliefs and attitudes, hostile to other entities, against which they act through violent and/or destructive modalities;

---

[350] Art. 252(2), Criminal Code of Kyrgyzstan.
[351] S. 6(1), 1997 Anti-Terrorism Act.
[352] Art. 83A, Criminal Code of the Netherlands [added emphasis].
[353] S. 131(2), Criminal Code of Norway.
[354] Art. 314, Criminal Code of Lebanon.
[355] Terrorist motivation thus pertains to predicate offences that are perpetrated 'in order to subvert the constitutional order or keep the population or a section of it in a state of collective anxiety, alarm, or panic'. Art. 133, Criminal Code of Bolivia.
[356] Art. 2(1), 2016 Terrorism Law, Law No. 13,260.
[357] S. 2, 1993 Internal Security Act.
[358] Art. 2, Law 45/2008 on countering terrorism.
[359] Art. 255, Criminal Code.

National Terrorism Legislation Worldwide

b) they are aimed at specific objectives of a political nature;
c) they concern human and/or material factors within the public authorities and institutions, the civil population or any other segment belonging to these;
d) they produce situations that have a deep psychological impact upon the population, which are meant to draw attention to the goals that they pursue.[360]

3.3.2.4 Compelling Conduct by a Foreign Government or an International Organization

Many States also include compelling conduct by an international organization as an alternative terrorism motivation, again reflecting the wording found in Article 2(1)(b) of the 1999 Terrorism Financing Convention. Some States are quite specific as to the harm that needs to be intended. In Finland, for instance, a terrorism motivation may be 'to cause particularly extensive damage to the finances or other fundamental structures of an international organisation'.[361]

Some States also consider actions to compel a foreign government to perform or not perform a certain act as a possible terrorist motivation. This is the case, for instance, in Afghanistan (with respect to a detainee),[362] Albania,[363] Australia,[364] Bosnia and Herzegovina,[365] and Monaco,[366] among others. In Kazakhstan, influencing the making of decisions by a foreign State is a terrorism motivation,[367] whereas in Bahrain, prejudicing the security of the international community more broadly is a terrorist motivation.[368]

3.3.2.5 Furthering Political, Ideological, or Religious Causes

Many States include furthering political, ideological, or religious causes as an alternative or, more often, as a *cumulative* requirement for terrorism motivation. Those that require this additional element beyond intimidating the population or seeking to compel government conduct include Antigua and Barbuda,[369] Australia,[370] Belize,[371] Canada,[372] the Central African Republic,[373]

---

[360] Art. 1, 2004 Law on Combatting Terrorism.
[361] S. 6, chap. 34(a), Criminal Code of Finland.
[362] 'If a person for the purpose of compelling the Government of Afghanistan, a foreign government, an international organization or a non-government foreign organization arrests or detains another person to carry out or avoid carrying out an action or threatens the person to death or physical torture or keeps the person in captivity and makes his/her release explicitly or implicitly conditional to carrying out or avoid carrying out an action.' Art. 12(1), 2008 Law on Combat against Terrorist Offences (unofficial translation).
[363] Art. 230, Criminal Code of Albania.
[364] S. 100.1, 1995 Criminal Code Act.
[365] Art. 201(1), Criminal Code of Bosnia and Herzegovina.
[366] '[D]irected either against the Principality of Monaco or against any other State or against an international organization'. Art. 391–1, Criminal Code of Monaco.
[367] Art. 255(1), Criminal Code of Kazakhstan.
[368] Art. 1, 2006 Law on the Protection of Society from Terrorist Acts.
[369] S. 2(1), 2005 Prevention of Terrorism Act.
[370] Australia requires that the action be done or the threat made with the intention of advancing a political, religious, or ideological cause as well as to intimidate the population or compel conduct by a State. S. 100.1, 1995 Criminal Code Act.
[371] S. 2C(1)(c), 2008 Money Laundering and Terrorism (Prevention) Act.
[372] S. 83.01(b)(i)(A), Criminal Code of Canada. The Canadian Supreme Court has upheld the constitutionality of the clause, reversing an earlier holding in the Court of Appeals in the *Khawaja* case. Supreme Court of Canada, *R. v. Khawaja*, 2012 SCC 69, para. 85.
[373] Art. 296, Criminal Code of the Central African Republic.

3.3 *National Definitions of Terrorism Offences* 105

China,[374] Eswatini,[375] Fiji,[376] Grenada,[377] Israel,[378] Jamaica,[379] Kiribati,[380] Lesotho,[381] Liberia,[382] Malawi,[383] Malaysia,[384] New Zealand,[385] Niue,[386] Palau,[387] St Lucia,[388] Sierra Leone,[389] the United Kingdom,[390] Vanuatu,[391] and Zambia.[392] Of course, the notion of a political cause overlaps with the motivation of compelling government conduct.

In Uganda, the 2002 Anti-Terrorism Act requires also 'a political, religious, social or economic aim'.[393] In Indonesia, it is violent acts perpetrated 'for reason of ideology, politics, or security disturbance' that is the purposive element.[394] For St Kitts and Nevis, action need only be 'taken or threatened for political, religious, or ideological purposes' to amount to terrorism if it is not an offence under any of the UN sectoral treaties listed in the 2002 law.[395] In Timor-Leste, terrorism is defined in the Criminal Code as an act whose goal is to achieve 'political, ideological, religious, or philosophical aims with a view to impairing national integrity or independence'.[396]

In Guyana, it is only offences intended to intimidate the public or a section of the public (and the alternative motivation of seeking to compel government conduct) where the additional purpose of advancing a political, ideological, or religious cause is required by the dedicated terrorism legislation.[397] Ghana specifies that predicate offences become terrorism when they are 'effected or performed in furtherance of a political, ideological, religious, racial, or ethnic reason'.[398] But the 2008 Act goes on to stipulate that a terrorist act *is also an act* intended to intimidate the public or compel conduct by a person, a government, or an international organization where that is carried out 'to advance a political, ideological or religious cause'.[399]

3.3.2.6 Undermining Sovereignty or National Unity or Destabilizing the Government

Beyond the political motivations discussed in the previous sections, legislation in certain States also sets undermining sovereignty or national unity, or destabilizing the government, as distinct

---

[374] The aim is 'of realising political, ideological and other purposes'. Art. 3, 2016 Counterterrorism Law.
[375] S. 2(1), 2017 Suppression of Terrorism (Amendment) Act.
[376] S. 2, Fiji 1969 Public Order Act.
[377] S. 2, 2012 Terrorism Act.
[378] The wording of a dedicated 2018 law is that the relevant act was carried out with a 'political, religious, nationalistic or ideological motive'. S. 2(a), 2018 Anti-Terrorism Law.
[379] S. 3(4), 2015 Terrorism Prevention Act.
[380] S. 3(2)(c), 2005 Measures to Combat Terrorism Act.
[381] S. 2(i)(iii), 2018 Prevention and Suppression of Terrorism Act, Act 3 of 2018.
[382] Art. 5(6), 2017 Amendment of the Liberian Criminal Code.
[383] S. 4, Penal Code of Malawi.
[384] S. 130B(2)(b), Penal Code of Malaysia.
[385] '[C]arried out for one or more purposes that are or include advancing an ideological, political, or religious cause'. S. 5, 2002 Terrorism Suppression Act.
[386] S. 4(2)(g)(ii), 2006 Suppression of Terrorism Act.
[387] S. 4202 (mm), Criminal Code of Palau.
[388] S. 2(ix) (ac), 2015 Anti-Terrorism Act.
[389] '[A]dvance a political, ideological, or religious cause'. S. 1, 2012 Terrorist Financing Act.
[390] S. 1, 2000 Terrorism Act.
[391] S. 3(1), 2005 Counterterrorism and Transnational Organized Crime Act.
[392] S. 2(1), 2018 Anti-Terrorism and Non-Proliferation Act.
[393] S. 7(2), 2002 Anti-Terrorism Act.
[394] Art. 1(2), 2018 Amendment to Terrorism Law.
[395] S. 2(b), 2002 Antiterrorism Act.
[396] Art. 131, Criminal Code of Timor-Leste.
[397] S. 2(B)(a), 2015 Anti-Terrorism and Terrorist Related Activities Act.
[398] S. 3, 2008 Anti-Terrorist Act.
[399] S. 3(3), 2008 Anti-Terrorist Act.

terrorism motivations. Thus, for example, Angolan law has as one of its multiple motivations for terrorism harming national integrity or independence. In Bahrain, prejudicing national unity is a specific terrorist motivation.[400] In Bangladesh, it is 'the purposes of threatening the unity, integration, public security or sovereignty of Bangladesh' that are considered terrorism motivations.[401] In Cabo Verde, a terrorism motivation is the intent to 'endanger the independence or territorial integrity of the country'.[402] In India, whoever does 'any act' with intent to threaten or which is likely to threaten 'the unity, integrity, security, economic security, or sovereignty of India' commits a terrorism offence.[403]

In Nepal, one requisite terrorist intent is 'to undermine or jeopardize the sovereignty and integrity of the Kingdom of Nepal'.[404] Oman's national law determines that threatening the regional stability or security of the country or its political unity or sovereignty is a terrorism motivation.[405] In Saudi Arabia, the 2017 terrorism law makes the intent 'to disturb public order, destabilize national security or State stability, endanger national unity' terrorism motivation.[406] In Sri Lanka, terrorism motivation includes 'causing harm to the territorial integrity or sovereignty of Sri Lanka or any other sovereign country'.[407]

In Türkiye, damaging the indivisible unity of the State with its territory and nation is a terrorism motivation.[408] The acts of carrying or hanging symbols, pictures, or signs that are related to a terrorist organization; chanting slogans; broadcasting; or wearing uniforms that carry symbols, pictures, or signs that are related to a terrorist organization are punishable by between one and five years in prison, regardless of whether these take place during a gathering or demonstration.[409] In Iraq, every criminal act that causes damage to public or private property with the aim of disturbing national unity is deemed terrorism.[410] The actus reus and mens rea of a terrorist crime are so broad under the 2005 law that they can be met by doing nothing more than, for example, daubing slogans on a building calling for an independent Kurdistan.

Linked to the notion of undermining sovereignty is the motivation of destabilizing the government in some manner. Afghanistan's 2008 Terrorism Law thus sets out terrorist motivation as acting 'to affect the political affairs of the Government of Afghanistan, a foreign Government, national or international organizations or to destabilize the Government system of Afghanistan or of a foreign government'.[411] In Bhutan, using or training another person to use a bomb or firearm is a terrorist act where it is conducted with 'intent to subvert the State'.[412] Finland refers to the intent to 'unlawfully abrogate or alter the constitution of a State or seriously destabilise the legal order of a State or cause particularly extensive damage to the central government finances or fundamental social structures of a State'.[413] In Sao Tomé and Principe, acting with the intent of 'harming national integrity and independence, or destroying,

---

[400] Art. 1, 2006 Law on the Protection of Society from Terrorist Acts.
[401] S. 6(1)(a), 2009 Anti-Terrorism Act (as amended).
[402] Art. 2(1), 2013 Terrorism Law, Law No. 27/VIII/2013 of 21 January.
[403] S. 15, India 1967 Unlawful Activities (Prevention) Act (UAPA). A series of predicate acts are listed in the law.
[404] S. 3(a), 2002 Terrorist and Disruptive Acts (Prevention and Punishment) Act.
[405] Royal Decree No. 8 of 2007 on combating terrorism.
[406] Art. 1(3), 2017 Law on Terrorism and Terrorist Financing.
[407] S. 3(1), 2018 Counterterrorism Act.
[408] Art. 1, 1991 Counterterrorism Law.
[409] Art. 7(3), 1991 Counterterrorism Law.
[410] Art. 1, 2005 Anti-Terrorism Law.
[411] Art. 3(1), 2008 Law on Combat against Terrorist Offences (unofficial translation).
[412] S. 329(a), Criminal Code of Bhutan.
[413] S. 6, chap. 34(a), Criminal Code of Finland.

3.3 *National Definitions of Terrorism Offences*

altering or subverting the functioning of the State institutions provided for in the Constitution' amounts to terrorist intent.[414]

3.3.2.7 Violating or Prejudicing Public Order or Security

Under Russian law, 'violating public security' is a terrorism motivation,[415] reflecting the text of the Shanghai Cooperation Organization (SCO)'s 2001 Convention on Combating Terrorism, Separatism and Extremism.[416] The same is true in Armenia[417] and Tajikistan.[418] China's counterterrorism law talks of 'undermining public security'.[419] In Bahrain, prejudicing public order is similarly a possible terrorist motivation.[420] In Cabo Verde, a terrorism motivation is to 'destroy, alter or subvert the constitutionally enshrined democratic rule of law, or to create a climate of agitation or social disturbance'.[421] In Nepal, one requisite intent is to 'undermine or jeopardize' the 'security or peace and order of the Kingdom of Nepal or any part thereof'.[422]

In Cameroon, a requisite motivation (rather than a predicate offence) is the intent to 'disrupt the normal functioning of public services or the delivery of essential services to the public to create a crisis situation among the public'.[423] Similar language is used in Chad's 2020 Terrorism Law.[424] Guatemalan law provides simply that terrorism involves criminal acts committed with the purpose of disturbing public order.[425] In Honduras, the crime of terrorism is committed by those who perpetrate attacks 'for political purposes against the security of the State' by carrying out a series of predicate acts.[426]

3.3.2.8 Promoting or Engaging in an Insurgency or Provoking an Armed Conflict

In Ukraine[427] and Uzbekistan,[428] the aim of provoking an armed conflict is specifically set as a terrorism motivation. In Cameroon, a requisite motivation is to 'create widespread insurrection in the country'.[429] In Belarus, explosions and arson perpetrated with the aim of provoking war amount to terrorism.[430] In Armenia, bombings or arson 'or other acts' in the territory of a foreign State comprise the distinct crime of *international* terrorism when perpetrated with the purpose of provoking war.[431] Engaging in a violent act or insurrection against Bhutan that is designed primarily to generate fear in a community or a substantial section of the society is

---

[414]   Art. 360(1), Criminal Code of São Tomé and Príncipe.
[415]   Art. 205(1), Criminal Code of Russia.
[416]   Art. 1(1)(1)(b), Shanghai Convention on Combating Terrorism, Separatism and Extremism; adopted at Shanghai, 15 June 2001; entered into force, 29 March 2003.
[417]   Art. 217(1), Penal Code of Armenia.
[418]   Art. 179(1), Criminal Code of Tajikistan.
[419]   Art. 3, 2016 Counterterrorism Law.
[420]   Art. 1, 2006 Law on the Protection of Society from Terrorist Acts.
[421]   Art. 2(1), 2013 Terrorism Law, Law No. 27/VIII/2013 of 21 January.
[422]   S. 3(a), 2002 Terrorist and Disruptive Acts (Prevention and Punishment) Act.
[423]   S. 2(1), 2014 Law on Repression of Acts of Terrorism. This is the official English version of the text, which translates 'populations' in French to 'public' in English.
[424]   '[T]o disrupt the normal functioning of public services, the provision of essential services to the populations, or to create a crisis situation within the populations'. Art. 2(1), 2020 Law on the Suppression of Terrorism.
[425]   Art. 391, Criminal Code of Guatemala.
[426]   Art. 335, Criminal Code of Honduras.
[427]   Art. 258(1), Criminal Code of Ukraine.
[428]   Art. 155, Criminal Code of Uzbekistan.
[429]   S. 2, 2014 Law on Repression of Acts of Terrorism.
[430]   Art. 3, 2002 Law on Terrorism.
[431]   Art. 389, Penal Code of Armenia.

a terrorism offence.[432] In Guinea, one terrorism motivation is to create a general insurrection in the country.[433]

In Côte d'Ivoire, however, an act that creates or is likely to create a crisis situation within the populations or a general insurrection is rather a predicate offence for terrorism than a purposive one.[434] In Iraq, as in many States, the fact of promoting a rebellion is a separate crime in its Criminal Code. In the United States, the crime of seditious conspiracy has been used to prosecute some of those involved in the Capitol violence on 6 January 2021.[435]

3.3.2.9 Xenophobia or Religious or Racial Discrimination as Terrorism

Brazil is almost alone in setting predicate acts as terrorism when they are perpetrated 'for reasons of xenophobia, discrimination or prejudice based on race, colour, ethnicity and religion'. The acts must further be committed 'for the purpose of causing social or generalized terror', and they must expose 'individuals, properties, public peace, or public safety to danger'.[436] In Comoros, though, terrorist acts are those that are committed 'to satisfy hatred towards *a community*, a country or a system',[437] while in Pakistan, 'advancing a religious, sectarian or ethnic cause' is an alternative motivation for terrorism.[438]

3.3.2.10 Harming Fundamental Political, Constitutional, Economic, or Social Structures

Numerous States, especially in Europe, set inflicting harm on the fundamental political, constitutional, economic, or social structures as one of the purposive elements of the crime of terrorism.[439] Thus, Austria has as one possible terrorism motivation 'seriously disturbing the fundamental political, constitutional, economic, or social structure of a State or international organization'.[440] Cyprus uses similar language[441] as do Bosnia and Herzegovina,[442] Italy,[443] Liechtenstein,[444] Luxembourg,[445] Malta,[446] and San Marino.[447] A number of States outside Europe use similar formulations. Tanzania is one,[448] and The Gambia[449] and Malawi[450] are others.

[432]   S. 329(c), Criminal Code of Bhutan.
[433]   Art. 574(1), Criminal Code of Guinea.
[434]   Art. 3, 2015 Anti-Terrorism Law.
[435]   18 USC 2384: Seditious conspiracy. See on this issue *infra* chap. 4, §4.2.
[436]   Art. 2(1), 2016 Terrorism Law.
[437]   Art. 255, Criminal Code of Comoros [added emphasis].
[438]   S. 6(1), 1997 Anti-Terrorism Act.
[439]   Thus, the preamble to the European Convention on the Prevention of Terrorism recalls that 'acts of terrorism have the purpose by their nature or context to . . . seriously destabilise or destroy the fundamental political, constitutional, economic or social structures of a country or an international organisation'. 2005 European Convention on the Prevention of Terrorism, ninth preambular para.
[440]   S. 278(c), Penal Code of Austria.
[441]   Art. 5, 2010 Combatting Terrorism Act.
[442]   Art. 201(1), Criminal Code of Bosnia and Herzegovina.
[443]   Art. 270(6), Criminal Code of Italy.
[444]   S. 278c, Criminal Code of Liechtenstein.
[445]   Art. 135(1), Criminal Code of Luxembourg.
[446]   Art. 328A(1), Criminal Code of Malta.
[447]   '[T]o destabilize or destroy the political, constitutional, economic, or social structures of the Republic, of a foreign State or of an international organisation'. Art. 1(1)(p), Measures to Prevent, Combat, and Repress the Financing of Terrorism, the Proliferation of Weapons of Mass Destruction and the Action of Countries that Threaten International Peace and Security, Law No. 57 of 29 March 2019.
[448]   S. 4(2)(b)(iii), 2002 Prevention of Terrorism Act.
[449]   Art. 2(b), 2002 Anti-Terrorism Act.
[450]   S. 4, Penal Code of Malawi.

3.3 National Definitions of Terrorism Offences

The aim of 'seriously destabilising or destroying the fundamental political, constitutional, economic or social structures' is used in Croatia's Criminal Code, with respect to 'international terrorism'.[451] There is also 'anti-State terrorism' in the Criminal Code, which concerns predicate offences whose aim is to 'endanger the constitutional order or the security of the Republic of Croatia'.[452] In Estonia, 'seriously interfering with or destroying the political, constitutional, economic or social structure of the State' is one of the terrorist motivations.[453] Germany's Criminal Code refers to intent to 'destroy or significantly impair the fundamental political, constitutional, economic or social structures of a State or an international organisation' where, given the nature or consequences of the predicate offences, they can 'seriously damage' a State or an international organization.[454]

Albania includes as a possible motivation for a terrorism offence destroying or seriously destabilizing substantial political, constitutional, economic, or social structures of the Albanian State, another State, or an international institution or organization.[455] In Serbia, the wording is similarly 'to seriously harm or violate main constitutional, political, economic or social structures of Serbia, a foreign country or an international organisation'.[456]

Angola's 2017 counterterrorism law includes acts to prevent, destroy, alter, or subvert the functioning of the State institutions provided for in the country's Constitution as a terrorism motivation.[457] Kenya's dedicated law uses the formulation 'destabilizing the religious, political, constitutional, economic or social institutions of a country, or an international organization'.[458] In Mauritania, the relevant purpose is to 'destabilize the constitutional, political, economic, or social structures and/or institutions of the Nation, or harm the interests of other countries or an international organization'.[459]

A person 'who, with the intention of endangering the constitutional system or the security of the Republic of Macedonia', commits any of a series of predicate offences has committed a terrorism offence.[460] In Andorra, one motivation for terrorism is 'the aim of subverting the constitutional order'.[461] Iceland's Criminal Code refers to action taken with a view to weakening or damaging the constitutional structure or the political, economic, or social basis of the State or international institution.[462]

3.3.2.11 Other Terrorism Motivations

As noted in the previous sections, Algeria considers environmental harm as a possible motivation for terrorism rather than a predicate offence. The same is true in Oman, which also considers 'preventing or obstructing the public authorities from exercising their duties' as a terrorism motivation.[463]

---

[451] The wording is: 'seriously destabilising or destroying the fundamental constitutional, political, economic or social structures of a state or an international organisation'. Art. 169(1), Criminal Code of Croatia.

[452] Art. 141, Criminal Code of Croatia.

[453] S. 237, Criminal Code of Estonia.

[454] Section 89c(1), Criminal Code of Germany.

[455] Art. 230, Criminal Code of Albania.

[456] Art. 391(1), Criminal Code of Serbia.

[457] Art. 23(1), 2017 Law on Preventing or Countering Terrorism.

[458] S. 2(b)(iii), 2012 Prevention of Terrorism Act.

[459] Art. 3, 2010 Counterterrorism Act.

[460] Art. 313, Criminal Code of North Macedonia.

[461] Art. 362(1), Criminal Code of Andorra.

[462] Art. 100(a), Criminal Code of Iceland.

[463] Royal Decree No. 8 of 2007 on combating terrorism.

National Terrorism Legislation Worldwide

Algeria similarly encompasses within the purposes of terrorist acts either the obstruction of State agencies or the provision of public services or the desecration of graves.[464]

3.3.3 *Jurisdictional Issues Pertaining to National Terrorism Laws*

Most often, when a terrorism offence is proscribed in a State's Criminal Code, its jurisdictional reach over location of act, perpetrator, and temporal issue does not differ from that pertaining to other crimes. But there are numerous exceptions to this general rule. Before turning to issues of geographical, personal, and temporal jurisdiction, additional jurisdictional elements *ratione materiae* are first considered. Beyond the material jurisdictional elements set out in the foregoing definitional analysis, two particular aspects call for review: whether the law, or a particular part of it, applies not only in peacetime but also in a situation of armed conflict; and whether (and if so, how) conduct in the exercise of fundamental human rights is excluded from consideration as a terrorism offence. As one might instinctively expect, State practice on these two issues is decidedly mixed.

3.3.4 *Jurisdiction ratione materiae: The Application of Offences in Armed Conflict*

3.3.4.1 A Carve-In for Unlawful Acts in Armed Conflict

A sizeable minority of States specifically apply a part of their terrorism legislation *in bello*. The focus of the 'carve-in' tends to be on terrorism as unlawful acts of violence against civilians or against soldiers or fighters who are *hors de combat*, consonant with the prohibitions and protections afforded under IHL. States opting to carve in often use part or all of the wording from Article 2(1)(b) of the 1999 Terrorism Financing Convention. Albanian law on terrorism, for instance, includes 'any other acts intended to cause death or serious injury to civilians or any other person who is not taking an active part in hostilities in a situation of armed conflict'.[465] In Bangladesh, the formulation becomes a final catch-all, mirroring the conventional approach by adding the following text to a list of enumerated offences and terrorism motivations:

> [A]ny other act intended to cause death or serious bodily injury to a civilian, or to any other person not taking an active part in the hostilities in a situation of armed conflict, when the purpose of such act, by its nature or context, is to intimidate a population, or to compel a government or an international organization to do or to abstain from doing any act; then the person, entity or foreigner shall commit the offence of 'terrorist activities'.[466]

A number of other States use a different formulation to address situations of armed conflict or have dedicated crimes *in bello*. In its Criminal Code, Czechia specifically criminalizes terrorism not only when it is perpetrated in peacetime[467] but also, and distinctly and without the need for special intent, when 'during a war or another armed conflict' a person 'terrorises the civilian population with violence or threat of its use'.[468] Colombia is another of the relatively few States to criminalize terrorism differently in peacetime and in armed conflict, in accordance with

---

[464] Art. 87 bis, Criminal Code of Algeria (as amended).
[465] Art. 230, Criminal Code of Albania.
[466] S. 6(1)(f), 2009 Anti-Terrorism Act (as amended).
[467] S. 311, Criminal Code of Czechia.
[468] S. 413(1), Criminal Code of Czechia.

international law. Its Criminal Code provides that anyone who, in the context of armed conflict, 'carries out or orders to carry out indiscriminate or excessive attacks, or makes the civilian population the object of attacks, retaliation, acts or threats of violence, whose main purpose is to terrorize it', commits an offence.[469] In Ecuador's Criminal Code there is likewise a specific prohibition of terrorizing the civilian population in armed conflict.[470] In Mali, a specific crime of terrorism concerns an unlawful act of violence committed in an armed conflict perpetrated against a civilian or any other person not participating directly in hostilities.[471]

In Uruguay, the definition of a terrorism offence is explicitly stated to include 'any act intended to cause a state of terror or general fear in part of the population or to cause death or serious bodily injury to a civilian or other person not directly participating in hostilities in an armed conflict'.[472] In 2018, Botswana amended its terrorism law adopted four years earlier in order to extend its application to situations of armed conflict for certain offences. Thus, a predicate offence in the amended law is similarly an act that 'causes or is likely to cause serious bodily injury to a person not taking an active part in hostilities in a situation of armed conflict'.[473]

Eritrea's definition of terrorism in its financing law, which specifically encompasses armed conflict,[474] could be used to determine the material jurisdiction of the crime of terrorism under its Criminal Penal Code. Mongolia's 2019 law on counterterrorism describes as a terrorism offence 'causing death or injury to a person not actively participating in armed conflict in pursuit of political, religious, ideological and other similar goals'.[475] In Mozambique, a terrorist act is defined in a glossary to the country's 2022 counterterrorism law as 'action intended to cause death or grievous bodily harm, committed against civilians or anyone who does not take a direct part in hostilities in a situation of armed conflict'.[476] In Myanmar, it is a distinct terrorism offence 'to cause fear among the public, to cause death of or severe pain to a civilian or any other person who is not involved in hostilities in the midst of armed conflict with the aim of forcing the government or a local or foreign organization to do an unlawful act or making them avoid acting lawfully'.[477]

3.3.5 A Carve-Out for Lawful Acts in Armed Conflict

It is also possible – and indeed desirable – to incorporate the core prohibitions and protections under IHL by means of a 'carve-out'. This is how many States, particularly in the Pacific, have

---

[469] Art. 144, 2000 Criminal Code of Colombia.

[470] Any person who during an armed conflict carries out any form of attack on a protected person for the purpose of terrorizing the civilian population will be sanctioned with a prison sentence of ten to thirteen years. Art. 126, Comprehensive Criminal Code of Ecuador. The reference to a 'protected person' could be construed as to limit the scope of application of the law to a situation of international armed conflict, as this is how the 1949 Geneva Conventions understands the term.

[471] Art. 3(2), 2008 Anti-Terrorism Law.

[472] Art. 17, 2019 Antiterrorism Law.

[473] S. 2(1), 2014 Counterterrorism Act (as amended). The general definition of armed conflict inserted in the law is not, though, one recognized by international law: 'a conflict involving the use of arms and ammunitions, NBC [nuclear, biological, chemical] weapons, explosives or other lethal devices'. New definitions of the two armed conflict classifications are also inserted in the amended law: '"international armed conflict" means a conflict involving two or more states'; and '"non international armed conflict" means a conflict between government forces and non government armed group and includes an armed conflict between two non government groups' [sic].

[474] 'An act intended to cause death or serious bodily to a civilian, or to any other person not taking an active part in the hostilities in a situation of armed conflict.' Art. 2, 2014 Proclamation on Terrorist Financing.

[475] Art. 3.1.4, 2019 Law on Counterterrorism.

[476] Annex (Glossary) to Law No. 13/2022: Lei que Estabelece o Regime Jurídico de Prevenção, Repressão e Combate ao Terrorismo e Proliferação de Armas de Destruição em Massa.

[477] Chap. 1(3)(13), 2014 Counterterrorism Law.

addressed the issue. The Cook Islands' 2004 law, for instance, uses a formulation to exclude from consideration as terrorism any act that would ordinarily be terrorism, but which 'occurs in a situation of armed conflict and is, at the time and in the place it occurred, in accordance with rules of international law applicable to the conflict'.[478] The same language is used in Kiribati's domestic legislation,[479] as well as in Lesotho's 2018 law,[480] Nauru's 2004 Terrorism Act,[481] New Zealand's dedicated 2002 terrorism law,[482] Samoa's 2014 counterterrorism law,[483] the Solomon Islands' 2009 Act,[484] Tonga's 2013 dedicated law,[485] Tuvalu's 2009 Act,[486] and Vanuatu's 2005 law.[487] The general application of these laws to situations of armed conflict is thus implicit by virtue of the carve-out. In Brunei, there is no general application in armed conflict, but the incorporation of a specific exception from the offence of a terrorist bombing for the acts of armed forces in armed conflict may reasonably be taken to imply that this is the case.[488]

In a small number of States, certain exemptions for humanitarian action, particularly in situations of armed conflict (and known as humanitarian 'carve-outs'), are incorporated into counterterrorism legislation. This is the case in Ethiopia, for instance, under Article 9 of its 2020 law. In the case of Chad, Article 1 of its 2020 law stipulates that nothing is the law shall be interpreted as derogating from IHL. These concerns are not merely theoretical. As Medécins sans Frontières reported in 2021:

> For frontline workers, the consequences of the ever-expanding war on terror have been brutal. MSF staff reported to us how they are beaten, harassed, insulted and accused of 'supporting terrorists' while carrying out their medical activities at the gates or in the wards of hospitals or in ambulances on the road. They are expected by security forces to refuse patients based on who could be considered a 'terrorist'.[489]

Guyana, which, as discussed in Section 3.3.8.1, has a narrow exemption from consideration as terrorism the exercise of certain human rights in peacetime, generally excludes conduct that 'causes death or serious bodily harm to a person taking active part in armed conflict in accordance with the applicable rules of international law'.[490] Trinidad and Tobago provides a similar carve-out from the definition of a 'terrorist act' in its 2005 law.[491] Canada's exemption from consideration as terrorism acts that comply with the law of armed conflict is a particular example of good practice. Thus, it is stipulated in its Criminal Code that an act of terrorism 'does not include an act or omission that is committed during an armed conflict and that, at the time and in the place of its commission, is in accordance with customary international law or conventional international law applicable to the conflict'.[492]

---

[478] S. 4(3)(b), 2004 Act on the Suppression of Terrorism (as amended).
[479] S. 3(3)(b), 2005 Measures to Combat Terrorism Act.
[480] S. 2(i)(iii)(aa), 2018 Prevention and Suppression of Terrorism Act, Act 3 of 2018.
[481] S. 3(3), 2004 Terrorism Act (as amended).
[482] S. 5, 2002 Terrorism Suppression Act.
[483] S. 3(2), 2014 Counter Terrorism Act.
[484] S. 2, 2009 Counterterrorism Act.
[485] S. 3(3)(b), 2013 Counterterrorism and Transnational Organised Crime Act, Act 23 of 2013.
[486] S. 4(3), 2009 Counterterrorism and Transnational Organised Crime Act.
[487] S. 3(2), 2005 Counter-terrorism and Transnational Organized Crime Act.
[488] S. 18(2)(a), 2011 Anti-Terrorism Order.
[489] J. Whittall and L. Saavedra, 'Our medics treat everyone, don't punish them for that', Press release, MSF Zimbabwe, 21 October 2021, at: https://bit.ly/42x04MA.
[490] S. 2, 2015 Anti-Terrorism and Terrorist Related Activities Act.
[491] S. 2(a), 2005 Counterterrorism Act.
[492] S. 83.01, Criminal Code of Canada.

3.3.6 Carve-In and Carve-Out

Ghana's 2008 Anti-Terrorism Act deems an act of terrorism in armed conflict to be one that by its nature or context is intended to *either* intimidate the population or compel conduct by a government or an international organization; *or* that is intended to cause death or serious bodily injury to a civilian not taking an active part in the hostility [*sic*].[493] It is further stipulated in the 2008 law that an act shall not be considered a terrorist act if it is in accordance with rules of international law applicable to the conflict.[494]

An equally idiosyncratic approach is taken by The Bahamas. Its 2018 Anti-Terrorism Act excludes an act 'done in the course of an armed conflict *for the defence of the Bahamas*'.[495] If a question arises as to whether an armed conflict existed at the salient time and whether an act was perpetrated in the course of that armed conflict, the relevant minister is to make the determination.[496] But other acts targeting civilians or other persons not taking a direct part in hostilities in armed conflict are deemed to be terrorism offences, when committed with the requisite intent.[497]

3.3.7 Terrorizing Civilians as a War Crime

Despite the findings of the Special Court for Sierra Leone and the International Criminal Tribunal for the former Yugoslavia,[498] only a very small number of States provide for acts of terror against civilians in detention (Geneva Law) or during the conduct of hostilities (the Hague Law branch of IHL) to be a war crime. Terrorizing civilians is a specific war crime under the Criminal Code of Bosnia and Herzegovina. The Criminal Code of Czechia provides for five to fifteen years' imprisonment for terrorizing the civilian population as a war crime where it is considered under the rubric of 'persecution of population'.[499] Slovakia's Criminal Code stipulates: 'Any person who, in time of war … terrorizes the helpless civilian population by violence or the threat of its use, shall be liable to a term of imprisonment of four to ten years.'[500]

In several States, the wording and context of the offence suggests it is specifically the criminalization of terror under the Geneva law branch of IHL that is being penally repressed. Thus, in Ethiopia, designated war crimes are measures of intimidation or terror against civilians in a situation of armed conflict.[501] Measures of terror and intimidation are also punishable as a war crime in a situation of armed conflict in Montenegro. A similar approach – and tariff – exists in Serbia's Criminal Code[502] – a minimum sentence is five years of imprisonment.[503] Lithuania's Criminal Code criminalizes a person who 'during an international armed conflict and in violation of norms of international humanitarian law uses means of intimidation or terror'. This is punishable by imprisonment for between three and fifteen years.[504]

---

[493] S. 4(1)(a) and (b), 2008 Anti-Terrorism Act.
[494] S. 4(2), 2008 Anti-Terrorism Act.
[495] S. 10(1)(b), 2018 Anti-Terrorism Act [added emphasis].
[496] S. 10(3), 2018 Anti-Terrorism Act.
[497] S. 14(1)(b), 2018 Anti-Terrorism Act.
[498] See further on this issue *supra* §2.6 and infra Chapter 9.
[499] S. 413(1), Criminal Code of Czechia.
[500] S. 431(2), Criminal Code of Slovakia.
[501] Art. 270(g), Criminal Code of Ethiopia.
[502] Art. 372(1), Criminal Code of Serbia.
[503] Art. 428(1), Criminal Code of Montenegro.
[504] Art. 104, Criminal Code of Lithuania.

3.3.8 *Jurisdiction* ratione materiae: *Exclusions for the Exercise of Human Rights*

3.3.8.1 A Limited Carve-Out for Acts in the Exercise of Certain Fundamental Human Rights

At least thirty States have explicit albeit limited carve-outs for the protection of certain fundamental rights, meaning that exercise of those rights, within set parameters, would not constitute terrorism. Albania, for instance, explicitly excludes strikes and assemblies from the purview of terrorist offences in the Criminal Code even if they disrupt an important public service.[505] Otherwise, the terrorist offence of interrupting electrical or water supply could be committed by utility workers going on strike. Canada likewise exempts conduct that causes 'serious interference with or serious disruption of an essential service, facility or system, whether public or private' as a result of 'advocacy, protest, dissent or stoppage of work' as long as the action or omission is not intended to result in physical harm.[506] The Cook Islands takes a similar approach.[507]

In Antigua and Barbuda, the law provides explicit exceptions for strikes and demonstrations except where they create a serious risk to the health or safety of the public.[508] Similar language is used in the law in Barbados[509] and Malaysia.[510] In Botswana, action must not be intended to damage property, result in any serious bodily harm to a person or endanger a person's life, or create a risk to human health or to public safety.[511] In the Solomon Islands, action must likewise not result in any serious bodily harm to a person or endanger a person's life but the risk to human health or to public safety must be 'serious'.[512] A similar approach is taken in St Lucian law,[513] in Tanzanian law,[514] in Vanuatu,[515] and in the repression of terrorism in the Seychelles.[516]

Ghana's 2008 law stipulates that a 'protest, demonstration or stoppage of work which disrupts an essential service' is not a terrorist act if the conduct does not result in serious physical harm or serious damage to property.[517] The same approach is taken in Kenya,[518] Kiribati,[519] and Sierra Leone.[520] Under Australian federal legislation, a terrorist act does not cover engaging in advocacy, protest, dissent, or industrial action where there is no intention to cause harm to others.[521]

---

[505] 'Actions that cause the disruption of an important service, system, public or private activity, as a result of protests, civil disobedience, or strikes, shall not be considered offences for terrorist purposes under the meaning of this Article.' Art. 230, Criminal Code of Albania.

[506] S. 83.01(b)(i)(E), Criminal Code of Canada. The first draft of the provision had excluded only 'lawful advocacy, protest, dissent or stoppage of work', but the word 'lawful' was removed after the Bill's second reading. K. Roach, 'Canada's New Anti-Terrorism Law', *Singapore Journal of Legal Studies*, Vol. 44, No. 1 (2002), 122–48, at p. 131.

[507] S. 4(3)(a), 2004 Act on the Suppression of Terrorism (as amended).

[508] Definition of 'terrorist act' in S. 2(1), 2005 Prevention of Terrorism Act.

[509] S. 3(1)(b)(D), 2002 Anti-Terrorism Act.

[510] S. 130B(4), Penal Code of Malaysia.

[511] S. 2(2), 2014 Counterterrorism Act.

[512] S. 2, 2009 Counterterrorism Act.

[513] An act which (i) disrupts any services, and (ii) is committed in pursuance of a protest, demonstration, or stoppage of work shall be deemed not to be a terrorist act within the meaning of the definition 'so long and so long only as the act is not intended' to result in any physical harm or risk of such harm or serious property damage. S. 2, 2015 Anti-Terrorism Act.

[514] S. 4(4), 2002 Prevention of Terrorism Act.

[515] S. 3(2), 2005 Counterterrorism and Transnational Organized Crime Act.

[516] S. 2, 2004 Prevention of Terrorism Act.

[517] S. 3(3), 2008 Anti-Terrorist Act.

[518] S. 2(b)(iii), 2012 Prevention of Terrorism Act.

[519] S. 3(3)(a), 2005 Measures to Combat Terrorism Act.

[520] S. 1, 2012 Terrorist Financing Act.

[521] S. 100.1, 1995 Criminal Code Act.

3.3 *National Definitions of Terrorism Offences*

Lesotho's approach is similar except that action must also not involve the use of weapons.[522] This is only the case under dedicated 2018 legislation, however, for no analogous exception for the exercise of human rights exists in the Criminal Code. Tonga's dedicated law similarly excludes from the exemption any use of weapons,[523] as does Tuvalu's.[524]

In Guyana, excluded from the definition of a terrorist act is an act that disrupts any service and which is committed in pursuance of a demonstration, protest, or stoppage of work, but which is not intended to result in 'loss of human life or serious bodily harm; damage to property; prejudice to national security or disruption of public safety, including disruption in the provision of emergency services or to any computer or electronic system or to the provision of services directly related to banking, communications, infrastructure, financial services, public utilities, transportation or other essential infrastructure'.[525] This means that in practice the human rights' exclusion is extremely narrow. A similarly restricted approach is taken in Liberia,[526] Malawi,[527] and Trinidad and Tobago.[528]

In contrast, one of the broadest exemptions is in Brazil's national terrorism legislation:

> The provisions of this article shall not apply to individual or collective conduct of people in political demonstrations, social movements, trade unions, religious, class or professional category movements, driven by social or claim purposes, aiming to challenge, criticize, protest or support, in order to defend rights, freedoms and constitutional guarantees, without prejudice to the criminal classification contained in law.[529]

One of Angola's counterterrorism laws likewise exempts action in the exercise of fundamental human rights from the application of the legislation.[530]

In Thailand, acts by demonstration, convocation, protest, argument, or movement demanding government support or justice do not constitute a terrorism offence. Nauru's approach differs materially: 'For the avoidance of any doubt, the fact that a person engages in any protest, advocacy, dissent, strike, lockout or other industrial action, is not, by itself, a sufficient basis for inferring that the person is carrying out an act with [a prohibited] outcome ... or terrorist act'.[531] The same language is used in New Zealand's 2002 law[532] and Ireland's approach is broadly similar.[533]

Indirectly, a number of other States might limit the impact on the exercise of fundamental rights by nuancing the motivation of coercing a change in government conduct. One of the

---

[522] S. 2(i)(iii)(aa), 2018 Prevention and Suppression of Terrorism Act, Act 3 of 2018.
[523] S. 3(3)(a), 2013 Counterterrorism and Transnational Organised Crime Act, Act 23 of 2013.
[524] S. 4(3), 2009 Counterterrorism and Transnational Organised Crime Act.
[525] S. 2, 2015 Anti-Terrorism and Terrorist Related Activities Act.
[526] The exemption in the 2017 law considers an act that 'is designed or intended to disrupt any computer system or the provision of services directly related to communications infrastructure, banking or financial services, utilities, transportation or other essential infrastructure' as not falling within the limited carve-out for the exercise of human rights. Art. 5(6), 2017 Amendment of the Liberian Criminal Code.
[527] S. 4, Penal Code of Malawi.
[528] S. 2(b), 2005 Counterterrorism Act.
[529] Art. 2(2), 2016 Terrorism Law.
[530] 'The provisions of this Law do not apply to individual or collective conduct of people in political demonstrations, social, union, religious, class or professional category initiatives, directed by social purposes or demands, aiming, peacefully to contest, criticize, protest or support, with the aim of defending rights, guarantees and fundamental freedoms.' Art. 5(1), 2017 Law on Preventing or Countering Terrorism (unofficial translation).
[531] S. 3(4), 2004 Terrorism Act (as amended).
[532] S. 5, 2002 Terrorism Suppression Act.
[533] The 2005 Anti-Terrorism Act clarifies that engaging in protest, advocacy, or dissent is not 'of itself a sufficient basis for inferring that the person is carrying out an act within the definition of 'terrorist activity'. S. 6(5), 2005 Criminal Justice (Terrorist Offences) Act.

116 National Terrorism Legislation Worldwide

phrases often encountered is 'unduly' compelling or coercing government action. This is the case, for instance, under the Criminal Code of Benin,[534] Bosnia and Herzegovina,[535] Denmark,[536] Lesotho,[537] Malta,[538] and Mauritius,[539] and the dedicated legislation in Cyprus[540] and Ireland.[541] Under Argentina's Penal Code, the fact that terrorism was committed during the exercise of human rights excludes the application of aggravating sentences that result from a terrorist offence.

3.3.9 *Jurisdiction* ratione loci

Where terrorism is repressed in a specific law, the jurisdictional reach *ratione loci* of those provisions varies widely beyond the territorial confines of the State where the offence (or a relevant mode of liability) occurs. Most reflect the extent of national criminal jurisdiction as ordinarily determined under international law, which typically also covers criminal acts perpetrated in an aircraft registered in the State, on a nationally flagged ship on the high seas,[542] or inside a State's diplomatic or consular mission abroad (which contrary to common perception is not that State's sovereign territory).[543] Some add the passive personality principle, where criminal acts are perpetrated against a national of the State, wherever in the world they may occur. Afghanistan's national terrorism law adds as a jurisdictional basis unlawful acts that are 'against the interests' of Afghanistan though this notion is not defined.[544]

A significant minority of States, however, provide for universal criminal jurisdiction for terrorism offences. Canadian terrorism law encompasses 'an act or omission, in or outside Canada'.[545] Botswana's 2014 Counterterrorism Act (as amended) similarly defines an act of terrorism as proscribed conduct which involves 'any act or omission in or outside Botswana'.[546] In Brunei, the 2011 Terrorism Order defines a terrorist act as encompassing 'an act or omission in or outside Brunei Darussalam which constitutes an offence within the scope of a counterterrorism convention', and it is further stipulated that any offence under the law committed abroad is punishable as if it had occurred in Brunei.[547] In Costa Rican law, it is stipulated that, irrespective of the provisions in force in the place where the offence is committed and the nationality of the perpetrator, the penalties provided for under Costa Rican law shall be imposed on any person who commits an act of terrorism or the financing thereof.[548]

Czechia's Criminal Code specifically provides for universal jurisdiction for terrorism,[549] as does Grenada's dedicated 2012 Terrorist Act.[550] Guinea's Criminal Code stipulates that the laws

---

[534] Art. 161, Criminal Code of Benin.
[535] Art. 201(1), Criminal Code of Bosnia and Herzegovina.
[536] S. 114(1), Criminal Code of Denmark.
[537] S. 96, 2010 Criminal Code of Lesotho.
[538] Art. 328A(1), Criminal Code of Malta.
[539] S. 3(b)(ii), 2002 Prevention of Terrorism Act.
[540] Art. 5, 2010 Combatting Terrorism Act.
[541] S. 4, 2005 Criminal Justice (Terrorist Offences) Act.
[542] See, e.g., C. Staker, 'Jurisdiction' in M. D. Evans (ed.), *International Law*, 4th ed., Oxford University Press, Oxford, 2014, p. 317.
[543] A. Clapham, *Brierly's Law of Nations*, 7th ed., Oxford University Press, Oxford, 2012, p. 207.
[544] Art. 4(2), 2008 Law on Combat against Terrorist Offences (unofficial translation).
[545] S. 83.01 (b), Criminal Code of Canada.
[546] S. 2(1), 2014 Counterterrorism Act.
[547] Ss. 2 and 56, 2011 Anti-Terrorism Order.
[548] Art. 7, Criminal Code of Costa Rica.
[549] S. 7(1), Criminal Code of Czechia.
[550] S. 2, 2012 Terrorism Act.

and penalties for terrorism also apply to acts perpetrated outside Guinean territory.[551] The same pertains to Guyana under dedicated legislation from 2015.[552] The Philippines' 2020 Terrorism Act defines the jurisdiction for prosecutable terrorism as 'any person who, within or outside the Philippines, regardless of the stage of execution'.[553] In St Kitts and Nevis, the 2002 Antiterrorism Act defines 'terrorist activity' as 'an action that takes places either within or outside of Saint Christopher and Nevis'.[554] A similar approach is taken in St Lucian law,[555] in the law in Sierra Leone,[556] in Trinidad and Tobago's domestic law,[557] under Tuvalu's dedicated 2009 Statute,[558] as well as under Zambian law.[559]

In Belize, the offences created by the 2008 Terrorism Act 'shall be investigated, tried, judged and sentenced by a court in Belize regardless of whether or not an offence occurred in Belize or in another territorial jurisdiction, but without prejudice to extradition where applicable in accordance with the law'.[560] Belize makes receiving training for terrorism an offence wherever it may occur.[561]

The Bahamas' national terrorism law stipulates that salient offences pertaining to weapons of mass destruction perpetrated abroad 'may for incidental purposes be treated as having been committed in any part of The Bahamas'. More generally, it is provided that terrorism acts may be conducted 'in or outside the Bahamas' for the purpose of criminal jurisdiction.[562] The same wording is used, mutatis mutandis, in the Barbados legislation.[563]

3.3.10 *Jurisdiction* ratione personae

Several States may prosecute their own citizens for terrorism offences perpetrated anywhere in the world. This is the case, for instance, in Bhutan,[564] Hungary,[565] and Rwanda.[566] In Argentina, the Criminal Code ordinarily applies to offences committed in Argentina, or which have effects on the territory of Argentina, or in other places subject to its jurisdiction. But the Code also applies to offences committed abroad by agents or employees of the Argentine authorities in the performance of their duties. In Bulgaria, the Criminal Code is applicable to Bulgarian citizens for crimes they commit outside the country as well as to foreign nationals who commit crimes outside the country where the crimes affect the interests of Bulgaria or its citizens. It also governs crimes committed by foreign nationals outside the country, when this is envisaged in an international agreement to which Bulgaria is a party.[567]

---

[551] Art. 13, Criminal Code of Guinea.
[552] S. 2, 2015 Anti-Terrorism and Terrorist Related Activities Act.
[553] S. 4, 2020 Terrorism Act.
[554] S. 2, 2002 Antiterrorism Act.
[555] S. 2 of the 2015 Anti-Terrorism Act pertains to 'an act or omission in or outside Saint Lucia'.
[556] S. 1, 2012 Terrorist Financing Act.
[557] S. 2, 2005 Counterterrorism Act.
[558] S. 4(3), 2009 Counterterrorism and Transnational Organised Crime Act.
[559] S. 2(1), 2018 Anti-Terrorism and Non-Proliferation Act.
[560] S. 10, 2008 Money Laundering and Terrorism (Prevention) Act.
[561] Art. 163(7), Criminal Code of Benin.
[562] Ss. 12 and 14(1), 2018 Anti-Terrorism Act.
[563] S. 3(1), 2002 Anti-Terrorism Act.
[564] S. 329, Penal Code of Bhutan.
[565] This applies generally to criminal offences under the Criminal Code and is thus not specific to terrorism.
[566] The 2008 law is extremely broad, applying to an 'act committed within or outside Rwanda by a Rwandan or a foreigner'. Art. 4(1), Law 45/2008 on countering terrorism.
[567] Art. 3(1), Criminal Code of Bulgaria.

In Australia, terrorist offences are, in general, only prosecutable if the conduct or result of the conduct occurs wholly or partly in Australia, or the person is an Australian citizen or resident, or the offence is an ancillary offence where the primary offence is intended to occur wholly or partly in Australia.[568] That said, the 1995 Criminal Code Act governs foreign recruitment for terrorism, prohibiting persons from engaging in hostile activity in a foreign country or preparing to do so. It is also an offence to enter, or remain in, a current declared area.[569]

Children may be prosecuted for terrorism offences under most national legislation. Often, however, dedicated tribunals may be accorded jurisdiction over suspected offenders, or at least the criminal procedures relating to juveniles may be applied. For instance, in the case of Afghanistan, if the offences set forth in the terrorism law are committed by juveniles, 'the proceedings for these offences' shall be carried out according to the Juvenile Code.[570] The 2005 Juvenile Code stipulates that children under the age of thirteen years are not criminally responsible.[571] In Mauritania, children ('minors') may be imprisoned for terrorist offences but at half the term imposable for adults and for no more than twelve years.[572] This would appear to be limited to children over fourteen years of age.[573]

In Azerbaijan, children from the age of fourteen years are criminally liable for acts of terrorism.[574] In El Salvador, in April 2022, however, the nation's Parliament adopted a new legislation to reduce the age of criminal responsibility for membership of terrorist groups from sixteen years to twelve years.[575] In Hungary, according to a 2016 amendment to the Criminal Code, terrorism is one of the crimes for which children between the ages of twelve and fourteen years are liable to criminal sanction, provided that they were able to recognize the consequences of the offence at the time of its commission. In Kyrgyzstan, the minimum age of criminal responsibility is specifically set at fourteen years in case of terrorism.[576]

3.3.11 *Jurisdiction* ratione temporis

A small number of laws stipulate that terrorism offences are not subject to a Statute of limitations. This is the case in Angola, for instance.[577] The same is true, albeit with respect to only limited terrorism crimes, in the Criminal Code of Croatia.[578] In Czechia, the exception to statutory limitation concerns terror as a war crime or a crime against humanity.[579]

3.4 THE IMPACT OF NATIONAL TERRORISM LEGISLATION ON FUNDAMENTAL HUMAN RIGHTS

While Chile's Constitution justly declares that terrorism is inherently ('por esencia') contrary to human rights,[580] legal action to counterterrorism may also breach fundamental human rights.

---

[568] S. 15.2, 1995 Criminal Code Act.
[569] S. 119.3, 1995 Criminal Code Act.
[570] Art. 5, 2008 Law on Combat against Terrorist Offences (unofficial translation).
[571] Art. 5(1), 2005 Juvenile Code.
[572] Art. 18, 2010 Counterterrorism Act.
[573] Art. 2, Ordonnance No. 2005–015 portant protection pénale de l'enfant.
[574] Art. 20(2), Criminal Code of Azerbaijan.
[575] Art. 2, Decree No. 342 of 2022.
[576] Art. 28(2), Criminal Code of Kyrgyzstan.
[577] Art. 129(4), 2020 Penal Code of Angola.
[578] Art. 81(2), Criminal Code of Croatia.
[579] S. 35(b), Criminal Code of Czechia.
[580] Art. 9, Constitution of Chile.

3.4 *Human Rights Impact of Terrorism Legislation*

Indeed, over the past decade there has been a marked tendency in legislatures to broaden definitions of terrorism and to strengthen powers to counter terrorism, usually to the detriment of fundamental human rights. Often new, more repressive laws follow horrific terrorist attacks, sometimes reflecting the age-old maxim of 'legislate in haste, repent at leisure'. A 2018 law in Indonesia thus erodes safeguards against arbitrary detention and ill-treatment and explicitly recognized that the Indonesian Armed Forces have a legitimate domestic counterterrorism role. The new law followed a series of deadly bombings, including terrorist attacks in Surabaya that included suicide bombings of mothers and their young children.[581]

The risks of violating the rights to freedom of expression and freedom of peaceful assembly are particularly acute in laws whose definitions of terrorism offences are particularly broad. Thus, for instance, as Chapter 4 considers, the law in Algeria has been used to prosecute human rights defenders, journalists, and peaceful activists. In Sri Lanka, the 1979 Prevention of Terrorism Act has been used to target peaceful protesters against the regime as recently as 2022.[582] The bill before Parliament that would replace this law raises continued human rights concerns.[583] In Uganda, Doreen Biira was arrested in 2016 for 'abetting terrorism' for filming and sharing videos of military brutality in western Uganda, in clashes that left more than seventy people dead.[584] The offence is punishable with seven years' imprisonment upon conviction. The UN Committee against Torture has stated with respect to the 2014 terrorism law in Saudi Arabia that:

> While recognizing the State party's concern about protecting its population from terrorist attacks, the Committee is concerned that the Penal Law for Crimes of Terrorism and its Financing adopted in 2014 contains an extremely broad definition of terrorism that would enable the criminalization of acts of peaceful expression considered as endangering 'national unity' or undermining 'the reputation or position of the State'.[585]

Human rights defenders are also at particular risk of being accused of terrorism. In Sudan, for instance, prior to the outbreak of armed conflict in 2023, a number of human rights organizations had observed that judicial harassment against human rights lawyers was made possible by an extensive interpretation of the country's Anti-Terrorism Act of 2001.[586] In 2019, Transparency International condemned the Zimbabwean government's crackdown on civil society and called for terrorism charges against seven activists arrested in May to be dropped immediately. The seven pro-democracy civil society activists were arrested after attending a non-violent training in the Maldives, which included sessions on strengthening civil society coalitions, engaging with the public, conducting advocacy, and improving communications.[587]

---

[581] G. Nabbs-Keller, 'Indonesia's Revised Anti-Terrorism Law', Blog post, Australian Institute of International Affairs, 26 August 2018, at: https://bit.ly/45sozbU.

[582] Human Rights Watch, 'Sri Lanka: End Use of Terrorism Law against Protesters', New York, 31 August 2022, at: https://bit.ly/3OE5XTk.

[583] See, e.g., Office of the UN High Commissioner for Human Rights, 'Call to Sri Lanka to revise anti-terrorism bill', Press release, Geneva, 19 January 2024.

[584] F. Namasinga Selnes, 'Anti-terrorism regulation and the media in Uganda', Verfassungsblog, 10 March 2022, at: https://bit.ly/43cGeWn.

[585] Committee against Torture, Concluding observations on the second periodic report of Saudi Arabia, UN doc. CAT/C/SAU/CO/2, 8 June 2016, para. 16.

[586] World Organisation Against Torture (OMCT), International Federation for Human Rights (FIDH), and African Centre for Justice and Peace Studies (ACJPS), *Sudan. Target one to silence a hundred: The repression of human rights lawyers in Sudan*, Joint Report, October 2018, at: https://bit.ly/3MC68Mh, p. 12, s. 4.1.2.

[587] Transparency International, 'Terrorism Charges against Zimbabwean Activists Are Unfounded', 6 June 2019, at: https://bit.ly/3N7lGci.

Numerous States use terrorism legislation to prosecute political opponents or those protesting against the regime. Bahrain has broad anti-terrorism laws that capture not only terrorists but also religious and political opponents to the regime. Its 2006 Anti-terrorism Law has thus been used to prosecute and convict Shia religious leaders, some of whom have been executed in recent years. In Belarus, six defendants belonging to the democratic opposition to President Lukashenko were convicted of terrorism and sentenced to between eight- and fifteen-years' imprisonment. Charges included throwing a stone at a window.[588] In Azerbaijan, terrorism charges have similarly been used against political opponents of the regime. It has been reported that, in October 2021, opposition activist Niyameddin Ahmedov was sentenced to thirteen years' imprisonment for sedition and financing terrorism on apparently politically motivated charges.[589]

Egypt has far-reaching legislation on terrorism that is used also to suppress domestic opposition to the regime. As the then UN Special Rapporteur on human rights and counterterrorism, Fionnuala D. Ní Aoláin, observed in relation to changes in Egyptian law in 2020: 'Legislative changes covering anti-terrorism, protests, association, and NGOs include extending the definition of "terrorist entity" and applying new measures against individuals, businesses, media outlets, and trade unions and provide for life sentences and capital punishment for funding terrorism. For example, trade unions could have assets seized and be added to the terrorism list'.[590]

Amendments to Austrian criminal law in 2021 are alleged by human rights organizations to have put at risk respect for the rights to freedom of religion, expression, and association. The European Center for Not-for-Profit Law (ECNL), for instance, criticized the incorporation in Criminal Code of a new criminal offence concerning the creation, leadership, financing or support in any form of a 'religiously motivated extremist association', or the promotion of 'religiously motivated extremist acts', given that the concepts were not clearly defined and articulated by the law and 'the interference with the rights of freedom of religion and freedom of expression goes beyond what is strictly necessary to achieve the objectives pursued'.[591]

In May 2022, a number of UN Special Rapporteurs wrote to the Israeli government to call for amendment of its 2018 Anti-terrorism Law. They stated:

> We are concerned that the present legal and regulatory framework for designating terrorist organizations lacks precision in key respects, infringes on critically important rights, and may not meet the required thresholds of legality, necessity, proportionality, and non-discrimination under international law. We are particularly concerned that the law may result in the unlawful infringement of, among others, the fundamental rights to freedom of peaceful assembly and association and freedom of opinion and expression, as well as fair trial rights and core social, economic, and cultural rights, including the rights to property, work, and participation in cultural life.[592]

---

[588] 'Authorities abuse criminal law by convicting dissidents of "terrorism"', Viasna, 19 October 2022, at: https://bit.ly/307KgAg.

[589] Freidrich Naumann Foundation for Freedom, 'Prisoner of Conscience: Niyameddin Ahmadov', 26 September 2022, at: https://bit.ly/302ORU6.

[590] 'Egypt's updated terrorism law opens the door to more rights abuses, says UN expert', Press release, 9 April 2020, at: https://bit.ly/42P50KI.

[591] ECNL, 'Austria: Anti-Terrorism Draft Law Not in Line with Human Rights Standards on Fundamental Rights', 2 February 2021, at: https://bit.ly/3Bw6ajw.

[592] Mandates of the Special Rapporteur on the promotion and protection of human rights and fundamental freedoms while countering terrorism; the Working Group on Arbitrary Detention; the Special Rapporteur in the field of cultural rights; the Special Rapporteur on the promotion and protection of the right to freedom of opinion and

3.4 Human Rights Impact of Terrorism Legislation

In the Philippines, under the law on terrorism, the crime 'shall not include advocacy, protest, dissent, stoppage of work, industrial or mass action, and other similar exercises of civil and political rights, which are not intended to cause death or serious physical harm to a person, to endanger a person's life, or to create a serious risk to public safety'.[593] Nonetheless, in 2022, the International Commission of Jurists published a critique of the application of anti-terrorism laws in the Philippines, accusing the authorities of using terrorism labels to attack human rights defenders in a process termed 'red-tagging'.[594]

---

expression; the Special Rapporteur on the rights to freedom of peaceful assembly and of association; the Special Rapporteur on the situation of human rights defenders; the Special Rapporteur on minority issues; the Special Rapporteur on the right to privacy; the Special Rapporteur on the situation of human rights in the Palestinian territory occupied since 1967; the Special Rapporteur on contemporary forms of racism, racial discrimination, xenophobia and related intolerance and the Working Group on discrimination against women and girls, UN Ref.: OL ISR 6/2022, 5 May 2022.

[593] S. 4, 2020 Terrorism Act.

[594] International Commission of Jurists, Danger in Dissent: Counterterrorism and Human Rights in the Philippines, Report, January 2022.

4

Prosecution of Terrorism Suspects in Domestic Courts

4.1 INTRODUCTION

There is a general duty to prosecute terrorists on all States. Indeed, as Trapp observes, the real impact of United Nations Security Council Resolution 1373 of 2001 is to impose an obligation on all States to bring terrorists to justice.[1] In the resolution, the Council decided unanimously that all States shall

> [e]nsure that any person who participates in the financing, planning, preparation or perpetration of terrorist acts or in supporting terrorist acts is brought to justice and ensure that, in addition to any other measures against them, such terrorist acts are established as serious criminal offences in domestic laws and regulations and that the punishment duly reflects the seriousness of such terrorist acts.[2]

Terrorism suspects are ordinarily prosecuted before domestic courts under national law. This includes the exceptionally rare cases of prosecutions for terrorism in peacetime mounted on the basis of universal jurisdiction for criminal acts committed abroad. Consonant with its Statute, the Special Tribunal for Lebanon mounted prosecutions for the murder of former Lebanese prime minister Rafik Hariri in 2005 purely on the basis of Lebanese domestic law. Otherwise, only when terrorism has been prosecuted as a war crime under international law has an international legal tribunal been the trial venue. This concerns the ad hoc International Criminal Tribunal for the former Yugoslavia (and, since the beginning of 2018, its Residual Mechanism)[3] and the hybrid Special Court for Sierra Leone.[4]

This chapter first summarizes the maximum sentences available to domestic courts around the world for the perpetration of acts of terrorism. In more than one-quarter of all States, this includes the death penalty. In a small number of these countries, imposition of capital punishment as the sentence upon conviction is mandatory, in violation of international human rights law. A further one-third of all States provide for imprisonment for life (or hard labour for life) as the maximum penalty for certain acts of terrorism. Other States set varying tariffs, ranging from short to very long terms of imprisonment to fixed terms of hard labour. A small number have

---

[1] Trapp, State Responsibility for International Terrorism, p. 249.

[2] UN Security Council Resolution 1373, adopted on 28 September 2001 by unanimous vote in favour, operative para. 2(e).

[3] See United Nations (UN) International Residual Mechanism for Criminal Tribunals, 'About', at: https://bit.ly/47VePLl.

[4] See for details of these trials infra Chapter 9.

minimum terms of imprisonment for any terrorism offence. Also considered are the penalties in selected States for the offences of funding terrorism, inciting terrorism or glorifying terrorists, and aiding or abetting acts of terrorism.

The remainder of the chapter describes the prosecution of terrorism suspects in selected domestic courts across the Americas, Africa, Asia and the Pacific, and Europe. Considered are the reasonableness of the charges laid, the fairness of the trials, and the legitimacy of the sentences imposed upon conviction. Some of those prosecuted for terrorism offences are children or women. The overwhelming majority, though, are men between the ages of eighteen and twenty-five years.

4.2 SENTENCES FOR TERRORISM IN DOMESTIC LAW

The sentences prescribed for the principal terrorism offences extend to the death penalty in more than fifty States upon conviction for certain acts of terrorism. In certain instances, assisting acts of terrorism may attract the same penalty as their perpetration. But, as the following description of State practice illustrates, the sentences prescribed for terrorism in national legislation differ very widely between States. This includes variance or consonance of sentences for differing modes of criminal liability. In almost every case, penalties for terrorism offences are set forth in either the Criminal Code or the legislation dedicated to the suppression of terrorism. Often, terrorism attracts additional periods of imprisonment over and above those foreseen for predicate offences when committed without a stipulated terrorism motivation.

4.2.1 The Imposition of the Death Penalty

In at least fifty-four States worldwide, those convicted of a terrorism offence may be executed.[5] In addition, in Cuba, Malaysia, Russia, Sri Lanka, and Tunisia, while capital punishment is imposable by law for terrorism offences, the sentence is not carried out, as a result of either a de facto or a de jure moratorium on executions. In Tunisia, a 2015 law expanded the number of offences for which the death penalty may be imposed. A sentence of death was imposed on convicted terrorists in January 2022,[6] but no execution has taken place since 1991 despite a public call by the president in 2020 for its reinstatement in practice.[7] Kuwait has the death penalty for State security crimes but not specifically for terrorism, while in China and Yemen many predicate offences are subject to capital punishment even though these do not specifically apply to terrorism offences.

In Cameroon, Comoros, and Libya,[8] capital punishment is obligatory as a sentence upon conviction for *any* terrorist act. In Iran, one form of terrorism – *fesad fel-arze* (offences against the

---

[5] Afghanistan, Bahamas, Bahrain, Bangladesh, Belarus, Botswana, Brunei, Cameroon, China, Comoros, the Democratic Republic of Congo, Egypt, Eritrea, Ethiopia, The Gambia, Guatemala, Guyana, India, Indonesia, Iran, Iraq, Japan, Jordan, Kazakhstan, Lebanon, Lesotho, Libya, Malaysia, Mauritania, Mali, Mongolia, Morocco, Myanmar, Niger, Nigeria, North Korea, Oman, Pakistan, Peru, Qatar, Saudi Arabia, Singapore, Somalia, South Korea, Sudan, Syria, Tajikistan, Thailand, Trinidad and Tobago, Uganda, the United Arab Emirates, the United States, Vietnam, and Zimbabwe.

[6] Agence France-Presse, 'Tunisie. Peine capitale pour neuf jihadistes ayant tué un soldat, selon des médias', Press release, 15 January 2022, at: https://bit.ly/4390p7C.

[7] Amnesty International, 'Tunisia: Presidential statement in favour of death penalty is shocking', 29 September 2020, at: https://bit.ly/420Dl3A.

[8] Art. 207, Criminal Code of Libya.

State, including criminal libel) – carries the mandatory death penalty as the sole punishment. This is also the case when death results from any terrorism offence under law in the Democratic Republic of Congo,[9] Mauritania,[10] Niger,[11] Nigeria (following its reintroduction as a sentence for terrorism in 2022),[12] Oman,[13] Uganda,[14] and the United Arab Emirates.[15] The mandatory death penalty violates international human rights law as it effectively precludes any appeal against sentence and prevents the particular circumstances of the offender being taken into account in deciding upon suitable punishment following conviction. Malaysia, which had in place the mandatory death penalty for any terrorism offence resulting in death,[16] abolished it, including for terrorism offences, in July 2023.[17]

The manner of execution may itself violate the right to life (as well as the prohibition on cruel or inhuman punishment). In Iran, *moharebeh* is 'drawing a weapon on the life, property or honour of people or threatening them, in such manner that results in insecurity in the environment'. The prescribed punishment for moharebeh is either death by hanging or death by crucifixion. Corporal punishment is an alternative to execution: amputation of the right hand and left foot.[18]

Also in violation of treaty and conventional human rights law is the imposition of the death penalty for other than the most grave crimes. Intentional killing is set by the UN Human Rights Committee as the minimum threshold for the possible imposition of capital punishment,[19] in accordance with Article 6(2) of the 1966 International Covenant on Civil and Political Rights (ICCPR).[20] In this regard, Bangladesh includes the death penalty as a possible sentence for property damage.[21] In both Bangladesh[22] and Cameroon,[23] the financing of terrorism also attracts the death penalty. In 2022, Belarus made 'attempted' terrorism a capital offence.[24]

Afghanistan has nine distinct terrorism offences, broadly construed, that may attract the death penalty. Not all of these require intentional killing. A terrorist offence under Afghan law may involve the infliction of serious injury on a person or it may concern endangering the safety of a ship or aircraft.[25]

---

[9] Art. 158, Military Criminal Code.

[10] Art. 17, 2010 Counterterrorism Act.

[11] Art. 399.1, Criminal Code of Niger.

[12] 2022 Terrorism (Prevention and Prohibition) Act.

[13] Royal Decree No. 8 of 2007 on combating terrorism.

[14] S. 7(1), 2002 Anti-Terrorism Act.

[15] Art. 5(3), 2014 Law on Combatting Terrorism.

[16] S. 130C, Penal Code of Malaysia.

[17] The Abolition of Mandatory Death Penalty Act 2023 (Act 846); entered into force, 4 July 2023. See Bernama, 'Abolition of Mandatory Death Penalty Act 2023 comes into force tomorrow', *New Straits Times*, 3 July 2023, at: https://bit.ly/3RgCsbF; and UN Special Procedures, 'Malaysia: UN experts hail parliamentary decision to end mandatory death penalty', Press release, Geneva, 11 April 2023, at: https://bit.ly/3MIkn2i.

[18] Art. 282, Criminal Code of Iran.

[19] Human Rights Committee, General comment No. 36 – Article 6: right to life, UN doc. CCPR/C/GC/36, 3 September 2019, para. 35.

[20] Art. 21, International Covenant on Civil and Political Rights; adopted at New York, 16 December 1966; entered into force, 23 March 1976. As of 1 January 2024, 173 States were party to the ICCPR.

[21] 2012 Terrorism (Amendment) Act.

[22] See International Federation for Human Rights (FIDH), 'Bangladesh: New Amendment to Anti-Terrorism Act gags Freedom of Expression', 14 June 2013, at: https://bit.ly/3MqZUQp.

[23] S. 2, 2014 Law on Repression of Acts of Terrorism.

[24] 'Belarus introduces death penalty for "attempted" terrorism', *France24*, 18 May 2022, at: https://bit.ly/3syXXdm.

[25] See inter alia Arts. 8(2), 9(2), and 11(4), 2008 Law on Combat against Terrorist Offences (unofficial translation).

4.2.2 *Maximum Sentences of Imprisonment*

In one-third of all States, life imprisonment is the maximum sentence for terrorism offences. This is the case in Albania,[26] Armenia,[27] Australia,[28] Azerbaijan,[29] Barbados (which removed the death penalty for terrorist offences in 2019), Belgium,[30] Belize,[31] Bulgaria (where death has been caused by a terrorist act),[32] Burkina Faso (which abolished the death penalty in 2018), Burundi (where death has been caused by a terrorist act),[33] Cambodia,[34] Canada, Chad (which removed the death penalty for terrorist offences in 2020),[35] Cyprus,[36] Czechia,[37] Denmark,[38] Djibouti,[39] Estonia,[40] Fiji,[41] Finland,[42] France,[43] Gabon,[44] Georgia,[45] Greece,[46] Grenada,[47] Guinea,[48] Hungary,[49] Iceland,[50] Ireland,[51] Italy,[52] Jamaica,[53] Kenya,[54] Kiribati,[55] Laos,[56] Latvia,[57] Liberia (which abolished capital punishment in 2022), Lithuania,[58] Luxembourg,[59] Malta,[60] the Marshall Islands,[61] Monaco, Nauru,[62] Nepal,[63] New Zealand,[64] North Macedonia,[65]

---

[26] Terrorist offences attract a term of imprisonment of at least fifteen years and up to life imprisonment. Art. 230, Criminal Code of Albania.

[27] Art. 104(2)9), Penal Code of Armenia.

[28] S. 101.1(1), 1995 Criminal Code Act.

[29] Where firearms or explosives are used in an act of terrorism or death or serious bodily harm results from the offence, the maximum term is life imprisonment. Art. 120.2.11, Criminal Code of Azerbaijan.

[30] Art. 138, Criminal Code of Belgium.

[31] S. 5(a), 2008 Money Laundering and Terrorism (Prevention) Act.

[32] Art. 108a(1), Criminal Code of Bulgaria.

[33] Art. 618, Criminal Code of Burundi.

[34] The 1992 Law generally specifies life imprisonment for terrorist offences that had an intended or actual fatal result. Art. 3, 1992 Law to Punish Terrorism.

[35] Art. 3, 2020 Law on the Suppression of Terrorism.

[36] Art. 5, 2010 Combating Terrorism Act.

[37] S. 54(3), Criminal Code of Czechia.

[38] S. 114(1), Criminal Code of Denmark.

[39] Art. 169, Criminal Code of Djibouti.

[40] S. 237(1), Criminal Code of Estonia.

[41] S. 12(A), 1969 Public Order Act. Harbouring a terrorist suspect can attract the same penalty.

[42] S. 1(8), chap. 34(a), Criminal Code of Finland.

[43] Art. 421–3, French Criminal Code.

[44] Art. 201, Criminal Code of Gabon.

[45] Art. 323(4), Criminal Code of Georgia. This is where homicide is involved. The general penalty for a terrorist act is imprisonment for between five and eight years. Art. 323(1), Criminal Code of Georgia.

[46] Criminal Code of Greece.

[47] S. 3(1), 2012 Terrorism Act.

[48] Art. 574, Criminal Code of Guinea.

[49] S. 314, Criminal Code of Hungary.

[50] Art. 100(a), Criminal Code of Iceland.

[51] S. 7, Criminal Justice (Terrorist Offences) Act 2005.

[52] The predicate offence of murder is subject to a maximum of life imprisonment but this is not limited to terrorist offences.

[53] S. 3(1), 2015 Terrorism Prevention Act.

[54] S. 4(2), 2012 Prevention of Terrorism Act.

[55] In the case of terrorist bombings. S. 39(2), 2005 Measures to Combat Terrorism Act.

[56] Art. 120, Criminal Code of Laos.

[57] S. 79(1), Criminal Code of Latvia.

[58] Art. 250(4), Criminal Code of Lithuania.

[59] Art. 135(2), Criminal Code of Luxembourg.

[60] Art. 328A(3), Criminal Code of Malta.

[61] S. 107, 2002 Counterterrorism Act.

[62] S. 10A, 2004 Terrorism Act (as amended).

[63] S. 10(1) and (2), 2002 Terrorist and Disruptive Acts (Prevention and Punishment Act).

[64] S. 6A(4), 2002 Suppression of Terrorism Act.

[65] Art. 394-b, Criminal Code of North Macedonia.

Palau,[66] St Kitts and Nevis,[67] Samoa,[68] Serbia,[69] the Seychelles,[70] Slovakia,[71] Solomon Islands,[72] South Africa,[73] Spain,[74] Suriname,[75] Sweden,[76] Switzerland,[77] Togo,[78] Tuvalu,[79] Ukraine,[80] the United Kingdom, Uzbekistan,[81] and Zambia.[82]

In addition, in Benin, life imprisonment is a *mandatory* sentence for all terrorism offences. The country effectively abolished the death penalty following a decision by its Constitutional Court in 2016.[83] Equatorial Guinea adopted a new Criminal Code in 2022, explicitly prohibiting terrorism for the first time and making life imprisonment the maximum penalty for a terrorism offence. The new law abolished the death penalty in Equatorial Guinea.[84] Those found guilty of committing terrorist acts in Haiti are subject to a term of imprisonment ranging from thirty years to fifty years and a heavy fine. But a repeat offence carries the punishment of life imprisonment.[85] In Israel, an attempt in 2015 to institute capital punishment for terrorists was defeated in the Knesset by overwhelming majority.[86] As already noted, in 2023, Malaysia abolished the mandatory death penalty, including for terrorism offences, following an earlier moratorium imposed on all executions.

4.2.3 Other Prison Sentences for Terrorism Offences

In Austria, a conviction for terrorism results in a sentence of imprisonment increased by one half compared to the penalty for the ordinary criminal offence.[87] The same approach is taken in Liechtenstein.[88] The penalty for the perpetration of a terrorist offence in Mexico is between fifteen and forty years in prison.[89] But the penalty for the predicate offence is increased by one half when the crime is committed against property to which the public has access; when damage or harm is inflicted on the national economy; or where, in the commission of the crime, a person is detained as a hostage.[90] In Mozambique, the penalty for the predicate offences may be

---

[66] S. 4205, Criminal Code of Palau.

[67] S. 24(2), 2002 Antiterrorism Act.

[68] S. 14(2), 15(2), 16(2) et al., 2014 Counter Terrorism Act.

[69] Art. 391(3), Criminal Code of Serbia.

[70] S. 4, 2004 Prevention of Terrorism Act.

[71] S. 419(1), Criminal Code of Slovakia. Subsection 2 makes the sentence of life imprisonment mandatory where the attack caused grievous bodily harm to a person.

[72] S. 3(1), 2009 Counterterrorism Act.

[73] 2022 Protection of Constitutional Democracy against Terrorist and Related Activities Amendment Act.

[74] Art. 573 bis (1), Criminal Code of Spain.

[75] Terrorist offences are prosecuted as ordinary criminal offences under the Criminal Code of Suriname.

[76] S. 4, 2022 Terrorist Offences Act (2022:666).

[77] Art. 260 ter, Criminal Code of Switzerland.

[78] Criminal Code of Togo.

[79] S. 4(3), 2009 Counterterrorism and Transnational Organised Crime Act.

[80] Art. 258(3), Criminal Code of Ukraine.

[81] Art. 155, Criminal Code of Uzbekistan. The minimum sentence under the Criminal Code is eight years in prison.

[82] S. 19(2), 2018 Anti-Terrorism and Non-Proliferation Act.

[83] Art. 166, Criminal Code of Benin.

[84] Law No. 4/2022 promulgating the Criminal Code of Equatorial Guinea.

[85] Art. 2, 2020 Decree for the Reinforcement of Public Security.

[86] L. Harkov, 'Knesset votes down death penalty for terrorists 94-6', *The Jerusalem Post*, 15 July 2015, at: https://bit.ly/45sdWc2.

[87] S. 278c, Penal Code of Austria.

[88] S. 278c, Criminal Code of Liechtenstein.

[89] Art. 139(I), Federal Criminal Code of Mexico.

[90] Art. 139(II), Federal Criminal Code of Mexico.

4.2 Sentences for Terrorism in Domestic Law

increased (without a specific tariff being imposed) when it concerns a terrorist offence.[91] The same occurs in the Netherlands under Dutch law.

In 2022, El Salvador increased the penalty for leading a terrorist group to forty-five years.[92] Colombia prescribes a term of imprisonment for the perpetration of terrorism in armed conflict of between twenty and thirty-nine years.[93] For terrorism in peacetime, the penalty is a prison term of between 160 and 270 months.[94] If the state of terror is caused by a telephone call, tape, video, cassette, or anonymous writing, the penalty is between thirty-two and ninety months in prison.[95] In Rwanda, any person, 'whether a principal author or an accomplice who joins or deliberately participates in the acts of a terrorism association', or a group 'which operates in building capacities of any association that conducts terrorist acts', is liable to a term of imprisonment of between twenty and thirty-five years.[96] The Criminal Code prescribes a penalty of either twelve to twenty-five years in prison for terrorist offences or the sentence for the predicate offence increased by one-third.[97]

In Andorra, the maximum sentence for terrorism is thirty years in prison.[98] The same upper tariff is set in Brunei[99] and the Dominican Republic.[100] Venezuela's 2012 law prescribes prison sentences of twenty-five to thirty years for the perpetration of acts of terrorism and fifteen to twenty-five years for the crime of terrorist financing.[101] Tanzania has a minimum sentence for terrorism of thirty years.[102]

In Brazil, the penalty under the 2016 law for terrorist offences is 'imprisonment, for a period of twelve to thirty years *in addition to the penalties corresponding for threats or violence*'.[103] In Norway, under the Criminal Code, the maximum penalty for terrorist offences is generally twenty-one years' imprisonment.[104] The penalty for 'aggravated' terrorist offences is imprisonment for a term not exceeding thirty years.[105] In Paraguay, the penalty for the commission of a terrorist offence is imprisonment for between ten and thirty years.[106] The standard penalty for terrorism in Panama is twenty to thirty years' imprisonment.[107] Honduras' Criminal Code stipulates that when terrorism offences involve weapons or explosives, the maximum penalty for the predicate offence can be increased by two-thirds.[108]

---

[91] Art. 11(3), 2022 Law on Countering Terrorism.

[92] Art. 2, Decree No. 337 of 2022, modifying the Criminal Code.

[93] Art. 144, 2000 Criminal Code of Colombia.

[94] Art. 343, 2000 Criminal Code of Colombia.

[95] Ibid.

[96] Art. 75, Law 45/2008 on countering terrorism.

[97] Art. 132(1), Criminal Code of Timor-Leste. A similar term of imprisonment is imposable for terrorist financing. Art. 133, Criminal Code of Timor-Leste.

[98] Art. 363(1), 2005 Criminal Code of Andorra (as amended).

[99] S. 3, 2011 Anti-Terrorism Order.

[100] Art. 435, Criminal Code of the Dominican Republic.

[101] Arts. 52 and 53, 2012 Law on Organized Crime and Terrorist Financing.

[102] S. 11A(c), 2002 Prevention of Terrorism Act, as amended by S. 55, 2016 Written Laws (Miscellaneous Amendment No.2) Act.

[103] Art. 2, 2016 Terrorism Law [added emphasis].

[104] S. 131(1), Criminal Code of Norway.

[105] In determining whether the terrorist act is aggravated, particular weight is given to whether it has caused the loss of several human lives or very extensive destruction of property or the environment, or an especially high risk thereof; has been committed using particularly harmful means; or has been committed by a person who by virtue of his or her position enjoys special trust which may be exploited to commit a terrorist act. S. 132, Criminal Code of Norway. Anders Breivik, who killed seventy-seven people in 2011 in a double gun and bomb attack, received only a twenty-one-year prison sentence for his crimes. P. Beaumont, 'Norwegian mass killer Anders Breivik appears before parole hearing', *The Guardian*, 18 January 2022, at: https://bit.ly/3q3mdTu. A parole hearing was heard in 2022.

[106] Art. 1, 2013 Law 4024 on Terrorism.

[107] Art. 293, Criminal Code of Panama.

[108] Art. 589, Criminal Code of Honduras.

Where a terrorist act results in death in Ecuador, the penalty on conviction is between twenty and twenty-six years in prison.[109] In Antigua and Barbuda, the maximum sentence is twenty-five years in prison.[110] If, in the course of committing a terrorism offence, the perpetrator intentionally deprives another person of his life, the punishment is to be at least ten years or 'long-term' imprisonment.[111] Tonga sets twenty-five years in prison as the maximum penalty for a terrorism offence[112] as do Turkmenistan[113] and Vanuatu.[114] In Dominica, which, at the time of writing, did not otherwise specifically punish terrorist acts, punishes the financing of terrorism with a maximum penalty of twenty-five years in prison along with a fine.[115] The maximum sentence for terrorist offences under St Lucian law is twenty-five years' imprisonment while no less than ten years in prison may be imposed for membership of a terrorist group.[116] Ghana's 2008 law provides for a term of imprisonment of not less than seven years and not more than twenty-five years upon conviction for a terrorist act.[117] In San Marino, the penalties range from fourteen to twenty-four years in prison.[118]

Considerably lighter sentences are imposable in a small number of States. Conviction for the commission of a terrorist offence carries a penalty of imprisonment of between ten and twenty years in Côte d'Ivoire.[119] St Vincent and the Grenadines' dedicated 2002 Act stipulates twenty years as the maximum penalty for terrorist offences.[120] Nicaragua's Criminal Code provides for prison terms of fifteen to twenty years for the perpetration of terrorist crimes.[121] The Cook Islands has a maximum sentence of twenty years in prison.[122] Generally, the punishment for a terrorist offence in Romania is imprisonment for between fifteen and twenty years; threatening a terrorist act carries a sentence of imprisonment from three to ten years.[123] Terrorist offences are generally subject to imprisonment for between three and fifteen years in Slovenia (although should the act involve intentional homicide, the *minimum* penalty is fifteen years in prison).[124]

The penalty for terrorist offences in São Tomé and Príncipe is imprisonment for between three and fifteen years or an increase in the penalty for the predicate crime by one-third (minimum and maximum limited).[125] The maximum penalty for the commission of a terrorist offence in Papua New Guinea is imprisonment for fourteen years.[126] In Angola, leading a criminal group, including for terrorist purposes, is punishable under a 2014 law with imprisonment for a term of between five and twelve years.[127] A 2017 law provides for terms of imprisonment of between five and fifteen years, which may be increased by one-third.[128] Under a 2012

[109] Art. 366(10), Comprehensive Criminal Code of Ecuador.
[110] S. 5, 2005 Prevention of Terrorism Act.
[111] Art. 201(3), Criminal Code of Bosnia and Herzegovina.
[112] S. 11(2), 2013 Counterterrorism and Transnational Organised Crime Act, Act 23 of 2013.
[113] Art. 271(3), Criminal Code of Turkmenistan.
[114] S. 5, 2005 Counterterrorism and Transnational Organized Crime Act.
[115] S. 5, 2003 Terrorist Financing Act.
[116] S.18(1), 2015 Anti-Terrorism Act.
[117] S. 1(2), 2008 Anti-Terrorist Act.
[118] Art. 340 quater, Criminal Code of San Marino.
[119] Art. 3, 2015 Anti-Terrorism Law.
[120] S. 7, 2002 United Nations (Anti-Terrorism Measures) Act.
[121] Art. 394, Criminal Code of Nicaragua.
[122] S. 16A, 2004 Act on the Suppression of Terrorism (as amended).
[123] Art. 32(2), 2004 Law on Combating Terrorism.
[124] Art. 108(5), Criminal Code of Slovenia.
[125] Art. 360(1), Criminal Code of São Tomé and Príncipe.
[126] S. 3, 1993 Internal Security Act.
[127] Art. 8(5), Law No. 3/2014 on Terrorist Financing.
[128] Art. 23(1), 2017 Law on Preventing and Countering Terrorism.

decree, the Holy See provides for prison sentences for the creation or leadership of terrorist groups of five to fifteen years.[129]

Cabo Verde's 2013 Terrorism Law generally criminalizes terrorist acts with imprisonment for between two and ten years.[130] That said, founding a terrorist group carries a penalty of eight to fifteen years in prison, while leading one is punishable by ten to twenty years imprisonment.[131] A similar penalty is envisaged for terrorism financing.[132] In Germany, criminal offences do not generally attract an additional penalty if they are committed for terrorist motives. Terrorist financing is punishable with imprisonment for between six months and ten years.[133]

4.2.3.1 Minimum Sentences of Imprisonment

Beyond the minimum sentences outlined in the previous section, Montenegro is extremely unusual in setting a minimum but not a maximum term of imprisonment for terrorism. The minimum penalty for the perpetration of a terrorist offence is five years' imprisonment.[134] Where a terrorist offence has caused the death of one or a number of persons or large-scale destruction, the offender is punished by imprisonment for a minimum of ten years.[135] Poland also sanctions terrorism with a term of imprisonment of at least five years.[136] Portugal's dedicated law sets the general penalty for terrorist acts as imprisonment for between two and ten years.[137] Should the predicate criminal offences be especially serious, the maximum penalty for those offences is increased by one-third when committed for a terrorism purpose.[138]

4.2.3.2 The Punishment of Hard or Forced Labour

A small number of States prescribe sentences of hard or forced labour for terrorism offences. Terrorism in Senegal is punished by forced labour for life. The penalty is also applied to preparatory acts for terrorism or participating in a group that is founded with a view to committing terrorism.[139] Acts of terrorism in the Central African Republic are criminalized under the Penal Code by a 'fixed term' of forced labour. Nuclear terrorism, however, is punishable with forced labour for life.[140] In Madagascar, hijacking or hostage-taking is punishable under the 2014 Counterterrorism Act with between five and twenty years of forced labour.[141]

In Jordan, in a case where the death penalty is not imposed as the sentence upon conviction, hard labour for life is the penalty for most terrorist acts.[142] In Lebanon, which also has the death penalty for terrorism offences, a terrorist act is punished by hard labour for life if it results in even

---

[129] Art. 4, Terrorism (Amendment) Decree of January 2012.
[130] Art. 4(1), 2013 Terrorism Law.
[131] Art. 4(2) and (3), 2013 Terrorism Law.
[132] Art. 6(1), 2013 Terrorism Law.
[133] Section 89c(1), Criminal Code of Germany.
[134] Art. 447(1), Criminal Code of Montenegro.
[135] Art. 447(4), Criminal Code of Montenegro.
[136] Art. 115(20), Revised Penal Code.
[137] Art. 4(1), 2002 Terrorism Law.
[138] Ibid.
[139] Art. 279–5, Criminal Code of Senegal.
[140] Art. 316, Penal Code of the Central African Republic.
[141] Arts. 2 and 6, 2014 Counterterrorism Act.
[142] Art. 7, 2006 Prevention of Terrorism Act.

partial destruction of a public building, industrial establishment, vessel or other facility, or in impediments to means of telecommunications, communications, and transport.[143]

4.2.4 *Sentences for Other Offences*

4.2.4.1 Funding Terrorism

In some instances the offence of funding acts of terrorism or terrorist groups is treated in the same way as the principal offence. This is so, for instance, in Albania,[144] Antigua and Barbuda,[145] and the Cook Islands.[146] Further to a 2012 amendment, the law in force in Bangladesh allows the imposition and execution of the death penalty for financial terrorism crimes.[147] In contrast, in Algeria, funding terrorism is, ordinarily, only punishable by five to ten years in prison,[148] compared to the death penalty imposable for the perpetration of terrorism offences. In Botswana, funding terrorism attracts a sentence of life imprisonment compared to the death penalty for the perpetration of terrorism.[149] Barbados has a maximum sentence of twenty-five years' imprisonment for providing funding or financial services for terrorism (compared to life imprisonment for acts of terrorism following the abolition of the death penalty).[150]

4.2.4.2 Attempted or Other Inchoate Offences

In many instances, attempting but failing to commit an act of terrorism attracts the same penalty as if the perpetrator had succeeded. This is the case, for instance, in Afghanistan,[151] in Benin (unless it was the defendant's action that precluded their successful perpetration),[152] and in Samoa.[153] The situation in Belarus has already been noted. In Honduras, attempted hijackings are punished with the penalty reduced by one-quarter.[154] In contrast, in the Bahamas, preparatory acts are punishable in the same way as completed acts of terrorism.[155]

4.2.4.3 Aiding or Abetting Terrorism

Complicity in acts of terrorism may also be prosecuted and sentenced with the same penalties as the acts themselves. This is the case in, for instance, Barbados.[156] In other States, a lesser penalty

---

[143] Art. 315, Criminal Code of Lebanon.
[144] In Albania, the 'provision or collection of funds, by any means, directly or indirectly, with the intent to use them or knowing that they will be used, in whole or in part: a) to commit offences for terrorist purposes; b) by a terrorist organisation; c) by a single terrorist' is thus punishable by a term of imprisonment of at least fifteen years and up to life imprisonment. Art. 230A, Criminal Code of Albania.
[145] S. 6, 2005 Prevention of Terrorism Act.
[146] Terrorist financing is subject to a penalty of twenty years in prison as is the perpetration of an act of terrorism. S. 11, 2004 Act on the Suppression of Terrorism (as amended).
[147] International Federation for Human Rights (FIDH), 'Bangladesh: New Amendment to Anti-Terrorism Act gags Freedom of Expression', 14 June 2013, at: https://bit.ly/3MqZUQp.
[148] Art. 87 bis 4, Penal Code of Algeria (as amended).
[149] S. 5(1), 2014 Counterterrorism Act.
[150] S. 4(1), 2002 Anti-Terrorism Act. Under the Act, for an act to constitute an offence it is not necessary to prove that the funds or the financial services were actually used to carry out the offence. S. 4(2), 2002 Anti-Terrorism Act.
[151] Art. 17(1), 2008 Law on Combat against Terrorist Offences (unofficial translation).
[152] Art. 169, Criminal Code of Benin.
[153] S. 15(2), 2014 Counterterrorism Act.
[154] Art. 335, Criminal Code of Honduras.
[155] S. 26, 2018 Anti-Terrorism Act.
[156] S. 3(2), 2002 Anti-Terrorism Act.

is incurred. But sometimes narrow distinctions between different forms of complicity are made. In Botswana, supporting terrorism by doing 'anything which will, or is likely to enhance the ability of another person to commit an act of terrorism, including to provide or offer to provide [*sic*] a skill or an expertise', is punishable with imprisonment for up to thirty years. This compares to the death penalty that is imposable for aiding or abetting a terrorist act.[157]

In Iceland, assisting or supporting terrorism is subject to a term of imprisonment of up to ten years (compared to life imprisonment as the maximum sentence for the perpetration of acts of terrorism).[158] In the United States, material support to terrorism can be punished by life imprisonment.[159] The offence is very broadly defined under the US Criminal Code to include, potentially, the teaching of international humanitarian law (IHL) to a proscribed group. This is so, even though dissemination of IHL is required under the customary and conventional law of war.[160]

4.2.4.4 Inciting or Glorifying Terrorism

The Bahamas, which has the death penalty for certain terrorist acts, provides for twenty-five years' imprisonment for inciting terrorism.[161] In Albania, inciting, calling publicly for, or distributing propaganda with the aim of supporting or committing one or more acts for terrorist purposes – 'if they do not constitute another criminal act' – are acts punishable upon conviction with imprisonment of between four and ten years.[162] In Algeria, knowingly issuing or publishing documents that support or justify terrorism is subject to between five and ten years in prison and a fine.[163] In Andorra, dissemination of ideology supporting or justifying terrorism or terrorist organizations is punishable with imprisonment for between three months and three years.[164]

In Angola, imprisonment of up to two years is imposable for the offence of disseminating propaganda for terrorism.[165] Public encouragement of terrorism in Iceland is punishable by up to six years in prison.[166] In Lithuania, a 'person who, by making public declarations orally, in writing or in the media, promotes or incites an act of terrorism or other crimes relating to terrorism or expresses contempt for victims of terrorism' is punishable by imprisonment for a term of up to three years.[167] Niger amended the law in 2016 to make justifying or inciting terrorism an offence under the Criminal Code subject to a penalty of between five and ten years in prison.[168]

Australia's Criminal Code makes it an offence, punishable by five years' imprisonment, to advocate the conduct of a terrorist act or offence, where the person is reckless as to whether another person will engage in that conduct as a result.[169] A person is deemed to be advocating terrorism if he or she 'counsels, promotes, encourages or urges the doing of a terrorist act or the

---

[157] Ss. 4(1) and (2) and 9(1)(a), 2014 Counterterrorism Act.
[158] Art. 100(b), Criminal Code of Iceland.
[159] US Code, Title 18, §2339A(a).
[160] US Supreme Court, *Holder* v. *Humanitarian Law Project*, 561 US (2010), Nos 08–1498 and 09–89, 21 June 2010, at: https://bit.ly/43ymT1w.
[161] S. 22, 2018 Anti-Terrorism Act.
[162] Art. 232A, Criminal Code of Albania.
[163] Art. 87 bis 5, Penal Code of Algeria (as amended).
[164] Art. 364(2), 2005 Criminal Code (as amended).
[165] Art. 167(2), 2020 Penal Code of Angola.
[166] Art. 100(b), Criminal Code of Iceland.
[167] Art. 250(1), Criminal Code of Lithuania.
[168] Art. 399.1.17 bis, Criminal Code of Niger.
[169] S. 80.2C, Criminal Code of Australia.

commission of a terrorism offence'. The standard of recklessness applies where the defendant is aware of a 'substantial risk' that another person would engage in terrorism, such that taking the risk was unjustifiable. This offence sets a lower bar than incitement of terrorism and may have adverse impacts on free speech.

4.2.4.5 Threatening to Commit Acts of Terrorism

Threatening to commit acts of terrorism typically attracts lower sentences as one would expect. In the case of Afghanistan, for instance, threatening to use nuclear material to kill or seriously injure a person or inflict enormous financial damage attracts a sentence upon conviction of at least six and not more than ten years in prison.[170]

4.3 THE PROSECUTION OF TERRORISM IN THE AMERICAS

This section addresses the prosecution – and occasional non-prosecution, at least for terrorism – of suspected or alleged terrorism crimes across the Americas. It covers a selection of relevant caselaw in Brazil, Canada, El Salvador, Mexico, and the United States. The United States has prosecuted more suspected terrorists than any other nation in the Americas; Brazil and Mexico the fewest. Canada's approach to the prosecution of terrorism has had to evolve significantly since its efforts to hold the perpetrators to account for the bombing of Air India Flight 182 in 1985 were bungled. The decision of El Salvador in 2015 to deem members of armed gangs as perpetrators of terrorism means that the number of terrorism convictions could skyrocket in that country over the coming years. In contrast, and despite the power and influence of the drug cartels, Mexico retains a far narrower conception of a terrorist group. At the time of writing, there was a proposal in the US House of Representatives and the Senate to add certain Mexican cartels to the list of designated Foreign Terrorist Organizations.

4.3.1 The Prosecution of Terrorism in Brazil

In March 2016, Brazil enacted a dedicated law on the repression of terrorism.[171] Brazil's Constitution had already stipulated that the law would preclude terrorism, along with illicit drug trafficking and the practice of torture, from being subject to clemency or amnesty.[172] But the notion of terrorism was not clearly defined in Brazilian law until the adoption of Law 13,260.[173] The first convictions under the new law were secured on 4 May 2017, when eight Brazilian citizens were found guilty of dissemination of Islamic State propaganda on social media.[174] The convictions were the result of 'Operation Hashtag', a law enforcement operation that had dismantled a loose, online network of supporters of Islamic State. Operation Hashtag had also seen the first arrests being made under the new terrorism law.[175]

[170] Art. 15(4), 2008 Law on Combat against Terrorist Offences (unofficial translation).
[171] Law No. 13,260, 16 March 2016, regulating the provisions of Section XLIII of Article 5 of the Federal Constitution, defining terrorism, dealing with investigative and procedural provisions and reformulating the concept of a terrorist organization.
[172] Art. 5(XLIII), Constitution of the Federative Republic of Brazil, 3rd ed. (2010).
[173] See, e.g., 'Brazil: New Anti-Terrorism Law Enacted', Library of Congress, United States, 15 April 2016, at: https://bit.ly/30GXT9I.
[174] Counterextremism Project, 'Brazil: Extremism and Terrorism', undated but accessed 1 June 2023, at: https://bit.ly/45I6b1E.
[175] US Department of State, *Country Reports on Terrorism 2017*, Bureau of Counterterrorism, Washington DC, September 2018, p. 198.

4.3 Prosecution of Terrorism in the Americas

Yet, as Chapter 3 described, the 2016 law is highly unusual on account of its focus on xenophobia and discrimination to the exclusion of violent efforts to secure political change. This poses a problem for prosecutors seeking to charge those supporters of Brazil's former president Jair Bolsonaro who stormed government buildings and institutions on 8 January 2023. Eight days after the inauguration of President Luiz Inácio Lula da Silva (commonly known as Lula), thousands of Bolsonaro supporters marched to Brasília's Three Powers Plaza, where they ransacked Brazil's Supreme Federal Court, Congress, and presidential offices.[176]

A joint statement from President Lula da Silva, Congressional leaders, and the Chief Justice of the Supreme Court condemned 'terrorist acts' in relation to the events in the capital. Brazil's Minister of Justice Flávio Dino similarly described the actions as terrorism, echoing rhetoric he had used when discussing a failed bomb plot at Brasilia's airport two weeks earlier.[177] The head of Brazil's federal police stated publicly that officials who intentionally undermined security ahead of the storming of the buildings had 'contributed to terrorist acts'.

The individual arrested on Christmas Eve 2022 for the airport bombing plot was named as George Washington de Oliveira Sousa. Mr de Oliveira Sousa, a fifty-four-year-old man, confessed to having assembled an explosive device that was later installed in a fuel truck near Brasilia Airport. Police found weapons and explosives in his apartment.[178] In referring to the incident, Mr Bolsonaro declared in his final presidential address: 'Nothing justifies an attempted terrorist act.'[179]

'We won't allow political terrorism in Brazil', Minister of Justice Dino declared.[180] But as Mr de Oliveira Sousa's motive was to provoke a state of emergency in the country in favour of Mr Bolsonaro and to reverse the election result, it was hard to see how that could be prosecuted as terrorism under Brazilian law. Although 'using or threatening to use, transporting, keeping, possessing, carrying or bringing explosives' are explicitly predicate terrorism offences under Law 13,260, and the requisite purpose of endangering public safety was equally satisfied, the statutory reasons for those actions and purpose of 'xenophobia, discrimination or prejudice based on race, colour, ethnicity, and religion'[181] were not. Indeed, when he came to trial four months later, Mr de Oliveira Sousa was not charged with terrorism offences but rather with endangering life through causing an explosion.[182] In May 2023, he was convicted and sentenced to nine years and four months in prison for the crimes of causing an explosion as well as causing a fire and unauthorized possession of a firearm. The police had alleged he was the person who had suggested the attack and produced the bomb.[183]

---

[176] D. Roy, 'Images Show the Extent of Brazil's Capitol Riots', Council on Foreign Relations, 12 January 2023, at: https://bit.ly/3WJiqak.

[177] 'IntelBrief: How Far Will Brazil Go to Prosecute Capitol Attacks?', The Soufan Center, 30 January 2023, at: https://bit.ly/3oJfXQx.

[178] M. Falcão and P. A. Neto, 'Bolsonarista que montou explosivo em Brasília foi autuado por terrorismo; em depoimento, disse que queria "dar início ao caos"', TV Globo and g1 DF, 25 December 2022, at: https://bit.ly/3OSxDUx.

[179] B. Chambers, 'Bolsonaro condemns "terrorist act" in Brasilia in last address as Brazil's president', Anadolu Agency, 30 December 2022, at: https://bit.ly/3qpgJTp.

[180] A. Romani and G. Stargardter, 'Bolsonaro's call to arms inspired foiled Brazil bomb plot, police are told', Reuters, 26 December 2022, at: https://bit.ly/3MOHI21.

[181] Art. 2(1), Law No. 13,260 (unofficial English translation).

[182] F. Vivas, M. Falcão and I. Caramori, 'Justiça aceita denúncia e torna réu trio acusado de montar artefato explosivo perto do Aeroporto de Brasília', TV Globo and g1 DF, 15 January 2023, at: https://bit.ly/3qtf5zT. The offence is set out in Article 251 of the Criminal Code.

[183] T. Viapiana, 'Bolsonaro supporter who planted bomb in truck found guilty and sentenced to 9 years in prison', Brazil Reports, 17 May 2023, at: https://bit.ly/3WOaswx.

134   *Prosecution of Terrorism Suspects*

A second defendant, Alan Diego dos Santos Rodrigues, a thirty-two-year-old man, was sentenced to five years and four months in prison for attempting to trigger the bomb inside the fuel truck, which did not fully detonate due to an error in assembling the device.[184] A third person accused of involvement in the bombing, Wellington Macedo de Souza, a politician who ironically had worked at the Ministry of Human Rights during the Bolsonaro administration,[185] was convicted in absentia in August 2023 by the Eighth Criminal Court of Brasilia and sentenced to six years' imprisonment. Mr Macedo de Souza had fled after the bombing attack.[186]

4.3.2 *The Prosecution of Terrorism in Canada*

In Canada, prosecutions for terrorism offences are the responsibility of the Public Prosecution Service of Canada and, more broadly, the Department of Justice Canada. The Royal Canadian Mounted Police (RCMP) investigates terror suspects, including 'Canadian Extremist Travellers' (CETs), in order to collect evidence with a view to laying criminal charges and supporting successful prosecutions. Prior to the 9/11 attacks in the United States, the authorities tended to rely on ordinary Criminal Code provisions to prosecute terrorist acts.[187] In 2001, Canada's Parliament adopted the Anti-Terrorism Act (ATA) to amend the Criminal Code, as well as other laws.[188] Between late 2001 and 2020, sixty-two individuals were charged with terrorism offences under the amended Criminal Code of Canada.[189]

Successful prosecutions include that of Momin Khawaja, who was convicted of involvement in a plot to plant fertilizer bombs in the United Kingdom.[190] He became the first person found guilty under the provisions introduced into the Criminal Code by the ATA based on his communications with the British Islamists plotting the attacks.[191] The fear expressed by the United Nations Office on Drugs and Crime (UNODC) in a 2004 report, that Canada's definition of terrorist activity, which is central to its definition of each terrorism offence, would be 'impossible to prove',[192] have thus proved unfounded. Based on their thoughtful review of terrorism prosecutions in Canadian courts, Nesbitt and Hagg conclude that the definition of 'terrorism activity' under the law 'looks relatively stable and settled'.[193]

---

[184] Ibid.

[185] Ibid.; and C. Silva, 'Bomb Plot Suspect worked for Bolsonaro Administration', *The Brazilian Report*, 16 January 2023, at: https://bit.ly/3oIx7xF.

[186] Lusa News Agency, 'Apoiante de Bolsonaro condenado por colocar bomba perto do aeroporto de Brasília Agência Lusa', *dnoticias.pt*, 19 August 2023, at: https://bit.ly/3KZIuto.

[187] M. Nesbitt and D. Hagg, 'An Empirical Study of Terrorism Prosecutions in Canada: Elucidating the Elements of the Offences', *Alberta Law Review*, Vol. 57, No. 3 (2020), 595–648, at: 595 note 3.

[188] These include the Official Secrets Act, the Canada Evidence Act, and the Proceeds of Crime (Money Laundering) Act. Parliament also enacted the Charities Registration (Security Information) Act. Government of Canada, 'About the Anti-terrorism Act', last modified 7 July 2021, at: https://bit.ly/3CaAUqD.

[189] Public Safety Canada, 'Terrorism Prosecutions', National Security and Cyber Security Branch (NCSB), 21 October 2020 (last modified 6 July 2021), at: https://bit.ly/3OP63Yl.

[190] On 12 March 2009, Mr Khawaja was sentenced to ten and a half years in prison. Eighteen months later, the Ontario Court of Appeals increased his sentence to life imprisonment. 'Appeal court hikes sentences for terror convictions', *Toronto Star*, 17 December 2010, at: https://bit.ly/43kfIKF.

[191] 'Khawaja "directly involved" in British bomb plot: Prosecutor', *CBC News*, 23 June 2008, at: https://bit.ly/3WQk4qG.

[192] UNODC, *Legislative Guide to the Universal Anti-Terrorism Conventions and Protocols*, UN, New York, 2004, p. 10, cited in Nesbitt and Hagg, 'An Empirical Study of Terrorism Prosecutions in Canada: Elucidating the Elements of the Offences', p. 596.

[193] Nesbitt and Hagg, 'An Empirical Study of Terrorism Prosecutions in Canada: Elucidating the Elements of the Offences', p. 613.

Public Safety Canada[194] was created in 2003 to ensure coordination across all federal departments and agencies responsible for national security and the safety of Canadians. Broadly speaking, it is Canada's equivalent of the Department of Homeland Security in the United States. Public Safety Canada works with the Department of Justice Canada and the Public Prosecution Service of Canada to coordinate efforts to prosecute terror suspects 'to the fullest extent of the law'.[195] Its view today is that so-called mega-trials, conducted in response to major terror attacks, 'pose significant challenges for the criminal justice system':

> For example, huge volumes of evidence need to be managed in a timely fashion, a task which is further complicated when the evidence involves sensitive information. Also, these trials frequently rely on expert and wiretap evidence for which there are complex court processes. Finally, these trials are generally accompanied by numerous preliminary motions. Because of how long they take, mega-trials may infringe on an accused's right to be tried within a reasonable time and therefore run a significant risk of collapsing under their own weight.[196]

4.3.2.1 The Bombing of Air India Flight 182

This contemporary view reflects the experience of the authorities in seeking to prosecute the worst terrorist attack in Canadian history: the bombing of Air India Flight 182 on 23 June 1985. The bomb placed on Flight 182 detonated as the aircraft neared the coast of Ireland, killing everyone on board. The attack, which was both planned and executed in Canada by Sikh extremists, claimed the lives of 329 innocent people, of whom 280 were Canadian nationals.[197] Until the 9/11 attacks, it was the single deadliest incidence of aviation terrorism.[198] A second bomb exploded at Japan's Narita Airport in Tokyo, killing two baggage handlers as they transferred cargo to another Air India plane. The bombings followed a crackdown on Sikhs fighting for an independent homeland, and those behind it were alleged to be seeking revenge for the storming of the Golden Temple in Amritsar by Indian troops in June 2014.[199]

The largest, most complex, and most expensive investigation ever undertaken in Canada failed to bring all those responsible for the bombing to justice. It led to the instigation of a Commission of Inquiry headed by Canadian Supreme Court Justice John C. Major, which reported its findings and recommendations to the government in 2010.[200] Inderjit Singh Reyat was the only person convicted of offences in relation to the bombing. Mr Reyat, a dual British-Canadian national, pleaded guilty in 2003 to manslaughter and was sentenced to fifteen years in prison for assembling the bombs.[201]

---

[194] Formally, the Department of Public Safety and Emergency Preparedness.

[195] Public Safety Canada, 'Terrorism Prosecutions'.

[196] Public Safety Canada, 'The Government of Canada Response to the Commission of Inquiry into the Investigation of the Bombing of Air India Flight 182', last modified 22 July 2022, at: https://bit.ly/3C8Or20.

[197] Ibid.

[198] S. Bell, 'Stewart 'Leadership and the Toronto 18', Chap. 6 in B. Hoffman and F. Reinares (eds.), *The Evolution of the Global Terrorist Threat: From 9/11 to Osama bin Laden's Death*, Columbia University Press, New York, 2014, p. 144.

[199] Agence France-Presse (AFP), 'Canada frees man convicted for 1985 Air India bombing that killed 329 people', *The Guardian*, 15 February 2017, at: https://bit.ly/420uGOK.

[200] Public Safety Canada, 'The Government of Canada Response to the Commission of Inquiry into the Investigation of the Bombing of Air India Flight 182.'

[201] In 2017, Mr Reyat was released from a halfway house following his move from prison a year earlier. Conditions of his release from prison still apply, which includes him having no contact with the victims' families or with extremists. He must also shun all political activities and take counselling for violent tendencies, a lack of empathy, and exaggerated beliefs. AFP, 'Canada frees man convicted for 1985 Air India bombing that killed 329 people', *The Guardian*, 15 February 2017.

136   *Prosecution of Terrorism Suspects*

According to prosecutors, his perjury in court helped to forestall convictions in the cases against his co-accused.[202] But investigatory failures were also partly to blame. The Commission report had concluded that a 'cascading series of errors' by the Government of Canada, the RCMP, and the Canadian Security Intelligence Service (CSIS) had allowed the terrorist attack to occur in the first place.[203] But in his written remarks presenting the final report to the Canadian government, Justice Major declared: 'The level of error, incompetence, and inattention which took place before the flight was sadly mirrored in many ways for many years, in how authorities, Governments, and institutions dealt with the aftermath of the murder of so many innocents: in the investigation, the legal proceedings, and in providing information, support and comfort to the families.'[204] For instance, one of the co-accused, Talwinder Singh Parmar, had been under surveillance by Canadian intelligence agents since 1982. After the bombing, Mr Parmar's communications were wiretapped by the CSIS, but an agent erased most of the tapes amid a fierce turf war with the RCMP.[205]

4.3.2.2 The Toronto 18

On 2 June 2006, counterterrorism raids in and around the Greater Toronto area resulted in the arrest of thirteen adults and four children who were suspected of involvement in a plot to attack targets in southern Ontario. A fourteenth adult was arrested two months later. Their plans were to detonate truck bombs, to open fire in a crowded area, and to storm the Canadian Broadcasting Centre, the Parliament of Canada building, the CSIS headquarters, and the parliamentary Peace Tower in order to take hostages and to behead the prime minister and other leaders.[206] The total number of arrests in the case – and their subsequent charging for terrorism offences – led to it being popularly referred to as the 'Toronto 18'.[207]

Seven adults pleaded guilty, including the two ringleaders: Fahim Ahmad, who was sentenced to sixteen years' imprisonment; and Zakaria Amara, who received a life sentence without the possibility of parole.[208] The five others received prison sentences of between seven and twenty years. Jahmaal James pleaded guilty in 2010 to having gone to Pakistan with the aim of receiving paramilitary training for the benefit of the Toronto 18 (which he did not get) and was freed after being sentenced to seven years but fully credited with time served.[209]

The courts convicted four other men, one of whom was a child at the time of his arrest. Nishanthan Yogakrishnan, aged seventeen years at the time of arrest, was sentenced to two and a half years in prison for conspiracy to commit terrorism. Mr Yogakrishnan, who had moved to Canada with his family from Sri Lanka in 1994, was the only child offender whose case went to trial. Following a camping trip to Orillia in Ontario, where training for the plots was organized, friends had suggested he should cut off the prime minister's head since he had enjoyed chopping wood so much.[210] Famously described by Mubin Shaikh, a CSIS undercover agent who testified

---

[202]   Ibid.
[203]   *Air India Flight 182: A Canadian Tragedy*, Volume One: The Overview, 2010, at: https://bit.ly/43mnMLa, p. 1.
[204]   Opening Remarks by the Honourable John C. Major, CC, QC on the release of the Report of the Commission of Inquiry into the Investigation of the Bombing of Air India Flight 182, 23 July 2010, at: https://bit.ly/3queqP2, p. 1.
[205]   Commission of Inquiry into the Investigation of the Bombing of Air India Flight 182, *Research Studies – Volume 1: Threat Assessment and RCMP/CSIS Co-operation*, 2010, at: https://bit.ly/3IUIQ32, p. 193; see also A. Mitrovica and J. Sallot, 'CSIS agent destroyed Air-India evidence', *The Globe and Mail*, 26 January 2000, pp. A1–A2.
[206]   CBC News, 'Toronto 18: Key events in the case', 4 June 2008 (last updated 4 March 2011), at: https://bit.ly/3IVoJyQ.
[207]   Ibid.
[208]   Mr Amara's Canadian citizenship was also revoked but later restored.
[209]   I. Teotonio, 'Toronto 18 terrorist freed after guilty plea', *Toronto Star*, 27 February 2010, at: https://bit.ly/3CaFp4z.
[210]   I. Austen, 'At Canada terror trial, the accused take on a less sinister cast', *The New York Times*, 25 September 2008.

in the case, as 'a few fries short of a happy meal', Mr Yogakrishnan is said to have suggested that the group convert the Aboriginal peoples in Canada to Islam, and then offer them control of Quebec city and Montreal in exchange for killing Quebecers.[211]

The jury trial of the three co-accused lasted for nine weeks and involved at least thirty pre-trial rulings. One pre-trial ruling divided one of the counts of the indictment (for participation in a terrorist group), as the original indictment had grouped together the co-accused who had splintered into new groups due to ideological rifts.[212] Charges against seven of the accused were stayed or dropped, largely as a result of sympathetic testimony by Mubin Shaikh.[213] A judge in the Ontario Superior Court of Justice (sitting as a Youth Justice Court) rejected suggestions by a prosecutor in the case that Shaikh had lied to protect the child defendants.[214]

4.3.3 The Prosecution of Terrorism in El Salvador

El Salvador adopted a dedicated terrorism law in 2006.[215] The law was modelled on the 2001 USA PATRIOT Act,[216] adopted in the aftermath of the 9/11 attacks in New York and Washington.[217] The then attorney general, Luis Antonio Martinez Gonzalez, proposed to use the law against gang members following the murder of an officer of the Anti-Extortion Unit in 2014.[218] In justifying such a change, he declared: 'Assassinating police officers, prosecutors, soldiers, judges, throwing grenades, assassinating hardworking and honourable people, it is not simply crime, it is terrorism. The gangs are causing terror in the population. That is why I have designated them as terrorists and that is how they should be treated.'[219]

Thus, in 2015, El Salvador redefined 'terrorist groups' to include those that use 'violent or inhumane methods with the express purpose of instilling terror, insecurity, or alarm within the population', or to 'assume the exercise of powers that belong to the sovereignty of the states or systematically affect the fundamental rights of the population or part of it'.[220] In response to a constitutional law challenge, the Supreme Court issued a ruling classifying Mara Salvatrucha (MS-13), La Mara 18 (also called Barrio 18 or 18th Street), and other gangs as terrorists due to their attempts to 'arrogate the exercise of legal authority' from the State.[221] In April 2022, it was made

---

[211] S. Pazzano, 'Students' insults upset spy', Sun Media, 4 July 2008, cited in H. Ramadan and J. Shantz (eds.), *Manufacturing Phobias: The Political Production of Fear in Theory and Practice*, University of Toronto Press, Toronto, 2016, p. 269.

[212] Nesbitt and Hagg, 'An Empirical Study of Terrorism Prosecutions in Canada', p. 596, note 10.

[213] CBC News, 'Toronto 18: Key events in the case'.

[214] Ontario Superior Court of Justice (sitting as a Youth Justice Court), R. v. N.Y., 2008 CanLII 51935 (ON SC), para. 175.

[215] Ley Especial Contra Actos de Terrorismo, Decree No. 108 of 2006.

[216] This is abbreviated from the formal title of 'Uniting and Strengthening America by Providing Appropriate Tools Required to Intercept and Obstruct Terrorism'.

[217] K. Martinez, '¿Marero o Terrorista? Examining the Supreme Court of El Salvador's Designation of Gang Members as Terrorists', *Georgia Journal of International and Comparative Law*, Vol. 47 (2019), 683–97, at p. 688.

[218] J. Bargent, 'El Salvador to Wield Terror Laws Against Gangs', Insight Crime, 16 April 2014, at: https://bit.ly/3qn9Baa.

[219] M. Melendez-Vela, 'Las maras son terroristas', *El Tiempo Latino*, 5 August 2015, at: https://bit.ly/3oKdjtW.

[220] M. Lohmuller, 'El Salvador Now Using Anti-Terrorism Law to Tackle Gangs', Insight Crime, 12 August 2015, at: https://bit.ly/3MRsPw7.

[221] 'Por esto, son grupos terroristas las pandillas denominadas Mara Salvatrucha o MS-13 y la Pandilla 18 o Mara 18, y cualquier otra pandilla u organización criminal que busque arrogarse el ejercicio de las potestades pertenecientes al ámbito de la soberanía del Estado –v. gr., control territorial, así como el monopolio del ejercicio legítimo de la fuerza por parte de las diferentes instituciones que componen la justicia penal–, atemorizando, poniendo en grave riesgo o afectando sistemática e indiscriminadamente los derechos fundamentales de la población o de parte de ella; en consecuencia, sus jefes, miembros, colaboradores, apologistas y financistas, quedan comprendidos dentro del concepto de "terroristas", en sus diferentes grados y formas de participación, e independientemente de que tales

explicit that the law on the repression of terrorism encompasses the many drug gangs that operate in the country.[222] In another decree issued that month, the Legislative Assembly reduced the age of criminal responsibility for membership of terrorist groups from sixteen years to twelve.[223]

El Salvador reported in 2019 that the Office of the Attorney General recorded 190 trials for terrorist crimes that resulted in convictions and sentences in 2018. Of this total, 179 cases concerned terrorist organizations in violation of Article 13 of the 2006 Special Law Against the Acts of Terrorism; 3 concerned terrorist acts committed with weapons or explosives (Articles 14 and 15 of the law); 3 concerned attacks against internationally protected persons or public officials (Article 5 of the law); 2 concerned threats (Article 27 of the law); 1 concerned conceal-ment (Article 30 of the law); another concerned preparatory acts, incitement, and conspiracy (Article 31 of the law); and the final case concerned the armed occupation of towns, villages, and buildings (Article 6 of the law).[224]

The number of trials has increased manifold times since the proclamation of a state of emergency in late March 2022.[225] Indeed, with nearly one in fifty of its adult population behind bars, El Salvador has the highest incarceration rate in the world.[226] Since its instauration and through to the end of May 2023, at least 68,000 people had been jailed in El Salvador on the basis of alleged gang membership or collusion. Of this, at least 1,600 were children.[227] In February 2023, about 2,000 accused members of the MS-13 and 18th Street gangs were moved to the 40,000-capacity 'Terrorism Confinement Centre' (Centro de Confinamiento del Terrorismo, or CECOT for short), considered to be the largest prison in the Americas.[228]

At the time of writing, the state of emergency, which was initially declared for a period of thirty days, was still in force, having been prolonged by the Legislative Assembly each month. The decision to institute a state of emergency was a direct response from the president to the killings of ninety-two people over a single weekend across the country, seemingly most if not all at the hand of gang members.[229] Under its terms, suspects can be detained for up to fifteen days without being charged, instead of the constitutionally mandated seventy-two hours.[230] Detainees no longer have the right to legal counsel and the authorities have unfettered access to private communications.[231] Once charged, there is mandatory pre-trial detention for an unlimited period.[232] Yet, despite these exceptional powers, Human Rights Watch has reported widespread violations of fundamental human rights by the police, including arbitrary arrests, enforced disappearances, torture and other ill-treatment of detainees, and significant due-process

---

grupos armados u organizaciones delictivas tengan fines políticos, criminales, económicos (extorsiones, lavado de dinero, narcotráfico, etc.), o de otra índole'. Constitutional Chamber of the Supreme Court, Resolution 22-2007AC, 24 August 2015, at: https://bit.ly/3ITZoIz, p. 44; and see '"We Can Arrest Anyone We Want". Widespread Human Rights Violations Under El Salvador's "State of Emergency"', 7 December 2022, at: https://bit.ly/3oNqSsz.

[222] Art. 1, Decreto No. 341 (2022); see Human Rights Watch, 'El Salvador: Sweeping New Laws Endanger Rights', 8 April 2022, at: https://bit.ly/43HK6Pd.

[223] Art. 2, Decree No. 342 of 2022.

[224] 'Measures to eliminate international terrorism', Report of the Republic of El Salvador pursuant to UN General Assembly Resolution 73/211, New York, 2019, at: https://bit.ly/3IRMYkg, p. 2.

[225] Office of the UN High Commissioner for Human Rights (OHCHR), 'El Salvador – State of emergency', Press Briefing Notes, 2 June 2023, at: https://bit.ly/3N8fVLo.

[226] Reuters, 'El Salvador opens one of Latin America's largest prisons', NBC News, 2 February 2023, at: https://bit.ly/3ITnPWy.

[227] OHCHR, 'El Salvador – State of emergency'.

[228] Reuters (San Salvador), 'El Salvador moves suspected gang members to 40,000-capacity "megaprison"', The Guardian, 25 February 2023, at: https://bit.ly/3OMiB2G.

[229] Human Rights Watch, '"We Can Arrest Anyone We Want".

[230] R. Romo, 'El Salvador's false dilemma', CNN, 11 March 2023, at: https://bit.ly/3qqXOaV.

[231] M. Charles, 'How a weekend of mass murder stripped a nation of its rights', Daily Telegraph, 23 April 2023.

[232] Human Rights Watch, 'El Salvador: Sweeping New Laws Endanger Rights', 8 April 2022.

violations. 'In addition, the circumstances of many deaths in custody during the state of emergency suggest State responsibility for those deaths.'[233]

As one example of policing operations, in June 2022, seventeen-year-old Katia Márquez was at school with her friends in the town of Osicala in the east of the country when the police arrived and arrested her. They handcuffed her and put her in a car without explanation. 'The police say Katia was involved in an illegal gathering', her mother, Veronica Márquez, told a journalist working for the *Daily Telegraph*. 'But how can that be if she was at school?' She said that the prosecutors told her to 'stop asking why they arrested my daughter otherwise they would arrest me too'. A few weeks earlier, police had come to search the farm where they lived along with her fifteen-year-old nephew, who was also detained for two weeks. They wanted information on local gang leaders. 'This was information we didn't have. We have nothing to do with gangs.' But the police did not believe them and threatened to take her daughter and nephew if she did not cooperate with them.[234]

It is sometimes suggested that while armed gangs and terrorist groups share 'common characteristics', they can – and should – be differentiated.[235] Writing on this issue specifically with respect to El Salvador, Martinez cites 'divergent motivations' as the basis for such a clear distinction: 'gangs are motivated by profit whereas terrorist organizations are motivated by politics'.[236] She further claimed: 'According to the United States, these gangs are not terrorists.'[237] While, arguably, this may have been true at the time of writing, it is certainly no longer the case. Thus, in February 2023, the US Department of Justice announced that three high-ranking MS-13 leaders had been arrested on terrorism (and racketeering) charges. The Justice Department stated that

> the defendants have engaged in a litany of violent terrorist activities aimed at influencing the government of El Salvador (GOES) policy and to obtain benefits and concessions from the GOES; targeting GOES law enforcement and military officials; employing terrorist tactics such as the use of Improvised Explosive Devices ('IEDs') and grenades; operating military-style training camps for firearms and explosives; using public displays of violence to intimidate civilian populations; using violence to obtain and control territory; and manipulating the electoral process in El Salvador. Several of these defendants have played prominent roles in MS-13's past and current negotiations with the GOES.
>
> Further, these defendants authorized and directed violence in the United States, Mexico, and elsewhere as part of a concerted effort to expand MS-13's influence and territorial control. As the leaders of the MS-13 transnational criminal organization, these defendants were an integral part of the leadership chain responsible for supervising MS-13 cliques in the United States that engaged in extreme violence, including countless murders, attempted murders, assaults, and related offenses.[238]

In a report issued in December 2022, Human Rights Watch called on the El Salvadorian authorities to end the state of emergency; to increase the age of criminal responsibility to fourteen years or above, 'consistent with international human rights standards'; to derogate the

---

[233]   Human Rights Watch, '"We Can Arrest Anyone We Want"'.
[234]   Charles, 'How a weekend of mass murder stripped a nation of its rights'.
[235]   See, e.g., G. I. Wilson and J. P. Sullivan, 'On Gangs, Crime, and Terrorism', *Indian Strategic Knowledge Online*, Vol. 9 (2007), 1–19, at: https://bit.ly/3CaD89u.
[236]   Martinez, '¿Marero o Terrorista?', p. 688.
[237]   Ibid., p. 689.
[238]   US Department of Justice, 'Three High-Ranking MS-13 Leaders Arrested on Terrorism and Racketeering Charges', Press Release, Office of Public Affairs, Washington DC, 23 February 2023, at: https://bit.ly/3P1E33A.

140 *Prosecution of Terrorism Suspects*

2022 reforms to the Special Law Against Terrorist Acts; and to narrow the definitions of terrorism.[239] There was, though, little evidence that any of these calls would be heeded.

4.3.4 *The Prosecution of Terrorism in Mexico*

In Mexico, domestic terrorism is considered to exist when anyone intentionally attacks the life or physical or emotional integrity of people, such that it produces 'alarm, fear, or terror in the population or in a group or sector of it'.[240] In contrast to El Salvador, however, Mexico has not sought to use or repurpose its terrorism laws to capture the salient actions of the drug cartels. At the time of writing, the pressure to do something towards this was mounting, at least indirectly, as a result of legislative action in its northern neighbour. On 8 March 2023, two US Senators, Rick Scott (Florida) and Roger Marshall (Kansas), introduced a Drug Cartel Terrorist Designation Bill,[241] aiming at the formal designation of certain Mexican drug cartels as Foreign Terrorist Organizations.[242]

Such a designation would make it an offence under US law knowingly to provide 'material support or resources' to the cartel to enter the United States as well as to prohibit any foreign citizen from entering the United States who was a member of one of the stipulated cartels, who was formally associated with the organization, or who had 'engaged in terrorist activity' relating to that organization.[243] The Bill's introduction followed the news that two of four American citizens kidnapped in Tamaulipas, a Mexican state over the border from Brownsville, Texas, had been killed by their captors.[244] Following the announcement of the proposed Bill, Brian Michael Jenkins, a Senior Adviser to the President of the RAND Corporation, observed that designating new terrorist organizations 'has become the go-to response to novel national security challenges in recent years' and questioned what law enforcement benefits such a designation would bring.[245]

Of greater concern was the proposal by Republican Senator for South Carolina, Lindsey Graham, that Congress should authorize the use of military force to destroy drug laboratories in Mexico. Jenkins observed that the Government of Mexico 'might be forgiven for not seeing the distinction between US destruction of drug labs and an invasion'. He acknowledged that such bellicose talk in Washington might encourage the Mexican government to do more to bring the situation within its own borders under control.[246] But he cautioned that US missile strikes 'could easily escalate into a broader conflict, making a terrible situation even worse. In response to attacks on their leadership and threats to their livelihood, any self-imposed constraints on attacking Americans will erode. Drug cartels could easily turn into real terrorist organizations.'[247]

---

[239] Human Rights Watch, '"We Can Arrest Anyone We Want"'.

[240] Art. 139(I), Federal Criminal Code of Mexico.

[241] R. Scott, 'Sens. Rick Scott, Roger Marshall Reintroduce Drug Cartel Terrorist Designation Act', Press release, Washington DC, 8 March 2023, at: https://bit.ly/45PrYVt.

[242] The same Bill was introduced a week later in the House of Representatives. C. Roy, 'Rep. Roy reintroduces bill to designate cartels as terrorist organizations', Press release, Washington DC, 13 March 2023, at: https://bit.ly/43K8AHm.

[243] The Reynosa/Los Metros faction of the Gulf Cartel; the Cartel Del Noreste faction of Los Zetas; the Jalisco New Generation Cartel; and the Sinaloa Cartel.

[244] J. Campbell, A. Alvarado, K. Suarez, C. Alvarado, and E. Levenson, '2 Americans kidnapped in Mexico found dead and 2 found alive, officials say', CNN, 8 March 2023, at: https://bit.ly/3qv8nJI.

[245] B. M. Jenkins, 'Should Mexico's Drug Cartels Be Designated Foreign Terrorist Organizations?', RAND Blog, 22 March 2023, at: https://bit.ly/3qvamOa.

[246] He recalled the unwritten rule among the cartels not to attack Americans. Indeed, following the attack in Matamoros, the Gulf Cartel delivered the five members allegedly responsible for the killing of two of the Americans to the police.

[247] Jenkins, 'Should Mexico's Drug Cartels Be Designated Foreign Terrorist Organizations?'.

4.3 Prosecution of Terrorism in the Americas

The US Department of State's 2021 Country Reports on Terrorism found 'no credible evidence indicating international terrorist groups established bases in Mexico, worked directly with Mexican drug cartels, or sent operatives via Mexico into the United States in 2021'.[248] This is not to understate the brutality of the drug cartels and the terror that they instil in the affected populations. In the ten years through to 2018, more than 100,000 people were killed in violence related to organized crime.[249] Writing on the issue that year, a US authority on terrorism, Phillips, while acknowledging that the cartels did carry out bombings and target political figures, acts which fit a classical definition of terrorism, preferred to talk of terrorist *tactics* and not terrorism per se.[250]

There have, however, been linkages between the drug cartels and the proposed prosecution of terrorism in Mexico under domestic law in the past. One of these was indirect. On 25 August 2011, Gilberto Martinez Vera and Maria de Jesus Bravo Pagola each posted information on social media saying that shootouts and kidnappings by drug gangs were happening near schools in Veracruz, the eponymous eastern coastal state's biggest city. 'I can confirm this, at the Jorge Arroyo school in the Carranza district, five children have been taken away by an armed group. Total psychosis in the area', Mr Martinez Vera, a forty-eight-year-old teacher, is said to have tweeted. He went on to say that he had confirmation of the kidnappings from his sister-in-law whose children attended the school. At the same time, according to the authorities, Ms Bravo Pagola, a former government official, allegedly wrote that a helicopter had opened fire at another school while the children were on their break. 'Confirmed and corroborated', her Facebook post reportedly said.[251]

The posts were later deleted. And none of those averred events proved to be true. But more than twenty car accidents happened amid the hysteria, according to the Secretary of the Interior for Veracruz State. The rumours about the drug gang attacks so angered Veracruz Governor Javier Duarte that he tweeted that he would be seeking terrorism charges against Mr Martinez Vera and Ms Bravo Pagola. On 26 August, they were both arrested and charged with 'terrorism and sabotage'.[252] The two defendants denied the charges, saying they had only resent information that was already circulating on social media sites. After the state legislature passed a new offence of 'disturbing public order' in direct response to the case, it was announced that the terrorism charges were being dropped. 'Since there is now legislation that defines the conduct of the two people who caused disturbances, prosecutors are dropping the criminal action', Governor Duarte wrote on his Twitter account. The maximum penalty for the terrorism charge would have been thirty years' imprisonment.[253]

But on the same day, as panic erupted in Veracruz, an arson attack by members of a drug cartel on a casino in the northern city of Monterrey killed fifty-two people. The then president of Mexico, Felipe Calderon, termed it an act of terror, declaring publicly that it was the work of 'true terrorists'.[254] That was the first time President Calderon had used such language in the drugs conflict, despite his heavily militarized response to the problem.[255]

---

[248] US Department of State, 'Country Reports on Terrorism 2021: Mexico', Bureau of Counterterrorism, Washington DC, 2022, at: https://bit.ly/3qvLKot.

[249] In 2019, the first year of the current federal government under President Andrés Manuel López Obrador, records were again broken in Mexico, with the most intentional homicides ever recorded: 29,458. P. Martínez, 'Calderón y Peña Ejercieron "Terrorismo de Estado": CNDH', *Corriente Alterna*, 14 December 2020, at: https://bit.ly/43iR5hA.

[250] B. J. Phillips, 'Terrorist Tactics by Criminal Organizations: The Mexican Case', *Perspectives on Terrorism*, Vol. 12, No. 1 (2018), 46–63.

[251] BBC, 'Mexico "Twitter terrorism" charges cause uproar', 6 September 2011, at: https://bit.ly/42ik1oE.

[252] Ibid.

[253] BBC, 'Mexico "Twitter terrorism" charges dropped', 22 September 2011, at: https://bit.ly/3MP1fzu.

[254] BBC, 'Six moments in the Calderon presidency', 30 November 2012, at: https://bit.ly/45LAuoa.

[255] BBC, 'Mexico "Twitter terrorism" charges cause uproar'. Indeed, in 2011, a famed Mexican poet, Javier Sicilia, speaking to cabinet members of the Calderón government on behalf of the Movement for Peace with Justice and

142 · *Prosecution of Terrorism Suspects*

Ten years later, though, Mr Calderon was himself the subject of terrorism allegations. In 2021, Mexican activist Flavio Sosa, the former president of the Popular Assembly of the Peoples of Oaxaca (APPO), filed a complaint against the former president for alleged treason and terrorism financing.[256] In January 2023, three years after being arrested, the trial of Genaro García Luna, Mexico's federal Secretary of Public Security during the Calderón administration, began in the Eastern District Court of New York. Mr García Luna's trial was taking place in the same courtroom where 'El Chapo' – Joaquín Guzmán – was sentenced to life imprisonment in 2019.[257] Mr García Luna was charged with cocaine trafficking, organized crime, and making false statements, charges that involved a minimum of ten years in jail and up to life imprisonment upon conviction. The District Attorney's Office claimed he had been collaborating with the Sinaloa Cartel for almost two decades. Mr Calderón said that he had no idea of any links between Mr García Luna and any drug cartel.[258] After a four-week trial, Mr García Luna was convicted on all five counts of the indictment.[259] None pertained to terrorism.

4.3.5 *The Prosecution of Terrorism in the United States*

The United States has prosecuted almost 10,000 people for domestic terrorism offences (including internal security cases that could constitute terrorism, such as the 6 January 2021 Capitol Breach) since 1998, as Figure 4.1 illustrates. There was a huge increase in the number of prosecutions in 2002 (from around 100 the previous year to more than 1,200), while prosecutions in 2021 and 2022 (at around 700) were the highest since 2005.[260]

A further 982 individuals have been prosecuted by the US Department of Justice for international terrorism since the 9/11 attacks, most of whom were charged with material support for terrorism. All but seven were either convicted or pleaded guilty to the charges.[261] More than one in three of terrorism defendants were caught in Federal Bureau of Investigation (FBI) 'sting' operations. Starting in 2014, there was a dramatic rise in terrorism prosecutions relating to Islamic State.[262] As discussed in Section 4.3.2.9, in October 2022, the first corporate prosecution for material support to terrorism resulted in a guilty plea from a French company in a New York district court.

Dignity, said: 'Your decisions [to use the military to fight drug trafficking], in addition to generating more violence and terror, are provoking the rise of paramilitary groups who, in this rarefied and atrocious atmosphere, feel authorized to practice, killing more Mexicans with impunity.' F. Rosen, 'The President, the PRI, and the Poet', Nacla, 18 October 2011, at: https://bit.ly/43F6gBw.

[256] Europa Press, 'Denuncian a Felipe Calderón por traición a la patria y terrorismo', Excelsior, 16 March 2021, at: https://bit.ly/3OYLTuW.

[257] E. Camhaji, 'Cartel trial of former Mexican security chief Genaro García Luna implicates ex-president Calderón', *El Pais*, 18 January 2023, at: https://bit.ly/420BfAH.

[258] Ibid.

[259] US Attorney's Office, Eastern District of New York, 'The Once-Highest Ranking Law Enforcement Official in Mexico Is Now a Convicted Felon', Press release, New York, 21 February 2023, at: https://bit.ly/430s2JZ; see also Reuters, 'Mexico's former drugs tsar Genaro Garcia Luna convicted for aiding El Chapo cartel', *The Guardian*, 21 February 2023, at: https://bit.ly/3NaQo4o.

[260] TRAC Immigration, 'Prosecutions for National Security/Terrorism and Domestic Terrorism Remain High in FY 2022', 10 March 2022, at: https://bit.ly/3IXP963.

[261] Of the total, defendants pleaded guilty to charges while 206 were found guilty at trial. Three were acquitted and four had the charges dropped or dismissed. 'Trial and Terror', The Intercept, Data last updated on 14 November 2022, at: https://bit.ly/3OYpA8K. For a useful review of how investigatory approach and policy prosecutorial have changed since 9/11, see C. A. Shields, K. R. Damphousse, and B. L. Smith, 'How 9/11 Changed the Prosecution of Terrorism', in M. J. Morgan (ed.), *The Impact of 9/11 and the New Legal Landscape: The Day that Changed Everything?*, Palgrave Macmillan, New York, 2009, 124–44.

[262] 'Trial and Terror', The Intercept, Data last updated on 14 November 2022.

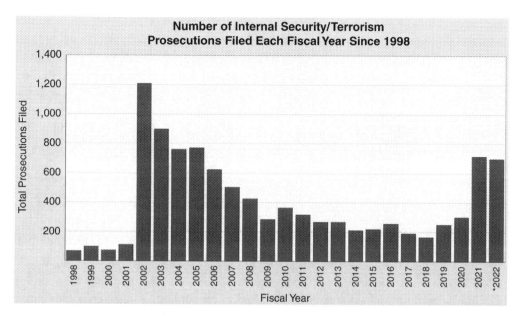

FIGURE 4.1 Recorded prosecutions for terrorism in the United States in 1998–2022

Writing in 2009, Shields, Damphousse, and Smith argued that the most profound policy change in relation to prosecutions was a redirection during the George W. Bush administration to intercepting and disrupting terrorist groups before they could launch attacks even if that meant the filing of lesser charges.[263] This led to a dramatic increase in federal terrorism prosecutions: more in the three years following the 9/11 attacks than in the previous twenty years combined.[264]

4.3.5.1 The Oklahoma City Bombing

Timothy McVeigh was executed by lethal injection on 11 June 2001, three months before the 9/11 attacks. Mr McVeigh, aged thirty-three years at the time of his death, was responsible for the – then – deadliest domestic terrorism attack in US history. His bombing of a federal building in Oklahoma City on 19 April 1995 killed 168 people and injured a further 680. The fatalities included nineteen children in a day-care centre on the second floor of the building.[265] McVeigh, a US army veteran who had fought in the 1991 Gulf War, wanted revenge against the federal government for, in particular, the 1993 siege at Waco, Texas, that resulted in the deaths of eighty-two Branch Davidians led by David Koresh.[266] The Oklahoma City bombing occurred two years to the day after the Mount Carmel Center at Waco burned to the ground.[267]

With the help of an accomplice, Terry Nichols, McVeigh constructed a 2,300 kg bomb composed of ammonium nitrate and nitromethane (a form of fuel oil). He drove a rented truck containing the bomb to the front of the Alfred P. Murrah Federal Building just as its offices

---

[263] Shields, Damphousse, and Smith, 'How 9/11 Changed the Prosecution of Terrorism', pp. 124, 130.
[264] Ibid., p. 140.
[265] FBI, 'Oklahoma City Bombing', undated but accessed 1 June 2023, at: https://bit.ly/3sdFEGB.
[266] History.com, 'Waco Siege', updated 21 August 2018, at: https://bit.ly/3IVPN3O.
[267] Mr McVeigh had travelled to Waco during the siege to show his support for those resisting the federal law enforcement agencies. Four federal agents were killed during the course of the siege.

were opening in the morning; he had already initiated the fuze. Just after 9 o'clock, a massive blast destroyed much of the front of the nine-storey building. The FBI's Oklahoma City Field Office, located five miles north-west, was shaken by the ferocity of the explosion.[268]

The investigation into the bombing would ultimately involve a total of 2,000 agents. The vehicle identification number of a rear axle found in the wreckage led the FBI to identify the rental truck and the agency in Junction city, Kansas. McVeigh had rented the truck using an alias but agency employees interviewed by FBI personnel helped a sketch artist to portray the named renter, 'Robert Kling'. When the sketch was shown to people in the area, the manager of a local motel identified it as McVeigh. In fact, he was already in the custody of law enforcement officials in Noble county, Oklahoma, having been arrested by a state trooper less than two hours after the bombing on unconnected offences: driving without licence plates and possession of an illegal firearm.[269]

On 10 August 1995, McVeigh was indicted on eleven federal counts in relation to the Oklahoma city bombing: conspiracy to use a weapon of mass destruction, use of a weapon of mass destruction, and destruction with the use of explosives; and eight counts of first-degree murder for the deaths of law enforcement officers. Thus, none of the charges specifically concerned terrorism.[270] The prosecution's case against Mr McVeigh was strong but not watertight, given serious mistakes in forensic analysis by the FBI. A report by the Department of Justice had concluded that an FBI forensic investigator lacked an adequate scientific basis for stating that the bomb comprised ammonium nitrate mixed with fuel oil. The report said that the investigator reached his conclusion in part by reasoning backward from the fact that a receipt for ammonium nitrate fertilizer had been found at Mr Nichols' house. The report also left open the question of whether Mr McVeigh's clothing might have been contaminated with nitroglycerine and PETN in the FBI laboratory.[271] The defence was also able to suggest a link to Islamic extremists. Indeed, as it followed the World Trade Center bombing in New York two years earlier, the media and many Americans assumed that the attack was the handiwork of Middle Eastern terrorists.[272] But in 1997, a jury in Denver first convicted McVeigh of the bombing and later sentenced him to death.[273]

The federal government had also charged Terry Nichols with advance knowledge of the bombing and participation in the plot. The judge in the case had ordered that McVeigh and Nichols were to be tried separately – the first time he had ever agreed to sever the cases of two defendants – with McVeigh's trial to begin first. After receiving authorization from Attorney General Janet Reno to do so, prosecutors announced that they would seek the death penalty in both cases. In 1998, Nichols, who had been convicted the previous year, a few months after McVeigh, was sentenced to life imprisonment without parole. The jury in his case had deadlocked on whether to order execution, perhaps swayed by his apparent remorse in court and owing to the fact that he was not in Oklahoma on the day of the bombing.[274]

---

[268] FBI, 'The Oklahoma City Bombing: 20 Years Later', 16 April 2015, at: https://bit.ly/3oOgqkA.

[269] FBI, 'Oklahoma City Bombing'.

[270] US Court of Appeals for the Tenth Circuit, *United States* v. *Timothy James McVeigh*, Case No. 97–1287 (decided 8 September 1998), at: https://bit.ly/3OYmS35.

[271] J. Collins, 'Oklahoma city: The weight of evidence', *Time*, 28 April 1997, at: https://bit.ly/430Nte5.

[272] FBI, 'Oklahoma City Bombing'.

[273] Fearing a fair trial was not possible in Oklahoma, US District Judge Richard Matsch had moved the trial from Oklahoma.

[274] D. O. Linder, 'The Oklahoma City Bombing & The Trial of Timothy McVeigh', University of Missouri, Kansas, 2006, at: https://bit.ly/3OXBHTF. In January 2000, Nichols was brought back to Oklahoma to face state charges: 160 counts of first-degree murder. He was convicted in 2004 on all charges but a jury again deadlocked on the death penalty.

Michael Fortier, another army friend of McVeigh, agreed to assist prosecutors in return for not facing conspiracy charges, a pledge of leniency for his admitted crimes, and the promise that his wife would not be charged.[275] He was convicted of failing to inform the authorities of the plot, lying to federal agents after the bombing, and selling stolen guns in order to help raise money to finance the attack. Fortier's role in helping to convict McVeigh was claimed to have been crucial to the prosecution case.[276] After serving ten-and-a-half years of a twelve-year sentence in a federal prison, Fortier was released and he and his wife went into witness protection.[277]

Despite considerable evidence linking a number of white supremacists to the bombing, no one else was prosecuted for what was, until 11 September 2001, the deadliest act of terrorism on American soil.[278] But after the bombing, the US Congress adopted new federal legislation allowing domestic terrorism to be subject to a sentence enhancement upon conviction.[279] The Criminal Code pertains to unlawful acts 'calculated to influence or affect the conduct of government by intimidation or coercion, or to retaliate against government conduct.'[280] A similar possibility of sentence enhancement already existed for international terrorism following the 1993 World Trade Center bombings,[281] which were carried out by, among others, Ramzi Yousef, said to be a nephew of Khalid Sheikh Mohammed. Yousef is serving a term of 240 years of imprisonment at the ADX 'Supermax' prison at Florence, Colorado.[282]

4.3.5.2 The Boston Marathon Bombings (2013)

On 15 April 2013, two bombs in pressure cookers placed near the finishing line of the Boston Marathon killed three people and injured at least 264.[283] The bombs had been filled with nails and ball bearings to increase the number and extent of injuries.[284] After an intensive investigation and search over the following four days, two brothers – Tamerlan and Dzhokhar Tsarnaev – were hunted by police.[285]

A chaotic shoot-out took place on 19 April in Watertown, a city in the Greater Boston area.[286] This followed a carjacking of an SUV by the brothers who had the owner hostage. He managed to escape and raise the alert when they stopped for petrol. In the exchange of fire, the two men

---

[275] His wife was aware of the planned bombing and had laminated the fake driver's license that McVeigh used to rent the truck in which he assembled the bomb.

[276] Grand jury indictments of McVeigh and Nichols came three days after Michael and Lori Fortier presented their testimony.

[277] '10 Years Later, OKC Bombing Figure Walks Free', Southern Poverty Law Center (SPLC), 2006 Spring Issue, 19 April 2006, at: https://bit.ly/3OXzDuz.

[278] Linder, 'The Oklahoma City Bombing & the Trial of Timothy McVeigh'.

[279] Invoking the terrorism enhancement typically adds about fifteen years in prison to a defendant's recommended sentence and sets the minimum calculation at seventeen and a half years.

[280] 18 USC §2332b(g)(5)(A), text at: https://bit.ly/3oQ8uPM.

[281] J. Gerstein, 'Why DOJ Is Avoiding Domestic Terrorism Sentences for Jan. 6 Defendants', Politico, 4 January 2022, at: https://bit.ly/3JoyI9c.

[282] CNN, 'Terror on Trial: Life in Supermax's "Bombers Row"', 2001, at: https://bit.ly/42mSVgh.

[283] CNN, 'Boston Marathon Terror Attack Fast Facts', updated 7 April 2023, at: https://bit.ly/3MWkSWm.

[284] J. Russell and T. Farragher, '102 Hours in Pursuit of Marathon Suspects', Boston Globe, 28 April 2013, at: https://bit.ly/3oWRQOi.

[285] In 2011, the Russian Intelligence Service, the FSB, had earlier warned the US authorities that Tamerlan Tsarnaev was a terrorist, following his travel to Daghestan and association with militants there. Reuters, 'Russia warned U.S. about Boston Marathon bomb suspect Tsarnaev: report', 25 March 2014, at: https://bit.ly/3qs2Gwc; and A. Taylor, 'The Mystery of Tamerlan Tsarnaev's Trip to Dagestan', Business Insider, 20 April 2013, at: https://bit.ly/3OZTfim.

[286] M. Schone, A. Blankstein, and T. Winter, 'Too Many Guns: How Shootout with Bombing Suspects Spiraled into Chaos', NBC News, 15 April 2014, at: https://bit.ly/468im8q.

threw four pipe bombs and a pressure-cooker bomb at local law enforcement officials and fired fifty-six rounds from a handgun. Law enforcement fired a total of 159 rounds at the two suspects, one of which hit a police officer.[287] Tamerlan, the elder brother, was seriously injured during the exchange of fire. Dzhokhar then drove over his seriously injured brother in making his escape from the scene.

Dzhokhar, nineteen years old at the time, was finally arrested that night. He had been hiding in a boat only two blocks away from the shootout. Law enforcement fired 100 rounds into the boat, wrongly believing Dzhokhar had either opened fire or waved a gun at them, seriously wounding him. Dzhokhar had scrawled a note on the interior of the boat claiming that the bombings were revenge for US military action in Afghanistan and Iraq, terming the victims of the bombing 'collateral damage', in the same way Muslims have been in the US-led wars.[288]

The conduct clearly fitted the definition in US law of domestic terrorism, although this was not among the charges first laid against Dzhokhar Tsarnaev. These concerned, initially, using a weapon of mass destruction and malicious destruction of private property that caused death, both federal crimes subject to the death penalty.[289] The prosecution eventually filed a total of thirty counts of federal terrorism charges and related crimes against Mr Tsarnaev.[290] These included the offence committed, 'after substantial planning and premeditation to cause the death of a person' and to commit 'an act of terrorism'. This serves as an aggravating factor for homicide under the US Criminal Code.[291] Federal charges were necessary for any sentence of death to be imposed upon conviction because Massachusetts law had abolished capital punishment for all crimes under state law.

Following his arrest, Mr Tsarnaev was taken to Boston's Beth Israel Deaconess Medical Center, the facility where several marathon bombing victims were recuperating from surgeries and amputations. Tsarnaev had multiple gunshot wounds and his injuries included being shot through the mouth.[292] Before either a lawyer was assigned to him or he was mirandized, he was questioned by FBI agents for twenty-seven hours. The agents told him he needed to answer questions before he would be allowed to speak with a lawyer, in order 'to ensure that the public safety was no longer in danger from other individuals, devices, or otherwise'.[293] As he was unable to speak because of his injuries and the surgery, he wrote his answers to the agents' questions.[294] When being questioned, he sought to invoke his right to a lawyer repeatedly.[295]

During interrogation, Tsarnaev disclosed that in the aftermath of the Boston Marathon bombing, he and his brother had intended to drive to New York City to bomb Times Square.[296] The

[287] Z. Enwemeka, 'DA: It's "Highly Likely" MBTA Officer Donohue Was Wounded by Gunfire from Fellow Officer', *WBUR*, updated 2 June 2015, at: https://bit.ly/43LVdGA.

[288] 'Boston Bombings Suspect Dzhokhar Tsarnaev Left Note in Boat He Hid in, Sources Say', *CBS News*, 16 May 2013, at: https://bit.ly/43qTXJj.

[289] G. G. Nathan, 'How the Boston Marathon Bombing Is a Federal Crime', Geoffrey G. Nathan Law Offices, undated but accessed 1 June 2023, at: https://bit.ly/3MRTYz4.

[290] *United States* v. *Tsarnaev*, Case No. 13-CR-10200-GAO-1 (D. Mass, 27 June 2013) (criminal docket).

[291] 18 US Code §3592(c)(9), text at: https://bit.ly/30OMohZ.

[292] B. Schwartzapfel, 'Tending to Tsarnaev', The Marshall Project, 11 March 2015, at: https://bit.ly/3Cidksi.

[293] *United States* v. *Tsarnaev*, Case No. 13-CR-10200-GAO (D. Mass, 7 May 2014), Defence's Motion to Suppress Statements, p. 5.

[294] Ibid., p. 4.

[295] B. Ching, 'Mirandizing Terrorism Suspects? The Public Safety Exception, the Rescue Doctrine, and Implicit Analogies to Self-Defense, Defense of Others, and Battered Woman Syndrome', *Catholic University Law Review*, Vol. 64, No. 3 (Spring 2015), 613–47, at: https://bit.ly/3Ph70cj, at p. 642.

[296] G. Botelho and J. Levs, 'Boston Bombing Suspects Planned Times Square Attack, Bloomberg Says', *CNN*, 26 April 2013, at: https://bit.ly/3OVrUoI.

4.3 Prosecution of Terrorism in the Americas

prosecution initially sought to use this and other statements he made in the hospital at his subsequent trial but relented before the judge ruled on a defence motion to suppress them.[297] The day after the first criminal charges were filed in the case, a federal magistrate informed Dzhokhar Tsarnaev, still in hospital, of the charges against him and gave him the Miranda warnings. By then he had been in custody for more than sixty hours, reportedly the longest period for any criminal suspect to be held without being advised of his Miranda rights.[298] Tsarnaev stopped speaking as soon as his rights were read to him.[299]

At the end of his trial on 8 April 2015, Dzhokhar Tsarnaev was found guilty on all charges and on 14 May the jury imposed the death sentence by lethal injection upon him.[300] In July 2020, however, the Federal Appeals Court for the First Circuit reversed the sentence, holding that the trial court had failed to adequately question jurors about their exposure to pre-trial publicity about the case and that the trial judge had unconstitutionally prevented Mr Tsarnaev's lawyers from presenting evidence supporting the mitigating circumstance that he had acted under the domination of his violent and radicalized older brother, Tamerlan. But on 4 March 2022, in a six-to-three decision authored by Justice Clarence Thomas, the Supreme Court reinstated Tsarnaev's multiple death sentences and remanded the case back to the US Court of Appeals for the First Circuit for renewed consideration.[301] The Supreme Court held that trial judges had significant discretion during voir-dire on the questioning of potential jurors and that the district court had acted within its discretion to exclude evidence that Tamerlan had previously murdered three people in Waltham, Massachusetts, in an act of violent jihad. He had done so as the evidence was 'without any probative value'.[302]

Reconsideration of the case at appellate level would still need to consider the fact that two of the jurors failed to disclose evidence suggesting that they were biased against Tsarnaev. That evidence showed that the forewoman had tweeted or retweeted about the bombing twenty-two times – including commenting on the psychological impact of being at work while her family was 'locked down' during the manhunt for Tsarnaev – and then concealed that information during jury selection when asked about her social media activity. At one point she had described Tsarnaev as 'that piece of garbage'.[303] A second juror had violated the court's order to stay off social media and had posted on Facebook the fact that he was in the jury pool for the case. In response, one friend urged him to 'play the part so u get on the jury then send him to jail where he will be taken care of', while another wrote, 'if you're really on jury duty, this guys [sic] got no shot in hell'. When the defence learned of those posts, Judge O'Toole refused to question the jurors about them and refused to remove them from the jury.[304] As of June 2023, more than ten years after the fatal bombing, Mr Tsarnaev was seeking to avoid the ultimate imposition of the

---

[297] Ching, 'Mirandizing Terrorism Suspects?', pp. 643–44.

[298] M. Clark, 'Now Charged, Boston Suspect Was Longest Held without Miranda Rights', *MSNBC*, 21 April 2013, at: https://bit.ly/3NggQtl.

[299] E. Fuchs, 'Judge Insisted on Miranda Rights for Boston Suspect and FBI "Was Not Happy"', *Business Insider*, 25 April 2013, at: https://bit.ly/3NenPDa.

[300] BBC, 'Boston bombing trial: Death sentence for Dzhokhar Tsarnaev', 16 May 2015, at: https://bit.ly/3CgBtzb.

[301] US Supreme Court, *United States* v. *Tsarnaev*, Certiorari to the United States Court of Appeals for the First Circuit, Case No. 20–443, decided 4 March 2022, at: https://bit.ly/42xQAil.

[302] Death Penalty Information Center, 'Supreme Court Overturns Appeals Court Decision Reversing Death Sentence in Boston Marathon Bombing', Washington DC, 7 March 2022, at: https://bit.ly/43mpqfl.

[303] Death Penalty Information Center, 'Federal Appeals Court Overturns Death Sentence in Boston Marathon Bombing', 3 August 2020, at: https://bit.ly/42HyIC5.

[304] Death Penalty Information Center, 'Supreme Court Overturns Appeals Court Decision Reversing Death Sentence in Boston Marathon Bombing'.

death penalty.[305] The case's return to an earlier stage of the appellate process was, though, thought likely to add 'years' to its journey through the courts.[306]

Law enforcement officials believed that the two brothers conspired alone, although two of their friends, both students from Kazakhstan, were convicted of obstruction of justice and conspiracy to obstruct justice. They had agreed 'to knowingly alter, destroy, conceal, and cover up tangible objects belonging to Dzhokhar Tsarnaev'. Dias Kadyrbayev was sentenced to six years' imprisonment at the beginning of June 2015,[307] while Azamat Tazhayakov was given three years' imprisonment as his sentence a few days later.[308] In addition, Robel Phillipos was found guilty in November 2014 on two counts of making false statements to federal investigators. He had denied seeing the two students removing the items.[309] He was sentenced to three years in prison. In 2018, upon release from prison, Dias Kadyrbayev was deported to Kazakhstan.[310] The wife of Tamerlan Tsarnaev was also investigated for her conduct leading up to the bombing,[311] although ultimately no charges were filed. The authorities suspected that Katherine Russell had gone with her husband to buy the pressure cookers used in the bombings.[312]

4.3.5.3 The US Capitol Breach (6 January 2021)

Five people died during or as a result of the violence in the Capitol on 6 January 2021. The violence has not – or at least not yet – resulted in terrorism charges, although the threat of a sentence enhancement has reportedly been wielded by prosecutors behind the scenes in some of the more serious cases.[313] But not every relevant charge against the rioters would even be subject to a terrorism enhancement. Under current federal law, fifty-seven offences are on this list, including hostage-taking, destroying an aircraft, using fire or explosives to destroy a building, and cyberattacks that create a threat to public health or impacts national security systems. Assaulting a police officer with a dangerous weapon, a felony charge which ordinarily carries a possible twenty-year sentence, is not included, nor is interfering with police during civil disorder, which can attract a five-year prison sentence on conviction.[314]

As of March 2023, more than two years after the violence, over 1,000 people had been indicted and charges against further individuals were expected.[315] On 8 March 2022, the first criminal trial of one of the leaders of the riot, Guy Reffitt, ended with a conviction. Mr Reffitt, a forty-nine-year -old Texan resident, never entered the Capitol buildings but was said by prosecutors to have helped to ignite the crowd into 'an unstoppable force'. His son, who had earlier tipped off the

---

[305] M. Casey, '10th anniversary of Boston Marathon bombing marked with somber ceremony', PBS Newshour, 15 April 2023, at: https://bit.ly/3MMPuJU.

[306] Death Penalty Information Center, 'Supreme Court Overturns Appeals Court Decision Reversing Death Sentence in Boston Marathon Bombing'.

[307] U.S. Attorney's Office, District of Massachusetts, 'Dias Kadyrbayev Sentenced to Six Years for Impeding the Boston Marathon Bombing Investigation', Press release, Boston, 2 June 2015, at: https://bit.ly/30TY6GE.

[308] R. Sanchez, 'Boston Marathon bomber's friends sentenced to prison', CNN, 5 June 2015, at: https://bit.ly/3WVIrU1.

[309] Ibid.

[310] Radio Free Europe/Radio Liberty, 'Boston Marathon Bomber's Friend Deported to Kazakhstan', November 2018, at: https://bit.ly/3MZ675d.

[311] M. S. Schmidt and S. F. Kovaleski, 'Investigators Obtain DNA from Widow of Bombing Suspect', The New York Times, 29 April 2013, at: https://bit.ly/3qHW1Os.

[312] B. Ross and M. McPhee, 'Boston Bombing Suspect's Widow under Investigation, Could Face Charges', ABC News, 4 March 2015, at: https://bit.ly/43DUzvu.

[313] Gerstein, 'Why DOJ is avoiding domestic terrorism sentences for Jan. 6 defendants'.

[314] Ibid.

[315] M. Anderson and N. McMillan, '1,000 people have been charged for the Capitol riot. Here's where their cases stand', NPR, 25 March 2023, at: https://bit.ly/3OTIlKB.

FBI about his plans, later testified against him.[316] Reffitt Sr was sentenced to seven years and three months in federal prison for civil disorder, obstruction of an official proceeding, entering and remaining on restricted grounds with a firearm, and obstruction of justice.[317] At the time of writing, the longest sentence for offences connected with the violence was given to ex-Proud Boys leader Enrique Tarrio, who was sentenced to twenty-two years' imprisonment for seditious conspiracy in September 2023. He had not been at the Capitol that day, having been arrested days earlier for vandalizing a Black Lives Matter banner at a historic Black church in Washington, DC, in 2020 but prosecutors argued that Mr Tarrio maintained command over Proud Boys members after his arrest and cheered on the group as its members stormed the Capitol.[318] The second longest sentence was given to Oath Keepers founder, Stewart Rhodes. He was found guilty of seditious conspiracy[319] in November 2022 and sentenced to eighteen years' imprisonment.[320]

The FBI continues to seek 'the public's assistance in identifying individuals who made unlawful entry into the US Capitol building and committed various other alleged criminal violations, such as destruction of property, assaulting law enforcement personnel, targeting members of the media for assault, and other unlawful conduct, on 6 January 2021, in Washington, DC'.[321]

4.3.5.4 Corporate Prosecutions for Terrorism

On 18 October 2022, the Department of Justice announced its first-ever prosecution of a corporation for material support to terrorism under Title 18 of the US Code, Section 2339B of the ATA. Lafarge SA, a French cement company, and its Syrian subsidiary, Lafarge Cement Syria SA, pleaded guilty to one count of conspiracy to provide material support to Islamic State and the al-Nusrah Front, both designated Foreign Terrorist Organizations, in connection with their business operations in Syria.[322] From August 2013 to October 2014, Lafarge made payments to Islamic State in order to be granted access to raw materials in territory under its control so that the company's cement plant at Jalabiyeh in northern Syria could continue to produce cement. Payments also allowed Lafarge employees and suppliers to pass safely through Islamic State and the al-Nusrah Front checkpoints on the roads leading to the plant. In addition, Islamic State agreed to impose costs on, and in some cases block the importation of, competing cement coming from Turkey.[323]

While most of the relevant conduct took place overseas, one of the payments was made through a New York intermediary bank. Lafarge attempted to conceal the scheme through

---

[316] BBC, 'The Capitol riot trial that tore a family apart', 2 August 2022, at: https://bit.ly/3qsVsbs.

[317] E. Neugeboren, 'Texan who prosecutors say "lit the match" of Jan. 6 riot sentenced to more than 7 years in prison', *The Texas Tribune*, 1 August 2022, at: https://bit.ly/3quEj15.

[318] I. Saric, 'Ex-Proud Boys leader Enrique Tarrio sentenced to 22 years in Jan. 6 case', Axios, updated 6 September 2023, at: https://bit.ly/3SAlZOr.

[319] 'If two or more persons in any State or Territory, or in any place subject to the jurisdiction of the United States, conspire to overthrow, put down, or to destroy by force the Government of the United States, or to levy war against them, or to oppose by force the authority thereof, or by force to prevent, hinder, or delay the execution of any law of the United States, or by force to seize, take, or possess any property of the United States contrary to the authority thereof, they shall each be fined under this title or imprisoned not more than twenty years, or both.' 18 USC 2384: Seditious conspiracy, at: https://bit.ly/43AWyjE.

[320] Associated Press, '2 more Oath Keepers are sentenced to prison terms for the Jan. 6 Capitol attack', *NPR*, 27 May 2023, at: https://bit.ly/3CedGjr.

[321] FBI, 'U.S. Capitol Violence', undated but accessed 1 June 202 at: https://bit.ly/3MUeAGD.

[322] See *United States* v. *Lafarge SA and Lafarge Cement Syria SA*, 22-CR-444 (Eastern District of New York, 2022), Docket No. 10 (Plea Agreement) and Docket No. 10–1 (Statement of Facts).

[323] Ibid., Docket No. 10, para. 15.

150   *Prosecution of Terrorism Suspects*

falsified records and the use of personal email addresses serviced by US-based providers.[324] In admitting its unlawful conduct, Lafarge SA agreed before the District Court for the Eastern District of New York to pay US$778 million in fines and forfeitures.[325] In a separate legal process in France, and after four years of litigation, the Paris Court of Appeal upheld the charges against the company for aiding and abetting crimes against humanity in May 2022, enforcing a French Supreme Court decision of September 2021.[326]

4.4 THE PROSECUTION OF TERRORISM IN ASIA AND THE MIDDLE EAST

4.4.1 *The Prosecution of Terrorism in Australia*

Under Australia's Criminal Code, a terrorist act is an act (or threat) that causes death or serious harm, or endangers a person, causes serious damage to property, causes a serious risk to the health or safety of the public, or seriously interferes with electronic systems affecting critical infrastructure. Any such act must be done both with the intention of advancing a political, religious, or ideological cause, and either to coerce or influence by intimidation the Government of Australia or another State, or to intimidate the public or a section of the public.[327] In December 2005, Parliament enacted the 2004 ATA, making a number of amendments to the formulation of certain terrorism offences and introducing new offences of providing training to or receiving training from a terrorist organization.[328]

Australia reported in 2015 that since the 9/11 attacks against the United States in 2001, thirty-five prosecutions of terrorism offences had been mounted in Australia, resulting in twenty-six convictions.[329] The maximum sentence for the commission of a terrorist act under the law is life imprisonment.[330] There are no mandatory minimum sentences.

4.4.1.1 *Faheem Khalid Lodhi* v. *Regina* (2007)

Faheem Khalid Lodhi was the first individual to be convicted under the amended terrorism laws in Australia's Criminal Code. An architect by profession, he was accused of a plot in October 2003 to bomb the national electricity grid and/or military installations in Sydney. In June 2006, Mr Lodhi was convicted by jury at the New South Wales Supreme Court of three of the four charges: two counts of preparing for a terrorist attack and one count of possessing terrorist manuals on how to manufacture poison, detonators, explosives, and incendiary devices. Justice Anthony Whealy imposed a sentence of twenty years' imprisonment for seeking chemicals for the construction of an improvised explosive device (with a non-parole period of fifteen

---

[324] A. Jeffress, D. Bernstein, and V. Ponomarov, 'Takeaways From First Anti-Terrorism Act Prosecution Of A Co.', Arnold Porter, 30 January 2023, at: https://bit.ly/3IZFOe5.

[325] US Department of Justice, 'Lafarge Pleads Guilty to Conspiring to Provide Material Support to Foreign Terrorist Organizations', Press release, Office of Public Affairs, Washington DC, 18 October 2022, at: https://bit.ly/3WPHn3Q.

[326] European Center for Constitutional and Human Rights (ECCHR), 'Lafarge in Syria: Accusations of complicity in grave human rights violations', at: https://bit.ly/45TvZZ4. See also Trial International, 'Lafarge SA, Eric Olsen and others', 17 April 2023, at: https://bit.ly/3J1y4rN.

[327] S. 100.1, 1995 Criminal Code Act. The law provides, however, that a terrorist act does not cover engaging in advocacy, protest, dissent, or industrial action where there is no intention to cause harm to others.

[328] S. 20, Anti-terrorism Act 2004, Act No. 104 of 2004 (an Act to amend the law relating to foreign incursions and recruitment, terrorism offences and proceeds of crime, and for related purposes). The provision amended the Criminal Code.

[329] Government of Australia, Review of Australia's Counterterrorism Machinery, Department of the Prime Minister and Cabinet, 2015, at: https://bit.ly/3Nh2LvH, p. iv.

[330] S. 101.1(1), 1995 Criminal Code Act.

4.4 Prosecution of Terrorism in Asia and the Middle East

years), with shorter sentences for the other two offences, to run concurrently. In his remarks upon sentencing, Justice Whealy said that Mr Lodhi sought to advance a political, religious, or ideological cause, 'namely violent jihad' in order to 'instil terror into members of the public so that they could never again feel free from the threat of bombing in Australia'.[331]

One of the issues in the case was the preservation of national security. A substantial amount of evidence was heard *in camera*, with some witnesses concealed from the defendant and who provided testimony under pseudonyms.[332] This clearly impinges on the defendant's chance of receiving a fair trial. Nonetheless, the Court of Appeal upheld both the convictions and the sentences.[333] After his non-parole period expired in 2019, Mr Lodhi began seeking release on parole.[334] His attempt to gain release by application to the Federal Court was, however, rejected in September 2020.[335] If no parole was authorized beforehand, he was due to be released from prison on 21 April 2024.

4.4.1.2 *The Queen v. Khazaal (2012)*

Another important prosecution of an inchoate terrorism offence involved the case that came before the High Court of Australia (on appeal) in 2012. It concerned a defendant, Belal Khazaal, who had been released on appeal from prison following his conviction for having authored an electronic book (e-book) entitled *Provisions on the Rules of Jihad: Short Judicial Rulings and Organizational Instructions for Fighters and Mujahideen Against Infidels.*[336] The e-book included advice on assassination techniques and listed categories of assassination targets, including in Australia.

The authorities appealed the decision to overturn his original conviction at trial. Mr Khazaal sought to rely on his status as an accredited journalist and researcher with an academic interest in Islam to justify the development of the e-book, arguing that this evidence suggested a reasonable possibility that the book was not intended to facilitate assistance in a terrorist act. The High Court of Australia, however, held that insufficient evidence was adduced to support his contentions and he was convicted with making a document connected with assistance in a terrorist act as proscribed under the Criminal Code.[337] The Court sentenced him to twelve years' imprisonment, with a non-parole period of nine years.[338]

Mr Khazaal was released from the Supermax jail at Goulburn Correctional Centre in August 2020, having served his full sentence. Upon his release, the authorities successfully applied for him to be subject to control orders, which required him to wear a tracking device and restricted his movements and freedoms while he was reintegrated back into society.[339] The control orders included a prohibition on him contacting anyone who was presently in jail. Police subsequently alleged that several months after being freed from prison he twice attempted to make contact with Ali Al-Talebi, the first Australian to be convicted of funding terrorism when

---

[331] Remarks reported in ABC, 'Sydney terrorism suspect jailed for 20 years', 23 August 2006, at: https://bit.ly/3qDT5Tm.

[332] N. J. Broadbent, 'Faheem Khalid Lodhi v Regina [2007] NSWCCA 360', Case Notes, *Australian International Law Journal*, 2007, 227–37, at: https://bit.ly/3Nl9Tak, p. 234.

[333] Ibid., p. 227.

[334] H. Parkes-Hupton, 'Faheem Khalid Lodhi: Terrorist pens letter from jail in latest parole bid', *The Australian*, 26 August 2020, at: https://bit.ly/3J5Vo7N.

[335] S. Zemek, 'Australia's first terrorist Faheem Lodhi loses parole court bid', *NCA NewsWire*, 28 September 2020, at: https://bit.ly/43SmXJK.

[336] *The Queen v. Khazaal* (2012) 246 CLR 601.

[337] S. 101.5(1), 1995 Criminal Code Act.

[338] High Court of Australia, *The Queen v. Khazaal* [2012] HCA 26, 10 August 2012.

[339] Federal Court of Australia, *Booth v. Khazaal* [2020] FCA 1241, No. NSD 859 of 2020, 26 August 2020, at: https://bit.ly/3P3mWyw.

he was found guilty of sending AUS$6,000 to Pakistan. Mr Al-Talebi was sentenced to twelve years' imprisonment in 2017.[340]

4.4.1.3 The 2017 Queanbeyan Stabbings

Sometimes it is challenging to determine with certainty whether an attack results from a terrorism motivation or as a consequence of an acute mental health issue. This was the case in April 2017 in New South Wales, when two boys aged fifteen and sixteen years went on a rampage in Queanbeyan, a city in the south-east of Australia. The elder boy brutally and fatally stabbed a service station attendant before using his victim's blood to scrawl the initials of Islamic State on a window, seemingly indicating an act of terrorism. The two teenage boys stole the cash register and went on to attack four other people over a period of more than twelve hours.[341]

According to the authorities, the sixteen-year-old had posted radical material online in the weeks leading to the attack. The Deputy Commissioner of New South Wales Police told the media: 'We have two teenagers in custody and sufficient information to believe the actions of one of those teenagers may be related to terrorism.'[342] Three years later, however, in sentencing the elder boy to thirty-five years in prison at the New South Wales Supreme Court, Justice Bellew said that while his actions and words were disturbing, he was not satisfied that he was motivated by extremism and said schizophrenia had contributed to the crime.[343] The boy, who was adjudged to be psychotic and addicted to drugs, said he heard a voice inside his head saying 'Kill him, kill him, kill him!' at the time. Justice Bellew said the teenager's preoccupation with Islamic State had not been behind the killing, and rather his use of methamphetamines – which the boy said made him a 'better criminal' – played a significant role in his offending.[344]

4.4.2 The Prosecution of Terrorism in China

China has very broad terrorism national legislation in place, contained in the general criminal law as well as in a dedicated terrorism law adopted in 2016 (and amended in 2018). Terrorism is defined in the counterterrorism law as 'any ideology or act that, by means of violence, sabotage, or danger, generates social panic, undermines public security, infringes upon personal and property rights, or menaces State authorities or international organizations, with the aim of realising political, ideological and other purposes'.[345] Although capital punishment is not prescribed per se for terrorist offences, many predicate crimes already attract the death penalty.

4.4.2.1 The Prosecution of Uighurs

The counterterrorism law has been used especially to target Muslim Uighurs in Xinjiang province as part of the broader crimes against humanity being perpetrated against Turkic

---

[340] S. Zemek, 'Sydney man convicted of terrorism offences fighting to be freed on bail', NCA NewsWire, 8 November 2021, at: https://bit.ly/3oO8wrz.

[341] ABC News, 'Queanbeyan stabbing: Counter-terrorism police investigate fatal rampage', 7 April 2017, at: https://bit.ly/3oUOqf7.

[342] Ibid.

[343] K. Fedor, 'Teenager jailed over murder of service station worker and writing "IS" in his blood in Queanbeyan in 2017', 9News, 1 May 2020, at: https://bit.ly/3WWhWxI.

[344] A. Thompson, '"Macabre and callous in the extreme": Teens jailed for service station murder', Sydney Morning Herald, 1 May 2020, at: https://bit.ly/3WVNHHb.

[345] Art. 3, 2016 Counterterrorism Law of the People's Republic of China.

Muslim minority groups.[346] In September 2022, Human Rights Watch calculated that half a million people had been prosecuted for offences in the province, including terrorism, since 2017. The Xinjiang High People's Procuratorate, which has continued publishing statistics, reported in February 2022 that a total of 540,826 people had been prosecuted in the region since 2017. 'Given that China's conviction rate is above 99.9 per cent, almost all of these 540,826 people would have been convicted.'[347]

In separate research published in May of the same year, the Associated Press found that in one county alone around one in twenty-five people had been sentenced to prison on terrorism-related charges, all of them Uighurs, a level of incarceration that equates to the highest in the world. A list obtained and partially verified by the Associated Press cites the names of more than 10,000 Uighurs sent to prison in just Konasheher county alone, one of dozens in southern Xinjiang.[348]

Human Rights Watch states that Chinese authorities have detained Turkic Muslims, including Uighurs, on the basis of the related crimes of separatism, terrorism, or religious extremism. They affirm that many of these arrests and detentions have been made in the absence of an evidentiary basis and without respect for the due-process rights of detainees. Detainees and their relatives interviewed by Human Rights Watch all reported that at no point did the authorities ever present them with a warrant, with evidence of a crime, or with any other documentation, nor were they ever informed of which authorities were responsible for their arrest.[349] Lawyers told the Network of Chinese Human Rights Defenders that defendants facing terrorism charges are not allowed to plead 'not guilty', and tend to be quickly put on trial and sentenced to prison terms.[350]

The Xinjiang authorities initiated a 'Strike Hard Campaign against Violent Terrorism' in 2014, but significantly escalated it in 2017. The crackdown followed a series of knifings and bombings perpetrated by a small number of Uighur militants. The Chinese government has defended the mass detentions that followed as both lawful and necessary to combat terrorism.[351] The corresponding sentences imposed upon conviction have been increasingly harsh. Prior to 2017, less than 11 per cent of people who were sentenced received terms of imprisonment of more than five years. In 2017, however, such sentences comprised 87 per cent of the total.[352] In July 2022, Chinese President Xi Jinping made his first trip to the Xinjiang region since ordering the Strike Hard Campaign. He visited a museum where he urged the 'better preservation' of the cultural heritage of minority groups.[353]

4.4.2.2 The Prosecution of the National Security Law in Hong Kong

In 2020, in the Hong Kong Administrative Region, the Chinese government introduced its National Security Law, which criminalizes 'separatism', 'subversion of State power', 'terrorism',

---

[346] L. Maizland, 'China's Repression of Uyghurs in Xinjiang', Backgrounder, Council on Foreign Relations, Washington DC, last updated 22 September 2022 at: https://bit.ly/46oloNw; and see generally BBC, 'Who are the Uyghurs and why is China being accused of genocide?', 24 May 2022, at: https://bit.ly/45VhK5T.

[347] Human Rights Watch, 'China: Xinjiang Official Figures Reveal Higher Prisoner Count', 14 September 2022, at: https://bit.ly/43NiKae.

[348] H. Wu and D. Kang, 'Uyghur county in China has highest prison rate in the world', *Associated Press*, 17 May 2022, at: https://bit.ly/3NnRb1W.

[349] Human Rights Watch, 'China: Free Xinjiang "Political Education" Detainees', 10 September 2017, at: https://bit.ly/43vQmtJ.

[350] Chinese Human Rights Defenders, 'Criminal Arrests in Xinjiang Account for 21% of China's Total in 2017', cited in Human Rights Watch, '"Break Their Lineage, Break Their Roots". China's Crimes against Humanity Targeting Uyghurs and Other Turkic Muslims', 19 April 2021, at: https://bit.ly/42tSmRT.

[351] Wu and Kang, 'Uyghur county in China has highest prison rate in the world'.

[352] Human Rights Watch, 'China: Xinjiang Official Figures Reveal Higher Prisoner Count'.

[353] 'Xi makes first Xinjiang visit since "strike hard" campaign', *The Japan Times*, 15 July 2022, at: https://bit.ly/3NphjcW.

Prosecution of Terrorism Suspects

and 'collusion with foreign or overseas forces to endanger State security'. Terrorism under this law involves a predicate offence that is perpetrated to cause grave harm to the society and with a view to coercing the Chinese government or the Government of the Hong Kong Special Administrative Region or to intimidating the public in order to pursue political agenda.[354] The predicate offences involve violence to a person, sabotage or disruption to transportation or State facilities, and 'other dangerous activities which seriously jeopardise public health, safety, or security'. The Law provides for a minimum of ten years in prison and a maximum of life imprisonment.

In theory, the National Security Law preserves the right of peaceful assembly and the right of expression under the Basic Law of Hong Kong.[355] Practice and caselaw has suggested otherwise.[356] The case of *Tong Ying-Kit* v. *Secretary of Justice* concerned Mr Tong, a twenty-four-year-old man who carried a protest flag during violent assemblies in 2020.[357] He had driven his motorcycle around lines of police officers causing them to jump out of the way and he ultimately collided into a group of officers, injuring three of them. He was convicted of terrorism and secession on 27 July 2021 and sentenced to nine years in prison, becoming the first person to be convicted of a crime under the National Security Law.[358] His appeal seeking a trial by jury had been earlier rejected by the courts.[359]

The injuries to the officers were the basis for his terrorism conviction. The High Court held that his flag contained a slogan which was 'capable of inciting others to commit secession', and therefore also a violation of the National Security Law.[360] The prosecution for secession was committed by the political banner he had pinned to his backpack which contained the words 'Liberate Hong Kong, Revolution of Our Time', referring to the Hong Kong protests in 2019. The judge found that Tong had 'incited other persons to organise, plan, commit or participate in acts, whether or not by force or threat of force, with a view to committing secession or undermining national unification' by promoting the independence of Hong Kong from China.[361]

Reacting to the judgment and sentence imposed on Mr Tong, Amnesty International's Asia-Pacific Regional Director Yamini Mishra said: 'The sentencing of Tong Ying-kit to nine years confirms fears that the national security law is not merely a tool to instil terror into government critics in Hong Kong; it is a weapon that will be used to incarcerate them.'[362]

---

[354] Art. 20, National Security Law.

[355] Art. 4, National Security Law.

[356] Amnesty International has reported that on 1 July 2020, the first full day of the law being in force, police arrested more than 300 protesters, including 10 on suspicion of violating the National Security Law. 'Since then, the government has continued to arrest and charge individuals under the NSL solely because they have exercised their rights to freedom of expression, peaceful assembly and association. . . . Worse still, people charged under the law are effectively presumed guilty rather than innocent, meaning they are denied bail unless they can prove they will not "continue to commit acts endangering national security"'. Amnesty International, 'Hong Kong: National Security Law has created a human rights emergency', Press release, 30 June 2021, at: https://bit.ly/43P8D4Q.

[357] High Court of the Hong Kong Special Administrative Region, *Tong Ying-Kit* v. *Secretary of Justice*, HCCC280C/2020 [2021] HKCFI 2239 (Reasons for Sentence).

[358] T. E. Kellogg and E. Yan-Ho Lai, 'The Tong Ying-Kit NSL Verdict: An International and Comparative Law Analysis', GCAL Briefing Paper, Center for Asian Law, Georgetown University, 20 October 2021, at: https://bit.ly/3NmIZyO, p. 4.

[359] Bernacchi Chambers, 'Tong Ying Kit v Secretary for Justice [2021] 2 HKLRD 1036, [2021] HKCFI 1397', Case Highlights, 20 May 2021, at: https://bit.ly/3X4m92f.

[360] Art. 21, National Security Law.

[361] High Court of the Hong Kong Special Administrative Region, *Tong Ying-Kit* v. *Secretary of Justice*, 27 July 2021, para. 141.

[362] Amnesty International, 'Hong Kong: Sentencing of Tong Ying-kit deals a hammer blow to free speech', Press release, 30 July 2021, at: https://bit.ly/3P4Mrzq.

4.4 Prosecution of Terrorism in Asia and the Middle East

Mr Tong initially filed an appeal against conviction and sentence, but later decided to drop it, for reasons unknown.[363]

4.4.3 The Prosecution of Terrorism in Iran

Iran has a very broad interpretation of terrorism in its domestic law, which it has used to prosecute opponents of the regime. Under the Penal Code, one form of terrorism is *moharebeh* – 'war against God' – which concerns the 'drawing a weapon on the life, property or honour of people or threatening them, in such manner that results in insecurity in the environment'.[364] The punishment for *moharebeh* is one of the following penalties, depending on the decision of the presiding judge: the death penalty (by hanging) or crucifixion, amputation of the right hand and left foot, or banishment.[365] Another form of terrorism is *fesad-fel-arze*, which comprises a range of offences against the State:

> [C]rimes against physical integrity and crimes against internal or external security of the country, criminal libel, a disorder in the state economic system, arson and annihilation, dissemination of toxic, microbial, and hazardous matters ... that cause severe disorder in the public order of the country, create insecurity or inflict substantial damage upon the physical integrity or persons or public and private properties'.[366]

The death penalty is the mandatory punishment for *fesad fel-arze*.

On 16 September 2022, a twenty-two-year-old Iranian woman, Mahsa Amini, died in a hospital in Tehran after being arrested and detained by the morality police, allegedly for not wearing the hijab in accordance with Iranian law.[367] The death, which the authorities implausibly claimed had resulted from natural causes, led to very widespread protests across Iran. The authorities detained and charged many people protesting against Ms Amini's killing with terrorism, the first of whom was convicted in November 2022. On 24 November, Volker Türk, the UN High Commissioner for Human Rights, speaking at a special session of the Human Rights Council on the human rights situation in Iran, called on the Iranian authorities to impose a moratorium on the death penalty.[368] But executions of convicted protesters began in December 2022. Mohsen Shekari, with the first to be killed, was convicted of *moharebeh* for having injured a member of the Basij militia.[369] Others were receiving long prison terms. On 13 December 2022, Iran's judiciary said 400 people had been sentenced to prison, including 160 to terms of between five and ten years.

In the middle of December 2022, Iran announced it had publicly hanged a twenty-three-year-old in what was the second execution linked to the anti-government protests. Majidreza Rahnavard had similarly been convicted of *moharebeh* after the Court found he had stabbed to death two members of the Basij. His execution took place just twenty-three days after his arrest.

---

[363] K. Ho, 'First Hong Kong activist jailed under national security law drops appeal in "surprise" move', Hong Kong Free Press, 13 January 2022, at: https://bit.ly/3qtf1jK.

[364] Art. 280, Criminal Code of Iran. The notion of honour refers to female members of the family.

[365] Art. 282, Criminal Code of Iran.

[366] Art. 286, Criminal Code of Iran.

[367] P. Wintour, 'Iran president says death in custody of Mahsa Amini must be investigated', The Guardian, 23 September 2022, at: https://bit.ly/3po5Oz8.

[368] UN, 'High Commissioner to Human Rights Council's Special Session: Iran Must Stop Violence against Peaceful Protesters, Release All those Arrested, and Impose a Moratorium on the Death Penalty', Press release, Geneva, 24 November 2022, at: https://bit.ly/43RDspB.

[369] Middle East Online, 'Iran executes first known prisoner arrested in protests', 12 December 2022, at: https://bit.ly/3p590JG.

Human rights groups warned repeatedly that protesters were being sentenced to death after sham trials without due process.[370] There were also regular and persistent reports of torture.

Executions continued into 2023, with two people executed in January[371] and a further three in May. That month, three UN experts urged the Iranian government 'to stop this horrific wave of executions'.[372] The three men executed in May 2023 had been convicted over their alleged involvement in a shooting that killed three security personnel in Isfahan the previous November.[373] In April 2023, the UN Human Rights Council had adopted a resolution expressing 'deep concern at the reported surge in the number of executions, including of individuals sentenced to death in relation to their alleged involvement in the recent protests'. It urged Iran to 'take all necessary legislative, administrative and other measures, in accordance with its international human rights obligations, to ensure that no one is sentenced to death or executed for offences that do not meet the threshold of the most serious crimes or for alleged offences committed before the age of 18 years'. It further called on the authorities to 'ensure that all criminal convictions and sentences are handed down by courts that are competent, independent and impartial, following proceedings that strictly respect fair trial guarantees'.[374]

4.4.4 The Prosecution of Terrorism in Iraq

Iraq's 2005 Anti-Terrorism Law defines terrorism in very broad terms as 'every criminal act committed by an individual or an organized group' that either targets people or damages public or private property. The terrorism motivations are either disturbing peace, stability, and national unity or provoking fear among people and creating chaos 'in order to achieve terrorist goals'.[375] The actus reus and mens rea of a terrorist crime are thus so broad that they can be met by doing nothing more than daubing slogans on a building calling for an independent state of Kurdistan. This could be deemed by a judicial authority to be disturbing the nation's stability and national unity. In 2022, the UN Committee against Torture declared that the broad definition of terrorism in the 2005 law 'falls short of international standards'.[376]

In the pursuit of justice and accountability for the domestic and international crimes perpetrated by Islamic State members and affiliates,[377] Iraq has repeatedly affirmed its commitment to uphold the right to a fair trial. In practice, it has fallen far short of this aim. From January 2018 to October 2019, the judiciary processed more than 20,000 terrorism-related cases. But in a report issued in January 2020, the UN Assistance Mission for Iraq (UNAMI) and the Office of the UN High Commissioner for Human Rights (OHCHR) found that basic fair-trial standards were not

---

[370]   See, e.g., P. Loft, 'Iran protests 2022: Human rights and international response', Research Briefing, House of Commons Library, London, 26 May 2023, at: https://bit.ly/43F4ZuD, §3.4.

[371]   Associated Press, 'Iran executes 2 more men detained amid nationwide protests', 7 January 2023, at: https://bit.ly/3P8Hx4y.

[372]   Javaid Rehman, Special Rapporteur on the situation of human rights in the Islamic Republic of Iran; Margaret Satterthwaite, Special Rapporteur on the independence of judges and lawyers; and Morris Tidball-Binz, Special Rapporteur on extrajudicial, summary or arbitrary executions. 'UN experts urge Iran to stop "horrific wave" of executions', Press release, 19 May 2023, at: https://bit.ly/3CoEmOy.

[373]   BBC, 'Iran executes three over anti-government protests', 19 May 2023, at: https://bit.ly/43F5ULB.

[374]   Human Rights Council Resolution 52/27: 'Situation of human rights in the Islamic Republic of Iran', adopted on 4 April 2023 by twenty-three votes to eight, with sixteen abstentions, operative para. 3. The Council members voting against the resolution were Bangladesh, Bolivia, China, Cuba, Eritrea, Kazakhstan, Pakistan, and Viet Nam.

[375]   Art. 1, 2005 Anti-Terrorism Law.

[376]   Committee against Torture, Concluding Observations on the Second Periodic Report of Iraq, UN doc. CAT/C/IRQ/CO/2, 15 June 2022, para. 18.

[377]   UN, '"No Shortage of Evidence" on Crimes Committed in Iraq by Da'esh, Special Adviser Tells Security Council, Noting Unified Repository of Digitized Information', UN doc. SC/15312, 7 June 2023, at: https://bit.ly/42DAvHZ.

generally respected in terrorism-related trials. Main areas of concern included ineffective legal representation, lack of adequate time and facilities to prepare a defence, and limited possibility to challenge prosecution evidence; an overreliance on confessions, with frequent allegations of torture or ill-treatment that were inadequately addressed by courts; and prosecutions under the anti-terrorism legal framework focused on 'association' with or 'membership' of a terrorist organization, without sufficiently distinguishing between those who participated in violence and those who joined Islamic State for survival and/or through coercion. This combined with harsh penalties for anyone convicted which failed to distinguish degrees of underlying culpability.[378]

Human Rights Watch similarly reported that criminal trials of defendants charged with terrorism in 2021, most often for alleged membership in Islamic State, were 'generally rushed' and convictions were based primarily on confessions, 'including those apparently extracted through torture'. The situation did not change in 2022, with some Islamic State-related counterterrorism cases still hearing forced confessions as the *only* evidence presented against the defendant.[379] There were also multiple reports of international and local aid workers being falsely charged with terrorism, as part of a broader campaign of harassment and intimidation.[380]

Although the accused have the right to presumption of innocence, in practice judges in Islamic State-related cases are said often to presume guilt based upon presence or geographic proximity to activities of the terrorist group, or upon a spousal or familial relationship to another defendant.[381] Furthermore, many defendants – children as well as adults – had been detained because their names appeared on wanted lists of questionable accuracy or because they were family members of listed suspects.[382] Sometimes, spouses and other family members of fugitives (mostly Sunni Arabs wanted on terrorism charges) were detained with a view to compelling the fugitives to surrender.[383]

Human Rights Watch found that authorities 'systematically violated the due process rights of suspects, such as guarantees under Iraqi law that detainees see a judge within 24 hours, have access to a lawyer throughout interrogations, and that their families are notified and be able to communicate with them'.[384] Instead, the authorities sometimes held detainees incommunicado, without access to defence counsel, presentation before a judge, or arraignment on formal charges within the legally mandated period.

Under anti-terrorism laws, the death penalty is mandatory for a wide range of acts that do not meet the 'most serious crimes' threshold. Even when they do, the death penalty was typically imposed following an unfair trial. As the US Department of State has observed, Iraqi courts routinely accepted forced confessions as evidence.[385] According to a Ministry of Justice statement in September 2021, authorities were detaining close to 50,000 people for suspected terrorism links, more than half of whom had already been sentenced to death.[386]

---

[378] UNAMI and OHCHR, *Human Rights in the Administration of Justice in Iraq: Trials under the anti-terrorism laws and implications for justice, accountability and social cohesion in the aftermath of ISIL*, Report, Baghdad, January 2020, at: https://bit.ly/43VZl7g.

[379] US Department of State, '2022 Country Reports on Human Rights Practices: Iraq', Bureau of Democracy, Human Rights, and Labor, Washington DC, 2023, at: https://bit.ly/3N4X82j, §1(C).

[380] Ibid., §5.

[381] Ibid., §1(E).

[382] Human Rights Watch, 'Iraq: Events of 2021', *World Report 2022*, at: https://bit.ly/3PeoqWK.

[383] US Department of State, '2022 Country Reports on Human Rights Practices: Iraq', §1(F).

[384] Human Rights Watch, 'Iraq: Events of 2021'.

[385] US Department of State, '2022 Country Reports on Human Rights Practices: Iraq', §1(E).

[386] Human Rights Watch, 'Iraq: Events of 2021'.

158

Those imprisoned for Islamic State affiliation reportedly include hundreds of foreign women and children, although children are not sentenced to death. Nonetheless, authorities can prosecute child suspects as young as nine years of age on terrorism charges in areas controlled by the central government and eleven years of age in the Kurdistan Region of Iraq.[387] In October 2022, a senior government official reported that the five juvenile correctional facilities held more than 100 per cent of their maximum capacity – an improvement from the more than 150 per cent of capacity recorded in 2021 – with more than half of juveniles held pursuant to terrorism-related convictions.[388]

4.4.5 *The Prosecution of Terrorism in Lebanon*

Lebanon has provisions governing terrorism in its Criminal Code. The definition of terrorism is very general: 'all acts intended to cause a state of terror and committed by means liable to create a public danger such as explosive devices, inflammable materials, toxic or corrosive products and infectious or microbial agents'.[389] Lebanon is thus one of the few States that does not overtly make efforts to compel or coerce government policy as a possible terrorism motivation in its definition of an act of terrorism. The maximum penalty for terrorist offences under Lebanese law is the death penalty, imposable where death results or a building in which people are present is destroyed or seriously damaged.[390]

4.4.5.1 The Special Tribunal for Lebanon

Lebanese domestic law was used to prosecute the alleged participants in the killing of former Lebanese prime minister Rafik Hariri on 14 February 2005, but before an international tribunal, not a domestic court. On the afternoon of that day, an explosion occurred in downtown Beirut 'so powerful that it left a crater at least ten metres wide and two metres deep in the street'. The explosion killed 22 people, including the former prime minister, and injured 226 others.[391]

The Special Tribunal for Lebanon was an ad hoc mechanism created by the UN Security Council in 2007 in relation to the bombing. As the Tribunal's website proudly declares, it was 'the first tribunal of international character to prosecute terrorist crimes'.[392] The Statute itself declared the killing to be a terrorist crime.[393] The statutory mandate issued by the Council explicitly stated that Lebanese law was to be the sole legal basis for the offences to be tried by the Tribunal.[394] This concerned, along other counts of the indictment, the offence of terrorism under Article 314 of Lebanon's Criminal Code.

---

[387] Ibid.

[388] US Department of State, '2022 Country Reports on Human Rights Practices: Iraq', §1(C).

[389] Art. 314, Criminal Code of Lebanon.

[390] Article 315 of the Criminal Code thus stipulates: 'The death penalty shall be imposed if the act leads to the death of a person or to the complete or partial destruction of a building in which one or more persons are present.'

[391] Special Tribunal for Lebanon, 'Ayyash et al. (STL-11–01)', undated but accessed 1 June 2023, at: https://bit.ly/34yXJa1.

[392] STL homepage, at: https://www.stl-tsl.org/en.

[393] Chapeau to the 2007 Statute of the Special Tribunal for Lebanon, annexed to UN Security Council Resolution 1757. See on the issue of assassination of Mr Hariri as terrorism B. Saul, 'Definition of "Terrorism" in the UN Security Council', *Chinese Journal of International Law*, Vol. 4, No. 1 (2005), 141–66, *esp.* at pp. 145–6.

[394] Art. 2, Statute of the Special Tribunal for Lebanon, annexed to UN Security Council Resolution 1757, adopted on 30 May 2007 by ten votes to nil with five abstentions (China, Indonesia, Qatar, Russia, and South Africa).

In its trial verdict issued on 28 August 2020,[395] Salim Jamil Ayyash, a Lebanese citizen born on 10 November 1963 and a member of Hezbollah,[396] was found guilty by the Special Tribunal on all counts. The charges were conspiracy aimed at committing a terrorist act; committing a terrorist act by means of an explosive device; intentional homicide of Mr Hariri with premeditation by using explosive materials; intentional homicide of twenty-one other persons with premeditation by using explosive materials; and attempted intentional homicide of 226 other persons. On 11 December 2020, the judges unanimously sentenced Mr Ayyash to five concurrent sentences of life imprisonment.[397]

In its trial judgment, the Tribunal acknowledged that the purposive element of the definition of terrorism in the Criminal Code – the *mens rea* of the offence – pertained to an intent to cause 'a state of terror'. It stated that Lebanese courts 'do not appear to consider that the perpetrator's sole or principal aim must be to cause a state of terror among the general public. Having the intent to cause terror in a particular area and or among a particular group has sufficed.'[398] Among the domestic caselaw cited by the Tribunal was the 1997 judgment by the Lebanese Judicial Council in the prosecution of Mr Samir Geagea for instigating terrorism.[399] The relevant acts were the attempted assassination of Minister Michel Murr on 20 March 1991 and a second car bomb operation on 29 March 1991 which 'involved the use of explosives, created panic among the population, killed and injured a number of persons, and destroyed residential and commercial buildings'.[400] The Tribunal noted that the Judicial Council did not elaborate further on the mens rea of this crime.[401] It did not, however, suggest – much less endorse – an alternative mens rea of compelling government conduct.

Nonetheless, in her separate opinion to the judgment, Judge Nosworthy noted that the chapter of the Code in which the offence of terrorism is a subsection is entitled 'Offences against State security'. Article 271 of that section provides: 'An attack on State security is made whether the act constituting the offence is complete, abortive or attempted.' She concluded, but without adducing firm evidence, that the notion of State security applied to all offences within the chapter and thus that the mens rea of the offence indirectly incorporated an attack on the State.[402] Her finding is highly questionable, as it imputes an alternative mens rea element into a capital crime and without supporting domestic jurisprudence.

The prosecution appealed the decision by the Tribunal to acquit two of Mr Ayyash's three co-defendants, Hassan Merhi and Hussein Oneissi.[403] On 10 March 2021, the Appeals Chamber reversed the acquittals of both men and convicted them of all counts against them, which included conspiracy to commit a terrorist act and being an accomplice to both intentional

---

[395] The verdict was originally set for 7 August, but was postponed until 28 August following the Beirut explosion (not a deliberate act of terrorism, but the unintended detonation of a large amount of ammonium nitrate stored at the Port of Beirut). Agence France-Presse, 'Lebanon Hariri tribunal judgement postponed after Beirut blast', *Arab News*, updated 5 August 2020, at: https://bit.ly/43Ei7Am.

[396] The judges in the STL Trial Chamber stated, however, that there was 'no evidence' that Hezbollah's leadership had any involvement in Mr Hariri's murder and 'no direct evidence of Syrian involvement in it'. STL, *Prosecutor v. Salim Jamil Ayyash and others*, Judgment, para. 787.

[397] STL, 'Accused', undated but accessed 1 June 2023, at: https://bit.ly/3qEEQO2.

[398] Special Tribunal for Lebanon, *Prosecutor v. Salim Jamil Ayyash and others*, Judgment (Trial Chamber) (Case No. STL-11–01/T/TC), 18 August 2020, para. 6177.

[399] Ibid., para. 6179.

[400] Lebanese Judicial Council, Judgement in the case concerning the attempted assassination of Minister Michel Murr, Judgment No. 2/97, 9 May 1997, p. 53.

[401] STL, *Prosecutor v. Salim Jamil Ayyash and others*, Judgment, para. 6179.

[402] STL, *Prosecutor v. Salim Jamil Ayyash and others*, Judgment, Separate Opinion of Judge Janet Nosworthy, para. 134.

[403] STL, 'Ayyash et al. (STL-11–01)', accessed 1 February 2022, at: https://bit.ly/34yXJa1.

homicide and attempted intentional homicide.[404] On 16 June 2022, the Appeals Chamber sentenced Mr Merhi and Mr Oneissi to five concurrent sentences of life imprisonment.[405] All three defendants were tried, convicted, and sentenced in absentia.

4.4.5.2 The Prosecution of Protesters as Terrorists

Lebanon has suffered numerous other acts of terrorism in the past decades but its domestic law has also been used to prosecute the actions of protesters during assemblies. In March 2021, Amnesty International called on the Lebanese authorities to 'immediately stop the use of terrorism-related charges to prosecute protesters, which marks a worrying new turn in the ongoing repression of activists and demonstrators'. The organization repeated earlier appeals to the authorities to 'immediately cease the practice of summoning civilians before military courts'.[406]

On 19 February 2021, Lebanon's military prosecutor had filed terrorism-related charges against at least twenty-three detainees, including two children, who had been involved in heated protests in the northern city of Tripoli. During the protests, both Internal Security Forces officers and civilians were injured and one civilian killed.[407] At the end of March 2021, four of the total of thirty-five charged in the case with criminal offences remained in detention but nineteen, including the children, were released. The authorities refused to identify the other twelve defendants, citing the 'secrecy' of the investigations.[408]

4.4.6 The Prosecution of Terrorism in Saudi Arabia

Saudi Arabia's 2017 dedicated law defines a 'terrorist crime' in very broad terms as any act committed with the intent to disturb public order, destabilize national security or State stability, endanger national unity, undermine State reputation or status, damage State facilities or natural resources, or compel conduct by the authorities.[409] Also included are any act intended to cause death or serious bodily injury to a civilian in order to intimidate a population or to compel government conduct, or which is contained in a terrorism treaty to which the Kingdom of Saudi Arabia is a State Party.[410]

The death penalty is imposable – and indeed has often been imposed and executed – for many terrorist offences in Saudi law. In March 2022, Saudi Arabia executed a record eighty-one people in a single day for terrorism-related offences. The convictions were for kidnapping, torture, rape, and smuggling weapons and bombs into the kingdom, among other offences. Of the eighty-one people put to death, seventy-three were Saudi citizens, seven were Yemeni, and the other condemned was a Syrian national.[411] Convictions and executions continued in 2023. By the

---

[404] STL, *Prosecutor v. Hassan Habib Merhi and Hussein Hassan Oneissi*, Appeal Judgment (Appeals Chamber) (Case No. STL-11–01/A-2/AC), 10 March 2022, at: https://bit.ly/3qzjZeN.

[405] STL, *Prosecutor v. Hassan Habib Merhi and Hussein Hassan Oneissi*, Sentencing Judgment (Appeals Chamber) (Case No. STL-11–01/S-2/AC), 16 June 2022, at: https://bit.ly/43VdPnH.

[406] Amnesty International, 'Lebanon: Authorities step up repression through use of terrorism charges against protesters', Press release, 8 March 2021, at: https://bit.ly/3q9id3V.

[407] Human Rights Watch, 'Lebanon: Tripoli Detainees Allege Torture, Forced Disappearance', 30 March 2021, at: https://bit.ly/3CuyyTy.

[408] Ibid.

[409] Art. 1(3), 2017 Law on Terrorism and Terrorist Financing.

[410] Ibid.

[411] 'Saudi Arabia executes record 81 people in one day for terrorism-related offences', *France24*, 13 March 2022, at: https://bit.ly/3X4mlOY.

middle of June, a total of twenty people had been executed for terrorism offences since the beginning of the year. This included three Saudi citizens convicted of having killed a security officer and creating a 'terrorist cell'. In a public statement, the Saudi Ministry of the Interior said the three men had killed an officer in Riyadh and burned his body by setting fire to his vehicle. The three were also convicted of financing terrorism and possessing weapons, ammunition, and 'material used in the manufacture of explosives'.[412]

The 2017 law also provides criminal penalties of between five and ten years in prison for portraying the king or crown prince, directly or indirectly, 'in a manner that brings religion or justice into disrepute', and criminalizes a wide range of peaceful acts that bear no relation to terrorism.[413] At the end of May 2023, two Bahrainis were executed for protest-related charges under the counterterrorism law. They had been tried and sentenced to death in Saudi's Specialized Criminal Court in October 2021 after being arrested in May 2015 and held incommunicado for more than three months.[414]

4.5 THE PROSECUTION OF TERRORISM IN AFRICA

While many States across Africa face a significant terrorism threat, some have also used domestic anti-terrorism laws to target lawyers, journalists, political opponents of the regime, and human rights defenders. This has especially been the case in Algeria, which has targeted each of these categories of individuals with terrorism charge. Kenya continues to suffer a sporadic but significant Islamist terrorism threat, in particular from al-Shabaab based in neighbouring Somalia. Niger is confronted with Boko Haram and its now more powerful offshoot, Islamic State West Africa Province.

4.5.1 *The Prosecution of Terrorism in Algeria*

Algerians have endured indiscriminate terrorist attacks stretching back many decades. They suffered grievously during France's attempt to suppress the insurgency that erupted in 1954 in favour of national liberation, with brutality and torture characterizing its counterinsurgency operations. This was still so, even as it became understood before de Gaulle's decision in 1962 to recognize Algeria's independence that French forces would be withdrawn.[415] But in the famous words of Voltaire, 'History never repeats itself. Man always does.' Thus, in the early 1990s, in suppressing a domestic Islamist insurgency, the Algerian army would reproduce against its own people many of the most serious human rights violations that had typified the latter years of French colonial rule. The period would be referred to as 'la décennie noire' or 'la décennie de terrorisme'.[416] As of April 2023, a former Algerian Minister of Defence was under active investigation for alleged war crimes committed between 1992 and 1994.[417] On 28 August 2023, the Office of the Attorney General of Switzerland filed an indictment in the

---

[412] Agence France-Presse, 'Saudi Arabia executes three convicted of slaying officer, founding "terrorist cell"', *Times of Israel*, 11 June 2023, at: https://bit.ly/42DGBYT.

[413] Human Rights Watch, 'Saudi Arabia: New Counterterrorism Law Enables Abuse', 23 November 2017, at: https://bit.ly/3MM7tQS.

[414] L. Saad, 'Saudi Arabia Executes Two Shi'a Bahrainis on Terrorism Charges', Human Rights Watch, 2 June 2023, at: https://bit.ly/3p5GMP9.

[415] See, e.g., A. Knapp, *Charles de Gaulle*, Routledge, London, 2021, pp. 221–33 and p. 202.

[416] See, e.g., P. Daum, 'Vingt ans après les massacres de la guerre civile Mémoire interdite en Algérie', *Le Monde Diplomatique*, August 2017, at: https://bit.ly/3NhDoKg.

[417] Trial International, 'Khaled Nezzar', 17 April 2023, at: https://bit.ly/3JpL8HZ.

Federal Criminal Court against Khaled Nezzar for war crimes and crimes against humanity perpetrated between 1992 and 1994. It is alleged that he knowingly and willingly condoned, coordinated, and encouraged torture and other cruel, inhumane, or humiliating acts, extra-judicial executions, and arbitrary detention.[418] Mr Nezzar died on 29 December 2023 before he could face trial.[419]

The Armed Islamic Group (le Groupe Islamique Armé, GIA) was one of the two main Islamist insurgent groups in the Algerian Civil War. According to the International Crisis Group, '[u]nlike the other armed groups, the GIA carried out indiscriminate attacks against civilians, abducted and killed foreigners, planted bombs in public spaces and committed massacres across the countryside'.[420] Tens of thousands died in the violence, with 2,000 killed by the GIA in 1998 alone.[421] In June 2023, Youcef M. was convicted of association with a terrorist group before the Sixteenth Correctional Court in Paris (which specializes in terrorism cases) and sentenced to five years' imprisonment. Youcef M. was accused of membership of Takfir wal-Hijra, a GIA dissident faction, in the 1990s and to have supported its activities. Having been convicted in absentia in a trial in France in 2001, he had spent much of the intervening twenty years in Ireland bringing up a family (and had acquired Irish citizenship).[422] In September 2021, however, he was arrested by the Garda and transferred to France pursuant to a European Arrest Warrant. He was retried on terrorism offences for the supply of weapons to the GIA and convicted despite protestations that he was only a petty thief and not a terrorist.[423]

4.5.1.1 The Kidnapping in the Desert (2003)

In February 2003, a unit of the Salafist armed group (le Groupe salafiste de prédication et de combat, GSPC) kidnapped a group of thirty-two European tourists in the Algerian Sahara.[424] The unit of the group under the command of Abderrazak El Para (also known as Amari Saïfi), a former soldier in the Algerian army who had deserted to join the GIA,[425] held all of the tourists for two months. Seventeen of the tourists were released in May while the remaining fifteen were detained for several more months until the German government reportedly paid €5 million in ransom.[426] One of the fifteen is said to have died in captivity from heatstroke.[427] El Para was captured in Chad in 2004 and handed over to the Algerian authorities.[428] Conspiracy theories

---

[418]   Swiss Federal Council, 'The Office of the Attorney General of Switzerland indicts former Algerian defence minister', Bern, 29 August 2023, at: https://bit.ly/45OB18k.

[419]   'Khaled Nezzar, general who brutally suppressed protests during Algeria's 'Black Decade' – obituary', Daily Telegraph, Obituary, 7 February 2024.

[420]   International Crisis Group, 'Islamism, Violence and Reform in Algeria: Turning the Page', *Middle East Report No. 29*, Cairo/Brussels, 30 July 2004, p. 11.

[421]   A. Boukhars, 'Political Violence in North Africa: The Perils of Incomplete Liberalization', Brookings Doha Center Analysis Paper No. 3, January 2011, at: https://bit.ly/3WZlbF.G, p. 20.

[422]   He is said to have arrived in Dublin hidden in a truck. Agence France-Presse, 'Cinq ans de prison pour un homme rejugé 20 ans après sa condamnation pour terrorisme', *Le Figaro*, 2 June 2023, at: https://bit.ly/3CgDgEt.

[423]   S. Seelow, 'Un terroriste algérien qui avait refait sa vie depuis vingt-trois ans en Irlande rattrapé et jugé par la justice française', *Le Monde*, 2 June 2023, at: https://bit.ly/3P11GcL.

[424]   The Salafist group was founded in 1998 as an offshoot of the GIA but later aligned itself with al-Qaeda, becoming known as al-Qaida in the Islamic Maghreb (AQIM).

[425]   Algeria Watch, 'What Happened to Hassan Hattab and Amari Saïfi (alias Abderrezak El Para)?', 13 December 2009 (Updated 31 May 2018), at: https://bit.ly/3WYoFny.

[426]   L. Kennedy Boudali, 'The GSPC: Newest Franchise in al-Qa'ida's Global Jihad', Combating Terrorism Center at West Point, West Point NY, 2007, at: https://bit.ly/3WUo3zk, pp. 1, 5.

[427]   Human Rights Watch, 'Algeria: Long Delays Tainting Terrorism Trials', 18 June 2012, at: https://bit.ly/42vPYdp.

[428]   S. Mellah and J.-B. Rivoire, 'Who Staged the Tourist Kidnappings? El Para, the Maghreb's Bin Ladin', *Le Monde Diplomatique*, 1 February 2005, at: https://bit.ly/42t1AgX.

swirled around the alleged links between El Para and the Algerian intelligence services, the DRS (le Département du Renseignement et de la Sécurité: the Department of Intelligence and Security).[429]

In 2012, Human Rights Watch reported claims that Amari Saïfi (El Para) was held in an undisclosed location, without access to a lawyer, for more than six years after his capture. Even though he was in Algerian custody from 2004, he was tried in absentia at the Algiers Criminal Court for having created an armed terrorist group and sentenced to life imprisonment. He was later sentenced to death at another trial, again in absentia but this time by Batna Criminal Court. The charges were membership of a terrorist group and premeditated murder, in violation of Article 87bis of the Criminal Code.[430] As Human Rights Watch observed, each of these convictions violated the right of a defendant to be present at his own trial. Saïfi was finally accorded a lawyer and brought before a judge in March 2011. But more than a year after that, he was still awaiting to exercise his right under Algerian law to have a new trial.[431]

In January 2013, two of the members of the unit involved in the kidnapping were prosecuted and sentenced to imprisonment, one for life and the other for seven years. The two had been held for six years by the Chadian authorities, who arrested them in 2004 before handing them over to the Algerians in 2010.[432] Four more members of the group were convicted in November 2013 and sentenced to twenty years' imprisonment.[433] But in 2014, the new trial for El Para was once again postponed. No new date was set for the trial to begin.[434]

4.5.1.2 Targeting of Journalists and Human Rights Defenders

In more recent years, the law has become an extension not only of Algerian counterterrorism efforts but also of internal repression, directed not only against those who are engaged in violence but also against lawyers, journalists, political opponents of the regime, and human rights defenders.[435] As Chapter 3 highlighted, the definition of acts of terrorism under contemporary Algerian law is exceptionally broad. New offences were added in 2021, enabling the prosecution of peaceful activists and critical voices.[436] Amnesty International reported that two journalists, Hassan Bouras and Mohamed Mouloudj, were subsequently charged with terrorism offences based on their online publications criticizing the authorities and their affiliations with two

---

[429]   Ibid.; and see Qantara.de, 'Interview with Jeremy Keenan: Mirage in the Desert?', 2010, at: https://bit.ly/45Qy2Nm.

[430]   Algeria Watch, 'What Happened to Hassan Hattab and Amari Saïfi (alias Abderrezak El Para)?'; and Human Rights Watch, 'Algeria: Long Delays Tainting Terrorism Trials'.

[431]   Human Rights Watch, 'Algeria: Long Delays Tainting Terrorism Trials'.

[432]   Agence France-Presse, 'Algerian jailed for life over 2003 kidnap of tourists', *AhramOnline*, 8 January 2013, at: https://bit.ly/3NhMW7X.

[433]   Atlas Info, 'L'énigmatique "Abderrezak El Para", l'absent-très présent du procès d'Alger', 25 November 2013, at: https://bit.ly/3P1Azy5.

[434]   Algeria Watch, 'Abderrezak El Para est-il au-dessus de la loi ?', 12 January 2014 (Updated 1 June 2018), at: https://bit.ly/3WVbdnv.

[435]   See, e.g., Human Rights Watch, 'Algeria: Events of 2022', World Report 2023, at: https://bit.ly/42n4c00; and Amnesty International, Algeria 2022', at: https://bit.ly/3MS129X; and Human Rights Committee, Concluding observations on the fourth periodic report of Algeria, UN doc. CCPR/C/DZA/CO/4, 17 August 2018, paras. 17 and 18.

[436]   On 27 December 2021, the UN Special Rapporteur on the promotion and protection of human rights and fundamental freedoms while countering terrorism, the Working Group on Arbitrary Detention, the Special Rapporteur on the promotion and protection of the right to freedom of opinion and expression, the Special Rapporteur on the right to peaceful assembly and freedom of association, and the Special Rapporteur on the situation of human rights defenders, in a joint communication, called on the Algerian authorities to review their counterterrorism legislation on the grounds that it contravenes international norms. Letter ref. OL DZA 12/2021, 27 December 2021, text at: https://bit.ly/42sfe47.

political organizations that opposed the government.[437] The terrorism offences the journalists faced included a provision in the Criminal Code defining terrorism as any act 'against State security, territorial integrity, [or] the stability and normal functioning of State institutions'.[438] The offences carry the death penalty.

Mr Bouras was a member of the Algerian Human Rights Defence League (Ligue algérienne pour la défense des droits de l'homme, LADDH). He was arrested on 6 September in front of his house in El-Bayedh district, before being transferred to Algiers. He was charged with a range of offences under the Criminal Code with 'membership of a terrorist organisation', 'endangering State security with the aim of regime change', justifying terrorism, assault on national unity, and dissemination of false information. At trial he was convicted and sentenced to one year in prison with an additional year imposed as a suspended sentence. He was released at the end of November 2022 on the basis of time served.[439]

Mr Mouloudj, who spent most of his career at the daily newspaper *Liberté* (since closed down by the authorities), was jailed by an investigating judge in the Algiers district of Sidi M'hamed on 14 September 2021. He was charged with 'membership of a terrorist organisation' and 'endangering State security' but was convicted only on the second charge. He was arrested over a text he sent on 27 April 2021 to Ferhat Mehenni, the head of the Movement for Kabylie's Self-Determination (MAK),[440] requesting an interview for an article for *Liberté* (the MAK had not even been proscribed as a terrorist organization at that time). Nonetheless, his text, which was deemed to be evidence of membership of a terrorist organization, was used as the basis for his pre-trial detention in Koléa prison for thirteen months. At trial he was convicted and sentenced to thirteen months' imprisonment.[441]

Prosecutions of those supporting the Kabylie self-determination movement have continued. In November 2022, fifty-four individuals were convicted of terrorism offences in mass proceedings and sentenced to death in connection with events in the Kabylie region in August 2021, which included the lynching of an activist. Among those sentenced to death, five were convicted in their absence, one of whom was a woman. At least six were prosecuted due to their association with the MAK. Five told the court they were subjected to torture or ill-treatment while in detention.[442]

4.5.2 *The Prosecution of Terrorism in Kenya*

The United Kingdom administered Kenya as a colony from 1920 until 1963, when it gained independence. The British colonial forces brutally suppressed a rebellion in the early 1950s by Mau Mau fighters, which it deemed terrorists. There was also widespread torture of those held in British detention camps, including rape of women.[443] In October 1952, the British government

---

[437] Amnesty International, 'Algeria: Stop using bogus terrorism charges to prosecute peaceful activists and journalists', 28 September 2021, at: https://bit.ly/3WSxkLg.

[438] Art. 87bis (as amended), Criminal Code of Algeria.

[439] A. Moussi, 'Condamné, le journaliste Hassan Bouras quitte la prison', *Interlignes*, 1 December 2022, at: https://bit.ly/3X1A083.

[440] The Kabyle people are ethnic Berbers from Kabylia in the north of Algeria, spread across the Atlas Mountains to the east of Algiers.

[441] Reporters without Borders, 'Algerian reporter got 13 months in prison for texting government opponent', 19 October 2022, at: https://bit.ly/3XoR7Zi.

[442] Amnesty International, 'Algeria: Mass death sentences marred by unfair trials, torture claims', 9 January 2023, at: https://bit.ly/3X1yYuf.

[443] On 6 June 2013, William Hague, the then Secretary of State for Foreign and Commonwealth Affairs, read a statement in the UK Parliament announcing an agreement to compensate 5,228 Kenyans who were tortured and abused during the insurrection. Each would receive about £3,800. 'The British government recognises that

declared a state of emergency in the colony. The Emergency Regulations of 1952 made possession of ammunition and firearms a capital crime and shifted the burden of proof of lawful authority or justification for possessing firearms or ammunitions onto the accused. The Regulations further declared the Mau Mau a terrorist organization, criminalizing all membership. A specialized court, the Court of Emergency Assize, set up to hear and expedite cases against suspects, conducted 1,211 trials between 1953 and 1958. A total of more than 2,600 suspects were tried on capital offences related to the group. At the issue of the trials, a total of 1,574 were sentenced to hang.[444]

As an independent State, Kenya also has been the target of international terrorism for several decades, beginning with al-Qaeda's 1998 US Embassy bombing and later at the hands of al-Shabaab. At the time of writing, most al-Shabaab activity in Kenya involved clashes with the security forces. This involved in one instance shelling of a Kenyan military base in Mandera county in 2022, the first time this had occurred since 2018.[445] As of June 2023, the Kenyan military continued to contribute troops to the African Union Transition Mission in Somalia (ATMIS). Kenyan troops are present in regions in the south of Somalia close to the Kenyan border.[446] ATMIS's term was due to expire in the course of 2024 when its responsibilities are to be handed over to Somali security forces.[447]

4.5.2.1 The 1998 US Embassy Bombing

Kenya was an early victim of al-Qaeda terrorism. The group carried out a massive suicide bombing in front of the US Embassy in Nairobi on 7 August 1998, killing a total of 213 people and injuring a further 4,000. Although the attacks were directed at US facilities, the vast majority of casualties were Kenyan citizens.[448] It was the worst ever terrorism attack on Kenyan soil. But the casualties could have been even higher had the local guards not refused to open the gates to the bombers who arrived in a truck at the outer perimeter.[449]

Two suspects, Mohammed Sadeek Odeh and Mohammed Rashed Daoud al-Owhali, were arrested in Kenya within twenty days of the bombings and rendered to the United States shortly thereafter.[450] Mr al-Owhali had thrown a stun grenade at Embassy guards from the truck containing the bomb before getting out and running off.[451] Both he and Mr Odeh were convicted for their roles in the bombing and sentenced to life in prison in the United States in October 2001.[452] Eight of the twenty-one individuals indicted by the United States for the

---

Kenyans were subject to torture and other forms of ill-treatment at the hands of the colonial administration', he said. Britain 'sincerely regrets that these abuses took place'. Press Association, 'UK to compensate Kenya's Mau Mau torture victims', *The Guardian*, 6 June 2013, at: https://bit.ly/3OWxOyc; and see also M. Parry, 'Uncovering the brutal truth about the British empire', *The Guardian*, 18 August 2016, at: https://bit.ly/3J29pTX.

[444] C. L. Mwazighe, 'Legal responses to terrorism: Case study of the Republic of Kenya', Master's Thesis, Naval Postgraduate School, Monterey, CA, December 2012, at: https://bit.ly/43Smd7H, pp. 55–6.

[445] ACLED, 'Context Assessment: Increasing Security Challenges in Kenya', 2 March 2023, at: https://bit.ly/43ox086.

[446] Ibid.

[447] M. Zeuthen, 'A New Phase in the Fight against al-Shabaab in the Horn of Africa,' International Centre for Counter-Terrorism, 21 September 2022; and 'UN Security Council approves African Union Transition Mission in Somalia', *Daily Nation*, 1 April 2022.

[448] CNN, 'Profiles of Americans killed in Kenya embassy bombing', 13 August 1998, at: https://bit.ly/42x96Yl.

[449] 'Bombings of the US Embassies in Nairobi, Kenya and Dar es Salaam, Tanzania on August 7, 1998', Report of the Accountability Review Boards, at: https://bit.ly/30R1H8m.

[450] FBI, 'East African Embassy Bombings', undated but accessed 1 June 2023, at: https://bit.ly/3uqMKdK.

[451] S. M. Katz, *Relentless Pursuit: The DSS and the Manhunt for the Al-Qaeda Terrorists*, Forge/Tom Doherty Associates, New York, 2002.

[452] FBI, 'East African Embassy Bombings'.

bombing[453] were ultimately imprisoned in the United States. All were given life sentences, except for Adel Abdel Bari, who received a twenty-five-year sentence after pleading guilty to charges that included conspiring to kill US nationals and conspiring to make a threat to kill, injure, intimidate, or to damage and destroy property by means of an explosive.[454] None of the suspects in the bombing was prosecuted in Kenya.

As of June 2023, only one of the twenty-one suspects who remained alive was not in prison. Saif al-Adel was a former colonel in the Egyptian army and an explosives expert. Mr al-Adel, who was allegedly residing in Iran, is said to have become the de facto leader of al-Qaeda following the killing of Ayman Al-Zawahiri in Kabul at the end of July 2022.[455]

4.5.2.2 The Attack on the Westgate Centre (2013)

Some of those responsible for the 1998 Embassy bombing later found refuge with al-Shabaab.[456] Following the seizure of Mogadishu by the Islamic Courts Union in June 2006, al-Shabaab grew swiftly to become the most powerful opposition armed group in Somalia. In October 2011, following the kidnappings that were claimed by al-Shabaab, Kenya invaded southern Somalia in Operation Linda Nchi (a move of highly questionable legality under the rules of *jus ad bellum*). In February 2012, Kenyan forces were integrated into the African Union Mission to Somalia (AMISOM), a peacekeeping mission endorsed by the UN Security Council.[457]

On 21 September 2013, militants aligned with al-Shabaab entered a shopping centre in Nairobi and over the course of three days sixty-seven people were killed and hundreds more injured.[458] The dead included the nephew of President Uhuru Kenyatta.[459] It was the deadliest terrorist attack in Kenya since the Embassy bombing. Four militants involved in the operation were killed within the shopping centre by Kenyan soldiers in a chaotic counterterrorism operation.[460] It remains unknown whether others managed to escape. In the aftermath of the attack, al-Shabaab formally claimed responsibility for the operation and pledged to 'strike Kenyans where it hurts', declaring that they would 'turn their cities into graveyards' and that 'rivers of blood will flow in Nairobi'. A statement from the group further announced that 'the Kenyan government's decision to keep its invading force in Somalia is an indication that they haven't yet learnt any valuable lessons from the Westgate attacks, warning that Kenya was 'inviting unprecedented levels of insecurity, bloodshed and destruction'.[461]

---

[453] District Court for the Southern District of New York, *United States* v. *Usama Bin Laden and others*, Indictment, Ref. S(9) 98 Cr. 1023 (LBS), at: https://bit.ly/3NjL4vG.

[454] R. Calder, 'Dad of "John the Beatle" suspect admits Osama terror plot', *New York Post*, 19 September 2014, at: https://bit.ly/3qCQAjR.

[455] E. M. Lederer, 'Who is Al Qaeda's new leader? U.N. experts say it's widely believed to be this man', *Los Angeles Times*, 14 February 2023, at: https://bit.ly/3NgrQXA.

[456] H. Malalo and G. Obulutsa, 'Kenya court convicts two for helping deadly jihadist attack on shopping mall', *Reuters*, 7 October 2020, at: https://bit.ly/43runDX.

[457] Council on Foreign Relations, 'Timeline: Al-Shabaab in East Africa, 2004–2022', at: https://bit.ly/3ChXsG5. UN Security Council Resolution 1744 was adopted on 20 February 2007 by unanimous vote in favour. Operative paragraph 4 authorized the Mission 'to take all necessary measures as appropriate' to support dialogue and reconciliation in Somalia by assisting with the 'free movement, safe passage, and protection' of all those involved in the peace process.

[458] BBC, 'Westgate attack: Two jailed over Kenyan shopping mall attack', 30 October 2020, at: https://bit.ly/43Q5nWK.

[459] P. Gathara, 'The Westgate Mall attack and Kenya's national amnesia', *Aljazeera*, 21 September 2021, at: https://bit.ly/3WVB12S.

[460] Soldiers and police fired at each other during the operations over four days and CCTV footage emerged of soldiers looting the complex amid bodies sprawled on the bloodstained floor. Malalo and Obulutsa, 'Kenya court convicts two for helping deadly jihadist attack on shopping mall'.

[461] Reuters, 'Al-Shabab: We will strike Kenyans where it hurts', *Mail & Guardian*, 2 October 2013, at: https://bit.ly/3Nh9V23.

A small number of criminal suspects were arrested over the subsequent days, months, and years. This included eight suspects detained with a week of the attack, of whom three were later released after questioning.[462] A ninth individual was arrested on 1 October 2013.[463] Ultimately, only four individuals were indicted in connection with the attacks.[464] Kenya amended its Prevention of Terrorism Act in 2014, the year after the Westgate attack, with a view to facilitating investigations and prosecutions for terrorism offences. But terrorism trials in Kenya 'often proceeded slowly and inefficiently' according to the United States. The US Department of State noted that in 2019, the three defendants in the Westgate Mall attack (all ethnic Somalis, of whom two were Kenyan citizens) were still on trial at the end of the year. 'Most delays are caused by crowded court dockets and the lack of continuous trials.'[465]

In October 2020, seven years after their indictment, two defendants were convicted by a court in Nairobi for having assisted the attack, while a third defendant, also charged under the Prevention of Terrorism Act, was acquitted. Chief Magistrate Francis Andayi held that the prosecution had proved its case against two of the accused on charges of conspiracy of committing a terrorism act and supporting a terrorist group.[466] The same month, a further suspect was arrested in Nairobi. The unnamed individual was a Somali refugee.[467]

In its annual report on terrorism and counterterrorism for 2021, the Department of State reported that a new secure, US-funded Kahawa Law Court opened in Nairobi. The courthouse is a dedicated resource for bringing suspected terrorists to trial. But the report also noted that

> [d]espite successes, challenges persist. Access to defense counsel for terrorism suspects is limited because the government has not fully funded the National Legal Aid Service. The Office of the Director of Public Prosecutions has been working to develop a uniform and consistent nationwide policy on plea negotiations. The use of plea agreements could provide a mechanism for cooperation of lower-level accomplices against higher-level terrorism suspects. Both [counterterrorism]-focused prosecutors and judges have begun using plea agreements in proceedings.[468]

4.5.3 The Prosecution of Terrorism in Niger

Niger's criminal justice system has, thus far, proved to be inadequate to the task of identifying and prosecuting terrorist suspects effectively, fairly, and in a timely manner. There are dedicated provisions on terrorism in its Criminal Code, many of which were introduced by an Order of 2011.[469] Severe sentences are prescribed for terrorism offences. The maximum sentence is the death penalty, whose imposition is obligatory when deaths result from an act of terrorism.[470] In 2019, in a report on legal counterterrorism efforts in Niger published by the

---

[462] Times of Israel staff and Associated Press, 'Kenya arrests eight suspects in mall siege', *Times of Israel*, 27 September 2013, at: https://bit.ly/43qIDgg.

[463] 'Kenyan police arrest another Westgate Mall raid suspect', *The Citizen*, 1 October 2013, at: https://bit.ly/3CjlIYw.

[464] CBS News, 'Kenya charges 4 Somalis over Westgate Mall attack', 4 November 2013, at: https://bit.ly/3WTaWl7.

[465] US Department of State, 'Country Reports on Terrorism 2019: Kenya', Bureau of Counterterrorism, Washington DC, 2020, at: https://bit.ly/3J2s1U4.

[466] Malalo and Obulutsa, 'Kenya court convicts two for helping deadly jihadist attack on shopping mall'.

[467] Countering Violent Extremism (CVE) Research Hub, 'Terror-Related Arrests', 9 October 2020, dataset accessed on 1 June 2023, at: https://bit.ly/43Oyg5S.

[468] US Department of State, 'Country Reports on Terrorism 2021: Kenya', Bureau of Counterterrorism, Washington DC, February 2023, at: https://bit.ly/3CibAix.

[469] Order No. 2011–12 of 27 January 2011 on the amendment of the Criminal Code.

[470] As Section 4.2 of this chapter recalled, the mandatory death penalty violates the right to life.

168   *Prosecution of Terrorism Suspects*

Institute for Security Studies, two barristers from West Africa called for the comprehensive abolition of the death penalty in Niger.[471]

The terrorism threat was initially the result of the evolution of the 'Boko Haram' movement into an armed terrorism group in neighbouring Nigeria in 2009.[472] The Diffa region where the terrorism threat was first concentrated borders the north-east of Nigeria to the south of the country as well as the north-west of Chad to the east. The later splintering of Boko Haram into two factions in 2016 led to the emergence of Islamic State West Africa Province (ISWAP), which has also gained a strong foothold in Niger. ISWAP has become the more powerful of the two groups.[473] In response to the threat from Boko Haram in the Lake Chad Basin, Niger has contributed troops to the Multinational Joint Task Force (MNJTF) since the Force's repurposing for counterterrorism operations in 2014. Nigerien forces serve alongside military personnel from Benin, Cameroon, Chad, and Nigeria.[474]

In September 2016, Islamic State in the Greater Sahara (ISGS) surfaced in Burkina Faso, launching its first major attack on a border post near the Burkinabe city of Markoye. ISGS has also moved into the west of Niger following clashes in 2020 with an al-Qaeda-linked collectivity, JNIM.[475] By the end of 2016, some 1,400 terrorism suspects were in detention and awaiting trial, of whom at least 70 were children. Trials have been hampered by the limited resources available in the Nigerien criminal justice system, despite the creation of a dedicated judicial network for counterterrorism efforts. And while Nigerien law formally prohibits torture and other ill-treatment in custody, the US Department of State notes reports that the security forces have beaten and abused detainees. 'Security officials reportedly inflicted severe pain and suffering on detainees in Diffa Region to secure information.'[476]

As is the case with many contexts in which denunciations of criminal suspects occur, a significant number of reported terrorists have not in fact engaged in any act of terrorism. Field research by the International Crisis Group (ICG) in the Diffa region in 2016 indicated that false or mistaken denunciations may even form the majority of cases: 'Accusations of collusion with Boko Haram allow people to settle personal scores, get rid of troublesome neighbours, business rivals and even, in a case reported to the ICG, of a jealous husband. According to some security sources, most accusations are false.'[477] As a consequence, in 2019 Cissé and Ngari called for the strengthening of human and material capacities for the field investigations in order to confirm allegations or discard records that were based on unfounded allegations.[478] The extent

---

[471] H. Cissé and A. Ngari, *Lutte contre le terrorisme au Niger: Offrir la garantie d'un procès équitable aux présumés terroristes*, Institute for Security Studies, 2019, at: https://bit.ly/464YAuu.

[472] The group is officially known as Jamā'at Ahl as-Sunnah lid-Da'wah wa'l-Jihād, but is commonly referred to as Boko Haram, meaning Western education is forbidden (the word 'boko' comes from the Colonial English word for book). The US Department of State designated Boko Haram a Foreign Terrorist Organization in November 2013. Office for the Director of US National Intelligence, 'Boko Haram', National Counterterrorism Center, undated but accessed 1 June 2023, at: https://bit.ly/43GSGh4.

[473] Congressional Research Service, 'Boko Haram and the Islamic State West Africa Province', updated 24 February 2022, at: https://bit.ly/43J37k6.

[474] MNJTF, 'About the Force', at: https://bit.ly/43u99pa.

[475] Center for Preventive Action, 'Violent Extremism in the Sahel', updated 27 March 2023, Council on Foreign Relations, at: https://bit.ly/3CfijUt.

[476] US Department of State, 'Country Reports on Terrorism 2016: Niger', Bureau of Counterterrorism, Washington DC, 2017, at: https://bit.ly/3WXYy37.

[477] International Crisis Group, *Niger and Boko Haram: Beyond Counter-insurgency*, Africa Report No. 245, 27 February 2017, note 57. The interviews were conducted with an administrator in Diffa and members of the security services in Niamey in May 2016.

[478] Cissé and Ngari, Lutte contre le terrorisme au Niger: Offrir la garantie d'un procès équitable aux présumés terroristes, p. 2.

to which this issue has been effectively addressed is unclear, but as of 2022, police and other security force members were still 'on occasion' rounding up individuals accused of being members of or supporters of terrorist groups based only on circumstantial evidence, subsequently holding them for months or even years.[479]

The International Crisis Group has also noted that an increase in arrests since February 2015 'has put pressure on the judicial and prison system. In the prisons, where inmates await a hypothetical trial, suspects arrested on the basis of denunciation mingle with hard-line, violent jihadists. They may therefore become a recruitment hotbed for armed groups that reject the state's authority'. The ICG called on the authorities 'to do more than isolate the most fervent preachers to counter this threat'.[480] The US Department of State reported that in 2022 terrorist and 'high-threat' offenders were duly separated from other criminal offenders but also observed that the authorities were holding pre-trial detainees with convicted prisoners. This detention could be exceptionally prolonged: the law allows pre-trial confinement of up to four years for terrorism offenses where the prison sentence, if ultimately convicted, could be a minimum of ten years (and even this upper limit was not always respected in practice).[481]

Meanwhile, the security situation has continued to deteriorate. By 2020, terrorist groups active in the country included Islamic State in the Greater Sahara, Boko Haram, ISWAP, and JNIM. The Department of State observed that Niger was the only country in the world with the presence of an Islamic State affiliate on three of its borders.[482] As a consequence, the extent of violence has continued to spiral. A report by the Africa Center for Strategic Studies in February 2023 noted a 43 per cent increase in violent events in Niger in 2022, rising to 214, although fatalities were cut in half compared to the previous year, dropping to 539 deaths.[483] Some of the unlawful violence is attributed to the army. With respect to 2022, the US Department of State noted 'numerous reports of arbitrary or unlawful executions by authorities or their agents. For example, the armed forces were accused of summarily executing persons suspected of fighting with terrorist groups in the Diffa and Tillaberi Regions'.[484]

In May 2023, the Nigerien army reported that it had detained 1,397 associates of Boko Haram, many of whom were women and children, who had fled into the south-east of Niger following clashes with ISWAP.[485] This would only add to the criminal justice burden, as well as the need for speedy rehabilitation and reintegration of those not engaged in violence. There were, though, some more positive signs emerging in the south-west of the country at the time of writing. Community mediation efforts in the Tillabery region led to the signing of a peace agreement between the Fulani and Zarma communities in January 2023. The South Africa-based Institute for Security Studies (ISS) considers the deal an important one, as violent jihadist groups have exploited decades-long conflicts between the two communities for the purpose of recruitment.[486]

---

[479] US Department of State, '2022 Country Reports on Human Rights Practices: Niger', Bureau of Democracy, Human Rights, and Labor, Washington DC, 2023, at: https://bit.ly/43KvYoa.

[480] International Crisis Group, *Niger and Boko Haram*, p. 23.

[481] US Department of State, '2022 Country Reports on Human Rights Practices: Niger'.

[482] US Department of State, 'Country Reports on Terrorism 2020: Niger', Bureau of Counterterrorism, Washington DC, 2021, at: https://bit.ly/3P7ne7L.

[483] Africa Center for Strategic Studies, 'Fatalities from Militant Islamist Violence in Africa Surge by Nearly 50 Percent', Infographic, 6 February 2023, at: https://bit.ly/3MZUZF3.

[484] US Department of State, '2022 Country Reports on Human Rights Practices: Niger'.

[485] Agence France-Press, 'Niger Says It Has Picked Up 1,400 Boko Haram Followers', *The Defense Post*, 10 May 2023, at: https://bit.ly/3J2n3qr.

[486] H. Koné and F. R. Koné, 'Is Niger's counter-terrorism approach an exception in the Sahel?', *ISS Today*, 5 April 2023, at: https://bit.ly/45TokcW.

The extent of detention of suspected terrorists and the inadequacies of the formal justice system have also led to greater discussion of the possibilities afforded by transitional justice mechanisms. There is varying perception and acceptance of transitional justice. In the view of an ISS researcher, some affected communities 'misconceive' it 'as a way to reintegrate former Boko Haram members that allows them to evade criminal sanctions for their atrocities'. The Institute reiterates that reintegration and reconciliation are both needed for peace, but acknowledges that 'victim-centric remedies' are 'crucial in getting transitional justice right'.[487] What is clear is that not everyone associated in some manner with a terrorist group can be prosecuted and that many of those held on the basis of suspicion alone should not be prosecuted.

4.5.4 *The Prosecution of Terrorism in Somalia*

Al-Shabaab – meaning 'the youth' – is an insurgent group formed in the early 2000s that seeks to establish an Islamic State in Somalia. It grew in strength after Ethiopia's invasion of Somalia in late 2006, subsequently gaining control of Mogadishu in the late 2000s, but a military campaign led by the African Union (AU) pushed the group's forces out of the major towns. The group has, however, proved 'resilient' and it still controls large parts of the south of Somalia with lethal attacks regularly mounted against international forces and civilians across the region.[488] At the end of October 2022, for instance, a massive twin car bombing in the capital killed at least 100 people and injured more than 300 others. Amnesty International termed Al-Shabaab's actions crimes under international law and declared it 'absolutely crucial that all those suspected of criminal responsibility for this crime face justice in fair trials'.[489]

Prosecutions of al-Shabaab members have been conducted in military courts. Colonel Hassan Ali Nur Shute, whose father was assassinated in 2018 in an act claimed by al-Shabaab, chairs the Somali National Armed Forces military court.[490] In 2017–21, he, and the eleven other military judges he supervises, tried a total of 659 alleged militants on charges of murder or terrorism (or both), as an article by a Voice of America journalist of January 2022 describes. Of those, 455 – mostly al-Shabab militants, but also a few individuals affiliated with Islamic State – were convicted. Seventeen of those convicted had been executed as of early 2022. These included Hassan Aden Isak, who coordinated a double truck bombing in Mogadishu on 14 October 2017 that killed 587 people. Mr Isak was executed exactly a year later. Ten other al-Shabaab fighters remained on death row.[491]

Somalia's system of military justice demands a panel of three judges for any trial. This rule applies irrespective of whether the defendant is an alleged militant or a member of the armed forces. The overwhelming majority of cases are heard in Mogadishu, but military judges also travel to other Somali regions and towns. The hearings are public – and are sometimes even televised – with attorneys for the prosecution and defence. Decisions to impose the death penalty

---

[487] A. Olojo and M. Mahdi, 'Transitional justice can give victims a voice in Lake Chad Basin', *ISS Today*, 27 April 2022, at: https://bit.ly/3Nv19yN.

[488] C. Klobucista, J. Masters, and M. Aly Sergie, 'Backgrounder: Al-Shabaab', Council on Foreign Relations, last updated 6 December 2022, at: https://bit.ly/3Nle5qI.

[489] Amnesty International, 'Somalia: Al-Shabaab must urgently stop carrying out attacks against civilians', 31 October 2022, at: https://bit.ly/3MVGUbT.

[490] 'Somalia: Al-Shabab kills father of military court chief', *Garowe Online*, 2 January 2018, at: https://bit.ly/3qrwGIy.

[491] H. Maruf, 'Al-Shabab Fears Somalia's Military Court, Judge Says', *Voice of America*, 14 January 2022, at: https://bit.ly/3CjXvBf.

as a sentence must be unanimous, and Colonel Shute must approve each one.[492] There is, however, no right of appeal.[493]

The jurisdictional basis for the military court to try al-Shabaab and other terrorism suspects is also strongly disputed. Human Rights Watch points out that the system of military justice is operating under a 2011 presidential decree that declared a state of emergency in parts of Mogadishu vacated by al-Shabaab. 'Although the state of emergency expired after three months, the military court has continued to try a range of defendants beyond those envisioned under the Military Code of Criminal Procedure.'[494]

But the system has continued. In 2020, the Independent Expert on the situation of human rights in Somalia wrote in his report to the UN Human Rights Council that this occurred 'despite serious rule of law and human rights concerns, especially in relation to the lack of fair trial and due process guarantees. Also of concern is the continuing practice of trying civilians in these courts'.[495] The same year, Human Rights Watch called for children to be explicitly excluded from the jurisdiction of the military courts.[496] Also prosecuted have been members of militia forces supported by the authorities to control al-Shabaab. In a report in March 2023, the International Crisis Group noted a case of a militia member being sentenced to death by the court for shooting a civilian at an ad hoc checkpoint.[497]

4.6 THE PROSECUTION OF TERRORISM IN EUROPE

The last two decades have seen many prosecutions for terrorism across Europe. In fifteen European Union Member States,[498] court proceedings for terrorist offences that concluded in 2022 resulted in a total of 427 convictions and acquittals for terrorist offences. The highest number of convictions and acquittals were reported by France (110), Belgium (81), and Germany (54).[499] In June 2022, as discussed further in Section 4.6.1.2, a French court sentenced the only surviving member of the terrorist cell that committed the deadly terrorist attacks on 13 November 2015 in Paris and Saint-Denis to life imprisonment with no possibility of parole. In December 2022, also in France, eight persons were convicted for their involvement in the terrorist attack on 14 July 2016 in Nice. Two were found guilty of participation in a criminal conspiracy with the purpose of preparing an act of terrorism and sentenced to eighteen years' imprisonment. According to the court, they knew about the radicalization of the perpetrator of the attack and his potential to commit a terrorist act. Another co-defendant was given a twelve-year prison term for providing a firearm to the perpetrator of the attack. The remaining five men were handed penalties between two and eight years' imprisonment.[500]

---

[492] Ibid.

[493] Legal Action Worldwide, 'Due Process and the Rule of Law in Somalia: Preliminary Key Findings and Recommendations', 2018.

[494] Human Rights Watch, 'The Courts of "Absolute Power": Fair Trial Violations by Somalia's Military Court', 21 May 2014, at: https://bit.ly/3X1ykxo.

[495] 'Situation of human rights in Somalia: Report of the Independent Expert on the situation of human rights in Somalia', UN doc. A/HRC/45/52, 24 August 2020, at: https://bit.ly/43RPE9Y, para. 55.

[496] Human Rights Watch, 'Submission to the Universal Periodic Review of Somalia', October 2020, para. 21.

[497] International Crisis Group, *Sustaining Gains in Somalia's Offensive against Al-Shabaab*, Africa Briefing No. 187, 21 March 2023, at: https://bit.ly/3NkrKy5, p. 9, citing Radio Dalsan, 'Military court sentences soldier to death for shooting minibus driver at illegal checkpoint', 4 December 2022.

[498] Austria, Belgium, Denmark, France, Germany, Greece, Hungary, Italy, Latvia, the Netherlands, Portugal, Romania, Slovakia, Spain, and Sweden.

[499] Some of the reported convictions and acquittals were final, while others were pending judicial remedy, as appeals have been filed by the prosecution, the defence, or both.

[500] Europol, *European Union Terrorism Situation and Trend Report*, Publications Office of the European Union, Luxembourg, 2023, at: https://bit.ly/3qKTOC8, p. 14.

Belgium's worst peacetime terrorism attack in Brussels left thirty-two dead and hundreds seriously injured. Belgium's largest ever criminal trial for those involved in planning and assisting the attacks in March 2016 ended with convictions in July 2023.[501] Many of those on trial in Belgium had participated in France's worst peacetime terrorism attack five months earlier in November 2015.

A report by the European Union Agency for Law Enforcement Cooperation (EUROPOL) published in 2023 stated that twenty-eight completed, failed, and foiled terrorist attacks were reported by the twenty-seven EU Member States in 2022. This was more than the previous year (eighteen attacks), but remained below the number of attacks reported in 2020 (fifty-six). In 2022, Italy experienced the highest number of attacks (twelve), followed by France (six), Greece (four), and Belgium (three). Germany, Slovakia, and Spain reported one attack each. Of the twenty-eight 'attacks', sixteen were completed.[502] Of the 380 individuals arrested in Member States in 2022 for terrorism-related offences, 266 were for violent jihadist offences, with most of these carried out in France (93).[503] The majority of the arrested suspects were charged with membership of a terrorist organization (ninety-five) and for planning or preparing an attack (forty-one). Other suspects were charged for disseminating propaganda (eighteen) and terrorism financing (fourteen). Most arrestees were male (176). The arrestees were between fifteen and seventy-five years old.[504]

In Russia, the Beslan school siege was a terrorist attack that started on 1 September 2004 and involved the taking of more than 1,100 people as hostages. It ended with the deaths of 333 hostages, 186 of whom were children. The only individuals ever prosecuted in relation to the attack, however, were the mothers of some of the victims who accused Vladimir Putin of failing to protect their children. Proceedings against local police officers for negligence in failing to prevent the attack were discontinued. In Ukraine, the Russian invasion that began on 24 February 2022 involved many incidents termed terrorism by the Ukrainian leadership. Prosecutions of captured Russians, however, were for war crimes and not terrorism.

The worst terrorist attack in Western Europe was the 'Lockerbie' bombing in December 1988 which killed 259 passengers and crew of Pan Am Flight 103 and 11 residents at Lockerbie in Scotland who were hit by the debris from the plane.[505] The attack resulted in the prosecution and conviction in 2001 before a special court convened in the Netherlands of a Libyan national and government intelligence officer, Abdelbaset al-Megrahi. In December 2022, Abu Agila Masud, also a Libyan national and alleged intelligence officer was arraigned before a court in Washington DC, also charged with involvement in the bombing, including the construction of the explosive device. In February 2023, he pleaded not guilty to two counts of destruction of an aircraft resulting in death and one count of destruction of a vehicle resulting in death.[506] In December 2023, it was revealed that his trial on federal offences was set to open on 12 May 2025.[507]

---

[501] EURACTIV.com with Agence France-Presse, 'Six years after bombings, Belgium readies for biggest trial', 29 November 2022, at: https://bit.ly/43YNULV.

[502] Europol, *European Union Terrorism Situation and Trend Report*, 2023, p. 9.

[503] Ibid., p. 10.

[504] Ibid., p. 11.

[505] US Department of Justice, 'Pan Am Flight 103 Terrorist Suspect in Custody for 1988 Bombing over Lockerbie, Scotland', Press release, Office of Public Affairs, 12 December 2022, at: https://bit.ly/43YR3vd.

[506] 'Lockerbie bombing suspect pleads not guilty in US court', *BBC*, 8 February 2023, at: https://bit.ly/43Ugz4E.

[507] C. Meighan, 'US sets date for trial against Lockerbie bombing suspect', *STV News*, 21 December 2023, at: https://bit.ly/3S0SFdq.

4.6.1 *The Prosecution of Terrorism in Belgium*

Belgium has detailed anti-terrorism legislation incorporated in its Criminal Code by the 2003 Terrorism Offences Act. Terrorism is generally defined in the Criminal Code as an offence that

> by its nature or context, may seriously harm a country or an international organization and is committed intentionally with the aim of seriously intimidating a population or unduly compelling a public authority or an international organization to perform or refrain from to do any act, or to seriously destabilize or destroy the fundamental political, constitutional, economic or social structures of a country or an international organization.[508]

Life imprisonment is the maximum sentence for the most serious terrorist offences under the Criminal Code. In 2013, a new law criminalized any person who diffuses ideas or messages with a view to inciting terrorist acts. The Criminal Code as amended also criminalized recruitment for terrorist purposes. In 2017, a new offence of travelling abroad for terrorist purposes was added. There is no carve-out in the Criminal Code for the exercise of fundamental human rights.

On 22 March 2016, a total of 32 people were killed and more than 300 injured in Brussels in coordinated terrorist attacks linked to Islamic State. As a proportion of its population, Belgium is said to have had more nationals fighting for Islamic State and other violent Jihadist forces in Syria than any other State in Western Europe.[509] According to the US Department of State, however, Belgium's greatest terrorism threat now comes from home-grown violence by lone actors, whether inspired by violent Islamist extremism or, to a lesser extent, violent right-wing extremism.[510] During the Covid-19 pandemic, the authorities in Belgium noted an increase in right-wing extremist propaganda, especially online.[511]

4.6.1.1 The 2016 Brussels Bombings

On 22 March 2016, two coordinated attacks were perpetrated in Brussels by adherents of Islamic State. Two suicide bombers detonated bombs at Brussels Airport and a third detonated a bomb on a train leaving Maelbeek underground station in the centre of the city. Najim Laachraoui, a twenty-four-year-old man, and Ibrahim El Bakraoui, a twenty-nine-year-old man, were later named as the suicide bombers at the airport. In 2010, Ibrahim El Bakraoui had shot and injured a police officer during an attempted robbery and had been sentenced to ten years in prison but was released early. Najim Laachraoui had been arrested in Turkey near the Syrian border in June 2015 and deported. He is believed to have made the bombs used in the November 2015 Paris attacks. Khalid El Bakraoui, aged twenty-seven, was Ibrahim's younger brother. He conducted the suicide bombing at Maalbeek. In 2012, he received a prison sentence for a violent carjacking and at the time of the Brussels attacks was being searched for by Belgian police for breaching his parole conditions.[512]

In December 2022, ten men went on trial in the Belgian capital charged with involvement in the attacks. The trial, which was expected to last six months, was taking place at a specially

---

[508] Art. 137, Criminal Code of Belgium.

[509] N. Elbagir, B. Naik, and L. Ben Allal, 'Why Belgium is Europe's front line in the war on terror', CNN, 24 March 2016, at: https://bit.ly/44hjoif.

[510] US Department of State, 'Country Reports on Terrorism 2020: Belgium', Bureau of Counterterrorism, Washington DC, 2021, at: https://bit.ly/3Na1qWn.

[511] US Department of State, 'Country Reports on Terrorism 2021: Belgium', Bureau of Counterterrorism, Washington DC, 2023, at: https://bit.ly/3qA2YRI.

[512] A. Chrisafis, 'The men in the top floor flat who sowed terror in Brussels', *The Guardian*, 24 March 2016, at: https://bit.ly/43XsleD.

constructed court at the former NATO headquarters.[513] Six of the ten defendants had already been found guilty of involvement in the terror attacks in Paris in November 2015 that killed 130 people (see Section 4.6.1.2). Salah Abdeslam, who was convicted of a leading role in those attacks, had been detained four days before the Brussels bombings. Another defendant is Mohamed Abrini, who prosecutors allege is the 'man in the hat' who was captured on CCTV fleeing the airport after his suitcase of explosives failed to detonate. On 29 June 2022, Abrini had been convicted of involvement in the Paris attacks and had been sentenced to life imprisonment with a minimum term to be served of twenty-two years. The eight other suspects are accused of supplying the attackers with weapons and logistical assistance or supporting the terrorist cell.[514] One defendant, Osama Atar, is believed to have been killed in Syria and was being tried in absentia.[515]

The long-delayed trial did not open in the most auspicious circumstances. In January 2023, *Le Monde* reported that controversy over the daily strip-search of the defendants was still disrupting the proceedings. Denounced by the defendants, who refused to appear at the trial, the searches had been deemed illegal by a civil court in Belgium but were still being carried out in the interest of security. Jonathan De Taye, lawyer for one of the accused, told the journalist for *Le Monde*: 'The French have given us an example of a perfect trial, here we're doing the opposite.'[516] There were even allegations from some quarters that key figures were deliberately sabotaging the trial. Some suggested the 'passivity' of the two prosecutors reflected the wish of the federal prosecutor's office to prove the impossibility of having terrorism cases tried by a jury. Other observers claimed that the Minister of Justice, a Flemish liberal, had no problem in seeing a francophone trial bogged down. The former member of a nationalist party was said to be in favour of regionalizing justice.[517]

In early April 2023, Salah Abdeslam, a thirty-three-year-old Frenchman and the sole surviving member of the unit that carried out the Paris attacks, pleaded not guilty to the charges against him.[518] He claimed that it was 'a great injustice' that he was 'sitting here in the dock'. He said he had not taken part in the activities of any terrorist group and noted that he had been in prison since 18 March 2016, claiming that the plans for the 2016 Brussels attacks were made the day after his arrest.[519] He told the court: 'The pilots of the planes over Raqqa and Mosul will never find themselves in the dock to answer for their abominable acts, they have been rewarded.'[520]

Mohamed Abrini, who first met Laachraoui in Syria in 2015, said that shortly before the attacks, he informed them that he wished to pull out. 'I saw women and children. I said I'm leaving; I'm not doing this.'[521] Abrini admitted that he did not attempt to convince Laachraoui or El Bakraoui to cancel the attack despite having already decided that he would not join them as they headed to the airport in a taxi. The only arguments they would listen to were 'religious', he

---

[513] BBC, 'Brussels attacks: Trial begins over 2016 attacks that killed 32', 5 December 2022, at: https://bit.ly/3Xd9xGk.

[514] Euronews with Associated Press, '2016 Brussels bombings: Ten men go on trial over airport and metro attacks', 10 December 2022, at: https://bit.ly/3JcvJdG.

[515] Ibid.

[516] J.-P. Stroobants, 'Belgian court struggling with the trial of the 2016 Brussels terrorist attacks', *Le Monde*, 10 January 2023, at: https://bit.ly/3JbTcvA.

[517] Ibid.

[518] Belga News Agency, 'Salah Abdeslam pleads not guilty in Brussels terror attack trial', 5 April 2023, at: https://bit.ly/3Nubueg.

[519] Ibid.

[520] RFI, 'Terror accused say Western bombing of Syria inspired 2016 Brussels attacks', 13 April 2023, at: https://bit.ly/3NrD1Mf.

[521] S. Rose, '"Man in the hat" Brussels 2016 bombing suspect minimises role in trial', *The National News*, 6 April 2023, at: https://bit.ly/3JcBoSw.

4.6 Prosecution of Terrorism in Europe

said, describing his knowledge of Islam at the time as 'close to zero'. His testimony also contradicted statements he made to police in 2018 whereby he wanted to follow Laachraoui 'until death'. Asked about this, he told the judge, 'Honestly, I don't remember.'[522]

A few days later, Sofien Ayari, a Tunisian national who had already been sentenced to thirty years' imprisonment for his involvement in the Paris attacks, went to fight with Islamic State in 2014 before being wounded and hospitalized in Syria. He told the court: 'What I experienced in Raqqa was not a war. It was something else. It was bombs falling on men, women, children. It was a tipping point for me. I had never felt such hatred, such incomprehension. I was mad with rage.' He added, 'I have the impression that only one side is being condemned.' Ayari went into hiding after the Paris attacks but was detained in Brussels just before the bombings.[523]

On 25 July 2023, after two weeks of deliberations by the jury, four of the eight accused were convicted of 'murder linked to terrorism'. Two other suspects – a Tunisian national, Sofien Ayari, and a Rwandan national, Herve Bayingana Muhirwa – were acquitted of murder but found guilty of participating in a terrorist group. Muhirwa was sentenced to 10 years in prison and Ayari to 20 years in September 2023. The two other accused, brothers Smail and Ibrahim Farisi, were both acquitted of all charges.[524]

4.6.2 The Prosecution of Terrorism in France

The proceedings of the largest criminal trial ever held in France opened on 8 September 2021. It involved 20 defendants, 330 lawyers, and 1,800 plaintiffs. On 13 November 2015, two suicide bombings occurred outside the Stade de France, where France was playing Germany in a friendly football match. This was followed by attacks on a series of bars and restaurants in the tenth and eleventh *arrondissements* by a unit of ten terrorists. The attacks culminated in a massacre inside a rock concert venue, the Bataclan. A total of 130 people died – 90 in the Bataclan – and more than 490 were injured in the attacks. The holding of eleven hostages inside the Bataclan by two terrorists was ended without loss of life among the hostages after a stand-off of more than two hours, thanks to the forcible intervention of specialist counterterrorism agents.[525] The government had specially constructed the biggest ever criminal courtroom on French soil in the thirteenth-century *Palais de Justice*, which was able to accommodate more than 550 people.[526]

Almost all of those directly responsible for the killings died in the attacks. Of the nine terrorists directly involved in the killings, seven died during the attacks and a further two were killed in a police raid five days later. But as already mentioned, Salah Abdeslam, a Brussels-born French citizen, the tenth member of the terrorist cell, survived to stand trial. His suicide vest was found dumped in a bin, with investigators saying it was 'defective'; Mr Abdeslam claimed that he backed out of the attack at the last minute and fled.[527]

---

[522] Ibid.

[523] Agence France-Presse, 'Brussels Attack Suspects Say Wests Bombing of IS Was "Tipping Point"', *Voice of America*, 12 April 2023, at: https://bit.ly/465cTza.

[524] 'Belgian court finds Paris attacker Salah Abdeslam guilty of murder in 2016 Brussels bombings', *France24*, 25 July 2023, at: https://bit.ly/44vrxNS.

[525] BBC, 'Paris attacks: Bataclan hostage held for hours by attackers', 21 November 2015, at: https://bit.ly/3p1yFTL; and A. Chrisafis, 'Bataclan survivors recall being held hostage as gunmen fired on crowd', *The Guardian*, 19 October 2021, at: https://bit.ly/3p2UVfU.

[526] I. Guenfoud, 'France's "trial of the century" begins over Bataclan terror attacks that killed 130', *abc News*, 8 September 2021, at: https://bit.ly/3p51mPI.

[527] A. Chrisafis, 'Paris attacks trial to conclude after 10 months of harrowing testimony', *The Guardian*, 29 June 2022, at: https://bit.ly/462Vabw.

176 *Prosecution of Terrorism Suspects*

Of the twenty defendants formally put on trial, fourteen appeared before the court. Six defendants were tried in absentia, including five Islamic State officials presumed dead in either Iraq or Syria. The trial heard ten months of harrowing testimony from the victims and the bereaved, which at times reflected more of a commission of inquiry than a trial. That is not to downplay the critical value of the trial as a platform for survivors to speak out about their experiences – some would later describe how the trial 'helped them piece together the fragments of their shattered lives', but it is not an approach that would be readily countenanced in the criminal court of a common law jurisdiction.[528]

On 29 June 2022, Salah Abdeslam was sentenced to life in prison without parole for murder and attempted murder in relation to a terrorist enterprise. His sentence, the toughest under French law, has only been pronounced four times in France: for crimes related to rape and murder of minors. The court found that his explosives vest had indeed malfunctioned, dismissing his argument that he ditched the vest because he decided not to follow through with the attack. He had nonetheless told the court that his profession was 'Islamic State fighter'.[529]

The special court also convicted nineteen other men for their involvement in the attacks, which were claimed by Islamic State. Eighteen of the defendants were convicted of various terrorism charges, while the nineteenth was convicted on a lesser fraud charge. They were given punishments ranging from suspended sentences to life in prison. Mohamed Abrini, who admitted to driving some of the attackers to Paris, was given a life sentence with twenty-two years as a minimum term. Swedish citizen Osama Krayem and Sofian Ayari were sentenced to thirty years' imprisonment with the possibility of parole after twenty years for helping to prepare the attacks. Mohamed Bakkali, a Belgian-Moroccan, was given the same sentence for his 'fundamental role' in preparing the Paris attacks.[530]

Muhammed Usman, a twenty-nine-year old Pakistani national, and Adel Haddidi, a thirty-four-year-old Algerian, were arrested in Greece as they travelled with the two jihadists who went on to blow themselves up outside the Stade de France. The two men were attempting to disguise themselves as refugees in the mass of people heading from Syria to Europe via Turkey, and had intended to take part in the attacks according to claims by prosecutors.[531] They were both sentenced to eighteen years in prison, with twelve to be served before the possibility of parole.[532] Ahmad Alkhald, age unknown, also known as Omar Darif, is a Syrian national, accused of making the suicide belts. Presumed dead, he was sentenced by the court to life in prison with no possibility of parole for thirty years for conviction for several offences, including complicity to terrorist murder.[533]

One of the suspected masterminds of the attacks, Oussama Atar, was tried in absentia but is presumed to have already died in either Syria or Iraq. He was convicted on charges that included directing a terrorist group and was sentenced to life with no parole. His younger brother, Yassine Atar, a thirty-five-year old, met with key suspects and his family had links to the jihadist cell in Brussels. A key to a hideout was found at his home. In his final statement, however, he said: 'I hope you've understood that I have absolutely nothing to do with Oussama Atar and nothing to

---

[528] Indeed, as the media report, never before had a French courtroom 'given so much time and space to the anguish of those who lost a loved one'. B. Dodman and A. Mazoue 'Salah Abdeslam sentenced to life in prison as Paris attacks trial winds up', *France24*, 29 June 2022, at: https://bit.ly/3XbCeDC.

[529] Ibid.

[530] Ibid.

[531] Ibid.

[532] BBC, 'Paris trial: Salah Abdeslam guilty as historic trial ends', 30 June 2022, at: https://bit.ly/42HeHvh.

[533] Associated Press, '20 convicted in Paris terrorist attacks trial: Who they are', 29 June 2022, at: https://bit.ly/3NccFgQ.

4.6 Prosecution of Terrorism in Europe

do with these attacks which I condemn firmly.'[534] He was sentenced to eight years in prison for criminal association with a terrorist enterprise.[535]

4.6.3 The Prosecution of Terrorism in the United Kingdom

4.6.3.1 The Prosecution of Terrorism Linked to the Troubles in Northern Ireland

The United Kingdom has a long experience of prosecuting terrorism cases from the thirty years of the 'Troubles' in Northern Ireland between 1968 and 1998. The violence saw 3,720 people killed[536] and more than 42,000 people injured.[537] Convictions were secured in Northern Ireland of some of the individuals responsible for the tens of thousands of individual acts of terrorism perpetrated in the province during the Troubles. But prosecutions also included several wrongful convictions for some of the gravest terrorism offences before juries on mainland Britain for terrorist bombings in England. These included convictions for the twin bombings in Guildford on 5 October 1974, which killed 5 people and injured 65 others along with the associated Woolwich bombings, which killed 3 people; and for the twin Birmingham pub bombings on 21 November 1974, which killed 21 people and injured 182 others. All these bombings were carried out by members of the Provisional Irish Republican Army (PIRA) but innocent people were convicted at trial instead. The so-called Guildford Four were cleared of all charges in 1989 after nearly fifteen years in prison.[538] The so-called Birmingham Six were similarly cleared of all charges and released in 1991 after sixteen years in prison.[539]

Within Northern Ireland itself many prosecutions were conducted before so-called Diplock Courts, where no jury was present to determine guilt. Rasnic pointed out some of the concerning features of the criminal justice approach that were adopted in response to fears that jury members would be intimidated by the loyalist or republican paramilitary groups. These included the possibility for a suspect taken into custody after arrest to be held for up to four weeks pending a first hearing before a magistrate; that a confession is presumed admissible in the absence of any *overt* evidence of the interrogator's deliberate effort to force the confession (with 'moderate degree of physical maltreatment' of the suspect explicitly permissible in order to obtain a confession); and the acceptance as 'credible' by the court 'the uncorroborated testimony of a known paramilitary terrorist who is under no obligation to cease his own illegal activities and who has not the reason nor the incentive to be candid and truthful'.[540] The Diplock court system processed a total of 418 persons, of whom 223 pleaded guilty, while 57 other defendants were found guilty by the presiding judge.[541] But acquittal rates before Diplock courts dropped

---

[534] Dodman and Mazoue 'Salah Abdeslam sentenced to life in prison as Paris attacks trial winds up'.

[535] Associated Press, '20 convicted in Paris terrorist attacks trial: Who they are'.

[536] D. McKittrick, S. Kelters, B. Feeney, C. Thornton, and D. McVea, *Lost Lives*, Mainstream, Edinburgh, 2007, p. 1552.

[537] Conflict Archive on the Internet (CAIN), RUC/PSNI statistics: Table NI-SEC-05: Persons injured (number) due to the security situation in Northern Ireland (only), data for 1968 to 1998, at: https://bit.ly/43ZRSnx.

[538] History, 'Guildford Four are cleared of IRA bombings', last updated 16 October 2020, at: https://bit.ly/3CtDGY6.

[539] R. Moore, 'Why the Birmingham Six's story must not be forgotten', *The Guardian*, 26 March 2022, at: https://bit.ly/43SklvA.

[540] C. D. Rasnic, 'Northern Ireland's Criminal Trials without Jury: The Diplock Experiment', *Annual Survey of International & Comparative Law*, Vol. 5, No. 1 (1999), Article 9, 239–57, at: https://bit.ly/3JekUrA, at: pp. 244, 248, 249, 250. See also K. L. H. Samuel and N. White (eds.), *Counter-Terrorism and International Law*, Routledge, Abingdon, 2017, p. xxvii.

[541] Rasnic, 'Northern Ireland's Criminal Trials without Jury, pp. 246–7.

178   *Prosecution of Terrorism Suspects*

significantly over time: from 53 per cent in 1984 to 29 per cent in 1993.[542] This is ascribed, at least in part, to the presiding judges becoming hardened so as to be biased against acquittals.[543]

In July 2021, the UK government announced it was effectively ending all prosecutions related to crimes committed during the Troubles. Described as a de facto amnesty for former British soldiers and former paramilitaries, the new Statute of limitations would apply to incidents prior to the signing of the Good Friday Agreement in 1998 that effectively ended the Troubles. Announcing the decision in the UK Parliament, the Secretary of State for Northern Ireland, Brandon Lewis, said: 'It's now a difficult, in fact painful, truth that the focus on criminal investigations is increasingly unlikely to deliver successful criminal justice outcomes, but all the while it continues to divide communities and it fails to obtain answers for a majority of victims and families.'[544] Less than a year later, the Secretary of State let it be known that terrorists who refuse to cooperate with authorities could still face prosecution for atrocities committed during the Troubles under the new proposed legislation designed to protect British troops.[545] At the time of writing, The Northern Ireland Troubles (Legacy and Reconciliation) Act, which was adopted in September 2023, was subject to legal contestation in the UK and potentially also before the European Court of Human Rights.[546]

4.6.3.2 The Conviction of Abdelbaset al-Megrahi for the Lockerbie Bombing

Western Europe's greatest loss of life from a peacetime act of terrorism was the bombing of Pan Am Flight 103 from London to New York on 21 December 1988. Explosives hidden in a cassette recorder in luggage placed in the hold of the aircraft were detonated by timer while the aircraft was flying over Scotland. A total of 270 people were killed, including 11 in the Scottish town of Lockerbie on which much of the wreckage of the Boeing 747 'Jumbo' aircraft fell. At the time, it was the greatest mass murder investigation in British history.

There were several candidates for the bombers: the Popular Front for the Liberation of Palestine-General Command (PFLP-GC), which had issued a threat against the United States and Israel and specifically their aircraft two years earlier, was an initial focus. Its head, Ahmed Jibril, had declared in a February 1986 press conference that '[t]here will be no safety for any traveller on an Israeli or US airliner'.[547] The PFLP-GC had also used the same Toshiba brand of cassette recorder – though not the exact model or timing device – to contain explosives in a bomb in preparation for other operations. Iran, which is suggested by some quarters to have paid the PFLP-GC to carry out the bombing, had a strong (and recent) motivation after the mistaken shooting down of commercial Iran Air Flight 655 by the USS Vincennes in July 1988.

Also linked with the bombings was Palestinian militant, Abu Nidal, the founder of Fatah: The Revolutionary Council. A former head of Iranian intelligence operations in Europe who

---

[542] J. Jackson and S. Doran, *Judge Without Jury: Diplock Trials in the Adversary System*, Oxford Monographs on Criminal Law and Justice, Clarendon Press, Oxford, 1995, p. 35.

[543] Rasnic, 'Northern Ireland's Criminal Trials without Jury, p. 252.

[544] D. Blevins, 'Prosecutions over crimes committed during Northern Ireland Troubles to end', *Sky News*, 14 July 2021, at: https://bit.ly/3XbkZlS.

[545] R. Mendick, 'Terrorists could be prosecuted for offences during the Troubles if they do not cooperate with authorities, Telegraph understands', *Daily Telegraph*, 6 February 2022.

[546] Northern Ireland Office, 'Government introduces amendments to NI Troubles legacy legislation', Press release, 8 June 2023, at: https://bit.ly/43JGCfw; and BBC, 'Troubles legacy bill enters law after receiving Royal Assent', 19 September 2023, at: https://bit.ly/3UsHuTT; and O. Wright, 'Troubles legacy bill: Ireland will take UK government to ECHR', The Times, 20 December 2023.

[547] M. Cox and T. Foster, *Their Darkest Day: The Tragedy of Pan Am 103*, Grove Press, New York, 1992, p. 28.

4.6 Prosecution of Terrorism in Europe

defected to Germany claimed that Iran had asked Libya and Abu Nidal to carry out the attack. Abu Nidal is even alleged to have confessed to the bombing before his death.[548] After the bombing, the US Department of State said that an unidentified person had telephoned the US Embassy in Helsinki on 5 December, sixteen days before the bombing, saying there would be a bombing attempt within two weeks against a Pan Am aircraft flying from Frankfurt to the United States. The caller claimed to belong to the Abu Nidal group, the Department of State said at the time.[549]

But the United States became convinced that Libya alone was behind the attack and was acting on its own initiative. Libya certainly also had motive, given the 14 April 1986 bombing of its territory by the United States in an operation named El Dorado Canyon. The air strikes, which were authorized and defended by US President Ronald Reagan on national television while they were ongoing, killed Colonel Gaddafi's fifteen-month-old adopted daughter and injured two of his young sons. Although he never admitted it publicly, it is speculated that Gaddafi was himself also wounded in the bombing. The US operation was in retaliation for the bombing of a dance hall known to be frequented by US servicemen in West Berlin nine days earlier, which was ascribed to Libya.[550]

In November 1991, the United States formally indicted and then demanded the extradition of two Libyan intelligence officers: Abdelbaset al-Megrahi and Lamen Khalifa Fhimah. Mr Fhimah, who worked for Libyan Arab Airlines on Malta, allegedly planted the suitcase on an Air Malta plane bound for Frankfurt where it was loaded onto a Pan Am feeder flight to London, and then at Heathrow Airport it was transferred to Pan Am 103. Mr Al-Megrahi, a Libyan intelligence officer, was accused of having prepared the suitcase containing the bomb, which was contained in a Toshiba cassette player.[551] Libya refused to extradite the two men but it did offer to put them on trial in Libya, as long as the relevant evidence was provided for prosecution. The United Kingdom and the United States refused the offer.[552] A similar reaction followed the offer to send the two men to Malta for trial there.[553]

Thanks in part to the mediation of Nelson Mandela,[554] it was eventually agreed that a trial would be held in the Netherlands, but that its proceedings would be governed entirely by Scottish law. The 'Scottish Court in the Netherlands', a special High Court of Justiciary with a three-judge panel, was created in a disused US Air Force base, Camp Zeist, in Utrecht.[555] An agreement between the United Kingdom and the Netherlands was needed to resolve key jurisdictional issues. These included the provision for transfer from Dutch jurisdiction to Scottish jurisdiction of the two defendants, given that on landing in the Netherlands the two defendants came within Dutch jurisdiction. There also needed to be a legal basis for the Scottish authorities subsequently holding the accused for the duration of their trial. Scottish law would

---

[548] N. Pyke, 'Aide says Nidal confessed to Lockerbie bombing', *The Guardian*, 23 August 2002, at: https://bit.ly/3NwzmOg.

[549] CBS News, 'Scots Dismiss Abu Nidal Report', 20 August 2002, at: https://bit.ly/3Nvsdxw.

[550] 'History, 1986: U.S. bombs terrorist and military targets in Libya', last updated 26 April 2023, at: https://bit.ly/3qDIYO8.

[551] Michael P. Scharf, 'Terrorism on Trial: The Lockerbie Criminal Proceedings', *ILSA Journal of International & Comparative Law*, Vol. 6 (2000), 355–61, at: https://bit.ly/3Cy35Qw, p. 356.

[552] Not unreasonably so, given its belief – rightly or wrongly – that Libya was responsible as a State for the bombing. Trapp, *State Responsibility for International Terrorism*, pp. 88–9.

[553] Scharf, 'Terrorism on Trial: The Lockerbie Criminal Proceedings', p. 357.

[554] C. P. Schneider, 'The Lockerbie Trial: A Unique Moment in International Justice and Diplomacy', Opinion Editorial, The Brookings Institution, Washington DC, 21 August 2009, at: https://bit.ly/3CzOnbG.

[555] A. Klip and M. Mackarel, 'Lockerbie Trial: A Scottish Court in the Netherlands', *International Review of Penal Law*, Vol. 70, Nos. 3–4 (1999), 777–818.

180 — Prosecution of Terrorism Suspects

have to provide for this and the Netherlands would have to agree to this exercise of foreign criminal jurisdiction on its territory.[556]

Michael Scharf contrasts the differing rules of criminal procedure under US federal law and Scottish law, some of which lessened the chance of conviction, while others increased it. Notably, for instance, Scottish law stipulates that no one may be convicted without corroboration. Thus, 'a single piece of evidence of guilt, no matter how compelling, cannot support a conviction'. That said, two eyewitness accounts suffice for this requirement and a single eyewitness account may be corroborated by circumstantial evidence pointing to the guilt of the accused. It is even possible for two pieces of circumstantial evidence to corroborate each other.[557] Of particular importance is the broader hearsay exception for unavailable witnesses under Scottish criminal procedure than in US law. An out-of-court statement may be introduced not only if the witness is dead or has disappeared (as is the case in the United States) but also if the witness simply refuses to appear in order to testify. This was important since the Scottish court sitting in the Netherlands lacked the power to compel the appearance of witnesses outside Scotland at Camp Zeist. Of lesser import, there was also no requirement under Scottish rules of criminal procedure that 'probable cause' be advanced and confirmed at a preliminary hearing.[558]

The two accused were charged with murder, conspiracy to murder, and breach of the 1982 United Kingdom Aviation Security Act. Both defendants pleaded not guilty to all charges. The trial on 3 May 2000 opened with the prosecution outlining the case against the accused. Significant material evidence and eyewitness testimony was provided, but their probity and reliability were very much open to question. On 31 January 2001, after thirty-six weeks of hearing the evidence, the judges announced their verdicts. Mr al-Megrahi was convicted of the charges and sentenced to life imprisonment with the possibility of parole after twenty years, while Lamen Khalifa Fhimah was acquitted and returned to Libya. In announcing the Scottish Court's judgment, Lord Sutherland said:

> While no doubt organisations such as the PFLP-GC and the PPSF [Palestinian Popular Struggle Front] were also engaged in terrorist activities during the same period, we are satisfied that there was no evidence from which we could infer that they were involved in this particular act of terrorism, and the evidence relating to their activities does not create a reasonable doubt in our minds about the Libyan origin of this crime.[559]

The Libyan narrative has, however, been widely challenged, both before the trial in the Netherlands and even more so since.[560] Professor Robert Black, the renowned emeritus professor of Scots law at Edinburgh University and the key architect of the non-jury setup at the Camp Zeist court, publicly declared not only his belief that Mr al-Megrahi was innocent but also that his murder conviction was the worst miscarriage of justice in Scots law 'for 100 years'.[561] A first appeal against the conviction of Mr al-Megrahi had been swiftly dismissed, but in 2007, after four years of review of the relevant case material, the Scottish Criminal Cases Review Commission

---

[556] D. R. Andrews, 'A Thorn on the Tulip – A Scottish Trial in the Netherlands: The Story behind the Lockerbie Trial', *Case Western Reserve Journal of International Law*, Vol. 36. (2004), 307–18, at: https://bit.ly/43K5WSj, at p. 315.

[557] Scharf, 'Terrorism on Trial', p. 358.

[558] Ibid.

[559] High Court of Justiciary at Camp Zeist, *Her Majesty's Advocate v. Abdelbaset Ali Mohmed Al Megrahi and Al Amin Khalifa Fhimah*, Opinion of the Court (Case No. 1475/99), 31 January 2001, at: https://bit.ly/43Ujtqi, para. 82.

[560] For a careful review of the evidence before and at trial by the journalist Paul Foot, see P. Foot, Lockerbie: The Flight from Justice, Special Report, Private Eye, London, May/June 2001.

[561] 'Why Robert Black won't let the Lockerbie trial lie', *The Scotsman*, 1 November 2005, at: https://bit.ly/3NzQr9S.

4.6 Prosecution of Terrorism in Europe

(SCCRC) referred his conviction to the Court of Criminal Appeal for a fresh appeal. This was based on six different grounds of appeal.[562] Diagnosed with terminal cancer, however, Mr al-Megrahi was offered early release on compassionate grounds on condition that he dropped this new appeal. On 20 August 2009, the Minister for Justice of Scotland announced al-Megrahi's release and he flew home to Tripoli from Glasgow Airport. He died in Libya in 2012. In 2020, the SCCRC declared that Mr al-Megrahi may have been the victim of a miscarriage of justice and ruled that his family could appeal his conviction over Pan Am bombing.[563]

In June 2023, however, things took another turn with the arraignment of Abu Agila Mohammad Mas'ud Kheir Al-Marimi (Mas'ud), now a seventy-one-year-old man, of Tunisian and Libyan nationality.[564] Mr Mas'ud had made his initial appearance in the US District Court for the District of Columbia on federal charges in December 2022. The criminal complaint, which was issued in December 2020, alleged that

> from approximately 1973 to 2011 Mas'ud worked for the External Security Organization (ESO), the Libyan intelligence service which conducted acts of terrorism against other nations, in various capacities including as a technical expert in building explosive devices. In the winter of 1988, Mas'ud was directed by a Libyan intelligence official to fly to Malta with a prepared suitcase. There he was met by Megrahi and Fhimah at the airport. Several days later, Megrahi and Fhimah instructed Mas'ud to set the timer on the device in the suitcase for the following morning, so that the explosion would occur exactly eleven hours later. Megrahi and Fhimah were both at the airport on the morning of Dec. 21, 1988, and Mas'ud handed the suitcase to Fhimah after Fhimah gave him a signal to do so. Fhimah then placed the suitcase on the conveyor belt. Subsequently, Mas'ud boarded a Libyan flight to Tripoli schedule to take off at 9:00 a.m.[565]

The charges against Mas'ud include 'destruction of aircraft resulting in death', which potentially attracts the death penalty upon conviction, although prosecutors said they do not plan to pursue the death penalty against him because the punishment was not constitutionally available in 1988 when the crime was committed.[566] The United States is now alleging that Mr Mas'ud is responsible for some of the conduct for which Mr al-Megrahi was originally convicted.

---

[562] BBC, 'Key Lockerbie witness Tony Gauci dies in Malta', 29 October 2016, at: https://bit.ly/3Xf6ZY3.

[563] M. Vella, 'Million-dollar reward for Malta Lockerbie witness was unfair to Libyan accused', *Malta Today*, 11 March 2020, at: https://bit.ly/42IXLV1.

[564] itvX, 'Lockerbie bomb suspect to appear in US court', 31 May 2023, at: https://bit.ly/3NeQHtT.

[565] US Department of Justice, Pan Am Flight 103 Terrorist Suspect in Custody for 1988 Bombing over Lockerbie, Scotland', Press release, Office of Public Affairs, 12 December 2022, at: https://bit.ly/43YR3vd.

[566] A. Sangal, M. Hayes, M. Chowdhury, and E. Hammond, 'The latest on the Lockerbie bombing suspect in US custody', CNN, 12 December 2022, at: https://bit.ly/43UmB5w.

5

Counterterrorism Action under International Law

5.1 INTRODUCTION

As noted in Chapter 2, States are required by customary and conventional international law to prevent terrorism and to prosecute terrorists both in peacetime and in situations of armed conflict. This inheres in the notion of sovereignty. Thus, in its General Comment 36 on the right to life, the Human Rights Committee reminds 'all States' – not merely those that are party to the International Covenant on Civil and Political Rights (ICCPR)[1] – of their 'responsibility as members of the international community to protect lives and to oppose widespread or systematic attacks on the right to life', which include 'international terrorism'.[2]

In its 2017 judgment in the *Tagayeva* case, the European Court of Human Rights reiterated its articulation of the specific duty to protect life where the authorities 'knew, or ought to have known at the time, of the existence of a real and immediate risk to the life of identified individuals from the criminal acts of a third party'. In such a circumstance, in particular when confronted by a looming terrorist attack, the authorities must take all reasonable measures 'within the scope of their powers' to 'avoid' such a risk.[3] These measures may demand the reinforcement of security measures in the face of an imminent threat to life.

More generally, it is required that States identify potential terrorists and then arrest suspects so as to prevent the perpetration of terrorism, where necessary using a reasonable measure of force to do so. Once in custody, criminal suspects should be interviewed without the threat or use of physical coercion in order to gather evidence to decide whether or not to it is right to engage a prosecution for terrorism (or other criminal offences). In certain circumstances, control orders or similar judicial decisions may limit the actions at large of an individual suspect with a view to protecting the public. Most controversial of all, preventive detention by the State may sometimes be necessary and lawful even where an individual has been convicted of no crime and is not being held on remand with a view to future prosecution.

This chapter addresses these issues in turn in peacetime (as well as when the acts of a terrorism suspect are unconnected to any ongoing armed conflict to which the State in question is a party). Of central relevance to the treatment of terrorist suspects are a range of fundamental human rights, in particular the rights to life, to freedom from torture and other ill-treatment, to liberty, and to privacy. The first two of these rights are non-derogable; the latter two are derogable in certain circumstances.

---

[1] International Covenant on Civil and Political Rights; adopted at New York, 16 December 1966; entered into force, 23 March 1976 (hereafter, ICCPR). As of 1 January 2024, 173 States were party to the ICCPR.

[2] Human Rights Committee, General Comment No. 36: Article 6: right to life, United Nations (UN) doc. CCPR/C/GC/36, 3 September 2019 (hereafter, Human Rights Committee General Comment 36 on the right to life), para. 70.

[3] European Court of Human Rights (ECtHR), *Tagayeva* v. *Russia*, Judgment (First Section), 13 April 2017, para. 482.

5.2 SURVEILLANCE AND DATA AND THE RIGHTS TO PRIVACY AND TO FAMILY LIFE

5.2.1 *The Rights to a Private and Family Life*

Roberts suggests that as much as 95 per cent of any counterterrorism effort consists of intelligence and police work. This includes identifying suspects, infiltrating movements, and collaborating with law enforcement agencies in other countries, and gathering evidence for trials.[4] Surveillance is an essential component in this effort. Protection of the fundamental rights to a private life and to a family life is therefore a key issue in any surveillance operation.

Article 17 of the ICCPR guarantees the right of every person to be protected against arbitrary interference with their privacy and their family as well as against unlawful attacks on their honour and reputation. The obligations imposed by Article 17 require each State Party to the Covenant to adopt legislative and other measures 'to give effect to the prohibition against such interferences and attacks as well as to the protection of this right'.[5] For any interference with privacy rights to be non-arbitrary, it must be provided for by law and necessary and proportionate to a legitimate aim being pursued; there must also be adequate safeguards to prevent abuse.[6]

5.2.1.1 The Lack of a Formal 'Terrorism' Exception

There is no mention in Article 17 of the ICCPR of an exception to the duty to respect privacy and family life rights for the preservation of national security, or more particularly terrorism. Indeed, the Human Rights Committee's brief General Comment on the provision, which dates back to 1988, did not even mention terrorism as a salient issue. Article 17 is a derogable right in 'time of public emergency which threatens the life of the nation and the existence of which is officially proclaimed'.[7] In fact, very few States have sought to derogate from their obligations to respect privacy rights.[8]

As Duffy has observed, there is little doubt that 'some encroachment into privacy rights' in order to meet the demands of counterterrorism is 'appropriate if not essential'.[9] Similarly, the 'targeted interception of communications can provide a valuable source of information for States to investigate, forestall and prosecute acts of terrorism'.[10] In contrast, the Human Rights

---

[4] A. Roberts, 'Countering Terrorism: A Historical Perspective', in A. Bianchi and A. Keller (eds.), *Counterterrorism: Democracy's Challenge*, Hart, Oxford, 2008, 3–41, at p. 19.

[5] Human Rights Committee, CCPR General Comment No. 16: Article 17 (Right to Privacy): The Right to Respect of Privacy, Family, Home and Correspondence, and Protection of Honour and Reputation, 8 April 1988 (Human Rights Committee General Comment 16), available at: https://bit.ly/46d9luP, para. 1.

[6] Human Rights Committee, *Van Hulst* v. *The Netherlands*, Views, 15 November 2005, paras. 7.6, 7.7, 7.8, and 7.10. See also H. Duffy, *The 'War on Terror' and the Framework of International Law*, 2nd ed., Cambridge University Press, Cambridge, 2015, p. 642.

[7] Art. 4(1), ICCPR. Any derogation must be consistent with a State's other international legal obligations and must not involve discrimination 'solely on the ground of race, colour, sex, language, religion or social origin'.

[8] Duffy, *The 'War on Terror' and the Framework of International Law*, 2nd ed., p. 641.

[9] Ibid.

[10] B. Emmerson, 'New Counter-Terrorism Measures: Continuing Challenges for Human Rights', in M. Nowak and A. Charbord (eds.), *Using Human Rights to Counter Terrorism*, Edward Elgar, Cheltenham, 2018, 125–65, at p. 133.

Committee's General Comment No. 16 stipulated that '[s]urveillance, whether electronic or otherwise, interceptions of telephonic, telegraphic and other forms of communication, wire-tapping and recording of conversations should be prohibited'.[11] Doswald-Beck criticized the Committee's formulation of the relevant passage for being 'not as well drafted as it could have been', but disputed whether this should be taken at face value so as to outlaw all secret surveillance of communications.[12] Certainly, a comprehensive interdiction does not reflect general State practice in the contemporary world.[13] That begs the question as to where the boundary of reasonable and lawful interference with a person's privacy should be situated (with everything on the other side of the line amounting to arbitrary interference)?

In any event, notwithstanding the seemingly strict nature of the General Comment, constraints on surveillance have been overtaken by technological advances, especially by electronic means. As a consequence, legal and political attention has favoured adequate safeguards, including independent oversight, rather than prohibition. As an example, in 2009, expressing concern over the wide powers proposed for the Government of Sweden to surveil electronic communications as a means of combating terrorism, the Human Rights Committee called on the authorities to 'guarantee that the processing and gathering of information be subject to review and supervision by an independent body with the necessary guarantees of impartiality and effectiveness'.[14]

Recognition of, much less compliance with, any general prohibition did not survive in the United States after the 9/11 attacks. This is despite the Fourth Amendment to the US Constitution, which bars the government from unreasonable search and seizure of an individual or their private property. A portion of the US approach to terrorism-related surveillance in the post-9/11 world breached both US domestic law and international law. Operation Stellar Wind was a programme of secret surveillance on US citizens (and others) initiated by the Bush administration, which the US Department of Justice (DoJ) deemed to be in violation of US domestic law. Indeed, the whistle-blower from the Federal Bureau of Investigation (FBI) who stumbled across the programme and informed *The New York Times* about it in 2004 said that an official working on the initiative freely admitted that 'the program' was 'probably illegal'.[15]

What was particularly concerning about Operation Stellar Wind was not only its warrant-less tapping of telephones but also its bulk collection of internet metadata. Hence, there was no targeting of terrorism suspects for the collection of the metadata but only a blanket gathering of data from all communications.[16] In March 2004, President George W. Bush reauthorized the programme despite the DoJ's formal conclusion that it was unlawful. James Comey, the Acting Attorney General, threatened to resign. Both John Ashcroft, the Attorney General who was seriously ill in hospital at the time, and FBI director Robert Mueller were

---

[11] Human Rights Committee General Comment 16, para. 8.

[12] L. Doswald-Beck, *Human Rights in Times of Conflict and Terrorism*, Oxford University Press, Oxford, 2011, p. 449, §16.4.1.

[13] Duffy, The 'War on Terror' and the Framework of International Law, 2nd ed., p. 642.

[14] Human Rights Committee, Concluding Observations on Sweden, UN doc. CCPR/C/SWE/CO/6, 7 May 2009, para. 18.

[15] M. Isikoff, 'The Fed Who Blew the Whistle: Is he a hero or a criminal?', *Newsweek*, 13 December 2008, at: https://bit.ly/3qMTNho.

[16] According to one analyst, 'despite the fact that intelligence failures related to 9/11 were primarily based not on a lack of data points but on an inability to connect the dots, the Bush administration launched an effort to *collect* dots on an unprecedented scale'. J. Laperruque, 'Secrets, Surveillance, and Scandals: The War on Terror's Unending Impact on Americans' Private Lives', Pogo, 7 September 2021, at: https://bit.ly/3PkSiRp [original emphasis].

said to be ready to do the same. President Bush ultimately backed down and the programme was briefly suspended.[17]

Nonetheless, the programme continued after being renewed under a different legal authority. Stellar Wind was succeeded by four major lines of intelligence collection in the territorial United States, which, together, were capable of spanning the full range of telecommunications. The best known was the PRISM programme, whose existence was revealed by former National Security Agency (NSA) contractor and whistle-blower Edward Snowden.[18] In 2006, the Human Rights Committee made known its concern in its Concluding Observations on the United States' third periodic report under the ICCPR that the United States, including through the NSA, 'has monitored and still monitors phone, email, and fax communications of individuals both within and outside the U.S., without any judicial or other independent oversight'. It called on the government to review Sections 213, 215, and 505 of the USA PATRIOT Act[19] 'to ensure full compatibility with article 17 of the Covenant' and further that any infringement on an individual's rights to privacy 'is strictly necessary and duly authorized by law'.[20]

The Human Rights Committee again expressed its concern about US surveillance programmes in its Concluding Observations on the United States' fourth periodic report under the ICCPR in 2014. The bulk phone metadata surveillance conducted by the NSA both within and outside the United States was authorized by the USA PATRIOT Act. Substantive surveillance was also conducted through PRISM, which involved the collection of communications content from US-based internet companies, while UPSTREAM garnered communications metadata and content by tapping fibre-optic cables carrying internet traffic.[21] These clearly had an 'adverse impact' on individuals' right to privacy in the Committee's view. The Human Rights Committee also drew attention to the fact that despite Presidential Policy Directive/PPD-28, which extended some safeguards to non-US citizens 'to the maximum extent feasible consistent with the national security', only 'limited protection' was provided against excessive surveillance. Those affected had 'no access to effective remedies in case of abuse'.[22]

5.2.1.2 The Position of the European Court of Human Rights

In contradistinction to the ICCPR, the 1950 European Convention on Human Rights specifically provides for the possibility of 'interference by a public authority' in the interests of national security. This is only so where the interference is 'in accordance with the law' and is necessary for that purpose 'in a democratic society'.[23] With respect to persons suspected of terrorism offences, the Grand Chamber of the European Court of Human Rights has held that governments must strike a 'fair balance' between the exercise by the individual of the rights to a private and family

---

[17] J. Sanchez, 'What the Ashcroft "Hospital Showdown" on NSA spying was all about', Ars Technica, 29 July 2013, at: https://bit.ly/3CyATo3.

[18] B. Gellman, 'U.S. surveillance architecture includes collection of revealing Internet, phone metadata', The Washington Post, 15 June 2013, at: https://bit.ly/3JkBTss.

[19] 2001 Uniting and Strengthening America by Providing Appropriate Tools Required to Intercept and Obstruct Terrorism Act.

[20] Human Rights Committee, Concluding Observations on the Third Periodic Report of the United States, UN doc. CCPR/C/USA/CO/3/Rev.1, 18 December 2006, para. 21.

[21] This was conducted under the authority of §702 of the Foreign Intelligence Surveillance Act (FISA) Amendment Act. FISA was originally adopted in 1978.

[22] Human Rights Committee, Concluding Observations on the Fourth Periodic Report of the United States, UN doc. CCPR/C/USA/CO/4, 23 April 2014, para. 22.

[23] Art. 8(2), Convention for the Protection of Human Rights and Fundamental Freedoms; adopted at Rome, 4 November 1950; entered into force, 3 September 1953.

life guaranteed under paragraph 1 of Article 8 and the necessity under paragraph 2 for the State to take effective measures with a view to preventing terrorism. In determining where this balance lies, the Court believes that a 'certain margin of appreciation' should be left to national authorities to decide what measures to take 'both in general and in particular cases'.[24]

In this regard, the Court has long accepted secret surveillance to enable States to counter-terrorism. Already in 1978, in its judgment in the *Klass* case, it held that domestic laws could allow for such surveillance under 'exceptional conditions' where this was necessary in the interests of national security. But this would only persist where there exist adequate and effective guarantees against abuse.[25] Moreover, the Court cautioned that States Parties to the European Convention on Human Rights did not enjoy 'unlimited discretion' to conduct secret surveil-lance subject on those within their jurisdiction. Acknowledging the danger of undermining 'or even destroying' democracy on the ground of defending it, the Court reiterated that States may not, in the name of the struggle against terrorism, adopt whatever measures they deem appropriate.[26]

The Court has held that surveillance of a suspected terrorist using a Global Positioning by Satellite (GPS) system along with processing and use of the data obtained by that manner will not necessarily violate Article 8 of the European Convention. Factors favouring legality were found in *Uzun* to be that surveillance of the target was carried out for a relatively short period of time (approximately three months) and, as in his visual surveillance by State agents, this affected him essentially only at weekends and when he was travelling in a particular individual's car. The fact that the target was not subjected to total and comprehensive surveillance was thus relevant. Moreover, the investigation justifying the surveillance concerned very serious crimes: the attempted murders of politicians and civil servants in bomb attacks.[27]

The Court has also accepted that the interests of national security and the fight against terrorism may prevail over the interest of concerned individuals to have access to information about them in the files of the security services or police. But prolonged retention of that information may amount to disproportionate interference in the right to privacy.[28] Moreover, whatever system of surveillance is adopted, the Court has repeated the need for adequate and effective guarantees against abuse.[29] But the permissible measures may be far-reaching in nature. Indeed, in June 2023, it was announced that the threat of terrorism (along with many other criminal offences) would allow intrusive surveillance software (spyware) to be introduced into journalists' mobile phones. France had criticized an immunity, proposed by the European Commission, that would exempt journalists from measures to 'intercept, subject to surveillance or search and seizure' unless 'justified by an overriding requirement in the public interest'.[30]

5.3 TACKLING TERRORIST SUSPECTS IN LAW ENFORCEMENT

The European Court of Human Rights has referred to the responsibility of an elected govern-ment in a democratic society to protect its citizens and its institutions against the threats posed by

---

[24] ECtHR, *Murray* v. *United Kingdom*, Judgment (Grand Chamber), 28 October 1994, paras. 90–1.

[25] ECtHR, *Klass* v. *Germany*, Judgment (Plenary of the Court), 6 September 1978, paras. 48 and 50.

[26] Ibid., para. 49.

[27] ECtHR, *Uzun* v. *Germany*, Judgment (Fifth Section), 2 September 2010 (rendered final on 2 December 2010), paras. 80 and 81.

[28] ECtHR, *Segerstedt-Wiberg and others* v. *Sweden*, Judgment (Second Section), 6 June 2006 (rendered final on 6 September 2006), para. 91.

[29] ECtHR, *Weber and Saravia* v. *Germany*, Decision on admissibility (Third Section), 29 June 2006, para. 106.

[30] B. Waterfield, 'Brussels to allow installation of spyware on journalists' phones and laptops', *The Times*, 21 June 2023.

'organized' terrorism.[31] As part of every State's duty to prevent terrorism, it is incumbent upon law enforcement agencies and the security services to identify and investigate terrorism suspects. Suspects must be arrested not killed (unless they resist arrest or threaten the public with potentially deadly force and other means short of deadly force are not feasible in the circumstances), and then interviewed when in custody without the use or threat of force. If sufficient evidence is gathered, the State must then charge suspects with relevant offences.

A high degree of competence is expected from the authorities in preventing and tackling terrorism. Regrettably, in many instances they have fallen short. The terrorism attacks in Paris on 13 November 2015 were one such instance. The attacks were carefully planned and carried out with a view to inflicting maximum casualties among the public. The scale of the attacks were almost unparalleled in peacetime in Western Europe, an exceptional challenge to the law enforcement authorities in the French capital, but their response inevitably came under scrutiny in the months that followed. While individual officers demonstrated immense courage, analysis of the response suggested that during substantial periods of time, the terrorists were able to operate with 'little or no hindrance' from the authorities. Part of the reason for this was France's 'top-heavy' chain of command, which had deprioritized neighbourhood patrols in favour of specialized units, which take more time to arrive on the scene and then to be instructed to intervene.[32]

The first police officer to reach the Bataclan music venue where 90 of the 130 victims were killed on the night of 13 November arrived roughly fifteen minutes after the attack had begun. Armed with only a service sidearm, he shot one attacker, blowing up the terrorist's suicide vest while sparing the victims around him. But he was ordered to withdraw in favour of a more specialized counterterrorism unit from the Research and Intervention Brigade (Brigade de Recherche et d'Intervention, BRI), which arrived half an hour after the massacre had begun inside. The BRI had initially been dispatched to sites where the violence had already ended as the attackers were mobile. What is more, another specialized unit stationed nearby was apparently never deployed.[33] During all this time, many lives were lost.

5.3.1 *The Conduct of Investigations into Terrorism Suspects*

Surveillance may lead the authorities to conclude that terrorism and other criminal offences have been committed. The significance of terrorism is such that the national authorities enjoy a wide margin of appreciation in matters relating to national security. In this regard, the European Court of Human Rights has declared that it will not supplant the evaluation of the national authorities at the time with its own armchair assessment of what might be the best policy in the field of investigation of terrorist crime.[34] The margin of discretion granted to States Parties to the European Convention by the European Court of Human Rights may even extend to the possibility of conducting searches in the absence of reasonable suspicion when this is authorized by counterterrorism legislation, but this can only be so where adequate safeguards are in place.

The 2019 *Beghal* case concerned the power given to police, immigration officers, and designated customs officers under UK terrorism legislation to stop, examine, and search all passengers at ports, airports, and international rail terminals. Although the Court acknowledged

---

[31] ECtHR, *Murray* v. *United Kingdom*, Judgment (Grand Chamber), para. 91.
[32] A. Nossiter, 'Response to Paris attacks points to weaknesses in French police structure', *The New York Times*, 31 December 2015, at: https://bit.ly/3JdKop7.
[33] Ibid.
[34] Ibid., para. 90.

188   *Counterterrorism Action under International Law*

the importance of controlling the international movement of terrorists, it held that the power in question was neither sufficiently circumscribed nor subject to adequate legal safeguards against abuse – in particular, the power of those authorities under the 2000 Terrorism Act to interrogate a person for up to nine hours where they would be compelled to answer questions without the right to have a lawyer present. This combined with only a limited possibility for subsequent judicial review of the exercise of their powers to render the powers 'in accordance with the law' in the understanding of Article 8(2) of the Act. The absence of any requirement of 'reasonable suspicion' contributed to this finding, but alone would not have been fatal to the lawfulness of the regime, the Court said.[35]

In its 2005 judgment in the case of *H. E. v. Turkey*, the Court recalled that, in the context of the fight against crime, States may deem it necessary to resort to searches and seizures in people's homes in order to establish material proof of offences and, where appropriate, prosecute the perpetrators.[36] Where the authorities suspect a terrorist attack is imminent, the legal latitude granted for searches and seizures may be exceptionally broad. In such a situation, the demands of counterterrorism and the urgency of the situation could justify a search based on terms that were wider than would otherwise have been permissible. In addition, the police should be accorded flexibility to assess which items found during a search might be linked to terrorist activities and to seize them for further examination. As the Court held: 'To impose under Article 8 the requirement that a search warrant identify in detail the precise nature of the items sought and to be seized could seriously jeopardise the effectiveness of an investigation where numerous lives might be at stake.'[37]

But legislation and practice must always provide adequate and sufficient safeguards against abuse. In the *Khamidov* case, the Court found against Russia on the basis that wide powers were vested in State agents by law but without defining with sufficient clarity the scope of those powers and the due manner in which they were to be exercised. The relevant legal provisions, which were formulated in vague and general terms, could not serve as a sufficient legal basis 'for such a drastic interference as occupation for a prolonged period of time of an individual's housing and property'.[38] The relevant legislation, Russia's 1998 Law on the Suppression of Terrorism, stipulated:

> On the basis of the legislation and within the limits established by it, damage may be caused to the life, health and property of terrorists, as well as to other legally-protected interests, in the course of a counter-terrorist operation. However, servicemen, experts and other persons engaged in the suppression of terrorism shall be exempted from liability for such damage, in accordance with the legislation of the Russian Federation.[39]

Even more serious is the destruction of civilian property on the basis that the occupants are deemed to be sympathetic to terrorists. The *Menteş and others* case concerned the burning of houses in a village in south-east Turkey in June 1993. The applicants blamed the security forces. They said they had pleaded with the gendarmes not to burn their houses but were told to remain

---

[35]   ECtHR, *Beghal* v. *United Kingdom*, Judgment (First Section), 28 February 2019 (as rendered final on 28 May 2019), para. 109.

[36]   ECtHR, *H. E.* v. *Turkey*, Judgment (Third Section), 22 December 2005 (as rendered final on 22 March 2006), para. 48.

[37]   ECtHR, *Sher and others* v. *United Kingdom*, Judgment (Fourth Section), 20 October 2015, paras. 174–5.

[38]   ECtHR, *Khamidov* v. *Russia*, Judgment (Fifth Section), 15 November 2007 (as rendered final on 2 June 2008), para. 143.

[39]   S. 21, Law on the Suppression of Terrorism of 25 July 1998.

5.3 Tackling Terrorist Suspects in Law Enforcement

quiet or they would be thrown on the flames. When asked why they were burning the houses, the gendarmes told the villagers that it was a punishment for helping the Kurdistan Workers' Party (PKK). In all, as many as thirteen houses in the lower neighbourhood were destroyed.

One woman said that her house was burned after she and her children had been thrown out and that she had been kicked and cursed at and a gun put to her face.[40] Only the arrival of a colonel who ordered the burning to stop had saved the upper village.[41] Turkey blamed the PKK, but neither the European Commission on Human Rights nor the European Court believed this claim.

5.3.2 *Arresting Terrorist Suspects and the Rights to Life and to Freedom from Torture*

In terrorism cases, as in all criminal cases, there is a duty on the authorities to protect the life and bodily integrity of a terrorist suspect[42] as well as, of course, the life and bodily integrity of the public and of all law enforcement officials.[43] The duty to protect applies particularly to those dedicated to counterterrorism operations while recognizing that greater risk inheres in their work.[44]

The law of law enforcement, which informs the interpretation of the rights to life and to freedom from torture and other ill-treatment, obligates State organs and agents to arrest terrorist suspects whenever it is reasonably possible to do so. Thus, in its consideration of the *Guerrero* case against Colombia, the Human Rights Committee found that a police unit that hid in a house to await the arrival of suspected kidnappers and then deliberately killed the seven people that arrived had violated their right to life. In its views on the communication, the Committee noted that the police action

> was apparently taken without warning to the victims and without giving them any opportunity to surrender to the police patrol or to offer any explanation of their presence or intentions. There is no evidence that the action of the police was necessary in their own defence or that of others, or that it was necessary to effect the arrest or prevent the escape of the persons concerned. Moreover, the victims were no more than suspects of the kidnapping which had occurred some days earlier and their killing by the police deprived them of all the protections of due process of law laid down by the Covenant.[45]

---

[40] ECtHR, *Menteş and others* v. *Turkey*, Judgment (Grand Chamber), 28 November 1997, paras. 19–20.

[41] Ibid., para. 73.

[42] The European Court of Human Rights has reiterated the absolute, non-derogable nature of the prohibition of torture and other ill-treatment under Article 3 of the European Convention on Human Rights in cases related to alleged acts of terrorism, stating that applicants suspected of or charged with terrorism-related activities have a right to be free from torture and inhuman or degrading treatment while in custody. ECtHR, *Martínez Sala and others* v. *Spain*, Judgment (Fourth Section), 2 November 2004, para. 120; and *Öcalan* v. *Turkey*, Judgment (Grand Chamber), 12 May 2005, paras. 179 and 192–6; see Office of the UN High Commissioner for Human Rights (OHCHR), *Istanbul Protocol: Manual on the Effective Investigation and Documentation of Torture and Other Cruel, Inhuman or Degrading Treatment or Punishment*, Professional Training Series No. 8/Rev. 2, UN, New York and Geneva, para. 88.

[43] Under international law, the term 'law enforcement officials' is construed broadly as including 'all officers of the law, whether appointed or elected, who exercise police powers, especially the powers of arrest or detention'. Art. 1, Code of Conduct for Law Enforcement Officials; adopted by UN General Assembly Resolution 34/169 (resolution adopted without a vote on 17 December 1979). The Code of Conduct makes it explicit that the term comprises the military, 'whether uniformed or not', as well as other State security forces, whenever and wherever they exercise such powers.

[44] ECtHR, *Ribcheva and others* v. *Bulgaria*, Judgment (Fourth Section), 30 March 2021 (as rendered final on 30 June 2021), paras. 156–60 and *esp.* 167.

[45] Human Rights Committee, *Guerrero* v. *Colombia*, Views (Communication No. R.11/45), 1982, paras. 13.2 and 13.3.

190   *Counterterrorism Action under International Law*

An arrest may certainly involve the use of force[46] under certain circumstances, namely in order to prevent or bring an end to the use or threat of violence by the suspect and to protect the law enforcement officials engaged in the operation as well as the public at large. But any use of force by law enforcement officials associated with the arrest of a terrorism suspect must comply with customary and general principles of necessity and proportionality.[47] The fact that a counter-terrorist operation is engaged does not alter that reality. A specific rule thus restricts the use of firearms and other deadly force against any criminal suspect, including anyone suspected of terrorist offences. Planned operations must respect the broader precautionary principle that derives from human rights law.

5.3.2.1 The Madrid Bombings (2004)

The Madrid bombings were the largest peacetime terrorist attack in European history in terms of total casualties.[48] On 11 March 2004, 193 people were killed and another 2,000 were injured when ten bombs were detonated by mobile phone on four trains in three stations in the Madrid area during the morning rush hour.[49] A number of other devices did not detonate. The government of the day, headed by José Aznar, quickly and unequivocally ascribed the attacks to the Basque separatist group ETA (*Euskadi Ta Askatasuna*, meaning Basque Homeland and Liberty). With general elections only three days away, Aznar did not want the attacks to be linked to Spain's involvement in the invasion of Iraq, which was extremely unpopular domestically. But the evidence quickly pointed to a violent Jihadist group.

Around noon on the day of the attacks, an audio tape, explosives, and detonators were found in a van parked outside Alcala train station in Madrid, from which the three bombed trains departed. The explosives were not of a type used by ETA and among the tapes one was in Arabic containing Quran verses. What is more, the scale and targets of the bombing did not fit the modus operandi of ETA and law enforcement had already degraded its ability to engage in a major terrorism attack. A letter purporting to be from al-Qaeda was sent to an Arabic newspaper in London in which the group claimed to be behind the attacks. The attacks were justified in the letter as retribution for old, unsettled debts in what was called the Spanish Crusade.[50]

Nonetheless, later that day, and prompted vigorously by Spanish diplomats, UN Security Council Resolution 1530 condemned 'in the strongest terms the bomb attacks in Madrid, Spain, perpetrated by the terrorist group ETA on 11 March 2004, in which many lives were claimed and people injured, and regards such act, like any act of terrorism, as a threat to peace and security'.[51]

---

[46]   The term 'use of force' in the context of law enforcement is not formally defined in international law. A useful 2017 publication by the UN Office on Drugs and Crime (UNODC) and the OHCHR defined the notion as 'the use of physical means that may harm a person or cause damage to property'. Physical means, they recall, 'include the use of hands and body by law enforcement officials; the use of any instruments, weapons or equipment, such as batons; chemical irritants such as pepper spray; restraints such as handcuffs; dogs; and firearms'. UNODC and OHCHR, *Resource Book on the Use of Force and Firearms in Law Enforcement*, Criminal Justice Handbook Series, United Nations, New York, 2017, at: http://bit.ly/2wAjBLH, p. 1. The use of force is not limited to kinetic impact of a weapon or projectile. Thus, the term 'use' should be interpreted broadly to encompass the action of aiming a firearm or conducted electrical weapon (e.g., a Taser) even if it is not discharged.

[47]   Human Rights Council Resolution 46/15: 'Torture and other cruel, inhuman or degrading treatment or punishment: the roles and responsibilities of police and other law enforcement officials', adopted on 23 March 2021 without a vote, operative para. 12; Human Rights Committee General Comment 36 on the right to life, paras. 12 and 14.

[48]   There were, however, more fatalities in the bombing of Pan Am Flight 103 over Lockerbie in December 1988.

[49]   History, 'Terrorists bomb trains in Madrid', last updated 10 March 2020, at: https://bit.ly/34HWQZs.

[50]   J. Finnegan, '11M: Lessons Learned from the Madrid Train Attacks', Transport Security International, 19 June 2022, at: https://bit.ly/3XjE19A.

[51]   UN Security Council Resolution 1530, adopted by unanimous vote on 11 March 2004, operative para. 1.

5.3 Tackling Terrorist Suspects in Law Enforcement

This swift attribution of responsibility proved to be factually and legally incorrect. An Islamist group loosely tied to and working in the name of al-Qaeda was responsible, later identified by the Spanish government as the Moroccan Islamist Combat Group.[52] On 16 March 2004, Spain's Ambassador to the United Nations in New York wrote to the Security Council explaining the Spanish government's insistence on blaming ETA, claiming it had acted mistakenly but 'in good faith'.[53]

The problems continued as the authorities searched for the bombers. While forensic science is ordinarily integral to the conduct of a professional criminal investigation, the human element can and does lead to critical mistakes. One notorious case was the use of fingerprint evidence to track down one of the individuals believed to have criminally enabled the 2004 Madrid train bombings. On 6 May 2004, following a flurry of arrests in the aftermath of the bombings, Brandon Mayfield, an US attorney, was arrested by the FBI in connection with the attacks. Mr Mayfield was incarcerated at Multnomah County Detention Center in Portland, Oregon, where he was kept in his cell for up to twenty-two hours per day. The FBI initially refused to inform either Mayfield or his family why he was being detained or where he was being held. His fingerprints had been identified by the FBI from latent prints on a bag containing detonators of the kind used in the attacks which had been found inside the van left near Alcala train station. The United States detained Mayfield as a material witness, describing him as a follower of Islam.[54] A Portland Assistant Attorney called Mr Mayfield's religious beliefs a 'mildly corroborating factor'.[55]

The use of latent fingerprints is, however, fraught with problems.[56] As two experts have observed, the probability that at least one fingerprint in the FBI Integrated Automated Fingerprint Identification System database (which contains more than 470 million fingerprints) matches a bomb site latent print is 0.93, which is significant enough to lead to a considerable risk of misidentification.[57] On 19 May, the Spanish police informed the FBI that it had identified an Algerian national, Ouhnane Daoud, as the true source of the fingerprint. After receiving Daoud's prints, the FBI laboratory did ultimately withdraw its original identification and the FBI apologized to Mr Mayfield and his family. Brandon Mayfield was released from detention on 20 May 2004 and the material witness order proceeding against him was formally dismissed four days later.

In March 2006, the US Department of Justice published 'A Review of the FBI's Handling of the Brandon Mayfield Case'. It concluded that while the degree of similarity between Mr Mayfield's prints and those of Mr Daoud was 'extraordinarily rare', confusing three FBI fingerprint examiners as well as a fourth external, court-appointed examiner, it also found errors in the examination procedure that contributed to the misidentification.[58] And although

---

[52] CNN, 'Spain Train Bombings Fast Facts', updated 1 March 2021, at: https://cnn.it/3ccovTB.

[53] UN, 'Spain explains reference to ETA in Security Council resolution after Madrid attacks', 16 March 2004, at: https://bit.ly/2SJvvDz. See on the issue of evidence in relation to the resolution T. O'Donnell, 'Security Council Resolution 1530, Evidence and the United Nations Security Council', *Proceedings of the American Society of International Law*, 29 March–1 April 2006, Vol. 100 (2006), pp. 47–51.

[54] CNN, 'Spain Train Bombings Fast Facts', updated 1 March 2021.

[55] DoJ, 'A Review of the FBI's Handling of the Brandon Mayfield Case', Report, Oversight and Review Division, Office of the Inspector General, March 2006, at: https://bit.ly/3vJ8wHp, p. 18.

[56] See, e.g., L. Spinney, 'Science in Court: The Fine Print', *Nature*, Vol. 464 (2010), pp. 344–6, at: https://go.nature.com/3g2XFgW.

[57] C. Su and S. N. Srihari, 'Latent Fingerprint Rarity Analysis in Madrid Bombing Case', in H. Sako, K. Y. Franke, and S. Saitoh (eds.), *Computational Forensics: International Workshop on Computational Forensics 2010, Lecture Notes in Computer Science*, Vol. 6540, Springer, Berlin, 2010, 173–84.

[58] DoJ, 'A Review of the FBI's Handling of the Brandon Mayfield Case', Report, p. 269.

Mr Mayfield's religion and his work as an attorney[59] were unknown to the examiners when they made the initial fingerprint identification, his contacts with other suspected Muslim extremists and the fact of his religion became known to the examiners and 'likely contributed' to their failure to reconsider adequately the identification after legitimate questions about it had been raised.[60] Ouhnane Daoud is said to have died later in Iraq while fighting Coalition forces.[61]

Several individuals were convicted of terrorism offences in connection with the Madrid train bombings. A trial in 2007 saw three individuals – Antonio Ivan Reis, Antonio Toro, and Sergio Alvarez Sanchez – convicted of distributing explosives. Explosives from a quarry are said to have been exchanged for hashish with the plotters. Nasreddine Bousbaa, Mahmoud Slimane, and Rafa Zouhier were convicted of aiding a terrorist organization. Nine others were convicted of belonging to a terror organization. Jose Milio Suarez Trashorras was convicted of being an accessory to 192 counts of terrorist murder. Jamal Zougam, Othman El Gnaoui, and Rabei Osman were convicted of 191 counts of terrorist murder. Six others were convicted in other countries or were dead or believed dead. Although the mastermind behind the attacks was not determined at the trial, Amer Azizi was connected to the operation and even presumed to be the group's leader. He was later killed in a drone attack in the mountains between Pakistan and Afghanistan in 2005.[62]

5.3.3 Necessity for the Use of Force against Terrorist Suspects

It may be necessary to use force to detain terrorism suspects. This is only true where a suspect is forcibly resisting arrest or the police reasonably suspect that he or she will resist arrest or otherwise put in danger their lives or the lives of the public. Thus, in its judgment in 2015 in *Bouyid* v. *Belgium*, the Grand Chamber of the European Court of Human Rights reiterated its long-standing position that 'in respect of a person who is . . . confronted with law-enforcement officers, any recourse to physical force which has not been made strictly necessary by his own conduct diminishes human dignity and is, in principle, an infringement' of the right to freedom from torture and inhuman or degrading treatment.[63] This rule applies a fortiori in the event that law enforcement officials use firearms.

Necessity is the fundamental principle governing the use of force by all law enforcement personnel, including counterterrorism police. The 1979 UN Code of Conduct for Law Enforcement Officials stipulates that the police may use force 'only when strictly necessary and to the extent required for the performance of their duty'.[64] This denotes the three core elements to necessity: that only minimum necessary force may be used, that the force used shall be for a legitimate law enforcement purpose, and that no further force may be applied once a suspect is safely in custody and not acting in a violent manner. Force used beyond the constraints of necessity is excessive or indiscriminate and therefore unlawful.

---

[59] Mr Mayfield had represented one of the so-called Portland Seven, a group of men who tried to travel to Afghanistan to fight for al-Qaeda and the Taliban against US and Coalition forces in a child custody case. He also worshipped at the same mosque as the militants. M. Harwood, 'The terrifying surveillance case of Brandon Mayfield', *Aljazeera*, 8 February 2014, at: https://bit.ly/3g4BvyB.

[60] DoJ, 'A Review of the FBI's Handling of the Brandon Mayfield Case', Report, p. 270.

[61] 'Spain arrests "terror" suspects', *Aljazeera*, 16 October 2008, at: https://bit.ly/3PmFpGk.

[62] Finnegan, '11M: Lessons Learned from the Madrid Train Attacks'.

[63] ECtHR, *Bouyid* v. *Belgium*, Judgment (Grand Chamber), 28 September 2015, paras. 88 and 100.

[64] Art. 3, Code of Conduct for Law Enforcement Officials.

5.3.3.1 The Minimum Necessary Force

In order to be lawful, any use of force against suspected terrorists must be no more than the minimum necessary.[65] The lawfulness of an intervention is judged at the moment of the use of force as the relevant officer or officers believed them to be.[66] This means that mistakes can be and are made, some resulting in tragedies, but without necessarily violating the principle of necessity (or proportionality). In the *McCann* case, the European Court of Human Rights' Grand Chamber held that use of force by agents of the State may be justified where it is based on an honest belief which is perceived, for good reasons, to be valid at the time but which subsequently turns out to be mistaken. To hold otherwise, the Court stated, 'would be to impose an unrealistic burden on the State and its law-enforcement personnel in the execution of their duty, perhaps to the detriment of their lives and those of others'.[67] The *McCann* case concerned the shooting to death of three Irish Republican Army (IRA) operatives who were on Gibraltar in 1988 to plant a bomb targeting members of the British armed forces.

5.3.3.2 Use of Force Only for a Legitimate Law Enforcement Purpose

An integral part of the principle is the rule that force may only be strictly necessary when it is applied for a legitimate law enforcement purpose.[68] Preventing the perpetration of an act of terrorism whose commission is reasonably believed to be imminent or arresting a suspect are legitimate purposes; police officers extracting bribes or seeking to punish suspected offenders for their prior actions are, of course, violative of the law. In its 2020 judgment in the *Kukhalashvili* case, the European Court of Human Rights considered that 'the use of lethal force for purely punitive, retaliatory purposes, even if those purposes target alleged members of the criminal underworld, cannot be justified'.[69]

5.3.3.3 Use of Force Only for as Long as Necessary

Once a terrorism suspect is safely in custody and not resisting, for instance when he or she is in handcuffs and under the control of a law enforcement official, no additional force is justified.[70]

---

[65] Sir Robert Peel founded the Metropolitan Police in London in 1829. Among the nine principles for policing that he promulgated at the time is one that holds that the Police should 'use physical force only when the exercise of persuasion, advice and warning is found to be insufficient to obtain public cooperation to an extent necessary to secure observance of law or to restore order, and to use only the minimum degree of physical force which is necessary on any particular occasion for achieving a police objective'. A copy of Peel's Nine Policing Principles is available at: https://bit.ly/3CwHuZ9.

[66] The margin of discretion accorded to police officers also extends to judgments they make at a specific instant but which, in hindsight, could have been better. Thus, for instance, the US Supreme Court held in its landmark 1989 judgment in *Graham* v. *Connor* that '[t]he calculus of reasonableness must embody allowance for the fact that police officers are often forced to make split-second judgments in circumstances that are tense, uncertain, and rapidly evolving – about the amount of force that is necessary in a particular situation'. US Supreme Court, *Graham* v. *Connor*, 490 US 386 (1989), Decided 15 May 1989, at 396–7.

[67] ECtHR, *McCann and others* v. *United Kingdom*, Judgment (Grand Chamber), 27 September 1995, para. 200; approved, inter alia, in *Armani da Silva* v. *United Kingdom*, Judgment (Grand Chamber), 30 March 2016, para. 244 *et seq.*

[68] The 2001 European Code of Police Ethics, for instance, stipulates that the police may use force 'only to the extent required to obtain a legitimate objective'. European Code of Police Ethics, adopted by the Committee of Ministers of the Council of Europe on 19 September 2001, para. 37, available at: https://bit.ly/3CuSbLM.

[69] ECtHR, *Kukhalashvili* v. *Georgia*, Judgment (Fifth Section), 2 April 2020, para. 151.

[70] Thus, for example, in September 2021, a UK police officer pleaded guilty to common assault for having tasered a vulnerable man four times when he was already handcuffed. In June 2023, a panel found the officer guilty of gross misconduct and dismissed him from Greater Manchester Police. The chair of the Panel stated: 'PC Smith lost his

Counterterrorism Action under International Law

The duty to refrain from ill-treatment demands that law enforcement officials do not beat or threaten detainees who are safely in custody and refraining from violence. They are also obligated by international human rights law to protect the suspects from attacks by others, such as other detainees.

5.3.4 *Proportionate Force in Tackling Terrorists*

The principle of proportionality places a ceiling on the permissible use of force in tackling a terrorist suspect. According to the 1990 UN Basic Principles on the Use of Force and Firearms by Law Enforcement Officials: 'Whenever the lawful use of force and firearms is unavoidable, law enforcement officers shall ... act in proportion to the seriousness of the offence and legitimate objective to be achieved.'[71] Thus, proportionality limits necessary force by reference to the harm expected to be inflicted on life or limb and to property when compared with the action taken to repel the threat. Proportionality thus may render unlawful force which may be (objectively as well as subjectively) deemed necessary to prevent crime in certain circumstances.

5.3.4.1 The Use of Firearms

The principle of proportionality is particularly important in regulating the use of firearms in law enforcement. The salient international rules are set out in Principle 9 of the 1990 Basic Principles,[72] which stipulates that firearms may be used where necessary to confront an imminent threat of death or serious injury (to either a law enforcement official or a member of the public).[73] Thus, use of firearms purely to protect property will not be lawful, nor may such use occur with a view to preventing a potentially serious injury that is not 'imminent'. Imminence implies a threat that will materialize in a matter of seconds at most.[74] All law enforcement officials, including counterterrorism police, should receive clear and precise instructions as to the manner and circumstances in which they should make use of firearms.[75]

---

temper – it was a gratuitous act to cause pain with no justification. PC Smith lost self-control and failed to show the victim respect.' M. Brown, 'Officer who Tasered vulnerable man six times in Greater Manchester sacked', *The Guardian*, 22 June 2023, at: https://bit.ly/43R1YHN. Although the case concerned the use of force against a suicidal man and not a terrorism suspect, the same principles apply to both situations.

[71] Principle 5, Basic Principles on the Use of Force and Firearms by Law Enforcement Officials; adopted at Havana by the Eighth UN Congress on the Prevention of Crime and the Treatment of Offenders, 7 September 1990 (hereafter, 1990 Basic Principles). In December 1990, the UN General Assembly welcomed the Basic Principles and invited governments to respect them. UN General Assembly Resolution 45/166, adopted without a vote on 18 December 1990, operative para. 4.

[72] The rules set forth in Principle 9 were most reaffirmed by UN Member States on the Human Rights Council in March 2021 in a resolution adopted without a vote. Human Rights Council Resolution 46/15, operative para. 14. The United States, which contests the customary law status of the UN Basic Principles in general, nonetheless co-sponsored the Council resolution along with Canada, Egypt, France, Georgia, Mexico, Turkey, and Ukraine. See Fifth Periodic Report submitted by the United States under Article 40 of the ICCPR, UN doc. CCPR/C/USA/5, 19 January 2021, para. 56.

[73] Human Rights Committee General Comment 36 on the right to life, para. 12.

[74] Ibid., p. 98.

[75] 'Governments should undertake to provide effective training to the police force with the objective of complying with international standards for human rights and policing. Furthermore, as indicated in many international documents ..., police should receive clear and precise instructions as to the manner and circumstances in which they should make use of firearms.' ECtHR, *Simsek and others* v. *Türkiye*, Judgment (Second Section), 26 July 2005 (as rendered final on 26 October 2005), para. 109.

5.3 *Tackling Terrorist Suspects in Law Enforcement*

Exceptionally, where a 'grave' and temporally proximate threat exists to life, an officer may also be entitled to use his or her firearm against a person. This is so even when the threat is not imminent.[76] This is particularly apposite in a case of suspected terrorism. In 1997, for instance, in its adjudication in the case of *M. D.* v. *Turkey*, the erstwhile European Commission on Human Rights deemed that the shooting of an escaping terrorist bombing suspect fell within an exception set out in the protection of the right to life under the European Convention on Human Rights,[77] namely 'to prevent the escape of a person lawfully detained'.[78]

In December 2015, a *gendarme* in Paris fired around ten shots when a driver refused to stop and then forced his way through the one of the main entrances of Les Invalides in the French capital. The incident took place at the complex where a remembrance ceremony had recently been held for the 130 people killed in the 13 November 2015 Islamist attacks across Paris.[79] (The driver, who survived, was subsequently sectioned under mental health legislation.) In March 2016, in Brussels, Salah Abdeslam, a prime suspect for involvement in the 2015 Paris terror attacks, was shot by armed police in the leg as he left a building that was surrounded by police officers. Belgian State prosecutor Eric Van der Sypt admitted that Mr Abdeslam was not armed, but said that he was shot when he did not immediately obey orders when confronted by the police.[80] Three days before his arrest Mr Abdeslam had fired on police officers; four were injured. He was subsequently convicted of attempted murder.[81]

A significantly higher international standard applies when a law enforcement official is shooting with intent to kill (as opposed to shooting to stop a criminal suspect). Principle 9 of the 1990 UN Basic Principles thus stipulates: 'In any event, intentional lethal use of firearms may only be made when strictly unavoidable in order to protect life.' Inhering in the phrase 'strictly unavoidable' are the notions of imminence and of absolute necessity. No other means must realistically be open to law enforcement officials to prevent loss of life. The heightened international legal standard for intentional killing typically concerns two scenarios: a hostage taker who is perceived to be on the verge of killing his or her hostage or a bomber just about to detonate an explosive device, whether or not it is body borne. Consequently, if the law enforcement official does not honestly and reasonably believe that a suspect is about to pull the trigger of a gun aimed at a hostage's head or to detonate a bomb, intentional lethal use of force cannot be said to be strictly unavoidable to protect life.

In the *McCann* case, the four British soldiers who shot to death the three IRA operatives in Gibraltar had acknowledged at an earlier inquest that their intent, once they opened fire, was to kill. 'They considered that it was necessary to continue to fire at the suspects until they were rendered physically incapable of detonating a device.'[82] The European Court's Grand Chamber accepted that the soldiers

> honestly believed, in the light of the information that they had been given, that it was necessary
> to shoot the suspects in order to prevent them from detonating a bomb and causing serious loss of

---

[76] 1990 Basic Principle 9.

[77] European Commission on Human Rights, *M. D.* v. *Turkey*, Decision, 30 June 1997.

[78] Art. 2(2)(b), European Convention on Human Rights.

[79] Associated Press, 'Police Open Fire on Car after Driver Tries to Ram Barrier at Paris's Invalides Monument', *Daily Telegraph*, 16 December 2015, at: https://bit.ly/3yYw3WX.

[80] J. Curtis and T. Wyke, 'Terror Mastermind Salah Abdeslam Escaped Police by Hiding in a Wardrobe Then Walked the Streets of Brussels Freely for Weeks before He was Captured in Sting Triggered by a PIZZA Delivery', *Daily Mail Online*, 20 March 2016, at: https://bit.ly/3g68uCD.

[81] « Salah Abdeslam reconnu coupable de tentative d'assassinat sur des policiers », *BFM TV*, 23 April 2018, at: https://bit.ly/3fQQ6PC.

[82] ECtHR, *McCann and others* v. *United Kingdom*, Judgment (Grand Chamber), para. 199.

life. ... The actions which they took, in obedience to superior orders, were thus perceived by them as absolutely necessary in order to safeguard innocent lives.[83]

In the aftermath of the Fishmongers' Hall terrorist incident in London on 29 November 2019, Usman Khan, a convicted terrorist who had already fatally stabbed two people, was cornered on London Bridge wearing what appeared to be a suicide vest.[84] Having received the order to kill him, he was shot to death by Metropolitan Police Service (MPS) officers.[85] The inquest into his death, held in May to June 2021, heard that twenty shots were fired at Mr Khan by firearms officers, at least nine of which struck him.[86] The officer who seemingly fired the fatal shots told the inquest that he noticed an improvised explosive device on the person on the floor. 'To me it looked viable and real', he said. 'To be honest, I did not think I was going home.'[87]

5.3.5 The Duty of Precaution and Operations to Tackle Terrorist Suspects

While a certain degree of operational latitude will be accorded to the authorities when dealing with a terrorist incident, a planned counterterrorism operation must still comply with the human rights duty of precaution. For it is important to take into account the broader context in order to adjudge the necessity for police use of force. What may have been necessary at the instant of use of force could have been avoided by better action upstream in the planning of a law enforcement operation. This duty was first identified by the European Court of Human Rights in its 1995 judgment in the *McCann* case.[88] The Court had to consider 'whether the anti-terrorist operation as a whole was controlled and organised in a manner which respected the requirements of Article 2 ... and whether the information and instructions given to the soldiers which, in effect, rendered inevitable the use of lethal force, took adequately into consideration the right to life of the three suspects'.[89]

The precautionary principle further demands that a plan be put in place for the medical treatment of terrorist suspects, in particular when they have been shot or otherwise seriously harmed. The *Finogenov* case concerned the occupation of the Dubrovka theatre in Moscow on 23 October 2002 by members of a Chechen separatist armed group. Several dozen heavily armed militants took around 1,000 people hostage. In resolving the crisis using significant levels of force, Russian special forces first pumped into the auditorium a narcotic gas (seemingly a derivative of the opiate, fentanyl) before storming the building. In addition to killing the hostage-takers, 129 or more of the hostages died from the effects of the gas, most as a result of choking on their own vomit or having suffocated because of a swollen tongue.[90]

As in its judgment in the *McCann* case, the European Court of Human Rights did not find a violation of the right to life on the basis of an unlawful use of force by the Russian authorities.

---

[83] Ibid., para. 200. Nonetheless, in its finding that the United Kingdom had failed in its duty of precaution towards the applicants' deceased relatives, the Court did mitigate that position (one might even say gainsaid if not reversed it) when referring to 'the automatic recourse to lethal force when the soldiers opened fire'. Ibid., para. 213.

[84] BBC, 'Fishmongers' Hall terror attack victim Jack Merritt's life "was a triumph"', 12 April 2021, at: https://bbc.in/3vSIxgU.

[85] D. Brown, 'Officers got "critical shot" permission for Fishmongers' Hall terrorist Usman Khan', *The Times*, 1 June 2021.

[86] BBC, 'Fishmongers' Hall: Terrorist shot at 20 times on London Bridge', 1 June 2021, at: https://bbc.in/3cemER9.

[87] D. Brown, 'Firearms officer at London Bridge terror attack thought Usman Khan was wearing suicide belt', *The Times*, 3 June 2021.

[88] ECtHR, *McCann and others* v. *United Kingdom*, Judgment (Grand Chamber), 27 September 1995.

[89] Ibid., para. 201.

[90] ECtHR, *Finogenov and others* v. *Russia*, Judgment (First Section), 20 December 2011 (as rendered final on 4 June 2012), paras. 24, 101.

The hostage-taking had come as a surprise 'so the military preparations for the storming had to be made very quickly and in full secrecy'. The Court further noted that the authorities were not in control of the situation inside the theatre. 'In such a situation', the Court accepted that 'difficult and agonising decisions' had to be made. It was prepared to grant the authorities 'a margin of appreciation, at least in so far as the military and technical aspects of the situation are concerned', even though, 'with hindsight', some of the decisions 'may appear open to doubt'.[91]

But the Court considered whether the authorities had taken 'all necessary precautions to minimise the effects of the gas on the hostages, to evacuate them quickly and to provide them with necessary medical assistance'. The lack of adequate planning and preparation, the refusal to tell the medical staff outside and in nearby hospitals which toxic chemical it had used, and the delay of an hour in evacuating the building of the victims led the Court to hold that they had not in fact taken the necessary precautions.[92] The duty to assist the injured applies even if the person or persons are themselves suspected offenders.

That said, on a domestic level, British police are authorized to leave behind seriously injured members of the public if a terrorist suspect is at large and potentially continuing to seek to kill or maim. The police may pursue the suspect and kill him or her if it is strictly necessary to do so to preserve lives. This change in policy followed the November 2015 terror attacks in Paris. Pat Gallan, MPS Assistant Commissioner for Special Crime and Operations, said: 'In asking them to go forward we are asking them not to give first aid to people injured and it might be their colleagues..... The most important thing is to actually get to the threat and stop them killing additional people, and that is why we've got to keep going forward and not tend to those that are injured at the time.'[93]

Misidentification of a terrorist suspect by the British police proved fatal for Jean-Charles de Menezes in July 2005. Mr de Menezes, a Brazilian electrician, was mistaken for a suicide bomber of Syrian origin about to detonate explosives on a tube train in the British capital and was shot to death by firearms officers from the MPS. Surveillance of the apartment buildings had been compromised as the officer most familiar with the suspect was relieving himself into a bottle in his surveillance van when Mr de Menezes came out on the morning of 22 July.[94] A first wave of bombings two weeks earlier had killed fifty-two people and injured hundreds more. The 7/7 bombings were the worst single terrorist atrocity on British soil.[95]

A second wave of bombings had been conducted on 21 July but only the detonators had exploded.[96] The following morning, while Mr de Menezes was killed as he innocently boarded a tube train at Stockwell underground station, the actual bomber being sought, Hamdi Issac Adus, an Ethiopian national claiming to be a Somali national, Hussain Osman, was on the south coast of England, preparing to flee the country.[97] Mr de Menezes was held by a police officer in a bear hug inside the tube train as he was shot seven times in the head and once in the shoulder in a total volley of eleven rounds. In its 2016 judgment in the case, the Grand Chamber of the European Court of Human Rights held that 'the principal question to be addressed' in such a circumstance is whether a police officer 'had an honest and genuine belief that the use of force

---

[91]   Ibid., para. 213.
[92]   Ibid., paras. 237, 254, 255, 257, and 266.
[93]   V. Dodd, 'UK Armed Police Told to Race to Stop Terrorists and Ignore the Dying', *The Guardian*, 2 December 2015, at: https://bit.ly/2S4YxgZ.
[94]   'The catalogue of errors that killed Jean Charles de Menezes', *The Conversation*, 21 July 2015, at: https://bit.ly/3z30sX6.
[95]   BBC, '7 July London bombings: What happened that day?', 3 July 2015, at: https://bbc.in/3yTxbuZ.
[96]   BBC, '21 July: Attacks, escapes and arrests', 11 July 2007, at: https://bbc.in/3pii9u4.
[97]   BBC, 'Profile: Hussain Osman', 9 July 2007, at http://bbc.in/2IW3DpB.

was necessary', even if that belief was in fact mistaken.[98] The broader intelligence failures of the operation had led to a situation where deadly force was highly likely, but the failure to take reasonable precautions in planning and conducting the operation was not effectively addressed by either the applicant or the Court.

In 2006, the Crown Prosecution Service found 'insufficient evidence to provide a realistic prospect of conviction against any individual police officer'. The challenge before the European Court of Human Rights did not find a violation of the right to life based on a failure to prosecute the officers responsible for his death. In 2007, however, the MPS was convicted of breaches of health and safety legislation and fined £175,000. In 2009, the Metropolitan Police paid significant compensation to the family who ended their civil suit against it.[99]

5.4 THE TREATMENT OF TERRORIST SUSPECTS IN CUSTODY

Once in custody, the right to freedom from torture and other inhumane treatment demands that all suspects be protected against harm, whether that may come at the hands of law enforcement officials, other detainees, or members of the public. Particular constraints on the use of force occur when a terrorist suspect is in custody. Torture and other ill-treatment (sadistic or excessive use of force or acts to humiliate a suspect fall within this category) are comprehensively prohibited. This does not change based on the perceived prevailing circumstances. The favoured scenario of those who would defend the practice of torture – the ticking bomb paradigm – is in practice not credible. If a bomb is about to go off and if it is believed that the suspect in custody knows when and where the bombing will occur – two big '*ifs*' – the last thing law enforcement needs is to be sent on a wild goose chase.

5.4.1 *Deaths in Custody*

Despite the law, the risk of terrorism suspects dying in custody is high. The risk of death from natural causes exists of course, but as the Human Rights Committee has stated, loss of life during custody in unnatural circumstances generates a presumption of arbitrary deprivation of life by the authorities. This presumption can only be rebutted on the basis of a proper investigation that establishes the State's compliance with its obligations under the right to life as codified in Article 6 of the ICCPR.[100] The appropriate conduct of such an investigation is described in the Minnesota Protocol on the Investigation of Potentially Unlawful Death (2016) published by the Office of the UN High Commissioner for Human Rights (OHCHR).[101]

The risk of ill-treatment inevitably rises when the police believe that they have arrested someone who has already engaged in acts of terrorism or is planning to do so. This issue arose in the *Satybalov* case, decided by the European Court of Human Rights in 2020. On the evening of 2 May 2010, Marat Satybalov and six friends were driving to the countryside for a barbecue in two cars in the Daghestan region of Russia. On the way there, Mr Satybalov and two others who were together in one car stopped at a pharmacy in the village of Dylym to get painkillers.[102] The pharmacist thought that Mr M. G. looked suspicious 'with his long beard' and called the

---

[98] ECtHR, *Armani da Silva* v. *United Kingdom*, Judgment (Grand Chamber), 30 March 2016, para. 248.
[99] H. Siddique, 'Who was Jean Charles de Menezes?', *The Guardian*, 30 March 2016 (Last updated 21 September 2017), at: https://bit.ly/34HzXFF.
[100] Human Rights Committee General Comment 36 on the right to life, para. 29.
[101] *Minnesota Protocol on the Investigation of Potentially Unlawful Death (2016)*, OHCHR, Geneva/New York, 2017, at: https://bit.ly/3aH8Yh7.
[102] ECtHR, *Satybalova* v. *Russia*, Judgment (Third Section), 30 June 2020, para. 6.

5.4 *The Treatment of Terrorist Suspects in Custody* 199

police.[103] Police officers from a district police station arrived and searched him at gunpoint before approaching the passengers in the car. The commander of the officers, Major A. S., dragged Mr Satybalov out of the car by his beard and hit him on the head with the butt of his machine gun. The officers then subjected Mr Satybalov and his two friends to beatings, hitting them with the butts of their machine guns and kicking them. Then they took them to the police station without telling them about the reasons for their detention.[104]

At the station, the three men were taken to the courtyard and subjected to beatings. They were punched, kicked, and hit with the butts of machine guns. They were then taken inside and asked repeatedly 'why they had long beards'. Major A. S. repeatedly pulled Mr Satybalov's beard, beat him, and continued to ask him about his beard. He filmed the ill-treatment of the three men on his phone while insulting them. The three men were released the next day after having been fined for failure to obey police orders.[105] Mr Satybalov's health worsened over the coming days. In the early hours of 6 May 2010, the applicants and their relatives took Mr Satybalov back to hospital, where he immediately underwent emergency surgery. He had lost a lot of blood owing to internal bleeding following the beatings on 2 May 2010. Doctors performed further emergency surgery and informed the applicants that Mr Satybalov was in a critical condition. He had punctured lungs, broken ribs, and damage to his heart and arteries. His kidneys, which were severely damaged, had stopped functioning. On 7 May 2010, Mr Satybalov died in hospital.[106]

The Court reiterated that the obligation on the authorities to account for the treatment of an individual in custody is particularly stringent where that individual dies. In the absence of an adequate explanation, the Court can draw inferences which may be unfavourable for the respondent government.[107] In fact, the government neither disputed the ill-treatment of Mr Satybalov nor that he had died as a result of the injuries inflicted during that ill-treatment.[108] Given that the authorities had failed to provide any explanation or justification for the use of force by the police against Mr Satybalov which led to his death, the Court held that his death could be attributed to the State and that Russia had violated his right to life.[109] Having found a violation of the right to life, as a result of the severity of the beatings, the Court went on to also hold that Russia had violated the prohibition on torture in Article 3 of the European Convention on Human Rights.[110]

Those charged with or convicted of terrorism offences must also be protected while they are incarcerated either following conviction or while awaiting trial. Should they resort to violence (rendering the use of force necessary), that force must still be proportionate to the threat. The *Neira Alegría* case concerned the violent repression of riots by the Peruvian military that took place on 18–19 June 1986 at the San Juan Bautista prison on the island of El Frontón.[111] Hundreds of prisoners in the Blue Pavilion area of the prison, most of whom were accused of belonging to the terrorist group Shining Path (*Sendero Luminoso*), rioted, seized hostages, and armed themselves with weapons. To resolve the situation the State's naval forces demolished the building and blew down the prison walls with explosives. In total, more than 110 people died

---

[103] Ibid., para. 7.
[104] Ibid., paras. 8–10.
[105] Ibid., paras. 11–16.
[106] Ibid., paras. 19–20.
[107] Ibid., para. 69.
[108] Ibid., para. 68.
[109] Ibid., paras. 69–70.
[110] Ibid., paras. 76–7.
[111] See, e.g., D. Willis, 'Scratched From Memory: The 1986 Prison Massacres and the Limits of Acceptable Memory Discourse in Post-Conflict Peru', *Journal of Latin American Cultural Studies, Travesia*, Vol. 29, No. 2 (2020), pp. 231–50.

(including the three victims in the case), of whom 97 could not be identified. Each of the three men had been charged with terrorist offences.

Amnesty International alleged that summary executions of surrendered rioters occurred at the prison after its storming.[112] It was also claimed that the final explosion that demolished the prison occurred not while an attack was in progress but afterwards, as a result of the blasting of the columns that sustained the building.[113] The Court accepted that those detained in the Blue Pavilion of the prison were 'highly dangerous and in fact armed', but held that this did not justify the amount of force that was used.[114] Indeed, a minority report on the operation by the Peruvian Congressional Commission found that 'the military force used was disproportionate in relationship to the actual danger present, and no precautionary measures were put into effect to reduce the human cost of crushing the riot'.[115] The Inter-American Court of Human Rights held that the right to life of each of the three men had been violated.[116]

5.4.2 *Extraordinary Rendition*

Several European nations participated in the unlawful 'extraordinary rendition' of detainees to the jurisdiction of the United States and sometimes witnessed and even engaged in the ill-treatment to which the detainees were subjected. In a number of instances, the victims sought redress through the European Court of Human Rights. The first such case was that of *El-Masri* v. *North Macedonia*, in which the applicant, a German national of Lebanese origin, alleged that he had been the victim of a secret rendition operation in early 2004.[117] Khaled El-Masri alleged he had been arrested, placed in solitary confinement, questioned, ill-treated in a hotel in Skopje for twenty-three days, and then handed over to US intelligence agents, who took him to an isolated and clandestine Central Intelligence Agency (CIA) prison in Afghanistan north of Kabul known as the 'Salt Pit', where he was subjected to further torture and other ill-treatment during a period of more than four months.[118] A CIA investigative document[119] revealed that the Agency 'quickly concluded he was not a terrorist', but justified his detention 'despite the diminishing rationale by insisting that they knew he was bad'.[120]

On 23 January 2004, Mr El-Masri was handcuffed and blindfolded, taken from the hotel where he was being detained by North Macedonian security officers, and driven to Skopje Airport. Placed in a room, he was beaten severely by several disguised men dressed in black. He was stripped and sodomized with an object. He was then placed in an adult nappy and dressed in a tracksuit. Shackled and hooded, and subjected to total sensory deprivation, he was forcibly marched to a CIA aircraft that was surrounded by North Macedonian security agents who formed a cordon around the plane. When on the plane, he was thrown to the floor, chained

---

[112] Inter-American Court of Human Rights, *Neira Alegría* v. *Peru*, Judgment (Merits), 19 January 1995, para. 43.

[113] Ibid., para. 52.

[114] Ibid., para. 74.

[115] Ibid., para. 62.

[116] Ibid., para. 76.

[117] For a migration law perspective on the case, see E. Guild, 'Terrorism and migration law', chap. 30 in B. Saul (ed.), *Research Handbook on International Law and Terrorism*, 2nd ed., Edward Elgar, Cheltenham, 2021, pp. 444–5.

[118] ECtHR, *El-Masri* v. *North Macedonia*, Judgment (Grand Chamber), 13 December 2012. At that time, North Macedonia was still known internationally as the former Yugoslav Republic of Macedonia.

[119] J. Dakwar, 'New CIA Torture Documents Confirm Chilling Details of Khaled El-Masri's 'Kafkaesque' Ordeal', ACLU, 27 June 2016, at: https://bit.ly/46czGch.

[120] See C. Carlyle, 'Bringing Human Rights Home: Rights to Reparations and Repair for CIA Extraordinary Rendition Survivors', University of North Carolina School of Law Human Rights Policy Lab, Chapel Hill, NC, 2021–2022, at: https://bit.ly/3CFFspu, p. 19.

down, and forcibly tranquillized.[121] The European Court of Human Rights found that the alleged ill-treatment had been established beyond any reasonable doubt,[122] and held North Macedonia responsible not only for this substantive violation of the prohibition in Article 3 of the European Convention during his detention in a Skopje hotel and his subsequent captivity in Afghanistan but also for the breach of the procedural obligation to investigate such allegations. The Court declared that Mr El-Masri's unacknowledged detention was a particularly serious violation of his rights to liberty and security.

Hari Kostov, the North Macedonian Minister of the Interior between November 2002 and May 2004 and prime minister between June and November 2004, gave a formal written statement on 4 March 2010 in which he declared:

> I am aware that the US authorities ultimately released Mr El-Masri, without charge, after several further months of detention. I understand that Mr El-Masri's situation resulted from a mistake. I maintain that if any mistake was made in Mr El-Masri's case, it was not Macedonia's mistake, and I do not believe there was any intentional wrongdoing on the part of the Macedonian authorities.[123]

Mr El-Masri's civil suit of 2006 against the CIA Director at the time of his ill-treatment, George Tenet, was dismissed by the US District Court for the Eastern District of Virginia as a result of the US government claiming 'State secrets privilege'.[124] An appeal against the dismissal was rejected by the US Court of Appeals for the Fourth Circuit. In October 2007, the US Supreme Court refused to review Mr El-Masri's case. On 9 April 2008, the American Civil Liberties Union (ACLU) filed a petition with the Inter-American Commission on Human Rights on his behalf. The Commission deemed the petition admissible in April 2016, and in November 2017, the ACLU filed a request for a hearing on the merits of the case. On 17 October 2018, the ACLU submitted its Final Observations on the Merits of Khaled El-Masri's case to the Commission.[125] At the time of writing, the Inter-American Commission on Human Rights had not heard the case.

5.5 FAIR-TRIAL RIGHTS

5.5.1 Terrorism Trials in Camera

If a prosecution is mounted, defendants against terrorism charges must be accorded all the rights of fair trial. Exceptionally, however, not all of the proceedings need be held in public when a

---

[121] ECtHR, *El-Masri* v. *North Macedonia*, Judgment (Grand Chamber), para. 205.

[122] His treatment – and blanket denials by the authorities – had been specifically documented by Dick Marty, the Special Rapporteur of the Council of Europe Parliamentary Assembly's Committee on Legal Affairs and Human Rights appointed to investigate allegations of extraordinary renditions in Europe. D. Marty, Committee on Legal Affairs and Human Rights, Council of Europe Parliamentary Assembly, 'Alleged secret detentions and unlawful inter-state transfers of detainees involving CoE member States', Part II, 7 June 2006, at: https://bit.ly/3fNgXvW, pp. 24–32.

[123] ECtHR, *El-Masri* v. *North Macedonia*, Judgment (Grand Chamber), para. 74.

[124] As the American Civil Liberties Union (ACLU), which represented Mr El-Masri in his lawsuit, has observed, although the State secrets privilege 'has existed in some form since the early 19th century, its modern use, and the rules governing its invocation, derive from the landmark case of *United States* v. *Reynolds*, 345 US 1 (1953). In *Reynolds*, the widows of three civilians who died in the crash of a military plane in Georgia filed a wrongful death action against the government. In response to their request for the accident report, the government insisted that the report could not be disclosed because it contained information about secret military equipment that was being tested aboard the aircraft during the fatal flight. When the accident report was finally declassified in 2004, it contained no details whatsoever about secret equipment. The government's true motivation in asserting the state secrets privilege was to cover up its own negligence.' ACLU, 'El-Masri v. Tenet: Background on the State Secrets Privilege', at: https://bit.ly/3uGsC3K.

[125] ACLU, 'Khaled El-Masri v. United States', last updated 6 November 2018, at: https://bit.ly/3g3HcNv. The text of the statement is available at: https://bit.ly/3fJTagg.

terrorism case truly endangers national security. This eventuality is recognized in Article 6 of the European Convention on the right to a fair trial[126] as well as Article 14(1) of the ICCPR.[127] In its judgment in the *Belashev* case, the European Court of Human Rights rebutted the claim by Russia that the presence of classified information in the case file automatically implies a need to close a trial to the public, without balancing openness with national security concerns. The Court recognized that it may be important for a State to preserve its secrets, but 'it is of infinitely greater importance to surround justice with all the requisite safeguards'. Accordingly, before excluding the public from criminal proceedings, courts 'must make specific findings that closure is necessary to protect a compelling governmental interest and limit secrecy to the extent necessary to preserve such an interest'.[128]

The *Khoroshenko* case heard by the Human Rights Committee in 2011 concerned membership of a criminal gang rather than a terrorist group.[129] But the principles underpinning the views of the Committee would hold good also for terrorism cases. That is to say, all trials in criminal matters must in principle be conducted orally and publicly and if one of the exceptions in Article 14(1) of the ICCPR is relied upon to justify an *in-camera* hearing for part of the trial, this must be explicitly justified.[130] Given that the author of the communication to the Committee had been sentenced to death following a trial held in violation of fair-trial guarantees, the Committee concluded that his right to life had also been violated.[131]

5.5.2 *Use of Evidence Obtained Using Coercion*

It will never be permissible to use evidence obtained using torture in proceedings against a terrorism suspect. It does not matter whether it concerns a confession from the suspect him- or herself or information extracted under torture from a third party.[132] Admitting evidence obtained by torture 'would only serve to legitimate indirectly the sort of morally reprehensible conduct' which is proscribed in international law.[133] It would 'afford brutality the cloak of law', in the words of the US Supreme Court in its judgment in 1952 in the *Rochin* case.[134]

The European Court of Human Rights has also made it clear that the use of information gleaned from detainees as a result of any ill-treatment against them, even when it does not amount to torture, may not lawfully be used in criminal proceedings against them.[135] But where it is a third party who is ill-treated (but not tortured), the use of evidence they provide as a result only contravenes the right to a fair trial where the violation influences the outcome of the

---

[126]   'Judgment shall be pronounced publicly but the press and public may be excluded from all or part of the trial in the interests of . . . national security in a democratic society.'

[127]   'The press and the public may be excluded from all or part of a trial for reasons of . . . national security in a democratic society'.

[128]   ECtHR, *Belashev* v. *Russia*, Judgment (First Section), 4 December 2008 (as rendered final on 4 May 2009), para. 83.

[129]   Human Rights Committee, *Andrei Khoroshenko* v. *Russia*, Views, 29 March 2011, para. 2.1.

[130]   Ibid., para. 9.11.

[131]   Ibid.

[132]   ECtHR, *Othman (Abu Qatada)* v. *United Kingdom*, Judgment (Fourth Section), 17 January 2012 (as rendered final on 9 May 2012), para. 267: 'the Court considers that the admission of torture evidence is manifestly contrary, not just to the provisions of Article 6 [of the European Convention on Human Rights], but to the most basic international standards of a fair trial. It would make the whole trial not only immoral and illegal, but also entirely unreliable in its outcome. It would, therefore, be a flagrant denial of justice if such evidence were admitted in a criminal trial'.

[133]   ECtHR, *Jalloh* v. *Germany*, Judgment (Grand Chamber), 11 July 2006, para. 105.

[134]   US Supreme Court, *Rochin* v. *California* 342 US 165 (1952), at p. 173.

[135]   ECtHR, *Ibrahim and others* v. *United Kingdom*, Judgment (Grand Chamber), 13 September 2016, para. 254.

proceedings, either by facilitating the person's conviction or by increasing the penalty that is imposed pursuant to a conviction.[136]

In August 2023, the confession made to federal agents by Abd al-Rahim al-Nashiri, who is accused of having led the attack on the USS Cole in 2000 which killed 17 American sailors, was thrown out as inadmissible by a judge at the US military commission at the Guantanamo Bay detention centre in Cuba. The judge held that his previous experiences of torture were still relevant. After his arrest in 2002, Mr al-Nashiri spent four years in secret CIA black sites where he was tortured. The judge ruled that the years of violent treatment, including waterboarding, would have been on his mind when he volunteered to be questioned again: 'Any resistance the accused might have been inclined to put up when asked to incriminate himself was intentionally and literally beaten out of him years before', Judge Acosta stated.[137]

5.6 PREVENTIVE DETENTION AND OTHER RESTRICTIONS ON TERRORISM SUSPECTS

It may not be possible to secure a conviction of a terrorism suspect, either because the evidence is lacking to secure a conviction or because the State is unwilling to prosecute (for a variety of reasons, including for fear of making public sensitive intelligence information).[138] In exceptional circumstances, the State may seek to either engage in preventive detention of those they fear will engage in terrorism in the future or impose a range of control orders or restrictions on those they suspect are liable to turn to terrorism. The most stringent restrictions should be imposed on preventive detention as it amounts to imprisonment without a fair trial as well as, effectively, to the denial of *habeas corpus*. The risk of arbitrary detention occurring is inherently greatly elevated. Less stringent controls will pertain to limitations on interaction with specified individuals or even to house arrest.

5.6.1 *Preventive Detention*

McLoughlin and others define 'preventive detention' (also termed security detention or administrative detention) as the 'detention or confinement of a person believed to pose a threat to national security or to public safety and order, or a person whose presence at a public proceeding is required but cannot be guaranteed'.[139] The purpose of the detention, they note, is to avoid the potential danger or absence rather than the punishment of a criminal offence. Hence, although many, if not most, of those held in preventive detention are in fact criminal defendants, others may not have been accused of a crime.[140] Such preventive detention is clearly distinguishable from remand pending trial, as no trial is envisaged in the instance of preventive detention.

---

[136] ECtHR, *El Haski* v. *Belgium*, Judgment (Second Section), 25 September 2012 (as rendered final on 18 March 2013), para. 85.

[137] M. Evans, 'Confession ruled out over past CIA torture at Guantanamo Bay', *The Times*, 28 August 2023.

[138] In 2005, in the debate on the Prevention of Terrorism Bill, the UK government claimed in the House of Commons that the allegations against certain individuals who posed a real and serious risk to the nation but that they could not be prosecuted 'because that would mean revealing sensitive and dangerous intelligence'. Statement of Hazel Blears, Minister of State in the Home Office for Policing, Security and Community Safety, House of Commons, 10 March 2005, text at: https://bit.ly/3XkVlew.

[139] J. McLoughlin, G. P. Noone, and D. C. Noone, 'Security Detention, Terrorism, and the Prevention Imperative', *Case Western Reserve Journal of International Law*, Vol. 40 (2009), 463–505, at: https://bit.ly/3NGBEdy, at p. 476.

[140] Ibid., citing US Supreme Court, *Hamdi* v. *Rumsfeld*, 542 US 517 (2004), at pp. 518–19.

In *A. and others* v. *United Kingdom*,[141] the issue was the preventive detention of foreign nationals who could not be deported because of the international legal rule of *non-refoulement*. After the 9/11 attacks in the United States, the British government believed that certain foreign nationals present in the United Kingdom had been involved in terrorist operations linked to al-Qaeda and that they threatened the security of the State. Those individuals could not be deported because there was a risk that they would be ill-treated in their respective State of origin. The government considered it necessary to allow the detention of foreign nationals, where the Secretary of State for the Home Department reasonably believed that the person's presence in the United Kingdom was a risk to national security and reasonably suspected that the person was an 'international terrorist'.[142]

The United Kingdom had formally derogated from Article 5 of the European Convention on Human Rights, the provision that guaranteed the right to liberty and prohibited arbitrary detention. The European Court of Human Rights' Grand Chamber considered that the detention of a person 'against whom action is being taken with a view to deportation or extradition' consonant with paragraph 1(f) of Article 5 could be justified only for as long as such proceedings were in progress, and which were being conducted with due diligence.[143] With respect to nine applicants, however, there was no realistic prospect of their being expelled without violating the international legal prohibition on *non-refoulement*. The Court therefore concluded that their detention breached Article 5, the derogation notwithstanding. A critical issue was the discrimination between nationals and non-nationals inherent in the measures taken by the United Kingdom. Moreover, the European Court noted that UK courts, including those that had studied 'closed' material that was classified secret, were not convinced that the threat from non-nationals was more serious than that posed by UK nationals.[144]

5.6.2 *Control Orders and House Arrest*

Control orders are not per se unlawful under international human rights law, despite views to the contrary.[145] But the extent of the restraints and the necessity for and proportionality of their imposition will determine whether they are lawful or not. In the United Kingdom, control orders have had a troubled history owing to poor formulation and disproportionate application. On 11 March 2005, the UK Parliament adopted the 2005 Prevention of Terrorism Act after a long debate. The new law introduced preventive control orders for terrorist suspects that replaced earlier administrative detention provisions, enabling the Executive to place far-reaching restrictions on the movement, communications, and work of individuals for renewable periods of twelve months. Control orders were issued upon 'reasonable suspicion' that an individual may pose a threat and were subject to judicial review. But in 2006, a High Court judge voided six

---

[141] ECtHR, *A. and others* v. *United Kingdom*, Judgment (Grand Chamber), 19 February 2009.
[142] Ibid., paras. 166 and 171.
[143] Ibid., para. 164.
[144] Ibid., paras. 188 and 189.
[145] Amnesty International, for instance, stated in 2007 its belief that the imposition of control orders 'is tantamount to charging, trying and sentencing a person without the fair trial guarantees required in criminal cases. The organization considers that the control order regime is intrinsically inimical to the rule of law, the independence of the judiciary and human rights protection in the UK. In particular, this regime runs counter to the principle of equality before the law; the right to be free from discrimination; and the right to a fair trial – including the presumption of innocence, equality of arms, access to counsel and the right to a defence – even more so when the conditions imposed on an individual are tantamount to deprivation of liberty.' Amnesty International, 'United Kingdom: As Law Lords hear key cases on control orders, Amnesty International calls on the UK government to abandon them', Press release, London, 5 July 2007, at: https://bit.ly/3CFIEkQ.

5.6 Preventive Detention and Other Restrictions

orders as being violative of the right to a fair trial.[146] The control orders at issue had confined six Middle Eastern men for eighteen hours each day in one-bedroom flats across the country after failing to bring charges under the Terrorism Act. Justice Sullivan writes in his judgment that the Secretary of State for the Home Department 'had no power to make them under human rights law'.[147]

The 2011 Terrorism Prevention and Investigation Measures Act replaced the system of control orders under the 2005 Act. The 2011 Act allows a series of constraints, reviewable in the courts, to be placed in the interests of public protection on persons whom the UK Home Secretary believes to have been involved in terrorism-related activity.[148] These new Terrorism Prevention and Investigation Measures (TPIMs) were intended to resolve the multiple issues of concern with respect to control orders. They failed to do so. Already in 2014, the House of Lords and House of Commons Joint Committee on Human Rights stated that their post-legislative scrutiny failed to find any evidence that TPIMs had

> led in practice to any more criminal prosecutions of terrorism suspects. This confirms the concerns we expressed in our scrutiny Reports on the Bill that the replacement for control orders were not 'investigative' in any meaningful sense. We believe TPIMs should be referred to as Terrorism Prevention Orders, or something similar, to reflect the reality that their sole purpose is preventive, not investigative.[149]

The Joint Committee agreed with the Independent Reviewer of Terrorism Legislation that 'serious restrictions on liberty, imposed outside of the criminal justice system, cannot be indefinite'.[150]

Depending on the conditions attached to it, a more limited form of house arrest is not, however, necessarily unlawful. In *De Tommaso* v. *Italy*,[151] the Grand Chamber of the European Court of Human Rights was considering the case of an individual who had been placed under special supervision by an Italian district court for two years. This involved reporting once a week to the police authority responsible for his supervision; starting to look for work within a month; living in a specific municipality and not changing his place of residence; not associating with persons who had a criminal record and who were subject to preventive or security measures; not returning home later than 10 pm or leaving home before 6 am; not keeping or carrying weapons; not going to bars, nightclubs, and amusement arcades or brothels; not attending public meetings; not using mobile phones or radio communication devices; and having with him at all times the document setting out his obligations ('carta precettiva') and presenting it to the police authority on request.[152]

The Court ruled that the measures imposed by the Bari District Court on the applicant did not amount to a deprivation of liberty under Article 5. There had been no restrictions on the applicant's freedom to leave home during the day, and he was able to have a social life and to

---

[146]   A. Travis and A. Gillan, 'New blow for Home Office as judge quashes six terror orders', *The Guardian*, 29 June 2006, at: https://bit.ly/3qT5oex.

[147]   Ibid.

[148]   Independent Reviewer of Terrorism Legislation, 'The Independent Reviewer's role', undated but accessed on 21 June 2023, at: https://bit.ly/43Nb2gI.

[149]   House of Lords and House of Commons Joint Committee on Human Rights, *Post-Legislative Scrutiny: Terrorism Prevention and Investigation Measures Act 2011*, Tenth Report of Session 2013–14, London, 2014, at: https://bit.ly/3Xk4kMN, p. 3.

[150]   Ibid., p. 5.

[151]   ECtHR, *De Tommaso* v. *Italy*, Judgment (Grand Chamber), 23 February 2017.

[152]   See Registry of the European Court of Human Rights, 'Terrorism', Guide to the case-law of the European Court of Human Rights, updated on 31 August 2022, pp. 28–29.

maintain relations with the outside world.[153] It did, however, find a violation of Article 2 of Protocol No. 4 to the European Convention on Human Rights on the basis that the applicable law[154] was drafted in 'vague and excessively broad terms'.[155] This provision in the Protocol stipulates that everyone lawfully within the territory of a State 'shall, within that territory, have the right to liberty of movement' and that restrictions placed on the exercise of the right must be in accordance with law and necessary in a democratic society in the interests of national security.[156]

5.6.3 *Revocation of Citizenship*

In certain instances, States have revoked or annulled citizenship for those convicted, or even only suspected, of terrorism offences. The revocation or annulment of citizenship as such is not incompatible with the European Convention on Human Rights,[157] but will be unlawful if it leaves a person stateless or if it is arbitrary in nature or application. Thus, in the *Ghoumid and others* case, the Court noted that the applicants all had another nationality, 'a fact to which it attaches some importance'. The decision to deprive them of their French nationality 'did not therefore have the effect of rendering them stateless'.[158]

The revocation of citizenship for an individual suspected of terrorism was considered by the European Court of Human Rights in the *K2* case against the United Kingdom. In 2000, the applicant, who was born in Sudan, became a naturalized UK citizen. In 2009, he was arrested and charged with a public order offence arising out of his participation in protests against Israeli military action in Gaza. He was released on bail but in October 2009, before the date on which he was required to surrender to his bail, he left the United Kingdom. He contends that he went directly to Sudan; however, according to the Secretary of State for the Home Department, the UK Security Service believes that he first travelled with two extremist associates to Somalia, where he engaged in terrorism-related activities linked to al-Shabaab, before travelling on to Sudan in April or May 2010.[159]

In June 2010, the Secretary of State wrote to the applicant declaring that she would be making an order pursuant to Section 40(2) of the 1981 British Nationality Act depriving him of his UK citizenship on the ground that to do so would be conducive to the public good. The Secretary of State signed the relevant order a few days later. She had also informed him of her decision to exercise the Crown's common law prerogative power to exclude him from the United Kingdom on the ground that he was 'involved in terrorism-related activities' and had 'links to a number of Islamic extremists'.[160] In rejecting the application by 'K2' as manifestly ill-founded, the Court

[153] ECtHR, *De Tommaso* v. *Italy*, Judgment (Grand Chamber), paras. 85 and 86.

[154] Act No. 1423 of 27 December 1956.

[155] ECtHR, *De Tommaso* v. *Italy*, Judgment (Grand Chamber), paras. 125 and 126. The European Court noted that 'the court responsible for imposing the preventive measure on the applicant based its decision on the existence of "active" criminal tendencies on his part, albeit without attributing any specific behaviour or criminal activity to him. Furthermore, the court mentioned as grounds for the preventive measure the fact that the applicant had no "fixed and lawful occupation" and that his life was characterised by regular association with prominent local criminals ("malavita") and the commission of offences'. Ibid., para. 118.

[156] Art. 2(1) and (3), Protocol No. 4 to the European Convention on Human Rights; adopted at Strasbourg, 16 November 1963; entered into force, 2 May 1968.

[157] ECtHR, *Usmanov* v. *Russia*, Judgment, 22 December 2020 (as rendered final on 22 March 2021), para. 65.

[158] ECtHR, *Ghoumid and others* v. *France*, Judgment (Fifth Section), 25 June 2020 (as rendered final on 25 September 2020) para. 50.

[159] ECtHR, *K2* v. *United Kingdom*, Decision on admissibility (First Section), 7 February 2017, paras. 4 and 5.

[160] Ibid., paras. 6 and 7.

held that an out-of-country appeal would not necessarily render a decision to revoke citizenship 'arbitrary' within the meaning of Article 8 of the Convention. It determined that the provision cannot be interpreted so as to impose a positive obligation on States Parties to facilitate the return of every person deprived of citizenship while outside the jurisdiction in order to pursue an appeal against that decision. Moreover, that he was out of the jurisdiction was due to his own act in skipping bail. Furthermore, the applicant was not rendered stateless by the decision to deprive him of his British citizenship, as he was entitled to – and had in fact obtained – a Sudanese passport.[161]

5.7 THE RIGHT OF BURIAL OF TERRORISM SUSPECTS

The Court has also addressed a State's policy of refusing to return the bodies of accused terrorists for burial. While recognizing that the State has an interest in protecting public safety, particularly when national security is involved, the Court found that the absolute ban on returning the bodies of alleged terrorists did not strike a proper balance between the State and the rights of the family members of the deceased under Article 8 of the European Convention on Human Rights.[162] The Court accepted that the authorities were entitled to act with a view to minimizing the informational and psychological impact of the terrorist act on the population and protecting the feelings of relatives of the victims of the terrorist acts. This could 'certainly' limit the 'ability to choose the time, place, and manner in which the relevant funeral ceremonies and burials were to take place or even directly regulate such proceedings'.[163] But a blanket ban was disproportionate and unjustified in the circumstances.[164]

In contrast, the refusal by the authorities in France to allow a convicted terrorist to attend the funeral of her father did not violate Article 8.[165] The Court declared itself to be 'aware of the problems of a financial and logistical nature caused by escorted leaves'. It noted that the national authorities had 'duly examined the applicant's profile, the seriousness of the crimes committed (punished by a long prison sentence), the context of the trip that would have to be organised, the factual considerations (in particular the geographical distance of almost 650 kilometres)'. It recognized that the authorities had concluded that the escort would have to be 'a particularly robust one'.[166]

---

[161] Ibid., paras. 57 and 60.
[162] ECtHR, *Sabanchiyeva and others* v. *Russia*, Judgment (First Section), 6 June 2013 (as rendered final on 6 September 2013), para. 147.
[163] Ibid., para. 142.
[164] Ibid., paras. 144–6.
[165] ECtHR, *Guimon* v. *France*, Judgment (Fifth Section), 11 April 2019 (as rendered final on 11 July 2019), para. 50.
[166] Ibid., para. 47.

6

Prosecution of Terrorism as an International Crime

6.1 INTRODUCTION

This chapter describes how terrorism is prosecutable under international criminal law. This body of international law holds natural persons – individuals – criminally responsible for the perpetration of international crimes. In describing international criminal law as 'a body of international rules designed to proscribe certain categories of conduct and which renders those who engage in such conduct criminally liable',[1] Cassese specifically cited 'international terrorism' as a distinct proscribed category.[2] In this, however, he was mistaken. As Cryer had already suggested, the better view was that individual acts of terrorism that do not fall within the definitions of war crimes, crimes against humanity, or genocide have not been directly criminalized by international law.[3]

Ambos and Timmermann argue that the special treatment of terrorism by the United Nations (UN) Security Council and the UN General Assembly 'demonstrates that terrorism is a "special" transnational offence that may come closer to a true international crime than "ordinary" transnational offences'.[4] But terrorism per se remains a transnational offence, despite suggestions to the contrary. Thus, for example, when it is claimed that the 2005 Nuclear Terrorism Convention defines nuclear terrorism as 'a crime under international law',[5] this delineates mandatory incorporation of an offence in domestic law with universal jurisdiction over offenders present within the territory, wherever their crime was committed, but not an international crime per se.[6]

A specific offence of terrorism is a notable absentee from the crimes falling under the jurisdiction of the International Criminal Court. This is despite support for its inclusion as a crime prior to the Rome Diplomatic Conference that adopted the Statute of the Court. In 1995, the Special Rapporteur of the International Law Commission on the 'Draft code of crimes against the peace and security of mankind, including the draft statute for an international criminal court', had recommended that the Court be given jurisdiction over an act of

---

[1] A. Cassese, *International Criminal Law*, 3rd ed., Oxford University Press, Oxford, 2013, p. 3.

[2] In 1994, the International Law Commission (ILC) also appeared to consider terrorism as an international crime per se, though without evidence. ILC, Commentary, para. 15 on draft Article 20, in Report of the International Law Commission on the work of its forty-sixth session, 2 May–22 July 1994, UN doc. 49/10, 1994, at: https://bit.ly/3YZrSaG.

[3] R. Cryer, 'International Criminal Law', in D. Moeckli, S. Shah, and S. Sivakumaran (eds.), *International Human Rights Law*, Oxford University Press, Oxford, 2010, p. 541.

[4] K. Ambos and A. Timmermann, 'Terrorism and Customary International Law', chap. 2 in B. Saul (ed.), *Research Handbook on International Law and Terrorism*, 2nd ed., 2021, p. 29.

[5] D. Joyner, 'Countering Nuclear Terrorism', at p. 234.

[6] Art. 2, International Convention for the Suppression of Acts of Nuclear Terrorism; adopted at New York, 13 April 2005; entered into force, 7 July 2007.

6.1 Introduction

international terrorism.[7] A year earlier, the proposal had been limited to cases that 'constitute exceptionally serious crimes of international concern'.[8] During the negotiations in Rome in 1998, a small number of States pushed hard for this to become a reality;[9] indeed, a number of proposed definitions of a discrete international crime of terrorism were formally tabled at the Conference.[10] The decision to omit the crime was, though, in part due to the inability to agree upon a definition and in part the result of opposition from the United States, which argued that the Court could obstruct its ability to investigate and penetrate terrorist groups effectively.[11]

Nonetheless, a Resolution adopted at the Rome Conference did explicitly recognize that 'terrorist acts, by whomever and wherever perpetrated and whatever their forms, methods or motives, are serious crimes of concern to the international community' and recommended that a Review Conference of the Statute consider terrorism 'with a view to arriving at an acceptable definition' and its inclusion in the list of crimes within the jurisdiction of the Court.[12] In preparation for the first Review Conference of the Rome Statute, the Netherlands proposed to add terrorism as a crime, but this did not attract widespread support.[13]

It remains true to say that no purely international court or tribunal 'has jurisdiction over a crime of terrorism as such'.[14] That said, 'acts of terrorism' within and outside situations of armed conflict have been prosecuted before a number of international and hybrid criminal tribunals. This is notably the case with the International Criminal Tribunal for Rwanda (ICTR) and the Special Court for Sierra Leone (SCSL), where the offence was inscribed in the relevant Statutes as a war crime.[15] Terrorizing civilians in the conduct of hostilities was deemed by a majority of judges in both the Trial and Appeals Chambers of the International Criminal Tribunal for the former Yugoslavia (ICTY) to be a war crime under customary international law. The 'internationalized' Special Tribunal for Lebanon (STL) contained the crime of terrorism within its Statute, but this concerned peacetime acts, and the crime as such was punishable only

---

[7] Draft Article 24, 'Draft Code of Crimes against the Peace and Security of Mankind', Thirteenth report on the draft code of crimes against the peace and security of mankind, by Mr. Doudou Thiam, Special Rapporteur, ILC, UN doc. A/CN.4/466, 1995, para. 111. Thiam's proposed wording with respect to 'an agent or representative of a State' who 'commits or orders the commission' of the following acts was exceptionally broad: 'undertaking, organizing, ordering, facilitating, financing, encouraging or tolerating acts of violence against another State directed at persons or property and of such a nature as to create a state of terror [fear or dread] in the minds of public figures, groups of persons or the general public in order to compel the aforesaid State to grant advantages or to act in a specific way'. Ibid., and *cf.* also para. 126.

[8] Draft Article 20(e) in Report of the ILC to the UN General Assembly, UN doc. A/49/10, 1994.

[9] Algeria, India, Israel, Sri Lanka, and Turkey. R. Arnold, 'Terrorism, War Crimes and the International Criminal Court', in B. Saul (ed.), *Research Handbook on International Law and Terrorism*, 2nd ed., p. 273. None of these States has adhered to the Rome Statute, although Algeria and Israel are signatories. Israel subsequently declared its intention not to ratify the Rome Statute.

[10] J. Van der Vyver, 'Prosecuting Terrorism in International Tribunals', *Emory International Law Review*, Vol. 24, No. 2 (2010), 527–47, at pp. 537–40.

[11] Ibid., pp. 535–56. For a discussion of the negotiations around the possible inclusion of terrorism as a distinct war crime, see G. Venturini, 'War Crimes' in F. Lattanzi and W. A. Schabas (eds.), *Essays on the Rome Statute of the International Criminal Court*, Il Sirente, Italy, 1999, pp. 180–81.

[12] Resolution E, Final Act of the UN Diplomatic Conference of Plenipotentiaries on the Establishment of an International Criminal Court, UN doc. A/CONF.183/10, 17 July 1998.

[13] The Netherlands proposed including 'terrorism' as a core crime within the jurisdiction of the Court, stating: 'The fact that there was no universally agreed definition of terrorism should not be grounds for the lack of jurisdiction of the Court over the crime.' Annexes to the Report on the Eighth Meeting of the Assembly of States Parties, at: https://bit.ly/3Bpl2PW, para. 41; and Appendix III; and see Van der Vyver, 'Prosecuting Terrorism in International Tribunals', p. 540.

[14] R. Cryer, H. Friman, D. Robinson, and E. Wilmshurst, *An Introduction to International Criminal Law and Procedure*, 3rd ed., Cambridge University Press, Cambridge, 2014, p. 343.

[15] Art. 4(d), Statute of the ICTR, at: https://bit.ly/3vsollD; and Art. 3(d), Statute of the SCSL, at: https://bit.ly/3vByDji.

on the basis of domestic Lebanese law.[16] Key cases, along with the definitions of the underlying crimes with which the defendants were charged, are described and discussed hereunder.

The chapter begins, though, by recalling the core components of international crimes, and the different 'modes of liability' by which individuals engaged in planning, ordering, assisting, or conducting such crimes can be held responsible. It then considers in turn terrorism as a war crime, as a crime against humanity, and as genocide. The prohibition of each of these international crimes is a peremptory rule of international law (*jus cogens*)[17] and thus 'the punishment of such crimes is obligatory pursuant to the general principles of international law'.[18] The chapter concludes with consideration of aggression as terrorism.

The prohibition of terrorism as such was not included in the non-exhaustive list of peremptory (*jus cogens*) rules previously identified by the International Law Commission (ILC), and which the ILC reiterated most recently in 2019. In a work published that year, however, the draft of which was referred to *en passant* by the ILC Special Rapporteur, Dire Tladi, in his fourth report on peremptory norms,[19] de Beer argues that the prohibition of terrorism has per se become a *jus cogens* norm.[20] She does so on four bases: first that the prohibition 'safeguards the fundamental values of humanity and human dignity'; second, that the global treaties against terrorism have approached universal adherence; third, that the international community of States as a whole has accepted and recognized that no derogation from the prohibition is permitted; and fourth, that the crime attracts universal jurisdiction.[21]

While the first and second of these assertions are true, the third is very much open to question given disputes among States as to the scope of the prohibition, in particular concerning the identity of potential perpetrators. In this regard, it remains unsettled whether, outside the conduct of hostilities in an armed conflict, members or associates of non-State armed groups that are fighting for the right of people to self-determination commit acts of terrorism.[22] With respect to universal jurisdiction, de Beer does not distinguish between the unequivocal, compulsory form of universal jurisdiction (*aut dedere, aut iudicare*) set forth in the treaties codifying war crimes and the modified forms of universal jurisdiction that exist under the global sectoral counterterrorism treaties.[23] The prohibition of terrorism as a war crime is a *jus cogens* norm; in no other instance is the prohibition of either domestic or international terrorism a peremptory norm of international law.[24]

---

[16] Art. 2, 2007 Statute of the Special Tribunal for Lebanon, at: https://bit.ly/3wFXPp2.

[17] Annex in Chapter V, ILC draft conclusions on peremptory norms of general international law (jus cogens), UN doc. A/74/10, 2019.

[18] Report of the Independent International Commission of Inquiry on the Syrian Arab Republic, UN doc. A/HRC/21/50, 16 August 2012, Annex II, para. 26, citing Inter-American Court of Human Rights, *Almonacid-Arellano and others* v. *Chile*, Judgment (Preliminary Objections, Merits, Reparations and Costs), 26 September 2006, para. 99.

[19] ILC, Fourth report on peremptory norms of general international law (*jus cogens*) by Dire Tladi, Special Rapporteur, UN doc. A/CN.4/727, 31 January 2019.

[20] A. C. de Beer, *Peremptory Norms of General International Law (Jus Cogens) and the Prohibition of Terrorism*, Brill, Leiden, 2019, chap. 2, pp. 61–102.

[21] Ibid., pp. 98, 99, 100. See also T. Weatherall, 'The Status of the Prohibition of Terrorism in International Law: Recent Developments', *Georgetown Journal of International Law*, Vol. 46, No. 2 (2015), 589–627, at pp. 600–01.

[22] The definition of terrorism also changes depending on whether the ambient context is peacetime or a situation of armed conflict, as this book has described. See *supra* Chapters 1 and 2.

[23] K. N. Trapp, *State Responsibility for International Terrorism*, Oxford University Press, Oxford, 2011, pp. 83–85. See, e.g., Arts. 5 and 6, International Convention against the Taking of Hostages; adopted at New York, 17 December 1979; entered into force, 3 June 1983; and Arts. 6 and 7, International Convention for the Suppression of Terrorist Bombings; adopted at New York, 15 December 1997; entered into force, 23 May 2001. For more on this issue, see Chapter 2 *supra*.

[24] Thus, the cherry-picking of evidence by De Beer and Tladi to support their claim in a 2017 article that the prohibition of 'terrorism' per se – and not merely international terrorism – was indeed a norm of *jus cogens* does not persuade.

6.2 ELEMENTS OF INTERNATIONAL CRIMES AND MODES OF LIABILITY

Consonant with the general understanding of a crime under domestic law, to secure any conviction for an international crime it similarly needs to be proven, beyond reasonable doubt, that an individual defendant had the requisite mens rea (culpable state of mind) at the time he or she committed the actus reus (culpable act) of the crime. The Rome Statute of the International Criminal Court stipulates that a person shall be criminally responsible and liable for punishment for a crime within its jurisdiction 'only if the material elements are committed with intent and knowledge'.[25] Intent means that, in relation to conduct, a person 'means to engage in the conduct' while in relation to a consequence, the person must either mean to cause that consequence or be 'aware that it will occur in the ordinary course of events'.[26] Knowledge demands awareness that either a circumstance exists or that a consequence will occur in the ordinary course of events.[27] There is thus an overlap between these two mens rea elements.

The requisite intent may be formed by deliberate action and, at least in certain other judicial fora, recklessness.[28] Certain international crimes – for instance, genocide – require specific intent (*dolus specialis*) while others – notably war crimes and crimes against humanity – are ordinarily perpetrated when the accused has knowledge of specific contextual elements. Thus, in the case of crimes against humanity, the accused must have knowledge of a widespread or systematic attack against a civilian population but it does not need to be shown that he or she 'had knowledge of all characteristics of the attack or the precise details of the plan or policy of the State or organization'.[29] In the case of war crime, it is not necessary to prove that the accused knew, as a matter of law, that an armed conflict was in progress and, a fortiori, the classification of that armed conflict. He or she must, though, be shown to have been aware of the 'factual circumstances' which 'established the existence of an armed conflict'.[30] Moreover, as noted in Chapter 2 and discussed further in Section 6.4.2, terrorism as a war crime in the conduct of hostilities is a crime of specific intent.

Details of the actus reus and mens rea elements of each of the crimes within the jurisdiction of the International Criminal Court are found in the Elements of Crimes adopted by the States Parties to the Rome Statute.[31] As these Elements of Crimes

---

A. de Beer and D. Tladi, 'The Prohibition of Terrorism as a Jus Cogens Norm', *South African Yearbook of International Law*, Vol. 42 (2017), 1–41, at: https://bit.ly/3SQModA.

[25] Art. 30(1), Rome Statute of the International Criminal Court; adopted at Rome, 17 July 1998; entered into force, 1 July 2002 (hereafter, Rome Statute).

[26] Art. 30(2), Rome Statute.

[27] Art. 30(3), Rome Statute.

[28] In the *Galić* case, the Appeals Chamber of the ICTY cited with approval the 1987 Commentary by the International Committee of the Red Cross (ICRC) on Article 85 of the 1977 Additional Protocol I, which describes recklessness as 'the attitude of an agent who, without being certain of a particular result, accepts the possibility of its happening', distinguishing it from negligence, which describes a person who 'acts without having his mind on the act or its consequences'. See ICRC Commentary on the 1977 Additional Protocols, para. 3474; see ICTY, *Prosecutor* v. *Galić*, Judgment (Appeals Chamber) (Case No IT-98-29-A), 30 November 2006, para. 140. The Trial Chamber in the *Galić* case held in relation to the offence of attacking civilians, 'the notion of "wilfully" incorporates the concept of recklessness, while excluding mere negligence. The perpetrator who recklessly attacks civilians acts "wilfully"'. ICTY, *Prosecutor* v. *Galić*, Judgment (Trial Chamber I) (Case No IT-98-29-T), 5 December 2003, para. 54. As to whether the International Criminal Court considers recklessness sufficient for an international crime within its jurisdiction, see, e.g., the discussion in S. Finnin, 'Mental Elements under Article 30 of the Rome Statute of the International Criminal Court: A Comparative Analysis', *The International and Comparative Law Quarterly*, Vol. 61, No. 2 (April 2012), 325–59, esp. pp. 344–49. Cryer et al. unequivocally reject the possibility. Cryer et al., *An Introduction to International Criminal Law and Procedure*, 3rd ed., pp. 382–83.

[29] Elements of Crimes for the Rome Statute, Introduction to Article 7: Crimes against Humanity, para. 2.

[30] Elements of Crimes for the Rome Statute, Introduction to Article 8: War Crimes.

[31] The original Elements of Crimes were contained in the Official Records of the Assembly of States Parties to the Rome Statute of the International Criminal Court, First session, New York, 3–10 September 2002, part II.B.

determine, existence of the requisite intent and knowledge can be 'inferred from relevant facts and circumstances'.[32] Each time a new crime is added to the Rome Statute, a corresponding text delineating the elements of that crime is also agreed upon.[33] At the time of writing, this had occurred most recently in December 2019, when States Parties to the Rome Statute added the war crime of intentionally starving civilians in a situation of non-international armed conflict to the list of crimes under the jurisdiction of the Court.[34]

6.2.1 Modes of Liability

Different 'modes of liability' exist for each international crime. While one or more persons may 'pull the trigger' and unlawfully kill a person and may therefore be convicted as murderers, often others will have planned the operation, ordered it, provided the weapon and/or the ammunition, and furnished the get-away vehicle. In a terrorist bombing, the components of the device must be procured and the bomb must be assembled, stored, fitted, and transported as well as, of course, detonated, either remotely or (in a suicide bombing) by the person carrying it. Here again, another individual entirely other than the person who detonated the bomb is likely to have planned the bombing. The killing or the bombing may be thwarted before it may occur, but nonetheless amount to a criminal attempt. In addition, in a military operation, a commander may not have ordered the perpetration of a terrorist act, but he or she may have wilfully failed in his or her duty of due diligence to prevent the commission of an international crime. This is a form of command responsibility that equally engages that commander's individual responsibility for an international crime.

Individual criminal responsibility in the International Criminal Court is delineated under Article 25 of the Rome Statute. This provides for the following modes of liability:

- Commission of a crime, 'whether as an individual, jointly with another or through another person, regardless of whether that other person is criminally responsible'[35]
- Ordering, soliciting, or inducing the commission of such a crime 'which in fact occurs or is attempted'[36]
- Aiding, abetting, or otherwise assisting in the commission or attempted commission of a crime, 'including providing the means for its commission'[37]
- In any other way contributing to the commission or attempted commission of a crime 'by a group of persons acting with a common purpose'[38]
- Attempting to commit a crime by taking a substantial step towards its execution but where the crime does not occur because of circumstances independent of the person's intentions.[39]

Thus, a set of accomplice and inchoate offences leading to the commission of the principal crime at issue are themselves punishable under international criminal law. This is so, in certain circumstances, even if that principal crime is not ultimately committed.

---

[32] Elements of Crimes for the Rome Statute, General Introduction, para. 3.
[33] Art. 9(1), Rome Statute.
[34] The crime was added as a new Article 8 (2)(e)(xix) relating to intentionally using starvation of civilians as a method of warfare by depriving them of objects indispensable to their survival, including wilfully impeding relief supplies. The elements of the crime mirrored, mutatis mutandis, those already set out in relation to Article 8(2)(b)(xxv) for the corresponding crime in international armed conflict under the jurisdiction of the Court.
[35] Art. 25(3)(a), Rome Statute.
[36] Art. 25(3)(b), Rome Statute.
[37] Art. 25(3)(c), Rome Statute.
[38] Art. 25(3)(d), Rome Statute.
[39] Art. 25(3)(f), Rome Statute.

The responsibility of commanders is set forth in a separate article of the Rome Statute. A military commander is criminally responsible for crimes within the jurisdiction of the Court committed by forces under his or her effective command and control as a result of his or her failure to exercise control properly over such forces. This is the case where the commander either knew or, owing to the circumstances at the time, *should have known* that the forces were committing or about to commit the crimes, but failed to take all necessary and reasonable measures to prevent them occurring.[40]

In respect of the specific crime of genocide, directly and publicly inciting others to commit genocide is also an international crime within the purview of the Court.[41]

6.3 TERRORISM AS A CRIME AGAINST HUMANITY

Crimes against humanity were first formally defined and then punished by the Nuremburg Tribunal that followed the end of the Second World War. This was seemingly, at the time, a progressive development of international law and it was even questionable whether the convictions of Nazi leaders for the murder and torture of minorities outside armed conflict violated the long-standing general principle of law, *nullum crimen sine lege*: that a crime may only be prosecuted if it was criminalized by law before the salient action or omission.

There is, as yet, no treaty that sets forth both the contours of crimes against humanity and the responsibility of States to prevent and repress them, although there has been increasing momentum in recent years towards the elaboration of just such a dedicated legal instrument.[42] In 2019, after five years of deliberation, the ILC submitted to the UN General Assembly its *Draft Articles on Prevention and Punishment of Crimes against Humanity*, recommending 'the elaboration of a convention by the General Assembly or by an international conference of plenipotentiaries on the basis of the draft articles'.[43] At the end of 2022, the General Assembly agreed to move towards drafting the Convention, after three years of delay.[44] Resolution 77/249, adopted without a vote on 30 December 2022, decided that its Sixth Committee would meet for one session in April 2023 and a further session in April 2024 'in order to exchange substantive views, including in an interactive format, on all aspects of the draft articles'. The sessions would also consider further 'the elaboration of a convention by the General Assembly or by an international conference of plenipotentiaries on the basis of the draft articles'.[45]

Crimes against humanity are, however, already punishable as international crimes before the International Criminal Court. They are defined as acts of violence perpetrated 'as part of a widespread or systematic attack directed against any civilian population, with knowledge of the attack'.[46] The essence of crimes against humanity is an attack of significant scale against civilians, which may occur in a situation of armed conflict or during peacetime.[47] When a crime against humanity is committed during an armed conflict, the same acts may also amount to war crimes.

---

[40] Art. 28(a), Rome Statute.

[41] Art. 25(3)(e), Rome Statute.

[42] See, e.g., M. George, 'Prospects for a Convention on the Prevention and Punishment of Crimes against Humanity', *OpinioJuris*, 8 October 2019, at: https://bit.ly/3oXaGR7.

[43] ILC, Draft articles on Prevention and Punishment of Crimes against Humanity, with commentaries, in UN doc. A/74/10, 2019, at: https://bit.ly/3odgLXD, para. 42.

[44] Human Rights Watch, 'UN Decision to Advance Crimes against Humanity Treaty. Resolution Breaks 3 Years of Inaction', 30 November 2022, at: https://bit.ly/454jzwr.

[45] UN General Assembly Resolution 77/249, adopted without a vote on 30 December 2022, operative para. 4.

[46] Art. 7(1), Statute of the International Criminal Court.

[47] ILC, Draft articles on Prevention and Punishment of Crimes against Humanity, with commentaries, para. 45, commentary para. 1.

Acts that may constitute crimes against humanity include the following:

- Murder
- Enslavement
- Imprisonment or other severe deprivation of physical liberty in violation of fundamental rules of international law
- Torture
- Rape, sexual slavery, enforced prostitution, forced pregnancy, enforced sterilization, or any other serious form of sexual violence
- Persecution against a group on political, racial, national, ethnic, cultural, religious, gender, or other unlawful grounds
- Enforced disappearance of persons.[48]

Many terrorist acts would thus amount to crimes against humanity when the contextual requirement of a widespread or systematic attack directed against any civilian population was met and when perpetrated with knowledge of that attack. It has, for instance, been widely argued that the 9/11 attacks against the United States amounted to a crime against humanity. According to Human Rights Watch, for example, the 11 September 2001 attacks were 'a crime against humanity that flouted the fundamental values of international human rights and humanitarian law'.[49] It is not, though, an 'either/or' question, as a number of commentators have suggested.[50] An attack can be, as a matter of law, both terrorist in nature and a crime against humanity.[51]

With respect to Islamic State, UN Security Council Resolution 2379 (2017) requested the UN Secretary-General to establish an Investigative Team to support domestic efforts to hold the group accountable for any crimes against humanity it may have committed in Iraq.[52] The Resolution condemned the commission of acts by Islamic State 'involving murder, kidnapping, hostage-taking, suicide bombings, enslavement, sale into or otherwise forced marriage, trafficking in persons, rape, sexual slavery and other forms of sexual violence, recruitment and use of children, attacks on critical infrastructure, as well as its destruction of cultural heritage, including archaeological sites, and trafficking of cultural property' and recognized that their commission was used by the group 'as a tactic of terrorism'.[53] On 18 September 2020, the Council, in a videoconference meeting (organized thus as a result of the Covid-19 pandemic), renewed the mandate of the UN Investigative Team to Promote Accountability for Crimes Committed by

---

[48] Art. 7(1)(a), (c), (e), (f), (g), and (i), Rome Statute.

[49] Human Rights Watch, 'September 11: One Year On', 11 September 2002, at: https://bit.ly/2QXKAki. Whether international humanitarian law was applicable is, however, open to serious question as it is doubtful that an armed conflict existed at that time between the United States and al-Qaeda.

[50] See C. Mallet, 'The Original Sin: "Terrorism" or "Crime against Humanity"?', *Case Western Reserve Journal of International Law*, Vol. 34, No. 2 (2002), 245–48, at: https://bit.ly/3frhXW3.

[51] Thus, for example, Arnold argued that certain terrorist acts could be prosecuted before the International Criminal Court, concluding that this might prove to be 'a valid alternative to the existing anti-terrorism law enforcement mechanisms, which have often proven to be impeded by the lack of international cooperation in penal matters, or by the hurdles created by extradition law'. Furthermore, since 'the heading on crimes against humanity is based on customary law . . . it is applicable universally. Thus, such acts could be prosecuted universally by every state who has adopted legislation on crimes against humanity'. R. Arnold, 'The Prosecution of Terrorism as a Crime Against Humanity', *Zeitschrift für ausländisches öffentliches Recht und Völkerrecht, Heidelberg Journal of International Law*, Max-Planck-Institut für ausländisches öffentliches Recht und Völkerrecht, Vol. 64 (2004), 979–1000, at: https://bit.ly/3wEyjko, at p. 1000.

[52] UN Security Council Resolution 2379, adopted on 21 September 2017 by unanimous vote in favour, operative para. 2.

[53] Ibid., fourth and fifth preambular paras.

Da'esh/ISIL (UNITAD) until 18 September 2021.[54] UNITAD's mandate was renewed until 17 September 2022,[55] and then until 17 September 2023.[56]

In its report of May 2021, UNITAD stated that the Iraqi Council of Representatives was considering draft legislation to establish a legal basis for the prosecution of Islamic State members for war crimes, crimes against humanity, and genocide. This draft legislation would provide a channel through which evidence collected by the UN Investigative Team could be used in such proceedings.[57] UNITAD expected that trials of Islamic State members in Iraq for international crimes could begin in 2022.[58] Instead, in May 2023, the UN Investigative Team was still 'confident in the future adoption of a domestic legal framework to prosecute Da'esh/ISIL members for genocide, war crimes and crimes against humanity'.[59]

Trials have, though, already occurred in Europe for the acts of Islamic State members. In April 2021, a German woman was convicted in Germany of war crimes and aiding and abetting crimes against humanity as a result of the 'purchase' of a Yazidi woman enslaved by Islamic State. The Higher Regional Court of Düsseldorf sentenced a thirty-five-year-old woman known as 'Nurten J.' to four years and three months in prison. Nurten J. had moved to Syria in 2015 and married a high-ranking Islamic State member. The judges held, based on the testimony of the Yazidi victim and the defendant herself, that Nurten J. had used a Yazidi woman who had been kidnapped and imprisoned by Islamic State for slave labour at her house. Nurten J. left Islamic State when the group lost its territory there and was arrested on her return to Germany in July 2020.[60]

In June 2023, Special Adviser and Head of the Investigative Team, Christian Ritscher, welcomed the German Higher Regional Court of Koblenz's conviction of Islamic State female member, 'Nadine K.', for the commission of genocide, crimes against humanity, and war crimes against a young Yazidi woman in Iraq. The Yazidi woman had been held as a slave for three years by the Islamic State couple, Nadine K. and her husband. Nadine K., a German national who joined the group with her husband in late 2014, was sentenced to nine years and three months in prison for membership of a terrorist organization abroad and for aiding and abetting genocide, crimes against humanity, and war crimes for the enslavement and abuse of the young Yazidi woman. In 2016, Nadine K.'s husband received the twenty-one years old Yazidi woman as a 'gift'. She was raped several times and the couple treated her as a private property.[61]

6.4 TERRORISM AS A WAR CRIME

Terrorism committed against civilians during and in connection with an armed conflict is prohibited under customary and conventional law, and is likely to amount to a war crime. The salient rules are found, distinctly, within Geneva Law (the body of international humanitarian law which protects persons in the power of the enemy) and within Hague Law (which

---

[54] UN Security Council Resolution 2544, adopted on 18 September 2020 by unanimous vote in favour, operative para. 2.
[55] UN Security Council Resolution 2597, adopted on 17 September 2021 by unanimous vote in favour, operative para. 2.
[56] UN Security Council Resolution 2651, adopted on 15 September 2022 by unanimous vote in favour, operative para. 2.
[57] Sixth Report of the Special Adviser and Head of the UN Investigative Team to Promote Accountability for Crimes Committed by Da'esh/Islamic State in Iraq and the Levant, UN doc. S/2021/419, 3 May 2021, para. 131.
[58] Ibid., para. 140.
[59] Tenth Report of the Special Adviser and Head of the UN Investigative Team to Promote Accountability for Crimes Committed by Da'esh/Islamic State in Iraq and the Levant, UN doc. S/2023/367, 22 May 2023, Summary.
[60] 'ISIS member convicted of crimes against humanity for aiding and abetting enslavement of a Yazidi woman', Doughty Street Chambers, Dusseldorf, 23 April 2021, at: https://bit.ly/34slnBF.
[61] UNITAD, 'UNITAD Welcomes German Court Conviction of ISIL Female Member for Aiding and Abetting Genocide against Yazidis', Baghdad, 26 June 2023, at: https://bit.ly/3qvnxiu.

216   *Prosecution of Terrorism as an International Crime*

regulates the conduct of hostilities). The ILC Draft Code of Crimes against Peace and the Security of Mankind, issued in 1996 and submitted to the UN General Assembly for its consideration, had stipulated as a war crime 'acts of terrorism' when committed in violation of IHL applicable in armed conflict not of an international character.[62] As such, there is no need for any international element as there is for international terrorism in peacetime.[63]

Acts of terrorism as a war crime includes hostage-taking, which, under the Rome Statute, is punishable in any armed conflict per se (so not as an act of terrorism). The elements of crime for hostage-taking in connection with a non-international armed conflict are as follows:

1. The perpetrator seized, detained, or otherwise held hostage one or more persons.
2. The perpetrator threatened to kill, injure, or continue to detain such person or persons.
3. The perpetrator intended to compel a State, an international organization, a natural or legal person, or a group of persons to act or refrain from acting as an explicit or implicit condition for the safety or the release of such person or persons.
4. Such a person or persons were either hors de combat, or were civilians, medical personnel, or religious personnel taking no active part in the hostilities.
5. The perpetrator was aware of the factual circumstances that established this status.
6. The conduct took place in the context of and was associated with an armed conflict not of an international character.
7. The perpetrator was aware of factual circumstances that established the existence of an armed conflict.[64]

6.4.1 *Acts of Terrorism against Persons in the Power of the Enemy*

Under the Fourth Geneva Convention of 1949 on the protection of civilians, which generally applies in international armed conflict, 'measures' of terrorism perpetrated against civilians in occupied territories are expressly prohibited.[65] The prohibition of 'acts of terrorism' under Article 4 of the 1977 Additional Protocol II[66] binds parties to non-international armed conflicts falling within the scope of that Protocol. The provision is broad in scope, applying to protect '[a]ll persons who do not take a direct part or who have ceased to take part in hostilities, whether or not their liberty has been restricted'.[67] Thus, exceptionally, acts of terrorism may be committed against those who formerly participated directly in hostilities (e.g., by taking part in fighting).

In the view of the ICRC, the term 'acts of terrorism' covers 'not only acts directed against people, but also acts directed against installations which would cause victims as a side-effect'.[68]

---

[62] Art. 20(f)(iv), ILC Draft Code of Crimes against the Peace and Security of Mankind, 1996, at: https://bit.ly/3vzkDH3. As with the other delineated war crimes, in order to attract material jurisdiction the criminal acts had to be committed 'in a systematic manner or on a large scale'.

[63] Cassese implied in 2006 that *international* terrorism in armed conflict was a sub-category of war crime. A. Cassese, 'The Multifaceted Criminal Notion of Terrorism in International Law', *Journal of International Criminal Justice*, Vol. 4 (2006), 933–58, at p. 943. He also claimed that there was a general prohibition of terrorism incorporated in the two 1977 Additional Protocols. Ibid., p. 944.

[64] Elements of Crime for Article 8(2)(c)(iii) of the 1998 Rome Statute: 'War crime of taking hostages'.

[65] Art. 33, Convention (IV) relative to the Protection of Civilian Persons in Time of War; adopted at Geneva, 12 August 1949; entered into force, 21 October 1950.

[66] Art. 4(2)(d), Protocol additional to the Geneva Conventions of 12 August 1949, and relating to the protection of victims of non-international armed conflicts (Protocol II); adopted at Geneva, 8 June 1977, entered into force, 7 December 1978 (hereafter, 1977 Additional Protocol II).

[67] Art. 4(1), 1977 Additional Protocol II.

[68] ICRC, Commentary on the 1977 Additional Protocols, at: http://bit.ly/2IGhscP, para. 4538.

6.4 Terrorism as a War Crime

Thus, for example, the deliberate destruction of civilian homes, schools, or medical facilities, as well as the murder or torture of civilians or those *hors de combat*, at least where the intent or effect was to terrorize the population, would be encapsulated by the prohibition.

6.4.1.1 Terrorism within the Statute of the ICTR

On 8 November 1994, the UN Security Council adopted Resolution 955 by majority vote, establishing 'an international tribunal for the sole purpose of prosecuting persons responsible for genocide and other serious violations of international humanitarian law committed in the territory of Rwanda and Rwandan citizens responsible for genocide and other such violations committed in the territory of neighbouring States, between 1 January 1994 and 31 December 1994'.[69] The Statute of the ICTR was annexed to the resolution.[70]

The provision in Article 4 of the 1977 Additional Protocol II that prohibited acts of terrorism against 'all persons who do not take a direct part or who have ceased to take part in hostilities, whether or not their liberty has been restricted' was included as a war crime under the jurisdiction of the ICTR.[71] Also prosecutable was a threat to commit an act of terrorism against any such person.[72] These acts could certainly have been sustained against many of the defendants before the Tribunal. None was, however, prosecuted and convicted for a threat or act of terrorism.

6.4.1.2 Terrorism as a War Crime in the Special Court for Sierra Leone

Similar provisions on threats or acts of terrorism as war crimes were included in the SCSL Statute.[73] The Statute was annexed to the Agreement between the United Nations and the Government of Sierra Leone on the Establishment of the SCSL, which was signed by the two parties on 16 January 2002.[74]

The armed conflicts in Sierra Leone in the late 1980s and the 1990s saw widespread use of terror tactics by non-State armed groups, in particular the Revolutionary United Front (RUF) and the Armed Forces Revolutionary Council (AFRC). These included widespread amputations of the arms of civilian women and children. In its report on a January 1999 offensive against the Sierra Leonean capital, Freetown, Human Rights Watch stated: 'Rebel forces in Sierra Leone systematically murdered, mutilated, and raped civilians during their January offensive'. Human Rights Watch documented 'how entire families were gunned down in the street, children and adults had their limbs hacked off with machetes, and girls and young women were taken to rebel bases and sexually abused.'[75]

The so-called AFRC judgment was issued by the Court in June 2007.[76] The indictment against the three defendants alleged that they ordered armed attacks to be carried out primarily

---

[69] UN Security Council Resolution 955, adopted on 8 November 1994 by thirteen votes to one (Rwanda) with one abstention (China), operative para. 1.

[70] See generally with respect to the Statute: M. P. Scharf, 'Statute of the International Criminal Tribunal for Rwanda', UN Audiovisual Library of International Law, May 2012, at: https://bit.ly/3c27RJm.

[71] Art. 4(d), Statute of International Tribunal for Rwanda (as amended), at: https://bit.ly/3vsollD.

[72] Art. 4(h), Statute of the International Tribunal for Rwanda (as amended).

[73] Art. 3(d) and (h), Statute of the Special Court for Sierra Leone, at: https://bit.ly/3vByDji.

[74] The text of the Agreement is available at: https://bit.ly/2R427aL.

[75] Human Rights Watch, 'Shocking War Crimes in Sierra Leone. New Testimonies on Mutilation, Rape of Civilians', 24 June 1999, at: http://bit.ly/3bcqDOy.

[76] SCSL, *Prosecutor* v. *Alex Tamba Brima, Brima Bazzy Kamara*, and *Santigie Borbor Kanu*, Judgment (Trial Chamber) (Case No. SCSL-04–16-T), 20 June 2007.

to terrorize the civilian population but also to punish the population for failing to provide sufficient support to the AFRC/RUF, or for allegedly providing support to the Kabbah government or to pro-government forces.[77] The indictment further alleged that as part of the campaign of terror and punishment, the AFRC/RUF routinely captured and abducted members of the civilian population, raped women and girls, and used many as sex slaves and as forced labour. It further alleged that men and boys who were abducted were also used as forced labour and that many abducted boys and girls were given combat training and used in active fighting. It alleged that the AFRC/RUF also physically mutilated men, women, and children, including amputating their hands or feet and carving 'AFRC' and 'RUF' on their bodies.[78]

In delineating the crime of terror under the Statute of the SCSL the Special Court borrowed from the jurisprudence of the ICTY relating to terrorizing the civilian population during the conduct of hostilities (a separate crime in IHL, as further discussed in Section 6.4.2). The Trial Chamber adopted a two-step approach to the examination of the crime of terror:

1. Were acts of violence particularized in the indictment wilfully directed against protected persons or their property by members of the AFRC?
2. If so, is there evidence that proves beyond a reasonable doubt that these acts were committed with the primary intent of spreading terror among the civilian population?[79]

But in setting out this test, the Court was transposing the elements of the IHL rule applicable in the conduct of hostilities whereby 'acts or threats of violence the primary purpose of which is to spread terror among the civilian population are prohibited',[80] rather than the Geneva Law prohibition on acts of terrorism under Article 4 of the 1977 Additional Protocol II. This is a flawed decision in legal terms. As Yoram Dinstein has observed, in its judgment in the *Fofana* case, the SCSL Appeals Chamber had portrayed the former rule as 'a narrower derivative' of the latter.[81] But this approach is 'not corroborated by general practice of States', and thus the two 'edicts have to be disencumbered from each other'.[82]

The recruitment of children under fifteen years of age was one of the potential acts of terror for which the defendants might be convicted under the terms of the Statute. Once recruited, child soldiers were, the Trial Chamber recalled in the *AFRC* case, forced to flog captured civilians, act as bodyguards, and amputate civilians. They were also used as human shields in certain cases.[83] But, the Trial Chamber found that the primary purpose of the conscription and use of child soldiers by the AFRC during the conflict in Sierra Leone was

> not to spread terror among the civilian population, but rather was primarily military in nature. Therefore, even where such acts may have occurred simultaneously with other acts of violence considered by this Chamber with regards to the crime of terror, the Trial Chamber is of the opinion that such acts cannot be considered to have been committed as part of any such campaign.[84]

---

[77] Ibid., para. 1431.

[78] Ibid., para. 1432.

[79] Ibid., para. 1440.

[80] Art. 13(2), 1977 Additional Protocol II.

[81] SCSL, *Prosecutor* v. *Fofana* et al., Judgment (Appeals Chamber) (Case No. SCSL-04–14-A), 28 May 2008, para. 348.

[82] Y. Dinstein, *Non-international Armed Conflicts in International Law*, 2nd ed., Cambridge University Press, Cambridge, 2021, p. 196, para. 547.

[83] SCSL, *Prosecutor* v. *Alex Tamba Brima*, *Brima Bazzy Kamara*, and *Santigie Borbor Kanu*, Judgment (Trial Chamber), para. 1447.

[84] Ibid., para. 1450.

6.4 Terrorism as a War Crime

This is to downplay the consequences of recruitment of the children (and of course, a fortiori, their subsequent treatment) as well as the impact on their families: all were terrorized as a result of the unlawful, ongoing act.

With respect to the commission of abductions and forced labour, the Trial Chamber similarly found that their primary purpose was not to spread terror among the civilian population, 'but rather was primarily utilitarian or military in nature'.[85] The Trial Chamber further held that 'in the particular factual circumstances before it, the primary purpose behind commission of sexual slavery was not to spread terror among the civilian population, but rather was committed by the AFRC troops to take advantage of the spoils of war, by treating women as property and using them to satisfy their sexual desires and to fulfil other conjugal needs'.[86] Again, this egregious failure to comprehend the impact on the victims in assessing criminality resulted in a failure of criminal justice.

With no military or 'utilitarian' purpose, the amputation of the limbs of civilians, the Court held, did amount to terrorizing the civilian population, and moreover that it was intended to do so. One AFRC operation, 'Operation Cut Hand', involved civilians being given the cruel choice of having either 'short sleeves' or 'long sleeves', meaning amputations of the arm at the bicep or of the hand at the wrist. Civilians whose hands were amputated by members of the AFRC were told to ask Sierra Leonean President Ahmad Tejan Kabbah for new hands.[87] The Trial Chamber noted that amputations were carried out primarily against unarmed civilians, in or near their homes, villages, and farms. It declared itself satisfied that the attacks 'could not have been primarily for military advantage'.[88] The amputations, regardless of the context in which they were committed, were thus 'acts of violence committed against protected persons with the primary purpose to terrorise protected persons'.[89]

Five years after the conviction of three AFRC leaders for acts of terrorism, Charles Taylor, the former president of Liberia, was prosecuted before the Special Court for his support to the AFRC and the RUC and his complicity in the atrocities they perpetrated. At trial, Count One of the indictment against Mr Taylor was of acts of terrorism. Mr Taylor was accused of having provided 'invaluable instruction, direction and guidance to the leaders of the AFRC/RUF alliance', which was 'often crucial to the continued survival of the alliance as a viable entity with the ability to continue carrying out the campaign of terror against the civilian population of Sierra Leone'.[90] The Trial Chamber, again drawing on jurisprudence from the ICTY relating to terrorizing the civilian population during the conduct of hostilities, determined that to secure a conviction for the crime of acts of terrorism each of the following three elements had to be proved beyond reasonable doubt:

- Acts or threats of violence directed against persons or their property
- The perpetrator wilfully made persons or their property the object of those acts and threats of violence
- The acts or threats of violence were committed with the primary purpose of spreading terror among protected persons.[91]

---

[85] Ibid., para. 1454.

[86] Ibid., para. 1459.

[87] Ibid., paras. 1460, 1461.

[88] Ibid., para. 1462.

[89] Ibid., para. 1464.

[90] SCSL, *Prosecutor v. Charles Ghankay Taylor*, Judgment (Trial Chamber) (Case No SCSL-03–01-T), 18 May 2012, para. 46.

[91] Ibid., para. 403.

220 Prosecution of Terrorism as an International Crime

Actual terrorization was not, the Trial Chamber held, a required element of the crime of terror, but it was necessary for the prosecution to prove that the spreading of terror was 'specifically intended'.[92] Furthermore, once again relying on jurisprudence within the ICTY, the actual infliction of death or serious bodily harm was not a required element of the crime of terror, but it had to be shown that the victims suffered grave consequences resulting from the acts or threats of violence, which might include death or serious injury to body or health.[93]

In the SCSL's judgment on appeal against conviction by Mr Taylor, the Appeals Chamber declared itself

> satisfied that the Trial Chamber's findings show that the RUF/AFRC used acts of terror as its primary modus operandi throughout the Indictment Period. The RUF/AFRC pursued a strategy to achieve its goals through extreme fear by making Sierra Leone 'fearful'. The primary purpose was to spread terror, but it was not aimless terror. Barbaric, brutal violence was purposefully unleashed against civilians because it made them afraid – afraid that there would only be more unspeakable violence if they continued to resist in any way, continued to stay in their communities or dared to return to their homes. It also made governments and the international community afraid – afraid that unless the RUF/AFRC's demands were met, thousands more killings, mutilations, abductions and rapes of innocent civilians would follow. The conflict in Sierra Leone was bloody because the RUF/AFRC leadership deliberately made it bloody.[94]

Overall, the SCSL was too narrow in its appreciation of the terrorization of civilians. The Court transposed a conduct of hostilities (Hague Law) requirement that violence has, as its primary purpose, the spreading of terror, to a situation where people were helpless and in the power of the enemy. They were violated in the most brutal manners imaginable. Imagine it being possible to argue on the basis of law that torture was not a war crime where its primary purpose was to extract critical military information.

6.4.2 Terrorism in the Conduct of Hostilities as a War Crime

6.4.2.1 Terrorism as a War Crime within the ICTY

Within the conduct of hostilities, the use of terror tactics against the civilian population is explicitly prohibited, in identical terms, by the two 1977 Additional Protocols to the four Geneva Conventions. Thus, it is stipulated that '[a]cts or threats of violence the primary purpose of which is to spread terror among the civilian population are prohibited'.[95] This is a customary rule, applicable to all armed conflicts.[96] The acts proscribed by the prohibition constitute, the ICRC avers, a 'special type of terrorism'.[97] According to the organization's commentary on the Additional Protocols, '[a]ir raids have often been used as a means of terrorizing the population, but these are not the only methods. For this reason, the text contains a much broader expression,

---

[92] Ibid., paras. 404, 405.

[93] Ibid., para. 407.

[94] SCSL, *Prosecutor* v. *Charles Ghankay Taylor*, Judgment (Appeals Chamber) (Case No SCSL-03-01-A), 26 September 2013, para. 300.

[95] Art. 51(2), 1977 Additional Protocol I; and Art. 13(2), 1977 Additional Protocol II.

[96] ICRC, Customary IHL Rule 2: 'Violence Aimed at Spreading Terror among the Civilian Population', at: http://bit.ly/2ONFTT7.

[97] Y. Sandoz, C. Swinarski, and B. Zimmermann (eds.), *Commentary on the Additional Protocols of 8 June 1977 to the Geneva Conventions of 12 August 1949*, Martinus Nijhoff, Geneva, 1987, para. 4538.

6.4 Terrorism as a War Crime

namely "acts or threats of violence" so as to cover all possible circumstances'.[98] The concept of 'terror' would be defined by the ICTY as 'extreme fear'.[99]

That said, the ICRC commentary notes that while acts of violence during conflict 'almost always give rise to some degree of terror among the population' and although 'attacks on armed forces are purposely conducted brutally in order to intimidate the enemy soldiers and persuade them to surrender', the Hague Law prohibition on terrorizing civilians is limited to acts of violence whose primary purpose is to spread terror among the civilian population 'without offering substantial military advantage'.[100] Thus, as Dinstein has observed, large-scale aerial bombardments that are 'pounding' military objectives and 'breaking the back of the enemy armed forces' are not unlawful according to this rule, even if they lead to the 'collapse of civilian morale'.[101]

Whether terrorizing civilians in the conduct of hostilities is a distinct war crime under customary international law is not entirely settled. In its judgment in the *Galić* case, the ICTY Appeals Chamber declared itself satisfied – though only by majority decision – that 'a breach of the prohibition of terror against the civilian population gave rise to individual criminal responsibility pursuant to customary international law at the time of the commission of the offences for which Galić was convicted'.[102] In his Dissenting Opinion at trial, Judge Rafael Nieto-Navia had argued that the crime of terror did not fall within the jurisdiction of the ICTY. He believed that the Trial Chamber had failed to establish that the offence of inflicting terror on a civilian population attracted individual criminal responsibility under international law.[103] Then in his Dissenting Opinion in the Appeals Chamber, Judge Wolfgang Schomburg declared there was no basis to find that 'terrorization against a civilian population' was penalized 'beyond any doubt under customary international criminal law at the time relevant to the Indictment'.[104] Judge Schomburg agreed that there could be 'no doubt' that the prohibition per se was part of customary international law.[105] But he questioned the State practice on which the majority of the Appeals Chamber relied, observing, inter alia, that none of the permanent members of the UN Security Council 'or any other prominent State' had penalized terrorization against a civilian population as a war crime.[106] He also considered it relevant that the Rome Statute did not have jurisdiction over such a war crime.[107]

The *Galić* case was the first time the ICTY had considered the charge of terror as a war crime. General Stanislav Galić, as commander of the Bosnian Serb army around Sarajevo, was accused of having 'conducted a protracted campaign of shelling and sniping upon civilian areas of Sarajevo and upon the civilian population thereby inflicting terror and mental suffering upon its civilian population'.[108] The Trial Chamber heard 'reliable evidence that civilians were targeted

---

[98] ICRC commentary on the 1977 Additional Protocols, para. 4785.
[99] ICTY, *Prosecutor* v. *Galić*, Judgment (Trial Chamber) (Case No. IT-98-29-T), 5 December 2003, para. 135. This holding was further confirmed in the judgment at trial in the *Blagojević* case two years later. ICTY, *Prosecutor* v. *Blagojević and Jokić*, Judgment (Trial Chamber) (Case No. IT-02-60-T), 17 January 2005, para. 590.
[100] ICRC commentary on the 1977 Additional Protocols, para. 1940.
[101] Y. Dinstein, *The Conduct of Hostilities under the Law of International Armed Conflict*, 4th ed., Cambridge University Press, Cambridge, 2022, pp. 168–69, para. 490.
[102] ICTY, *Prosecutor* v. *Galić*, Judgment (Appeals Chamber) (Case No. IT-98-29-A), 30 November 2006, para. 86.
[103] ICTY, *Prosecutor* v. *Galić*, Judgment (Trial Chamber), Dissenting Opinion of Judge Nieto-Navia, paras. 113, 114.
[104] ICTY, *Prosecutor* v. *Galić*, Judgment (Appeals Chamber), Dissenting Opinion of Judge Wolfgang Schomburg, para. 2.
[105] Ibid., para. 7.
[106] Ibid, paras. 8–12, 18.
[107] Ibid, para. 20.
[108] ICTY, *Prosecutor* v. *Galić*, Judgment (Trial Chamber), paras. 65, 66.

222   *Prosecution of Terrorism as an International Crime*

during funerals, in ambulances, in hospitals, on trams, on buses, when driving or cycling, at home, while tending gardens or fires or clearing rubbish in the city'.[109] The majority at trial were convinced by the evidence that civilians in government-held areas of Sarajevo were 'directly or indiscriminately attacked' from Bosnian Serb-controlled territory, and that, as a result and 'as a minimum, hundreds of civilians were killed and thousands others were injured'.[110]

General Adrianus Van Baal, Chief of Staff of the United Nations Protection Force (UNPROFOR) in Bosnia and Herzegovina in 1994, testified before the Trial Chamber that sniping in Sarajevo was 'without any discrimination, indiscriminately shooting defenceless citizens, women, children, who were unable to protect and defend themselves, at unexpected places and at unexpected times'.[111] This led him to conclude, the Trial Chamber noted, 'that its objective was to cause terror; he specified that women and children were the predominant target'.[112]

The ICTY Trial Chamber, by majority, rejected the submissions by both Defence and Prosecution that actual infliction of terror was an element of the war crime of terror. It did so on the 'plain wording' of Article 51(2) of the 1977 Additional Protocol I, as well as on the basis of the *travaux préparatoires* of the Diplomatic Conference.[113] The key issue was the intent of the perpetrator. Accordingly, the Trial Chamber and the Appeals Chamber found, by majority, that for the war crime of terror to be established, the following specific elements need to be proven:

1. Acts or threats of violence were directed against the civilian population or individual civilians not taking direct part in hostilities causing death or serious injury to body or health within the civilian population
2. The offender wilfully made the civilian population or individual civilians not taking direct part in hostilities the object of those acts of violence
3. The above offence was committed with the primary purpose of spreading terror among the civilian population.[114]

General Galić was convicted at trial and his conviction was upheld on appeal, inter alia for seeking to terrorize the civilian population as a war crime.

In its trial judgment against Radovan Karadžić in 2016, the ICTY (citing the *Galić* appeal judgment) extended the scope of the crime to potentially encompass also indiscriminate attacks: 'as is the case with unlawful attacks on civilians, the acts or threats of violence constituting terror need not be limited to direct attacks on civilians or threats thereof, but may include indiscriminate or disproportionate attack'.[115] The Trial Chamber reaffirmed its view that the mens rea of terror consists of both general intent and specific intent. To have the general intent, the perpetrator must wilfully make the civilian population or individual civilians the object of acts or threats of violence. The specific intent for the crime is the intent to spread terror among the civilian population.[116] Mr Karadžić was convicted of terror, a violation of the laws or customs of war (and thus a war crime).

---

[109]   Ibid., para. 584.
[110]   Ibid., para. 591.
[111]   Ibid., para. 573.
[112]   Ibid.
[113]   Ibid., para. 134.
[114]   Ibid., para. 133; ICTY, *Prosecutor v. Galić*, Judgment (Appeals Chamber), paras. 100, 101.
[115]   ICTY, *Prosecutor v. Radovan Karadžić*, Judgment (Trial Chamber) (Case No. IT-95–5/18-T), 24 March 2016, para. 460.
[116]   Ibid., paras. 463, 464.

6.4 Terrorism as a War Crime

In June 2021, in adjudicating the appeal against conviction of Ratko Mladic, the Residual Mechanism of the ICTY that followed the Tribunal's closure once again addressed the issue of whether terrorizing civilians in the conduct of hostilities was a war crime under customary law. Mr Mladic had asserted that the prohibition of spreading terror among the civilian population did not extend to its criminalization under customary international law, at least when the Siege of Sarajevo was ongoing, 'due to insufficient evidence of settled, extensive, or uniform state practice'.[117] The Residual Mechanism rejected his assertion.[118] It therefore appears that indiscriminate attacks on populated areas, such as during a siege, as well as directly attacking civilians in such a context may indeed amount to the war crime of terror. This is so, where the primary purpose is to spread terror among the civilian population. It remains to be seen whether other international criminal tribunals will follow the approach of the ICTY.

6.4.3 *Terror in a Situation of Armed Conflict: Other International Practice*

6.4.3.1 The 9/11 Attacks

In 2008, before the US District Court for the Southern District of New York, Khalid Sheikh Mohammed and four others were charged with a series of counts, including conspiracy to commit acts of terrorism transcending national boundaries and acts of terrorism transcending national boundaries, in violation of US federal law.[119] But in April 2011, following the enactment of the National Defense Authorization Act by President Barack Obama, the US Attorney General announced that the five defendants would face military trial on war crimes charges. On 31 May 2011, Khalid Sheikh Mohammed and the other four accused were charged for their involvement in the 9/11 attacks by the Criminal Investigation Task Force with conspiracy to commit terrorism, and hijacking an aircraft.[120]

Hence, the war crimes charges laid against the 9/11 planners in 2011, in particular Khalid Sheikh Mohammed, are, by their nature, predicated on the existence of a prior armed conflict. This is a significant obstacle to securing a conviction. As David Glazier has observed, if the conduct had been treated as acts of terrorism under US domestic law,

> virtually every aspect of the 9/11 attack constitutes validly prosecutable crimes. The hijacking of four aircraft, the killing of each passenger and crew member onboard, the attacks on the World Trade Center and Pentagon, and every resulting death or injury on the ground can each constitute separate federal counts. Liability for related inchoate offenses of solicitation, conspiracy, and attempted commission is well established, as well as various forms of participations such as being an accessory before or after the fact. If treated as 'ordinary' terrorists, the defendants would essentially be limited to challenging the admissibility and factual sufficiency of the evidence against them. Military commission use, in contrast, renders virtually every aspect of the unproven trial procedure and substantive law open to judicial challenge, and permits the assertion of unique law of war defenses.[121]

---

[117] International Residual Mechanism for Criminal Tribunals, *Prosecutor* v. *Ratko Mladic*, Judgment (Appeals Chamber) (Case No. MICT-13–56-A), 8 June 2021, para. 280.

[118] Ibid., para. 287.

[119] US Code Title 18, S. 3592(c)(9). US District Court for the Southern District of New York, *United States* v. *Khalid Sheikh Mohammed and others*, Indictment (S14) 93 Cr. 180(KTD), at: https://bit.ly/3uDmucE.

[120] International Crimes Database, '*United States* v. *Khalid Shaikh Mohammad* et al.', undated but accessed 1 June 2021 at: https://bit.ly/3uxxBUr.

[121] D. Glazier, 'Destined for an Epic Fail: The Problematic Guantánamo Military Commissions', *Ohio State Law Journal*, Vol. 75, No. 5 (2014), 903–67, at pp. 960–61.

The charge against Khalid Sheikh Mohammed and his co-defendants of conspiracy to commit war crimes was dropped by the US authorities in early 2013, recognizing a 'legal flaw'.[122] The conviction of material support to terrorism as a war crime against Osama Bin Laden's driver, Salim Ahmed Hamdan, had been struck out the previous October by the US Court of Appeals for the District of Columbia (after Mr Hamdan's release from prison) as similarly not reflecting the international law of war.[123] The Court stated that 'the Executive Branch acknowledges that the international law of war did not – and still does not – identify material support for terrorism as a war crime. Therefore, the relevant statute at the time of Hamdan's conduct – 10 USC §821 – did not proscribe material support for terrorism as a war crime'.[124]

It remains to be seen whether other prosecutions will be secured for terrorism as a war crime in connection with the 9/11 attacks. The 2009 Military Commissions Act defined the crime as:

> Any person subject to this chapter who intentionally kills or inflicts great bodily harm on one or more protected persons, or intentionally engages in an act that evinces a wanton disregard for human life, in a manner calculated to influence or affect the conduct of government or civilian population by intimidation or coercion, or to retaliate against government conduct . . .
>
> The term 'protected person' means any person entitled to protection under one or more of the Geneva Conventions, including civilians not taking an active part in hostilities, military personnel placed out of combat by sickness, wounds, or detention, and military medical or religious personnel.[125]

The reference in the mens rea to 'a manner calculated to influence or affect the conduct of government or civilian population by intimidation or coercion' brings in the language of the sectoral treaties – none of which institutes international crimes in peacetime let alone armed conflict – instead of using the specific intent required by applicable international humanitarian law. This breaches the fundamental criminal law principle of *nullum crimen nulla poena sine lege*.[126]

The military commissions are a hybrid of the military court-martial and federal criminal court systems. The judge and jury, called a panel, are members of the US military. While both the prosecution and the defence teams are required to have military lawyers on their teams, civilian lawyers have for many years done the bulk of the work. The prosecution will have to prove that an armed conflict existed on or before 11 September 2001, no mean feat if the law is applied correctly. The attack on the Pentagon concerned the targeting of a military objective and US military personnel, who are not protected as such by the Geneva Conventions. As of July 2023, no date had been set for the trials of the principal accused to begin.[127]

Indeed, there were ongoing discussions about a plea bargain at the time of writing. Prosecutors had initiated negotiations in March 2022, and for more than a year had been

---

[122] J. Bravin, 'Conspiracy charges dropped for 9/11 suspects', *The Wall Street Journal*, 9 January 2013, at: https://on.wsj.com/3z2nBWG.

[123] In October 2012, the Court held that providing material support for terrorism had never been classified as a war crime before 2006, when Congress listed it among triable offences under the Military Commissions Act. See further P. Margulies, 'Defining, Punishing, and Membership in the Community of Nations – Material Support and Conspiracy Charges in Military Commissions', *Fordham International Law Journal*, Vol. 36, No. 1 (2013), at: https://bit.ly/3x07J5h. The law of war is US preferred parlance for IHL/the law of armed conflict.

[124] US Court of Appeal for the District of Columbia, *Hamdan* v. *United States*, Judgment on Petition for Review from the US Court of Military Commission Review (Case No. 11–1257), 16 October 2012, at: https://bit.ly/3yQWMV3, p. 5.

[125] §950t(24), 2009 Military Commissions Act.

[126] B. Saul, *Defining Terrorism in International Law*, Oxford University Press, Oxford, 2006, pp. 310–11. Although Saul was writing about an earlier 'Instruction', the same problems persisted in the reformulated crime.

[127] C. Rosenberg, 'Trial Guide: The Sept. 11 Case at Guantánamo Bay', *The New York Times*, 10 July 2023, at: https://bit.ly/3YqlcSx.

seeking an answer from the Biden administration on whether it endorses certain assurances sought by Khalid Shaikh Mohammed and his four co-defendants. Under the proposal, the men would plead guilty to their roles in the attacks in exchange for a maximum sentence of life in prison, rather than the possibility of the death penalty. The defendants also asked not to be placed in solitary confinement and were requesting the establishment of a civilian care programme to treat the effects of their torture during the years they were held in CIA detention before their transfer to Guantánamo Bay in September 2006.[128]

In the view of one legal authority, plea deals would offer benefits to the authorities in these particular cases:

> Two factors underscore the particular utility of pleas at Guantanamo. First, the Guantanamo military commissions, which were initially designed to avoid procedural safeguards and other legal constraints, continue to suffer from shortcomings and questions about their legitimacy despite numerous rounds of reform. Plea agreements are a way to avoid deciding critical, unanswered questions surrounding the commissions, including the use of evidence obtained through torture and lesser forms of coercion, the legal validity of several war crimes charges (which turn, for example, on when the armed conflict with al Qaeda started), and the application of certain provisions of the Constitution itself, including the Sixth Amendment's Confrontation Clause, which the government has long contested.[129]

But in August 2023, more than 2,000 family members of people who died in the 11 September 2001 terror attacks signed a letter to President Joe Biden protesting against a potential plea agreement. For some, it was the lack of the death penalty that was most significant; for others, the lack of a trial and the absence of transparency from the US and Saudi governments was the most hurtful aspect.[130]

6.4.3.2 Direct Attacks on Civilians and Indiscriminate Bombardment in Syria

The frequent link between acts carried out during armed conflict with a view to terrorizing civilians, such as bombardment, and crimes against humanity was frequently witnessed in Syria. In 2014, the UN-mandated International Independent Commission of Inquiry on Syria found that the government had employed a military strategy targeting the civilian population, combining long-lasting sieges with continuous air and ground bombardment. In neighbourhoods around Damascus, civilians were targeted on the basis of their perceived opposition to the government. Merely living in or originating from those neighbourhoods led to their attacks.[131] The Commission concluded that the Syrian regime 'has carried out a widespread and systematic attack against the civilian population of Aleppo to punish and terrorize civilians

---

[128] C. Rosenberg, 'Judge Delays 9/11 Hearings While Awaiting Defendant's Competency Exam', *The New York Times*, 5 June 2023, at: https://bit.ly/3QtNuJU. Ironically, part of the plea deal under discussion involved the US authorities keeping the detention centre at Guantánamo Bay open as the defendants preferred life there to the one awaiting them in a supermax prison, such as at Florence, Colorado. Ramzi Yousef, a nephew of Khalid Sheikh Mohammed, is held at the ADX facility in Florence.

[129] J. Hafetz, 'Accountability at Guantanamo? A Negotiated Plea for the 9/11 Defendants', Blog post, Just Security, 15 November 2022, at: https://bit.ly/3KXOTEX. The Sixth Amendment includes the right to a 'speedy' trial.

[130] E. Stokols and J. Haberkorn, 'Sept. 11 families make emotional plea to Biden', *Politico*, 22 August 2023, at: https://bit.ly/45uYuLU.

[131] Report of the Independent International Commission of Inquiry on the Syrian Arab Republic, UN doc. A/HRC/27/60, 13 August 2014, para. 104.

226   *Prosecution of Terrorism as an International Crime*

for supporting or hosting armed groups, in an apparent strategy to erode popular support for those groups'.[132]

In its seventh report, in 2014, the Commission stated:

> The terror that the Government's barrel-bombing campaigns generate should not be underestimated. Barrel-bombs, particularly when dropped from high altitudes, cannot be properly targeted. Nor is it likely that anyone at the impact site would survive the initial blast. The Government does not provide early warning of attacks and there is little chance of being able to move from the area once a barrel bomb is released from a helicopter overhead. Victims of barrel bombs emphasized the extreme fear and mental suffering they felt as they came under attack. Survivors and witnesses consistently described that as a result of the barrel bombing campaign, much of the civilian population lived in a state of terror.[133]

Attacks also included the use of chemical weapons, a means of warfare manifestly intended to terrorize. In the early hours of 21 August 2013, attacks using chemical weapons targeted two suburbs of Damascus. Several rockets loaded with sarin struck Eastern Ghouta and, a few hours later, Western Ghouta, causing mass casualties among the civilian population.[134] Two days later, the UN Secretary-General Ban Ki-moon said that the use of any chemical weapons in Syria would amount to a crime against humanity, pledging 'serious consequences' for the perpetrators.[135] In March 2021, lawyers representing survivors announced that they had filed a criminal complaint in France against Bashar al-Assad, alleging that the regime had carried out chemical attacks outside of Damascus in August 2013.[136] France is home to thousands of Syrian refugees, and its investigating judges have a mandate to determine whether crimes against humanity were committed anywhere in the world.[137]

6.5   TERRORISM AS GENOCIDE

Genocide, the so-called crime of crimes,[138] was formally prohibited by the 1948 Genocide Convention.[139] Its prohibition has 'assuredly' attained the status of a norm of *jus cogens* in the words of the International Court of Justice.[140] Acts of genocide may be committed within and outside a situation of armed conflict. Genocide means

---

[132]   Ibid.

[133]   Report of the Independent International Commission of Inquiry on the Syrian Arab Republic, UN doc. A/HRC/25/65, 12 February 2014, Annex VI: Use of barrel bombs, para. 7.

[134]   'Swedish Criminal Investigation of Chemical Weapons Attacks in Syria', Open Society Justice Initiative, 19 April 2021, at: https://bit.ly/30uc2Eo.

[135]   UN, 'Use of chemical weapons in Syria would be "crime against humanity" – Ban', UN News, 23 August 2013, at: https://bit.ly/3spFHPB.

[136]   'Chemical attack victims file a criminal complaint against the Syrian regime', TRT World, 3 March 2021, at: https://bit.ly/3GEwR60.

[137]   J. Irish, 'Syrian victims of chemical attacks file case with French prosecutors', *Reuters*, 2 March 2021, at: https://reut.rs/30vJcmt.

[138]   See, e.g., W. A. Schabas, 'National Courts Finally Begin to Prosecute Genocide, the "Crime of Crimes"', *Journal of International Criminal Justice*, Vol. 1, No. 1 (2003), 39–63.

[139]   Convention on the Prevention and Punishment of the Crime of Genocide; adopted at Paris, 9 December 1948; entered into force, 12 January 1951. As of 1 January 2024, 153 States were party to the Convention.

[140]   International Court of Justice, *Case Concerning Armed Activities on the Territory of the Congo* (New Application: 2002) (*Democratic Republic of the Congo v. Rwanda*), Jurisdiction of the Court and Admissibility of the Application, Judgment, 3 February 2006, para. 64.

6.5 Terrorism as Genocide

any of the following acts committed with intent to destroy, in whole or in part, a national, ethnical, racial or religious group, as such:

(a) Killing members of the group;
(b) Causing serious bodily or mental harm to members of the group;
(c) Deliberately inflicting on the group conditions of life calculated to bring about its physical destruction in whole or in part;
(d) Imposing measures intended to prevent births within the group;
(e) Forcibly transferring children of the group to another group.[141]

The crime of genocide thus requires that the perpetrator have a special intent to destroy, in whole or in part, a protected group. Perpetrators who have this *dolus specialis* to destroy a protected group may also be fuelled by multiple other motives such as capture of territory, economic advantage, sexual gratification, and spreading terror.[142] This does not preclude a conviction for genocide.

To date, terrorism has not been successfully prosecuted as an act of genocide, although there is no reason why this should not occur in the future. The best candidate for such a precedent is in relation to the actions of Islamic State in Iraq and Syria. In May 2021, Karim Khan, the head of the UN team investigating atrocities in Iraq (and now the Prosecutor of the International Criminal Court), said that 'clear and compelling evidence' had been found that Islamic State extremists committed genocide against the Yazidi minority in 2014.[143] This followed the finding by the UN Commission of Inquiry on Syria in 2016 that Islamic State was in the throes of committing genocide against the Yazidis in Syria.[144] The Yazidis are a religious group falling within the protection of the prohibition on genocide.[145] Islamic State fighters were said to commonly refer to the Yazidis as infidels and 'dirty kuffar'.[146] The group engaged in forced conversions of Yazidis.

In August 2014, Islamic State fighters summarily executed hundreds of Yazidi men and adolescent boys when the victims refused to convert to Islam or were captured with weapons in their possession. Mass killings occurred in Kocho and Qani villages.[147] While most of the killing of Yazidis occurred in Iraq, Islamic State fighters who had purchased Yazidi women and children in Syria also committed intentional killings in Syria. An Islamic State fighter in Aleppo killed several children after a failed escape attempt by their mother, after which he beat her for crying over the deaths of 'kuffar children'.[148]

Islamic State's sexual enslavement of Yazidi women and girls was an act of sexual violence that constituted serious bodily and mental harm also falling within the definition of genocide.[149] Islamic State fighters severely beat captured Yazidi women and girls if they resisted rapes, attempted to escape, refused orders to carry tasks for the fighters and their families, or tried to

---

[141] Art. 6, Rome Statute.

[142] Independent International Commission of Inquiry on the Syrian Arab Republic, '"They came to destroy": ISIS Crimes against the Yazidis', Conference Room Paper, UN doc. A/HRC/32/CRP.2, 15 June 2016, para. 10.

[143] 'UN experts: Islamic State committed genocide against Yazidis', *The Independent*, 11 May 2021, at: https://bit.ly/3i2KumQ.

[144] 'UN Commission of Inquiry on Syria: ISIS is committing genocide against the Yazidis', Press release, Office of the UN High Commissioner for Human Rights, 16 June 2016, at: https://bit.ly/3wVhO3p.

[145] Independent International Commission of Inquiry on the Syrian Arab Republic, '"They came to destroy": ISIS Crimes against the Yazidis', para. 105.

[146] Ibid., para. 104.

[147] Ibid., para. 107.

[148] Ibid., para. 109.

[149] Ibid., para. 122.

228 *Prosecution of Terrorism as an International Crime*

prevent Islamic State fighters from removing their children or siblings from their care.[150] Yazidi women and girls, captured by Islamic State and registered and sold in Syria and Iraq, were subjected to organized sexual violence on a massive scale occurring in the context of their sexual enslavement. Women and girls suffered multiple – sometimes hundreds – of the rapes by their various fighter-owners.[151] These acts amounted to acts causing serious bodily or mental harm to members of the Yazidis and the deliberate infliction on the group conditions of life calculated to bring about its physical destruction in whole or in part. Objectively, the Islamic State members terrorized Yazidis, in particular in 2014–16, as war crimes, as crimes against humanity, and as part of their sustained campaign of genocide.

6.6 TERRORISM AS A DISTINCT INTERNATIONAL CRIME IN PEACETIME

The STL was established under an agreement between the United Nations and the Lebanese Republic pursuant to UN Security Council Resolution 1664 of 29 March 2006. This responded to the request of the Government of Lebanon for the establishment of a tribunal of an international character to try all those who are found responsible for the 'terrorist crime' which killed the former Lebanese prime minister Rafiq Hariri and others on 14 February 2005.[152]

The Tribunal was established by Security Council Resolution 1757 of 30 May 2007,[153] annexed to which was the Statute of the Special Tribunal. Resolution 1757 noted in a preambular paragraph that the Council was 'mindful of the demand of the Lebanese people that all those responsible for the terrorist bombing that killed former Lebanese Prime Minister Rafiq Hariri and others be identified and brought to justice'.[154] Article 2 of the Statute dealt with the 'applicable criminal law'. Therein, it was stated that 'the provisions of the Lebanese Criminal Code relating to the prosecution and punishment of acts of terrorism' would be applicable to the prosecution and punishment of the crimes within the Tribunal's mandate.[155]

In 2011, the Appeals Chamber of the Special Tribunal issued a decision in which it claimed that international terrorism during peacetime was already defined under customary international law and that it comprised the following three key elements:

(a) The perpetration of a criminal act (such as murder, kidnapping, hostage-taking, or arson), or threatening such an act

(b) The intent to spread fear among the population or to coerce a national or international authority to take some action or to refrain from taking it

(c) When the act involves a transnational element.[156]

Yet, given that the adoption of the Comprehensive Convention on International Terrorism remains precluded by lack of agreement on the definition, the holding by the Special Tribunal was not persuasive.[157] Indeed, in the Tribunal's own judgment against four accused, issued in August 2020, the Trial Chamber affirmed not only that the Appeals Chamber's

---

[150] Ibid., para. 130.

[151] Ibid., para. 140.

[152] Statute of the Special Tribunal for Lebanon, 2007, at: https://bit.ly/3wFXPp2, opening para.

[153] UN Security Council Resolution 1757, adopted on 30 May 2007 by ten votes to none with five abstentions (China, Indonesia, Qatar, Russia, and South Africa), operative para. 1.

[154] UN Security Council Resolution 1757, ninth preambular para.

[155] Art. 2(a), 2007 Statute of the Special Tribunal for Lebanon.

[156] Special Tribunal for Lebanon (STL), *Interlocutory Decision on the Applicable Law: Terrorism, Conspiracy, Homicide, Perpetration, Cumulative Charging* (Case No. STL-11–01/I), 16 February 2011, para. 85.

[157] See, e.g., M. Milanovic, 'Special Tribunal for Lebanon Delivers Interlocutory Decision on Applicable Law', *EJIL Talk!*, published on 16 February 2011, at http://bit.ly/3gb00Zo.

6.7 TERRORISM AS AN ACT OF AGGRESSION

'lengthy (41 page)' consideration of the 'apparent existence of a customary international law definition of terrorism' was 'obiter dicta', the Trial Chamber was also 'not convinced that one exists'.[158]

While commentators differ as to the robust nature of Judge Cassese's earlier affirmation in the Appeals Chamber, the (far) better view is that there is no definition of terrorism under customary law, much less one that exists for a dedicated international crime under customary international criminal law. As Guénaël Mettraux has written, the Special Tribunal's 'discovery' of an international crime of international terrorism 'fails to convince'.[159]

6.7 TERRORISM AS AN ACT OF AGGRESSION

The Special Tribunal's legerdemain notwithstanding, this does not mean that terrorism cannot be committed as an international crime, as this chapter has sought to demonstrate with respect to war crimes, crimes against humanity, and genocide. There is one more possible international crime that may involve an act of terrorism. Under *jus ad bellum*, aggression is a serious violation of the prohibition on inter-State use of force. Under the Charter of the United Nations, for instance, the Security Council is obligated to determine the existence of any act of aggression and is further required to make recommendations, or decide what measures shall be taken to maintain or restore international peace and security.[160]

As Chapter 2 observed, in 2005, the then UN Secretary-General Kofi Annan declared: 'It is time to set aside debates on so-called "State terrorism". The use of force by States is already thoroughly regulated under international law.'[161] This statement is legally incorrect and morally questionable. Terrorism can be committed by organs or agents of the State domestically (where *jus ad bellum* does not ordinarily apply) and in a situation of armed conflict under IHL without reference to *jus ad bellum*. Trapp too rejects the notion of State terrorism, preferring the moniker of 'State sponsorship of terrorism'.[162] This is similarly unpersuasive. Where a State, through its organs or agents, commits an act of terrorism, it is a perpetrator, not a sponsor. That it may also be in violation of the prohibition on inter-State use of force does not change that fact.

Aggression is now also punishable as an international crime within the purview of the International Criminal Court. It is the first time that this has been possible since the International Military Tribunal established in 1945 to punish the Nazis for the planning and launching of an aggressive war and subsequently the Tokyo Tribunal with respect to the actions of the Japanese were prosecuted as crimes against peace.[163] Under the amendment to the Rome Statute, which was adopted by the 2010 Review Conference in Kampala,

---

[158] STL, *Prosecutor v. Salim Jamil Ayyash and others*, Judgment (Case No. STL-11–01/T/TC), 18 August 2020, para. 6192. See also on this issue the Separate Opinion of Judge Janet Nosworthy, who asserts, but without adducing sufficient evidence, that the definition was *de lege ferenda* as custom as of 2005. See paras. 124–25.

[159] G. Mettraux, 'The UN Special Tribunal for Lebanon: Defining International Terrorism', chap. 40 in B. Saul (ed.), *Research Handbook on International Law and Terrorism*, 2nd ed., p. 598.

[160] Art. 39, Charter of the United Nations; adopted at San Francisco, 26 June 1945; entered into force, 24 October 1945.

[161] 'In larger freedom: towards development, security and human rights for all', Report of the Secretary-General, UN doc. A/59/2005, 21 March 2005, para. 91.

[162] K. N. Trapp, *State Responsibility for International Terrorism*, Oxford University Press, Oxford, 2011, p. 24.

[163] Art. 6, 1945 Charter of the International Military Tribunal, at: https://bit.ly/3nfdN78. See with respect to the Tokyo Tribunal: M. Ediger, 'Prosecuting the Crime of Aggression at the International Criminal Court: Lessons from the Tokyo Tribunal', *New York University Journal of International Law and Politics*, Vol. 51, No. 1 (2019), 179–210, at: https://bit.ly/3UxM9nl.

[f]or the purpose of this Statute, 'crime of aggression' means the planning, preparation, initiation or execution, by a person in a position effectively to exercise control over or to direct the political or military action of a State, of an act of aggression which, by its character, gravity and scale, constitutes a manifest violation of the Charter of the United Nations.[164]

For the purpose of this provision, '"act of aggression" means the use of armed force by a State against the sovereignty, territorial integrity or political independence of another State, or in any other manner inconsistent with the Charter of the United Nations'.[165] Although assassination of a foreign leader is not listed as one of the acts constituting aggression, it is hard to conceive of a more manifest violation of the political independence of another State.[166] As already noted, the Tribunal's Statute has declared the killing a terrorist crime.[167] The question thus arises as to whether the Syrian regime was responsible for Mr Hariri's killing.

In its verdict in August 2020, Salim Jamil Ayyash was found guilty by the STL on numerous counts for the killing of Mr Hariri in Beirut on 14 February 2005. Mr Ayyash is not a Syrian national but a member of the Lebanese group, Hezbollah. The judges in the STL Trial Chamber stated, however, that there was 'no evidence' that Hezbollah's leadership had any involvement in Mr Hariri's murder. It further held that there was 'no *direct* evidence of Syrian involvement in it',[168] leaving the door ajar if not entirely open to the possibility that Syria might have been involved. This issue is addressed further in Chapter 7.

---

[164] Art. 8 *bis* (1), Rome Statute of the International Criminal Court, text available at: https://bit.ly/34lgyO4.

[165] Art. 8 *bis* (2), Rome Statute of the International Criminal Court.

[166] Thus, while Gilbert is correct, in fact, to say that an act of terrorism is 'unlikely' to ever constitute the crime of aggression, this is not always the case. Indeed, while terrorism does indeed focus on the 'means and methods of violence', it also concerns itself with targets, in particular leading figures within a State's executive. G. Gilbert, 'Terrorism and international refugee law', chap. 29 in B. Saul (ed.), *Research Handbook on International Law and Terrorism*, 2nd ed., p. 429.

[167] Chapeau to the 2007 Statute of the Special Tribunal for Lebanon, annexed to UN Security Council Resolution 1757. See on the issue of assassination of Mr Hariri as terrorism Saul, 'Definition of "Terrorism" in the UN Security Council', 141–66, *esp.* at pp. 145–46.

[168] STL, *Prosecutor* v. *Salim Jamil Ayyash and others*, Judgment, para. 787 [added emphasis].

7

State Responsibility for Terrorism

7.1 INTRODUCTION

While people may instinctively think of a member of a non-State armed group as a potential terrorist, as this book has already illustrated, many States are also responsible for acts of terrorism. In 1984, the United Nations (UN) General Assembly adopted a resolution entitled the 'Inadmissibility of the policy of State terrorism and any actions by States aimed at undermining the socio-political system in other sovereign States'.[1] The resolution, which was focused on non-intervention in other States, rather than terrorism per se, nonetheless 'resolutely' condemned 'policies and practices of terrorism in relations between States as a method of dealing with other States and peoples'. It urged all States 'to respect and strictly observe, in accordance with the Charter of the United Nations, the sovereignty and political independence of States and the right of peoples to self-determination'.[2]

The notion of State responsibility goes to the heart of respect for international law. Its fundamental tenet is that each State bears legal responsibility for the acts (and omissions) of its organs and agents. International law attributes to the responsible State the obligation to make reparation for the harmful consequences flowing from that act.[3] Thus, every State must take concrete action to repair the damage it has wrought by violating international law. The duty to make reparation is implemented through a series of actions and measures, as this chapter explains. This responsibility, which is of a delictual not a criminal nature, is without prejudice to the criminal responsibility of individuals, including members of State organs and State agents.[4]

The principle of State responsibility encompasses every branch of international law – international human rights law, international humanitarian law (IHL), and international counterterrorism law, among others – with each violation of international law giving rise to the duty to repair. While the focus is on inter-State reparation, the rules cover all the

---

[1] UN General Assembly Resolution 39/159, adopted on 17 December 1984 by 117 votes to nil with 30 abstentions (Australia, Austria, Belgium, Brazil, Canada, Chile, Colombia, Denmark, Finland, France, Germany, Honduras, Iceland, Ireland, Israel, Italy, Japan, Luxembourg, Malawi, Netherlands, New Zealand, Norway, Paraguay, Portugal, Spain, Sweden, Turkey, United Kingdom, United States, and Venezuela).

[2] Ibid., operative paras. 1 and 3.

[3] Commentary, para. 2, on Part II: 'Content of the International Responsibility of a State', Draft articles on Responsibility of States for Internationally Wrongful Acts, with commentaries, 2001; Text adopted by the ILC at its fifty-third session, in 2001, and submitted to the UN General Assembly in UN doc. A/56/10, at http://bit.ly/32A30cT (hereafter, 2001 ILC Draft Articles on State Responsibility).

[4] Trapp, State Responsibility for International Terrorism, pp. 231, 232 n 9. As Trapp observes, France tried – unsuccessfully – to claim that its admission of State responsibility for the destruction of the Rainbow Warrior and associated homicide relieved its agents of criminal responsibility. Ibid., p. 100.

international obligations of the State and not only those owed to other States. Thus, State responsibility extends to human rights violations as well as other breaches of international law 'where the primary beneficiary of the obligation breached is not a State'.[5]

With respect to terrorism and counterterrorism, a violation of international law can, most obviously, occur at the hands of a soldier on the battlefield or an aerial drone operator acting remotely; be perpetrated by a police officer in the street or a corrections officer in a prison; result from abusive interrogation by an intelligence agent; or arise from the biased actions of a judge sitting over the trial of a defendant accused of a criminal offence.[6] Some unlawful acts are defended by the State in question as 'counterterrorism'. It is not, though, the labelling of an act that is determinative but rather the nature of the conduct: what was done (or not done) and in what manner.

Having set out first the key components of State responsibility under international law, this chapter then uses a series of case studies to demonstrate the parameters of that responsibility in practice. This first entails responsibility for a State's negligent failure to prevent a terrorist attack, considering the acts and omissions of the Russian authorities with respect to the school siege at Beslan in 2003. Whereas of course the Chechen separatists who took as hostages the teachers and schoolchildren were first and foremost criminally liable for terrorism under domestic and international law, the European Court of Human Rights held Russia also responsible for failing to take even minimal steps to prevent the attack. This was so despite foreknowledge by the authorities of some of the critical details of the terrorists' plans.

Three cases have been chosen to exemplify the direct perpetration of terrorism by a State. The first case is the bombing by French agents of the Greenpeace boat, *Rainbow Warrior*, by French agents in New Zealand in 1985. A Portuguese photographer on the boat drowned as a result of the bombing, which was said to have been personally authorized by the French president of the day, François Mitterrand.[7] Two of the agents involved in the operation were detained by New Zealand police and convicted of manslaughter. The second case involves certain acts of the Syrian Arab Republic following the protests related to the Arab Spring, in particular the widespread and systematic torture and summary execution of opponents of the regime. The third case is the conduct of Russian forces in Ukraine following its invasion on 24 February 2022. To the rape and murder of civilians in occupied towns is to be added the terror bombing of other towns and cities across Ukraine.

Even when non-State armed groups do not operate as the agents of a State – or when the existence of a proxy relationship cannot be fully supported by the available evidence[8] – a State may serve as an accomplice to an act of terrorism. On this particular issue, the draft articles on State responsibility for internationally wrongful acts proposed by the International Law Commission (ILC) to the UN General Assembly in 2001 may seem rather lacking. The 2001

---

[5]   Commentary, para. 3, on Draft Article 28, 2001 ILC Draft Articles on State Responsibility.

[6]   According to paragraph 1 of Draft Article 4 ('Conduct of organs of a State'): 'The conduct of any State organ shall be considered an act of that State under international law, whether the organ exercises legislative, executive, judicial or any other functions, whatever position it holds in the organization of the State, and whatever its character as an organ of the central Government or of a territorial unit of the State.' Art. 4(1), 2001 ILC Draft Articles on State Responsibility.

[7]   M. Simons, 'Report Says Mitterrand Approved Sinking of Greenpeace Ship', *The New York Times*, 10 July 2005, at: https://bit.ly/441WrgH.

[8]   There is State responsibility where paramilitary or other armed groups act under instruction from an organ or agent of the State. Thus, Draft Article 8 stipulates that 'the conduct of a person or group of persons shall be considered an act of a State under international law if the person or group of persons is in fact acting on the instructions of, or under the direction or control of, that State in carrying out the conduct'.

ILC Draft Articles on State Responsibility duly foresee the responsibility of a State for its aid or assistance to another State which enables the latter to violate international law,[9] but do not explicitly countenance the situation where it is a non-State armed group that is the perpetrator.[10]

Two case examples of State responsibility as accomplices to acts of terrorism are proffered. The first is the unquestionable responsibility of Liberia for the actions of the Revolutionary United Front (RUF) in neighbouring Sierra Leone during the civil war. Charles Taylor, who was the Liberia's president at the salient time, was convicted by the judges of the Special Court of Sierra Leone many years later of assisting the perpetration of war crimes (including acts of terrorism) and crimes against humanity. In May 2012, Mr Taylor was sentenced to fifty years in prison for his crimes. He is serving his sentence, which was confirmed on appeal the following year, in a Category A (high security) prison in County Durham in England.[11] The second case is the potential responsibility of Syria for the murder of former Lebanese prime minister, Rafik Hariri, in Beirut on 14 February 2005.

The final section of the chapter considers the ongoing case of Myanmar and the labelling and treatment of political opposition as terrorists. Despite the vagaries of legal definitions of terrorism, an issue considered in detail in Chapter 2 of this book, such a labelling may itself amount to a violation of international law entailing the responsibility of the State. A politicized label will assuredly have grave human consequences, but it may also generate legal liability. Where State responsibility arises from a failure to implement in good faith the obligations in a UN sectoral treaty, the compromissory clauses in those treaties provide for recourse to the International Court of Justice (ICJ).[12]

7.2 THE KEY COMPONENTS OF STATE RESPONSIBILITY

As noted in the previous section, the primary instrument pertaining to State responsibility under international law is the 2001 ILC Draft Articles on State Responsibility. The Draft Articles overwhelmingly reflect customary international law applicable to all States. Their focus is on the secondary rules of State responsibility: 'the general conditions under international law for the State to be considered responsible for wrongful actions or omissions, and the legal consequences which flow therefrom'.[13] That is to say, when a State is responsible under international law for a violation of international law and how that responsibility must be discharged.

Article 2 of the Draft Articles stipulates that there is an internationally wrongful act of a State when conduct consisting of an action or omission is attributable to the State under international law, where that conduct 'constitutes a breach of an international obligation of the State'. An internationally wrongful act is thus, simply put, any violation of an applicable rule of

---

[9] Art. 16, 2001 ILC Draft Articles on State Responsibility.

[10] That said, the European Court of Human Rights has duly recognized the potential responsibility of a State even when it does not have effective control of non-State actors present in its territory. In its 2012 judgment in the *Catan* case, the European Court's Grand Chamber stated that although Moldova had no effective control over the acts of the self-styled 'Moldavian Republic of Transdniestria', a breakaway entity controlling territory in Transnistria, 'the fact that the region is recognised under public international law as part of Moldova's territory gives rise to an obligation, under Article 1 of the Convention, to use all legal and diplomatic means available to it to continue to guarantee the enjoyment of the rights and freedoms defined in the [European] Convention [on Human Rights] to those living there'. European Court of Human Rights (ECtHR), *Catan and others* v. *Moldova and Russia*, Judgment (Grand Chamber), 19 October 2012, para. 110.

[11] K. Southern and L. Hill, 'Sean Mercer, The Yorkshire Ripper and Ian Huntley: We look at HMP Frankland's notorious prisoners', Chronicle Live, 13 November 2018 (updated 22 May 2020), at: https://bit.ly/3OvODyc.

[12] Trapp, *State Responsibility for International Terrorism*, pp. 6 n 36, 136–47.

[13] General Commentary, para. 1, 2001 ILC Draft Articles on State Responsibility.

international law by a State – a long-standing position in international law.[14] It applies whether the salient rule is set forth in a treaty to which the relevant State is party, is part of the corpus of customary law, or if it reflects a general principle of international law. The ILC preferred the term 'internationally wrongful act' to others that have been used in international law in the past, such as 'tort'[15] or 'delict'.[16]

Attribution of conduct to a State occurs even if the conduct of members of the armed forces, law enforcement agencies, or other security forces acting in the course of their duties goes beyond – or even is in breach of – the instructions they are given by other State agents. The Draft Articles thus stipulate: 'The conduct of an organ of a State or of a person or entity empowered to exercise elements of the governmental authority shall be considered an act of the State under international law if the organ, person or entity acts in that capacity, even if it exceeds its authority or contravenes instructions.'[17]

And, as Draft Article 2 makes explicit, an internationally wrongful act includes not only a positive action by a State organ or agent but also an omission. For instance, an omission may amount to arbitrary deprivation of life and thereby violate the right to life when the authorities fail to provide food and water to a suspected terrorist held in custody or do not ensure the provision of medical treatment and care when needed, resulting in death or a life-threatening or life-altering condition.[18] The failure to investigate the potentially unlawful death of any person, including a suspected terrorist, is a violation of the procedural element of the right to life and similarly a violation of international law.[19]

The consequences for a State of being responsible for an internationally wrongful act are potentially manifold. The 2001 ILC Draft Articles on State Responsibility identify a number of these legal consequences. In particular, the State responsible for an internationally wrongful act is under an obligation to cease that act (if it is continuing) and to offer 'appropriate assurances and guarantees of non-repetition, if circumstances so require'.[20] An omission that is violative of international law must similarly be rectified by appropriate positive conduct.[21] Thus, if the omission is the failure to conduct an effective investigation into an alleged violation of the right to life of a suspected terrorist, an investigation meeting international standards must still be carried out as part of the State's international legal responsibility.[22] Guarantees of non-repetition involve preventive measures to be taken by the responsible State designed to avoid repetition of the breach.[23]

---

[14] Permanent Court of International Justice (PCIJ), *Phosphates in Morocco case* (*Italy* v. *France*), Judgment, 14 June 1938, *PCIJ* Series C, No. 84 (1938), 10, at p. 28.

[15] See, e.g., C. L. Bouvé, 'Russia's Liability in Tort for Persia's Breach of Contract', *American Journal of International Law*, Vol. 6, No. 2 (April 1912), p. 389.

[16] In its first judgment, in the *Corfu Channel* case in 1949, the International Court of Justice (ICJ) had referred to '*corpora delicti*'. ICJ, *Corfu Channel case* (*United Kingdom* v. *Albania*), Judgment (Merits), 9 April 1949, *ICJ Reports 1949*, 4, at p. 34.

[17] Art. 7, 2001 ILC Draft Articles on State Responsibility. See further on this point Inter-American Court of Human Rights, *Velásquez-Rodríguez* v. *Honduras*, Judgment (Merits), 29 July 1988, para. 170.

[18] S. Casey-Maslen, *The Right to Life under International Law*, Cambridge University Press, Cambridge, 2021, p. 613, para. 32.07.

[19] Ibid., paras. 32.47–32.52.

[20] Art. 30, 2001 ILC Draft Articles on State Responsibility.

[21] Commentary, para. 2, on Draft Article 30, 2001 ILC Draft Articles on State Responsibility.

[22] These standards require that an investigation be prompt, effective, and thorough, and carried out with independence, impartiality, and transparency. See *Minnesota Protocol on the Investigation of Potentially Unlawful Death* (2016), Office of the UN High Commissioner for Human Rights (OHCHR), Geneva/New York, 2017, at: https://bit.ly/3aH8Yh7, paras. 22–33.

[23] Commentary, para. 12, on Draft Article 30, 2001 ILC Draft Articles on State Responsibility.

Naturally, the duty to repair demands that a responsible State make 'full reparation for the injury caused by the internationally wrongful act'.[24] This general principle of international law, which is of exceptionally long-standing nature, binds all States. As stated by the Permanent Court of International Justice in 1928: 'It is a principle of international law that the breach of an engagement involves an obligation to make reparation in an adequate form. Reparation therefore is the indispensable complement of a failure to apply a convention and there is no necessity for this to be stated in the convention itself.'[25] Reparation involves both material and moral damage.[26] Material damage concerns damage to property or other interests of the State and its nationals that is assessable financially. Moral damage includes pain and suffering and the loss of loved ones.[27] Full reparation for the injury caused by the violation of international law must take the form of restitution, compensation, and satisfaction, 'either singly or in combination'.[28]

7.3 THE DUTY TO PREVENT TERRORISM

The nature of the duty to prevent terrorism involves the taking of all reasonable measures by the State and its organs and agents with a view to preventing the perpetration of acts of terrorism.[29] Such measures of due diligence encompass the promulgation of dedicated domestic law as well as the development of law enforcement capacity, including specific counterterrorism expertise. It would encompass surveillance of those reasonably suspected to be planning terrorism, as and where this is lawful, and prosecution where evidence of the commission of a crime exists. Terrorist funding must be interdicted. Terrorists must also be prevented from accessing weapons, and especially any weapons of mass destruction.[30]

7.3.1 *The Beslan School Siege*

The siege that occurred at Beslan school in North Ossetia on 1–3 September 2004 ended with the deaths of more than 300 teachers and children as a result of the storming of the school by Russian forces. The pupils and their teachers had been taken hostage by the Riyadus-Salikhin Reconnaissance and Sabotage Battalion of Chechen Martyrs,[31] an Islamist armed group that had been designated as terrorist by the UN Security Council more than a year earlier.[32]

---

[24] Art. 31(1), 2001 ILC Draft Articles on State Responsibility.

[25] PCIJ, *Case concerning the Factory at Chorzów* (*Germany* v. *Poland*), Judgment (Jurisdiction), No. 8, 1927, *PCIJ* Series A, No. 9, at http://bit.ly/2GaUDwF, p. 21.

[26] Art. 31(2), 2001 ILC Draft Articles on State Responsibility.

[27] Commentary, para. 5, on Draft Article 31, 2001 ILC Draft Articles on State Responsibility.

[28] Art. 34, 2001 ILC Draft Articles on State Responsibility.

[29] See for a discussion of due diligence obligations under UN Security Council Resolution 2396 (2017) and their normative status under international law: I. Österdahl, 'Due Diligence in International Anti-Terrorism Law', chap. 14 in H. Krieger, A. Peters, and L. Kreuzer (eds.), *Due Diligence in the International Legal Order*, Oxford University Press, Oxford, 2020, 234–51.

[30] Under UN Security Council Resolution 1540, States are required to refrain from providing any form of support to non-State actors that seek to develop, acquire, manufacture, possess, transport, transfer, or use nuclear, chemical, or biological weapons and their means of delivery. UN Security Council Resolution 1540, adopted on 28 April 2004 by unanimous vote in favour, operative para. 1.

[31] Mapping Militant Organizations, 'Riyadus-Salikhin Reconnaissance and Sabotage Battalion of Chechen Martyrs', Center for International Security and Cooperation (CISAC), Stanford University, last modified 17 August 2018, at http://stanford.io/32118F1.

[32] On 4 March 2003. The full list is available at: http://bit.ly/321NkyH.

236 *State Responsibility for Terrorism*

In its 2017 judgment in the *Tagayeva* case, the European Court of Human Rights held that Russia had failed in its duty of due diligence to prevent the terrorism attack at the school.[33] The applicants to the Court had argued that the Russian authorities had known of a real and immediate threat to life but had failed to take reasonable preventive measures available to them. The *Tagayeva* judgment was the first time the European Court had held that a Contracting State to the European Convention on Human Rights had failed to meet its due diligence obligations to protect the right to life from a terror attack.

The basis for the Court's decision was that the authorities had learned of a planned attack on an educational institution in the region but had not stepped up security – indeed it had been reduced – nor had they warned schools, teachers, or pupils of the danger. Expert testimony provided to the Court concluded that while no security measures could serve as a guarantee against the attackers' success, the presence of security personnel on the roads and at potential targets would have acted as a deterrent and could have substantially impeded the attackers. The fact that a group of more than thirty armed terrorists had been able to travel along local roads to Beslan, having encountered only one police roadblock that was manned by a single officer, demonstrated 'the extent of failure' on the part of the authorities 'to act upon the information available to them'.[34]

In its assessment, the Court confirmed that it was 'acutely conscious of the difficulties faced by modern States in the fight against terrorism and the dangers of hindsight analysis'. It was clear that as a judicial body, it would need to differentiate between the 'political choices made in the course of fighting terrorism, that remain by their nature outside of such supervision', and 'other, more operational aspects of the authorities' actions that have a direct bearing on the protected rights'.[35] But the information known to the authorities before the Riyadus-Salikhin Reconnaissance and Sabotage Battalion of Chechen Martyrs took all those hostages at Beslan school had confirmed the existence of a real and immediate risk to life.[36]

At least several days in advance the authorities had sufficiently specific information about a planned terrorist attack in the areas in the vicinity of the Malgobek District in Ingushetia and targeting an educational facility on 1 September. The intelligence information likened the threat to major attacks undertaken in the past by the Chechen separatists, which had resulted in heavy casualties. In the face of a threat 'of such magnitude, predictability, and imminence', it could reasonably be expected that preventive and protective measures would be directed to all educational facilities in the concerned districts and further that other security steps would be taken to 'detect, deter and neutralise the terrorists as soon as possible and with minimal risk to life'.[37] Although several preventive measures were taken, these were inadequate. The terrorists were, the Court recalled, able successfully to 'gather, prepare, travel to and seize their target, without encountering any preventive security arrangements'. There was no single structure at a sufficiently high level tasked with handling the situation, allocating resources, ensuring that the at-risk target group were defenced, and that the threat was effectively contained.[38]

The Court thus concluded unanimously that the information available to the authorities was clear as to the nature, imminence, and (general) location of the attack, and therefore Russia was

---

[33] ECtHR, *Tagayeva* v. *Russia*, Judgment (First Section), 13 April 2017, paras. 482, 492, 639, 659.
[34] Ibid., para. 439.
[35] Ibid., para. 481.
[36] Ibid., para. 491.
[37] Ibid., para. 486.
[38] Ibid., para. 491.

7.4 STATE PERPETRATION OF TERRORISM

under an obligation to take suitable measures to prevent the taking of hostages.[39] In the prevailing circumstances, the Court found a breach of the positive obligations to protect the right to life of all the applicants in the case.[40] The Court imposed a duty upon Russia to pay €2.9 million in damages resulting from its State responsibility. Russia was not granted leave to appeal the decision to the Grand Chamber but it pledged, at the time, to comply with the ruling.[41]

7.4 STATE PERPETRATION OF TERRORISM

State organs or agents[42] may perpetrate acts of terrorism both during peacetime and during armed conflict, and in either scenario terrorism may occur on sovereign territory and/or extraterritorially. This section comprises three case studies of State terrorism, the first of which occurred during peacetime. It was perpetrated by France in 1988 against a Greenpeace vessel engaged in protests against French nuclear testing in the Pacific. The bombing of the *Rainbow Warrior* by covert French secret service agents resulted in the death by drowning of a photographer. It was a clear use of force in violation of the rules of *jus ad bellum* but it was also an instance of State terrorism.

The second case involves torturing to death by government officials in Syria of thousands of political opponents of the regime following the Arab Spring that spread across much of the Arab world in the early 2010s. What began as government repression in peacetime, including the use of torture to terrorize opponent of the regime, became war crimes amid the many armed conflicts that broke out across the country beginning in 2012. While these were not examples of international terrorism *stricto sensu* as that term is understood in the UN sectoral treaties, they represented multiple international crimes, first as crimes against humanity and then, once armed conflict existed in Syria, also as war crimes. The third case concerns the acts of Russian forces in Ukraine in the conduct of hostilities since the invasion that began on 24 February 2022. Increasingly, the targeting of civilians and the indiscriminate bombing of towns and cities – themselves war crimes – are also war crimes of terror.

7.4.1 *The Rainbow Warrior Bombing*

Opération Satanique[43] was a plot by the French authorities to sink the Greenpeace boat *Rainbow Warrior*[44] while it was moored at the port city of Auckland on New Zealand's North Island. The converted fishing trawler was being used by Greenpeace to confront French nuclear testing on Moruroa atoll in the Pacific. France conducted 193 nuclear test detonations between 1966 and 1996 at Moruroa and Fangataufa atolls in French Polynesia.[45] During the 1970s, Greenpeace

---

[39] S. Galani, '*Hostages and Human Rights at the European Court of Human Rights: The Tagayeva and Others v. Russia Case*', University of Bristol Law School blog, Posted 8 May 2017, at http://bit.ly/2vE1Blo.

[40] ECtHR, *Tagayeva v. Russia*, Judgment, para. 493.

[41] BBC, 'Beslan Siege: Russia "Will Comply" with Critical Ruling', 20 September 2017, at http://bbc.in/2OM9bmr.

[42] As Trapp observes, acts of international terrorism are rarely carried out by organs of a State: they are more likely to be conducted through private persons or groups that act on its behalf. Trapp, *State Responsibility for International Terrorism*, p. 37.

[43] One of the agents involved in the Operation later claimed that all French Secret Service operations at that time were codenamed to start with the letters S and A after the agency's 'Service Action'. Field,

[44] The vessel was named after a North American Cree Indian prophecy: 'When the world is sick and dying, the people will rise up like Warriors of the Rainbow.' Greenpeace, 'The bombing of the Rainbow Warrior', Greenpeace Aotearoa, 2023, at: https://bit.ly/3OQanWI.

[45] J. Henley, 'France has underestimated impact of nuclear tests in French Polynesia, research finds', *The Guardian*, 9 March 2021, at: https://bit.ly/3rnBn3o.

238 *State Responsibility for Terrorism*

had sent yachts into the area to try to disrupt the tests, leading to the French navy holding the boats and once beating up several of the protesters. But the *Rainbow Warrior*, which was much bigger than the yachts previously used, would be harder to stop and intimidate.[46]

On 10 July 1985, after three months of planning, two divers attached two packets of plastic-wrapped explosives to the Greenpeace boat below the waterline, one by the propeller and the second to the outer wall of the engine room. The first bomb blew a large hole in the hull. On-board photographer Fernando Pereira was below deck gathering his camera equipment when the second bomb detonated. The *Rainbow Warrior* sank four minutes later and Mr Pereira, a father of two who had recently celebrated his thirty-fifth birthday, drowned in his cabin.[47]

While a gas explosion was initially suspected, New Zealand navy divers later discovered the blasts had come from explosives attached to the hull. In the words of one newspaper article, 'Sleepy New Zealand suddenly had its first ever international terrorism inquiry'.[48] At first, French officials publicly decried the bombing as an act of terrorism. They tried to blame British intelligence for the sinking in a campaign of 'misinformation and smears'.[49] In fact, the two divers and other personnel in the Operation's three teams belonged to the French secret service, the DGSE: the Direction générale de la sécurité extérieure (the General Directorate for External Security).[50] The role of the French authorities became increasingly evident to the police as their investigation progressed.[51]

Two of the agents were caught by New Zealand police, in part due to incompetence and in part as a result of hard luck. At a marina a few miles from the harbour, boat owners had been watching the site after a spate of thefts. One had seen a frogman dragging a dinghy ashore two hours before the bombing. He was picked up by a campervan, whose registration number they wrote down and provided to detectives. The van was traced to a local car hire firm and alert staff at the firm called the police inquiry hotline to tell them that sitting in their office were the young couple who had hired the van and who were returning it a day early.[52] The couple were ostensibly Swiss newly-weds, Alain and Sophie Turenge, on honeymoon in New Zealand. But their passports were subsequently revealed to be high-quality forgeries[53] and, under questioning, the stories they told the police about picking up the man as a 'hitchhiker' was wholly unconvincing.[54]

---

[46] C. Freeman, 'Why the French bombed Greenpeace's Rainbow Warrior: "The goal wasn't to slaughter"', *Daily Telegraph*, 2 March 2023, at: https://bit.ly/3qqQSuA.

[47] Greenpeace, 'Murder in the Pacific: The sinking of the Rainbow Warrior and what happened next', 1 March 2023, at: https://bit.ly/45opUlY.

[48] Freeman, 'Why the French bombed Greenpeace's Rainbow Warrior'.

[49] R. Evans and P. Brown, 'France blamed MI6 for Rainbow Warrior', *The Guardian*, 28 November 2005, at: https://bit.ly/45hI8X3.

[50] The DGSE's strapline today is: 'We act in utmost secrecy to defend the vital interests of our nation.' DGSE website, 'Who we are', at: https://bit.ly/45rlooF. The site does not make any reference to *Opération Satanique*.

[51] One French source cited by James Belich in his partial history of New Zealand said that the DGSE agents had left a trail so Gallic, 'the only missing clues were a baguette, a black beret, and a bottle of Beaujolais'. J. Belich, *Paradise Reforged: A History of New Zealanders from the 1880s to the Year 2000*, University of Hawai'i Press, Honolulu, 2001; and see also J. Wilson, 'The sinking of the rainbow warrior: Responses to an international act of terrorism', *Journal of Postcolonial Cultures and Societies*, Vol. 1, No. 1 (2010), 58–70, at p. 61.

[52] Freeman, 'Why the French bombed Greenpeace's Rainbow Warrior'.

[53] As he wrote later, Alain Mafart, the French agent whose alias was Alain Turenge, realized at the time that the choice of Swiss passports was a high risk. A. Mafart, *Carnets Secrets d'un Nageur de Combat*, Albin Michel, Paris, 1999, p. 146.

[54] The police wisely questioned the two separately and asked them simple questions such as where did the man sit? Different answers from the two – one said the front seat, the other said the back – made it clear they were not being truthful about what had happened.

7.4 State Perpetration of Terrorism

Separately, a forestry worker who had seen the campervan rendezvous 'mysteriously' with an estate car also provided the police with the number plate of that other car. It had been rented from Avis by four Frenchmen, who wrote on the rental form that they had come to New Zealand on the *Ouvea*, a yacht. The men were detained by Australian police but later released without charge. They made good their escape before forensic tests determined that traces of explosive on board the yacht matched those used in the bombing of the *Rainbow Warrior*, which would have led to their prolonged detention in police custody and likely extradition to New Zealand.[55]

But although most of the agents managed to escape, pressure continued to mount on the French government, with a journalist at *Le Monde*, Edwy Plenel, playing a crucial role in uncovering the truth.[56] Finally, on 22 September 1985, after two months of repeated denials by the authorities, the French Prime Minister Laurent Fabius publicly admitted France's responsibility to the world: 'The truth is cruel. Agents of the DGSE sank this boat.'[57] This public admission obviated the obvious legal problem vis-à-vis State responsibility that secret service personnel are rarely operating openly 'under colour of authority'.[58]

New Zealand demanded compensation for what Prime Minister David Lange termed 'an affront to sovereignty'.[59] Prime Minister Lange declared that the sad aspect of the admission of French responsibility 'is that the bombing is not fortuitous Beau Geste, but instead a sordid act of international State-backed terrorism'. France never formally apologized for the operation. It would, though, later pay an undisclosed amount of compensation to Mr Pereira's family and around £7 million to Greenpeace for the loss of the *Rainbow Warrior*.[60] The French Minister of Defence, Charles Hernu, was forced to resign while the head of the secret service, Admiral Pierre Lacoste, was sacked. But while both were certainly culpable, President Mitterrand, who had authorized the operation, denied all knowledge and stayed in post.

The two agents detained by New Zealand police, whose real identities were Major Alain Mafart and Captain Dominique Prieur – both French citizens – were sentenced to ten years' imprisonment for their role in the bombing. They denied charges of murder but pleaded guilty to manslaughter (and wilful damage) before the High Court in Auckland on 3 November 1985.[61] Captain Prieur had been responsible for logistics, including delivery with Major Mafart of the explosives to the two divers,[62] and then to organize the escape of the agents from New Zealand after the bombing.[63] Following their convictions, a United Nations arbitration ruling in July 1986 led to both agents being transferred to Hao atoll, a French military base in French Polynesia. Both were released and returned to France (without the approval of the New Zealand government) within two years, first Major Mafart and then Captain Prieur.

A ruling by the UN Secretary-General required that France pay US$7 million to New Zealand as reparation.[64] New Zealand later complained before an international arbitration tribunal that France had threatened to disrupt New Zealand trade with the European

---

55 Ibid.
56 See, e.g., '1985 : le sabordage du "Rainbow-Warrior" dans les eaux troubles de la raison d'État', *Le Monde*, 27 November 2004, at: https://bit.ly/447ENIx.
57 He had previously and personally denied that the bombers were in the employ of the French secret service.
58 Trapp, 'Terrorism and the International Law of State Responsibility', 31–46, at pp. 37–38.
59 C. Page and I. Templeton, 'From the archive, 24 September 1985: French inquiry into Rainbow Warrior bombing', *The Guardian*, 24 September 2014, at: https://bit.ly/453YH8r.
60 Freeman, 'Why the French bombed Greenpeace's Rainbow Warrior'.
61 BBC, 'On this day: 3 November 1985: Agents plead guilty in Rainbow Warrior trial', at: https://bit.ly/3KApSj9.
62 Mafart, *Carnets Secrets d'un Nageur de Combat*, p. 153.
63 C. Field, 'Saboteur spills the French beans', *New Zealand Herald*, 30 June 2000, at: https://bit.ly/3s9V8iM.
64 'Rainbow Warrior', *International Law Reports*, Vol. 74 (1987), 241 at p. 256.

Community unless the two agents were released.[65] The tribunal of three experts applied the law of treaties and the law of State responsibility in order to reach its decision.[66] It held by majority decision that Major Mafart's initial evacuation to France, notwithstanding that it was effected without New Zealand's consent, was not internationally wrongful, since subsequent examinations showed that the major did indeed require medical treatment not available in Hao. The Tribunal held unanimously, however, that France's decision not to return him to Hao after he had recovered following his treatment was in breach of its obligations.[67] In the case of Captain Prieur, the Tribunal held unanimously that France had committed a material breach of a written agreement with New Zealand by not endeavouring in good faith to secure consent to Captain Prieur's immediate repatriation as well as by failing to return Captain Prieur to Hao. The fact that Captain Prieur might have been entitled to leave under French military law was no justification, since under the law of treaties a State is not entitled to rely upon its own domestic law as grounds for failure to comply with its international obligations.[68]

DGSE agent Lieutenant Christine Cabon had infiltrated Greenpeace in New Zealand under the assumed name of Frederique Bonlieu. She had even helped Greenpeace to draft a letter to the French president to ask him to halt nuclear testing. Lieutenant Cabon left for Israel before the attack, then fled to France just as police were about to arrest her. She was awarded the *Legion d'Honneur*, France's highest order of merit, and later became a local councillor at a village in south-west France. Speaking to media in 2017, Ms Cabon felt no remorse for her actions.[69] Two years earlier, however, one of the two divers in *Opération Satanique* who had placed the bombs, Jean-Luc Kister, voiced his personal regrets in an interview with a media agency. 'We are not assassins and we have a conscience. I have the weight of an innocent man's death on my conscience. ... It's time, I believe, for me to express my profound regret and my apologies', he said.[70]

7.4.2 *Syrian Regime Infliction of Torture as Terrorism during the 'Arab Spring' in Syria*

The Arab Spring began with a self-immolation by a young Tunisian on 17 December 2010 in protest against police harassment. Mohamed Bouazizi died almost three weeks later from his injuries but his gesture had already gone viral on social media, sparking protests against the cost of living and the country's authoritarian president, Zine El Abidine Ben Ali. President Ben Ali's twenty-three-year-rule ended ten days later when he fled to Saudi Arabia, becoming the first leader of an Arab nation to be ejected from power by popular protests.[71]

Egypt was the next Arab nation to experience the force of the Arab Spring. On 25 January 2011, thousands of Egyptians marched in Cairo and Alexandria, demanding the departure of President Hosni Mubarak, who by then had been in power for thirty years. On 11 February, with more than a million protesters in the streets, President Mubarak resigned and handed control to the military. Protests in Bahrain broke out on 15 February, but were swiftly repressed by force by

---

[65] France-New Zealand Arbitration Tribunal, *Rainbow Warrior (New Zealand v. France)*, Decision of 30 April 1990, *International Law Reports*, Vol. 82 (1990).

[66] Summary of the decision available at: https://bit.ly/3KDsjBr.

[67] Ibid., pp. 557–60.

[68] Ibid., pp. 560–66.

[69] C. Meier and K. Dennett, 'Rainbow Warrior spy tracked down in France 32 years after bombing', *The Sydney Morning Herald*, 9 July 2017, at: https://bit.ly/3Kzo4qy.

[70] K. Willsher, 'French spy who sank Greenpeace ship apologises for lethal bombing', *The Guardian*, 6 September 2015, at: https://bit.ly/3cgjoUe.

[71] Aljazeera, 'What is the Arab Spring, and how did it start?', 17 December 2020, at: https://bit.ly/3sc3pmo.

7.4 State Perpetration of Terrorism

the authorities. In Libya, however, a sit-in against the government in the second city, Benghazi, which was also forcibly repressed, led to an armed uprising. That insurgency would later be supported by NATO forces operating under – and later beyond – the remit of UN Security Council Resolution 1973.[72]

On 6 March 2011, a dozen teenagers tagged the wall of their school in southern Syria with 'Your turn, doctor', referring to President Bashar al-Assad, a trained ophthalmologist. The torture of the youths sparked mainly peaceful protests at first along with calls for democratic reform. In 2011, prior to operations to stop civilian demonstrations, military commanders told their units, falsely, that they were going to fight 'terrorists', 'armed gangs', or Israelis.[73] This spurred excessive use of force in the dispersal of peaceful assemblies. But the abuse did not end there, with arbitrary detention of thousands of protesters by the authorities.

Many detainees were subjected to severe beatings with batons and cables. They endured prolonged stress positions for hours or even days in a row, were subject to electric shocks, and were deprived of food, water, and sleep. The victims included children, some of whom were tortured to death. One witness saw a thirteen-year-old boy, Thamir Al Sharee, lying on the floor bleeding profusely from his ear, eyes, and nose on 3 May. He was calling out to his mother and father for help when he was hit with a rifle butt on the head. He died during detention.[74]

Several testimonies reported the practice of sexual torture used on male detainees. Men were routinely made to undress and remain naked.[75] Several former detainees testified reported beatings of genitals, forced oral sex, electroshocks, and cigarette burns to the anus in detention facilities, including those of the Air Force Intelligence in Damascus, the Military Intelligence in Jisr Al Shughour, the Military Intelligence and the Political Security in Idlib and Al Ladhiqiyah, and the intelligence detention facilities in Tartus. Several detainees were repeatedly threatened that they would be raped in front of their family and that their wives and daughters would also be raped.[76] A number of cases were documented of injured people who were taken to military hospitals, where they were tortured during interrogation. Torture and killings reportedly took place in Homs Military Hospital by security forces dressed as doctors, said to be acting with the complicity of medical personnel.[77]

Torture was thus a feature of the Syrian regime's response to the protests from the very beginning, despite the constitutional prohibition of the practice,[78] and notwithstanding Syria's earlier adherence to the 1966 International Covenant on Civil and Political Rights and the 1984 Convention against Torture and Other Cruel, Inhuman or Degrading Treatment or Punishment. Torture is always terrorizing to its victims, but the systematic nature of the practice in Syria was intended to terrorize the population as a whole.[79] Detainees reported being tortured whether or not they confessed.

---

[72] Ibid.

[73] First Report of the Independent International Commission of Inquiry on the Syrian Arab Republic, para. 104.

[74] Ibid., paras. 61 and 62.

[75] As the Istanbul Protocol explains, 'Nudity enhances the psychological terror of every aspect of torture, as there is always the threat of potential sexual torture or ill-treatment, including rape.' OHCHR, *Istanbul Protocol: Manual on the Effective Investigation and Documentation of Torture and Other Cruel, Inhuman or Degrading Treatment or Punishment*, Professional Training Series No. 8/Rev. 2, UN, New York and Geneva, para. 455.

[76] First Report of the Independent International Commission of Inquiry on the Syrian Arab Republic, para. 66.

[77] Ibid., para. 50.

[78] See, e.g., Art. 53(2), 2012 Constitution of the Syrian Arab Republic (unofficial English translation): 'No one may be tortured or treated in a humiliating manner, and the law shall define the punishment for those who do so.'

[79] The practice of torture was also not new in Syria. As the Independent International Commission of Inquiry on the Syrian Arab Republic observed in its first report in November 2011, during the previous four decades, suspected

When use of torture as terror by the government failed to achieve its objective of pacification of the opposition, peaceful protest turned into violent resistance and then inexorably into civil war.[80] A series of non-international armed conflicts erupted over the ensuing twelve months across the country. Ultimately, a plethora of non-State armed groups would be fighting the regime (and sometimes each other) for territorial control over the next five years. The conflicts and the violence created more than five million registered refugees and over six million internally displaced persons (IDPs).[81]

Human Rights Watch has carefully documented the practice of torture in Syria since the beginning of the uprising. In a report issued in 2015, the organization wrote: since the beginning of the uprising in Syria, an untold but very high number had died in detention facilities run by the government's security agencies (*mukhabarat*). In 2012, Human Rights Watch identified and mapped twenty-seven detention centres around the country, many located in Damascus. But while accounts by former detainees and defectors consistently indicated that torture was 'rampant' and that many detainees were dying in the different facilities, the scale of abuse and deaths in detention remained unknown.[82]

In 2014, however, a defector left Syria with tens of thousands of images, many showing the bodies of detainees who died in Syria's detention centres. The defector, code-named 'Caesar', was an official forensic photographer for the Military Police who, under instruction, had personally photographed bodies of dead detainees and helped to archive thousands more similar photographs. Caesar smuggled more than 50,000 images out of Syria on discs and thumb drives until he defected. According to the dates on the files, the photographs were taken between May 2011 and August 2013, the month he left. Caesar entrusted the images to the Syrian National Movement (SNM), an opposition political movement, and in March 2015, the SNM gave 53,275 unique files to Human Rights Watch. The largest category of photographs (28,707 images) are the photographs of people understood to have died in government custody, either in a detention facility or after they had been transferred to a military hospital. The photographs were believed to correspond to at least 6,786 deceased persons. They are only a portion of those who died while in the custody of the Syrian authorities.[83]

In 2014, UN Security Council Resolution 2139 had strongly condemned the arbitrary detention and torture of civilians in Syria.[84] In an interview with *Foreign Affairs* the following January, President Bashar al-Assad responded to allegations that prisoners had been tortured and abused by Syria, saying: 'if there's any unbiased and fair way to verify all those allegations, of course we are ready. That would be in our interest'.[85] Seven years later, the pervasive nature of torture was met with the adoption by the government of a law on 30 March 2022 formally banning the

---

opponents of the government suffered torture, detention, and long prison sentences imposed under vaguely defined crimes relating to political activity. First Report of the Independent International Commission of Inquiry on the Syrian Arab Republic, UN doc. A/HRC/S-17/2/Add.1, 23 November 2011, para. 17. In 2010, the UN Committee against Torture reported widespread, routine torture of prisoners in detention. Committee against Torture, Concluding Observations on the Initial Report of Syria on Its Implementation of the Convention against Torture, UN doc. CAT/C/SYR/CO/1, 25 May 2010, para. 7.

[80] Aljazeera, 'What is the Arab Spring, and how did it start?', 17 December 2020.

[81] K. Robinson and W. Merrow, 'The Arab Spring at Ten Years: What's the Legacy of the Uprisings?', Article, Council on Foreign Relations, 3 December 2020, at: https://bit.ly/455qIMW.

[82] Human Rights Watch, 'If the Dead Could Speak: Mass Deaths and Torture in Syria's Detention Facilities', Report, 16 December 2015, at: https://bit.ly/3QSolpN.

[83] Ibid.

[84] UN Security Council Resolution 2139, adopted on 22 February 2014 by unanimous vote in favour, operative para. 11.

[85] Human Rights Watch, 'If the Dead Could Speak: Mass Deaths and Torture in Syria's Detention Facilities'.

practice from April 2022 onwards.[86] A researcher for Human Rights Watch declared that it was 'not an April Fools' joke', but in 'an announcement that might have appeared as satire', the Syrian State News Agency (SANA) had reported the passage of the law which makes torture a crime subject to a minimum penalty of least three years' imprisonment, and up to the death penalty where the torture results in death or involves rape. The new law also prohibits any authority from ordering the torture of anyone, and states that evidence gathered through torture is invalid.[87]

Security Council Resolution 2139 had reaffirmed that 'terrorism in all its forms and manifestations constitutes one of the most serious threats to international peace and security, and that any acts of terrorism are criminal and unjustifiable, regardless of their motivation, wherever, whenever and by whomsoever committed'.[88] At the time of writing, however, no senior-level State agent had been prosecuted, much less convicted of the practice in Syria. The authorities have claimed that a total of ninety-five individuals had been 'held accountable' for torture or mistreatment of detainees between 2016 and 2020. The figures appear to refer exclusively to police personnel, of whom forty-nine were referred to the courts and forty-six were subject to 'disciplinary measures'.[89] The report does not, however, refer to any publicly available information on the outcome of those court processes, nor to whether the individuals were convicted or acquitted, nor what measures were taken in terms of restitution for survivors of such conduct or their families. Indeed, no sources have reported a situation in which a survivor or surviving family has been compensated or provided other forms of reparation for torture or ill-treatment or for deaths in custody resulting from such treatment.[90]

But universal jurisdiction in other countries offers a route to some measure of individual accountability. The first trial on State torture in Syria began in Germany in April 2020. The defendants were Anwar Raslan[91] and Eyad Al-Gharib, two former officials of President Bashar al-Assad's security apparatus. In February 2021, the Koblenz Higher Regional Court sentenced Mr Al-Gharib to four and half years in prison for having aided and abetted crimes against humanity in at least thirty cases of deprivation of liberty and torture. In January 2022, the conviction of Mr Raslan followed, with a sentence of life imprisonment imposed on the defendant for torture as a crime against humanity.[92] German prosecutors had charged Raslan with having ordered the torture of detainees between late April 2011 and early September 2012 in his capacity as head of the investigations section at the General Intelligence Directorate's al-Khatib detention facility in Damascus, known as 'Branch 251'.[93]

The Independent International Commission of Inquiry on the Syrian Arab Republic was established on 22 August 2011 by the UN Human Rights Council through its Resolution S-17/1. The mandate of the Commission is to investigate all alleged violations of international human rights law since March 2011 in the Syrian Arab Republic and to present public reports on its findings. The Human Rights Council also tasked the Commission with establishing the facts

---

[86] Law No. 16/2022 of 30 March 2022.

[87] S. Kayyali, 'Torture in Syrian Prisons Is Not a Joke: Syria Passes Law Criminalizing Torture', Human Rights Watch, 1 April 2022, at: https://bit.ly/3sczpXa.

[88] UN Security Council Resolution 2139, operative para. 14.

[89] Fourth periodic report of Syria to the Human Rights Committee, UN doc. CCPR/C/SYR/4, 2021, paras. 39–40.

[90] Independent International Commission of Inquiry on the Syrian Arab Republic, '"No End in Sight": Torture and Ill-Treatment in the Syrian Arab Republic 2020–2023', UN doc. A/HRC/53/CRP.5, 10 July 2023, at: https://bit.ly/3Kxo1IH, paras. 81 and 85.

[91] See Trial International, 'ANWAR RASLAN', 17 March 2023 (last modified 30 March 2023), at: https://bit.ly/3OUAcoR.

[92] European Center for Constitutional and Human Rights (ECCHR), 'First criminal trial worldwide on torture in Syria before a German court', accessed 1 August 2023, at: https://bit.ly/3s74GuH.

[93] Human Rights Watch, 'Germany: Conviction for State Torture in Syria', 13 January 2022, at: https://bit.ly/3QB2Nk1.

244 State Responsibility for Terrorism

and circumstances and to support efforts to ensure that all perpetrators of violations, including of crimes against humanity and war crimes, are identified and held accountable.[94]

Its first report had set forth Syria's State responsibility for the perpetration of crimes against humanity, in particular torture. Its report of March 2021 documented government forces' commission of torture and other ill-treatment on a massive scale since 2011:

> At least 20 different horrific methods of torture used by the Government have been extensively documented; they include administering electric shocks, burning body parts, pulling out nails and teeth, mock executions, folding detainees into a car tyre (*dulab*) and crucifying or suspending individuals from one or two limbs for prolonged periods (*shabeh*), often in combination with severe beating with various tools such as sticks or cables. Torture methods were both physical and mental, and had severe long-term consequences for detainees, and frequently led to their death. Inhuman conditions documented across government detention centres often in and of themselves amounted to torture.[95]

The report cited a former prisoner of the government's security forces in Homs as saying: 'They tortured me …, then the interrogator told me "We can kill you here and now, nobody will ever know"'.

The Commission's most recent report at the time of writing was dedicated to documenting the prevalence of torture in Syria. The conference report of July 2023, entitled 'No End in Sight', highlights the continuing widespread and systematic patterns of torture in detention facilities in Syria between 1 January 2020 and 30 April 2023. With respect to the government of Syria, the report focuses on the four main intelligence directorates in whose detention facilities torture and ill-treatment are most often reported: Military Intelligence, Air Force Intelligence, the Political Security and General Intelligence Directorates, and the Police's Criminal Security department.[96]

Torture as terror in Syria shows precious little sign of abating, whatever domestic law might say. Syria has made no reparation to the survivors or the families of the victims of torture as international human rights law[97] and the rules of State responsibility more broadly demand.[98] It has not investigated alleged torture as the law requires.[99]

7.4.3 Russian Terrorism in Ukraine since the 2022 Invasion

Since Russia's invasion of Ukraine on 24 February 2022 – a serious and manifest act of aggression amounting to an ongoing international crime[100] – allegations of terrorism have been made

---

[94] OHCHR, 'Independent International Commission of Inquiry on the Syrian Arab Republic: Mandate', at: https://bit.ly/3sbIFuC.

[95] Report of the Independent International Commission of Inquiry on the Syrian Arab Republic, UN doc. A/HRC/46/55, 11 March 2021, para. 20.

[96] Independent International Commission of Inquiry on the Syrian Arab Republic, 'No End in Sight'.

[97] See, e.g., Art. 14, Convention against Torture and Other Cruel, Inhuman or Degrading Treatment or Punishment; adopted at New York, 10 December 1984; entered into force, 26 June 1987. Syria adhered to the Convention against Torture in 2004.

[98] Basic Principles and Guidelines on the Right to a Remedy and Reparation for Victims of Gross Violations of International Human Rights Law and Serious Violations of International Humanitarian Law; adopted on 15 December 2005 by UN General Assembly Resolution 60/147, at: https://bit.ly/47TuxGU.

[99] As the Istanbul Protocol stipulates: 'The purposes of effective investigation and documentation of torture and ill-treatment include clarification of the facts and establishment and acknowledgement of individual and State responsibility for victims and their families.' *Istanbul Protocol: Manual on the Effective Investigation and Documentation of Torture and Other Cruel, Inhuman or Degrading Treatment or Punishment*, para. 191(a).

[100] See Art. 8 *bis* (1) and (2)(a), Rome Statute of the International Criminal Court; adopted at Rome, 17 July 1998; entered into force, 1 July 2002.

frequently by each party to the international armed conflict against the other.[101] It is unquestionably the case that Russia has launched many terror attacks against Ukrainian cities and towns. The primary purpose of many missile attacks has been to spread terror among the civilian population through direct attacks on the Ukrainian civilian population and civilian objects as well as through indiscriminate attacks on populated areas. In addition, a much smaller number of unlawful attacks have been launched by Ukraine against Russian cities. But not every allegation made by the Ukrainian government (or, for that matter, by international experts and non-governmental organizations) does indeed describe a terror attack as that term is understood in contemporary IHL and international criminal law.

As Chapters 1 and 6 have described,[102] the test for terror attacks *in bello* is clearly set out in conventional and customary IHL as follows: 'Acts or threats of violence the primary purpose of which is to spread terror among the civilian population are prohibited.'[103] This rule ordinarily encompasses a series of attacks whose primary purpose is to terrorize the civilian population,[104] but it would also prohibit an individual attack of great severity, in particular one that involved the use of a weapon of mass destruction or the carpet bombing of a city or town. The rule does not prohibit attacks whose primary purpose is to damage or destroy lawful military objectives, even if civilians are terrorized as a result. To fall within the prohibition, therefore, the attacks must be either directed against civilians or the civilian population as such or must amount to indiscriminate attacks. This demands a dispassionate application of IHL to a set of facts and especially resistance to sweeping statements about the illegality of particular means or methods of warfare.

In this regard, the conclusion of the Independent International Commission of Inquiry on Ukraine that the 'relentless use of explosive weapons with wide area effects in populated areas', which have killed and injured 'scores of civilians and devastated entire neighbourhoods', is not reflective of IHL. Such a blanket assertion is not legally robust because under IHL attacks that cause civilian harm are not per se unlawful. In its first report to the UN General Assembly of October 2022, the Commission of Inquiry stated that 'the type and number of munitions used in the attacks impacted civilians and civilian objects in a wider area, beyond the apparent military objective. They therefore constituted indiscriminate attacks'. It also documented indiscriminate attacks with the use of cluster munitions, 'which affect a large area and are therefore indiscriminate when used in populated areas'.[105] Neither conclusion is, however, grounded in law. While there is some evidence that certain cluster munitions may have indiscriminate effects, a similar holding at trial by the ICTY in the *Martić* case, which concerned the use of cluster munitions against Zagreb in 1995, was duly amended on appeal. What the trial chamber called 'an

---

[101] See, e.g., A. Osborn, 'Russia talks of retaliation after "Ukrainian drone strike" near Moscow army HQ', *Reuters*, 25 July 2023, at: https://bit.ly/3QCmRCJ.

[102] See *supra* §§1.4 and 6.4.

[103] Art. 51(2), 1977 Additional Protocol I; and International Committee of the Red Cross (ICRC), Customary IHL Rule 2: 'Violence Aimed at Spreading Terror among the Civilian Population', at: http://bit.ly/2ONFTT7.

[104] In the case of the siege of Sarajevo, in 2003, the International Criminal Tribunal for the former Yugoslavia (ICTY) convicted General Stanislav Galić, the commander of the Bosnian Serb army around Sarajevo, of terror attacks for having visited 'a protracted campaign of shelling and sniping upon civilian areas of Sarajevo and upon the civilian population thereby inflicting terror and mental suffering upon its civilian population'. The majority at trial were convinced by the evidence that civilians in government-held areas of Sarajevo were 'directly or indiscriminately attacked' from Bosnian Serb-controlled territory, and that, as a result and 'as a minimum, hundreds of civilians were killed and thousands others were injured'. ICTY, *Prosecutor v. Galić*, Judgment (Trial Chamber) (Case No. IT-98-29-T), 5 December 2003, paras. 65, 66, and 591.

[105] Report of the Independent International Commission of Inquiry on Ukraine, UN doc. A/77/533, 18 October 2022, paras. 47 and 48.

indiscriminate weapon' became – more accurately in law – 'use as an indiscriminate weapon' in the holding of the Appeals Chamber.[106]

In its subsequent report to the UN Human Rights Council of March 2023, the Commission of Inquiry on Ukraine continued its analysis of Russian attacks. It stated as follows:

> When objects of military value that might have been the intended targets of the attacks were present in the vicinity of some of the impact sites, the Commission has generally found that Russian armed forces used weapons that struck both military and civilian objects without distinction. It has identified four types of weapons, the use of which in populated areas led to indiscriminate attacks: unguided bombs dropped from aircraft; inaccurate long-range anti-ship missiles of the Kh-22 or Kh-32 types, which have been found to be inaccurate when striking land targets; cluster munitions, which, by design, spread small submunitions over a wide area; and multiple launch rocket systems, which cover a large area with inaccurate rockets.[107]

The first conclusion, that unguided bombs dropped from aircraft amount to indiscriminate attacks, does not depict IHL accurately either. As it stands, the law does not require the use of precision-guided munitions in the conduct of hostilities.[108] The use of gravity ordnance is thus not per se a violation of the law. That said, if a specific attack might otherwise be expected to cause excessive civilian harm, using such 'smart' munitions may be the only lawful means to achieve the military mission without violating IHL.[109]

The Commission's second conclusion, pertaining to 'inaccurate long-range anti-ship missiles of the Kh-22 or Kh-32 types, which have been found to be inaccurate when striking land targets', is also highly questionable, at the least when the assertion is made in such sweeping terms. The Kh-22 Burya ('Storm') was originally a Soviet nuclear-tipped anti-ship missile developed during the Cold War. But subsequently developed were versions with 1,000 kg conventional warheads and intended for a ground attack role, which were the missiles used against Ukraine. While their guidance systems were an upgrade on the original nuclear missiles, they are not reliable for precision strikes.

Russia had reportedly launched more than 210 Kh-22 missiles against Ukrainian targets by January 2023. 'This missile proved to be very inaccurate, especially in [the] urban environment. Missiles were missing their targets by several hundred meters and were often hitting civilian targets.'[110] This failure to hit the target also does not necessarily amount to an indiscriminate attack. After use of five of the missiles against Dnipro in January 2023, a spokesperson for the Ukrainian Air Force, Yuriy Ihnat, told the media: 'This missile with a 950 kg warhead, which is called an "aircraft carrier killer", is designed to destroy aircraft carrier groups at sea. It can be equipped with a nuclear element. And such a missile was used to hit a densely populated city. There is no explanation or justification for this terrorist act'.[111] If it

---

[106] ICTY, *Prosecutor v. Milan Martić*, Judgment (Trial Chamber) (Case No. IT-95-11), 12 June 2007, para. 463; and ICTY, *Prosecutor v. Milan Martić*, Judgment (Appeals Chamber) (Case No. IT-95-11-A), 8 October 2008, para. 247.

[107] Report of the Independent International Commission of Inquiry on Ukraine, UN doc. A/HRC/52/62 (Advance Unedited Version), 15 March 2023, para. 30.

[108] US Department of Defense, *Law of War Manual*, June 2015 (Updated December 2016), §5.2.3.2, citing the military manuals of Australia, Canada and Germany; and see also Y. Dinstein, *The Conduct of Hostilities under the Law of International Armed Conflict*, 3rd ed., Cambridge University Press, Cambridge, 2016, p. 170, para. 454.

[109] Casey-Maslen, *Hague Law Interpreted*, p. 203, citing Dinstein, The Conduct of Hostilities under the Law of International Armed Conflict, p. 167, para. 447; and p. 169, para. 453.

[110] Military Today, 'Kh-22', accessed 13 August 2023, at: https://bit.ly/47sPSqw.

[111] S. Tiwari, 'Russia's Kh-22 Missile "Devastates" Ukraine; Kyiv Admits Helplessness against Carrier-Killer Missiles', *The Eurasian Times*, 17 January 2023, at: https://bit.ly/45pfe6H.

7.4 State Perpetration of Terrorism

is true, as has been alleged, that one of the missiles hit a purely residential area of the city, far from any military objective,[112] this specific attack would likely be indiscriminate and potentially also amount to a terror attack.

The Kh-32 missile is a significantly improved and more capable version of the Kh-22. It was designed to overcome the US air defence systems that emerged in the early 1980s and is equipped with an improved guidance system, making it far more accurate.[113] In November 2022, Ukrainian Pravda stated that Russia was using the longer range missiles to attack 'civilian infrastructure',[114] which if true would certainly be a serious violation of IHL. In June 2022, the UK Ministry of Defence had identified the Kh-32 as 'highly likely' to have been the missile that struck a shopping centre in Kremenchuk on 27 June.[115] The attack,[116] which killed a reported eighteen civilians and injured scores of others, was either indiscriminate[117] or more likely a direct attack on civilians, and may amount to a war crime[118] and a terror attack under customary international criminal law. Given the accuracy of the weapon, the shopping centre and particularly the civilian shoppers would appear to have been the target and not its incidental victims. Yulia Gorbunova, senior Ukraine researcher at Human Rights Watch, said in the aftermath: 'The Russian missile that directly hit an open and busy civilian shopping center on June 27 caused devastating loss of civilian life. The incident should be investigated as a potential war crime, and if the Russian authorities don't, the International Criminal Court and other investigative bodies should.'[119]

The Commission was on much stronger ground in its general assertion that 'multiple launch rocket systems, which cover a large area with inaccurate rockets' are indiscriminate when used in densely populated areas. The issue should have been addressed as such by the ICTY in the *Gotovina* case (including by the prosecution), but instead the Trial Chamber held that based primarily on the testimony of expert Geoffrey Corn, it believed that although multiple-barrelled rocket launchers (MBRLs) 'are generally less accurate than Howitzers or mortars', their use by the Croatian army against of Knin on 4 and 5 August 1995 was 'not inherently indiscriminate'.[120]

The case concerned the use of MBRLs by the Croatian army in their assault on Knin in the context of Operation Storm in May 1995. An *amicus curiae* brief annexed analysis by a former US artillery expert, retired Lieutenant-General Shoffner, noted that the 122 mm forty-tube BM21 MBRL, with a firing range of up to twenty kilometres, was introduced into operational service with the Russian Army in 1963 and was 'widely used throughout the world'. Owing to its 'high volume of fire and large area coverage', he asserted that it is 'well suited for use against troops in the open or for use in artillery preparations'. He cautioned, however, that because the weapons have

[112] Tweet by the journalist Euan MacDonald cited in ibid.

[113] Military Today, 'Kh-22'.

[114] S. Pohorilov, 'Russia confirms using Kh-32 cruise missiles to attack Ukraine's civilian infrastructure', *Pravda*, 2 November 2022, at: https://bit.ly/3OFE6Rc.

[115] Tweet reported and reproduced in T. Kadam, 'Russian Tupolev Bombers Firing New Kh-32 Anti-ship Missiles to Attack Ground Targets in Ukraine – State Media', *The Eurasian Times*, 2 November 2022, at: https://bit.ly/3OWbQep.

[116] L. Tondo and P. Sauer, 'At least 16 dead as Russian missile hits shopping centre in Ukraine', *The Guardian*, 28 June 2022, at: https://bit.ly/444SmbO.

[117] Report of the Independent International Commission of Inquiry on Ukraine, UN doc. A/HRC/52/62 (Advance Unedited Version), 15 March 2023, para. 31.

[118] Art. 8(2)(e)(i), Rome Statute of the International Criminal Court.

[119] Human Rights Watch, 'Ukraine: Russian Missile Kills Civilians in Shopping Center. Investigate Attack in Kremenchuk as Potential War Crime', 30 June 2022, at: https://bit.ly/456eW54.

[120] ICTY, *Prosecutor* v. *Gotovina and others*, Judgment (Trial Chamber) (Case No. IT-06–90-T), 15 April 2011, para. 1897.

a large circular error probable (CEP), 'they are not suited for attacks against point targets'.[121] He estimated the weapon's CEP at 300 metres, with a consequent figure for 3 CEP of 900 metres. This means that almost half of a volley of rockets fired would be expected to land between 300 and 900 metres from their target. This rate of dispersion renders an attack indiscriminate and their widespread use forms the basis for a terror attack under IHL and international criminal law.

7.5 STATE COMPLICITY IN ACTS OF TERRORISM

Aiding or assisting another State to commit an internationally wrongful act is also itself an internationally wrongful act under customary law.[122] This primary rule of State responsibility, as set forth in the ILC Draft Articles, determines that unlawful aid or assistance occurs where the assisting State does so with knowledge of the circumstances of the internationally wrongful act by the assisted State, but only if the act would also be internationally wrongful if committed by the assisting State.[123] Thus, the assisted act must violate international law and the rule that is violated must also be applicable to the assistor.

There are also specific treaty obligations not to assist another State or armed non-State actor to violate international law. Most notably, this principle is at the heart of the UN Arms Trade Treaty, where arms may not be transferred by a State Party to anyone else where they would be used to commit a range of international crimes, nor where there is an overriding risk they would be used to commit or facilitate a serious violation of IHL or international human rights law, or to 'commit or facilitate an act constituting an offence under international conventions or protocols relating to terrorism to which the exporting State is a Party'.[124]

In his commentary on the provision, James Crawford suggested that a third condition exists: that the aid or assistance is given with intent to facilitate the commission of the unlawful act.[125] This miscasts the state of international law and has not been validated subsequently. Thus, in its 2007 judgment in the *Bosnian Genocide* case, the ICJ affirmed that the prohibition of complicity for genocide required knowledge and not intent: 'there cannot be a finding of complicity against a State unless at the least its organs were aware that genocide was about to be committed or was under way. ... In other words, an accomplice must have given support in perpetrating the genocide with full knowledge of the facts'.[126] The Arms Trade Treaty similarly stipulates that a State Party 'shall not authorize any transfer of conventional arms ... *if it has knowledge at the time of authorization* that the arms or items would be used in the commission of genocide, crimes against humanity, grave breaches of the Geneva Conventions of 1949, attacks directed against civilian objects or civilians protected as such, or other war crimes as defined by international agreements to which it is a Party'.[127]

---

[121] Comments by Lt.-Gen. (ret.) Wilson A. Shoffner on The Report by Major General Robert H Scales on Croatian Army ('HV') Use of Artillery and Rockets on Targets Based in Knin, Croatia, August 4–5, 1995, p. 3, in ICTY, *Prosecutor* v. *Gotovina* (Appeals Chamber) (Case No. IT-06–90-A), Application and Proposed Amicus Curiae Brief Concerning the 15 April 2011 Trial Chamber Judgment and Requesting that the Appeals Chamber Reconsider the Findings of Unlawful Artillery Attacks during Operation Storm.

[122] International Court of Justice (ICJ), *Case Concerning the Application of the Convention on the Prevention and Punishment of the Crime of Genocide (Bosnia and Herzegovina v. Serbia and Montenegro)*, Judgment, 26 February 2007, para. 419.

[123] Art. 16, ILC Draft Articles on State Responsibility.

[124] Arts. 6(3), 7(1)(i), (ii), and (iii), and 7(3), Arms Trade Treaty; adopted at New York 2 April 2013; entered into force 24 December 2014. As of 1 January 2024, 113 States were party to the Arms Trade Treaty.

[125] Commentary, para. 3, on Art. 16, ILC Draft Articles on State Responsibility.

[126] Ibid., para. 432.

[127] Art. 6(3), Arms Trade Treaty [added emphasis].

7.5 State Complicity in Acts of Terrorism

If it is unlawful to aid or assist another State to violate international law, a fortiori it must be unlawful to assist a non-State armed group to do so through a terror attack. Thus, States have agreed it is a principle of international law that:

> Every State has the duty to refrain from organizing, instigating, assisting or participating in acts of civil strife or terrorist acts in another State or acquiescing in organized activities within its territory directed towards the commission of such acts, when the acts referred to in the present paragraph involve a threat or use of force.[128]

Despite criticism of the distinction,[129] in its judgment on the merits in the *Nicaragua* case, the ICJ held that providing training or arms to a non-State armed group operating unlawfully on the territory of another State and which was 'participating in acts of civil strife' amounted to a threat or use of force by the assisting State, whereas the funding of such a group only breached the customary rule of non-intervention.[130] Thus, even where terrorist conduct is not attributable to a State (such as when the State does not direct or have effective control over the salient act of terrorism by a non-State actor) a State's 'support for such conduct may nevertheless amount to a prohibited use of force if the support is military in nature'.[131]

7.5.1 Liberia's State Responsibility for Acts of Terror in Sierra Leone

Charles Taylor's support for the RUF and the paramilitary Armed Forces Revolutionary Council (AFRC) in Sierra Leone was both material and significant to their campaigns of terror. He was found to have supplied arms and ammunition to the RUF in knowledge of the crimes the armed non-State group was committing in neighbouring Sierra Leone. Mr Taylor was also accused before the Special Court for Sierra Leone of having provided 'invaluable instruction, direction and guidance to the leaders of the AFRC/RUF alliance' which was 'often crucial to the continued survival of the alliance as a viable entity with the ability to continue carrying out the campaign of terror against the civilian population of Sierra Leone'.[132]

Charles Taylor's conviction at the Special Court for Sierra Leone made him the first former Head of State to be convicted of international crimes by an international criminal court since Admiral Karl Doenitz was convicted of war crimes and the crime of aggression by the International Military Tribunal at Nuremburg.[133] The Special Court for Sierra Leone made its final major decision on 26 September 2013 when its Appeals Chamber upheld the fifty-year sentence imposed upon Mr Taylor.[134] But while Charles Taylor is personally paying a price for his crimes by virtue of his fifty-year prison sentence, the question remains as to the responsibility under international law of Liberia *qua* State for his acts as president.

---

[128] Principle 1, para. 9, Declaration on Principles of International Law Concerning Friendly Relations and Co-operation among States in Accordance with the Charter of the United Nations, annexed to and approved by UN General Assembly Resolution 2625 (XXV), adopted without a vote on 24 October 1970, para. 1.

[129] See, e.g., Trapp, *State Responsibility for International Terrorism*, §2.1.2.

[130] ICJ, *Military and Paramilitary Activities in and against Nicaragua (Nicaragua v. United States)*, Judgment (Merits), 27 June 1986, para. 228.

[131] Trapp, 'Terrorism and the international law of state responsibility', p. 33.

[132] SCSL, *Prosecutor* v. *Charles Ghankay Taylor*, Judgment (Trial Chamber) (Case No SCSL-03–01-T), 18 May 2012, para. 46.

[133] Slobodan Milosevic, the former president of the Federal Republic of Yugoslavia, had been indicted by the ICTY, but he died before the case was concluded and judgment was issued. The President of Côte d'Ivoire, Laurent Gbagbo, was prosecuted before the International Criminal Court but acquitted at trial on 15 January 2019, a decision confirmed on 31 March 2021 by the Appeals Chamber (again by majority decision).

[134] L. Gberie, 'The Special Court for Sierra Leone rests – for good', *Africa Renewal*, April 2014, at: https://bit.ly/45uFxbY.

250 *State Responsibility for Terrorism*

The Statute of the Special Court allowed the Trial Chamber, in addition to the imposition of a term of imprisonment, to 'order the forfeiture of the property, proceeds and any assets acquired unlawfully or by criminal conduct, and their return to their rightful owner or to the State of Sierra Leone'.[135] It did not, however, have the power to order reparations to be made by a convicted person for the crimes they had committed as does the Rome Statute of the International Criminal Court.[136] Liberia has not formally accepted its responsibility for crimes committed with its aid and assistance in Sierra Leone. Instead, attention was being paid to putting on trial individuals responsible for crimes within Liberia during the civil war in that country.[137]

7.5.2 *Syria's Role in the Assassination of Rafik Hariri*

There remain serious questions as to the role played by Syria in the death of former prime minister of Lebanon, Rafik Hariri, in Beirut in 2005. The Special Tribunal for Lebanon was created by the UN Security Council in 2007 in relation to the bombing: 'the first tribunal of international character to prosecute terrorist crimes'.[138] The Statute of the Tribunal declared the killing to be a terrorist crime.[139] The indictment of suspects for the offence of terrorism concerned a violation of Lebanese domestic law.[140] In its trial verdict issued on 28 August 2020, Salim Jamil Ayyash, a Lebanese citizen born on 10 November 1963 and a member of Hezbollah, was found guilty by the Special Tribunal on all counts. The judges in the Trial Chamber stated that there was 'no evidence' that Hezbollah's leadership had any involvement in Mr Hariri's murder but only that there was 'no *direct* evidence of Syrian involvement in it'.[141]

In the verdict, the Tribunal suggested that the assassination was politically motivated as it was perpetrated after discussions to end the Syrian army presence in Lebanon.[142] On 1 February 2005, Syrian Deputy Minister of Foreign Affairs, Walid al-Muallem, had met with Prime Minister Hariri, who told him that 'Lebanon will not be ruled by Syria forever', as it was 'unacceptable' that he could 'bear no more orders'.[143] On 2 February 2005, the third 'Bristol Group' meeting occurred at the Bristol Hotel in Beirut in which the participants (who included allies of the prime minister) agreed there should be an immediate and total withdrawal of Syrian forces from Lebanese territory.[144] The assassination took place twelve days later.

In mid December 2005, the chief UN investigator into the assassination, Detlev Mehlis, a former German state prosecutor, declared for the first time his belief that the Syrian authorities were behind the killing. 'The Syrian authorities are responsible', he said in comments published

---

[135] Art. 19(3), Statute of the Special Court for Sierra Leone.
[136] Art. 75, Rome Statute of the International Criminal Court.
[137] Human Rights Watch, 'Q&A: Justice for Civil Wars-Era Crimes in Liberia', 1 April 2019, at: https://bit.ly/3QBm6tx.
[138] STL homepage, at: https://www.stl-tsl.org/en.
[139] Chapeau to the 2007 Statute of the Special Tribunal for Lebanon, annexed to UN Security Council Resolution 1757. See on the issue of assassination of Mr Hariri as terrorism B. Saul, 'Definition of "Terrorism" in the UN Security Council', *Chinese Journal of International Law*, Vol. 4, No. 1 (2005), 141–66, *esp.* at pp. 145–46.
[140] Art. 314, Criminal Code of Lebanon.
[141] STL, *Prosecutor v. Salim Jamil Ayyash and others*, Judgment (Trial Chamber) (Case No. STL-11–01/T/TC), 18 August 2020, para. 787 [added emphasis].
[142] Jusoor for Studies, 'The effects of the Rafik Hariri Assassination Verdict on the Syrian regime and its Allies', In Focus, 26 August 2020, at: https://bit.ly/47KuTjh.
[143] STL, *Prosecutor v. Salim Jamil Ayyash and others*, Judgment, para. 6498.
[144] Ibid., para. 678.

in the *Al-Sharq al-Awsat* newspaper.[145] Mr Mehlis' report to the UN Security Council in October was more nuanced, delineating only 'converging evidence' of Syrian involvement.[146] After reviewing Mr Mehlis' report, the UN Security Council in its Resolution 1636 took note of the finding that it 'would be difficult to envisage a scenario' in which 'such a complex assassination plot' could have been perpetrated without the knowledge of the Syrian authorities, and that there was 'probable cause to believe' that the decision to assassinate Mr Hariri 'could not have been taken without the approval of top-ranked Syrian security officials'.[147] The Council further determined that 'Syria's continued lack of cooperation to the inquiry would constitute a serious violation of its obligations under relevant [Security Council] resolutions'.[148] By then, four Lebanese generals had been arrested on suspicion of murder; they would be detained by Lebanese authorities for four years.[149]

In late December 2005, Syria's former vice president, Abdul Halim Khaddam, said that Syrian President Bashar al-Assad had threatened Mr Hariri months before his death. Mr Mehlis also said several sources had reported being told by Mr Hariri that Mr Assad had threatened 'to break Lebanon over [his] head' if he did not support the extension of Lebanese President Emil Lahoud's term in office.[150] Mr Hariri's own son, Saad, made, but then in 2010, following several visits to Damascus, withdrew, allegations that the Syrian regime was responsible for his father's killing.[151]

7.6 THE LABELLING OF POLITICAL OPPOSITION AS TERRORIST

In especially repressive regimes, the label terrorist is frequently applied to political opposition with a view to encouraging or justifying internal repression. Such action may violate the duty to prevent terrorism, the prohibition on the perpetration of terrorism, and amount to encouraging acts of terrorism by ostensibly non-State actors. At the time of writing, these violations were occurring notably in Myanmar. On 9 June 2021, Myanmar's military rulers branded a national unity government formed by members of parliament (MPs) forced to flee in the wake of the military coup a terrorist group, blaming it for bombings, arson, and killings as part of a propaganda campaign in State-controlled media. Myanmar's army overthrew the elected government on 1 February 2021 and detained elected leader Aung San Suu Kyi, sparking months of protests during which hundreds of people have been killed by the security forces. In response, local militias have been formed to confront the army while anti-junta protests have continued across the country with strikes paralyzing the economy.[152]

---

[145] CBC (Canada), 'UN investigator says Syrians responsible for Hariri assassination', 17 December 2005, at: https://bit.ly/459kLyz.

[146] UN, 'Head Investigator into Killing of Former Lebanese Prime Minister Rafik Hariri Briefs Security Council, Describes "Converging Evidence" of Syrian Involvement', Press release SC/8535, 25 October 2005, at: https://bit.ly/3KIb029.

[147] UN Security Council Resolution 1636, adopted on 31 October 2005 by unanimous vote in favour, sixteenth preambular para. and operative para. 2.

[148] Ibid., operative para. 5.

[149] E. MacAskill, R. McCarthy, and B. Whitaker, 'Middle East tension rises as UN prepares to accuse Syria of Hariri assassination', *The Guardian*, 23 September 2005, at: https://bit.ly/3OZmUaI.

[150] BBC, 'Hariri "threatened by Syria head"', 30 December 2005, at: https://bit.ly/3DUEjuv.

[151] Agence France-Presse, 'Hariri retracts accusations against Syria in ex-premier's death', *France24*, 6 September 2010, at: https://bit.ly/45q7Qbi. Lebanon's Prime Minister Saad Hariri said that it was 'a mistake' to accuse Syria of involvement in the 2005 murder of his father, and declaring that his statements at the time were politically motivated.

[152] 'Myanmar junta labels opposition government of ousted MPs a "terrorist" group', *The Guardian*, 9 May 2021, at: https://bit.ly/3g1GcsY.

State television MRTV announced that a committee of ousted lawmakers known as the CRPH (Committee Representing Pyidaungsu Hluttaw) would be covered by Myanmar's counterterrorism law, saying: 'Their acts caused so much terrorism in many places.' The counterterrorism law, drafted in 2013[153] and enacted on 4 June 2014,[154] bans not only membership of the groups but also any contact with them. The junta had previously accused its opponents of treason.[155]

One of the victims of the repression was Zaw Myat Lynn, a teacher and activist with the National League for Democracy, the party of deposed leader, Aung San Suu Kyi. Zaw had been at the forefront of local anti-coup protests, sharing graphic videos online of soldiers beating and shooting peaceful demonstrators. In Facebook posts, he termed the Tatmadaw 'terrorists' and 'dogs', stating that 'people should fight the army even if it costs our lives'. He was detained by soldiers on 8 March 2021. The following day, his wife was contacted and told to come to a military hospital in Mingarlardon township, in north Yangon, to identify his body. The official post-mortem report she was given claimed that Zaw had fallen nine metres onto a sharp metal fence while trying to escape from custody. His injuries included a stab wound to the abdomen seemingly made by a cross-sectional knife. The wound, which may have been the cause of death, appears to have been inflicted while he was still alive. Severe bruising could be seen on the sides of his body.[156]

By late April 2021, more than 4,400 people had been detained by Myanmar's security forces since the coup. One nineteen-year-old who was detained by the military in a compound was repeatedly beaten by the guards, who used cables, the butts of guns, and glass bottles. He said: 'They beat me with a cable wire, they used a big cable wire and they braid it with two cable wires to make it bigger. They forced us to be on our knees, with our backs straight, and punched and kicked us. When we fell on the ground, they hit us with the cable wire. It hurt so much. I even told them to kill me instead of torturing me it was that painful.' Three weeks after his ordeal, the youth remained in hiding. His wounds were healing, he said, but he still has difficulty walking and cannot properly fasten his buttons. Zaw Win of human rights group, Fortify Rights, said: 'People arrested by the security forces are more likely to be subjected to torture or ill treatment in detention. ... The military tactics of arrest and ill treatment are creating an environment of terror and anxiety among the public. Yet, protesters are still going to the streets to call for an end to military rule.'[157]

In June 2023, in its latest report (at the time of writing), the Independent Investigative Mechanism for Myanmar established by the Human Rights Council declared it had eyewitness accounts of mass executions of civilians or fighters *hors de combat* in the custody of the Myanmar military forces 'or their affiliates'.[158] The Mechanism had also 'collected more and more evidence concerning torture, sexual violence, and other forms of severe mistreatment at numerous detention facilities'. Some of these facilities were being run by the military; others by the police or the Myanmar Prisons Department.[159]

[153] Radio Free Asia, 'Myanmar Drafts New Anti-terror Law', 21 October 2013, at: https://bit.ly/3pmlvfW.
[154] Measures to eliminate international terrorism, Report of the Secretary-General, UN doc. A/75/176, 17 July 2020, para. 70.
[155] 'Myanmar junta labels opposition government of ousted MPs a "terrorist" group', *The Guardian*, 9 May 2021.
[156] L. Harding, 'Outrage in Myanmar after activist allegedly tortured to death', *The Guardian*, 15 March 2021, at: https://bit.ly/34LQdWb.
[157] H. Regan, S. Sidhu, and C. Ward, '"I thought I would die". Myanmar protesters describe torture they suffered in detention', *CNN*, 28 April 2021, at: https://cnn.it/3gcrf7y.
[158] Report of the Independent Investigative Mechanism for Myanmar, UN doc. A/HRC/54/19, 30 June 2023, para. 28.
[159] Ibid., para. 32.

7.6 The Labelling of Political Opposition as Terrorist

The Mechanism's latest report followed a press release by several UN Special Rapporteurs in March 2023 accusing the military junta of orchestrating an online campaign of terror and weaponizing social media platforms to crush democratic opposition. 'Online rhetoric has spilled into real world terror, with military supporters using social media to harass and incite violence against pro-democracy activists and human rights defenders', the experts said.[160] They noted that women are often targets of 'doxxing': the act of publishing private information, including names and addresses, about individuals without their consent. These attacks are frequently accompanied by calls for violence or arrest by junta forces. Doxxed women have also been accused of having sexual relations with Muslim men or supporting the Muslim population – a common ultranationalist, discriminatory, and Islamophobic narrative in Myanmar. 'Failing to cement its grip on power by locking up political prisoners and gunning down peaceful protesters, the junta has escalated its ruthless suppression of dissent to virtual spaces', the experts said. They explained that the junta was terrified of women's power to mobilize resistance to military rule in online spaces.

---

[160] 'Myanmar: Social media companies must stand up to junta's online terror campaign, say UN experts', Press release, OHCHR, Geneva, 13 March 2023, at: https://bit.ly/3OpstO5.

8

The Outlook for International Counterterrorism Law

It is known that in contemporary international law there is no autonomous concept of terrorism and, if the internal law of different States shows the existence of regulations on this, comparative study shows that the meaning differs. If we have not at the international level defined the basic concept of terrorism, how is it possible to describe unlawful actions or sets of actions as a type of terrorism the illegality of which is a consequence of internationally established laws and principles, and not a consequence of innovative concepts which have no internationally accepted legal basis?

These words were spoken as part of a declaration before the UN General Assembly in 1984 by Honduras.[1] While a portion of its affirmation remains true today – as the review in Chapter 3 of the widely diverging practice across 197 States demonstrated – in other respects it is an overly pessimistic assessment of contemporary law. True, the UN Comprehensive Convention against International Terrorism[2] has remained an unconcluded draft for the past two decades and more, and prospects for its adoption in the near future are poor. There is no customary definition of international terrorism in peacetime either, much less an international crime under customary international law. But the absence of these two important elements does not detract from an important corpus of international law we can now call international counterterrorism law.

Outside the context of armed conflict, sectoral treaties govern international terrorism involving a range of tactics and targets, notably hostage-taking, bombings, hijackings, and nuclear terrorism, as well as attacks on foreign diplomats and, under a treaty-approaching universality, the financing of international terrorism. The distinction with terrorism in a situation of armed conflict in these treaties should, however, have been drawn far more sharply. This would have enhanced clarity and coherence while reducing the unwelcome fragmentation of international law. It defies logic, for instance, that a Ukrainian civilian who forcibly resists Russian aggression by targeting a Russian soldier in the ongoing armed conflict should be designated by international law an international terrorist. The same is true of anyone else targeting the military forces of an illegal occupier or colonizer. That does not make their actions immune from prosecution, but it should not attract under colour of law the epithet of terrorist.

Domestic terrorism is often defined too broadly in national law but is restrained by the dictates of international human rights law (albeit far more in legal theory than in practice). Terrorist intent – to cause fear in the civilian population or a segment of it or to seek unduly to coerce conduct by a State or international organization – should always be an integral component of any terrorism offence in domestic or international law, as Resolution 1566 indicates. In their

---

[1]   Statement of Honduras as recorded in the report on discussions on 17 December 1984 in Summary Records of UN General Assembly Plenary Meetings, UN doc. A/39/PV.I02, New York, 1984, p. 1905, para. 73.

[2]   Draft comprehensive convention against international terrorism (Consolidated text prepared by the coordinator for discussion), Appendix II to Letter dated 3 August 2005 from the Chairman of the Sixth Committee addressed to the President of the General Assembly, UN doc. A/59/894, 12 August 2005.

254

national criminal law, some States do exempt the exercise of certain fundamental human rights, notably the right to strike and to freedom of peaceful assembly, from consideration as acts of terrorism, as human rights law demands. But they are still far too few in number. Thus, Saul's assertion that exempted from terrorism on the basis of State practice is 'advocacy, protest, dissent or industrial action which is not intended to cause death, serious bodily, or serious risk to public health or safety' is welcome but not persuasive.[3]

Acts with direct nexus to armed conflicts are directly regulated by international humanitarian law (IHL). Despite regrettable fragmentation owing to overlap from the peacetime sectoral treaties, the definitions of terrorism in armed conflict are clear. As Gasser observed, within the scope of IHL, 'terrorism and terrorist acts are prohibited under all circumstances, unconditionally and without exception'.[4] Thus, prohibited *in bello* are unlawful acts or threats aiming to, or which do in fact, terrorize detainees under the Geneva Law branch of IHL; and in the conduct of hostilities (Hague Law), acts of threats of violence whose primary purpose is to spread terror among the civilian population. When perpetrated with the requisite specific intent (*dolus specialis*), these violations of IHL are war crimes.

But otherwise, consensus on the definitional issue eludes the international community. In 2004, the UN Security Council adopted Resolution 1566, in which it

> [r]*ecalls* that criminal acts, including against civilians, committed with the intent to cause death or serious bodily injury, or taking of hostages, with the purpose to provoke a state of terror in the general public or in a group of persons or particular persons, intimidate a population or compel a government or an international organization to do or to abstain from doing any act, which constitute offences within the scope of and as defined in the international conventions and protocols relating to terrorism, are under no circumstances justifiable by considerations of a political, philosophical, ideological, racial, ethnic, religious or other similar nature, and calls upon all States to prevent such acts and, if not prevented, to ensure that such acts are punished by penalties consistent with their grave nature.[5]

Saul approves of the general thrust of this element of the resolution, which makes specific intent an integral part of terrorism, but regrets that the targeting of buildings and infrastructure is omitted from the actus reus. 'More pressingly', he argues, the definition is too narrow because it confines terrorism to the scope of the existing convention offences. 'While these cover some common terrorist methods (particularly hostage taking and bombings), they were developed reactively and do not cover all forms of terrorism – or even the most common, such as attacks by small arms. Many are also limited to transnational not domestic terrorism, yet the Council also requires action on the latter.'[6]

Two months after the passage of Security Council Resolution 1566, the High-Level Panel on Threats, Challenges and Change reported back to the UN Secretary-General on the results of their work. In turn, Kofi Annan transmitted the report to the UN General Assembly. The Panel called for rapid completion of the negotiations on a comprehensive convention on terrorism and proposed that 'terrorism' be defined as follows:

> Any action, in addition to actions already specified by the existing conventions on aspects of terrorism, the Geneva Conventions and Security Council resolution 1566 (2004), that is

---

[3] Saul, Defining Terrorism in International Law, p. 66.

[4] H. Gasser, 'Prohibition of Terrorist Acts in International Humanitarian Law', *International Review of the Red Cross*, No. 253 (1986), 200–12, at: https://bit.ly/3R3M4WR, at p. 212.

[5] UN Security Council Resolution 1566, adopted on 8 October 2004 by unanimous vote in favour, operative para. 3.

[6] Saul, 'The Legal Black Hole in United Nations Counterterrorism'.

intended to cause death or serious bodily harm to civilians or non-combatants, when the purpose of such an act, by its nature or context, is to intimidate a population, or to compel a Government or an international organization to do or to abstain from doing any act.[7]

The High-Level Panel rejected the argument that any definition of terrorism should include States' use of armed forces against civilians on the basis that 'the legal and normative framework against State violations is far stronger than in the case of non-State actors'.[8] The members did, though, acknowledge that attacks that specifically target 'innocent civilians and non-combatants' must be 'condemned clearly and unequivocally by all'.[9] The terror effected by the United States in torturing detainees in the early years of the 'Global War on Terror' was only weakly and obliquely referred to in the Panel's report.[10] Surprisingly, little heed was also paid to the concerns of those promoting the *jus cogens* right of peoples to self-determination.[11]

As a consequence, the proposal of the Panel for a 'consensus' definition foundered on its lack of original thinking, offering little more than a composite of existing definitions and without a constructive solution to the ideological impasse that persists to this day. What is more, since the Panel's deliberations, which concluded in November 2004, new terrorism threats have emerged. Cyberterrorism was not even mentioned by the Panel, nor were armed drones, much less fully autonomous weapons, whose potential use as a terror weapon in counterterrorism operations outside armed conflict is significant. The current UN Secretary-General's call for a negotiated prohibition on fully autonomous weapons by 2026[12] is likely to fall on many deaf ears among the major military powers.

Just as there is no universally agreed definition of terrorism (at least in peacetime), so too the notion of counterterrorism may be disputed. Nonetheless, already in 2006 the UN General Assembly adopted the Global Counterterrorism Strategy for the global organization and its Member States in the form of a resolution[13] and an annexed Plan of Action.[14] The Strategy is composed of four pillars, namely:

– Addressing the conditions conducive to the spread of terrorism
– Measures to prevent and combat terrorism
– Measures to build States' capacity to prevent and combat terrorism and to strengthen the role of the UN system in that regard
– Measures to ensure respect for human rights for all and the rule of law as the fundamental basis for the fight against terrorism.[15]

---

[7] 'A more secure world: Our shared responsibility: Report of the High-level Panel on Threats, Challenges and Change', UN doc. A/59/565, 2 December 2004, para. 164(d).

[8] Ibid., para. 160.

[9] Ibid., para. 161.

[10] Ibid., para. 147.

[11] In this regard, Saul argues: 'Unless a pacifist position is accepted, any international definition of terrorism must ensure that legitimate forms of violent resistance to political oppression are not internationally criminalized.' Saul, Defining Terrorism in International Law, Oxford University Press, Oxford, 2006, p. 317.

[12] UN Secretary-General, 'Our Common Agenda: A New Agenda for Peace', Policy Brief 9, July 2023, at: https://bit.ly/47RevgX, p. 27.

[13] UN General Assembly Resolution 60/288, adopted without a vote on 20 September 2006.

[14] As Cockayne observes, the motivation for some of the Member States to elaborate a global strategy was a perceived 'overreach' on counterterrorism by the Security Council as well as the desire to counterbalance the more 'robust' enforcement approach favoured by the Council. J. Cockayne, 'Challenges in United Nations Counter-Terrorism Coordination', pp. 602, 603. For a thoughtful discussion of the problems with the Strategy, see, e.g., N. Quénivet, 'You Are the Weakest Link and We Will Help You!', 371–97.

[15] UN, 'UN Global Counter-Terrorism Strategy', accessed on 1 February 2022, at: https://bit.ly/3uq8K8l.

The Outlook for International Counterterrorism Law

In June 2023, the General Assembly adopted its eighth review of the Strategy. In the preamble to the relevant resolution, UN Member States reaffirmed

> that the acts, methods and practices of terrorism in all its forms and manifestations are activities aimed at the denial of human rights, fundamental freedoms and democracy, at threatening the sovereignty, territorial integrity and the security of States, at impeding the enjoyment of political, civil, economic, social and cultural rights, including the right to life, liberty and security, and at destabilizing Governments.[16]

The resolution reiterated the General Assembly's 'strong and unequivocal condemnation of terrorism in all its forms and manifestations, committed by whomever, wherever and for whatever purposes', despite their inability to agree upon a definition. Member States called on the international community once again to 'enhance cooperation to prevent and combat terrorism in a decisive, unified, coordinated, inclusive, transparent and human rights-based, gender-responsive manner, addressing the conditions conducive to terrorism'.[17] Aside from the contorted language, the plethora of aims and recommendations made in the 123 operative paragraphs of the resolution are hugely ambitious and many are far from commanding general agreement, let alone consensus.

One call is for Member States to ensure that any measures taken or means employed to counter terrorism, including the use of remotely piloted aircraft (i.e., armed drones), 'comply with their obligations under international law'.[18] Another, and despite widespread contrary practice, is the reiteration that arbitrary deprivation of liberty can never be justified by invoking security or counterterrorism purposes.[19] The resolution expressed concern over the potential use of new and emerging technologies for terrorist purposes and exhorts all Member States to consider 'additional measures' to counter the use of artificial intelligence and 3D printing for terrorist purposes.[20] The resolution further called on States to ensure that their surveillance and interception of communications and their collection of personal data comply with the right to privacy,[21] while also expressing concern at the 'increasing and rapidly evolving use' by terrorists of the internet and other media to 'commit, incite, recruit for, fund or plan terrorist acts'.[22]

As one might expect from a body of 193 States, the resolution is more of a menu than a strategic review (as indeed largely is the Strategy itself). Furthermore, the discussions in the General Assembly in 2023 were at times heated,[23] belying the notion of a 'unified' and 'coordinated' counterterrorism response. Indeed, in the aftermath of the resolution, India slammed the co-facilitators of the review, affirming that they 'not only disregarded the strong support and trust offered' by its delegation, but also asserting that the Canadian and Tunisian diplomats acted in a 'non-transparent, non-consultative and partial manner'.[24]

In assessing the review and its outcome, Kessels and Lefas suggested that the resulting document is 'largely a technical roll-over with minimal changes, raising questions about

---

[16] UN General Assembly Resolution 77/298, adopted without a vote on 22 June 2023, eighth preambular para.
[17] Ibid.
[18] Ibid., operative para. 112.
[19] Ibid., operative para. 108.
[20] Ibid., operative para. 41.
[21] Ibid., operative para. 111.
[22] Ibid., operative para. 40.
[23] E. Kessels and M. Lefas, 'The Cost of Consensus in the Eighth Review of the UN Global Counter-Terrorism Strategy', Blog post, Just Security, 17 July 2023, at: https://bit.ly/3swxEUZ.
[24] Statement by Ambassador Ruchira Kamboj, Permanent Representative of India to the UN, General Debate: Adoption of Review Resolution of the Global Counter Terrorism Strategy (GCTS), UN General Assembly, 23 June 2023, at: https://bit.ly/3YZ8Dht, para. 7.

whether international consensus on the counterterrorism agenda has reached its limits'.[25] In their article entitled 'The Cost of Consensus', they argue that this approach has 'prevented the kind of structural change needed to promote and protect human rights and the rule of law, meaningfully engage with diverse civil societies, and mainstream gender across UN counter-terrorism efforts'.[26] In sum, the counterterrorism agenda is still fraught, just as it was more than fifty years ago when efforts to devise a definition and a comprehensive prohibition by treaty were being devised in the United Nations. International counterterrorism law, if applied coherently, dispassionately, and humanely, offers meaningful progress towards the elimination of the politically motivated but ideologically bereft murder and torture of civilians and intentional destruction of civilian infrastructure. 'Set against the vain hope of pounding terrorists into oblivion through war, the criminal law offers the promise of restraint', in Saul's wise words.[27] But to recite the proverb, the road to hell is paved with good intentions. And, as the writer Mohsin Hamid cautions, '[w]hen terrorism strikes, divisive anger is a natural response'.[28]

---

[25] Kessels and Lefas, 'The Cost of Consensus in the Eighth Review of the UN Global Counter-Terrorism Strategy'.
[26] Ibid.
[27] Saul, *Defining Terrorism in International Law*, p. 316.
[28] M. Hamid, 'Bound by sorrows', *The Guardian*, 29 November 2008, at: https://bit.ly/3qUznmE.

Index

9/11 attacks, 3, 6, 14, 16–17, 59, 184, 214, 223–25, *see also* al-Qaeda

Abdeslam, Salah, 174, 175, 176

Achille Lauro *hijacking*, 38

Additional Protocol I to the Geneva Conventions (1977), 47, 222

Additional Protocol II to the Geneva Conventions (1977), 48, 72, 216, 217, 218

Afghanistan, 80, 85, 88, 91, 94, 95, 103, 104, 106, 116, 118, 124, 130, 132

African Charter on Human and Peoples' Rights (1981), 81

African Union, 63–64, 170

   Mission to Somalia (AMISOM), 166, 170

   Peace and Security Council, 64

Aggression, 75, 229–30

Aircraft hijacking, 89–90, *see also* Hague Aircraft Hijacking Convention (1970)

Air India Flight 182, bombing of, 135–36

al-Assad, Bashar, 226, 242, 251

al-Baghdadi, Abu Bakr, 17

Al-Marimi, Abu Agila Mohammad Mas'ud Kheir (Mas'ud), 181

al-Megrahi, Abdelbaset, 178–81

al-Nashiri, Abd al-Rahim, 203

al-Nusrah Front, 149

al-Qaeda, 1, 14, 16, 17, 75, 165–66, 168, 191

al-Shabaab, 166–67, 170–71

al-Zarqawi, Abu Musab, 17

Albania, 84, 86, 88, 91, 96, 102, 104, 109, 110, 125, 130, 131

Algeria, 80, 94, 96, 109, 110, 119, 130, 131, 160–64

   Algerian Human Rights Defence League, 164

Algiers Convention (1999), 63

   Protocol (2005), 64, 73–74

Ambos, Kai, 208

Amini, Mahsa, 155

Ammunition, 95–96

Amnesty International, 154, 160, 163, 200

Andorra, 94 n237, 95, 100, 103, 109, 127, 131, 127, 131

Angola, 82, 83, 84, 86, 100, 106, 109, 115, 118, 128, 131

Annan, Kofi, 229

Antigua and Barbuda, 92, 94, 104, 114, 128, 130

Apartheid, 99

Arab Convention on the Suppression of Terrorism (1998), 64–65

Arab League, 64–65

Argentina, 116, 117

Armed conflict, 22, 28, 46–50, 58, 71–73

   International, 25, 26, 46–47

     Geographical jurisdiction, 25

   Jurisdictional issues in national legislation, 110–12

   Non-international, 47–48

   Provoking (as terrorism), 107–08

Armed Forces Revolutionary Council (AFRC), 217, 218

Armenia, 89, 101, 107, 125

Arms, 95–96

Arms Trade Treaty (2013), 248

Arson, 89, 141

Ashcroft, John, 184

ASEAN Convention on Counter Terrorism (2007), 65

Australia, 91, 92, 101, 104, 114, 118, 125, 131, 150–52

Austria, 27, 84, 86, 93, 97, 102, 108, 120, 126

Ayari, Sofien, 175

Ayyash, Salim Jamil, 159, 230, 250

Azerbaijan, 89, 91, 102, 118, 120, 125

Aznar, José, 190

Bahamas, The, 83, 84, 87, 88, 93, 113, 117, 130, 131

Bahrain, 83, 84, 98, 104, 106, 107, 120

Bangladesh, 81, 86, 91, 102, 106, 110, 124, 130

Barbados, 83, 85, 101, 114, 117, 125, 130

Barrel bombs, 226

Barthou, Jean Louis, 3

Belarus, 89, 97, 102, 107, 120, 124

Belgium, 84, 86, 90, 93, 102, 125, 172, 173–75

Belize, 83, 91, 92, 101, 104, 117, 125

Benin, 93, 116, 126, 130

Beslan School Siege, 235–37

Bhutan, 80, 106, 107, 117

Biden, Joe, 255

bin Laden, Osama, 166 n453

Biological weapons, 87–88

Black September, 16

Blumenau, Bernhard, 55

Bolivia, 96, 102, 103

Bolsonaro, Jair, 133

Boko Haram, 168, 170

Bosnia and Herzegovina, 14, 86, 87, 89, 104, 108, 113, 116

Boston Marathon Bombings (2013), 145–48

Botswana, 85, 86, 111, 114, 116, 130, 131

Bouazizi, Mohamed, 240

260   *Index*

Brazil, 81, 87, 92, 98, 103, 108, 115, 127, 132–34
Breivik, Anders, 127 n105
Brunei, 87, 92, 94, 101, 112, 116, 127
Bulgaria, 102, 117, 125
Burkina Faso, 100, 125
Burundi, 24, 94, 99, 125
Bush, George W., 184

Cabo Verde, 82, 101, 106, 107, 129
Calderon, Felipe, 141, 142
Cambodia, 102, 125
Cameroon, 91, 98, 100, 107, 123, 124
Canada, 27, 90, 94, 104, 112, 114, 116, 125, 132, 134–37
   Royal Canadian Mounted Police (RCMP), 134, 136
   Security Intelligence Service (CSIS), 136
   Toronto 18, the, 136–37
Carlos 'the Jackal', 16
Cassese, Antonio, 40, 41, 208
Central African Republic (CAR), 92, 101, 104, 129
Chad, 100, 107, 112, 125
Chemical weapons, 87–88, 226
Chicago Convention (1944), 58
Children (as perpetrators), 118, 139, 171
Child soldiers, 218–19
Chile, 84, 118
China, 22, 91, 102, 105, 107, 123, 152–55. *see also* Hong Kong
Citizenship, revocation of, 206–07
Cluster munitions, 245
Colombia, 110–11, 127
Combatant's privilege, 45, 51
Committee Against Torture. *see* United Nations
Committee of Public Safety, 11
Commonwealth of Independent States (CIS), 66
   Treaty on Cooperation CIS in Combating Terrorism (1999), 66
Comoros, 86, 94, 99, 103, 108, 123
Comprehensive Convention against International
      Terrorism (draft), 5, 20, 33–36, 44, 56, 254
Congo, Democratic Republic of, 79, 81, 99, 124
Congo, Republic of, 78
Constitutional law prohibition of terrorism, 80–82
Control orders, 204–05
Convention for the Prevention and Punishment of
      Certain Acts of International Terrorism (1972
      draft), 21–22
Convention for the Prevention and Punishment of
      Terrorism (1937), 21, 76
Convention for the Suppression of Unlawful Acts against
      the Safety of Maritime Navigation (SUA), 38–39, 60, 61
   Protocol for the Suppression of Unlawful Acts against
      the Safety of Fixed Platforms located on the
      Continental Shelf (1988), 61
   Protocol to the 1988 Protocol(2005), 62
   Protocol to the SUA Convention (2005), 39, 61
Convention on the Law of the Sea. *see* United Nations
Convention on the Prevention of Terrorism (2005), 67, 102, 108 n439
   Protocol (2015), 67

Convention on the Rights of Persons with Disabilities
      (2006). *see* United Nations
Convention on the Suppression of Terrorism (1977), 66, 67
   Protocol (2003), 66, 67
Cook Islands, 88, 101, 112, 114, 128, 130
Corporal punishment, 124
Corporate prosecutions for terrorism, 149–50
Costa Rica, 116
Côte d'Ivoire, 82, 100, 108, 128
Council of Europe, 66–67
Covenant (International) on Civil and Political Rights
      (1966), 124, 182–86, 198, 202, 241
Covenant (International) on Economic, Social and
      Cultural Rights (1966), 44
Crawford, James, 248
Crimes against humanity, 213–15
Croatia, 89, 109, 118
Crucifixion, 9
Cryer, Robert, 208
Cuba, 92, 93, 100, 123
Customary international law, 112. *see also Jus cogens* norm
Cyberterrorism, 84, 92–93
Cyprus, 102, 108, 116, 125
Czechia, 90, 110, 113, 116, 118, 125

Death penalty, 123–24
   Mandatory, 77, 124
Degrading national honour (as terrorism), 97
de Beer, Aniel, 210
de Menezes, Jean-Charles, 197–98
Democratic People's Republic of Korea. *see* North Korea
Denmark, 84, 116, 125
de Oliveira Sousa, George Washington, 133
Desecration of graves (as terrorism), 110
Di Filippo, Marcello, 31
Dinstein, Yoram, 31, 49, 218, 221
Diplock Courts, 177–78
Diplomats, 4
Djibouti, 125
Dolus specialis, 83
Domestic terrorism, 43–46
Dominica, 78, 95, 128
Dominican Republic, 82, 87, 127
Dresden, bombing of, 49
Drones, armed, 17, 192, 232
Duffy, Helen, 44, 183
Duty to prevent terrorism, 73–74, 235–37
Duty to prosecute terrorism, 122
Duty to punish terrorism, 76–77

Ecuador, 111, 128
Egypt, 32, 99, 120, 240
Einsatzgruppen, 13, 47
El Chapo. *see* Guzman, Joaquín
El Para, 162–63
El Salvador, 118, 127, 132, 137–40
Environmental harm (as terrorism), 94
Equatorial Guinea, 81, 126
Eritrea, 78, 84, 111

Eritrea-Ethiopia Claims Commission, 25
Estonia, 99, 109, 125
Eswatini, 105
ETA (Euskadi Ta Askatasuna), 190
Ethiopia, 112, 113
European Center for Not-for-Profit Law (ECNL), 120
European Commission on Human Rights,
   M. D. v Turkey case, 195
European Convention on the Prevention of Terrorism
   (2005). see Convention on the Prevention of
   Terrorism (2005)
European Court of Human Rights, 8, 73, 185–89, 192, 198–99, 202–03
   A. and others case, 204
   Beghal case, 187–88
   Belashev case, 202
   Bouyid case, 192
   Catan case, 233 n10
   De Tommaso case, 205
   El-Masri case, 200
   Finogenov case, 196
   H. E. v. Turkey, 188
   Khamidov case, 188
   Khoroshenko case, 202
   Kukhalashvili case, 193
   McCann case, 193, 195, 196
   Mentes case, 198–99
   Saadi case, 8 n44
   Satybalov case, 198–99
   Tagayeva case, 74, 182, 236–37
European Union, 43, 67
   Framework Decision on Terrorism (2002), 43
Extortion (as terrorism), 97

Ferencz, Benjamin, 13
Fiji, 79, 105, 125
Financing (of terrorism), 94–95, 130
Finland, 30, 102, 106, 125
Firearms, use of,
   Default international legal rule, 194–96
   Rule on intentional lethal use of, 195
France, 4, 27, 94, 97, 99, 125, 171, 175–77, 186, 226, 237–40
   Brigade de Recherche et d'Intervention (BRI), 187
   Directorate for External Security (la DGSE), 28, 238
French Revolution, 10, see also La Terreur

Gabon, 81, 94, 100, 125
Galić, Stanislav, 73, 221–22
Gambia, The, 92, 101, 108
Geneva Conventions (1949), 26, 46–47, 216
   Grave breaches, 26
Geneva Law, 46–48, 72
   acts of terrorism, 47
   Customary rule, 47
Genocide, 14–15, 226–28
   As an international crime, 14, 226
   Definition, 227
   Dolus specialis, 227
Georgia, 89, 101, 125

Germany, 4, 27, 94, 102, 109, 129, 215, 243
Germany, Federal Republic of, 4, 24
Ghana, 105, 113, 114, 128
Gilets jaunes, 43
Graham, Lindsey, 140
Great Britain. see United Kingdom
Great Purge, The, 13
Greece, 86, 89, 90, 94, 125
Grenada, 92, 105, 116, 125
Groupe salafiste de prédication et de combat (GSPC), 162–63
Guatemala, 4, 14, 15, 85, 90, 107
   Commission of Historical Clarification, 15
Guinea, 88, 94, 100, 102, 108, 116, 125
Guinea-Bissau, 84
Gulag, 13
Gulf Cooperation Council, 68
   Convention for the Suppression of Terrorism (2004), 68
Gunpowder Plot (1605), 10
Guyana, 105, 112, 115, 117
Guzman, Joaquín, 142

Hague Aircraft Hijacking Convention (1970), 89
   1988 Montreal Protocol, 90
Hague Law, 48–50, 72–73
Haiti, 89, 93, 96, 97, 126
Hamburg, bombing of, 49
Hamdan, Salim Ahmed, 224
Hariri, Rafik, 40, 122, 158, 228, 250
Hezbollah, 230, 250
Hiroshima, nuclear bombing of, 49
Holocaust, The, 13, 14
Holy, 66, 79, 95, 128–29
Homicide, 84–85
Honduras, 82, 86, 97, 107, 127, 130, 254
Hong Kong, China, 58 n39, 102, 153–55
Hostage-taking, 4, 5, 16, 43, 85–87, see also Hostage-Taking
      Convention
   Definition, 26
Hostage-Taking Convention (1979), 25–27, 44, 55–56
Human rights
   carve-out for in national legislation, 114–16
   impact of terrorism legislation on, 118–21
Human Rights Committee. see United Nations
Human Rights Watch, 80, 138, 153, 157, 163, 171, 214, 217, 242
Hungary, 81, 117, 118, 125

Iceland, 86, 89, 90, 91, 109, 125, 131
India, 81, 86, 100, 106, 257
Indiscriminate bombing, 49
Indonesia, 94, 105, 119
Institute for Security Studies (ISS), 169
Inter-American Court of Human Rights, 199
   Neira Alegría case, 199
International Civil Aviation Organization, 4, 58
International Commission of Jurists, 121

International Committee of the Red Cross (ICRC), 29, 47, 48, 72, 73, 76, 216, 220, 221
International Court of Justice, 60, 82, 248
  Armed Activities case (2005), 75, 226 n140
  Bosnian Genocide case, 248
  Nicaragua case, 249
  Questions Concerning the Obligation to Prosecute or Extradite (*Belgium* v. *Senegal*) (2012), 53 n7
  Wall case (2004 Advisory Opinion), 75
International Criminal Court, 208, 209, 211–12, 229–30, 250
International criminal law, 208–30
  Modes of liability, 212–13
International Criminal Tribunal for Rwanda (ICTR), 14, 209, 217
International Criminal Tribunal for the former Yugoslavia (ICTY), 5–6, 21, 113, 122, 209, 220–23, 247
  Blagojević case, 48 n222
  Galić case, 21, 48, 73, 221–23
  Gotovina case, 247
  Martić case, 245
  Prlić case, 49
  Tadić case, 22 n17
International Crisis Group (ICG), 168
International humanitarian law (IHL), 21, 22, 25, 28, 31, 33, 45, 58, 59, 63, 71–73, 87, 111, 113, 131, 245, 247, 255
International human rights law, 44, 73–74, 77, *see also* human rights
  Right of peoples to self-determination, 256
  Right to a fair trial, 201–03
  Right to freedom from torture, 44, 241
  Right to liberty of movement, 206
  Right to freedom of peaceful assembly, 44, 114–15
  Rights to liberty and security, 44
  Right to life, 44, 241
  Right to private and family life, 182–86, 207
International Law Commission (ILC), 210, 248
  Draft Articles on State Responsibility (2001), 232–34, 248
International Maritime Organization (IMO), 38, 58, 90
International Military Tribunal at Nuremburg, 13,
International terrorism, definition of, 40–42
Internationally Protected Persons Convention (1973), 23–25, 55, 88
  internationally protected person, definition of, 24
Iran, 27, 93, 97, 100, 123, 124, 155–56
Iraq, 14, 18, 24, 80, 81, 82, 108, 156–58, 214
Ireland, 115, 116, 125, 162
Irish Republican Army (IRA), 177, 193
Islamic State, 1, 14, 17–18, 132, 149, 156, 157, 170, 175, 176, 214, 227, 228
Islamic State in the Greater Sahara (ISGS), 168
Islamic State West Africa Province (ISWAP), 168, 169
Israel, 24, 88, 98, 105, 120, 126
Istanbul Protocol, 189 n142
Italy, 24, 27, 92, 108, 125

Jamaica, 92, 101, 105, 125
Japan, 27, 79, 85, 102
Jenkins, Brian Michael, 15, 140
Jordan, 32, 36, 79, 98, 129
Jurisdiction (in national legislation), 110–118

Geographical, 116–17
Material, 110–16
Personal, 117–18
Temporal, 118
Jus ad bellum, , 52, 56, 74–75, 81
Jus cogens norm, 35, 210, 226, 256

Kabuga, Félicien, 14
Karadzic, Radovan, 222
Kazakhstan, 81, 89, 99, 104
Kenya, 96, 101, 109, 114, 125, 164–67
Khan, Karim, 227
Khan, Usman, 196
Khazaal, Belal, 151–52
Khmer Rouge, 15
Khowaja, Momin, 134
King Alexander I, 3
Kiribati, 105, 112, 114, 125
Klinghoffer, Leon (murder of), 38
Kurds, 14
Kuwait, 78, 95, 123
Kyrgyzstan, 89, 102, 118

Lafarge SA, 149, 150
Laos, 93, 95, 98, 125
La Terreur, 1, 10, 11, *see also* Committee of Public Safety
Latvia, 88, 89, 90, 91, 125
Law enforcement, 34
  officials, 43
League of Arab States, 24
League of Nations, 2, 3–4
  Convention for the Prevention and Punishment of Terrorism, 2, 3–4
Lebanon, 82, 100, 103, 129–30, 158–60, 250
Lemkin, Raphael, 14
Lesotho, 105, 112, 115, 116
Levée en masse, 30
Liberia, 105, 115, 125, 250
Libya, 60, 123, 178, 179, 241
Liechtenstein, 85, 90, 91, 93, 95, 108, 126
Lithuania, 83, 87, 89, 98, 113, 125, 131
'Lockerbie' bombing, 172, 178–81
Lula da Silva, Luiz Inácio, 133
Luxembourg, 83, 108, 125

McVeigh, Timothy, 16, 143–45
Macedo de Souza, Wellington, 134
Macron, Emmanuel, 43
Madagascar, 83, 129
Madrid Bombings (2004), 190–92
Malawi, 105, 108, 115
Malaysia, 105, 114, 123, 124, 126
Maldives, the, 119
Mali, 83, 86, 111
Malta, 108, 116, 125
Mandela, Nelson, 179
Mara Salvatrucha (MS-13), 137, 139
Maritime terrorism, 36–39, 60–62, 90
Marshall Islands, 79 n17, 90, 123, 125
Martić, Milan, 245

Index

263

Mauritania, 109, 118, 124
Mauritius, 116
Mayfield, Brandon, 191–92
Medécins sans Frontières, 112
Metropolitan Police (London), 193 n165, 196, 197, 198
Mettraux, Guénaël, 229
Mexico, 92, 100, 126, 132, 140–42
Micronesia, 78
Milch, Erhard, 46
Minnesota Protocol on the Investigation of Potentially
    Unlawful Death (2016), 198
Mladic, Ratko, 73, 223
Mohammed, Khalid Sheikh, 223
Moldova, 85, 89
Molotov cocktails, 29
Monaco, 97, 101, 104, 125
Mongolia, 111
Montenegro, 95, 113, 129
Montreal Convention (1971), 60
Morocco, 98
Moroccan Islamist Combat Group, 191
Mozambique, 111, 126
Mueller, Robert, 184
Munich Olympic Games (1972), 16, 21
Myanmar, 14, 81, 83, 90, 95, 111, 251–53

Nagasaki, nuclear bombing of, 49
Namibia, 32, 95, 101
National liberation movement, 22, 24
Nauru, 112, 115, 125
Nazis, 1, 13, 47, see also Einsatzgruppen
Nepal, 86, 101, 106, 107, 125
Netherlands, the, 27, 103, 127, 179
New Zealand, 88, 105, 112, 115, 125, 237–40
Nezzar, Khaled, 162
Ní Aoláin, Fionnuala, 42, 120
Nicaragua, 128
Nichols, Terry, 143, 144
Nieto-Navia, Rafael, 221
Niger, 124, 131, 167–70
Nigeria, 97, 124
Niue, 26 n46, 105
Non-Aligned Movement (NAM), 19, 23, 35, 54
non-refoulement, rule of, 52, 59, 204
Non-State armed group, 98
North Macedonia, 82, 85, 89, 109, 125, 200–01
North Korea, 87
Norway, 103, 127
Nosworthy, Janet, 41
Nuclear explosive devices, 87–88, see also Nuclear weapon
Nuclear Terrorism Convention (2005), 5, 32–33, 44, 57
Nuclear weapons, 39, 61, 62, 95

O'Donnell, Daniel, 28, 29, 34, 36
Oklahoma City bombing, 16, 143–45
Oman, 82, 91, 106, 109, 124
Operation Barbarossa, 13
Operation Cut Hand, 219
Oradour-sur-Glane, 47
Organization of African Unity (OAU), 24

Organization of American States (OAS), 24, 68–69
    Convention to Prevent and Punish the Acts of
        Terrorism (1971), 68–69
    Inter-American Convention against Terrorism (2002), 69
Organisation of Islamic Cooperation (OIC), 35
    Convention on Combating International Terrorism
        (1999), 69
Organization of the Petroleum Exporting Countries
    (OPEC), 16

Pacta sunt servanda, 50
Pakistan, 30, 32, 97, 103, 108
Palau, 86, 105, 126
Palestine, 79
Panama, 89, 93, 127
Pan Am Flight 103, bombing of, 172, 178–81
Papua New Guinea, 81, 103, 128
Paraguay, 94, 127
Paris terror attacks (2015), 175, 187, 195
Peaceful protest, criminalization of, 18
Peremptory norm. see Jus cogens norm
Permanent Court of International Justice (PCIJ), 235
Peru, 81, 82, 91, 199–200
Philippines, the, 89, 117, 121
Piracy, 37, 61, 70, 90
PKK (Kurdistan Workers' Party), 189
Poland, 83, 129
Policing powers. see Law of law enforcement
Pol Pot, 15
Popular Front for the Palestine Liberation Front (PLF), 38
Portugal, 27, 82, 88, 89, 129
Powell, Colin, 17
Preventive detention, 203–04
Privateering, 37
Propaganda, 131, 172, 173, 251
Property damage (as terrorism), 91
Public order (offences), 96
Putin, Vladimir, 97

Qatar, 83

Rainbow Warrior, bombing of, 28, 35, 237–40
RAND Corporation, The, 140
Raslan, Anwar, 18
Revolutionary United Front (RUF), 217–18
Right of peoples to self-determination, 35, 36, 47, 64
Riyadus-Salikhin Reconnaissance and Sabotage Battalion
    of Chechen Martyrs, 235
Roberts, Adam, 1
Robespierre, Maximilien, 1, 11, 12
Roach, Kent, 42
Rohingya, 14
Roman Empire, 9
Romania, 103–04, 128
Russell, Katherine, 148
Russia, 30, 66, 67, 89, 97, 107, 123, 172, 188, 196–97, 235–37,
    244–48
    Federal Security Service (FSB), 145 n285
Russian Federation. see Russia
Rwanda, 14, 103, 117, 127

Index

Saint-Just, 12
St Kitts and Nevis, 105, 117, 126
St Lucia, 105, 114, 117, 128
St Vincent and the Grenadines, 83
Samoa, 112, 126, 130
Samuel, Katja, 36
San Marino, 108, 128
São Tomé and Príncipe, 85, 89, 106, 128
Saudi Arabia, 27, 97, 106, 119, 150–61
Saul, Ben, 20, 28, 30, 40, 41, 258
Schama, Simon, 11
Scharf, Michael, 180
Second World War, 4
Senegal, 100, 129
Serbia, 109, 113, 126
Seychelles, the, 114, 126
Shanghai Cooperation Organization (SCO), 71, 107
  Shanghai Convention on Combating Terrorism,
      Separatism and Extremism (2001), 71, 107
Sierra Leone, 78, 85, 93, 105, 114, 117, 217
Simma, Bruno, 75
Singapore, 91
Slovakia, 95, 113, 126
Slovenia, 85, 90, 128
Solomon Islands, 112, 114, 126
Somalia, 80, 170–71
  National Security and Intelligence Agency, 80
South Africa, 98, 99, 126
  Protection of Constitutional Democracy against
      Terrorist and Related Activities Act (2004),
      44
  Protection of Constitutional Democracy against
      Terrorist and Related Activities Amendment Act
      (2022), 45, 99
South Asian Association for Regional Cooperation
    (SAARC), 70
  Regional Convention on the Suppression of Terrorism
      (1987), 70
  Additional Protocol (2004), 70
South Korea, 85, 87, 90
South Sudan, 82, 101
Soviet Union, 13, 89
Spain, 27, 82, 89, 99, 126
Spanish Inquisition, 10
Special Court for Sierra Leone (SCSL), 72, 113, 122, 209,
    217–20, 249, 250
Special Tribunal for Lebanon (STL), 40–42, 89, 122,
    158–60, 209, 228–29
Sri Lanka, 95–96, 97, 98, 106, 119, 123
Stalin, Joseph, 13
Starkey, David, 10
State Responsibility, 231–45
Sudan, 14, 100
Suriname, 78, 126
Suu Kyi, Aung San, 251
Sweden, 126, 184
Switzerland, 81, 126
Syria, 17, 18, 32, 49, 50, 102, 149, 150, 225–26, 240–44

Tajikistan, 89, 107
Tanzania, 108, 114, 127
Tarrio, Enrique, 149
Taylor, Charles, 219, 220, 233, 249–50
Terrorism, definition of
  Lack of, 20
  Etymology, 8, 10, 12
  In armed conflict, 46–50, 72–73, 110–113, 216,
      217–26
Terrorism Financing Convention (1999), 30–32, 44, 62–63,
    83, 95, 99, 101, 103, 110
Terrorist Bombings Convention (1997), 5, 27–30, 36, 43,
    44, 56
  other lethal device, definition of, 27
Thailand, 115
The Troubles (in Northern Ireland), 177–78
Timor-Leste, 65 n97, 105
Tladi, Dire, 210
Togo, 84, 85, 90, 91, 126
Tokyo Convention (1963), 58
Tomás de Torquemada, 10
Tonga, 112, 115, 128
Tong, Ying-Kit, 154–55
Transnational Organized Crime, 39–40
Transparency International, 119
Trapp, Kimberley, 122, 229
Trinidad and Tobago, 112, 115, 117
Tsarnaev, Dzhokhar, 145–48
Tsarnaev, Tamerlan, 145, 146, 147
Tunisia, 85, 98, 99, 123
Turkey. see Türkiye
Türk, Volker, 155
Türkiye, 106, 188–89
Turkmenistan, 89, 97, 128
Tuvalu, 112, 115, 117, 126

Uganda, 105, 119, 124
Uighurs, prosecution of, 152–53
Ukraine, 29, 30 n76, 89, 107, 126, 244–48
United Arab Emirates, 85, 124
United Kingdom, 4, 24, 27, 60, 105, 126,
    177–82
  House of Lords, 10
  Secretary of State for the Home Department, 204,
      205, 206
  Supreme Court, 45
United Nations
  Assistance Mission for Iraq (UNAMI), 156
  Basic Principles on the Use of Force and Firearms
      (1990), 194–96
  Charter (1945), 75, 231
  Code of Conduct for Law Enforcement Officials
      (1979), 192
  Committee Against Torture, 156
  Convention against Transnational Organized
      Crime, 40
  Convention on the Law of the Sea (1982),
      37, 58

Declaration on Principles of International Law
    concerning Friendly Relations and Co-operation
    among States (1970), 76
Definition of Aggression (1974), 76
General Assembly
    Global Counterterrorism Strategy, 256–57
    Resolution 3034 (XXVII), 23
    Resolution 39/159, 231
    Resolution 46/51, 36
    Resolution 51/210, 53 n5
    Resolution 55/158, 53 n5
    Resolution 60/1: 'World Summit Outcome', 6
    Resolution 76/169, 77
    Resolution 77/75, 6 n42
    Resolution 77/77, 6 n41
    Resolution 77/113, 6 n40
Human Rights Committee, 44, 73, 124, 182, 183, 185,
    189, 198
    General Comment 16, 183–84
    Guerrero case, 189
Human Rights Council, 155, 156, 171, 243, 246, 252
    Resolution S-17/1, 243
Independent International Commission of Inquiry on
    the Syrian Arab Republic, 17, 49, 50, 225–26, 243
Independent International Commission of Inquiry on
    Ukraine, 245, 246
Independent Investigative Mechanism for
    Myanmar, 252
Office of the United Nations High Commissioner for
    Human Rights (OHCHR), 156
Secretary-General, 5, 23, 56 n27, 58, 72, 214, 226, 229,
    239, 255, 256
Security Council, 2, 20, 40, 73, 208, 235, 251
    Resolution 579, 2 n4
    Resolution 955, 217
    Resolution 1368, 75
    Resolution 1373, 6, 20, 62, 73, 75, 122
    Resolution 1530, 75, 190
    Resolution 1540, 33, 59
    Resolution 1566, 42, 254, 255
    Resolution 1757, 228
    Resolution 1973, 241
    Resolution 2139, 242, 243
    Resolution 2379, 214
    Resolution 2195, 39
Special Rapporteur on the promotion and protection of
    human rights and fundamental freedoms while
    countering terrorism, 42
UNITAD, 214–15
United States, 27, 60, 108, 131, 142–50, 184–85, 223–25
    Air Force, 15, 49
    Capitol Breach (6 January 2021), 148–49
    Central Intelligence Agency (CIA), 200, 201, 203

Department of Defense, 246 n108
Department of Justice, 184, 191
Department of State, 157, 169, 179
Federal Bureau of Investigation (FBI), 142, 144, 146,
    149, 191
Operation Stellar Wind, 184, 185
PRISM (programme), 185
Seditious conspiracy, 108
Supreme Court, 202
UPSTREAM (programme), 185
USA PATRIOT Act, 185
University of Pretoria
    Centre for Human Rights, 7 n44
    Institute for International and Comparative Law in
      Africa (ICLA), 7 n44
Uruguay, 111
Uzbekistan, 107, 126

V-1/V-2 rockets, 49
Vanuatu, 94, 105, 114, 128
Venezuela, 85, 90, 112, 127
Vienna Convention on Diplomatic Relations (1961),
    25
Vienna Convention on the Law of Treaties (1969),
    24 n29
Vienna Convention on the Physical Protection of Nuclear
    Material (1979), 57
    amended Convention (2005), 58
Vietnam, 15, 85, 98
Vlad 'the Impaler', 9, 10
von Spreti, Karl, 4

Wahnich, Sophie, 11 nn63, 64
Waldheim, Kurt, 33
War crimes (terrorism as), 215–26
    Hostage-taking, 216
Washington Treaty. *see* North Atlantic Treaty
Webster, Noah, 12
Westgate Centre, attack on (2013), 166–67
WMD (weapons of mass destruction), 87–88
World Trade Center bombing (1993), 144, 145
World War II, 49

Xenophobia (as terrorism), 108

Yazidis, 14, 17, 215, 227, 228
Yemen, 45, 78, 123
Yousef, Ramzi, 145

Zagreb, 245
Zambia, 94, 105, 117, 126
Zimbabwe, 84, 119
Zuckerberg, Mark, 42

Printed in the United States
by Baker & Taylor Publisher Services